I0820046

# AMERICAN POPULIST

THOMAS E. PATTERSON

# AMERICAN POPULIST
# Huey Long
# OF LOUISIANA

LOUISIANA STATE UNIVERSITY PRESS
BATON ROUGE

Published with the assistance of the V. Ray Cardozier Fund

Published by Louisiana State University Press
lsupress.org



Manufactured in the United States of America
First printing

DESIGNER: Kaelin Chappell Broaddus
TYPEFACES: Miller Text Roman, text; HT Osteria, Mostra Nova, and Neutra Text, display.
PRINTER AND BINDER: Sheridan Books

JACKET IMAGE: Senator Huey P. Long rests after a long filibuster on the Senate floor in August 1935. Photograph by Harris & Ewing, Prints and Photograph Division, Library of Congress.

Map and line graphs created by Mary Lee Eggart.

Cataloging-in-Publication Data are available at the Library of Congress.

ISBN 978-0-8071-8299-4 (cloth) | ISBN 978-0-8071-8386-1 (pdf) | ISBN 978-0-8071-8387-8 (epub)

# Contents

# Acknowledgments

I am grateful to Mary Devlin, Brady Banta, Jack McGuire, Stephen Ortiz, Donna Barnes, Michael Martin, William Dolan, Bill Craven, David Baumheckel, Audra McCardell Snider, and anonymous reviewers for reading all or parts of drafts and making editorial suggestions; to Faye Consuela for obtaining articles and pictures and permissions to reproduce the same, and for creating the bibliography and list of abbreviations; to Srdjan Savic for collecting magazine articles; to John Eckenstein, Jeff Crawford, Tim Landry, Sophie Popovich, Sarah Deas, and Brent Baughan, who worked on particularized research projects, Mr. Eckenstein most extensively; to the editorial and marketing team at LSU Press, Alisa Plant, Rand Dotson, Catherine Kadair, Neal Novak, copyeditor Stan Ivester, James Wilson, Mary Lee Eggart, and Sunny Rosen for their invaluable assistance with the text, the charts, and the pictures; to Jessica Freeman for creating the index; to those who gave permission to cite their research and pictures; to Shonna Moss and Justin Cotton at the Political Hall of Fame in Winnfield, Louisiana, for sharing their knowledge and memorabilia; to Mrs. Kristan Green, who showed me Huey's first law office.

I am also grateful to the personnel at the following libraries for their help with my research: LSU Hill Memorial Library (especially Germain J. Bienvenue); the Howard-Tilton Memorial Library at Tulane University; the Franklin D. Roosevelt Presidential Library and Museum; the Library of Congress; the Chicago Public Library; the Charlotte Mecklenburg Library; the Nashville Public Library; the UCLA Film Library; the UW-Madison Libraries; the DePaul University Rinn Law Library; the Princeton University Library, Department of Special Collections; the Robert W. Woodruff Library, Emory University, especially E. Kathleen Shoemaker; and the Maureen and Mike Mansfield Library, University of Montana.

I must also thank Parrain's Seafood Restaurant in Baton Rouge and Pêche Seafood Grill and ACME Oyster House in New Orleans for sustaining me during much of my research, Mary Mac's Tea Room in Atlanta for serving potlikker, and my parents, Jack and Sara, my wife, Zully, my son, Tom, my stepdaughter, Christina, my brother, Dan, my sister, Jackie, and my colleagues at the Patterson Law Firm, who were generous in their encouragement and support.

If I have forgotten to thank anyone, it is due to the long period of time since this project began (2014), and I regret it. Any errors are my responsibility. I would be grateful to anyone who diplomatically points them out and I will list them on my website, www.pattersonbooks.com.

Some famous quotes by Huey or about him have been omitted for reasons of space, but many of them and more pictures can be found on the website www.hueylong.com.

# AMERICAN POPULIST

# INTRODUCTION

Whenever deconstruction finds a nutshell—a secure axiom or a pithy maxim—the very idea is to crack it open and disturb this tranquility.
**—John D. Caputo, *Deconstruction in a Nutshell* (1997)**

Invited to a Rotary Club lunch during a frenetic political campaign, the host instructed the speaker to avoid controversial issues. For the first time in his life, the speaker was stumped for something to say. After an uncomfortable moment, someone rescued him with a question: Would he ever stop fighting for those things in which he believed? He would always fight for his ideals, he replied, and then he quoted poetry:

I burn the candle at both ends,
It will not last the night,
But oh my foes, and oh my friends,
It sheds a lovely light.

The speaker was the most fascinating and perhaps the greatest American politician of the twentieth century, Huey Pierce Long Jr. No one would deny that he burned his candle at both ends. The extent to which he shed a lovely light is the subject of this book.

Without graduating from high school, Huey left home at age sixteen to work as a traveling salesman for four years, covering territories from Tennessee to Texas. When business soured, he attended law school for two semesters and then studied for and passed the Louisiana bar examination to become a licensed lawyer at age twenty-one. In Winnfield, Louisiana, his brother was a leader of the ruling political faction and district attorney for two adjoining parishes (counties). With his brother, Huey started his law practice in Winnfield. As a first-year lawyer, he led a grassroots campaign to liberalize Louisiana's workers' compensation laws and sued the biggest bank in Winnfield. Two years later, he defended with his brother a local state senator that the federal government indicted during World War I for antiwar views. Each of these efforts was successful, and Huey then won election to the Railroad Commission in 1918 at age twenty-five.

Plantation owners and a corrupt New Orleans machine ruled Louisiana. Immediately upon his election, however, Huey astounded the state by regulating railroads, utilities, and oil companies for the first time. On behalf of independent oil drillers, he took on Standard Oil Company. He forced a phone company to write refund checks to its customers throughout the state after he argued the case in the U.S. Supreme Court, winning compliments from one of the justices along with the case. These efforts made him popular, and Huey won the governorship of Louisiana on his second try in 1928.

Huey's accomplishments as governor are legendary. His legislation gave free schoolbooks and bus rides to secondary school students. He sponsored education classes that taught 125,000 illiterate adults to read. School enrollment accordingly increased by 20 percent, and adult illiteracy decreased by 10 percent. His free-schoolbooks law artfully provided them to Catholics in private schools without violating the First Amendment. He shifted the tax burden from the poor to the wealthy. He took Louisiana out of the mud, building roads, bridges, an airport, a state capitol, and a governor's mansion. Even opponents admitted to the high quality of his building projects.

Huey radically improved Louisiana State University (LSU), beginning with the creation of a large marching band, an improved football team, and a new medical school, doubling the supply of doctors. He expanded the free Charity Hospital in New Orleans, and its death rate was reduced. LSU's accreditation rating went from C to A. Enrollment exploded. New buildings, courses, and first-rate faculty accompanied the expansion. Tuition was cheap, and many students obtained state jobs. LSU attracted applicants from all over the South during the Great Depression.

Elected U.S. senator, Huey advocated the redistribution of wealth by means of high taxes upon the wealthy. This was one of Franklin Delano Roosevelt's promises in his 1932 campaign, during the third year of the Great Depression. Believing that Roosevelt was progressive, Huey helped him win the presidency. Huey strengthened the early New Deal Banking Act so that it rescued state as well as federal banks and insured bank deposits. With these changes, it was the most successful of the early New Deal programs. Yet Huey and Roosevelt could not get along.

In February 1934, Huey started a movement called the Share Our Wealth Society. Anyone could organize one. The societies sought a more equitable distribution of wealth by taxing the rich and guaranteeing everyone else a minimum income, a home, college and vocational education, and an old-age pension. He advocated shortening the hours of work, increasing the money supply, a unique farm program, and generous veteran benefits, too. Share Our Wealth's platform was set forth in a thirty-two-page pamphlet. The mission of the societies was to develop a voting majority for his economic proposals and elect Huey president. Their growth was stunning. There were an estimated nine million members in September 1935. This threatened Roosevelt so much that he endorsed or sponsored legislation in the so-called Second New Deal of 1935—Social Security, progressive taxation, the Labor Act, and aid to college students, among them—to "steal his thunder."

Roosevelt did not rely on stolen thunder alone to fight Huey. He abused the IRS and the FBI to investigate or prosecute him and his allies, and he expanded and politicized governmental relief expenditures in Louisiana to defeat him. William Ivy Hair calls this the "dark side" of Roosevelt's presidency.[1]

In response, in a series of special legislative sessions that passed laws with frightening speed, Huey cannibalized every governmental job in the state, including local governments and school boards. This increased his patronage without raising the total tax load of the state. It was done while he was a U.S. senator and lacked any official role in Louisiana's government. If that were not unusual enough, he dominated Louisiana legislative sessions in person, explaining the legislation and instructing his followers how to vote. Many thus thought that he was an incipient fascist, the first potential dictator of the United States.

Louisiana at the time had a history of violence. Huey's revolutionary program of taxing the wealthy to provide services to everyone else, his ruthless control of patronage from the state government down to local school boards, his humiliation of the old aristocrats, and his continued electoral success provoked violent reactions. In one congressional election, armed gangs opposed to Huey hijacked state trucks and burned the ballots they carried. An organization of armed men who had formed to overthrow Huey was routed by tear gas fired by the National Guard. Advocacy of armed revolt against the "dictator" Long appeared in newspapers. Huey was threatened publicly with whipping, hanging, and kidnapping. The mayor of Shreveport said he would swing the rope. The lieutenant governor said he would pardon the kidnappers.

Conspiracies to assassinate him were common. Thirty years later, one of the plotters reminisced that Huey was a "dictator just like the Kennedys." We "would all have killed him, he said with relish."[2] The bodyguards Huey surrounded himself with added to the sense of drama and danger.

On September 8, 1935, a brilliant young doctor shot Huey in the Louisiana State Capitol. Huey's bodyguards riddled the assassin with bullets. The circumstances provoked conspiracy theories that are still asserted today. Two days later, Huey died age forty-two.

People have asked me, with different emphases, why are you writing about him? Huey's story was fun to write. Beyond the interest in the traits that made him successful and the drama of his success against unreasoning and violent opponents, he had an exuberance that is hard to dislike, even when he misbehaved. He bragged that he bought a legislator like a "sack of potatoes"; was indicted; was impeached; caused an international incident when he received a foreign government official in his pajamas; appointed his mistress to be secretary of state; allegedly kidnapped a man who might have charged him with infidelity on the eve of an election; started a humorous national debate over whether the cornpone biscuit should be dunked or crumbled into potlikker (soup broth left over after cooking greens); was punched in the eye after a drunken encounter in a country club restroom; composed football songs, designed the LSU band uniforms, and led the marching band of LSU during parades and concerts; subsidized all of the LSU students so they could travel by train to a football game in Tennessee; composed and sang a campaign song, and had it sung by famous musicians during a radio speech and on newsreels; brought a New Orleans bartender up to New York City to teach the proper method of making a Ramos gin fizz; gave nicknames such as "Bang Tail" (to a politician who liked horse races), "Whistle Britches" (to a man subject to flatulence), and "Turkey Head" (to a man with a long neck, a small, bald head, and a beak nose) to political opponents; described the CEO of the United Fruit Company as a banana peddler; and conducted a fifteen-and-one-half hour-long filibuster, one of the longest and most entertaining on record. His self-bestowed nickname was the Kingfish, after the humorously scheming head of the Mystic Knights of the Sea Lodge on the popular *Amos 'n Andy* radio show.

Paradoxes made ultimate judgments about Huey difficult. He was careless with the facts when he described opponents but kept his campaign promises and gave the people real, lasting benefits. He extorted kickbacks from patronage workers and state contractors, but his machine was thereby independent from the oligarchy that had previously ruled the state. The money was taken for political goals and, while he lived a hectic lifestyle that cost a lot of money, he did not accumulate much. His machine was thereby corrupt, but opponents believed even in retrospect that he kept it within reasonable bounds.[3] Patronage appointees signed undated resignations to ensure their loyalty. Yet he appointed some opponents to positions and sometimes intervened to prevent political interference. He accumulated political power but abolished the poll tax so that more people could vote. Voter participation increased because the elections meant something. In the service of real ideals, he was cynically realistic.

Huey's intense exertions to fulfill his goals were sometimes undone by a manic exuberance or vindictiveness. An existential objectivity and sense of comedy and showmanship advanced and occasionally undermined his goals. He was usually kind to ordinary people and had a gift for making them feel important. He could invest a sense of occasion, ceremony, and fun to the ordinary. Exhibiting the full range of human characteristics, he got the most out of his forty-two years of life and is well worth knowing for that reason alone.

At least six novels, ten biographies, one Ken Burns documentary, plays and movies, and an opera have been based on Huey's life and career. The best novel, *All the King's Men* by Robert Penn Warren (recruited to LSU during Huey's reign), presented the ethical question of whether the ends justify the means, the historical issue of the influence of "great men" on history, and the drama of leadership in a democracy when a ruling class neglects the interests of the people. Warren won a Pulitzer Prize for his novel, and it was made into an Oscar-winning movie in 1949 (and remade in 2006). In 1969, T. Harry Williams's biography won the Pulitzer Prize and the National Book award. Without diminishing their achievements, some credit they received belongs to Huey because of his compelling life.

Because of Warren and Williams, I read all the later biographies. Most of them criticized Williams in whole or in part. Who was right? After authoring a book for lawyers published by the American Bar Association in 2009, I was looking for a new project. I learned that Huey's personal and law practice papers at LSU had not been available to Williams and were not used much by later biographers. Recent economic scholarship about the Great Depression had not been integrated into the history books. The Internet provided new material about Huey, material that could not have been easily available to prior biographers. I finally decided to spend the time with the primary and secondary sources to get my own answers.

The patterns of Huey's career have a shockingly similar structure that was easier to deconstruct than his personality. It resembles a fractal, both as to his own development and the environment's response to him. The personal characteristics that led to his success and the flaws that led to certain of his defeats can be detailed. His plans can be analyzed. They are worth studying.

Nationally, Huey has been universally considered as a genius but, according to critics, a corrupt and intolerant one, a dangerous rival to Roosevelt who might have become a fascist dictator. Roosevelt hung the devastating label of "dangerous" on him. This is myth and caricature. Historian Arthur Schlesinger Jr. said that Huey was not a politician with a program: he should be viewed as a political boss interested only in power and graft. As brilliant as Schlesinger was, this pithy maxim is wrong. It is a mistake to view him as anything but a politician with a program.

During the boom times of World War I and the roaring 1920s, the Kingfish advocated the same principles. It is impossible to conclude that his program was a product of Great Depression opportunism. If he had advanced more conservative or irrelevant and demagogic views, as other popular politicians have done, or if he had supported Roosevelt, as most Democratic politicians did, he would have obtained a lot more power and money.

The history books also misdescribe Huey's split with Roosevelt. When Huey disagreed with Roosevelt, his reasons were ideological, and Huey was more progressive. Huey's criticisms of the New Deal—especially of the National Industrial Recovery Act and Roosevelt's inhumane cuts to veteran benefits—were biting but true. While Roosevelt wrote Huey off in 1933, Huey did not break with Roosevelt until January 1935. The psychology of the two men dovetails with the ideological and is riveting.

The derivation of Huey's idea that wealth should be redistributed can be traced to his family and his hometown, to the Bible, to Tulane Law School, to a local state senator, and to William Jennings Bryan, Theodore Roosevelt, Woodrow Wilson, and other national leaders at the time Huey came of age. Within that master frame, he developed subsidiary frames before he reached the national stage.

Huey exhibited an enormous and unappreciated intellectual growth during his Louisiana career and after he became a national leader. Ultimately, he conceived of an economic ecosystem different from the corporate-state characteristics of the New Deal, laissez-faire capitalism, or socialism. It eliminated outliers of rich and poor, but promoted competition and free markets, the essence of capitalism, and ensured a more equal opportunity to compete. It would counteract the trend he perceived toward a modern economic feudalism, in which wealthy families dominated the economy and government.

Government actions during World War II—the war contracts that employed the previously unemployed and underemployed—caused the redistribution of wealth that Huey advocated without a war. The debate over inequality then stopped while liberals and conservatives argued about productivity, considered to be the key to the economy and the cure to poverty.

Yet, nine years after Huey died, the famous GI Bill of 1944 conferred farm, home ownership, and education benefits that "matched nearly exactly those found in Huey Long's Share Our Wealth program."[4] Shortly before and in the wake of the Great Recession of 2008, scholars and others revived the inequality debate that was the centerpiece of Huey's contentions. Scholars, politicians, and business leaders advocate Huey's other proposals—taxing wealth, free college and vocational education, a shortened workweek, educational sabbaticals, and minimum incomes—today. Ninety years after his death, he still has something to say.

While I owe an enormous debt to prior biographers and scholars, there is something fresh in every chapter of this book from unused primary sources, other authors, unpublished thesis writers, or my own ideas. Robert Heilman wrote: "We have not yet a key for whatever center may be assumed to lie behind [the] centrifugal outpourings of [Huey's] personality. We are bound to keep looking for it: Huey's challenge to the imagination is a strong one. He died young, but he makes a strong impact on the psychic centers from which flow the arts of historical and literary interpretation."[5] I have been looking at Huey on and off for fifty years, and this book is my effort to find that key.

Before we consider the genesis of his ideas, the traits that made him successful, the patterns of his career, and his effect on his state and nation, however, we should review the conditions of the United States, Louisiana, his hometown of Winnfield, and the family into which he was born in 1893.

# One

## A SINGULARITY

It is fitting that Huey Pierce Long Jr., who had such an impact on the economics and politics of the Great Depression, the worst of the twentieth century, was born on August 30, 1893, during the worst depression of the nineteenth century. In 1893, life was nasty, brutish, and short. There were no automobiles, telephones, televisions, radios, refrigerators, washing machines, or vacuum cleaners. For most families, there was no running water, plumbing, electricity, or central heating.

While aspirin, morphine, and quinine were reliable medicines, opium, cocaine, heroin, and alcohol were sold as miracle cures. Folk remedies were common and no more useless than many medicines. Prescriptions were not required. Doctors were difficult to reach without a phone, likely to arrive too late in the absence of paved roads or automobiles, and often diploma-mill quacks. Hospitals were dumping grounds for the sick poor, where, without antiseptics, they often contracted infections and died.[1]

Out of a population of 63,000,000 people, 40,227,401 Americans lived in rural areas and 22,720,223 lived in cities.[2] Isolation, endless toil, and subsistence living were the rule for farmers. They plowed their fields with mules or horses. Farm housewives lugged water in pails from streams or cisterns into the house for cooking, baths, and cleaning, and then lugged the dirty water back outside—in one year hauling thirty-six tons of water 148 miles. Cooking took hours because it was done from scratch, the stove depending on wood that had to be chopped, stacked, and then brought inside to turn into ashes that had to be shoveled into bins and discarded. Bathrooms were outdoor privies. Kerosene lamps lit the homes despite their poor light and the danger of burns and fires.[3] City dwellers lived in small houses or smaller tenement flats and worked long hours for low pay, often in dangerous factories. Their children worked, too. The adult Huey recalled that any man of brawn could make his way.[4]

In 1901, the average working family had four members, earned $651, and spent an aggregate of $618 on food ($266), clothing ($80), rent-household ($112), heating fuel ($35), and sundries ($124). The railroad depot was the center of small towns and cities, from which businesses and the residential area radiated. The telegraph office was adjacent to the depot. Nearby hotels provided lodging for the occasional visitor and salesman. Transportation was by foot, horse and buggy, horseback, or trains. Horses were expensive but could be rented from the local livery stable. Most roads were muddy, rutted, and filled with horse manure.

Not that this is any consolation, but farmers lived longer than city dwellers. Their food was fresh. They breathed clean air. Crowded and unsanitary conditions bred disease in the city. Milk, beer, and other foods were often adulterated. Bad milk was the suspected cause of early infant deaths. Lack of sewer systems, the prevalence of rats, and the proximity of city dwellers—unaware of germ theory—spread disease.[5]

Laws enacting income taxes, prohibiting child labor, setting minimum wages or maximum hours of work, and fighting monopolies in business were deemed unconstitutional. Jim Crow laws, passed to exclude Black people from equal opportunities, were judged constitutional.[6]

Before concluding that events in such a primitive environment could teach us nothing, consider that Huey lived during forty-two years of change—spectacular technological, industrial, and legal innovations—and its pace since then has accelerated. Forty-two years before starting this book, there were no portable personal computers, smartphones, or Internet. People were lucky to have one car and one landline phone. They drank coffee in their homes and drove to stores to buy books. Innovations have given us new problems—including mass shootings of civilians and students and the risk of nuclear war—that will make our time appear primitive to future generations. How Huey's generation dealt with their conditions and their changes might help us deal with our own.

Technological change and industrialization in Huey's time produced fortunes for a few. The top two hundred or so families near to or soon after the time of Huey's birth—Vanderbilt, Whitney, Carnegie, Harriman, Morgan, Rockefeller, and so on—were worth at least $20 million, "fortunes with few parallels in history,"[7] until today. Now, the impact of modern technology, rapid change, and the enormous wealth and power of the economic elite bear a striking resemblance to the world that shaped Huey. Not every problem we face is new.

A similar inequality of wealth and opportunity existed in Louisiana. But it preceded that of the northern states and was more related to the plantation economy than to technological change or industrialization. "Rural planters and the men of commerce in [New Orleans], though comprising but 3 percent of the free people of the state, controlled the greater part of the economic wealth and political power of ante-bellum Louisiana."[8]

North of the junction of the Red and Mississippi rivers, Louisiana's climate facilitated growing cotton. The Lowlands bordered the Mississippi River (the eastern border of the state) and the Gulf of Mexico to the south, saved from floods, most of the time, by levees. The soil there was rich. While the plantation owners were wealthy, sharecroppers were in hock to financiers, grocers, and dry goods stores. Floodwaters during May and June of 1893 ruined cotton fields in northeast Louisiana and left forty thousand farmers—most of them Black—homeless. A drought in the summer hurt crops in northwest Louisiana. Cotton picking in the broiling sun—bending over for twelve hours a day to grab the little cotton boll from among the sharp bracts and filling a hundred-pound sack—was the lot of poor white farmers and all Black field hands.

The heavy rainfall and tropical heat south of Rapides Parish supported crops of rice, citrus fruits, and sugarcane. The big sugarcane plantations were comparable to the big cotton plantations, and the work was no easier. A cane knife (like a machete but with a curved blade at the end) was used to cut the cane, which when grown resembles a small bamboo tree. The workers, most of them Black, would advance over the cane field in rows, singing or chanting to keep the cutting in rhythm. They stayed fully clothed despite the heat because the cane juice attracted bugs. Carts followed to collect the cut cane, which was transported to the mill—generally one per plantation—where it was ground and granulated. The Audubon Sugar School was founded in 1891 and promoted improved methods of manufacture. Weather risks also afflicted southern Louisiana. A hurricane in October 1893 killed twenty-five hundred people in the marshes south of New Orleans.

Unique among the southern states, the southern half of Louisiana was Catholic. Creoles were descendants of Native Americans and Spanish, French, and African settlers.[9] The Cajuns were descendants of the French Acadians who fled religious persecution in British Nova Scotia in the mid-eighteenth century, when Spain owned Louisiana and gave them sanctuary. White Creoles comprised part of the urban aristocracy in New Orleans. Cajuns in south Louisiana lived modestly at best and often off the land on the banks of rivers and bayous, in swamps and marshes, and on western prairies. Both Creoles and Cajuns tenaciously maintained their ethnic identities.[10]

Louisiana farmers attended cooperative work parties and revival meetings with singing, preaching, and picnicking. The occasional circus, minstrel show, or vaudeville act was prized entertainment. Most amusements, however, were self-generated: letters to write and receive, playing the piano, singing, reading poetry, and one-act plays. Playing checkers at the store, taking a buggy ride, hunting, fishing, or shopping rounded out the available diversions. Cajuns enjoyed Saturday night dances, horse racing, cooking, gambling, fairs and religious festivals, group camping, and hunting and fishing expeditions.[11]

Louisiana also owned the distinction of New Orleans, then the largest and most powerful city in the South. It was the second busiest port in the United States, trailing only New York. Cotton was shipped and financed through New Orleans, whose banks were the largest and most important in the South. The city had twice the economic activity of Dallas, the second wealthiest city in the South, and double or triple the activity of Houston, Atlanta, Memphis, Louisville, Richmond, or Birmingham.[12] The city was cosmopolitan, with French, Spanish, Portuguese, African, Caribbean, Catholic, Jewish, and Protestant inhabitants, tolerant of unconventional lifestyles, and corrupt. Drinking, gambling, horse racing, vaudeville, music, theater, and prostitution flourished.

The Civil War decimated the southern agricultural economy. The former plantation owners and their allies lost political control to Republicans during Reconstruction. The Republicans ended slavery and enfranchised Black people with the Thirteenth, Fourteenth, and Fifteenth amendments to the Constitution. With their votes and backed by federal troops, the Republicans ran Louisiana until 1876.

Terrorism sponsored by the Ku Klux Klan and others fought Republican rule. A riot in New Orleans in 1866 killed 34 African Americans. In Caddo

Parish (Shreveport, in the northwestern part of the state) in 1868 only one vote was cast for a Republican, and this voter was shot to death the next day. In 1872, after a contested election, a court declared the Republicans victorious, and they accordingly showed up to serve at the Colfax courthouse. Armed Democrats gathered outside and ordered them to leave. Between 50 and 70 Blacks surrendered under a white flag of truce. They were allowed to leave and then murdered. When the rest failed to leave, the courthouse was set on fire, and they were killed in the fire or shot while trying to escape. In 1874, the White League in New Orleans fought a pitched battle against Republican troops. Sixteen White Leaguers were killed and 45 wounded. Louisiana's militia suffered 11 dead and 60 wounded.[13] White Leaguer Edward White was later appointed to the U.S. Supreme Court. Between the end of the Civil War and 1874, 2,141 Black people were murdered and 2,115 were wounded by Klan attacks in Louisiana.[14] In 1876, Republicans supporting Rutherford B. Hayes for president agreed to end Reconstruction in exchange for the electoral votes of states (such as Louisiana) where election-day violence precluded an accurate vote count.

An oligarchy of sugar and cotton plantation owners, allied with New Orleans politicians, governed Louisiana after Reconstruction. The planters set the policy and tone: "government by gentlemen," a term coined by Roger Shugg, or, as T. Harry Williams revised it, "government by goatee." New Orleans furnished most of the officeholders and lawyers.[15]

Dislike of Republican rule during Reconstruction—exploited by the oligarchy—became equated with hostility to progressive legislation in general, allowing continuation of the government by gentlemen. "In no other post-Reconstruction state did the planters so effectively dominate the political process."[16]

Southerners celebrated, memorialized, and ritualized the Lost Cause of the Civil War, its military heroes, and its traditions. Huge funeral celebrations and eulogies of Confederate General P.G.T. Beauregard and Confederate President Jefferson Davis (his body was moved from New Orleans to Richmond, Virginia) in 1893 portrayed them as Christian saints whose cause was holy. The nostalgia perpetuated by the churches and mythmakers translated into a broader religious and cultural conservativism.

In 1893, Southern Baptists, the most populous religious group in northern Louisiana, taught that slavery was a benefit to the slaves and was justified by the Bible; that the Bible was the literal word of God; and that personal salvation was required, memorialized by a baptism requiring the dunking of the whole person in a pond or stream. Baptists protested the Chicago World's Columbian Exposition of 1893 because it was open on Sundays and displayed nude artwork. Their standards required temperance and forbade gambling and race mixing.

Catholics, in contrast, made home altars and lawn statuaries, prayed the rosary, ate fish on Friday, drank wine and spirits, and tolerated gambling, even supporting a state-chartered lottery company, causing a controversy that divided northern and southern Louisiana. Catholics celebrated the Way of the Cross with a procession and a Mardi Gras festival that had a "certain aura of outlawry."[17]

The thunder and vengeance of God could be twisted in the southern culture of honor, by the tradition of terrorism during Reconstruction, the religious belief in the Lost Cause of the Civil War, and the perceived moral and intellectual inferiority of Black people into mob violence. In a carnage over decades after the Civil War that is painful to contemplate, Black people (and, less frequently, others) were regularly lynched. A careless look, an unguarded remark, or an unfounded rumor could unleash a violent outpouring of emotion—mob insanity, or the flip side or dark side of an ecstatic impulse—sufficient to cause a Black man's lynching, sometimes with body parts sliced off and distributed as souvenirs. Some onlookers praised God during lynchings as if they were purging evil from their midst.[18] Religious leaders condemned lynching, but they often gave more prominence to the cause and explanation of it—the crime of the lynched victim or the slow pace and uncertain result of the legal system—in their discussion.

Eleven Italians were lynched in New Orleans in 1891. One of the mob leaders later became governor. Legendary preacher and Lost Cause devotee Benjamin M. Palmer preached a sermon justifying the slaughter in the largest Presbyterian Church in New Orleans.[19]

Among whites of all religions, the culture of honor, mingled with the God of vengeance, tolerated no evil and manifested violence. Calling someone a "son of a bitch" would provoke a fistfight. Insulting a man's wife might warrant a gunshot. A man who could not or would not fight was not respected. The southern murder rate exceeded that of northern states, and Louisiana led the South in homicides. Only the frontier towns of the Wild West were more dangerous.[20]

The consequences of concentrated power exercised foolishly—the decision to join the Confederate rebellion, the inability to cope with change in its aftermath, and the extrajudicial violence—can be seen in compelling statistics. Louisiana's farmland values plummeted from $247.9 million in 1860 to $110.4 million in 1890. Total manufactured products in Louisiana in 1900 were $121,181,683, ranked twenty-second in the nation; New York led with almost twenty times that amount, $2,175,766,900.[21] Louisiana's share of the cotton market had declined from 20 percent in 1860 to 7.7 percent in 1890. In the United States, 28 percent of all farmers were tenant farmers in 1890; in the South, the figure was 38 percent; in Louisiana, the percentage was 44 percent. The percentage of farmers who owned their farms had decreased from 1880 to 1890, in several regions by more than 25 percent.[22] In 1890, Louisiana's educational system spent $26.66 per white pupil and $8.29 per Black pupil. The length of the school year was approximately ninety days. The public schools of Louisiana and the rest of the southern states "could be charitably described as backward."[23]

Huey was born in the north central town of Winnfield in Winn Parish, cotton country, but Winnfield's main crop was dissent. Before the Civil War, Winn voters were Jacksonian Democrats, not Whigs, and were at political odds with the wealthy planters and urban New Orleans. Jacksonian Democrats talked the language of egalitarianism but opposed big government and public works projects.

At the convention to consider secession in January 1861, the Winn Parish delegate opposed the Civil War, dissented from the vote to secede, and refused to sign the resolution after it was passed. Many residents of the "free state of Winn" served with "General Green," hiding out in the woods until the Civil War concluded.[24]

Winn Parish cotton crops were barely profitable in good years because the soil was lousy. The town lacked public utilities and running water. Only a few stores had electricity. Chickens roamed the streets. No sidewalks.

Some members of different ethnic groups—Italians operating fruit stands, Mexican sawmill laborers, Jewish businessmen, Syrian peddlers, French Cajuns, Black people, and Chinese families who ran a laundry—added "patches of alien and colorful culture." They "intrigued the natives, without necessarily awakening feelings of understanding or respect."[25]

The deterioration of the agricultural economy led to the formation of farmer pressure groups: the Louisiana Farmers Union (LFU) in 1888, the Colored Farmers Union (CFU), and, finally, the Populist Party in 1890. The Populists advocated government-sponsored easier and cheaper credit for farmers. Leaders of both the Democratic and Republican parties scorned them. But they were popular in Winn Parish. A Populist bought the only newspaper in Winn, the *Winnfield Comrade,* in 1890. In 1892, the Populist candidate for governor, Richard L. Tannehill, was from Winn. In 1894, the *Winnfield Comrade*'s editor, B. W. Bailey of Winnfield, was a Populist candidate for Congress. Hardy Brian represented Winnfield at the LFU national convention and became the Populists' first secretary, chairman of its state central committee, and editor of the *Louisiana Populist.*[26]

In 1896, the Populists allied with Republicans. Their support was highest in the small farmer parishes such as Winn and in the sugar section that was angry at the low-tariff policy advocated by the national Democratic Party. Their candidate, John N. Pharr, was favored to win the January 1896 election.

To meet this threat, the Caddo Parish newspaper said that it was the "religious duty of Democrats to rob Populists and Republicans of their votes. . . . Rob them! You bet!" Pharr lost to Murphy Foster, the Democrat, despite carrying Winn Parish. Armed violence and intimidation and open, notorious, and unapologetic election fraud caused Pharr's defeat. Pharr got 43 percent of the vote nevertheless, from parishes that decades later supported Huey.

Outraged by the fraud and intimidation that caused Pharr's defeat, Hardy Brian called for a farmer's march on Baton Rouge to take over the state government by force. State officials mobilized in anticipation of the assault. Cooler heads then prevailed, and Pharr conceded defeat.[27]

Populist Party candidates carried Winn Parish in every election until 1900. In 1908, the Socialist Party elected half the officials of Winn. In the 1912 presidential election, Socialist Eugene V. Debs won 36 percent of the vote in Winn.[28]

In the presidential election of 1896, Winn was a stronghold for William Jennings Bryan, who co-opted populists, becoming the candidate of the Democratic and Populist parties, but he lost the election to William McKinley.[29] Bryan advocated inflating the money supply by coining silver as well as gold; imposing a progressive income tax; regulating railroads and banks; strengthening labor rights; granting voting rights for women; avoiding international disputes; enacting antitrust laws; prohibiting child labor; eliminating tariffs (free international trade); providing government insurance of bank deposits; prohibiting the sale of alcohol; and teaching creationism rather than evolution in public schools. The 1896 election was the height of his electoral strength, but he earned the Democratic presidential nomination again in 1900 and 1908, and his brother was the Democratic vice-presidential candidate as late as 1924.[30]

While Bryan advocated many progressive and well-meaning ideas, history has dwelled on his misguided and regressive ones. Woodrow Wilson's biographer wrote: "history has treated few more unfairly than William Jennings Bryan."[31]

When in 1896 Bryan advocated coining silver to expand the money supply and thus defeat the Depression of the 1890s, for example, conservatives of both parties considered him a radical who would destroy the economy.[32] Even a *favorable* biography about Bryan, written in 1925, stated that he was wrong.[33] But in 1971, economist Milton Friedman declared that Bryan was right. Increasing the money supply in 1896 would have ended the Depression and improved the economy. The economy later revived because new supplies of and means of refining gold were found, increasing the money supply, as Bryan advocated, but without using silver.[34]

The Longs settled in Winnfield in or before 1859.[35] James Long had lived in Maryland in the 1800s and had worked as a physician and Methodist minister. A call of the church led him to Ohio, where his son John was born. The family moved to Tunica, in Smith County, Mississippi, in 1841 when John was sixteen. John moved from Mississippi to Winn Parish in 1859. John never served in the Civil War. Either he was realistic about its likely failure, had a hernia and could not serve, or—having been raised in Ohio—had Union sympathies, but was smart enough to keep his mouth shut. John's wife was a temperance advocate.

John's third son, Huey Pierce Long Sr. (Old Hu), who was sixteen when the family moved to Louisiana, supervised his father's farm operations, and then took them over—abandoning his original plan to become a doctor—when his father became ill. Old Hu's brother George was the president of Winnfield Bank.

In 1875, Old Hu married fifteen-year-old Caledonia Tison, whose parents had died and who was living with two half-sisters, perhaps out of pity more than love. Caledonia's father had been a successful dairy farmer, and her family had lived in Louisiana longer than the Longs. They had been wealthy enough to own slaves (the Longs never did), and their ancestors included at least one remarkable, stubborn, and powerful man, James Mackie, who was one of the original organizers of Winn Parish, and an ancestor of Texas representative Martin Dies.[36]

Caledonia was frail but had a disciplined mind and an excellent—maybe photographic—memory. She stood five feet, five inches tall and weighed less than one hundred pounds. She had hazel eyes and coal-black hair. Old Hu was six feet tall, big boned, had flashing brown eyes, and a roaring, dominating voice. Daughter Lucille said he was a better and wittier public speaker than any of his sons.[37] Old Hu may have had the roaring voice, but his wife ruled the home.[38]

The first four children were born on a farm southeast of Winnfield, the parish seat: Charlotte, Julius, Helen (who died at eighteen months), and George (called Shan as an adult). In 1886, Old Hu bought 320 acres of land closer to Winnfield and moved the family into a large, cold, and drafty log house. Two more girls, Olive and Clara, were born before 1893, when, on August 30, Huey Pierce Long Jr. was born. About a year after Huey's birth, Old Hu moved the family into a smaller, warmer saltbox house, where they lived for thirteen years, and where Earl, Caledonia, and Lucille were born.

Because the Winnfield soil was too poor to raise much cotton, Old Hu also raised cattle and hogs. His farm was self-sustaining, growing small quantities of fruits and vegetables, but it produced little cash.

Around the turn of the century, however, Winnfield boomed because the lumber companies exploited the rich timber nearby. Roads and railroad lines were built into the town. A stave-manufacturing plant, two hotels, seven brick downtown buildings, and a brickyard were established in Winnfield by 1910, when its population grew to almost three thousand. The consequent demand for housing allowed Old Hu to sell off some of his land, including a lot located in what is now the town, at a good profit. The sale proceeds allowed the family to build a large, colonial style house of two stories, sixteen rooms, a big porch, with "waterworks and lights," when Huey was fourteen, one of the best houses in Winnfield. The family took in lodgers. A domestic servant helped with the home chores, children, and boarders. Worried about the effect of the free and easy lifestyle of sawmill laborers on Huey, his father bought another farm about ten miles out of town so that Huey could work there, away from the town.[39]

Winnfield lacked a library, but the Long family acquired books and subscribed to the *Saturday Evening Post*, the *Progressive Farmer*, and *Youth's Companion* magazines. The family discussed politics at the dinner table. The governing body of Winn Parish, the police jury, sometimes met at the Long home.[40]

All the Long children received higher education, unusual for their time and place. Julius became a lawyer; George became a dentist in Oklahoma; Earl attended Polytechnic, plus Louisiana State University and Loyola University in New Orleans. The girls became teachers; Olive earned a master's degree from Columbia University and served on a college faculty.

Old Hu ran for the state senate in 1900 as an Independent Democrat opposed to corporate control of the government and in favor of a strong school system, but came in third, behind a regular Democrat and a Populist candidate, the first time a Populist had lost the race since 1888. In 1910, Old Hu ran last in a six-man race for alderman. In this latter race, Old Hu emphasized his property holdings, a poor strategy.[41] Old Hu might not have been as intelligent or as friendly as some related. Maybe Huey inherited his father's voice and constitution but his mother's brains.

The Longs perceived themselves as part of the upper crust[42] and were among the elite of Winnfield, but, as a matter of economics and status, they dwelt far below the planter and business aristocracy that ruled the state. After building his grand house, Old Hu lacked the money to send Huey to college. Late in life, Old Hu reviled wealthy planters to a magazine reporter.[43]

Huey later mythologized his humble beginnings—infuriating his status-conscious sisters—because he was aware of his low status and to identify with his constituents, delighted in the humiliation of rich people, and always advocated programs that struck at their interests.[44] Other politicians have faced similar childhood deprivations and social or political ostracism or isolation (think Richard Nixon or Lyndon Johnson), but no other politician in American history was raised in an environment such as Winnfield, in a family as resentful of its lack of status, and with the ability to exact revenge.

The abilities Huey displayed as an adult had antecedents in childhood. Descriptions of Huey as a child include disputatious, officious, bossy, ornery, curious, energetic, impudent, eager, smart, a show-off, contemptuous of rules, "a pesterance." Huey began walking at nine months. Before he learned to walk, he perfected a way of rolling off the front porch, unlatching the gate, crawling to the road, and parking himself there to observe passersby. The underside of trains interested him at age eight and, once, bystanders pulled him out just before the train left. His father said that Huey would jump down a well if he could to see what it looked like. "[Huey] was the most restless [of his children]," he said, "the most enterprising one."[45] Olive was the sibling assigned to watch him. A frequent cry in the family was "Run, Ollie, run! There he goes again."

One of his neighbors said that, if there were a parade, Huey would throw a rock at the elephants just to get attention. If he couldn't pitch, he wouldn't play. If old-timers in town were playing checkers, he would interject and suggest moves. When his father told a story, Huey would interrupt and finish it for him.[46]

Huey would sneak over to the Baptist Church and ring its bell, in the absence of a church service or fire.[47] The appearance of telephones was an event, with Huey's pals goading him into trying the new device that had been purchased by a shop owner. In response to the operator's "Number please," Huey could only say that he wanted to see how it sounded: "Sounds funny, don't it?" When the owner of the phone suddenly appeared, Huey, frightened, took off running.[48]

Neighbors recalled seeing Huey's mother herding him to school with a peach tree switch. In response to a suggestion that she whip him into submission, she sighed that she would have to whip him to death. Twice he ran away from home, once traveling fifty miles by train. Remembering the story of the Prodigal Son, he expected a warm reception from his family upon his return. Instead, his sister in a shrill voice shouted, "Welcome home, tramp!"[49]

Within his family, Huey was closest to his younger brother, Earl, but idolized his oldest brother, Julius. Julius was fourteen years older than Huey, attended college and then law school, and became a lawyer. Julius brought books home from college for Huey and considered himself Huey's mentor.

Huey read Shakespeare, several Victor Hugo novels, the works of the Romano-Jewish scholar Josephus, the autobiography of Renaissance artist Benvenuto Cellini, Dickens, Poe, Longfellow, Balzac, Scott's *Ivanhoe,* Goldsmith's *The Deserted Village, The Count of Monte Cristo* by Dumas, biographies of Napoleon, Caesar, and Frederick the Great, Ridpath's *History of the World,* the *Saturday Evening Post,* Henley's poem *Invictus,* and the racist novels of Reconstruction by Dixon, an exceptional reading list for his time and place.[50] Cellini's rollicking romantic and business adventures and his resourcefulness in meeting challenges can be enjoyed today, and Huey told one friend that Cellini was the greatest man who ever lived.[51] Huey liked to copy "really elegant sentences" from books that he read and write them in the back of each book by page number, and then he would "go back and get them fairly well in mind." Huey typed excerpts from Cellini's autobiography, proof that he considered them important. Some excerpts:

(1) Even so it may be seen that God keeps account of the good and the bad and gives to each one what he merits.
(2) He was the most loyal friend, the wisest, the most worthy, the most discreet, the most affectionate that I have ever known.

(3) Cats of a good breed mouse better when they are fat than starving; and likewise honest men who possess some talent exercise it to far nobler purport when they have the wherewithal to live abundantly. . . . genius and talent, at their birth, come into this world lean and scabby.
(4) Know then, that men like Benvenuto, unique in their profession, stand above the law.
(5) Laws cannot be imposed on him who is the master of the law.
(6) From this incident we may learn to know how evil fortune exerts her rage against a poor right-minded man, and how the strumpet, luck, can help a miserable rascal.
(7) As for dying, I knew for certainty that die I must; a little earlier or a little later was a matter of supreme indifference to me.

An advertisement about Julius Caesar found among Huey's papers noted that Caesar amassed great power through force of personality. Huey underlined that sentence.[52]

Brother Earl was slower mentally but physically bigger and tougher than Huey. The two boys slept and played together, with Huey planning their activities, often goading neighborhood boys into confrontation. Once Huey provoked two boys who began to beat him up. Earl liked to fight, and he stepped in to help. But when Earl looked up, Huey was disappearing down the road in a cloud of dust. Huey avoided hog-killing time because "he had an aversion to seeing anything killed." Earl, to the contrary, was always on hand to help.

Called a physical coward for most of his life, Huey nevertheless provided an exception to prove the rule. Having developed a crush on a schoolgirl, Huey waited outside the school for her and carried her books home with her for several days. A rival for her affections decided not to wait outside, but to go in and get her books, co-opting Huey. Enraged, the next day Huey bumped his rival, the challenge to a fight. Another classmate intervened to formally promote the fight, complete with ticket sales, a referee, and timed rounds. The two pugilists took turns bloodying each other's faces and knocking each other down until the referee called the fight a draw. The ticket seller made money. The girl married someone else.[53]

Baptist religious services dominated Sunday mornings and nights. Wednesdays were committed to prayer meetings. Family members read at least a chapter of the Bible daily at dinner. Huey accepted all religious obligations, including making a "decision for Christ." He was baptized by full immersion in Crawford's Pond, attended services, and took the temperance pledge (several times), but confessed in his autobiography that he did so under "compulsion."[54]

Huey's mother hoped he would become a preacher. Credited as a pillar of the local church, she sent Huey on charitable missions with food to support other families (Black and white) who were having financial difficulty. Huey was capable of charitable acts, once giving his entire week's wages of three dollars to the church for three straight weeks after he was baptized.[55] He once rigged a candy-weighing machine so he got twice the candy that he paid for, but guilt made him give all the candy away.[56] Religion didn't prevent Huey from smoking and chewing tobacco at a young age. Sharing a buggy ride with his father, a plug of tobacco escaped Huey's pocket. His father took it away from him and said, "If you stay alive until you are twenty-one, it will be the wonder of this world."[57]

None of the Long men internalized what we would think of as normal religious virtues, even though Huey studied the Bible and could quote it by chapter and verse. Julius, Shan, Huey, and Earl all gambled or were criticized for corruption, drinking, or adultery. The religion of *The Count of Monte Cristo* might be a clue to Huey's theology. In this revenge fantasy, an unjustly imprisoned man escaped and found a buried treasure. As a "superman" who stood above all governments and societies, aided by servants who obeyed his every command, the self-created Count exacted revenge against those who had imprisoned him. As an adult, Huey once told a friend that the Count knew how to hate and, "until you know how to hate, you'll never get anywhere in this world."[58] The Count's hatred was deep and patient, forged from the injustice of his long imprisonment. He meticulously planned and executed his revenge, manipulating the financial markets of the day, cooperating with the criminal underworld, arranging a kidnapping, and deceiving even those who loved him, all done with the assistance and approval of Divine Providence.

The church afforded Huey the chance to sing. With his sister, Olive, he often performed at family gatherings, belting out "Rose Marie," "Three Little Words," "Pretty Red Wing," "Old Black Joe," and other songs of the time. The first time Edmund Talbot remembers seeing Huey as a boy, he was singing at an auction outside a country store.[59] As an adult, Huey claimed never to have suffered from stage fright. Some family members thought he would become a great performer.

In his autobiography, Huey implied that he worked on his father's farm, hating it: "In the field, the rows were long; the sun was hot; there was little companionship. . . . Rising before the sun, we toiled until dark." His "every sympathy" went out "to those who toil," in part because, at age eight, he witnessed a farm foreclosure auction. The farmer pleaded for one more chance to grow another crop. No one would bid for the farm. Right before the auction closed, however, the debt holder bid the amount of the debt and the farmer was ousted from his farm. "It seemed criminal," Huey wrote.[60]

Huey's siblings reported, however, that Huey avoided farm work and that it was all he could do to plow to the end of a single row.[61] Once, Old Hu promised each child a cash reward for picking one hundred pounds of cotton. All his siblings did it, but Huey couldn't or wouldn't, and didn't, and the others had to pitch in and fill his sack. One farmer refused to pay the young Huey by weight of cotton picked because he caught Huey slipping a hooked watermelon into his cotton sack. There was nothing to do after each hard day on the farm, said the adult Huey, except eat supper, listen to the whip-poor-wills, and go to bed.[62] His siblings, however, wondered if Huey had ever spent a hard day working on the farm.

Huey worked hard at jobs away from home and the farm, however. Huey got a job as a bakery-truck driver and worked thirteen-hour days, six days a week, for three dollars per week. He carried water to bricklayers at a construction site until a falling brick knocked him unconscious and out of the job. Huey once sawed wood for the winter at the farm, his industriousness attributed to a hired man also assigned to the task.[63] The man was a great storyteller, and that was enough to keep Huey interested and productive. Once Shan told Huey that Chinese people liked to eat rats. The enterprising Huey therefore brought a wheelbarrow full of dead rodents to the local Chinese laundry. But he had been misled: the proprietor chased him out of the shop and threw his flatiron at him, yelling, "Git out. Git out. Chinee no eat rats!"[64]

When he was thirteen, Huey worked as a printer's devil, apprenticed to mix ink and fetch type, for the *Baptist Monthly Guardian,* and then the *Southern Sentinel.* The editor let him smoke and supplied the tobacco and 75 cents for eleven hours of work each day.[65] Type was set by hand. With his excellent memory Huey could set four galleys a day, whereas three was normal. He wrote some news items. Whatever interest Huey had in becoming a newspaper journalist or publisher was not sustained, although he applied for a journalist job when he was eighteen and once inquired about the cost of buying a newspaper.[66] In a story that may be apocryphal, Rupert Peyton says that Huey once set type for a "shirt sale" but left out the "r"; the advertisement had to be cut out of the paper before it was distributed.[67]

Huey once told his pals that he could sell anything to anybody, and convinced his audience when, on the spot, he launched into a sales pitch for a second-hand coffin to an elderly Black man. The man was convinced to follow him to his barn, where the coffin was located. There Huey ended the experiment because the coffin was imaginary.[68] Huey expressed no remorse at fooling the man.

Huey's best boyhood friend was Harley Bozeman. Bozeman's family moved to Winnfield in 1905. He met Huey in a shoe store. Huey advised against a purchase of shoes advertised as waterproof because the merchant was a cheat, and the shoes would leak. Bozeman bought the shoes anyway. Huey subjected him to a barrage of questions: What's your name? Is that your family's house being built? What grade are you in? What books have you read? They became best friends.[69]

When Huey was about fifteen, a Texas bookseller came to Winnfield. He had advertised for an auctioneer and was momentarily nonplussed when Huey met him at the train station, saying, "I'm the man you're looking for." Joining an impressive list of predecessors such as John James Audubon, Jay Gould, Bret Harte, Rutherford B. Hayes, and Daniel Webster,[70] Huey and Harley assisted him and took their pay in books. When the bookseller concluded his efforts, Harley and Huey read and then peddled their consignment, riding trains or driving a rented horse and buggy to other towns, lugging the books in big trunks, and staying in hotels, going door to door during the day and holding auctions at night. Success was small until Huey traded a book for a mandolin plus lessons on how to play it. Mastering it in an afternoon just outside of town under the shade of a big tree, he then attracted a crowd for the auction by playing tunes he knew, singing, and telling jokes. Then they sold every book that they didn't want to retain, quite a feat considering Louisiana's illiteracy rate.[71] Huey also traveled to the neighboring town of Dodson to date teachers years older than he was, "paining the mores"[72] of that community.

Looking back, Huey explained his entrance into politics simply: the first he knew about it, he was in it. Julius may have used the teenage Huey as a helper in the political campaign of 1908, but Julius later denied it.[73] Huey helped an older friend in Winnfield win office as a tick inspector.[74] Old Hu used Huey as his lieutenant to defeat a railroad tax proposal to have the town pay some of the cost of extending a line into the town. Something about this "smelled," said Old Hu, who thought the railroad would pocket the tax money and abandon the railway or that it would build the railway anyway without the tax money. With Huey's help, Old Hu defeated the railroad's proposal, and this railroad and its owner earned Huey's undying enmity.[75]

In school, Huey did brash things such as signing his name "The Honorable Huey P. Long" and pinning a sign to his arm after a vaccination: "Don't touch this arm. Vaccinated." He once read a governor's Thanksgiving Proclamation substituting his name for the governor's, after which his nickname was "Governor." He suggested that one girl kiss him so that she could say the famous Huey Long kissed her.[76]

Harley said that he and Huey received top grades, and that they skipped the seventh grade.[77] Despite protests of classmates, the teacher, a bit of a maverick, allowed them to skip the grade after they correctly answered her qualifying questions. In a remark also attributed to Julius, Huey said that maybe he wasn't so smart; maybe there were just a lot of dumb people in the world.[78]

Once, Huey improperly obtained the teacher's manual of a Latin short-story book and memorized the translation. When asked to translate a chapter, Huey perpetrated what Williams aptly noted was a brutal yet entertaining affront to the rules of the school: he gave the translation, perfectly, but the teacher noticed that, while reciting, his book was shut. Questioning him how he translated with his book closed, he gave a smart aleck answer: "I got x-ray eyes." She asked him to start on the next chapter and he did; then asked him to skip several chapters ahead, but he hadn't memorized that far and said nothing. "What happened to your x-ray eyes?" said the teacher. "I must've blown a fuse," Huey replied.[79]

Eschewing contact sports, Huey enjoyed track, but put most of his extracurricular efforts into public speaking and debate, also an interest of Harley Bozeman. Huey and Harley were chosen by the town to debate traveling socialist lecturers when Huey was fifteen. The debaters traveled to the debate site and boarded in the same house. Huey continued his argument with the socialist well into the night. Returning to school the next day, Huey proclaimed victory: "Vini, vidi, vici."[80]

The two of them also competed in the state speech tournament. In 1909, they lost in the preliminaries. Next year Huey signed up for speech and Harley for debate. Leading Baton Rouge citizens hosted the contestants. Huey stayed with the superintendent of education, T. H. Harris, and predicted that he would win if he got "justice." He got everyone up at 6 a.m., left his clothes on the floor, arrived late for every meal, left his luggage for others to carry, and introduced himself to the entire family and the cook. Despite practice in the woods of Winnfield and his selection of an oration of Henry W. Grady, advocate of the "New South," he lost again in the preliminaries. Incensed, he sought out Harley, who was getting ready to debate whether women should have the right to vote. While explaining the injustice of his loss to three girls to Harley, he got the idea to enter the debate, reasoning that women had too many rights now, which was why no boy could win the tournament. He then pulled one of the judges into the hallway and talked him into letting him enter the debate despite the rules that forbade it. In the debate, he gave an impromptu speech against women's rights that brought down the house and won third place.

When he left, he promised to return the Harrises' kindness when he was governor, U.S. senator, and president of the United States. After an absence of eighteen years, he met Harris again at his gubernatorial inaugural ball, reminded him of his promise, and asked by name about each of his four children, and the cook, Lily.[81]

The third-place finish entitled Huey to a scholarship to Louisiana State University, which he said he loved, but couldn't use. Huey never graduated from high school, a precondition to enrollment at LSU. The principal of Winnfield's high school had added a twelfth grade and required completion of it to qualify for graduation. This was contrary to the direction of the State Board of Education. Huey rebelled and circulated a petition in town, calling for the principal's removal. The principal was removed, but his requirements stood. Huey never graduated.[82] Huey also lacked the money for living expenses at LSU. One wonders whether Huey resented his father spending money on a big house when just two years later he lacked the funds to send him to college. Huey decided to leave home, age sixteen. He would have to support himself, but how?

## *Two*

# EARLY PATTERNS

## CRAZY OR A GENIUS

Between the turn of the century and World War I, modern salesmanship was born. Salesmen were agents of change, bringing new products from the modern, urban centers to the rural, isolated ones. Peddlers gave way to drummers, then salesmen.

Systematized techniques of selling were taught. The sales structure was to attract attention, maintain interest, and create desire. Flirting, humor, wit, curiosity-inducing statements, and public relations events attracted attention. Words were malleable, language was expedient, but ideally concise, direct, forcible, and descriptive. A "circus whirl" of talk could "build a fence" around a customer and create desire. Spontaneity and improvisation were essential.

Experts studied the characteristics of a good salesman. Enthusiasm was a prized trait, a powerful economic force. It was compared with and may have been conceived from observing evangelism. Enthusiasm was associated with other desired traits of boldness, confidence, energy, optimism, hustle, pluck, and grit. Salesmen read peoples' faces, were good mixers, engaging, and knew the latest jokes and stories.

Good salesmen excited fascination, even amid doubts about their claims. But the trend was against one-shot sales of the peddler and in favor of repeat business, which necessitated the development and maintenance of relationships and trust.[1]

Traveling salesmen then were "lustrous figures of the day, who wore the latest cuts of tight trousers [and] had a way with the ladies."[2] They faced and overcame travel hardships. They knew about new distribution methods and brand development that threatened the wholesaler and how credit worked. Worried about salesmen on the road, the Gideons in 1908 began their Bible-placement program in hotel rooms.[3]

James Guild wrote the earliest sales journal in 1818. It recorded his reasons for entering the profession: his "disposition would not allow [him] to work on a farm."[4] Huey was similarly disinclined to farmwork.

The records don't show what Huey did immediately after school in 1910. But Bozeman found a job selling Cottolene, cooking oil made from cottonseed oil and beef suet. The N. K. Fairbank Company of Chicago made Cottolene, along with Gold Dust washing powder and bath and laundry soaps. Cottolene was advertised in magazines. The company published a cookbook featuring recipes using Cottolene.[5] Bozeman had taken a training course at company facilities in New Orleans, probably learning a sales script that reflected the standard sales structure. The company sent him on the road as a junior salesman.

Cottolene salesmen solicited orders from grocers and from housewives door to door. Grocers would fill the orders obtained from the housewives. Posters and cookbooks were offered for display at the grocery stores. Most housewives at the time used lard or butter, so a good deal of resistance to this new product had to be overcome to make a sale.[6]

Victor Thorssen was Bozeman's supervisor. His team of junior salesmen worked northern Louisiana, earning salaries that started at nineteen dollars per week, less hotel fare. In July 1910, two of the crew quit. Bozeman recommended Huey as a replacement. Huey joined them in Monroe, in the northeastern part of Louisiana, on a Sunday without decent clothes and with his possessions in a shoebox. Thorssen was dubious. Bozeman promised to buy Huey decent clothes. Thorssen reluctantly agreed to a one-week tryout.

Thorssen took the newly tailored Huey and another trainee, Louis Grieff, out on the road to teach them his techniques. After three or four house calls, Huey abruptly told Thorssen that he had gotten "the hang of this selling racket. How about cutting me loose, working one side of a street and you and Mr. Grieff the other side?" Thorssen agreed. At the time, the company considered fifteen orders a day good and twenty orders outstanding. At the end of the day, Huey turned in twenty-six orders; Grieff and Thorssen had fourteen. Twenty-five years later, Thorssen, an accountant living in Indiana, vividly recalled Huey: a gangling boy, not very attractive, fresh off the farm, very well read, with a gift of gab and a lot of nerve. Everyone remembered him after one meeting.[7]

Huey led Thorssen's crew in sales. He liked overcoming resistance. He knew the habits, beliefs, and manners of his customers. It is likely that Huey improvised beyond any sales script offered by the company. Sometimes he interpreted the Bible to forbid cooking with lard but not eating pork, whereas Cottolene was pure and not blasphemous. Huey sometimes cooked dinner for families to secure an order. Grieff was good at display advertising, so Huey went with him to stores early to set up displays. Grieff wasn't as good at door-to-door selling, and Huey would split his sales orders with him. Grieff had theatrical training. In the evenings, Huey listened to his dramatic readings.[8]

When the crew reached Alexandria, the company suggested that Thorssen hold baking contests to promote Cottolene. The company asked Thorssen to solicit prizes from local merchants in exchange for advertising at the event, a task that the gentle and timid Thorssen delegated to Huey. Huey accepted the challenge because "gall was one of his specialties, and rebuffs did not affect him at all." He collected bags of flour, a ham, buckets of coffee, a rocking chair, a floor lamp, and an electric iron, among other grocery items. Thorssen was master of ceremonies, Huey was the judge, and the contests were successful.

Huey met his future wife at a baking contest. Rose McConnell was a stenographer for an insurance company. She had learned to cook from her mother, who was originally from southern Louisiana and had mastered French cooking. Huey's approach wasn't suave, but it was nervy and characteristically confrontational: "I bet you didn't bake this cake," he said. When she said she did, he asked her for a date to "prove it."[9] Huey awarded a prize to Rose and, diplomatically, another one to her mother.[10]

Rose liked Huey's quick mind and excellent memory. Huey liked her looks and told her she had qualities that he lacked: the practical, common touch. They both loved music. Huey told Bozeman he had discovered his future wife. Their courtship lasted over two years, however. Rose disliked Huey's controlling nature: at parties he prohibited her from having too much fun with others and would rush across a room to grab a drink from her hands. She learned not to argue with him because he pouted until he got his way.[11] After giving her a tiny—the size of a pinpoint, not a pin—diamond ring, Huey requested its return, saying he wanted to date another girl. Later he returned it, saying the other girl didn't look the same. Years later, Huey told a friend that he had loved a girl of the upper class, but she wasn't able to follow his destiny or understand his crudeness. Political calculation motivated both the breakup with the upper-class girl and the courtship of Rose.[12]

In September 1910, Huey became unable to support a wife or even a girlfriend. The company terminated Thorssen and everyone else except Huey and Harley. The teenagers thought they were destined for promotion from junior to regular salesman (which would let them sell the other products rather than just Cottolene) and a raise to $175 a month. They redoubled their efforts. At Thanksgiving, the company dismissed them.[13] The *Southern Sentinel,* which had taken over the *Winnfield Comrade,* welcomed Huey home and congratulated him for making good.[14]

Julius recommended that Huey complete high school and then attend law school. Huey refused to reenroll in Winnfield. The family arranged for him to go to Shreveport, instead, in January 1911, where he stayed with an aunt, attended high school, and continued his courtship of Rose. When the chemistry teacher asked Huey for an example of a chemical compound, he answered Cottolene, and then recited his sales pitch.[15] But the school told him that he couldn't graduate because he had not attended the fall semester. Huey nevertheless stayed in Shreveport, attending school only during the morning, and got a job in the afternoon.

Notwithstanding that he lacked any knowledge of shorthand, Huey became a stenographer for a plumbing company. When his boss doubted his qualifications, Huey proposed a tryout, invented symbols, used a notepad for effect, and relied on his memory and writing skills to produce letters. The plumber opined that "them letters" Huey produced were the best he had ever written.

In February 1911, Bozeman got an offer to sell for the Houston Packing Company. It sold cured meats, lard, and canned goods to wholesalers. Before going to Houston, Bozeman went to Shreveport to see Huey. Huey asked Bozeman to get him a job there, too, if he could, since he was making only nine dollars per week as a stenographer. Bozeman racked up so many orders that the company asked him to recommend others with similar talents. Bozeman suggested Huey. Huey left Shreveport for the job as soon as he got the offer.[16]

Originally working in Austin, Huey performed so impressively that the company sent him to Little Rock to supervise sales in Arkansas. For the first time in his life, Huey felt he "had hit a bed of ease."[17] He stayed in the best hotels in Arkansas or with farmers outside of town to save money, traveling by foot, train, or horse and buggy. He recorded the names and addresses of his friends and customers.[18]

The company thereafter expanded into Memphis and assigned Huey to its new office. He resided in the luxurious Gayoso Hotel. But the cotton crop and therefore all business were poor that year. Huey secured no significant orders. At the end of August, he was terminated. In his autobiography, Huey claimed that he turned in a good volume of orders but charged too many expenses and was "summarily discharged" after not heeding warnings to trim them,[19] confessing to insubordination and padded expense accounts rather than failure.

Huey also wrote that he returned to Houston to seek reinstatement and, when that failed, sought other employment in Houston. When that failed, he sought work again in Memphis. Williams says he remained in Memphis, continued to live at the Gayoso, and looked for another job. Finding none, his money dwindled.

Huey moved into a cheaper rooming house but still could not find work. Prevailing on the proprietor for credit, he lasted a few more days at the rooming house, giving up his suitcase of clothes as security. Two days later, still unemployed, he couldn't pay for his room and was physically kicked out of the premises, denied even the courtesy of getting clean clothes from his suitcase: "Git going, you little bum, I don't never want to see no more of you."[20]

Now Huey struggled to survive. He slept in parks, depots, and railroad yards, and ate free food sometimes offered by bars. Once he convinced a company to hire him as a painter despite his lack of overalls or equipment. He started to paint the wall from the bottom up. The supervisor told him he admired his gumption but couldn't employ him. A kindly policeman rousted him from a park bench one night and referred him to the Salvation Army home, where he stayed for several nights. Getting a job breaking up boxcars—back-breaking work—proved too physically taxing, so he finally did the unthinkable, asking his family and Bozeman for help.

His mother proposed divinity school. His older brother, Shan, lived in Shawnee, Oklahoma, where he practiced dentistry, and where Oklahoma Baptist University was located. Shan agreed to supply the money and Huey agreed to attend the university, so he traveled to Shawnee late in September, without money, with a frayed suit, and with his few personal items wrapped in a newspaper. When he arrived, he bragged that he was on his way back up.

While he may have attended classes at the university, there is no record of his enrollment. During the Christmas holidays, he told Shan that he didn't want to be a preacher and asked him for money to take law-school classes at the University of Oklahoma at Norman. Shan provided a hundred dollars.

Years before, Huey's brother Julius had won the money for his law-school tuition in a gambling house. Probably wanting to emulate this success, Huey stopped at Oklahoma City on his way to Norman. Playing roulette at a local gambling den on New Year's Eve, he lost his money. On New Year's Day, 1912, Huey woke up broke, without money to pay for registration, books, or hotel.

Desperate, he looked for a job. The owner of Dawson Produce Company, Mr. K. W. Dawson, a "serious but kindly faced gentleman," moved by Huey's ambition to attend law school, agreed to hire him on January 2 to solicit orders for produce in Norman and a few other towns, and gave him his produce price list. Even after pawning his overcoat to pay his hotel bill, Huey lacked the money to take the train to Norman, so he walked eighteen miles in the January cold—while "snow and sleet covered the ground" and the wind "was cold and cutting"—without an overcoat, arriving about midnight, warming himself by a stove at an oil mill, and grabbing a few hours of sleep in a cottonseed bin.[21]

Early on January 3, spending his last three nickels on breakfast, he ventured forth to sell produce. At the store of S. H. McCall, he secured an order for a carload of potatoes. Trying to place the order with a collect call, it was declined. Pawning a leather purse that "had been put to no use whatever," Huey obtained coins to place the phone call. When his call went through, Dawson blithely told him he didn't have any potatoes and couldn't fill the order. Having "walked" and "starved" and "disposed of everything of value [he] had on the face of the earth,"[22] Huey exploded: "The list you gave me yesterday has got spuds on it. If you did not have any spuds, why didn't you mark them off the list? You caused me to spend my last two bits on this damn phone call."[23] Luckily, McCall was listening and offered to buy other items that were on the list. This appeased Dawson, who otherwise might have fired Huey on the spot. But because Huey would not receive the commissions immediately, he was still penniless.

At the railroad depot, Huey started a conversation with a "well groomed, rather stout looking gentleman," a stranger named R. O. Jackson. He told Jackson that he lacked the funds to travel by train, that he had walked into town, and that he planned to study law and work part-time for Dawson. Moved, Jackson offered Huey a loan of twenty dollars. Huey said he could survive with five dollars and, if he couldn't repay him, he would at least have saved Jackson fifteen. After securing the five dollars from Jackson, Huey told his brother that unexpected expenses had left him short, and his brother sent another seventy-five. Jackson used his influence with the local merchants to help Huey make sales and persuaded his brother-in-law to extend credit to Huey so he could purchase law books.[24]

In describing this low point in his life, Huey's autobiography omitted the requests to his family and Bozeman, the plan to attend the Baptist University, and Shan's provision of funds. Huey described the events involving Dawson and Jackson, in contrast (although he omitted cursing Dawson). They were friends for the rest of his life. When Huey wrote his autobiography twenty years later, he inscribed a copy for Jackson: "To my dear old friend R. O. Jackson with my love and appreciation for a real favor which can never be repaid by me—Sincerely Huey P. Long."[25] And when Jackson thereafter fell on hard times, Huey got him a job in Louisiana.[26] Dawson hosted a reception for Huey in Oklahoma City days before Huey's death.

Once he settled in at law school, Huey had some happy times. He made lifetime friends. They nicknamed him "Hugh Hanna Honolulu" because he decorated his room with lights. The job with Dawson paid about a hundred dollars per month, although he worked hard for his money. Sometimes he walked nine miles to the outlying towns, which made him late for or miss classes. On weekends he traveled to Oklahoma City and renewed his gambling contacts, with better results. One of the gambling houses hired him as a dealer and dice man. The money he made from gambling supplemented his commissions from Dawson.

Omitted from his autobiography—but not from other interviews Huey gave as an adult—was his entry into campus politics. The campaign of 1912 for the Democratic presidential nomination pitted Woodrow Wilson, governor of New Jersey and former president of Princeton University, against Missourian Bennett Champ Clark, Speaker of the House of Representatives. The fraternities on campus lined up for Wilson. The independents lacked the leadership to do anything until Huey issued a circular charging that Wilson was a complete failure as a lawyer and successful only as a schoolteacher. Huey called for a mass meeting of the independents to organize for Clark. Enough independents showed up to form a club, and they elected Huey president.

The fraternity leaders called for a campus-wide convention to demonstrate Wilson's support. Huey was outnumbered. He called his friends from town to swell his delegate count, but the fraternity leaders recognized the trick and insisted on a roll call. Huey then bolted the convention and formed his own rump caucus, but he left a few of his delegates behind to vote until the end for William Jennings Bryan. Thus, the public perceived Huey's group as unanimous for Clark, but the fraternity convention, divided, with a mere plurality for Wilson. In a political fight, when you've got nothing on your side, Huey advised, "start a row in the opposition camp."[27]

Huey audited some law courses and received Cs in others. Later Huey said that gambling diversions distracted him from learning law.[28] In his autobiography, Huey said that, at the end of the spring 1912 semester, he took another selling job, intending to return in the fall, but incurred certain other, unnamed obligations that prevented it, which caused "much grief and heartache."[29]

At the end of the spring term, Huey stayed with Shan, who had moved to a nearby town, and helped a congressional candidate that Shan supported by writing and distributing circulars. When Wilson won the Democratic Convention, which ended July 2, 1912, Williams reports that Huey joined with the fraternity leaders to start the first Young Democrats organization and was elected as its vice president. This might be an error, however, because school was not in session in July and Huey never returned in the fall.

It may be that Huey left Oklahoma because he observed that all lawyers and politicians there were broke or because he was discouraged by the lengthy process to get a degree. Huey asked Bozeman to get him a job. Huey wanted to make money.

Bozeman was working for the Faultless Starch Company of Kansas City and obliged Huey by asking his supervisor, John Nesbitt, to hire him. Nesbitt was considering opening a Memphis office, met Huey in Texarkana for a tryout of two weeks, and was sold almost immediately, saying he had never worked harder in his life and that Huey was "the damndest character I ever met. I don't know whether he is crazy or a genius."[30]

Once he got the job, Huey promptly returned to the Gayoso Hotel and directed a crew of salesmen and advertising men who covered four states. Huey's salary climbed to $125 a month plus expenses, his highest compensation yet. Only once did he participate in politics, fighting in an election-eve brawl in Memphis in November 1912. He fought on behalf of the Democratic machine boss of Memphis, Ed Crump, who bailed him out of jail and promised to return the favor someday.[31]

During the Christmas holiday, Huey visited Shreveport to ask Rose to marry. What happened next remains a mystery. The police arrested Huey and charged him with carrying a concealed weapon in the African American red-light district of Shreveport. Bozeman bailed him out, and Julius, who was then a district attorney in Winnfield, got the charges dropped. In his autobiography, Huey claimed an alibi: he was attending *Lohengrin* with

Rose. Her retention of the theater ticket stubs and statements from witnesses seated near them secured his release.[32] According to author Hair, however, *Lohengrin* only played on December 16, four days before the incident. In newspaper reports in 1928, Huey said that a boyhood friend who resembled him admitted that he had done it but asked Huey not to expose him. This "double" fled to Texas where he became a successful businessman. As a loyal friend Huey proudly refused to divulge the man's name.[33]

Bozeman's account of the incident—that the charges against Huey were a frame-up—rings truer than Hair's. Although newspapers reported the arrest in 1928 and Huey included it in his autobiography in 1933, no political opponent ever mentioned it, nor did his brother Julius, who, in later years, accused Huey of every other vice. Hair speculates that Rose refused to marry him then in part because of this incident,[34] but Williams says the false charges drew them closer together, so Huey invited Rose to meet his family.

Visiting his family, Rose underwent the "critical scrutiny of his mother and his sisters." The family advised Huey not to marry so young. Rose decided to wait. Huey went back to Memphis irritated. Rose was hurt. Friends thought the relationship was over.

Later in the spring, however, Huey renewed his entreaties with telegrams and letters. Rose thought he was drinking and went to save him from himself. This time he won her hand, and they married in Memphis on April 12, 1913, the day she arrived.[35]

The preacher who officiated at the wedding said Huey had a "stirring personality."[36] Huey had borrowed money from a friend to pay for the ring and the marriage license and had nothing left to pay the preacher. Rose stepped up with the money. Unlike Huey, Rose was gentle, tactful, calm, classy, and disciplined with money. She remained in the background of the man with the stirring personality.

After they married, they took an apartment in Memphis, where they stayed until October. Again, Huey's company suffered economic reverses (the price of cotton dropped when World War I started in Europe) and eliminated the Memphis office, assigning Huey to go on the road in Texas, Oklahoma, and south Louisiana.[37] And Huey's mother died at age fifty-two of typhoid fever. Huey and Rose moved back to the Long home in Winnfield.

In 1914, the owner of Faultless Starch died. All company activities ceased while his estate was settled. Huey obtained another job immediately but for a company that left him open to ridicule.

The Chattanooga Medicine Company sold patent medicines, including

Wine of Cardui to eliminate menstrual cramps and stimulate the blood, and Black Draught, a laxative. According to the American Medical Association, Wine of Cardui consisted of 40 proof alcohol and was a "vicious fraud," one of many perpetrated on the public in the era before regulation by the Food and Drug Administration. The AMA lost a defamation suit brought by the company, but the damages awarded were 1 cent. In south Louisiana, the company employed Dudley LeBlanc, later Huey's political rival and still later founder of the patent medicine Hadacol.[38] Economic conditions worsened, however, and the company released Huey soon after he was hired.

Out of a job and with a wife to support, Huey called Julius in a panic. Julius took a train that afternoon to Alexandria to meet him. The prospects for another selling job were slight. Julius advised law school at Tulane in New Orleans. He promised to loan Huey the money to attend. This pledge by "a brother" was even acknowledged in his autobiography.[39] Huey decided to change course, this time for good.

The term "fractal" describes a shape or object that has the same structure regardless of its size; that is, whether it is microscopic or the size of a continent, breaking off any piece of it shows it to be the same structurally. Huey's career—not just his personal characteristics, but also how his environment interacted with him—is as close to a fractal as any human being is likely to get. Aspects of his selling career recurred: early success based on talent, gall, and confidence; bad luck, overconfidence, or carelessness resulting in a crisis or reverse; the resilience, guile, and energy to surmount it; a willingness to change course; and personal growth.

It is not possible to know whether Huey selected particular sentences from Cellini because they confirmed his previously existing thoughts or whether Cellini's ideas were so powerful that they made an impression on Huey. Either way, one can see the relationship between those sentences and the way Huey lived, the things he did, and his thoughts about his life and career.

Similarly, no one knows how many salesmanship principles Huey was taught, even though the writings advocating techniques of salesmanship and desired characteristics of salesmen were extensive by the time he entered the profession; how many he learned on his own from trial and error; or whether he was a born salesman. Whether salesmanship was encoded in his DNA or learned, all his life he used the techniques and lived the lifestyle of a salesman.

A salesman initiates cold calls; Huey the lawyer and politician initiated cold calls on political leaders, newspapermen, and other influential people. As a salesman, Huey enjoyed hotel life; as a politician, he spent more time in hotels away from his family than he did in houses that he owned. Once while working as a lawyer, he was so engrossed in a case that he moved out of his house and into a hotel for two months so he could concentrate on it.

The type of humor and publicity stunts Huey produced as a public figure were the kind that someone hanging around a hotel would display and owed something to the flair of the cake-baking contests he conducted. The social skills he developed were those of a hotel lodger. Poems he wrote about bedbugs in various hotels amused his friends. He knew how to mix drinks and "cure" someone's hangover. He was a good dancer. As a salesman for Cottolene, Huey cooked dinner for families; the adult Huey would demonstrate how to fix salads or cook potlikker.[40]

A prized skill for a salesman was reading peoples' faces. Years later as a senator, Huey was a dinner guest at Senator Burton K. Wheeler's house. Over the protests of Wheeler's daughter, Huey insisted on removing the flower centerpiece from the dining table so that he could see the faces of those he was talking to.[41] Speaking to newspaper reporters before a speech to ten thousand farmers, Huey said: "I watch faces when I speak. . . . I will study them until I can tell just what every man will do for two hours after he leaves."[42]

The adult Huey was enthusiastic, optimistic, confident, and humorous. He excited fascination amid doubts about his claims. In private conversations, he would tell stories about his salesman days in which he made himself the rascal, beguiling his listeners, both by the stories and because he would tell them. People who disliked him because of his reputation could be charmed upon meeting him once they realized that he was a showman and they decided to enjoy the theatrics.[43] Jokes and stories enlivened the opening of his speeches, much as a salesman tries to develop a rapport to interest someone in buying. Publicity stunts akin to cake-baking contests generated interest in him, attracting the attention he needed so that he could make meaningful presentations.

Huey could overwhelm people with a circus whirl of talk, building a verbal fence around them until they had to agree with him. In part it was a function of energy, in which he would simply outtalk others, wearing away their resistance. In part it was a function of instantaneously analyzing what promise would appeal to a prospect or what his objections were, rebutting each objection or minimizing them by stressing other relevant benefits, an argumentative structure of a salesman.

Huey's most significant characteristics were grit, resiliency, and dedication. Any salesman faces rejection. A good salesman recovers from it and goes on to the next prospect and sometimes returns to the rejecter and tries again. Huey was disappointed by defeat but unfazed: "evil fortune" could rage at a good man, and the "strumpet, luck," could help a rascal. There are many examples of Huey's continued efforts to win over political opponents and rebound from defeat.

Huey's later political campaigns combined modern print and display advertising theories with personal speechmaking as in an advertising campaign. Marketing personnel today emphasize promising benefits, not attributes,[44] and using specific language.[45] Huey made political promises in specific language of benefits. Running for governor, he didn't just advocate support for education, he promised free schoolbooks for children.

His written election material—Huey wrote his own circulars as well as his own speeches—possessed the characteristics of the most effective advertising of his time. In particular, he wrote long headlines and long copy as, for example, Claude Hopkins and David Ogilvy advocated.[46] If they could read, his constituents had the time to read them and, if they didn't read them, nevertheless they knew that Huey had set forth a lot of facts in support of what he was doing.

As a salesman, whether from other political speeches, Mr. Grieff's declamations, or from the Victor Hugo literature that he read, Huey incorporated abstract, educated, or poetic appeals. The adult Huey asserted, "He who falls in this fight falls in the radiance of the future," and he compared the suffering of Louisiana's people to the unrequited love of Longfellow's Evangeline. Huey didn't originate the idea that he needed to speak in the language of his audience *and* above their heads,[47] but this feature of his speeches was effective.

Apart from the personal characteristics he displayed or developed, the four years Huey spent on the road were invaluable. He had traveled all over Louisiana and in other southern states. He met other salesmen, farmers, and merchants and recorded the names of people of all types. He learned, too, that the French Cajuns of southern Louisiana resisted sales pressure and preferred to relax and socialize before doing business.

Huey read the political speeches of popular politicians while still in high school.[48] As a salesman in Arkansas, Huey talked to associates of Arkansas senator Jefferson Davis who, although past his prime, denounced corporations and "potbellied" bankers and asked for the votes of "rednecks" and "hillbillies."[49] (None of the rednecks and hillbillies took offense.) Huey may have seen

Davis's speeches when Davis won reelection in 1912. In Mississippi, Huey may have observed virulent racist and isolationist Senator James K. Vardaman, who dressed in immaculate clothes. (No one resented Vardaman's expensive garb. Vardamen's supporters identified themselves as rednecks and wore red neckerchiefs to his rallies.)[50] He was elected to the U.S. Senate in 1911.[51]

Mississippi's Theodore Bilbo repulsed Huey but used one technique that Huey later adopted. In each town, Bilbo would denounce the richest, most powerful personality. The crowd paid attention to these attacks, and then in the rest of his speech Bilbo aroused their envy and, ultimately, their support. Bilbo had run for lieutenant governor as an ally of Vardaman in 1911.[52]

Senator John Sharp Williams of Mississippi was polished, scholarly, and dignified. Professor Williams reports that he spoke in unmistakable language and had a sharp wit that Huey admired. Given the dates of his campaigns, the only time Huey could have heard him speak was in September 1912, when, as a member of Wilson's Executive Campaign Committee in the East, he delivered eight lectures on Thomas Jefferson at Columbia University in Jackson, Mississippi. The voters reelected Senator Williams in 1916 without opposition, but Huey was off the road by then.[53] It may be that Huey *read* accounts of Senator Williams's (and maybe the other politicians') speeches before, during, and after his sales career.

Law school was a big change from selling. Thinking like a lawyer is a unique way of looking at problems, relationships, and society. Law school and law practice gave Huey additional tools beyond those of a salesman. But the money pledged by Julius for law school wouldn't last forever. Huey had to learn the law fast before his money ran out.

## *Three*

# POLITICAL TRENDS HUEY MEASURED AS HE CAME OF AGE

Law school usually lasts for three years, but Huey had neither the money nor the high-school diploma to take the three-year course. He was enrolled as a special non-credit student, and the plan was for him to take classes for two semesters and study on his own until he could pass the bar. Most Louisiana lawyers at the time passed the bar without graduating from law school.[1]

Julius loaned Huey $400, and state Senator S. J. Harper loaned him another $250. Julius imposed conditions for his loan: the budget was $50 per month and Rose had to accompany him to New Orleans to control the checkbook. Julius probably didn't know that Huey had borrowed money from Harper.

Harper was a Winnfield character, a politician, cotton buyer, and amateur scholar, which, Williams says, qualified him "as an eccentric." An opponent of corporate domination of government, high heels for women, and the Bible, as well as an antiwar isolationist and a believer in the Protocols of the Elders of Zion (fraudulent papers that supposedly documented the secret plan of Jews for world domination), it is surprising that he was elected to anything. Harper loaned Huey the money, he told his daughter, because Huey had a brilliant mind and needed help and, besides, he might need a lawyer someday.

Rose vetoed Huey's selection of a flat on Prytania Street for $25 a month as too costly. They chose a dingy, two-room apartment on Carrollton Avenue for $15 a month. The kitchen was also their study and sitting room. The breakfast room doubled as their bedroom.

The law consists of constitutions (the U.S. Constitution and, for Louisiana lawyers, the Louisiana Constitution), statutes passed by the U.S. Congress and state legislatures, and the written opinions of judges in past controversies. Scholars collect in textbooks by subject the most relevant judicial opinions from past cases to illustrate the points of law. Subjects include torts (personal injury actions), contracts, constitutional law, wills and estates (succession), property (real estate), criminal law, and corporations, plus courses in procedure (how to file a lawsuit and proceed to trial), evidence (how to introduce competent proof in a trial), and other more specialized subjects. Professors lecture about the various principles but also engage in Socratic dialogue, in which the implications of the principles are explored by argument and discussion in class.

In Louisiana, much of the law is contained in statutory codes (based on the Napoleonic Code of France), so students had to learn the codes. Constitutional provisions were similarly studied. Judicial decisions decided disputes for which the codes or constitution lacked a definitive answer, and these cases were analyzed.

Having a good memory allows the recall of the cases and the arguments that should be made. An analytical mind correctly applies the memorized principles to the facts. The class load Huey took was lighter than a regular student but only because he had to read most textbooks outside of class. He did not take examinations.

Notwithstanding Huey's tight budget and inability to register as a regular student, he had some advantages that other would-be lawyers lacked. He had already attended several law classes at the University of Oklahoma. Because Julius had studied law, passed the bar, and was a practicing lawyer, he could and did recommend what to study.[2] Rose was a big help. Huey would take notes of lectures, read the textbooks, case decisions, and law review commentaries recommended by Julius or professors and then dictate an abstract to her. She typed them up and then Huey memorized them. Several of these abstracts are in his papers at LSU. Typed on eight-and-one-half-by-fourteen-inch paper, single-spaced, Huey's abstract for constitutional law was twenty-two pages long. Some of his headings or commentary were typed in red. As in most abstracts of this type, they had more meaning to Huey than they do to a reader today.[3] But they represent diligent study and impeach Professor Jeansonne's claim that Huey relied on impressions and intuition rather than study, that he was too impatient to observe accurately, and that he was neither disciplined nor educated.[4] His schooling left him uneducated on some topics. But Huey's abstracts of "elegant sentences" from literature and his law abstracts prove that Huey studied and diminish the perception that he relied on a photographic memory.

Huey attended classes at Tulane for about seven months and was an active student. He peppered the professors with questions, always, as one student remembered, asking one more question after the bell rang, and sometimes contradicted them to stimulate more discussion or test his argumentative powers. Once telling the dignified but dour professor Charles Fenner that "he could not believe that was the law," Fenner replied, "Mr. Long, for the benefit of your future clients, tell them that is the law and reserve your opinions to yourself." Equally harsh was the debate coach: Huey waved his arms and yelled too much.[5]

Considering his undisciplined habits of spending, of study, and of conduct up to this point, his intense effort while at Tulane and afterward preparing for the bar examination was an amazing about-face, the first of several in which he suddenly altered his habits and imposed his will—on himself. Aside from the law courses and one political science course that he audited, he read from sixteen to twenty hours a day, beginning when he woke up and stopping only to attend class or to eat and sleep. At midnight, he would end his day and walk around the block with Rose or buy a pitcher of beer and drink it to sleep. He was about five feet, ten inches tall, but his weight declined to 112 pounds.[6]

Yet he made friends in New Orleans. Clark Shaughnessy was a football coach at Tulane and met Huey while he attended Tulane or afterward when he was studying for the bar exam. They became friends. In the following years, he helped Shaughnessy recruit football players to Tulane.[7]

In the course on estates, Professor Fenner lectured that Louisiana law required each child of a deceased person to inherit equal shares of his property. English law, in contrast, allowed it all to be inherited by the oldest boy. The Louisiana law had the social benefit of minimizing the concentration of wealth, Fenner explained. Huey hopped on a streetcar with Fenner to continue the discussion with him after class. While the evils of concentrated wealth were a chief topic in Winnfield and included in Ridpath's history, "now it was brought before [Huey] in a peculiarly authoritative way."

Then or later, Huey decided that the Law of Moses was the foundation for all law. This included not just personal injury or criminal law, which have obvious antecedents there, but also the economic principles set forth in Leviticus 25, where every fifty years a jubilee is declared, and property outside towns and cities must be returned to the original family that owned it. Loans likewise could not last for a term decided freely by the borrower and the lender. Debts had to be canceled every seven years. To Huey, this disallowed a financial aristocracy established by inherited wealth.

Years later, a young man sought out Huey while he was governor and explained that he wanted to be a lawyer but was too poor to attend law school, so Huey sketched out a program of self-study on his hotel's stationary. He listed the required subjects and recommended that he synopsize each written case in the textbooks, record what the parties' contentions were, explain the court's decision, and state his own opinion. Huey sprinkled encouragement to study hard, article by article, for example, and twice he "revealingly wrote: 'don't get discouraged.'" Included in his program was advice to study the Bible because Hebrew Law was the basis of all law and to read some good books so his head would "stay open to absorb." He suggested three Victor Hugo novels, *The Count of Monte Cristo,* and Shakespeare's *Julius Caesar, Hamlet,* and *The Merchant of Venice.*[8]

When Huey neared the end of his studies, he engaged Charles J. Rivet, a smart and newly licensed lawyer, to prepare him for the bar examination. Rose went home to her mother. Huey took a room in a boardinghouse. Rivet visited Huey there several nights a week and coached him on likely questions and gave him helpful tips. Always miss part of the questions asked by examiner Edward T. Merrick, said Rivet, for example, so that Merrick could correct him.

Rivet and Huey argued over whether Huey could take the bar examination in New Orleans. Rivet explained that Huey had to pass the bar examination in Shreveport, near Winnfield, where Huey intended to practice. Huey told him to concentrate on the coaching and he would take care of the bar examination.[9]

When he was ready, Huey convinced first Chief Justice Frank A. Monroe of the Louisiana Supreme Court and then the examining committee to give him an early examination in New Orleans, probably omitting that he intended to practice in Winnfield. Huey answered the committee's questions accurately and seriously, with one exception. When the expert on admiralty law, George H. Terriberry, asked him what he knew about his area of expertise, Huey answered "nothing." When Terriberry asked him what he would do if a client needed help in this area, Huey answered that he would "associate Mr. Terriberry with me and divide the fee with him."[10] Huey passed the examination and was sworn in by the Louisiana Supreme Court on May 15, 1915, when he was twenty-one.

Huey told Rose that he had planned his political career. First, he would win election to a secondary state office, then the governorship, then a U.S. Senate seat, and then the presidency. "It almost gave you the cold chills to hear him," she said, "shivering slightly even as she looked back from a perspective of half a century. He was measuring it all."[11]

Napoleon said that, to "understand a man, look at the world when he was twenty."[12] Give or take a few years, the effect of the political trends measured by Huey between his birth and the start of his law and political career are distinct. Theodore Roosevelt became president in 1901 when President William McKinley was assassinated, was elected on his own in 1904, and served until 1908. A progressive, he advocated government action to reduce the influence of big business trusts, preserve the environment, and safeguard food and medicine. In foreign policy, he caused a revolution to take what is now Panama away from Colombia to build the Panama Canal.[13] Yet he won the Nobel Peace Prize in 1906 for helping Russia and Japan mediate a serious international dispute.[14]

Roosevelt gave a speech that year which included this remarkable comment: "[W]e shall ultimately have to consider the adoption of . . . a progressive tax on all fortunes, beyond a certain amount, either given in life or devised or bequeathed upon death to any individual—a tax so framed as to put it out of the power of the owner of one of these enormous fortunes to hand on more than a certain amount to any one individual."[15] Roosevelt handpicked his successor, William Howard Taft (1908–12), but in 1912, Roosevelt decided that Taft was not progressive enough and formed a third party, called the Progressive Party or the Bull Moose Party because Roosevelt said he felt as strong as a Bull Moose at the start of the campaign. In the campaign, he proposed a New Nationalism[16] that would employ Hamilton's concept of a powerful central government to implement the Jeffersonian ideals for the common man. Only a powerful central government could regulate big business, he thought.

The Democratic nominee in 1912 was Woodrow Wilson. As president of Princeton University, he eliminated social barriers between rich and poor students, stating that those who inherit money would be doomed to obscurity.

Backed by party bosses and elected governor of New Jersey despite his vow to be independent, he implemented a progressive platform that made him a presidential candidate soon after he was elected governor.

As a prospective candidate in 1910, he said the "most serious thing facing us today is the concentration of money power in the hands of a few." He met William Jennings Bryan, writing that Bryan "has extraordinary force of personality, and it seems the force of sincerity and conviction. . . . A truly captivating man, I must admit." He supported Bryan's efforts to have the democratic national convention chaired by a progressive. Bryan then helped him win the nomination.[17]

Wilson believed that tariffs were the principal cause of the unequal distribution of wealth. The Democratic platform of 1912 therefore promised to reduce them. It also pledged to toughen the antitrust laws, prohibit corporate campaign contributions, limit individual campaign contributions, publicize those contributions that were made, and opposed imperialism.[18]

Wilson and Roosevelt believed in many of the same things.[19] Roosevelt once said that Wilson was "a less virile me." Wilson believed that government power and accountability should be concentrated and that politicians should personally identify with the causes in which they believed. They should report to the people often, be transparent, and practice politics the year-round. Wilson's "New Freedom" differed from Roosevelt's "New Nationalism," however, in that Wilson believed in small businesses competing. Attacks on monopolies would keep competition, whereas Roosevelt would tolerate monopolies and have the government regulate them.[20]

Roosevelt's third party split the Republican vote and elected Wilson. As president, Wilson got Congress to enact a tariff-reduction bill. The revenue lost from tariffs was replaced by an income tax, "a redistribution of wealth, with the rich paying more than the poor." Later, in 1916, the graduated tax was even more pronounced, and "critics gasped at this redistribution of wealth." Between 1912 and 1916, passage of the Federal Reserve Act reduced the power of Wall Street bankers and trusts, asserted the government's power to issue currency, and made the supply of money more plentiful and credit easier to get, especially by farmers, as the populists had requested decades earlier.[21] "[Wilson's] middle-class program for the control of big business was embodied in the Clayton Act, which was meant to implement the Sherman Anti-Trust Act, and in the creation of the Federal Trade Commission. . . . [T]he Clayton Act exempt[ed] unions from harassment by anti-trust suits, and . . . [Wilson passed] an eight-hour day for railroad workers in interstate commerce, a child-labor act . . . and a compensation law for Civil Service workers."[22] Seventy-five million dollars were allocated to match state funding for highways.[23]

In 1913, when Huey was twenty, Wilson appointed a new chairman of the Commission on Industrial Relations. Formed in the wake of violent industrial strikes, the commission issued an eleven-volume report in 1916 that blamed industrial unrest primarily on the unequal distribution of wealth. It stated that 2 percent of the people owned 60 percent of the wealth; 33 percent of the people owned 35 percent of the wealth; and the remaining 65 percent of the people owned 5 percent of the wealth. It recommended limiting inheritances, graduated income taxes, an eight-hour workday, collective bargaining, and a minimum wage. The report helped justify increased graduated income tax rates. The *Saturday Evening Post* summarized the report on September 23, 1916. Huey read this article and never forgot it.[24]

Wilson won reelection in 1916 in part for keeping the United States out of World War I. The country was then drawn into war in April 1917, with an attendant war hysteria, suppression of free speech, and government control over the economy. It concluded on November 11, 1918, with total victory for the Allies.

These national trends were reflected in Louisiana, but its geography, population, constitution, and business interests created some unique characteristics. After the violent Louisiana gubernatorial election of 1896, a constitutional convention was held in 1898. The delegates drafted a constitution that created a Railroad Commission to govern railroads and utilities and other agencies to regulate banks and support agriculture. It provided a one-term limit on governors. The primary aim of the convention, however, was to disenfranchise as many poor Blacks and whites as possible. "[F]our classes of men would be allowed to vote: (1) literates; (2) tax-paying property owners; (3) sons of property owners; and (4) men who had voted in 1867, or their descendants."[25]

Political self-interest combined with racism made this possible. Recognizing Blacks' value as a workforce, the oligarchy was less overtly racist and more protective of the physical safety of Black people. Excluding Blacks from the primary excused the planters from having to continue to appeal to, intimidate, or fraudulently cast Black votes.[26] Poor white representatives and voters agreed to exclude Black voters because their appeals to Black voters' interests had not outweighed the jobs and protection or the intimidation and fraud of the oligarchy. Produced by prevailing racism, these decisions reflected "one of the paradoxes of Southern history": political "democracy for the white man and racial discrimination for the Black were often products of the same dynamics. . . . The barriers of racial discrimination mounted in direct ratio with the tide of political democracy among whites."[27]

Eliminating Black voters from the general election destroyed the Republican Party in Louisiana, and the adoption of some Populist ideas by William Jennings Bryan and other Democratic leaders destroyed the Populist Party. No future John Pharr would be able to add poor white votes to Black Republican votes in a general election.

If somehow the poor whites were able to elect a sympathetic governor, the planters could frustrate him in the legislature. Legislative seats were apportioned based on *total* population. Black field hands thus gave the planters a weighted legislative influence in which they lacked any share. The one-term limit, moreover, made governors lame ducks as soon as they took office.

The New Orleans version of Tammany Hall met in the Choctaw Club of New Orleans and ruled the city, supported by payoffs from the vice interests, extorted contributions from patronage workers, and a political police force. This political machine was known as the Choctaws, the Ring or, later, the Old Regulars. New Orleans contained about 20 percent of the state's population but contributed about 30 percent of the state's vote, controlled by the Old Regulars.

Outside New Orleans, parish jobs supplied the incentive to organize. One sheriff told Williams that he possessed duties that were "not defined by law or confined by law."[28] You can almost see him winking as he said it. Local police interfered with or controlled local voting. At the time, a poll tax was required to vote (one dollar, or about twenty-five dollars in today's money). Political machines or candidates who were wealthy or backed by the wealthy would pay the poll taxes of impecunious voters and control their vote.[29]

The local sheriffs exercised political autonomy within the framework of government by gentlemen. Candidates would tour the parishes to try to collect the support of as many sheriffs as possible. The politicians made no permanent alliances, however, so every four years the same tours by different candidates resulted in a unique, one-time combination of support that elected a governor.

The one constant was the New Orleans Ring. Its controlled vote generally was enough to guarantee success if it waited until a candidate with a lot of support elsewhere in the state developed and then negotiated to support him. The non-endorsed candidates would then run against the corrupt city machine, notwithstanding that often they did so only after the Ring refused them support. From 1900 to 1920, the Old Regulars dominated Louisiana gubernatorial elections.[30]

Statewide, religious differences divided the state, with Catholics mistrusting Protestants and vice versa. Rural voters distrusted the city politicians of New Orleans. Whether to prohibit the sale of liquor divided the northern parishes (dry) from the southern parishes (wet). Whether to permit gambling was a similarly divisive issue.[31] Politicians of all regions exploited racial prejudice, even after Black voters were disenfranchised.

The sugar parishes would have been Republican because they believed in tariffs, but their racism would not abide the Black members of that party. Businessmen in New Orleans supported government public works to pave streets, control floods, and improve the port docks on which many businesses depended. The planters along the Mississippi River wanted big federal flood-control projects. Northern small farmer parishes believed in limited government.

These differences should have weakened the governing elite and created political opportunities for reform. One wonders whether the power of the planters was more assumed than real and whether the Old Regulars' domination depended on their skill in navigating the divisions among voters in the rest of the state, a talent that could be outmaneuvered. The absence of significant progressive legislation before 1920 might have been caused in part by the staid traditions of an agricultural economy, inertia, or lack of imagination, ambition, and skill by other political leaders.

The national reform movements included supporters in Louisiana, however, and they had some impact on the politics of the state. Municipal takeover of utilities was authorized, support for education was given, and the populist-oriented fire-insurance regulation plan of Texas was adopted. But the gubernatorial administrations of Sanders (1908–12), Hall (1912–16), and Pleasant (1916–20), respectively, were described as reactionary, frustrated, and caretaker.[32]

In 1910, John M. Parker formed a "Good Government League" to fight corruption in New Orleans. Parker owned a plantation north of Baton Rouge and a cotton-factoring business, thus embodying plantation and business characteristics of the elite, and had been involved in politics since 1891. In that year, he signed the call that led to the lynching of eleven Italian Americans in New Orleans. Friendly with Theodore Roosevelt since 1898 (he couldn't join Roosevelt's Rough Riders because of asthma), Parker told the lynching story at a White House dinner to an attentive and appreciative audience.[33] In a 1907 hunting expedition with Parker into Tensas Swamp, the president had enjoyed meeting legendary wilderness guide Ben Lilly.

In 1912, Parker backed Judge Luther Hall as a reform candidate for governor. The northern hill parishes supported local educator Dr. James Aswell, who ran a populist-themed campaign, and the Choctaws backed Secretary of State John T. Michel against Hall but miscalculated. Hall won the governorship with 43 percent of the vote, Michel got 37 percent, and Aswell 20 percent.

Parker supported Theodore Roosevelt and the Progressive Party later in 1912, opposing the low-tariff position of Woodrow Wilson. Roosevelt polled 12 percent of Louisiana's vote, mostly from New Orleans and southern Louisiana. To understand how radical Parker's support of Roosevelt was, consider that Roosevelt had invited Booker T. Washington, who had distinguished himself as a scientist, to the White House and ate dinner with him. A storm of racist denunciation was issued from Louisiana and other southern newspapers because Roosevelt dined with an African American. Roosevelt never repeated the gesture.[34]

After Roosevelt lost in 1912, Wilson and the Democrats alienated the sugar-plantation areas of Louisiana by reducing tariffs on sugar. Of the five Democrats who deserted Wilson on the tariff bill, four were from Louisiana.[35] The Democrats there bolted from the Democratic Party and voted to continue Roosevelt's Progressive Party. They elected a Progressive congressman from their district in 1914. Parker envisioned that the Progressive Party would support tariffs, civil service, governmental efficiency (concentrated authority and accountability), conservation, and the incremental expansion of state government services in education, health care, and road building. Parker was suspicious of ethnic groups and opposed union strikes and Black voting rights, however. He had opposed William Jennings Bryan's monetary expansion principles. He exemplified the middle-class or businessman's progressivism as opposed to the Bryan-style labor-and-farmer populism. Had the party survived, however, Louisiana would have had a two-party system.

Parker agreed to be the Progressive Party's candidate for governor of Louisiana in 1916 and had solid support in the southern region of the state. His opponent was Ruffin Pleasant, who had won the Democratic primary in January 1916.

Pleasant's supporters attacked Parker as Roosevelt's friend and thus for endangering white supremacy. This was only politics, for Parker was a virulent racist privately, but he despised demagogic appeals to racism and the Ku Klux Klan. In the northern hill parishes, opponents attacked him as a rich planter, but he obtained some of the Populist-leaning vote there because he was fighting the New Orleans Ring and offered a progressive platform. Parker lost the election, 80,801 votes to 48,068. Sixteen sugar-plantation parishes gave Parker a majority, however, and elected several state legislators who ran as Progressives.

Later in the year, the Progressive Party nominated Parker for vice president on its national ticket. But Roosevelt, over Parker's public and bitter objections, maneuvered a rapprochement with the Republican Party. Without Roosevelt, the Progressive Party collapsed. Roosevelt returned to the Republicans; Parker returned to the Democrats. Democrats in Congress revised the tariff laws to regain support in the sugar parishes. President Wilson appointed Parker as food administrator for Louisiana in 1917, during World War I.[36]

The beliefs of Roosevelt and Wilson on concentrated wealth matched Huey's own views. How much he was influenced by the progressives' belief in concentrated governmental power and accountability is speculative, but his later actions fell within this principle. Huey lived Wilson's belief that politicians should personally identify with the causes in which they believed and that they should report to the people often, be transparent, and practice politics the year-round. Huey lacked the distaste some Progressives such as Parker felt for different ethnic groups and supported the labor movement and other Bryan policies more than Progressives. Huey must have been impressed with south Louisiana's dedication to tariffs at the expense of loyalty to any political party and the opposition throughout the state to the corrupt politicians of New Orleans.

Upon measuring these trends, Huey decided how to practice law and enter politics. While some of his actions as a lawyer capitalized on unanticipated events, most of what he did resulted from a plan. It was a bold plan to oppose and defeat the oligarchy's domination of Louisiana and to create a career for himself. It started with his law practice.

After Huey obtained his law license, he returned to Winnfield to live in the Long family home and joined Julius as a junior partner, an enviable way to start practicing law. Julius had clients, law books, forms for practice, and would be available as a mentor. Julius was influential in Winn Parish. In 1912, he and ally Cass Moss ran for district attorney and judge, respectively, and won a hard-fought campaign that extended to two parishes. He planned to run for reelection in 1916. Both Louisiana U.S. senators knew him and would take his telephone calls.

Julius believed in Huey's potential and thought he had nurtured it. Being fourteen years older, more experienced, and having invested in Huey, however, he planned to supervise him and gain a return on his investment. When he was younger, Huey admired and emulated Julius, but now, consciously or unconsciously, he wanted to exceed Julius, and a closer acquaintance with Julius and his own maturation allowed him to understand Julius's limitations and his own talent.

Most people suppress their undiplomatic observations about others, especially their bosses and family members. According to Julius, Huey suppressed nothing. He represented defendants that Julius prosecuted as Winnfield's district attorney;[37] tried to steal Julius's clients; read a brief Julius wrote, said it was not worth a damn, and tore it up. Huey never denied or admitted these charges publicly. In later letters, each charged the other with economic exploitation, but the real nub of the problem was one of authority, control, deference, and respect. It is impossible to tell from their letters or Williams's interviews who was right: whether Julius belittled Huey, required too much deference, treated him as a clerk, or required too much control, or whether Huey was rude to or belittled Julius to his face or to others.[38]

When the final blow-up occurred about three months after he began to practice law, Huey and Rose moved out of the Long household and in with a neighbor, and Huey moved out of Julius's office and set up his own, a small eight-by-ten-foot anteroom in Uncle George's bank building for four dollars a month, with the bank trusting him for it. It lacked electric lights and a telephone and had only one window. On credit he bought law books, a typewriter, a typewriter table, and a filing cabinet. A converted dry goods box served as his desk. Rose installed curtains on its sides. His overhead was about thirty-four dollars a month. A fifty-cent tin sign advertised his name. A shoeshine stand next door promised to let Huey use its phone.[39]

Almost as soon as Huey was licensed, the court recessed for the summer. According to Huey, before their split Julius only allowed him to earn fees of two dollars in his first three months. Julius had paid his grocery bills, but this wasn't enough to support a wife. He hadn't measured or planned for this.

## Four

# REBUKES, RIDICULE, AND REPRIMANDS

Seriously needing money, Huey become a commission salesman again, this time for Never-Fail kerosene home oilcans. He hit the road by horse and buggy and sold a lot of oilcans over the summer of 1915.[1] He planned to continue selling them during court recesses or political travels. To facilitate his travel, he asked the company to let him buy a car from it over time by deducting 50 percent of his commissions. The proprietor, J. A. Harps, was reluctant, but acquiesced after Huey wrote him a four-page single-spaced letter in October 1915,[2] explaining that he would need to travel and sell for the next five years while he built his reputation and law practice.

Rose's brother David gave him driving lessons on the secondhand Model T Ford. Knowing nothing about the mechanics of the car ("What is the radiator?") or its limitations, he was a difficult pupil to teach and an erratic driver. He carried a bottle of bootleg whiskey to offer farmers when he needed help to pull his car out of the mud. Money was still tight. He earned about sixty dollars per month but thought he needed to make a hundred per month.[3]

Huey seriously overestimated the time he could devote to selling the oilcans and the time it would take to build a successful law practice. Sales ceased, but he used the car. In a series of monthly letters starting in March 1916, Harps complained to Huey about the lack of orders in a hectoring tone (individuals "offering excuses are weak") that, however deserved (Huey offered a series of excuses), must have been irritating to read. In September, Harps requested the car's return. Huey returned it, writing his regrets at losing the money he had paid for the car and the lack of time he had to sell. When Harps recovered the car, he was livid at its poor condition and blistered Huey with a letter: "Now if there is a spark of manhood in you, come back at me with your defense!"[4] No response to this blast is contained in Huey's papers.

The time and effort Huey spent building his practice were large, but his early cases were small. Julius gave him collection cases for a 10 percent contingent fee, probably because they were too small for Julius.[5] Divorce cases; personal injury or workers' compensation; real estate, including timber, mineral, and oil drilling rights; and succession (probate) cases rounded out his early practice.

Included in his files was Julius's complaint filed against someone who stole "four spotted sows worth $25." A claim against a railroad sought $53.06 for a cow that died while being shipped. A hay supplier contracted to send a carload of hay for $51.50, and then failed to send it but offered a refund. Huey wrote, "You certainly don't think we would stand for you taking this money and when hay went up to the ceiling you will get out by just paying the money back do you?"[6]

Huey's practice was so small that he overdrew his checking account. When he visited his uncle's Bank of Winnfield to fund the check, the officer said the bank wouldn't cover overdrafts or wait for its office rent. "Now I understand you," Huey muttered. "Well, if you understand that," the officer replied, he should understand that they might evict him and take his belongings, except that in his office, "there ain't anything to move."[7]

A few days later, a widow, Mrs. DeLoach, consulted Huey about suing the Bank of Winnfield. After her husband's death, she obtained $2,000 of insurance money. A member of the Louisiana Fire Prevention Bureau, William Campbell, had an office at the Winn Parish Bank, was a stockholder, and used his influence to get deposits for the bank in exchange for their referral of insurance business. "Soon after the death of Mr. DeLoach," he "went down to her home and solicited the deposit" of her insurance money, and directed the president of Winn Parish Bank, a Mr. L. Rogers, to press the request. She agreed. Rogers put her money in a bank deposit box, embezzled it, and paid her monthly interest as if it were held in the bank. The Bank of Winnfield later bought all assets of Winn Parish Bank, and Rogers became a vice president. When payments stopped, DeLoach engaged an attorney, and they managed to recover in a settlement meeting about $1,700, all but $276 of what she was owed. Rogers gave a note for $276, but DeLoach's attorney warned her that it was probably uncollectible. The Bank of Winnfield lawyers had the settlement money technically come from Rogers and claimed they represented only Rogers at the meeting. At this meeting, Rogers and his attorney refused to give her the $1,700 unless she surrendered the original checks that showed his forgery and embezzlement. Luckily, her lawyer had secretly made a photocopy. Rogers got indicted for embezzlement but fled the state; she was still owed $276. Other lawyers in town rejected the case to avoid alienating the bank, because of the risk of losing it, or because of its small size.[8]

Having just been insulted by the bank, albeit with some justice, Huey must have enjoyed filing the lawsuit. A bond had to be posted against the costs that would be incurred in the case, and the bank insisted that Huey deposit $100. Huey couldn't find a lender until midnight, when his law school benefactor—his "one great friend" in Winnfield—state Senator S. J. Harper, loaned him $75. The court let Huey post $25 for the bond until the costs exceeded that amount.[9]

The defense was that Bank of Winnfield purchased Winn Parish Bank's assets and DeLoach's insurance money had never been deposited in Winn Parish Bank, was not included on its books, and therefore was not purchased as an asset. Asset purchases often don't transfer the seller's liabilities to the buyer, but there are exceptions depending on the jurisdiction and whether and how the acquiring company continues the prior business. Harper, a director of the Bank of Winnfield, testified that banking continued as usual after the acquisition. Even the old Winn Parish Bank checks were honored. Many Bank of Winnfield stockholders, including its president, provided their stock to those Winn Parish Bank shareholders who wanted stock rather than cash for the acquisition, but they were careful to say that these were individual transactions between stockholders rather than between the two banks. A stock-for-stock transaction would transfer the liabilities.

About a month before trial, showing some insecurity, Huey wrote to the Louisiana attorney general and, separately, to his old law professor Fenner asking for their advice. No replies exist in his file. The opposing lawyer objected to Huey's questioning at the beginning of the trial, a common testing tactic against a young lawyer. Huey got more confident and skilled as the trial progressed. He made the current bank president, B. W. Bailey, look foolish when he testified that the Bank of Winnfield did not buy every asset of Winn Parish Bank:

Q: Is the statement authorizing and ratifying the sale made by the Winn Parish Bank to the Bank of Winnfield of its entire assets correct or incorrect?
A: *I have answered that question as conclusively as I know how.*
Q: I want you to answer the question YES or NO. Mr. Bailey?
A: *The word entire as used—*
Q: I object to anything—I want you to answer yes or no and I don't want any explanation.
A: *I undertook to answer your question. I am not trying to dodge at all.*
Q: I don't want any information except what my question called for.
A: *The word entire as used is susceptible of such a broad interpretation until it is difficult for me to understand just exactly the import or the scope that is sought to be covered. . . .*
Q: Mr. Bailey, do you know of anything that the Winn Parish Bank owned that you didn't buy—do you know of anything?
A: *Just at this time I don't know as I could answer the question.*

DeLoach's settlement lawyer, Mr. E. E. Kidd, called by the bank as a witness, on cross-examination by Huey, said the bank's lawyer admitted to him that he had been "fooled" by Kidd's photocopying of the checks.

Huey said he won the case "very easily,"[10] but the trial was hard fought. Julius's political ally Cass Moss was the judge who ruled in Huey's favor, handwriting a decision of one paragraph. "Widow and orphan" cases often get favorable treatment, perhaps because of biblical injunctions, and sometimes with the result of bending the law. The full set of circumstances smelled, however: the rush to get her money, the embezzlement and forgery by the president, and the settlement meeting structured to avoid implicating the bank and to shield Rogers. The bank's lawyer, supposedly acting only for Rogers at the settlement meeting, didn't ask for a release of the bank, probably to avoid telling her the bank was responsible, but thought that, by demanding the originals of the insurance checks in exchange for the partial payment, he would prevent her ability to prove she had deposited the money. The bank's cross-examination of DeLoach mainly revealed her poverty, a counterproductive tactic in a case against a widow. Huey may have brought her raggedly dressed children into the courtroom for additional sympathy.

The Bank of Winnfield thereafter declined to offer Huey customary courtesies with respect to drafts or checks or to notify or forward them to him.[11] A vice president sought out Harley Bozeman to beg Huey to stop attacking the bank. Huey replied that the bank should feel complimented that it was big enough to deserve his attacks.[12]

DeLoach was the first of Huey's many challenges to the biggest, closest target at hand. In 1917, he represented employees against a big company taking illegal deductions from their wages. Huey left it up to the "boys" what they wanted to pay him. Such attacks elevated his stature, and the DeLoach case—her husband was a train conductor—and those for injured workmen earned the gratitude of labor unions.[13] As he went to the drugstore to celebrate his win, a man asked him to represent his family in another—and bigger—case, exemplifying how a notable success results in additional business.

Williams described another early case. One Black man asked for two divorces, one from his wife and the other from his common-law wife, whom he wanted to marry legally. Huey only charged him for one, so the client believed he had gotten a bargain and referred all his friends to Huey. But Huey got in trouble handling divorce cases. No-fault divorce was not the law at the time, so Huey used an accessory, someone to point to as an adulterous partner. Huey systematically used the same man in multiple cases, earning a "notable judicial rebuke" and a warning against using this man ever again.[14]

The early Winnfield lawsuits Huey discussed in his autobiography—an eclectic group—revealed that he valued brevity, trustworthiness, and energy. When an "able lawyer" in Winnfield asked Huey to write an appeal from an adverse judgment, Huey wrote a brief that was only four pages long and wondered if he shouldn't write more. The lawyer told him, "That is the law and that's enough."[15]

After winning a hard-fought lawsuit for the title to land against a lumber company (the case he obtained after the DeLoach victory), the company's owner told Huey that, in any future cases, he should send him a deed with the amount of the conveyance filled in by Huey and he would send the money. Huey later sent him deeds, the man paid the amounts Huey demanded, and Huey never sued him again.[16]

Another case won in the Louisiana Supreme Court, at a cost of hundreds of dollars, involved a dispute over $22.50. The key to building a practice, Huey wrote, was the energy to prosecute every case regardless of its size. But he also had another case for the man and may have taken this one to keep him happy.[17]

His law files reveal that he was courteous to opposing counsel, sympathetic to his clients, conscious of trying to gain a reputation for prompt payments and honest dealings, dropped clients who malingered or lost cases where his client made a poor impression during the trial,[18] got irritated with and dropped clients who consulted with another lawyer after consulting him,[19] or who rejected reasonable compromises,[20] protected his rights to his own fees but sometimes compromised them or delayed taking them,[21] displayed the pressure of a volume practice and his political duties by writing short letters[22] and briefs, occasionally faced biased judges in other cities (getting "hometowned"),[23] loaned clients money, advised clients to save the money he won them and sometimes kept money from clients for fear that they would spend it all,[24] got discouraged when they didn't save it,[25] had some ungrateful clients,[26] and early on made some mistakes with respect to rules of pleading and procedure, especially in federal court.[27]

He made definite statements to clients, telling them when he thought he had a strong case and how to make it stronger, when he did not think they could win, and confessed when he was too busy to manage cases or was delayed in doing so. Sometimes he couldn't find papers or admitted that his office, having been neglected while campaigning, was in a "furor" or a "storm."[28]

The real estate, timber, and oil cases often required a detailed study of conveyances of property by virtue of their legal description through a course of years, and assignments of fractional shares of timber or royalties. In a 1919 assignment, he carefully abstracted the record in pencil on eight-and-one-half-by-fourteen-inch unlined paper.[29] In personal injury cases, no deep knowledge of the law was required. "Huey would ask, 'Is this a leg or arm case?' and then he'd go to bat."[30] In some cases, he represented Black workers who were injured, but declined one case for Black workers who were being whipped and bullied at a lumber mill. He believed them, but taking the case would "merely injure" him and they "would never get anything" out of a lawsuit.[31] When he did represent Black people, he often advised them to locate white witnesses.

Many files show rulings of relevant cases in handwriting, sometimes on scraps of paper. His pleadings generally went through more than one draft.

Eventually, he handled as many cases as the rest of the Winnfield bar combined, sometimes two or three trials a day, and worked through the night to take advantage of the opportunities.[32] A next-door neighbor who didn't like him nevertheless respected how often he saw him working at 1:00, 2:00, or 3:00 a.m. Huey told a colleague that 3:00 in the morning was no different to him from 3:00 during the day. After researching a point of law late into the night, he said, "We've got them beat before they've opened their eyes."[33]

---

Williams attributes Huey's success as a lawyer to his ability to inspire the confidence of clients, judges, and juries, a conclusion easily drawn from, and consistent with, his personality as a salesman; his insistence on organizing the facts of a case chronologically; his retentive mind, allowing him to cite case facts and legal cases from memory, without notes, which impressed clients and judges; his ability to bring facts outside the courtroom into it, providing context to a case; use of picturesque phrases, proverbs, and metaphors, making his ideas easier to recall and more persuasive; analytical ability, cutting to the heart of a case without getting distracted by tangential facts; and energy.[34]

Gamesmanship must be added to Williams's list. Huey would subpoena the president of a corporation in a personal injury suit and then cross-examine him for not knowing anything about an accident. He revealed his witnesses at the last moment before the trial so that his opponents couldn't influence their testimony. In a routine motion that required a representation that it was not made for purposes of delay, Huey wrote that it had been made only to delay, but no one read his motion until long after it was granted. In one case he won because his opponent had violated the rules of procedure. Judge O'Niell dissented from the ruling of his colleagues, saying that rules of procedure should not be used to prevent determinations on the merits. Huey's gamesmanship won the case but—appreciating the goal of justice—Huey wrote a letter to Judge O'Niell complimenting him on his dissent.[35]

A story told by Charles Rivet revealed a peculiar trait. He found Huey in the clerk's office while his opponent was arguing Huey's case. Rivet told Huey he better get in there, but Huey said he never listened to his opponent's argument; he concentrated on his own presentation.[36]

Huey liked the practice of law and was committed to producing a high-quality work product. He spent a lot of his meager funds on law books. Lawbook purchases continued throughout his career until many thought that he had the finest private law library in the United States. He paid high wages to stenographers. Most of his letters were neatly typed at a time when many established men still wrote letters by hand. The road, a "splendid place" to study, was where he learned most of his law, he said.[37] Huey enjoyed locking himself up with law books for days to attack a legal problem.[38]

While Williams's list of Huey's skills is accurate, it is difficult to assess whether his talent exceeded that of other lawyers in Winnfield. A lawyer's oral and written rhetoric is important, but case and theme selection are more outcome-determinative. It is impossible to know now what his clients told him, what investigation and research Huey performed, what factors made him accept an assignment, or how he decided whether to settle or take a case to trial.

Easier to evaluate are what practicing as a trial lawyer added to Huey's skill set. Some of his sales abilities transferred to his legal practice. Thus, a salesman will often make his product the hero of his sales pitch, and a lawyer will make his client the hero of his trial presentation. Some sales-questioning techniques—probing a prospect to determine a winning sales promise—are like questioning a witness or a potential client. Either through argument or questions, a "circus whirl" of talk can build a fence around a witness or even around a judge or jury. Lawyers and salesmen can use similar strategies to deal with objections: easy objections can be rebutted directly; difficult objections can be minimized by stressing other relevant principles.

Learning the law and practicing as a lawyer supplemented the skills Huey already had. In argument, lawyers appeal to authority, urging the judge to rule in their favor because of other judges' decisions in similar circumstances. Huey's political speeches often cited and appealed to authorities: laws in other states, the Bible, and government reports. Lawyers organize their presentations by stating the issue, citing the applicable rule or other authority, applying that rule to the facts, rebutting the arguments of the opponent, and then concluding with a request for a favorable ruling. Huey used this structure in his political speeches.

Famous presidential advisor Clark Clifford attributed his success to his experience as a trial lawyer: "A trial lawyer must confront an enormous amount of facts, sift through them, and identify the most salient. Then he must organize them logically and present them articulately and persuasively in order to convince the jury. Such courtroom experience was priceless. . . . Substitute the President or Cabinet members for the jury; in both cases, the key art to be mastered was the art of persuasion."[39] Such was the case with Huey.

In politics, Huey often clowned and joked. In court during an argument, he was serious. Several times as governor Huey represented the state or himself in court, an unusual circumstance. Jules Fischer, a local power in southwest Louisiana, became a supporter after observing Huey argue one of his court cases.[40]

Intelligent career planning was as responsible for the meteoric success of his law practice as the DeLoach victory or the skills mentioned. Huey decided not to accept any case against a poor man. He would represent a rich man against another rich one or a poor man against a rich one, but never the reverse.[41] Lincoln never made such a decision—he represented the powerful railroads—and was not disadvantaged by it. Having this criterion, however, made decisions easier, both for Huey and for prospective clients. It showed goal coherence in his professional and political life. When a bank association wanted to list him in a directory as an attorney for banks, he declined the listing because he did not want to be identified as a bank attorney. He wanted to be free to judge whether to accept an individual case even if it meant forgoing large retainers.[42] He declined to represent lumber companies in suits against ordinary people.[43]

Lawyers then could not advertise. Politics, however, gave Huey an excuse to initiate contact with other lawyers, political figures, or potential clients, which indirectly but inevitably promoted his practice. John Overton, mayor of Alexandria, thanked Huey for encouraging him to run for governor.[44] Huey wrote Harry Gamble, a prominent campaign manager, that he was disappointed Gamble had not been a candidate in a recent election.[45] Huey shared political intelligence with Judge John Sandlin, who contemplated a run for Congress.[46]

Hair concludes that Huey, who ignored the gubernatorial and presidential races of 1916, was "uncharacteristically detached" from politics.[47] In reality, Huey had an almost myopic focus on himself, a trait that Robert Penn Warren labeled "genius."[48]

Huey instead selected an issue to champion, one appropriate for his status and influence, one that reflected his sympathy for the laboring man and advanced his law career. There was a grumbling sentiment among personal injury lawyers and labor unions against Louisiana's workers' compensation law. Huey subscribed to the *American Railway Employees' Journal.* He wrote to its editors on February 6, 1916, to see what law they would recommend. Huey drafted proposed amendments that month and showed them to state Senator Harper. Harper agreed to sponsor them in the legislature.[49]

Huey rallied public support in an extensive public relations campaign. Form letters explained the injustice of the existing laws and his rationale for change. Huey wrote newspaper articles carried on the front pages of smaller newspapers. He sent his letters and reprints of the newspaper articles to lawyers and friends he knew and to public officials he didn't know, asking them to support changes to the law.

Railroad and timber executives denounced him. In response, Huey wrote form letters stating that "when a man stands up and criticizes the looting and stealing by presidents and managers of railroads and lumber companies . . . he is soon called a demagogue and an anarchist, while the man who stands up . . . in favor of the criminal rich and big business of this state is called . . . a statesman."[50]

By May, he had collected four hundred letters from supporters of his views and offered them to Governor Pleasant while asking for his aid to repeal the unjust law.[51] By that time, unsurprisingly, his practice was doing better.[52]

When Huey's bills came before the appropriate legislative committee, he accompanied Harper to urge passage. A rude reception, however, awaited him in the statehouse. A legislator asked Huey whom he represented. "Several thousand common laborers," Huey replied. "Are they paying you anything?" "No," Huey said. The legislator administered his coup de grâce: "They seem to have good sense." The audience guffawed.[53]

Huey had the last laugh. He denounced the committee for denying a laborer's family only $300 for a life upon whom they depended, even though it was lost in the "honest discharge of duty. . . . Those seeking reforms have, from necessity, bowed their heads in regret and shame when witnessing the victories of these corrupting influences at this capitol. . . . [T]here are those here representing the combined corporations, who declare that they merely seek justice. What a subterfuge!"[54]

While Huey's amendments were voted down in the committee, the full legislature adopted them. Huey had either prompted the reversal by his attack and the public pressure he brought to bear or benefited from popular, progressive sentiment in 1916 that compelled it anyway. He also drafted legislation making it a crime to provide an unsafe workplace, and this bill became law.

After Woodrow Wilson was elected governor of New Jersey, one of the laws that established him as a progressive contender for the presidency liberalized that state's workers' compensation law.[55] As an unelected private lawyer, Huey obtained a like result. The elements of Huey's plan were simple: he recognized a grievance, researched and framed a solution, recruited allies in a massive mobilization campaign, and strategically and dramatically confronted his opposition.[56] If it were so simple, why didn't anyone else do it?

The passage of these laws in 1916 supports the thesis that progressives and populists had an impact in Louisiana and that the oligarchy either was not blind to all social issues or all-powerful. Moreover, while historians accurately portray Huey as a friend of farmers with a strong base in rural Louisiana, his early political and legal efforts earned the gratitude of labor unions and industrial workers, the base of urban reformers.

The publicity must have influenced laborers to consider hiring Huey to sue for their injuries. The newspaper articles Huey circulated identified him as a "leading lawyer," omitting that he was in his first year of practice. His speech to the legislative committee was printed (including his picture) and circulated at Senator Harper's expense.[57]

Julius and Huey cooperated in handling some of each other's cases, and Huey supported Julius in his reelection campaign for district attorney in September 1916. Julius supported the improvement of the workers' compensation law. The state fire marshal, William B. Campbell (the same man who testified for the bank in the DeLoach case), was hired as a lobbyist by insurance companies to defeat Julius.[58] Oscar K. Allen—one of Huey's first clients—was running for assessor, and Huey also backed him. Julius and Allen won.

Huey also became a correspondent for several newspapers. The articles he wrote were small items, however, unhelpful politically or to his law career. He lacked the time to devote to the job and frequently traveled, which made him miss some local events. The papers complained. Eventually Huey quit or was terminated from these jobs.[59]

By 1917, Huey was ready to get out of Winnfield. His classmates, 90 percent of whom were doing nothing with their lives, Huey perceived as a hindrance. I speculate that Huey wanted to get out of Julius's shadow. Shreveport was then the second largest city in Louisiana and enjoying an oil boom. Huey thought it was three times the size of Alexandria with ten times the practice, without many capable lawyers. The impetus to move to Shreveport was calculated and realistic, capitalizing on the opportunity presented by the oil boom and to move to a bigger city.[60] When he was a U.S. senator, a teenager asked him for life advice. He replied, "make the most of your opportunities."[61] Julius lacked the insight to move to Shreveport or was satisfied with his status in Winn Parish.

When in 1917 a new U.S. attorney was about to be appointed for the district that included Winnfield and Shreveport, therefore, Huey sought the job. Julius talked to Senators Joseph Ransdell and Robert Broussard about getting Huey the appointment. The office would be in Shreveport. The senators assured Julius that, if Huey could get sufficient endorsements, he would get the job.[62]

Huey and Julius mobilized a public relations campaign to secure the job. They wrote letters to lawyers and political leaders and often asked them to write to others soliciting support. Most of them complied enthusiastically, and Huey promised to return all favors.[63]

The senators—Ransdell and Broussard—first wrote that the decision on the appointment would be up to the U.S. attorney, not them.[64] This was false. They then wrote that they had decided for equitable reasons of patronage to award the position to a resident of the Seventh rather than the Eighth Congressional District.[65] Huey and Julius mobilized support in the Seventh Congressional District. Friends there wrote letters to the senators that they supported Huey even though he was a resident of the Eighth District. Finally, the senators stated in no uncertain terms that the position would go to another candidate who resided in the Seventh District.[66]

In Huey's autobiography, he wrote that he was disappointed in losing the appointment, could not cast it from his mind, and awaited the opportunity for a political contest.[67] This is sometimes cited as evidence of a vindictive nature. After being misled about the likelihood of the appointment and undertaking the massive campaign, however, it would be a rare person who could forget or forgive the dissembling senators. Julius was livid at being misled and vented his undiplomatic disgust to one of the senators.[68] Opposition to Huey and Julius by the timber interests and "the strutting, white-haired" Congressman James "Chicken Jim" Aswell caused his defeat. Huey asked several people to run against Ransdell in 1918, but no one did.[69]

At the end of 1917, a new Winnfield Courthouse was going to be built. The Bank of Winnfield wanted the architectural contract to be awarded to W. L. Stevens. Early in the year, Stevens had offered Huey a retainer, but Huey refused. When a public meeting was held at the end of the year, Huey disclosed the offer as an attempt to bribe him. The resulting ruckus was reported—with Huey providing the news—even in New Orleans newspapers.[70]

When the United States entered World War I in April 1917, "war fever" gripped the country. A vocal minority protested. Disregarding the First Amendment, Congress passed laws—most notoriously the Espionage Act—that allowed war dissenters to be jailed. State Senator Harper opposed the war, blamed it on Wall Street and, once it was declared, argued that conscripting the profits of the rich should finance it. A pamphlet outlined his views. In part to curry favor with President Wilson, Congressman Aswell supported the war. Harper announced his candidacy for Congress to oppose Aswell. (In 1912, Harper had opposed Aswell's gubernatorial candidacy.) Aswell then instigated Harper's indictment for opposing the war on February 13, 1918.[71]

The case was set for trial in federal court in Alexandria, just four miles from Camp Beauregard, one of the largest military camps in the South, an inhospitable venue for such a trial.[72] Harper faced thirty years in jail and a

$30,000 fine if convicted.[73] Julius and Huey agreed to represent Harper, notwithstanding the unpopular views he expressed, and that Huey was planning to run for office. Harper's views had so enraged Deputy Sheriff Cupp that he socked Harper in the jaw and knocked out three of his teeth. Huey filed a lawsuit against Cupp, alleging that he was a "notorious bully" frequently hired by corporations to quell labor strikes. Cupp paid $200 to settle the case[74] but became the government's chief witness in the criminal trial.

A government investigator noted that Julius led a strong antiwar political faction in Winnfield. The three-member draft board was composed of one avowed pacifist and a chairman (also the sheriff) who said he would protect anyone who didn't want to be drafted.[75]

Before the Harper trial, Huey wrote a letter to the editor—printed in two major newspapers—urging a redistribution of wealth, citing the *Saturday Evening Post* of 1916. The sincerity of his interest in this topic cannot be denied,[76] but it set forth views like Harper's and must have been designed at least in part to influence people who might serve on Harper's jury.

Huey and Julius opposed every effort to delay the trial, fearing the buildup of patriotic publicity. Huey gave so many statements to the press denouncing Harper's indictment that the judge reprimanded him.[77] During the trial, Huey and Julius exposed the system that led to the indictment and claimed that Cupp had a vendetta against Harper. The jury "was liking the exposure," Huey said later, but the judge was so hostile to Huey that Julius gave the closing argument.

Huey was proud of the judge's reprimand. In his autobiography, he wrote: "To the devil with a reprimand as far as we were concerned! All we wanted was a chance to clear our client."[78]

The Long brothers may have won the case by a clever ruse. Government agents spied on the potential jurors. Huey decided which jurors were likely to favor the prosecution and (with the more lax standards of the time) arranged to meet them for drinks or meals, where he engaged them in whispered, intimate conversations about everything except the Harper case. During jury selection, the government lawyers asked if they had discussed the case with Huey. They all truthfully denied it. The government didn't believe them, however, and exercised their right to excuse them, exactly what Huey and Julius wanted.[79]

On March 19, 1918, the jury deliberated for roughly seven minutes before acquitting Harper. Huey believed this was the only wartime acquittal under the Espionage Act. The judge, a friend and ally of Aswell, was furious, blistered Harper with a long posttrial statement carried in the newspapers, and ordered Harper to turn over the pamphlets to the U.S. marshal to be burned. Public outrage forced Harper's resignation from the legislature. But Huey had kept faith with his "one great friend" in Winnfield. In gratitude, Harper bought Huey the most expensive suit he could find, at a cost of $37.50.[80] Often critical of Huey, Hair wrote that the Harper representation was the most courageous and selfless act of Huey's life.[81]

The plan Huey confided to Rose did not specify the minor state political office he intended to win first. The Louisiana Railroad Commission, with three commissioners, regulated passenger and freight railroad, telephone and telegraph, steamboat, and other watercraft companies with respect to rates, safety, and related matters.[82] There was no age requirement to run for commissioner, Huey said, so he could run at age twenty-four.[83]

Bozeman claims he told Huey that in states where commissioners were elected, the position was a springboard to higher offices.[84] Huey was aware of the commission because he represented people who sued railroads and depended on them to ship goods. There are only hints as to when he decided to run for commissioner. In a letter of April 17, 1917, he commented on the efforts of Congressman Aswell to "crush" him "for a time" by denying him the assistant U.S. attorney position and said he would "go to the people directly the next time, about next year." A January 21, 1918, letter to the *Daily States* of New Orleans solicited their involvement in an issue under consideration by the incumbent. A letter to the incumbent dated February 7, 1918, suggests that Huey was trying to set him up or size him up.[85]

However the Railroad Commission came to Huey's attention, Huey announced his campaign for commissioner in the summer of 1918. He talked to clients about running for the office and let some of them think they suggested it. Bozeman reported that Huey had begun writing to elected officials and defeated candidates for two years before his candidacy, but he must have been thinking of the workers' compensation or assistant U.S. attorney campaigns, because these are the types of letters included in Huey's papers.[86] Huey rejected a suggestion that he run for the state senate.[87]

A friend wanted to run against him. They argued about who would win. Huey said, "Let's write down the names of a hundred men we know and ask them which of us they would prefer to have as a candidate." "All right," his friend agreed. "Shall I write 50 and you write 50?" "No," replied Huey, "you can write them all." The friend gave up after writing ten or fifteen names, tore up his list and said, "you win." Years later Huey chuckled that "There ain't a politician in the world who can name a hundred men he's absolutely sure of—except me."[88]

Huey's campaign literature emphasized that he represented injured laborers. Posters were plastered everywhere he and brother-in-law Dave McConnell could tack them up. Instead of traveling by horse-driven carriage, Huey wanted the electorate to think he was somebody and drove his car over the twenty-eight parishes of the district. Each day, he wore the same expensive, white linen suit bought for him by the grateful state Senator Harper.[89]

Conventional handshaking tours and speeches were made, but Huey also stopped at farmhouses in the middle of the night and woke up the occupants to ask for votes. Farm families were so isolated that they appreciated the social contact and being deemed important enough to be called on for their views and vote regardless of the hour. Reporting this, one newspaper said it might be wise to elect this insane candidate: "he might start something."

At Shooter's Station, Huey timed his speech for when the Cannonball train roared down the tracks without stopping. He looked up innocently and exclaimed with mock surprise, "you mean to tell me that the Cannonball don't stop at Shooter's Station?. . . . [Y]ou elect me and that'll be changed." At another location he trudged up to a man and said he was thirsty from the long walk from the station, anticipating that the man would expound on his grievance that the station was located far away from his property. Huey promised that the station would be moved. After his election, Huey never did it. "The old bastard wasn't entitled to it to start with."[90] Apparently you can't lie to a greedy man.

Some attacked him for his defense of Harper. Huey said he was loyal to a friend. He got more votes by that defense than his attackers got by bringing it up.[91]

No one attacked Huey for dodging the draft. Rose had given birth to their daughter, Rose, on April 13, 1917. Huey applied for an exemption on grounds that he had a wife and child, and supported his father, and under the public official exception, on the ridiculous grounds that he was a notary public. The draft board exempted Huey on the first ground, but not the second. Years later, the chairman of the draft board issued a statement defending his decision to exempt Huey but added this improper reason: Huey had borrowed money from him.[92]

Huey supported the Red Cross, temperance societies, and women's suffrage[93] and spoke at public forums to help sell war bonds. While some reported that he appeared on one such platform with a war-hero imposter, the man was mentally disturbed from injuries received in the war.[94]

After the war ended and congressional hearings revealed the extent of war profiteering, many people concluded, cynically, that the war was fought only to swell big fortunes and that all the patriotic rhetoric in support of the war was rubbish. The best writers of the generation wrote books "filled with passionate contempt for the statements of conviction, of purpose and of belief on which the war of 1914–1918 was fought."[95] At that time, Huey more boldly said he didn't serve in the war because "he wasn't mad at anybody over there."[96] In 1918, however, while the war raged and he campaigned, he said nothing like this.

While Huey was out campaigning, wife Rose, then pregnant with their second child, Russell,[97] mailed political literature to the voters from their home. Her father's house was the campaign headquarters. Family and neighborhood friends helped stuff envelopes. She would carry suitcases full of them to the post office. Family members, hers and his, all campaigned. Julius was the campaign manager. Earl campaigned while traveling as a salesman for a baking powder company.

Julius Long wrote his campaign literature and put the organization that elected him district attorney behind Huey. Clients O. B. Thompson, O. K. Allen, and others contributed money. At a critical point, returning from a campaign trip out of money, Huey received a cash contribution from O. K. Allen. John H. Overton of Alexandria was then mayor and running for the U.S. Senate; he endorsed Huey. Huey spent more money than any other candidate, placed four times more newspaper advertisements than the incumbent, and claimed endorsements from the *Monroe Star*, the *Macon Ridge Journal*, the *Lake Providence Banner Democrat*, and several sheriffs and assessors.[98]

Incumbent Burk A. Bridges was Huey's main opponent. A traveling salesman before running for the commission, he had alliances with merchants in some of the larger cities who had been his customers and with courthouse politicians. Dignified but not dynamic, Bridges probably did not realize the extent of Huey's imaginative campaign, which concentrated on the rural areas.

Even with Huey's exertions, Bridges got 6,979 votes to Huey's 5,515 on Election Day (September 15, 1918).[99] The votes cast for the other candidates deprived Bridges of a majority and thus compelled a runoff. Huey had made deals with other minor candidates in the race that he would support them if they made the runoff if they supported him if he made it.[100]

In the subsequent runoff, Huey's personal contacts, visits, mailings in the rural areas, and endorsements from three defeated candidates overcame Bridges's strength in the urban centers, and Huey squeaked by to victory, 7,286 to 6,651 votes, a 635-vote margin.[101] Julius obtained court orders, and his uncle Albert Long rode all over the district serving those court orders to ensure that the votes were counted.

Only 14,000 votes were cast, less than 50 percent of the eligible voters, for a position that represented twenty-eight parishes and one-third of the state. This was equivalent to the votes of three or four out of the seventeen New Orleans wards. The Spanish flu pandemic and a liberty loan drive may have reduced the vote. Huey took out a full-page newspaper advertisement congratulating Bridges on a manly campaign and promising a conservative approach to the commission.[102]

The runoff took place in November 1918, three months after Huey's twenty-fifth birthday, and three and one-half years after Huey was licensed as a lawyer. He was sworn in when Bridges's term ended in December 1918. Beforehand, statewide publicity about Huey was episodic or nonexistent. Now, the entire state would be exposed to his new approaches to law, economics, government, and politics. Either close to the end of the runoff election or in the interim between it and his swearing in, an issue erupted that gave his term a dynamic start.

# Five

# REFUSING TO PLAY IT SAFE

Oil was discovered in Caddo Parish (Shreveport) in the early 1900s, but technical problems impeded production. By World War I, however, these obstacles had been overcome and Caddo enjoyed a great economic boom, with "feverish trading in leases, land and oil stocks." Some of the new millionaires, "knowing no other way to the enjoyment of wealth, bought two and three automobiles, all in a high state of red enamel and brass fittings." Huey represented Banks Oil Company, Bayou Oil Company, and Claiborne Oil Company. He acquired stock in these companies, but his holdings are difficult to value. The biggest was Banks, owned by O. K. Allen and O. B. Thompson. Huey had dreams of great wealth.

A primary oil field was at Pine Island. By 1918, 113 independent operators were producing 25,000 or more barrels of oil per day. Standard Oil, Gulf Refining, and the Texas Company bought and transported to their refineries the oil from the independents through pipelines they owned for $1.55 per barrel.[1]

At the end of the war in November 1918, the military contracts for oil were cancelled, so the demand for oil dropped. On December 1, 1918, Standard Oil announced that as of December 10 it would no longer purchase Pine Island oil at any price, and Gulf Refining and the Texas Company followed suit. The oil refineries, however, continued to import about seven thousand barrels of oil every day from Mexico by tanker up the Mississippi River.[2]

The price of Pine Island oil dropped to 50 cents per barrel. The alternatives of the independents were limited. They lacked their own pipelines and refineries. They couldn't stop the gushing oil. To store the oil that couldn't be sold, the drillers dug primitive storage pits in the ground. They leaked, causing substantial environmental damage and the risk of fires. Every stream and bayou carried a glistening film of oil. Plowed farm-field furrows filled up with oil from the saturated soil. The cost to Caddo Parish's economy was over $15 million in the first six months after the embargo.[3]

The independents organized an association and met with the Standard Oil group at the Shreveport Chamber of Commerce, but no agreement was reached. The faces of the Standard Oil group bore "expressions of self-content. About these men there was that undefinable something that betokens freedom from money cares and anxiety. . . . But the faces of the men in the independent group told a different story. Care, and in some cases, desperation, was written in every line." Huey denounced the big oil companies for the freeze-out, saying they would "never hear the last of it."[4] Facing economic ruin, many independents sold out cheap to Standard Oil, meaning they had taken the risk of drilling a dry hole and then were robbed of profits when they drilled a gusher.

The U.S. Interstate Commerce Commission in 1915 had ruled that interstate oil pipelines were "common carriers," requiring them to transport between states any company's oil for standard fees approved by the Interstate Commerce Commission. This prevents freeze-outs or price discrimination for oil shipped between states. In Oklahoma, for example, Standard Oil took all the crude produced in Ohio at more than a dollar a barrel but bought only part of Oklahoma's production at half that price. To remedy price discrimination within the state, Oklahoma made its intrastate pipelines common carriers, complementing the rules for interstate pipelines established by the Interstate Commerce Commission.[5]

In Louisiana, intrastate pipelines were only deemed common carriers if they transported oil for "consideration" (money). When Standard Oil bought oil in Louisiana, it piped it for nothing to avoid common carrier regulation.[6] In 1915, the Railroad Commission ordered Standard to file its tariffs for the intrastate transportation of oil in its pipelines, but Standard refused because, under the law, it was not a common carrier. The commission backed down.[7]

Huey asked the independents to testify at a February 1919 meeting of the Railroad Commission. Based on their testimony, he wrote a report that criticized the freeze-out and recommended new legislation: first, that pipelines be required to carry everyone's oil as a common carrier; second, that they purchase without price discrimination and subject to commission regulation all oil offered to them as a common purchaser; and third, that pipeline-company ownership be separated from the oil companies.[8]

The proposal required the insight of a good lawyer to diagnose the legislation that was needed and to recognize the power of the commission to conduct a hearing and collect evidence on an issue over which it lacked but wanted jurisdiction. The Oklahoma law provided precedent for Huey's proposal.

Huey's political instincts were equally acute. Representing small businessmen against a monopoly aligned him with the underdogs, but they were capitalist underdogs, businessmen who competed in the marketplace for profit. Regulation to protect them was an achievable, practical solution to their difficulty. Having a constitutionally established state commission issue a report based on evidence and recommend new legislation was more credible than having a private citizen or a solitary officeholder do so.

At the next commission meeting in March in Baton Rouge, Huey obtained the concurrence of the two other commissioners to his report in executive session (away from the oil-company lobbyists). The commissioner representing the district that included New Orleans, John T. Michel, was a descendant of sugar-plantation owners from Normandy, France. Originally a stenographer for a criminal court, he worked his way up to become a ward leader in the New Orleans Ring. A colorless career politician, "short, dumpy, and inarticulate," he had nevertheless been elected secretary of state four times.[9]

The other commissioner was Shelby Taylor, a former mayor of Crowley, who since 1908 had represented the second district and home of Standard Oil. Paunchy and moon-faced, he lacked backbone.[10] The commission also had a secretary, Henry Jastremski, who became Huey's ally, and a legal counsel, Wylie M. Barrow, from the attorney general's office.

After the release of Huey's report, Standard Oil lobbyists and their allies attacked the commission. Taylor and Michel, ordinary politicians, retreated. Taylor even tried to retract his concurrence by asking Jastremski to hand over the report so he could "tear it up."[11]

But Huey escalated his advocacy. He urged Governor Pleasant to call a special session of the legislature to enact pipeline legislation. Pleasant aspired to a U.S. Senate seat, however, and didn't want to ruffle feathers.[12] Standard Oil pressed its case with newspaper ads explaining that market forces—it claimed it had tried but failed to find new markets for Pine Island crude—were to blame for the difficulties at Pine Island. Huey responded with issue-advocacy ads of his own on May 10 and May 21 in the *Shreveport Times*. On June 7, Huey spoke at a rally urging support for a special session, arguing that Standard Oil's freeze-out was designed to destroy and then absorb the independents.[13]

When Pleasant declined to call a special session, Huey charged Pleasant with being a tool of Standard Oil. In response, Pleasant had a secondary official, state fire marshal William Campbell, Julius's political enemy from 1916 and a witness for the bank in the DeLoach case, denounce Huey. Campbell accused Huey of asking the legislature to benefit his personal oil-stock holdings, a "stock jobbing deal," and challenged Huey to respond at a statewide political rally at the Hot Wells resort the next month. Four gubernatorial candidates were scheduled to speak there on July 4, 1919, in front of a statewide audience. Huey got permission to answer the charges.

Newspapermen from all over the state arrived to evaluate the candidates. Those with no hope of the Ring's endorsement denounced the Ring. Those with some hope of Ring support discussed other issues. None of their speeches were any good. The crowd was bored. Last on the program was Huey. He walked over to the newsmen right before he ascended the platform and warned them that some of what he was going to say couldn't be printed.

On the platform, Huey looked awkward and rustic, but he gave a fiery speech. He didn't have a dime and didn't care if he had a political future. Governor Pleasant was a "criminal who disgraces the gubernatorial chair." Campbell, the man who had challenged him, was a "barfly." Standard Oil was an octopus out to control the state. It consisted of "the nation's most notorious and leading criminals" who were thrown out of Texas, ousted from Kansas, and forced to terms by the Oklahoma pipeline bill. Pleasant's crime was refusing to call the legislature into session to enact a pipeline regulation bill. Louisianans interested in "commercial freedom" should oppose Standard Oil just as they would fight a "cattle thief" or a "highway bandit."

The chairman said Huey's speech was as hot as the Hot Wells boiling springs. One newspaper announced that Long was a "sensation." Others said his speech was "vicious." A common question afterward was "[W]ho the hell is he?"[14]

Huey wrote his brother Shan that he had now recovered from the initial shock of being "complimented, cartooned and ridiculed." He followed up his attacks with a big Labor Day speech sponsored by a union. Julius fed anti-Campbell information to the newspapers. Huey privately complained that he was being asked about the gubernatorial race and had denied any ambition for it even though the real reason was his age, his handicap, he said, for the last fifteen years.[15]

Huey's oil stocks lost value because of the Pine Island freeze-out, but by how much is difficult to determine. Huey said his seven thousand shares of Claiborne Oil Company stock were worthless after the freeze-out.[16] Deutsch and Williams thought that Huey and O. B. Thompson traveled to New York to sell Banks Oil Company for only 10 percent of their investment.[17] This is a myth.

The freeze-out only lasted until July 1919. First the Texas Company and then Standard Oil lifted the embargo. Oil prices rose to $0.75 per barrel and then to $1.25 by December 1919. Huey's advocacy helped force this, or perhaps the big companies had absorbed the independents by this time,[18] but the freeze-out afterward caused no *additional* distress.

The story of Banks Oil Company, moreover, is more complicated than the myth. Huey put most of his time in the second half of 1919 and much of 1920 into the affairs of Banks, complaining to O. K. Allen that he was wasting the best years of his life and neglecting his family to do so.[19] But Huey still had dreams of great wealth, infected as he was by an oil-industry propaganda pamphlet: "Riches are today being powered into the laps of men who yesterday had just the bare necessities of life"; the opportunity has "never been equaled in the history of the world." Huey called this fifteen-page pamphlet a "marvel."[20]

In March 1919, after the freeze-out began but before it ended, Huey worked on a plan to change the capitalization of Banks from $80,000 to $1,500,000. A New York firm, H. L. Mandeville, was engaged to sell the additionally issued shares. If it could raise investor money, Banks could build a refinery and drill more wells.[21] A prospectus was issued, and rosy financial prospects for the "famous" Pine Island field were outlined. Mandeville asked for more and more information and for Banks to pay dividends to make its shares more attractive. Mandeville dribbled out excuses why it had not hit the big stock sales that Huey was counting on and that he had assured his Louisiana stockholders were coming.[22] Banks's primary shareholders had to loan the company $50,000 to keep it afloat at one point. It weathered a Federal Trade Commission inquiry and newspaper articles wondering whether investing in oil companies was a good idea. Banks counted on a well in Homer. Huey and O. K. Allen gave glowing reports about the drilling progress to Mandeville.[23]

The Homer well failed.[24] The shaft hit plenty of gas, and company officials believed that oil was right below it, but a kerosene lantern caught fire one night, injuring a workman and then water flooded the well for reasons no one could explain. Contemporaneously, Standard Oil, probably by taking over independents, drilled Pine Island gushers. Eventually a trade magazine wrote that it doubted Banks paid dividends from profits but probably only from the sale of its stock.[25] This is characteristic of a Ponzi scheme and killed future stock sales.

Unable to pay creditors, Banks then merged with American National Oil Company, getting stock and a promise to pay $650,000 to drill wells in exchange for its real estate and leases. Huey didn't negotiate this deal but wrote that it was splendid. The acquiring company was financially strong and its chief official, J. L. Payne, wealthy and successful.[26]

Huey was wrong. The company never spent the money to drill and, when sued, filed for bankruptcy. Creditors began hounding Huey. He developed an "oppressed feeling, which constant door knocks cause." When he got Payne on the witness stand in a bankruptcy hearing, Payne fought off Huey's cross-examination and accused Banks of misrepresenting the properties it provided to his company, thus excusing his obligation to pay the $650,000 to drill. Banks had listed a few properties it did not own in the list of assets to be acquired, probably an innocent mistake, and had offered substitute properties when it was discovered. To excuse his company's obligations, Payne—probably in bad faith—refused to accept them or ask for anything else.

Huey believed that, unlike a Ponzi scheme, the Banks properties were valuable, and he tried to reacquire them, but he couldn't raise the necessary funds. The "swindler" Payne—as Huey called him—became Huey's "nemesis," and he could never "put his finger" on him to rectify the situation. In court, Huey lost a motion to remove Payne and appoint a receiver for Banks. Banks's stockholders then lost interest in continuing a fight that Huey was unable to win.[27]

Two gubernatorial candidates survived the pre-campaign maneuverings. Frank P. Stubbs of Monroe had just returned from the war, had lined up support in northern Louisiana, and had won the Ring's endorsement. Stubbs's endorsement by the New Orleans Ring was masterminded by its leader, Martin Behrman. Since 1904, Behrman had served as mayor of New Orleans. He was born to a poor Jewish couple who had moved from New York to New Orleans when he was an infant. His father died soon after the move.

His mother died when he was twelve. Surviving as a street waif, he worked in grocery stores and went to school at night. When he was twenty-two, he converted to Catholicism, got married, and became a partner in a grocery store. Working his way up the Fifteenth Ward organization, he was cordial and polite, known by his saying, "let's get togedder." Behrman worked with all white ethnic groups, primarily Irish and Italians. He disliked silk-stocking, patrician reformers such as John M. Parker. With a few exceptions, the Ring under Behrman favored business interests. The cost of electricity from a regulated electric company was the highest in the country.[28]

Prostitution flourished in the Storyville area under Ring protection until the federal government closed it down in 1917, after which it spread to the rest of the city, as Behrman predicted: "You can make prostitution illegal, but you can't make it unpopular."[29] Another gem: "most people remember what you did to them rather than what you did for them."[30]

The Ring had made a few decisions that came back to haunt it in 1919. It had refused to back Jared Y. Sanders, a former lieutenant governor, governor, and congressman, each time elected with Ring support, in a recent race for the U.S. Senate. Jilted, Sanders now attacked the Ring. Behrman also had somehow managed to infuriate sitting governor Pleasant, who turned on him and fired thousands of the Ring's patronage workers. The Ring then splintered. The renegades formed the Orleans Democratic Association. Behrman sensed that much of the population, maybe influenced by veterans returned from World War I, was tired of politics and corruption as usual and was "wild" for reform.

Behrman's anointed candidate, Frank Stubbs, therefore, drew an opponent in the Democratic primary scheduled for January 1920: none other than John M. Parker. Parker already had support in the sugar parishes from his race in 1916 and in New Orleans from his Good Government League. Much of Parker's appeal resulted from his opposition to corruption. Parker also advocated, however, a severance tax to fund construction of modern highways and better schools, expansion of the state university, destruction of the New Orleans Ring, bringing natural gas to New Orleans, conservation of natural resources, women's suffrage, protection of independent oil drillers, and convening a constitutional convention to modernize Louisiana's constitution.[31] He was less specific than Huey, however, in advocating legislation regarding oil pipelines. Parker drew support from the Orleans Democratic Association, J. Y. Sanders, and other groups that splintered from the Ring, many of whom were not reform minded.[32]

Huey originally decided to sit out the race and break his neck to earn money.[33] But at a Labor Day rally in Shreveport, Huey drew from Stubbs an expression of sympathy for independent oil drillers and a pledge of support for an equitable pipeline-regulatory law. Stubbs balked at divorcing the oil companies from ownership of oil pipelines. Huey then wrote Parker asking for his position.[34]

On September 18, Parker pledged to protect independent oil interests. Huey described a meeting with Parker, who said he sympathized with victims of Standard Oil.[35] In public, Huey said he was satisfied with both candidates' answers, but he backed Parker, because Stubbs was supported by the Ring and Standard Oil.[36]

Parker's worst electoral showing four years earlier was in northern Louisiana. If Huey could change that, Parker might be elected, and Huey should be influential with a new administration. Most pundits, however, did not think Stubbs could be defeated.

Campaigning all over northern Louisiana for seventy days and neglecting his law practice,[37] Huey promised that Parker would pass a pipeline bill and criticized the New Orleans Ring for vice and corruption. He spoke in venues politicians hadn't visited in years. He contributed $2,200 to the campaign, a lot of money, considering his income. Julius backed Stubbs, but Huey enticed many of Julius's leaders to support Parker instead.[38] Huey couldn't deliver the entire north Louisiana vote to Parker. But he delivered a small majority of it, enough for Parker to win the January 1920 primary: 78,868 to 65,685 votes.[39]

No one thought Huey could help elect Parker. He won so many bets—suits and hats being a common wager—that his "mind was crowded as to a method of disposing them in a legitimate manner." One man sent him $100 to settle. Another bought him a new suit, now his most expensive one, at a cost of $95.[40] What would Huey do with his new clout?

Parker held a conference with five hundred oil-industry representatives and government officeholders in February 1920. The independents asked that all pipelines be declared common carriers and required to operate as common purchasers, and that ownership of oil and pipeline companies be separated. By April, however, the independents had prepared two weaker bills. Both bills were endorsed by Gulf Refining and Texas Company. In a press release written by their press agent, T. O. Harris, the independents denied there was anything radical in their proposals.

Huey wrote to Parker to oppose the independents' bills, arguing that price discrimination should always be prohibited, and that ownership of pipelines and oil companies should be separated. Huey claimed that Pine Island now was 95 percent controlled by the big oil companies, which explained the weaker legislation (drafted by Texas Company) they proposed.[41]

The new governor kept his distance. When the independents introduced their bill, however, Huey supported it. If a pipeline carried oil other than the oil of the pipeline's owner—subject to certain minimums—it would be judged a common carrier, and its rates set by the Railroad Commission. It passed the lower house by two votes. The opponents then asked for a gubernatorial conference.

The independents agreed to the conference, but Huey published a circular for the legislators charging that Standard Oil was now part of the legislative process of the state and that, regardless of the electoral results, the same old politicians wrote the legislation. His autobiography set forth his frustration: "Those of us, zealous for reform and who had exhausted ourselves in the election, hied back to our work to give attention to our several neglected affairs. The crowd of wiseacres, skilled at flattery and repartee, surrounded our newly elected governor. . . . When the slaves of the campaign had the time to visit him, the element we had expected to oust were needed to introduce us to our late candidate."[42] In private correspondence, Huey said Parker was a weakling who had to be flattered daily. To Julius, he wrote that "politics is the sorriest of all sorry games."[43]

On July 2, 1920, the conference was held. As a spectator, Huey remarked that certain independents had sold out. The governor and the big oil companies confronted Huey: did his circular refer to them? Huey replied that something peculiar was going on, but he was not referring to anyone personally. The conference negotiations produced a compromise bill.

The bill passed—not as good as the Oklahoma bill—and broadened the definition of a common carrier pipeline to include those carrying oil for consideration and those that may be legally held to be common carriers from the nature of the business conducted or from the way the business was carried on. Everyone agreed with this compromise except Huey.[44]

Huey had solid precedent on his side. Having the courts declare a pipeline as a common carrier on a case-by-case basis under the amorphous standards set forth would be slow. The delay and expense of litigation—especially if this took place in the middle of a freeze-out—would inhibit effective relief. Further litigation (initiated by Huey) was required to establish the commission's right to regulate the pipelines.

From then on, Parker, T. O. Harris, and Standard Oil's spokesman, Hunter Leake, were Huey's enemies. Leake issued statements and made speeches "skinning" Huey.[45] Parker hired detectives to see if Huey violated the Mann Act (anti-prostitution legislation) [46] on his commission trips.

Huey also fought Parker on the issue of a severance tax on natural resources such as oil, natural gas, lumber, salt, and sulfur. The existing law was poorly drafted, produced little revenue, and was inadequately enforced. Parker called a conference of industry representatives and asked them to agree on a new severance tax of 2.5 or 3.0 percent to raise revenue for the state university and other institutions. They refused. Standard Oil and its allies agreed to accept a rate of 1.0 percent, but no more.

Parker compromised and suggested 2 percent, but no less. He stood firm at this rate over a period of weeks. If the industry leaders refused to agree, Parker promised to propose that rate anyway and take his chances with the legislature.

In a separate meeting, the lumber interests agreed to the 2 percent rate but worried about subsequent increases. Parker pledged not to increase the tax during his term. The lumber agreement broke what had been a solid industry front of opposition. In a separate visit, Standard Oil agreed to the 2 percent rate, and Parker again agreed to prevent later increases. It asked who was going to draft the bill. "Basking in the glow of his success and the company of fellow aristocrats," Parker "gave a fantastic reply." He told them they could write the bill.

This stupidity "followed" Parker "like an evil specter for the rest of his administration." At various times he said he was "joking," that the state's lawyers had checked their work, or that he was justified by the need to obtain the additional tax revenue for the state. The "joking" defense was just a lie; Standard Oil wrote the bill as a temporary license tax on industries severing natural resources from the state. The best defense was that he wanted to avoid litigation over the bill, but this was not agreed to, and the oil industry challenged the severance tax in court.

In compromising on 2 percent, Parker misjudged the strength of support for a higher rate. Having faced down the industry in support of his 2 percent rate, he now tried to face down those who wanted a higher rate.[47] His honor was at stake. Huey allied with those who asked for a higher rate, but they lost, and the 2 percent rate was enacted.

Because of Parker's pipeline and severance tax positions, Huey opposed Parker's call for a constitutional convention. He thought the corporations would dominate it. Huey's district agreed with him, but the voters in south Louisiana and New Orleans overwhelmed his opposition. Huey's popularity was growing: he won his own election by 635 votes, carried his district for Parker in the gubernatorial election by 1,500 votes, and obtained a 6,000-vote margin against the constitutional convention.[48]

In the same month, Cumberland Telephone and Telegraph Company applied to the commission for a 25 percent increase in telephone rates. The company omitted from its application data on its costs and details of a promised expansion and gave its suggested rate schedule to commission counsel Wylie Barrow, not Chairman Taylor. Huey used this harmless breach of etiquette to goad Taylor into opposing the company. At the hearing, Huey and Taylor asked hostile questions of the company's lawyer, Hunt Chipley, whose cigarette holder and mannerisms connoted an English duke. Why had they bypassed the chairman? Why hadn't they submitted specific supporting data to justify their request? What was the increase going to cost a subscriber in Winnfield? The hearing adjourned until December for the company to submit supporting data.[49]

In December 1920, Cumberland provided the data. In the interim, municipalities converged on the commission to protest. Three days of testimony were taken. The commission took the application under advisement. Then New Orleans requested that the case be reopened so that it could present testimony from an expert accountant. Huey skipped the meeting to consider this on February 24, 1921. Statistical testimony was offered. The commission again took the case under advisement.

Just one day after the hearing and two days before the constitutional convention was to convene, Taylor and Michel granted the rate increase. Roused from his sleep at home by a reporter on the Saturday night the decision was issued, Huey charged that he was offered legal work if he would vote for the increase and that Taylor repudiated a promise to him to vote against it. Municipal officials were angry.

Strange and suspicious behavior was manifest. The opinion was issued on Saturday after the hearing concluded on Friday, and therefore was probably written before the hearing took place.[50] New Orleans opposed the rate increase, but its faithful ward leader and representative, Michel, voted for it. Huey charged that Michel was a tool of one of the company's lawyers. Originally, Taylor was hostile to the increase. Why did he change his mind? Huey's behavior in skipping the meeting is equally strange, however, considering that he usually sought out the scene of action. Did he secretly want the increase granted so he could dissent and dramatize a fight against a big corporate foe?

On behalf of Taylor and Michel, commission counsel Barrow wrote a defensive opinion. It supported the company's right to a return on its investment of 8 percent, omitted any discussion of Cumberland's ownership by two larger companies, and exhorted its customers to recall the number of years that Cumberland had operated without a rate increase. In his dissenting opinion, Huey denounced the 8 percent rate, considering the economic circumstances of Cumberland's 80,000 customers, and emphasized that Cumberland was owned (94 percent) by the Bell Telephone System, which was in turn owned (100 percent) by AT&T. AT&T owned 97 percent of Western Electric Company, which furnished Cumberland with its equipment. Thus, there was an opportunity to manipulate the ostensible costs to Cumberland that underlay its requested return.

Public sentiment forced the commission to consider requests to reopen the case in March. A large crowd attended to protest the increase. At its conclusion, one of the speakers, egged on by Huey's suggestive comments that he "leave the personalities for later" and that the decision was written "before the testimony closed," rushed over to Taylor and punched him twice in the face. The man was arrested and jailed. Huey bailed him out upon payment of a small fine. Two weeks later, the commission reopened the case to collect more evidence. Over Huey's objection, it allowed the approved and increased rates to be collected in the meantime.[51]

Huey now had three issues—the pipeline controversy, the severance tax, and the telephone-rate case—and a big political event (the constitutional convention) upon which to promote his views. Further cementing his brand as the champion of the people, in January 1921, he had won a lawsuit (later reversed on appeal) holding that the Shreveport ordinance raising streetcar fares to 6 cents from 5 cents was improper. This was front-page news in the *Shreveport Journal* and the *Shreveport Times*. The Central Trades and Labor Council congratulated him.[52]

At the constitutional convention, many delegates wanted to increase the severance tax rate to 3 percent and include that in the constitution, rebating some to the parishes from which the resources were taken. Governor Parker appeared before the taxation committee of the convention and asked its delegates to honor his gentlemen's agreement with Standard Oil, despite their mandate from their constituents and Parker's prior promise to exert no influence over the convention.

The debate culminated with a front porch conference. Delegates visited Parker to seek his views on a compromise severance tax provision for the constitution. Parker excused himself to telephone Standard Oil's treasurer and invited him to join them. After this, Parker addressed the convention. To fulfill his gentlemen's agreement, he urged that the severance tax be kept at its present level. To avoid hamstringing future legislatures, Parker advocated leaving the rate out of the constitution but, instead, letting future legislatures set the rate. The delegates followed this wise recommendation but set aside some portion of the tax for the parishes.[53] Standard Oil escaped having a 3 percent rate assessed against it; the parishes got some portion of the tax dedicated to them; and proponents of the higher rate got the chance to enact an increase at the next legislative session.

The new constitution contained a few desirable features. It renamed the Railroad Commission the "Public Service Commission" and broadened its authority. It empowered the legislature to regulate working conditions for women and authorized juvenile courts. The constitution was long and convoluted, however, and included many features detested by progressives. Effective authorization for an income tax was denied. Bonds to construct highways were forbidden. All highways had to be constructed on a pay-as-you-go basis, funded by taxes on gasoline and truck licenses.[54] Former governor Pleasant, a delegate to the convention, refused to sign the document because, he said, it was produced by corrupt corporate forces.[55]

Governor Parker was still influential, however. Reform candidate Andrew McShane, backed by Parker and the leader of the Orleans Democratic Association, John Sullivan, defeated New Orleans mayor Behrman in 1921. Parker and Sullivan were incongruous allies. Sullivan owned gambling interests and had split from and wanted to supplant the Ring and wield its power. In his obsession to defeat the Ring, Parker used patronage—the spoils system he had pledged to eliminate—to defeat the Ring's candidate. Huey applauded the victory.[56]

In his own district, Huey ran the campaign of John Land for the Louisiana Supreme Court. Brother Julius supported Land's rival. No one thought Land could win on his own, but he was credited with enough brains to engage Huey as his campaign manager. Huey was charged with being the "official mud slinger of the Land campaign" but had to defeat prejudice against Land's Christian Science religious beliefs. Land's victory left Huey still undefeated in his district.[57]

A special session of the legislature convened in September 1921. Proponents of the 3 percent severance tax rate—led by former governor Pleasant—again pressed their position. Governor Parker again relied on his gentlemen's agreement to oppose it.

Huey issued three circulars (on September 27 and 28, and October 1) to the legislators. They charged that Standard Oil, previously an invisible empire, was now visibly running the Parker administration: Parker let Standard Oil draft the severance tax bill; repudiated his promise to back an oil-pipeline bill; appointed the son of Standard Oil's lawyer to be superintendent of the state Charity Hospital in New Orleans after pledging that no lobbyists would be maintained at Baton Rouge; and pledged noninterference with the constitutional convention but then intervened to protect Standard Oil. Huey told the newspapers that Shelby Taylor was corruptly influenced to vote in favor of the Cumberland rate increase.[58] And he charged that a relative, Wade Long, had offered Huey a bribe.[59]

In response, legislators denounced Huey, demanded an investigation, and considered impeachment. One state representative suggested that a sanity commission be appointed to examine him. Another wanted to try him for contempt and put him in jail. Only one member exhibited intelligence. He proposed that everyone ignore Huey.

The House began hearings on Huey's charges. Called to testify, Huey explained that Cumberland's attorney, James C. Henriques Sr., had promised to throw legal work his way if he voted for the telephone-rate increase. In the presence of Paul Maloney, an Old Regular leader, Taylor had told Huey that he would vote against the rate increase. Henriques and Taylor responded that Huey lied. Huey asked to cross-examine Henriques; the chairman of the committee ruled that he could, but Henriques hustled to his seat, saying he didn't "even want to talk to such a liar as you are."[60] The committee chairman reversed himself and blocked Huey from asking Henriques any questions. The chairman also declined to call Paul Maloney to the stand—even though he witnessed the conversation of Huey and Taylor and would have either confirmed Huey's testimony or impeached it—and closed the hearing.[61]

A Parker ally tried to have the incumbent members of the Railroad Commission removed incident to the creation of the new Public Service Commission. At Huey's direction, one member rose to suggest that all three commissioners should resign and be made to stand for reelection. Another member said he was authorized to say that Huey would accept this arrangement. An opposition member stumbled into the trap: "But Long's the only one who would be reelected." At the end of this farce, the House voted to impeach all three members of the commission but never took any action to remove them.[62]

Right before those proceedings, Parker one-upped the House. He swore out affidavits charging Huey with criminal libel. If Huey's charges were true, Parker said, he was unfit to be governor but, if they were false, then Huey should be jailed. The sheriff of Caddo Parish served the writs. Huey traveled to Baton Rouge—far from home, into the domicile of Standard Oil, he complained—to post bond. Borrowing $5,000 from James G. Palmer of Shreveport, and hiring Palmer, Robert R. Reid of south Louisiana, and his brother Julius to represent him, Huey swaggered into Baton Rouge and posted the bond, saying "I figured you boys might be short of ready money down here." Huey's third child was born during this crisis, and he named him Palmer Reid Long, after his two attorneys. Palmer wanted to run for governor. Huey implied that he might support him.[63]

The criminal libel trial was scheduled almost immediately after the House concluded its investigation. Autobiographies rarely provide a fully accurate insight into the personality of their authors. But at the time of this trial, Huey revealed an insight into his personality, something that made him great, first by letter to his lawyers, and then to the public by reprinting it twelve years later.

Huey's lawyers advised him to play it safe before the trial or to seek some adroit way out. Playing it safe means to keep your mouth shut, because anything you say can and will be used against you. An adroit resolution would entail some face-saving compromise. Huey rejected this advice. The *Saturday Evening Post* had published an article on Lost Leaders that Huey quoted in his letter to his attorneys:

> There is real pathos about a certain class of politicians to be found in every capitol. They are men, public servants, of marked and acknowledged ability, whose inborn talents would have made them first-raters if they could have mustered a little more courage, a little sterner devotion to principle (rather than expediency), a sense of duty a little higher; *if they could only lose their heads at the right time and refuse to play it safe;* if, in short, *they could have brought themselves to pay the price* that the truest success exacts even of genius itself. Their status is not that of men who are naturally qualified to lead, but who deprive the world of their best services because *they grudge the price* that leadership costs.

Huey concluded that it was too late to play it safe; too much depended on standing his ground.[64] He stood for the trial.

Judge Harney F. Brunot presided over the six-day trial. Parker testified with a flushed face and in an emotional voice, admitting to his numerous contacts with Standard Oil, that he made an agreement with it, and that its representatives in fact drafted the severance tax statute. Huey testified that he was not trying to save Parker's personal soul and that he had made a political attack to help the people of the state. Asked to explain how the invisible empire of Standard Oil had become visible, he pointed to Parker's admissions of his meetings with Standard Oil representatives, his appointment of Standard Oil spokesman Hunter Leake and others connected to Standard Oil to state positions, and their drafting of the tax bill.[65]

The trial split public opinion and friends of Huey and Parker. Reid reported that sentiment in Baton Rouge was strongly divided. Many who wanted a higher severance tax rate and criticized Parker's decision to back off the higher rate disliked Huey's attacks. Some thought Parker was honest but too befuddled to take a principled position. These same men thought Huey was sincere. John Overton, for example, thanked Huey for saying that Parker should have had Overton draft the bill. But he took pains to tell him that Parker had asked him to review the severance tax bill, that he viewed it as admirably drafted, and that he considered the controversy lamentable. Huey was helped because former governor Pleasant, like Huey, complained of Parker's interference at the behest of Standard Oil. Likewise, many delegates or legislators admitted that they wanted to vote for a higher severance tax rate but felt Parker's stand was a steamroller, a bitter pill, which constrained them to vote as he wished.[66]

Before the trial, it was rumored that Judge Brunot would rule against Huey. And he did, finding Huey technically guilty on both counts. Lecturing Huey that he had an impulsive nature given to ill-considered and indiscreet utterances, sentencing was set at thirty days in jail on the first count and a fine of one dollar on the second count. The jail term was suspended. In a grandstand play, Huey refused to pay the fine. So, Palmer paid it. Parker claimed vindication.

Although Huey walked out of court smiling and claiming victory, he was enraged. Huey demanded that his lawyer, Reid, oppose Brunot for the next Supreme Court election the following year. In a restaurant after the verdict, J. Y. Sanders stopped by his table to chat, and Huey was heard to say, "Brunot will never go to the supreme bench." In fact, Reid defeated Brunot in the next election.

After the trial, Huey issued a press release full of bravado. Corporate control of the state had been exposed. The power of the people would make the corporations accountable. "The fight is just beginning," he said. A south Louisiana politician told a New Orleans newspaper reporter that an "awful illogic" had infected the people. "They don't know Huey Long. They never saw him and would not know him if he stepped off the train at our station. But they know him in name and you can't make them believe he is not their defender."[67]

The power of the people caused Parker and Standard Oil to end their gentlemen's agreement in January 1922. Parker announced that he would recommend a 3 percent severance tax rate in the May legislative session. Huey charged that Parker only agreed to the increase to avoid a recall election.[68]

Nevertheless, Huey remained a minority on the Public Service Commission. If he stayed in the minority, he could continue to verbally attack the big corporations but could never strike a blow against them or confer a benefit on his constituents. Fate intervened, however, to give him that chance.

# Six

# GETTING THINGS DONE

John T. Michel died at his home on November 22, 1921. Governor Parker scheduled an election for March 1922 to replace him. The Ring's candidate was Stuart Seelye, and his biggest opponent was Francis Williams. Williams was backed by John P. Sullivan, head of the Orleans Democratic Association that had supported Parker for governor and McShane for mayor. The group renamed themselves the New Regulars.

Sullivan was six feet, four inches tall and weighed 260 pounds. He flunked out of West Point because of a weakness in mathematics, but not before engaging in twenty-seven fights prompted by his refusal to be hazed. He dressed in expensive silk shirts, tailored suits, and smoked 90-cent cigars, also tailor-made, was a gambler, and had ties to racetracks and liquor interests despite Prohibition. With Parker's backing, a civil service provision for New Orleans had been passed by the constitutional convention. Under pressure from McShane and Sullivan, Parker never asked for legislation to implement it.[1]

Williams was also big with curly reddish hair but more handsome than Sullivan. An urban progressive, he and his brother Gus affiliated with Sullivan to get Francis elected to the Public Service Commission. He promised to vote against telephone-rate increases. Huey did not campaign for Williams but offered helpful advice.[2] Williams won.

Huey went to New Orleans after the election, and he and Williams reached an agreement by which Huey would become chairman and they would control the commission. They took over on April 28, 1922. Williams then moved, with Huey's support, to require Cumberland to attend the May 2 meeting of the commission—four days later—to show cause why the rate increase granted the previous year should not be stopped pending a rehearing.

The hearing on May 2 was attended by Cumberland (represented by Hunt Chipley, James C. Henriques Sr., and J. Blanc Monroe) and the City of New Orleans (represented by Ivy Kittredge). Monroe was New Orleans's leading attorney: direct, tenacious, fierce, charming, arrogant, and cold, a race imperialist, and proud of his ancestors on both sides of the family, James Monroe and James K. Polk. His father was a justice on the Louisiana Supreme Court and had served as president of the Louisiana Club, the most exclusive private club in New Orleans, and as Comus, the monarch of the city's most socially elite Mardi Gras Carnival Krewe.[3]

Monroe moved to recuse Williams, saying he had prejudged the case, having campaigned to deny the rate increase. Huey shouted: "Don't read the motion! We will not allow the motion to be read at this time nor will we entertain it. There is no provision in the law to recuse a member of the [Public Service Commission], regardless of what kind of campaign pledges he makes." Monroe repeated himself, adding that Huey had not consulted the other members in making his ruling. Huey interrupted again and directed the stenographer to show nothing on the record other than what he said and again overruled the recusal motion. Monroe then had a failure of perception (he had made his motion, preserved the record, but was overruled) and presumed to dictate again what the record would show. Now Huey threatened him with jail for contempt. Monroe subsided.

After two days of evidence, the case was taken under advisement. Huey took the record to Shreveport and drafted an opinion and order that continued the rehearing and suspended the rate increases granted the previous year until a final decision was reached. This was announced and adopted on May 13 by a two-to-one vote. A final hearing was scheduled for June.

Cumberland then went to court, declaring an emergency. It asked the U.S. District Court, Judge Rufus E. Foster, to prevent the commission from enforcing its order. Judge Foster granted an injunction, but Cumberland overreached. Huey and Williams voted to make Huey counsel for the commission, and he appealed the order to a three-judge panel of the same court, which included Foster, on procedural grounds: a single judge was not allowed to enjoin a state agency. Only a three-judge panel could do it. The panel agreed with Huey and voted two-to-one to overrule Foster.

Cumberland appealed this decision and asked Judge Foster to reinstate his injunction while it did so. Huey was confident that he could defeat this maneuver, saying "Judge Foster cannot revive a dead body." But he was wrong. Foster reinstated it.

Huey moved to dissolve Foster's order in the U.S. Supreme Court. Traveling to Washington, DC, Huey again argued that Judge Foster could not himself enjoin the commission. Monroe argued that Huey's rollback of the rate increase was ruinous. The Supreme Court agreed with Huey by opinion issued November 20, 1922.[4]

Exactly why Cumberland's lawyers, all well-established members of the bar, would embark on an expensive and fruitless procedural challenge is unclear. Perhaps they wanted to wear down Huey, or did not think he would realize their error, or have the confidence to appeal when Judge Foster ruled against him. Why they failed to ask a three-judge district court to enjoin the suspension of the rate increase while they appealed is also difficult to fathom. Perhaps from their prior loss, they knew that Foster was their only sympathetic judge, reflecting that their position on the merits was weak.

Cumberland's lawyers picked the fight—they chose to appear before Judge Foster only, to seek an injunction at that point, and to maintain their position after a three-judge panel told them they were wrong—and Huey beat them. Years later, Chief Justice William Howard Taft of the U.S. Supreme Court said he had seldom seen a lawyer with a greater legal mind or a better capacity to argue a legal point than Huey.[5]

When the case was remanded, the commission set the final hearing for January 11, 1923. Municipal representatives, civic groups, and political leaders now urged compromise. Cumberland presented a revised rate proposal; the City of New Orleans pushed for a lower one. Cumberland's Chipley, "no longer looking so ducal," begged for compromise. Two days later, Huey and Williams allowed rate increases of about half the company's original proposal but required it to refund its customers 100 percent of the increase levied after the commission's May order. A specified construction program was outlined. If it failed to fulfill the program, the commission reserved the right to reopen the case. Cumberland had to pay the commission's lawyers, too. Huey warned that, if Cumberland refused to accept the decision, it would be fought "to the bitter end." Two days later, the company accepted. It then refunded $467,000 to eighty thousand people across the state and paid Huey a fee of $10,000.

Huey became a state hero overnight. Telephones were new and prized devices. The idea of a politician forcing a large corporation, represented by a team of expensive lawyers, to issue actual refund checks must have been thrilling to the powerless Louisiana population, even to those who at the time lacked phones. Huey was later criticized for considering higher rates or for retracting an agreement to issue a smaller rebate. Huey was a normal, pragmatic politician, Professor Williams said; he made his play for principle and then settled reasonably. Huey said he donated his fee to the sanitarium that cared for his sick sister.[6] But Huey was exhausted and temporarily depressed after the victory: "As blue as indigo," he said.[7]

After winning his appeal in the Cumberland case but before the compromise, Huey attacked another corporate opponent, his longtime nemesis from the Pine Island freeze-out, Standard Oil. On December 5, 1922, the commission ordered Standard Oil to explain why it shouldn't be judged a common carrier, why a uniform scale of rates for the transportation of oil should not be prescribed, and why it should not be prohibited from owning oil wells.

Because the company had recently extended its pipelines into Arkansas and thus was now subject to the Interstate Commerce Commission's common carrier rules, it had already decided to put its pipelines into a separate company. Huey's announcement sped up their plans. Standard Oil declared in January 1923 that it had divested its pipeline properties, thinking this would moot the order. The commission nevertheless set a hearing date in February.[8]

At that meeting, Standard Oil objected to the jurisdiction of the commission over it because it no longer owned pipelines. Huey overruled the objection but directed that the new pipeline company be added as a party. The pipeline company submitted proposed rates, which Huey rejected. With everyone waiting for his rate decision, the commission issued a report in April that was all history and no decision. The report recounted the Pine Island freeze-out; explained the necessity for a combined state and federal regulation of the entire oil industry; and charged that Standard Oil misused its power to hurt the small farmer, independent oil operator, and chance-taking capitalist. Later in the month, the commission asked the pipeline companies to submit data necessary to prescribe rates and to show cause why it should not be judged a public utility. It also issued a subpoena to inspect Standard Oil's books.

Standard Oil asked Judge Brunot to prevent this. Emphasizing Huey's personal antipathy to the company, it alleged that he had announced at a hotel that he was going to put Standard Oil's officers in jail for contempt. Brunot granted the order. Huey immediately appealed, writing a twenty-eight-page legal brief in four hours. Huey's simultaneous orders and threats to declare Standard Oil a public utility must have poisoned the court. It denied Huey's appeal *in toto* the same day it was filed.

In a hearing the next day, Huey said the injunction was illegal, but the commission would adhere to it until it was dissolved, and Huey's application to dissolve the injunction would be filed shortly. Meanwhile, testimony on the rates that should be charged by the pipeline company would be heard, after which a schedule of rates would be prescribed. Testimony was taken, and the matter was taken under advisement.

The very next day, May 5, Huey issued a scale of rates that was insanely low. The pipeline company took issue with every finding, every theory of calculation, and with Huey's hostility, and asked for and obtained an injunction from Judge Brunot forbidding enforcement of the rates. After Brunot made it final, Huey appealed the judge's prior order forbidding the commission from declaring Standard a public utility or examining its books. He won the right to examine Standard Oil's books but lost the right to declare it a public utility. Huey claimed victory.[9]

Huey overreached the commission's authority and never requested legislation that would allow it to declare that the oil or pipeline company was a utility. By prescribing a ridiculous rate structure, he let the company and the court prescribe them. He was correct in demanding access to Standard Oil's books and records because that information would be relevant to establish the rates for the pipeline companies but, then, after winning his point, he never inspected them. The newspapers that applauded his fight against the telephone company denounced him for his actions in the Standard Oil case.

The Cumberland and Standard Oil fights aroused great popular interest and made Huey a household name. With his work and publicity from smaller cases, however, he would still have been a notable public figure.

Huey forced a railroad company to build a new depot at Monroe, after conducting a personal inspection. The commission ordered the repair or installation of a new cistern at Bordelonville and directed that platforms at Bayou Sara and Plattenburg be raised. The commission initially denied Southwestern Gas and Electric Company's rate request, after which a moderate increase was permitted. The Shreveport Railway Company had its first request denied, too, after which a moderate increase was allowed.

Huey informed himself of the regulatory practices in other states and researched the law. One hostile commentator conceded that Huey knew more than the railroad lawyers who practiced before the commission about what had been done and the relevant legal authority.[10] Huey intended to become active in the National Association of Railway and Utility Commissioners, but after getting appointed to study the capitalization of railroads, had to resign the assignment because of his political duties.[11]

He also had an instinctive empathy for people in trouble and enjoyed exercising power to help them. A salesman who had not voted for Huey needed a phone to keep in touch with his household while he traveled. He called Huey who, in two separate phone calls to the telephone company one week apart, profanely and emphatically demanded a phone. An independent logger couldn't get a railroad to transport his logs. He called Huey. Huey told him to get the logs ready and he would have a freight train pick them up that evening. The man doubted until the logs were retrieved as promised. The man's wife thought Huey must be a dictator. "What's the difference," her husband said, "he gets things done."[12]

Compulsive follow-up was a key reason he got things done. Ira Gleason complained to Huey that a load of his lumber had rotted because of the absence of railroad spurs, so Huey promised to have the railroads construct them. Each week for three weeks Huey wrote Gleason to see whether construction had started. After the third week, construction began.[13]

Every month, Huey's name appeared in a newspaper somewhere in a favorable light based on some good deed done, some problem being investigated, some beneficial order issued: "Long to Fine Rails That Don't Give Service," "Long Wins Rate Fight For Sugar," "Long Answers Farmers' Plea," "Long Calls Lines to Consider Cut in Freight Rates," "Long Has Issued Warning About Louisiana Sugar Rate Increase," "Long Leads Fight on Rates in Orleans," "Long Condemns Missouri Pacific as Flouting Law."[14] Sometimes he was gruff and threatening; sometimes he was charming and affable; it depended on what he thought would work.[15]

The newspapers created some favorable press coverage, but Huey induced stories, too. Henry Jastremski circulated press releases as Huey directed. Huey would bring a reporter his press release and weigh it down with a jar of moonshine whiskey on the man's desk.

Huey could act vindictively. The railroad run by the Edenborns, the same family that tried to get Winnfield to impose a tax to support its railroad line into Winnfield which Old Hu and Huey had foiled, was subjected to a running campaign of criticism.

Gamesmanship livened other hearings. Charles Dunbar was one of Huey's old law professors. Dunbar was also on retainer by a railroad that had a case up before the commission. On the pretext that some interesting legal issues were going to arise, Huey invited Dunbar to the hearing. The professor was startled when, at the hearing, Huey said that the eminent Dunbar's attendance "shows the [railroad's] interest in this case, but we will win."[16]

Stalwart member of the bar Edward T. Merrick suffered the indignity of Huey's interruption in the middle of an argument: "Damn it, sit down!" Later Huey apologized to Merrick, telling him he had to "impress these people." Offended by Huey's ideas and conduct, Merrick complained to fellow lawyer Charles Rivet about "that creature" Long, wondering how he ever got admitted to the bar. Rivet told Merrick that he had been on Huey's examining committee. Merrick checked his examining committee records and then, in shock, wondered how Huey had fooled so many people.[17]

After his election to the Railroad Commission, Huey moved his law practice to Shreveport in January 1919. Lumber magnate, oil man, friend, and client, O. B. Thompson, a big, rugged, handsome man who radiated confidence, had suggested the move, and found Huey a great office location.[18] His practice grew even faster than it had grown in Winnfield. His doctor ordered him to get some exercise, so he joined a local baseball team, playing every position, in his spare time.[19] Juggling his law clients, business interests, and political duties left him in a "deranged mental state at the end of each week." By September 1919, he was making good money from investments in oil companies and legal fees. He declined to advise his brother Shan about whether or how to invest in the oil business, however, because money was easy to lose as well as easy to make.[20] In October, he asked Julius to take over his cases outside of Shreveport because he only wanted to practice there.[21]

Because of the Banks Oil recapitalization and other oil business, Huey traveled to New York about every five weeks. He stayed in the Hotel Pennsylvania, the largest hotel in the world,[22] a hangout for many oil-industry executives and entrepreneurs. Meeting people who could invest in oil companies or provide the capital to drill wells, Huey acted like a typical capitalist. In fact, he was not anti-capitalist, but rather against the Standard Oil monopoly and in favor of the independent entrepreneurs. Huey sent New Orleans cigars to one New York entrepreneur, writing that they were far superior to any he could obtain in New York.[23] To a California businessman, he offered two gallons of cane syrup fresh from southern Louisiana.[24] In one prophetic letter, he wrote that, from the discussions he witnessed, the tax burden of the country was going to be shifted in the coming years from the rich to the poor.[25]

Huey asked Julius to join him in Shreveport as a partner. Huey said Julius could be the nominal senior partner, but neither should be the supreme ruler, both should treat each other with respect, and Huey could not be treated as a clerk or junior partner in any joint trials they conducted; his reputation couldn't stand diminishment, even from a single incident. Julius was the district attorney in Winnfield, however, and he declined, without bitterness. One year later, Huey wrote him without rancor that it was "useless for you and I to ever talk about practicing law together."[26]

While Huey's practice grew, Julius's fortunes declined. In 1920, Huey critiqued Julius's support for incumbent congressman James Aswell, recalling Aswell's sins from 1917.[27] Julius decided to run for district judge against his former ally, Cass Moss. Huey advised against opposing Moss, not because of any regard for Moss, but because the position was a dead end. At the end of eight years, Huey said, Julius wouldn't have a law practice and would have to start over. Better to spend half the time he had spent on politics educating himself about the law. Better to have a law practice than to engage in politics, with its uncertainty.[28] Julius ran anyway but lost.

On June 19, 1920, Huey again offered Julius a partnership in Shreveport.[29] This time Julius accepted. Huey wrote a friend that he was looking forward to having Julius join him because he was one of the best lawyers in the state.[30] They drafted a partnership agreement that reflected prior problems more than it effected a solution, however. Each promised not to disrespect the other in front of clients or enter the other's office without permission.[31]

This was no more successful than their partnership in Winnfield, with violent arguments and long periods of the silent treatment. The final precipitating event that ended their partnership was political, arising from Huey's support of Judge Land for the Supreme Court. Julius backed Land's opponent. Huey had an awful argument with Julius about it, and Huey literally kicked him out of his office. Huey wrote sister-in-law Aline McConnell that his offices "are pretty now" with "large nice rugs on all three floors. . . . Only the name 'Huey P. Long' adorns these offices. I am governor, mayor, king and clerk. No . . . other authority has a right even to be heard."[32]

In September 1921, Julius wrote a terrible letter to Huey, accusing him of numerous misdeeds, and Huey replied with violent denials and countercharges and demeaning characterizations of Julius: Huey had taken him in as a "broken-down, impoverished, and past-handed politician" whose demeanor destroyed the positive impressions Huey tried to create about Julius. Two months later, they reconciled. Huey wrote that he knew Julius was motivated by good faith, and that he appreciated his recent "brotherly interest" and help on one of Huey's cases and offered to reciprocate. It was unfortunate, Huey said, that their "mutual faults and temperaments" deprived each of their mutual support, and he was "only too sorry for it." A year later, Huey again wrote Julius with antipathy.[33] Huey chortled to family members that, when the brothers settled their accounts, Julius left with more money from their partnership than he had made in the previous three years.[34]

Huey concentrated on his lucrative volume personal injury and workers' compensation practice. He stopped taking divorce and collection cases.[35] The workers' compensation cases often required periodic payments, necessitating a lot of paperwork as small checks arrived and had to be divided to account for attorney fees. He preferred to negotiate a lump sum payment after an award was made.[36] When he couldn't, the companies would sometimes reopen the case years later, arguing that the plaintiff had recovered.

It is difficult to determine Huey's winning percentage and would not indicate much. Sometimes he won an award at the trial level and appealed to get more, and his opponents often appealed to reduce the award he obtained at the trial level or to throw it out. He won and lost some of these cases. He took an aggressive approach in case selection, did his best, and let the chips fall where they may. In those cases where one can see how he examined witnesses, he got right to the point with a concise examination that covered the essential points. He pushed the envelope with leading questions.

With the liberalization of workers' compensation laws and his political notoriety, Huey capitalized on an expansion of this type of work. He systematized his practice. He often used his personal physician, Dr. E. L. Sanderson, as an expert witness to testify about his clients' injuries but thought he was trusted by his opponents to issue an honest opinion. His exploitation of these factors can be compared to those lawyers who, in more recent times, capitalized on advertising or class actions for mass torts (such as asbestos or tobacco).

Huey sued the corporations he regulated as a member of the Public Service Commission: Standard Oil, Cumberland, Southwestern Gas, railroads, and others. The commission's counsel opined that this was permissible.[37] It wouldn't be today.

Huey was the richest Long at this point.[38] His notion of friendship, sense of family, or fear of God required him to be generous, and to get things done for his friends and family. This "soft side of [Huey's] nature was visible to but a few people and would have been unbelievable to the many who knew him only as the ruthless ruler of politics. It is unbelievable to many even today."[39]

In a land title case, he beat some of the best lawyers in the state, convincing the fact finder that the rich and powerful Urania Lumber Company had either never obtained the signature of poor and innocent Hattie D. Wheelus or had obtained her signature by fraud. The owner of Urania believed Huey's presentation was unscrupulous, a common reaction from defendants who lose. Walking with Bozeman on the night of his victory past an open-air tabernacle at which a preacher was taking up a collection, Huey marched down the aisle and wrote the astonished preacher a check for $150, one-tenth of his Wheelus fee. Then he left, fast.[40]

One of his friends from the University of Oklahoma visited New Orleans and lost all his money at the racetrack. Huey wired him the money and said he would do the same for any of his Oklahoma friends.[41] Street panhandlers were given money.[42] Once he broke down and wept while talking to a client and told his partners to fight twice as hard for half of the fee.[43] He kept a charity jar of coins on his desk to donate to needy people. He tried to get one man to give up drinking by giving him a dollar for every day he was sober. After thirty days, he was so pleased that he bought the man a new suit, hat, shirt, tie, and shoes. The man pawned the clothes to go on a bender.[44] A fellow salesman who had loaned him money when they were both down and out in Memphis six years earlier was sent fifteen dollars; Huey spent months to track him down.[45]

Sister Caledonia was afflicted with tuberculosis and went to live in Arizona at a sanitarium. Huey supported her for years and followed her progress. At times, Huey believed she was taking advantage of him and not concentrating on getting well. While he told many friends that his law practice was doing well and that he was making considerable money, there were various times when he had "troubles" that prevented him from sending the sanitarium money.[46] When Rose's mother got sick, Huey paid for her recuperation out of state at a sanitarium without complaint.[47]

Huey administered the estate of Mrs. Jennie K. Bankston's husband, which was set up to benefit his two boys. The older boy, Wyatt, contracted tuberculosis and was admitted to a sanitarium in Texas. Williams credits Huey for regularly writing him encouraging letters as if he were the boy's father and giving him quite a bit of his own money.[48] Tempering Williams's praise, Huey administered the estate because he settled the case for the death of Mrs. Bankston's husband for $4,000, with $1,000 of this going for legal fees, without having to file a lawsuit. John Overton represented the defendant, and the company told Huey it did not want to fight it. Wyatt's brother made a bigger sacrifice, giving up his share of the wrongful death award to help his brother recuperate. Huey gave about $160 of his own money. When

Wyatt was cured, Huey asked Senator Broussard to get him a civil service job. In 1927, he told Wyatt (and others) that he had no more money to give because of his gubernatorial campaign.[49]

Rose's sister Aline, called "Peaches," was also a victim of tuberculosis and a beneficiary of Huey's extended generosity. Admitted to a sanitarium run by Huey's cousin Arthur Long, in Texas, Huey unstintingly paid her expenses of $125 per month, and he offered her more spending money than she requested. She adored him. Some War Department order threatened the survival of the sanitarium after the war, but Huey, working through his friend and now congressman, John Sandlin, got the order modified.[50] Eventually, he thought the sanitarium was not effecting a cure and he advised her to go elsewhere at his expense.[51]

A war hero that some said was an imposter who spoke in favor of war bonds with Huey in 1918 was a bona fide hero with a mental illness—at least Huey thought so. The man traveled under aliases, passed bad checks, and ran up bills that he never intended to pay. Huey wrote letters over months to investigate his whereabouts. When he learned that the man was in a Texas prison, Huey collected statements and affidavits from people to support his request to the Texas governor for a pardon. He was "paid by no one" and was "taking this up as a humane duty."[52]

At various times, his brothers, his wife's brothers, his father, and his own family irritated or wearied him. They all wanted to borrow money or share his, he complained.[53] Huey didn't support Earl's law-school ambitions because he doubted his character. He denied Old Hu a loan to buy additional land to raise hogs. His old man should "piddle around with what he had." When Old Hu remarried and moved, Huey wrote that in this new community he would be able to "find several hundred people who will be glad to listen to him talk at all hours of the day or night." His brother Shan asked to borrow $500. Huey feared that, when it came time to repay the loan, Shan would invent some prior instance in which he had performed an uncompensated service for Huey that would excuse repayment.[54] That is what Shan did.[55] On Thanksgiving 1920, Huey was even reluctant to go home to his family. He had planned to attend an Elks Club event, but Rose forbade it. To gather and restore his "sinews" to go home to his family, he stayed in his office and wrote a friend first.[56]

Williams wrote that Huey's new home city, Shreveport, ostracized him because he didn't associate with the "nice people." In 1921, a newspaper reported a legislator's comment that Huey got drunk in Baton Rouge.[57] Huey issued a detailed statement accounting for his activities on the day in question—he was conducting public hearings—and listed the people who witnessed his conduct to rebut the charge.[58] He threatened a libel suit. When Huey saw the editor on the street, he attacked him. They ended in the gutter rolling around until bystanders separated them. On two other occasions Huey was accosted by Shreveport lawyers angered about something he said. One of them gave Huey a black eye. Another elderly lawyer assaulted Huey with an umbrella. The city's "acidly expressed disapproval did not faze Huey in the slightest.... [H]e hurled every insult with obvious relish."[59]

Yet Huey insinuated himself into leadership in Shreveport. A mass meeting called to investigate police cruelty to prisoners resulted in the appointment of a committee including Huey and Judge James G. Palmer to investigate. They recommended convening a grand jury to take evidence. Huey was active representing labor unions, dissolving injunctions issued against strikers, fighting to prevent railroads from reducing laborers' wages, and contributing to union members on strike.[60]

As his law practice grew, Huey partnered with a succession of junior lawyers. One of them was William Denman, in Arkansas. The two of them could sometimes choose which state's law was best for their clients—depending on where their client lived, where the injury occurred, and where the injury-causing company was located—and file lawsuits in the most favorable state. When he gave Denman a copy of his autobiography, he inscribed: "To a friendship that survived a law partnership."[61]

Williams ends his description of Huey's law career with another lawsuit against a bank. Once again, other lawyers declined to take the case. Again, Huey was consulted as a last resort. But this time the amount in controversy was a lot more than $276, and the client was a lot more prominent than a poor widow. A former mayor of Shreveport, Ernest R. Bernstein, had also been a vice president of Commercial National Bank, responsible for approving loans, and had approved a loan to an oil company in which he owned an interest. The company later defaulted. Bank officials lauded Bernstein in their board meetings but secretly excoriated him to the comptroller of the currency. The comptroller thereupon opined that Bernstein approved the loan to enrich himself, even though Bernstein had not profited personally. The backstabbing officers had made similar loans to the same company when Bernstein was absent from the bank. The officers hired a detective to impersonate a law enforcement officer who, with the comptroller's report, confronted Bernstein, who, under this duress, guaranteed the loan's repayment up to $70,000. They concealed from Bernstein that the comptroller's opinion was based on their own misrepresentations and that the law enforcement official was their hired imposter. The bankers prepared a pamphlet criticizing Bernstein and distributed it in Louisiana and other states.

Huey filed a defamation lawsuit seeking $500,000 and cancellation of the guaranty. It was fraudulently obtained because of the conspiracy and false statements of the bank officials, he alleged. He printed his complaint so it could be distributed to counteract the bad publicity Bernstein received. The bank filed two countersuits seeking damages from Bernstein on guarantees provided months later. (It was difficult to claim that these latter guarantees were obtained by the earlier fraudulent acts.) A younger lawyer, Robert A. Hunter, assisted Huey, but Huey did most of the work himself, initially at home to get away from office distractions and then at a hotel to avoid household distractions. Huey lost a procedural motion in 1922 that he successfully appealed. The trial in 1924 took two months, the longest trial in the history of Caddo Parish. He lost again and appealed. On appeal, the Louisiana Supreme Court, in a decision written by Winston Overton, John Overton's brother, ruled that Bernstein was defamed and awarded him $5,000 (about $125,000 today), a large defamation verdict, plus he was excused from the $70,000 guaranty (about $1.2 million today). It was front page, banner headline news in the Shreveport newspapers.

The case was unlike the volume-practice personal injury work. There were numerous detailed court papers filed and many witnesses. A thorough study of banking rules and regulations was required. Huey obtained certified copies of Department of Treasury documents and issued subpoenas in other states. The abstract of the trial testimony was typed on long paper and was almost one inch thick. His first brief on appeal was almost two hundred pages long, and his reply brief was almost half that size. Lawyers from other states requested copies of his briefs. A month later, the two related lawsuits filed against Bernstein for the later guarantees were settled for $85,000, or 47 percent of what was claimed. This made the front page of the Shreveport papers but without the banner headlines.[62]

The president of Commercial National Bank was so enraged at Huey's legal attacks that he accosted Huey in downtown Shreveport, pulled a knife, and dared him to say something. Huey was asked how he responded: "What would you do if a man held a knife to your throat and dared you to say something? I didn't say nothing."[63] Huey saved Bernstein over $150,000, plus his reputation. In 1926 Bernstein paid Huey over $38,000, a huge sum for the time.[64]

There is an appealing symmetry in bracketing the study of Huey's legal career with a case against two banks, one that launched his law practice, and the other—"Huey's last important case" that paid him "the only big fee of his legal career"—shortly before he won the governorship.[65] In Huey's autobiography, he said that, after the corporations and the millionaires "fell out with each other," he "was able to accept highly remunerative employment from one of the powerful to fight several others which were even more powerful. Then [he] made some big fees." Only after Williams published his book were the documents relating to Huey's law career found, which showed that he had multiple cases for businessmen and corporations.[66]

Huey made $70,000 gross as a lawyer in 1926.[67] With these huge fees, Rose convinced Huey to buy their first house. They built a Spanish-style structure of white brick that cost $40,000. Huey moved into the house, the construction of which he had compulsively planned and impatiently supervised, the night before the rest of the family arrived, and slept on the floor. The balcony featured wrought-iron grillwork. Huey took the architect down to the Commercial National Bank and had him copy the bank's grillwork to remind everyone how he had defeated the bank, changing only the monogram to "HPL."[68]

Before the big fees were earned in 1926, Huey was considering a gubernatorial run, especially after his victory in the Cumberland case and during his controversy with Standard Oil.

He was strongest in north Louisiana, where he had campaigned for himself in 1918, for Parker in 1919, against the constitutional convention in 1920, and for Supreme Court justice John Land in 1921. Huey's wealthy former attorney, James G. Palmer of Shreveport, wanted to run for governor but could not get the Old Regulars or the New Regulars in New Orleans to support him. Huey pointed out that Palmer had represented a Standard Oil subsidiary and had denied to the press that he was running as a Huey Long candidate. Fighting a single battle on his side, Huey said, was not enough to earn his endorsement.[70]

Huey wanted the support of the New Regulars. They were not a cohesive group. There were reformers allied or previously allied with Parker, gambler-spoilsman John Sullivan, the Williams brothers, and others.

The Ku Klux Klan complicated everyone's political calculations. In the twentieth century, aided in part by the "Red Scare" led by U.S. attorney general Mitchell Palmer against communists, the 1920s were the time of the Klan's greatest strength. It branded itself as standing for "Americanism." Its mission was to rid communities of moonshiners, bootleggers, immoral women, foreigners, Catholics, Jews, and Black people who didn't know their place, and any white person who associated with undesirables.

In Louisiana, the northern and central parts of the state—areas of Huey's greatest support—provided many Klan recruits. One Klan rally in Shreveport attracted twelve thousand people. New Orleans was too cosmopolitan and southern Louisiana was too Catholic to tolerate the Klan, except for the Florida parishes, Lake Charles, and certain areas bordering Texas.[71] Even so, however, in 1921, New Orleans Klan politicians helped defeat legislation to require disclosure of Klan membership lists and prohibiting masks except during Mardi Gras.[72]

Huey's political enemy, Lee Thomas, was elected mayor of Shreveport in 1922 with Klan support and over the opposition of Huey and Governor Parker. By August 1922, the Klan controlled Shreveport, Alexandria, and Monroe, and appeared dominant throughout northern Louisiana. Huey's friend and client, O. B. Thompson, was a member, as was Huey's cousin and backer Swords Lee. Huey's brother Shan was a Klan member in Oklahoma.

On December 22, 1921, Huey wrote Shan that he was "not a member" and had never "taken a hand either way." He had instructed some of his "good friends" who were members to ensure that he was not asked to join. Noting that there were about two thousand members in Shreveport, "some of the most prominent men we have," he asked Shan to tell him about it.[73]

Morehouse and Richland parishes and the city of Bastrop were particularly strong Klan enclaves, leading Louisiana in lynchings per capita. In 1921, Morehouse elected J. K. Skipwith—almost eighty and a veteran of the Confederate Army—as the local "Exalted Cyclops." In separate incidents, white men were flogged, undesirable women put on trains to Arkansas, and a Catholic teacher terminated from her school. Outside of Morehouse Parish, a Shreveport white man was tarred and feathered and then escorted out of town; a Beauregard Parish white Methodist minister was tarred and feathered; a month later (March 1922), four members of a white family, including girls thirteen and fourteen years old, were kidnapped from their Vernon Parish home and flogged.

Mer Rouge was Morehouse Parish's second largest town. The Klan resented certain Mer Rouge residents for cohabiting with Black women, gambling, and drinking. The feud was vicious and the situation volatile. On August 24, 1922, fifty masked men invaded and removed five men from a car. One of the men had threatened the local Cyclops that, if the Klan ever showed up at his place again, "scaring my n——, I'll make it a personal matter." Of the five men, one was released, two were beaten, and two went missing. Klan members insisted the men were alive.

The wife of one of the missing men wrote Parker for help. Parker's wife was Catholic, and he despised the secrecy and lawlessness of the Klan. He offered a reward for evidence of what happened and contacted local law enforcement, who were uncooperative. Klan members read his mail and tapped his phone. Parker sent his attorney general, a Catholic, to Washington to ask the Justice Department for help. They dispatched two agents to investigate. The agents confirmed the crimes and the Klan's involvement, but they were harassed by local officials and decided it was a local matter. Parker requested that the president intervene because conditions were "beyond the control of the Governor of this State," gave an interview about it, and went to Washington to press his request. Congressman Aswell, Senator Ransdell, and others denounced Parker for libeling Louisiana. For fear of compromising the investigation, Parker withheld the facts that justified his request, leaving his opponents unopposed in the media.

Parker's dander was up now, however, and he declared war against the Klan. He denied them political appointments and fired them when he could. He sent troops to Morehouse Parish to protect investigating detectives. Morehouse's sheriff was removed after a shortfall was discovered in municipal accounts.[74] Divers were sent to search for the bodies in Lake Lafourche and Lake Cooper. Learning of this, the Klan dynamited Lake Lafourche, trying to further conceal the two bodies of their victims. Instead, they rose to the surface. The men had been tortured and castrated.

One of the murdered men, Watt Daniel, had been accused of moonshining and cohabiting with a Black woman. Daniel was the son of a wealthy planter also abducted and beaten in the attack, a veteran of World War I, and a graduate of LSU. He was probably killed because he tore the mask off a Klansman and recognized him. Even after agents of the newly formed FBI were sent to Morehouse, three more persons were removed from their homes and flogged.

A public hearing orchestrated by Parker was held at the courthouse. It was guarded by the National Guard, manning a machine gun. Klansmen claimed it was a Catholic inquisition, that the bodies could not be identified, and that Parker was a traitor to the white race. Initially experts said the bodies were not decomposed enough to have been dead for more than a few days, thus damaging the state's presentation, but other experts later explained that alluvial deposits at the bottom of the lake preserved the bodies. Some of the state's witnesses were intimidated and thus failed to appear at the hearing. A later Grand Jury in Bastrop, nine of twelve of whom were Klan members, as was the district attorney, failed to or refused to identify the kidnappers.[75]

Catholic politicians from southwestern Louisiana, urban and patrician progressives varying from Governor Parker to the Williams brothers, all loathed the Klan. Jules A. Dreyfus, a representative from Iberia Parish, endorsed a new masking law because "if the fact that I am a Jew makes it impossible for me to be 100 percent American, then I want to be 100 percent dead."[76]

Obsessed with defeating the Klan, Parker backed his Catholic lieutenant governor, Hewitt Bouanchaud, for the governorship. "[S]hort, spare, and swarthy," Bouanchaud was a successful lawyer from southwest Louisiana. He spoke French and English fluently. Friendly in individual meetings, he was stiff and stilted giving speeches. Sullivan said he was a "cold drink of water." Another French politician, Dudley Guilbeau, announced his candidacy but dropped out and became Bouanchaud's campaign manager. Bouanchaud's major proposal was a new anti-masking law to oppose the Klan. Catholics had rarely been elected governor. "Only a politician of Parker's impracticality and integrity could have placed such a candidate on such a platform."

Henry Fuqua opposed him. Governor Pleasant had appointed Fuqua to run the state prison at Angola; Parker had retained him. A former hardware merchant in Baton Rouge, not a dynamic public speaker but a conservative, stable, friendly businessman who didn't say much, Fuqua had support among conservatives in the northern parishes but favored a moderate anti-masking law. He was a Protestant, but from southern Louisiana. The combination of support in the North and his business values led the Old Regulars to endorse him.

If the Old Regulars were going to endorse Fuqua, the New Regulars couldn't. Because Sullivan disliked Huey and had broken with the Old Regulars, he had nowhere else to go and nothing else to do but support Bouanchaud.

Either because he was pressed to make an anti-Klan statement and refused, or because the Williams brothers couldn't induce the New Regulars to support him, Huey lacked support in New Orleans. Before the Old Regulars formally settled on Fuqua and the New Regulars formally decided on Bouanchaud, therefore, Huey announced in May 1923 that he was not going to be a gubernatorial candidate. "To some a political career may seem like a bed of roses, but there are lots of thorns," he said. Huey had not given up, however. Developments in New Orleans shortly allowed him to reconsider.[77]

## Seven

# ELECTION DAY RAIN

On June 7, Francis and Gus Williams seceded from the New Regulars and formed the Independent Regulars. Joining them were John St. Paul Jr., heir of an aristocratic Creole family and the son of a Louisiana Supreme Court justice, Thomas I. O'Connor, superintendent of the Courthouse Building, and Richard Dowling, judge of a criminal district court. This induced Huey to reconsider his gubernatorial candidacy, but all the "political wiseacres enjoyed a hearty laugh."[1]

On August 17, 1923, Huey revealed that he would announce his candidacy on his birthday, August 30, at the Elks Club, the only fraternal organization of which he was a member.[2] He wanted to defeat the predatory corporations that ruled Louisiana.

Seven sheriffs supported him, compared to fourteen for Fuqua and ten for Bouanchaud. No major state officials endorsed him, whereas former governors Pleasant and J. Y. Sanders supported Fuqua, and Parker backed Bouanchaud. Friends such as John Overton, his lawyer Robert Reid, and others were undecided.[3] Eighteen newspapers supported Fuqua, fifteen Bouanchaud, and six Huey. The *New Orleans Item* called Huey "The Prince of Piffle," pictured in cartoons as a jester accompanied by two little girls, representing Francis and Gus Williams.[4]

Huey reprinted excerpts from past news stories and editorials complimenting his work on the Public Service Commission, especially on the Cumberland case. He mailed an estimated 100,000 envelopes with these circulars right before his announcement.[5]

Huey's opening statement was not as well considered. It was a polysyllabic bunch of platitudes, such as: "Our present state of government has descended into one of deplorable, misunderstood orgy, of frequent corporate dictations, mingled with bewildering cataclysms of various criminations and recriminations amongst the personal satellites of the governor and the beneficiaries of the immense public plunder which he has dispensed." The *Times-Picayune* ridiculed this in an editorial headlined "Boom! Boom!" There was a "warlike spirit in the polysyllabic Huey." The enthusiasm from World War I had "contaged him finally," seven years after the conflict's conclusion.[6]

Two days later, Huey presented his platform in Shreveport. It advocated road construction, free textbooks for schoolchildren, enlargement of the court system, warehouse and cold-storage facilities for farmers' crops (so they could be stored to wait for a favorable market), the right of labor to organize, natural gas for New Orleans, pensions for the indigent, flood control, restrictions on lobbyists, and improved state services, all to be paid for by eliminating wasteful government spending. Huey attacked concentrated wealth, Governor Parker's decision to move the agricultural college (Louisiana State University) from its old buildings to teach "fancy" ways to farm, the use of injunctions in labor disputes, and secret orders and super-governments of all kinds (labor, capital, or Klan).[7]

Traveling by himself by automobile all over the state, occasionally accompanied by his wife's brother, Dave McConnell, Huey put up campaign posters and handed out literature and buttons himself. His posters were often torn down, until he bought a long-handled hammer and stood on the roof of his car to tack them up beyond reach. When he asked permission to put his posters in store windows, it was often granted, only to be removed later when he was out of sight, so he learned to bring helpers. Once permission to put them up was given, the helpers glued them on before the proprietor could react.[8]

While Huey had less money than his two opponents, his cousin Swords Lee raised and contributed thousands of dollars; Will Henderson, the owner of a radio station, raised $10,000 and contributed free radio time; client Ernest Bernstein contributed $4,600; the Independent Regulars contributed; John St. Paul Jr. gave $2,000. Julius Long, Earl Long, Harley Bozeman, O. K. Allen, and O.B. Thompson contributed money, among others in Winnfield. How he attracted the support of Will Henderson with his pro-labor platform is a mystery, given Henderson's strong anti-union beliefs. "Huey is not as bad as a lot of them say and not all they say of him is true," Henderson said.

Huey scheduled about 120 meetings, interspersed with shaking hands, distributing literature, tacking up posters, and conferring with local supporters. He got up before dawn and ended at one or two o'clock in the morning. Where he had local leaders, they publicized his visits, drawing a bigger crowd. In his strongholds, his appearances drew record, overflowing crowds. In south Louisiana, however, only small groups attended.

As a public speaker, Huey gesticulated too much, raised his voice to a raucous pitch when excited, paced the stage in a "panther tread," took off his coat or loosened his tie, and scratched his left buttock. One observer wrote that "I liked [Huey], but I was worried. I didn't know what he was going to take off next."[9] Congressman Overton Brooks heard Huey speak and thought he lacked coherence; he and Huey's campaign manager thought he used too many expletives.[10] Rose accompanied Huey to some speeches to mingle with the crowd and gauge its reaction, but most of the time she stayed home and stuffed and mailed envelopes. Huey had acquired a secretary who helped with the campaign. Alice Lee Grosjean was pretty, with hazel eyes and stylishly cut black hair, intelligent, and discreet. Married at fifteen but separated from her husband shortly thereafter, she had joined Huey at eighteen.[11]

Huey's initial speeches were attacks: on the richest men in towns, on the New Orleans Ring, on Standard Oil, on the newspapers, and on the bureaucracy and waste of government. Huey believed that the most powerful man in the community controlled about 40 percent of the vote, and if he denounced him, he would pick up 40 percent of the vote that disliked the man, and then he would have to horse-trade his opponents out of the remaining 20 percent.[12] Huey's announcements said, "public speaking—no reading." Standard Oil was importing oil from Turkey, favoring the "Crescent over the children of Moses," and sending its vice president, C. K. Clarke, all over the state to instruct businessmen to oppose Huey. Wall Street owned the *New Orleans Item*. Wall Street and Esmond Phelps, attorney for the Western Union Telegraph Company and the Texas and Pacific Railroad, owned the *New Orleans Times-Picayune*. *Item* editorial writer Marshall Ballard was the "Imperial Wizard of Pen-pushers." Fuqua had lost money while running the Angola prison, failed to build flood levees despite having the machinery to do so, eliminated the striped prison uniforms that made prisoner identification easier and thus increased prisoner escapes, and armed some prisoners to guard others. While state institutions needed money, the state Conservation Department employed fifty-three "coon chasers" to harass poor men during hunting season.[13] There were "inspectors" for each "coon" and "inspectors of inspectors."[14] C. K. Clarke compared Huey's speeches to the "braying of an ass or the yelping of a locoed coyote." Former governor Pleasant said Huey was "a pompous, inflated, chesty, loose-mouthed, rattletrap" guilty of Bolshevistic tendencies, that he was suspected of treason during World War I and shadowed by the Secret Service, and that he had obtained a campaign contribution from the Southwestern Gas Company while its rate increase request was under consideration by the Public Service Commission. Huey's rebuttal called him a political corpse, stated that he was only shadowed by Standard Oil while in New York, and that attorney fees received from Southwestern Gas were administered through the state. Newspapers opined that he was a demagogue, careless with the truth and irresponsible, but neither Fuqua nor Bouanchaud spent much time attacking him because they didn't take his candidacy seriously.[15]

In September, Huey was embarrassed three days before his first speech in New Orleans. A patrolman stopped a speeding car leading from the red-light district of the West End. Gus Williams was a passenger and asked if he could pay the fine of his "chauffeur" without being arrested, but the officer took the men to the station and booked the driver, named "Harold Swan."

Williams paid the fine. Unfortunately for Huey, the same patrolman worked on the night of Huey's speech and asked a friend to point him out. When this was done, he scoffed and said that was Harold Swan, the chauffeur: "I ought to know. I arrested him the other night."

Williams concocted a story about eating fish at the Moulin Rouge restaurant. He forgot an engagement with his wife and asked his chauffeur to speed so he wouldn't be late. Williams borrowed Huey's car because his own needed repairs. Newsmen weren't going to fall for that, and they found witnesses who placed Huey at the Moulin Rouge restaurant. He had been drinking and table-hopping to invite other diners to his inaugural ball.

The *Item*'s cartoonist drew a Swan with Huey's face, and its editors wrote a poem about it:

> That demon chauffeur, who was he?
> On this the public disagree;
> Some give his name as "Harold Long."
> And others say 'twas "Huey Swong."

Huey's only response was "Go to Hell! I have only that answer for all questions by newspapers."[16]

In Baton Rouge, the wife of Standard Oil's president clapped at the wrong times during his speech. Another dissenter managed only one "boo" before being thrown down a staircase. On Armistice Day (November 11), Huey honored the soldiers who had defeated the Germans, but hecklers chanted "Where were you then? Where were you then?" Huey yelled, "Well I can take care of you anyway." One of his supporters jumped up and added "And if he can't there's plenty here that can."[17]

Huey had a sound truck drive up near one Bouanchaud rally and pull the crowd: Huey talked to 1,000 people while Bouanchaud's crowd dropped to 150. He timed another speech in a Catholic municipality to occur right after a Catholic mass but during an Episcopal service. Huey often donated $25 or $50 to country preachers. Many led their church part-time after spending all week in the fields, so they appreciated the donation.

Professor Williams's favorite story about Huey related to his first campaign speeches in Catholic southern Louisiana. Huey recounted that, every Sunday as a boy, he would hitch his horse to the wagon and take his Baptist grandparents to church. Then he would return and drive his Catholic grandparents to mass. A leader exclaimed to Huey later that he didn't know Huey had Catholic grandparents. "Don't be a damn fool," Huey replied, "we didn't even have a horse."

As the campaign progressed, Huey outlined his economic program. His ideas echoed Parker's of four years earlier, but no other candidate offered a program.[18] Bouanchaud's main issue was the Klan, but he also opposed Prohibition and efforts to close New Orleans's racetrack. Fuqua avoided specifics. He supported Prohibition and avoided Klan denunciations.[19] This was the sum and substance of their campaigns.

There were about twenty-five thousand Klansmen in the state. Huey's speeches tried to diminish the Klan, saying: Bouanchaud wanted to hang Klansmen; Fuqua wanted Klansmen to vote for him first and then hang them. In Huey's papers are some undated statements about the Klan: He didn't depend on other leaders but went over their heads directly to the people, so he would get most Jews, Baptists, Methodists, Catholics, Klan, and anti-Klan votes because of his program. Mob action could take place without masks. The attorney general, a Catholic, said there already was an anti-masking law on the books. If the law were good, it ought to be enforced and, if it were not good, why add another one? He would convene a conference of experts to review existing laws and consider new ones to prevent people from taking the law into their own hands. Religious bigotry was a step backward toward the Middle Ages. Armies could kill millions in the name of religion and not change a single person's beliefs. George Washington, a Protestant, the Catholic nation of France, and Robert Morris, Jew (he wasn't), all contributed to the American Revolution. Everyone should follow the Golden Rule and leave each to his or her own beliefs.[20]

In his autobiography, Huey said the corporations and the newspapers fomented religious controversies to manipulate divisions among the people.[21] The divisions were exacerbated in November, right in the middle of the campaign, when the Morehouse murderers were convicted on only minor charges and fined ten dollars each. In disbelief that he had been convicted of anything, the leader muttered, "What's this world coming to?"[22]

Huey compounded the problem by trying to have it both ways. For example, he let his brother Shan join his campaign. Fresh from resigning from the Oklahoma legislature on suspicion of getting bribed and having been elected to that post with Klan support, Shan called on local klaverns for Huey. His brother was innocent of the charges in Oklahoma, Huey said, he wasn't responsible for organizations his brother had joined, and he was only riding with him. Shan was dismissed when Huey traveled to south Louisiana. In other towns, Huey played up support from Civil War veterans as a means of showing solidarity with the Lost Cause.[23]

In a ruse concocted by Fuqua supporters, copies of a forged Klan certificate with Huey's name on it were circulated in north Louisiana shortly before the election. The Klan then took out a full-page advertisement to accuse Huey of perpetrating the forgery to get the Klan vote. In the closing days of the campaign, the Klan pushed for Fuqua, over the opposition of Huey's backers O. B. Thompson and Swords Lee.[24]

In Huey's view, Fuqua and Bouanchaud were both members of the oligarchy, and neither would benefit the people. Huey invented a story about a man who wanted to breed out the incessant cackling of guinea hens, who were otherwise superior egg producers, by putting the eggs of the guinea under turkeys until they hatched. But when the eggs hatched, the man's experiment had failed. They still had the same old guinea cackle. Because Fuqua was a Parker appointee and Bouanchaud Parker's lieutenant governor, both candidates came from the Parker nest, and they would each have the Parker cackle, cluck, and strut. Bouanchaud and Fuqua backed out of a final campaign joint appearance, so Huey told his story without his opponents as props.[25]

The New Orleans newspapers predicted a dismal vote for Huey. The *Item* forecast that Huey would get only 2,500 votes in New Orleans and would carry only six parishes. Based on a poll, the *Picayune* predicted that Bouanchaud would get 77,000 votes, Fuqua 63,000, and Huey 49,000.[26] The *Item* later revised its projection to Bouanchaud: 95,000, Fuqua: 92,000, and Huey: 53,000.

The results of the election on January 15 must have been a shock to these newspapers: Bouanchaud 84,162; Fuqua 81,382; Huey 73,985.[27] Huey blamed the result on heavy rains on Election Day that cost him 15,000 rural votes. While this was a "fortifying myth" useful to explain temporary defeats and keep one's followers optimistic,[28] the *Times Picayune* conceded that Huey lost one-third of his votes due to rain. It thought this was balanced by rain in New Orleans, however, that depressed the urban vote.[29]

The "dominance of religious, rather than class, issues,"[30] and the lack of votes in New Orleans and southern Louisiana were the real causes of Huey's defeat. The Independent Regulars obtained only 12,000 votes for him in New Orleans. Fuqua got 33,000 votes there, and Bouanchaud got 23,000. The southern parishes went strong for Bouanchaud: he got a majority vote in twenty-two such parishes and a plurality in one. Huey took twenty-one small farmer parishes by a majority vote and a plurality in seven more. Fuqua had a majority in only six parishes and a plurality in seven more, all including cities with significant populations.

Huey wanted to blister the Klan in a post-election statement, but O. B. Thompson talked him out of it. "We have only begun to fight," Huey said instead, "We will march forward next time organized."[31] Some newspaper writers wrote off Huey after his defeat, but they were "whistling in the dark."[32] The wiser of them noted that Huey had aroused districts whose voters had been hibernating for thirty years. "We may just as well try and charge hades with a bucket of water as to try and stop Huey P. Long." A road contractor who had backed Fuqua said that he was now prepared to support Huey because "We can't raise enough money to beat him again!"

Huey endorsed neither candidate in the runoff election but couldn't stop his leaders from taking sides. Bouanchaud stole Huey's idea to provide free textbooks. The Williams brothers backed Bouanchaud. They must have known Bouanchaud would lose, but they could not abide backing the Ring's candidate. Picking up most of Huey's support in north Louisiana without Huey's endorsement, Fuqua won the runoff 125,880 to 92,006.[33]

---

The road to change has been mapped by academics studying political revolutions (rebellions resulting in a major change in government) and social movements (group action to achieve a social or political goal) for decades. Their "theories are tools of simplification" that might not explain everything but can generate "useful insights."[34] Revolution and social movement theories now overlap because theorists acknowledge that revolutions can occur without violence. A book reviewing Louisiana populists according to social movement theories delivered a definitive analysis.[35]

*Grievances* describes the reasons people desire change.[36] There were quite a few reasons Louisianans wanted change in the 1920s. They resulted from economic growth, technological advances, and the maldistribution of the benefits from that growth and advancement. From 1870 to 1970, the United States experienced startling economic growth, and technological change accompanied or drove it. Telephones, automobiles, radios, record players, motion pictures, and household conveniences were invented and adopted with staggering speed. People who could not acquire them wished they could. Farmers in the 1920s "were restless with the feeling that they had been bypassed by modern progress." The cities were "full of excitement and popular culture," whereas on the farm "'economic distress, population decline, and psychological doubt and despair seemed to sap the lifeblood of the countryside.'"[37] Consider the following charts from Professor Robert J. Gordon's *The Rise and Fall of American Growth.*

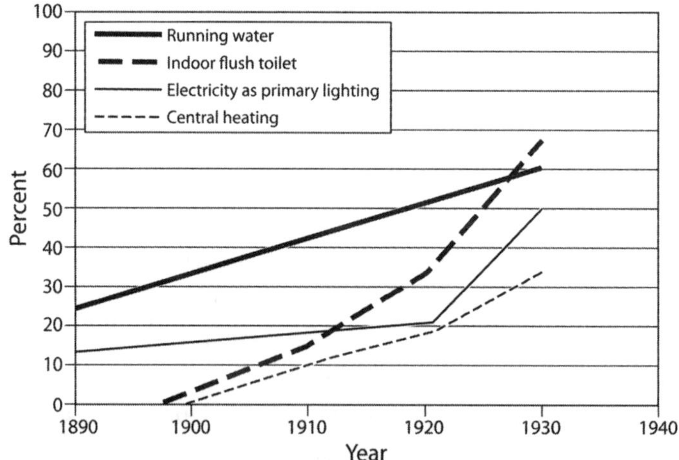


Diffusion of Modern Conveniences, 1890–1940.
Adapted from Gordon, *The Rise and Fall of American Growth*, fig. 4-1.

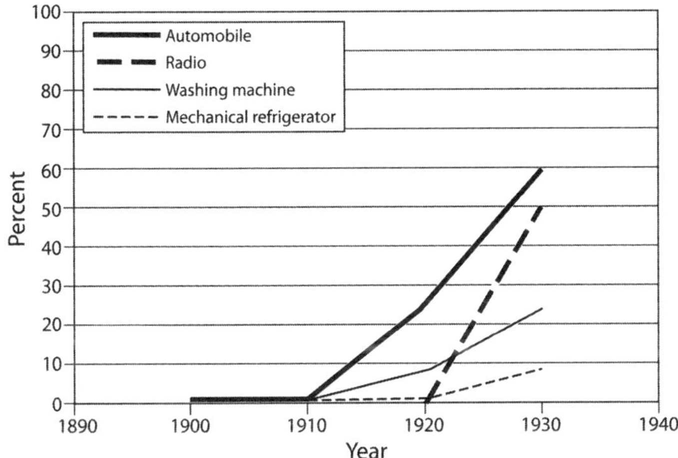


Diffusion of Modern Appliances and Automobiles, 1890–1940.
Adapted from Gordon, *The Rise and Fall of American Growth,* fig. 4-2.

In Louisiana, there was substantial economic progress and growth: manufacturing value increased sevenfold from 1900 to 1920, leading the South, although lagging the rest of the country. From 1890 to 1930, Louisiana's population doubled to over 2,100,000 people, as had New Orleans, to almost 500,000. The number of laborers doubled. Unions were weak, however. Wage rates were low. The illiteracy rate was high, and state spending for education and social services was low. In 1900, "73 per cent of the population had lived in rural areas and 21 per cent in urban, but by 1930 the rural figure had decreased to 60.3 per cent and the urban had risen to 39.7 per cent." Moreover, compared to other states, "Louisiana ranked . . . forty-third in the value of farm property, forty-fourth in the number of farms with piped water; forty-fifth in the number of farms with electric lights; and forty-seventh in the number of farms with electric motors."[38]

Radios, telephones, automobiles, and roads were prized because they diminished farmers' isolation. Roads improved their ability to get their crops to market. Farmers more easily *perceived* the decline in their status, income, and opportunity because of inventions that made communications faster. Louisianans owned 73,000 automobiles and trucks in 1920, 178,000 in 1924, and 264,000 in 1928.[39] The most optimistic estimate of the number of roads in Louisiana before 1928 was 296 miles of concrete roads, 35 miles of asphalt roads, and 5,728 miles of gravel roads. Contemporaneous state Highway Commission reports noted very few concrete roads, but other governmental entities might have constructed some that were omitted from its reports.[40] There were only three bridges over the big Louisiana rivers, at Shreveport, Alexandria, and Monroe. There were no bridges over the Mississippi or Atchafalaya rivers, only ferries. It took at least six hours to drive fifty miles from Opelousas to Baton Rouge.[41]

North Carolina, Virginia, Louisiana, and Mississippi showed a similar growth in automobile and vehicle licenses. These same states reported on their paved roads under state maintenance. In 1924, the difference between the construction of paved roads in North Carolina and Louisiana was about 1,500 miles of roads. By 1928, the difference was about 3,200 miles of roads. Louisiana was the worst of these four states before 1928 (see chart on page 113). The federal government reports of state contributions to highway construction for the years 1924–26 (excluding federal contributions) confirms the differential between them (see chart on page 113).

One can see that Louisiana's lack of paved roads was not inevitable and not a characteristic of every southern state. When considering the maldistribution of the benefits of progress in Louisiana, Professor Sindler concluded that the "gentlemen" in control of Louisiana "ruled more in the image of unenlightened self-interest than [in] a broader public interest."[42] The government by goatee failed to alleviate the maldistribution of the benefits of progress and, in the case of paved roads, failed to progress at all.

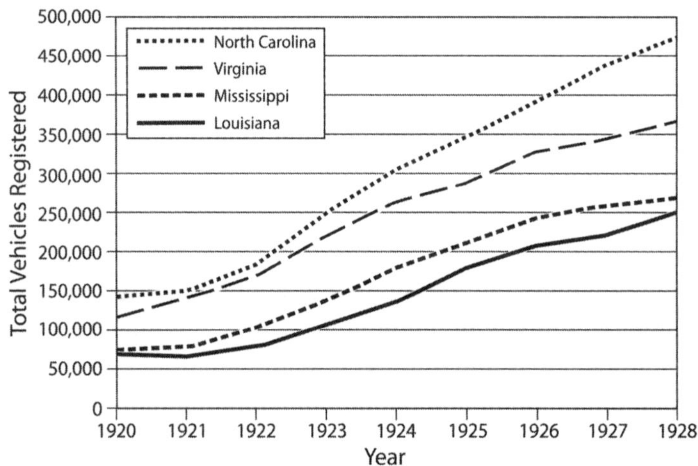


Registered Vehicles by State, 1920–1928.

Federal Highway Administration, State Motor Vehicle Registrations, by Years, www.fhwa.dot.gov>ohim>summary95/mv200.pdf.

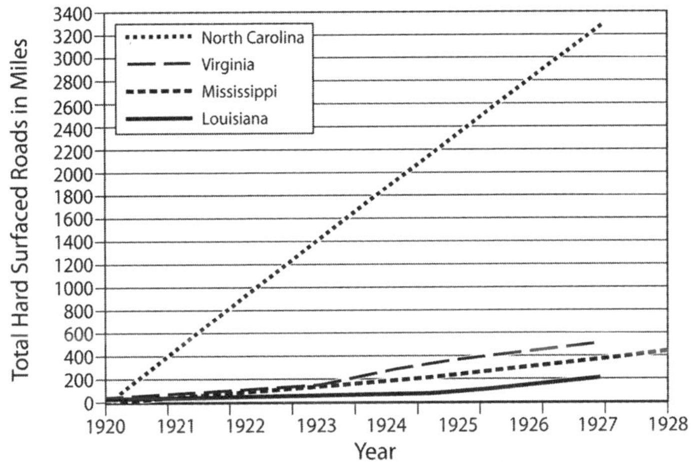


Hard-Surface Roads (concrete or asphalt) under State Maintenance, 1920–1928, in North Carolina, Virginia, Mississippi, and Louisiana.

Source for North Carolina: Biennial Reports, 1922–1928; for Mississippi: Biennial Reports, 1923–1929; for Virginia: Annual Reports, 1921–1927; for Louisiana Biennial Reports, 1922–1928.

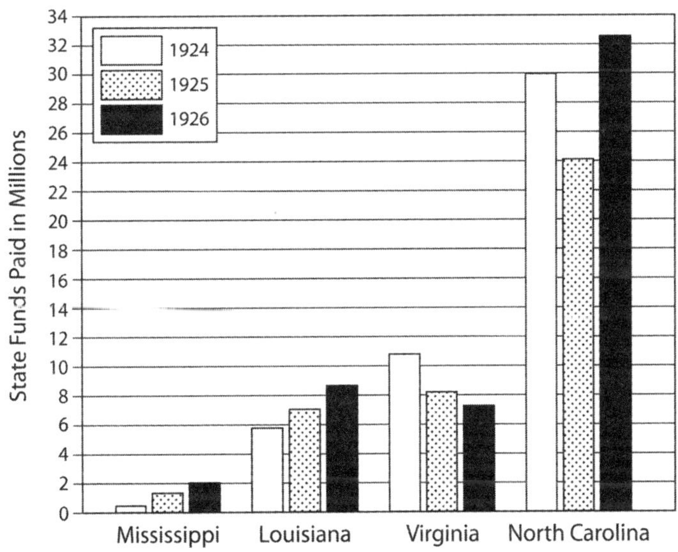


State Funds Paid for Roadwork in Excess of Federal Funding from 1924 to 1926.

Source: Annual Reports of the Department of Agriculture, 1925–1927.

The measurement of grievances hasn't predicted social movements or revolution, however. Paved roads, literacy, unemployment, or foreclosures can be calculated, but the measured amount necessary for a social movement to take root or that would lead to revolution is impossible to compute.[43] Autocratic seizures of power, for example, are often accompanied by a promise to improve literacy because it is "valued by recipients and create[s] loyalty that ideology and promises alone could not elicit."[44] Grievances might prompt change or constitute an "inert backdrop."[45]

The modern theories assert that the failure to manage change or the presence of grievances can create a revolutionary "situation." A revolutionary situation can lead to varied revolutionary "trajectories" and "outcomes." Social movement and revolution theories discuss several concepts to analyze whether or how a reform or revolutionary movement capitalizes on grievances to implement change.[46]

First, there is the cognitive or framing mechanism. Reformers have to frame the issues: to diagnose the problem, propose a solution, and create an identity.[47] Appeals to shared values and understandings; the use of evocative phrases, metaphors, and slogans; the development of symbols and myths, songs and narrative; and appeals to reason (with evidence, common experiences, shared values) and emotion (religious, injustice, unfairness) are all necessary to convince people that they are right and that there is an enemy or opponent. The identity of the movement depends on the framing articulated by its leaders and the choice ("agency") of the individuals who join it.[48]

Second, they must organize and mobilize to recruit adherents, sympathizers, and allies. This takes money, access to media, and networks of family, friends, fraternal organizations, clubs, business associations, civic or interest groups (such as the Good Roads Association), and, of course, political organizations.[49]

Third, there is the political "environment" or, alternatively, "political opportunities."[50] Cultural, political, and economic barriers can impede a social movement or revolution. In Huey's time the constraints were the power of the planters, the poll tax, literacy tests for voters, the New Orleans Ring and, in 1924, the Klan. The poll tax and literacy tests kept the poor, the likely reform constituency, from voting, or the incumbent leaders would pay the poll tax for them and control their vote. The Ring gave the incumbents a head start of controlled votes, a political police force, and the money to campaign, extorted from patronage workers or corrupt payoffs from the vice interests.

Whether the elite leadership is divided or unified, perceived as corrupt, and able to use force are key factors in gauging political opportunity. The divisions between Catholics and Protestants, those for and against Prohibition or gambling, the disputes over civil service, tariffs, monetary policy, and access to credit, paving New Orleans roads, and improving New Orleans docks, demonstrated that the government of gentlemen and the goateed were not always united. There were or should have been political opportunities for someone who could exploit their divisions. While the sheriffs acted within the construct of government by gentlemen, their independence created political opportunities. The notorious corruption of the Old Regulars also did, as evidenced by Parker's victory in 1920.

The framing, mobilization, and leadership of the reformers must be examined in comparison to that of the status quo, over time. Incumbents can frame their own diagnoses for grievances (for example, market forces, not a freeze-out, caused the price decline of Pine Island oil) or problems with the solutions proposed by reformers (for example, socialism has never worked). The rhetoric of reaction often claims that the reforms proposed will jeopardize a class of people, constitute an exercise in futility, or will have perverse consequences.[51] Their resources can counteract reform mobilization, make use of the constraints of the status quo, and foment irrelevant divisions among the likely reform constituency. Corruption or leadership divisions can plague either the reformers or the incumbents.

In 1924, the Klan was an impediment to reform—beyond the Old Regulars, poll taxes, and the remaining elements of the oligarchy—that could not be overcome. Bouanchaud and Huey couldn't or wouldn't combine forces, so the potential reform vote split.

After he was elected, however, Fuqua and his supporters never considered that they should enact the proposals that—absent the distraction of the Klan—were supported by most voters. To consider only roads for the moment, while there was a proposal for $27 million of bond financing for roads in 1921, the constitutional convention convoked by Parker in that year forbade it.[52] Conservatives successfully advocated only pay-as-you-go road construction, and Parker constructed gravel roads rather than paved roads.[53]

In an article hostile to Huey, John W. Scott argues that between 1920 and 1924 Parker created a modern state highway system and deserved the credit for taking Louisiana out of the mud. He imposed a new tax on gasoline and automobile license fees. The 6,000 miles of roads, 89 bridges, and 500 miles of highways under construction as of 1928 were an overlooked achievement.[54]

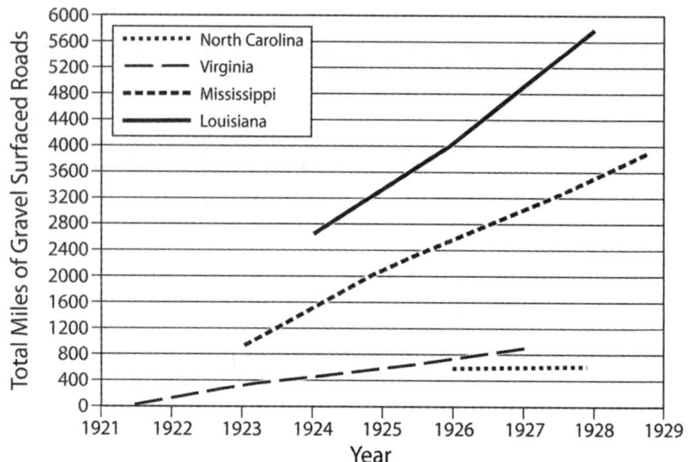


Total Miles of Gravel-Surfaced Roads in North Carolina, Virginia, Mississippi, and Louisiana.

Source for North Carolina: Biennial Reports, 1926 and 1928; for Mississippi: Biennial Reports, 1923–1929; for Virginia: Biennial Reports, 1921–1929; for Louisiana: Biennial Reports 1924–1928.

By the end of Parker's term in 1924, gravel roads connected every parish's municipal seat.[55] If only gravel-surfaced roads are considered, Louisiana was a leader (see chart above).

Scott admits, however, that "The highways built by Parker increased exponentially the demand for motor vehicles in Louisiana, spurring enormous traffic growth, in turn focusing public interest on more and better roads throughout the 1920s."[56] Expanding on Scott's paper, Karen J. S. McKinney details the coalition seeking good roads in Louisiana.[57] The consensus was broad-based, implying that Huey has obtained too much credit for leadership on this issue. She points out that Huey opposed an increase in the gas tax to fund the pay-as-you-go construction in 1926. McKinney describes the paradoxical problem of Louisiana's progress constructing gravel roads that induced more automobile travel: "[G]reater numbers of vehicles on the roads caused greater deterioration at a faster rate than contemporary funding could pay for timely repairs. Congested sections of roads carrying up to 3,500 vehicles per day well exceeded the five hundred per day expected on gravel roads."[58]

Parker's gravel roads thus created rising expectations. The sentiment for paved roads accelerated exponentially while only gravel roads were constructed at a moderate linear rate. This is one of the classic patterns of revolution.[59] Before the French Revolution, Louis XVI implemented moderate reforms, the nobles squelched them, and the people revolted. Interrupted rising expectations of reform hastened the revolt.[60]

In the events that follow, compare Huey to the oligarchy with respect to issue framing, voter mobilization, and political opportunities, including whether the leadership of the competing forces was united or perceived as corrupt. Would the oligarchy reform or repress? Could Huey improve his framing or mobilization? Could he exploit the rising expectations paradigm?

*Eight*

# WINNING THE GOVERNORSHIP IN 1928

Because 1924 was a presidential year, delegates to the Democratic National Convention had to be selected. Behrman, Fuqua, and J. Y. Sanders preselected a delegate slate that they expected the convention of 716 elected delegates to ratify. Huey objected, but a chorus of boos and yells prevented his being heard, and Chairman Behrman gaveled for order so hard that he broke the marble podium. On a roll call, Huey was outvoted 536 to 180. Behrman also ruled that only resolutions passed by an appointed committee that he controlled could be considered by the convention. One delegate proposed to denounce the Klan, but this caused pandemonium and his resolution was defeated on a voice vote. Another wanted to repeal Prohibition, but Behrman shoved him off the rostrum while a mob of delegates cheered.

Huey also objected to the slate of four at-large delegates. Striding to the podium and waiting five minutes for silence, he denounced bossism and proposed to enlarge the at-large slate to eight persons, each with a half vote, the extra positions to be filled by representatives of the people. This proposal had no chance, and Huey's request for a roll call was denied. The convention adjourned. Huey and his supporters "were swept aside like chaff before the wind," said the *Times-Picayune*. The *Item* said he was finished. The revolutionary was repressed.

In September, Huey ran for reelection to the Public Service Commission and U.S. Senator Joseph Ransdell stood for reelection. Despite the cooperation between the Old Regulars and J. Y. Sanders at the convention, the Old

Regulars endorsed Ransdell, not Sanders, who wanted to replace him. The Old Regulars did not want to break a pledge to support Ransdell or substitute the Protestant Sanders for him just after electing a Protestant governor over a Catholic candidate. In consolation, Behrman promised to support Sanders in 1926 against Senator Broussard (also a Catholic).[1]

Born on a plantation nine miles south of Alexandria, in central Louisiana, Ransdell moved to Lake Providence in northeastern Louisiana to study law. He practiced there for fifteen years, twelve of them as district attorney. A delegate to the Constitutional Convention of 1898, he promoted the poll tax and the single-term limit for the governor's office. Running for Congress, he supported the whites-only primary. In several early campaigns, his Catholicism was an issue. Many of his speeches were given to extol religion or promote outstanding Catholics: "The Patriotism of Catholics"; "Christian Life Maintained in the Course of Our Earthly Pilgrimage by the Eucharist—the Sacrament of Perseverance." Elected to the Senate in 1912 and reelected in 1918, he had the support of the press and the Old Regulars in 1924.

Then Shreveport mayor Lee Thomas gave Huey a break. He opposed Ransdell and criticized him for advocating parochial schools and, more obliquely, for his religion. Sanders, still smarting from his rejection by Behrman, and Fuqua, for reasons unknown, decided to support Thomas and oppose Ransdell. The Klan criticized Ransdell, although Thomas denied any connection to it.[2] Lack of cohesion in the incumbent elite equals weakness.

Originally, Huey had declared neutrality because both candidates had supported Fuqua against him but, about a week before the election, he changed his mind and endorsed Ransdell. Huey sent speakers to southern Louisiana to publicize his support and campaigned with Ransdell in northern Louisiana. Huey had to campaign in northern Louisiana anyway as he was running for reelection. State Senator Walter L. Bagwell opposed Huey and obtained Fuqua's endorsement.

The Klan had receded in influence. The national Klan wanted its Louisiana membership to oppose anti-masking and enrollment laws passed during Fuqua's administration, not appreciating that the legislation gave members time to transfer their memberships out of state before enrollment disclosure. The Monroe Klan defied the national Grand Wizard, Hiram Evans, by refusing to oppose the reelection of popular Arnold Bernstein, a Jew, for mayor. Infuriated, Evans reorganized Klan leadership in Louisiana, creating a triumvirate, one of whom was Swords Lee. Two contradictory stories emerged about the Klan's actions in Huey's race: one, that it had decided to help Huey by pulling out another potential opponent; the other, more likely given the Klan's diminished power, that the Klan refused to oppose Huey to avoid a humiliating defeat.[3]

Huey was confident that he would defeat Bagwell and only joked about him. Bagwell was tall with a long neck and small head, and wore a high, stiff standing collar. In one joint speaking appearance, Huey said Bagwell's collar was so high, he had to tiptoe to spit over it. In urging Ransdell's election, Huey developed a story about Shreveport mayor Thomas. During revival meetings, when babies cried, a sugar teat (pacifier made from cloth and moistened sugar) would be put in the baby's mouth to stop its crying. Huey accused Thomas of having had the sugar teat of public office in his mouth for three decades—and still he cried for more.

Thomas retaliated with his own story. A man went to hell and saw a locked box there. The devil warned him not to open it, for inside was Huey Long, and he would take charge of hell if let loose.[4] When Mayor Thomas attacked Ransdell for having written a polite letter to Black Republican leader Walter Cohen, Huey sprang to Ransdell's defense, playing on the same prejudice. Thomas must have gotten the letter from Cohen, Huey said, and therefore was a hypocrite: a white Louisianan seeking campaign help from a Black Republican; Thomas had taken Cohen to his bosom and "snuggled" with him on a political bed.[5]

Huey won his own race with over 80 percent of the vote, carrying every parish in his district: 45,000 votes to 8,600 votes for Bagwell. Huey's *margin*[6] was bigger than the *total vote* commanded by the Ring.[7] Huey also helped reelect Ransdell, who won by more than 20,000 votes.[8]

Now Huey turned to New Orleans. The mayoral election was scheduled for February 1925. Francis Williams announced his own candidacy. Fresh from electing Fuqua, Behrman sought the mayoralty, too, and looked unbeatable, campaigning on the slogan "Papa's Coming Home."[9] When the Old Regulars met in caucus to anoint Behrman, however, Paul Maloney challenged him. With City Attorney Ivy Kittredge, he had led the fight against Cumberland's telephone-rate increase in New Orleans. Maloney was popular enough to defy the reform wave and win a seat as commissioner of public utilities in 1920, the only machine politician to win.

The recent vote totals showed that, if Bouanchaud's gubernatorial vote (23,000) were added to Huey's (12,000), Behrman (33,000 for Fuqua) could be defeated. On December 15, 1924, Huey wrote a letter to Williams, with a copy to Robert Ewing, publisher of the *New Orleans States* and the *Shreve-*

*port Times*, but told Ewing not to let the letter out of his sight. Ewing had a bristling white mustache that resembled “an angry schnauzer,” and had been a newspaper power in Louisiana for decades, at times affiliated with the Ring. If Francis Williams had a chance to win, Huey wrote, he would support him, but he wanted Williams to withdraw because they should not lead their followers into a slaughter. Nor did Huey want Williams to bargain with each side. They would lose their existing reputation with the voters as vanquished (in the governor’s race) but principled.[10]

Williams withdrew and endorsed Behrman’s challenger, Maloney. Huey also visited John Sullivan. Sullivan had his New Regulars back Maloney. Ewing’s newspapers recommended Maloney.

Maloney came close to an upset. Incumbent reform mayor Andrew McShane entered the race as a third candidate at the last minute, obtained only 4,000 votes, but took them all from Maloney. Some ballot boxes from a Maloney stronghold were lost overboard while on a ferry on the way to being counted.[11] The Old Regulars then paid off one of Maloney’s leaders to defect. After that betrayal, Maloney withdrew, electing Behrman. Sullivan’s New Regulars nevertheless captured some offices that gave them patronage; it was “in no sense a rout.”[12] Having established a coalition of Maloney, Sullivan, the Williams brothers, and Ewing, Huey thought he had formed an effective New Orleans organization.

The Public Service Commission soon considered two matters that became relevant to Huey’s gubernatorial chances.[13] Because New Orleans is surrounded by water, the increased popularity of the automobile necessitated bridges. A 1918 constitutional amendment authorized the state to build a free bridge in one location over Lake Pontchartrain, but no legislation ever implemented the amendment. In 1924, instead, the legislature authorized the state Highway Commission to contract with private firms to build toll bridges.[14]

Two insiders offered proposals. The Watson-Williams syndicate employed former governor J. Y. Sanders as its lawyer, whereas a rival firm hired former governor Pleasant. The two firms each proposed a separate route, each different from the authorized free bridge route.

Huey opened a public assault on New Year’s Day, 1925. Claiming that only the Public Service Commission had the power to award a bridge franchise, he attacked J. Y. Sanders and the Watson-Williams proposal in a series of statements: the state should not be bartered away, Sanders was exploiting the state, the people had authorized a free bridge and should not pay Sanders a big fee to get a toll bridge, and the proposed bridge would cost the people "multiplied millions" of dollars. Huey instructed his supporters in the city to first help ex-governor Pleasant show up ex-governor Sanders and then help Sanders show up Pleasant.[15] By the time the controversy concluded, Huey calculated that he would be governor and would build a free bridge.

Sanders argued that it was better to have private interests risk their capital and have the costs borne by tourists and pleasure seekers and people who could afford to pay for the privilege of a short cut. "Apparently it never occurred to the old aristocrat that people who could not afford to pay the charges might also like to tour and seek pleasure and enjoy the convenience of a short route."[16]

"Luncheon clubs passed resolutions. . . . The Association of Commerce took a formal poll. All [showed] an overwhelming majority in favor of free bridges."[17] Ignoring Huey's attacks and this overwhelming sentiment, the Highway Commission in February awarded the franchise to Watson-Williams. It would cost $5.5 million.[18]

The Public Service Commission authorized Huey to file a suit to annul the bridge contract because it was a public utility and the Public Service Commission had not authorized its scale of rates. Huey lost the suit, but there was no other lawsuit alternative that would have resulted in victory. Its purpose was to arouse public opinion in time to stop the toll bridge. The legislature in May took some account of the protest and altered the legislation so that the state could purchase the toll bridge at any time.

The company began to sell its bonds. It omitted mention of the state's right to build a free bridge parallel to its route. When construction began, Huey again sued, as a citizen, as a bondholder, as a taxpayer, and on behalf of the Public Service Commission, to halt construction or for the right to set the toll rates.[19] He lost again. But the court recognized the right of the state to construct the free bridge. Huey therefore warned the company that it was "building the most expensive buzzard roost . . . in the United States."[20] Huey lost the legal battle but exposed two ex-governors and their elite allies grabbing for money and imposing tolls that people detested. The elite were divided and perhaps corrupt.

The second controversy was the Galveston rate case. The federal Interstate Commerce Commission reduced the railroad shipping rates for wheat and oil into Galveston, which would help Galveston develop its port but hurt New Orleans. New Orleans businessmen and allied civic and governmental groups protested. The Public Service Commission appointed Huey to travel to Washington, DC, to argue the inadequacy of Galveston's port, the superiority of New Orleans's port, and the impropriety of the Interstate Commerce Commission's order.

Changing the minds of Interstate Commerce Commission members was like pulling teeth, he said later. But Huey persevered and obtained reversal of the order. In the bridge controversy, Huey lost the court cases but won public opinion. In the Galveston rate case, he won a reversal, but the business community he had aided was ungrateful and he lost his ally on the Public Service Commission.

One business group wrote him a thank-you letter, but most blamed him for not anticipating the order or suggested that he wanted the order issued so he could claim credit for its revocation. This whipsaw of criticism was unfair, but whereas an "awful illogic" gripped his supporters, a converse illogic gripped his opponents.

Proof of the ingratitude occurred at the opening banquet of the new Roosevelt Hotel in downtown New Orleans, attended by twelve hundred leading businessmen. One businessman invited Huey. The master of ceremonies unexpectedly asked Huey to stand and be recognized. As he stood up, the crowd booed him, and he sat down. Huey believed the incident was planned to embarrass him.[21]

Francis Williams chimed in that he had done the hard work on the Galveston case, but Huey stole the credit, and then charged that Huey withheld support for a Union Station project in New Orleans that Williams sponsored. By the end of 1925, Huey and Francis were allies no more. Huey responded in mournful tones to Francis's criticisms, but behind the scenes he forged an alliance with his former opponent on the Public Service Commission, Shelby Taylor, so he remained as chairman.[22]

The split between Huey and Williams was caused by clashing egos. It could have portended a problematic division of reform forces, inhibiting voter mobilization for reform. While Huey had done nothing for Williams except urge him to withdraw from the 1924 mayoral contest, Williams had not done much for Huey in New Orleans, either. Huey must have believed that he had traded up by backing Maloney, with his superior mobilization capability.

The election of 1926 for U.S. senator gave Huey one more opportunity to add to his support outside northern Louisiana. He liked to say "It ain't enough to get the breaks. You gotta know how to use them."[23] He got a break in 1926, and he used it.

Recall that, in 1924, Behrman wouldn't support J. Y. Sanders against

Ransdell but promised to back him in 1926. Even though Behrman, the promise maker, had died, Arthur O'Keefe, Behrman's successor, now endorsed Sanders. Edwin S. Broussard was the incumbent senator, a Catholic from southwest Louisiana. His brother Robert had held the Senate seat before him. Affectionately known as "Coozan Bob," he was popular. Edwin was not as friendly or as good a speaker, but he was known as "Coozan Ed." Since Ransdell had made it an issue in 1912,[24] Louisiana had one senator from the north and the other from the south. Ransdell was from the north. Normally, then, "Coozan Ed" would have not feared reelection.[25]

With J. Y. Sanders as his opponent, however, Coozan Ed had a lot to fear. Described as a "virile . . . clean, brainy, fearless white man's man, [Sanders] advocated good schools for white children, gravel roads funded on a pay-as-you-go plan, and white supremacy."[26] J.Y. had been governor from 1908 to 1912 but had run for the U.S. Senate in 1912 and 1920 and was defeated first by "Coozan Bob" and then "Coozan Ed." He had lacked Old Regular support in 1912, and the Old Regulars were weak in 1920. After each defeat, he moved, in 1914 from Franklin to Bogalusa, and in 1920 from Bogalusa to Hammond. The French said, "Dat Broussard family, dey goin' make a gypsy outta ol' J.Y. yet."[27]

Ironies of the campaign included the Ring's support for Sanders even though Sanders favored Prohibition while the Ring wanted repeal. Broussard supported repeal, but the Ring endorsed Sanders. Governor Fuqua also endorsed Sanders. Sanders supported challenger Dudley LeBlanc against incumbent Shelby Taylor in their Public Service Commission race, even though LeBlanc supported Broussard.[28] To Sanders, deposing Huey as Public Service Commission chairman was worth endorsing an opponent. The *Times Picayune*, a previous supporter of Sanders, now faulted him as a pawn of the special interests, perhaps because, as Sanders charged, one of its directors owned land in the pathway of the rival bridge deal. Former governor Pleasant joined the *Times Picayune* to endorse Broussard because, Sanders alleged, Pleasant lost out on the bridge deal. Paul Maloney and John Sullivan, allies from Maloney's mayoral race, endorsed Broussard to oppose the Ring. Maloney's other ally from the mayoral race, Francis Williams, supported Sanders, a stain on his reform credentials.

Huey was the last leader to endorse a candidate. Reporter Deutsch observed that Sanders had patronage (because of Fuqua and the Old Regulars), was strong in northern Louisiana, and was a good speaker. Broussard lacked patronage, was weak in northern Louisiana, and was an indifferent speaker. "On paper, Sanders could not lose. So, Huey Long . . . chose Broussard."[29]

But Huey must have kept abreast of the views of his allies from the recent mayoral race: Sullivan and Maloney. Long negotiations took place before Huey was comfortable announcing his choice. He wanted a commitment from Broussard to campaign with him in southern Louisiana, Broussard's home turf, and to endorse him for governor in 1928. Broussard agreed to campaign together but refused to promise an endorsement in 1928. Broussard's *leading supporters*, however, made the necessary agreement to back Huey for governor.[30] While Huey had backed the Catholic Ransdell two years previously, he had not campaigned in southern Louisiana with any leader like Broussard who had a popular following there. Now, he was guaranteed a warm welcome—and a seasoned organization for 1928.

Huey's tour of south Louisiana with Broussard was a triumph. His humor, dynamic speeches, and association with their hero Broussard caused the people to nickname him Huey Polycarp Long, Polycarp being the name of a Christian martyr revered among the French. The "long-legged sapsucker" Sanders's sins, according to Huey, included (1) leading the bridge syndicate, (2) having Valentine Irion, commissioner of conservation, corruptly issue a carbon-black permit for a company represented by Sanders, (3) influencing Governor Fuqua to keep cheap natural gas out of New Orleans, (4) controlling patronage in state departments, and (5) causing decreased expenditures by the state for the "deaf and dumb asylum" so that more money could be allocated for the patronage-rich "coonservation" department, with "all those coon-chasers and possum watchers and squirrel counters."[31]

The carbon-black[32] permit had been controversial for months in 1925 and 1926. Governor Fuqua in 1925 removed the conservation commissioner, W. J. Everett. Everett charged this was done at Sanders's direction on behalf of the carbon-black interests. In mid-1926, Huey joined some legislators who demanded a ban on carbon black, the manufacture of which wasted natural gas and caused environmental problems, but this proposal failed. In 1926, Commissioner Irion was fired. Irion challenged his removal in court in a big battle featuring lawyers Hugh Wilkinson for the governor against Edward Rightor and Rene Viosca for Irion. Despite a trial court finding that he was incompetent, Irion won the case. During a court argument, Rightor made this ugly comment: "Nine out of ten of those Cajans [*sic*] will lie. They will lie about anything. Those Cajans [*sic*] are of a low order of mind and morals. One of them that took the witness stand looked like a monkey."[33]

After their tour of southern Louisiana, Huey took Broussard into northern Louisiana. They faced some hostile audiences, but mostly whenever Huey saw a group of people, he would leap from his car and announce himself as Huey Long. They would say "we knew that." Then he would introduce his friend Senator Broussard, standing for reelection, and ask them to support him, and they said they would. Huey presented Broussard as the man who was standing with him against the toll-bridge syndicate and the New Orleans Ring, ignoring his Catholicism and his support for Prohibition's repeal. Because it was backing Broussard, the *Times Picayune* now liked Huey's speeches, calling them conservative, constructive, and picturesque.[34]

Robert L. Prophit was a legislator attacked by Huey for holding a job in the Conservation Commission. He was short, had lost a leg during childhood, and used a cane. With the cooperation of the local sheriff, J. E. McClanahan, Prophit planned to assault Huey at a campaign appearance. If Huey fled, he would reveal himself as a coward, afraid of a small, disabled man.

When Huey arrived, he saw Prophit and said, "Hello, Bob." Prophit whacked him. Huey ran away, and Prophit swung his cane at him. Friends of Huey formed a circle around Prophit, after which Huey returned and swung a wild blow at him that missed by two feet. Prophit was booked for assault and paid a small fine. Huey obtained a piece of Prophit's broken cane and showed it to the crowd the next night, saying: "I had no trouble finding a conservation agent in Columbia."[35]

Whereas Huey's alliance in the New Orleans 1924 mayoralty election had failed by an eyelash, his alliance in the 1926 Senate race succeeded by a whisker. Broussard was elected with a statewide margin of only thirty-four hundred votes. Huey had only been able to convince a fraction of his supporters to vote for the Catholic and wet Broussard, but they were votes that Broussard never would have obtained otherwise. Broussard carried New Orleans, too, however, because of Ring defections over Prohibition.[36]

Dudley LeBlanc beat Shelby Taylor, however, and then joined with Francis Williams to depose Huey as Public Service Commission chairman. "With two members always ready to vote against me for Chairman, it is only now that any two have ever been able to assemble where one would vote for the other," Huey said.[37]

Williams became chairman. He and LeBlanc rescinded the order against Standard Oil and adopted the company's rates. Williams and LeBlanc lacked Huey's technical knowledge of cases he was managing before his removal. They were forced to ask him to represent the commission in a few of them. In one, Huey said he would, but only if they confessed their "incompetency to fill the position to which they elected themselves." In another, he said he wouldn't, even though they were not "competent," because they had elected themselves to do it. He also urged them to keep meetings public.[38]

The elite may have considered this an effective curtailment of Huey's power, but it allowed him to concentrate on making money and his next objective: the governorship. While he had to withstand some adverse publicity for the huge fees he had earned in workers' compensation lawsuits because of a movement to limit them, there was no other counterattack by the elite. Huey was dubbed the man to beat in 1928.[39]

Unlike Martin Behrman, who died after savoring his mayoral comeback victory, Henry Fuqua died on October 11, 1926, after feeling the sting of J. Y. Sanders's senatorial defeat. Lieutenant Governor Oramel Simpson—who along with Maloney had backed the winner Broussard—succeeded Fuqua. Huey wrote that 1926 was disastrous to his political fortunes because Fuqua's death allowed Simpson to run to succeed himself, and because LeBlanc's election caused the loss of Huey's Public Service Commission chairmanship.

A dumpy little man, Simpson had an undistinguished career. With Fuqua's death, however, he saw his main chance. He moved to construct the free bridge authorized by the constitutional amendment of 1918 and put a free-schoolbooks plank in his platform. Commentators said he was stealing Huey's clothes while he was swimming, but Simpson's stratagem was too obvious. Huey offered to let Simpson use all his ideas.[40]

Simpson's supporters included conservatives such as Shreveport mayor Lee Thomas. But his primary supporter revealed one of two ironies in the campaign lineups. The Ring dissident, Paul Maloney, supported Simpson despite Huey's (indirect) help in 1924. But Broussard's leaders backed Huey even though Simpson had supported Broussard in 1926. Maloney never explained why he chose Simpson, an uninspiring speaker, "booze hound,"[41] and horse-racing gambler (a liability in north Louisiana).[42]

Simpson and Maloney's opposition to the Old Regulars in the 1925 mayoral race and in the Senate race in 1926 made the Ring hunt for a candidate. Fresh from his narrow defeat in 1926, J. Y. Sanders declined to run.[43] Congressman Aswell was asked to run but refused.[44] A natural disaster helped the Ring discover a candidate.

Before Hurricane Katrina, the biggest natural disaster in Louisiana history was the Great Mississippi Flood of 1927. Two million acres of land were flooded, and 750,000 people were left homeless. New Orleans's elite directed certain levees to be dynamited to save New Orleans. When the levies were blown up, two parishes below the city were flooded. City leaders promised compensation to the flood victims of the two parishes but, led by lawyer J. Blanc Monroe, minimized the compensation afterward. President Coolidge sent secretary of commerce Herbert Hoover to coordinate relief work. John M. Parker assisted him. Overcome by tales of human cooperation in the face of disaster, one newspaperman wrote: "businessmen, doctors, prisoners, lawyers and negroes worked side by side."[45]

Congressman Riley Joe Wilson had served for fourteen years, since 1914. Orphaned at an early age, Riley Joe had pulled himself up by his bootstraps. He attended school and studied law. After the flood, he helped pass legislation to build new flood-control systems at federal, not state, expense.[46]

The Old Regulars hailed him as the savior of the hour and decided that Riley Joe should be governor, ignoring his colorless personality and incompetence as a public speaker. Even a newspaper supporting him said he should loosen up. His own driver called him a tightwad.[47]

The Old Regulars organized a convention to nominate him on July 11. It was a prearranged, bossed gathering. J. Y. Sanders dramatically announced that he would support the choice of the convention. The delegates spent more time denouncing Huey than applauding Riley Joe. Huey responded, "Give 'em rope."[48] Privately, he wrote that the convention was a "stench in the nostrils of the good people."[49] Days after the convention, J. Y. Sanders, politically blind, filed a suit to stop construction of the free bridge for New Orleans.

Simpson favored free schoolbooks but only if it could be done without raising taxes or by raising taxes on racetracks. Wilson stressed his record on flood control, opposed free schoolbooks, but agreed he would give them to poor parents if it could be done without embarrassing them; opposed paving roads because it would cost too much; and stressed low taxes and limited government.

Huey disclosed his candidacy on July 17 and held his opening rally in Alexandria on August 3, where the Wilson convention occurred. The banner across the stage said, "Every Man a King, but No One Wears a Crown." Huey denounced the Ring. J. Y. Sanders, instead of John Parker, was now the directing force behind it. Free schoolbooks and access to education for every child, paved roads, warehouses to aid farmers in storing their crops, vocational training for the deaf, mute, and blind, and an expanded court system were all elements of his program to modernize Louisiana. Huey promised to make Angola prison self-sustaining. The crowd was estimated at eight thousand people, three thousand in the auditorium and five thousand immediately outside, one of the largest gatherings ever assembled in Alexandria.[50]

Aristocratic lawyer John Overton—respectable, honest, idealistic—gave the best speech at the rally. Satirizing the convention that nominated Wilson, he compared his selection to the birth of a crown prince, attended by lords and dukes and earls in their Lincoln limousines, Rolls-Royce automobiles, and Pullman palace cars. The political stork then arrived with the "Imperial Crown Prince, Riley, of Ruston!" The babe thus presented was not old enough to stand alone, much less to walk, and by election time it would not know how to run.[51] Huey told Overton: "Think yourself up another speech, John. I'm going to use yours."[52]

Huey's campaign was unlike his 1924 contest in money, in organization, and in leaders. He had more money than any other candidate.[53] Road contractors awoke to the possibilities of a governor who wanted to expand road construction. Having no jobs to award, Huey could promise them all, five times over. Family and friends again contributed, this time in larger amounts: Julius and Earl Long ($10,000), Huey's cousin and road contractor, Swords Lee ($30,000), Will Henderson, and Ernest Bernstein. Nicholas Carbajal contributed $10,000 and presided over the state campaign headquarters in New Orleans. Mike Moss, who later secured all the highway bonding business for the state, was a contributor. Wealthy Shreveport businessman Leon Kahn sent a large amount.[54]

The wealthiest, Robert Maestri, was a new supporter from New Orleans, and may have been the largest contributor ($40,000). Probably introduced to Huey by John Sullivan, he made a fortune in the red-light district of New Orleans in hotels and furniture. Prostitutes frequented the hotels. When they were raided, he reclaimed the furniture and resold it to the hotels when they reopened, a maneuver called "perpetual motion." With only a third-grade education, he didn't speak much and, when he did speak, listeners doubted he had any education at all.[55] A shrewd businessman nevertheless, Maestri is an example of how a socially restrictive elite can induce the wealthy to support change. Sullivan and his other gambling acquaintances contributed substantial sums, in cash. The main stash was kept in a safe. Alice Lee Grosjean held what was needed on a day-to-day basis in her brassiere.[56]

With this money, Huey no longer tacked up campaign posters himself. Advertising trucks toured the state under the direction of Earl Long and Frank Odom, an expert in display advertising. The trucks themselves had pictures of Huey on their sides. They crisscrossed the state, letting Huey concentrate on writing the circulars they distributed and giving speeches. The circulars were printed on paper that people could "use on their backsides" after reading it. "Don't use any of that damn smooth stuff," Huey ordered.

Language a six-year-old could understand was the appropriate level for writing circulars, Huey thought.

Senator Ransdell's brother endorsed Huey, denying that Huey was a radical. Likewise, Senator Broussard's followers backed Huey. Harvey Ellis, a lawyer from a small town (Mandeville) and member of a long-standing, respected, aristocratic family, was named Huey's state campaign manager. John Sullivan led his cause in New Orleans. Newspaper publisher Robert Ewing endorsed him, after talking to Congressman Aswell about running, giving Huey the support of the *Shreveport Times* and the *New Orleans States*. Twenty other weekly papers supported Huey. Jeff Snyder of Madison Parish, wealthy and, along with Swords Lee, one of the triumvirate that governed the Louisiana Klan, supported Huey.[57]

Problems developed. Carbajal was resentful of Sullivan and Maestri, who elbowed him aside in New Orleans. After his appointment, Harvey Ellis abruptly resigned as campaign manager in a public letter that attacked Sullivan: Sullivan was crooked and only stood for racing, gambling, and whiskey. Huey denied ever gambling and then named a new campaign manager, Sheriff Charles L. Pecot of St. Mary Parish, southwest of New Orleans.

Huey's organization in the rural parishes might be the most significant difference from his 1924 campaign. In the intervening four years, he had met with leaders of the various parishes, north and south, offering flattery and promises—implicit or explicit—to improve the state or grant patronage. Many of Huey's leaders now were the richest men in their parish. The Fisher family of Jefferson Parish, near New Orleans, was rich from the fur trade, fishing, and canning industries. Sugar-plantation manager Clay Dugas supported Huey and was promised the directorship of the state penitentiary. Clarence Savoie owned several plantations. Williams lists many more leaders he either interviewed or researched. One can appreciate how much time and effort Huey devoted to recruiting them. "The Long movement might represent the aspirations of the common people, but in 1927 many of its leaders were of the upper classes."

A combination of factors caused this. Intransigent leadership by the remaining members of the oligarchy contrasted with the appeal of Huey's road building and other promises (issue framing); the split between the state machine (Simpson/Maloney) and the Old Regulars (O'Keefe) (mobilization); and the salesmanship of Huey. The split within the elite caused some of them, notably Senator Ransdell's brother and Jeff Snyder, embarrassment. When they shared a platform with Huey, he denounced their friends supporting Wilson, much to their discomfort.[58]

One leader made this crucial point: "[Huey] taught [the voters] to think. He educated them to him."[59] It had taken ten years, but he had finally prepared them, with his speeches, his attacks, his lawsuits, his press agentry, and his victories, to give him the power that they had to give.

Huey ran as part of a ticket that included candidates for lieutenant governor (Paul Cyr, a dentist from southwestern Louisiana, who spoke fluent French, and who was Bouanchaud's candidate for lieutenant governor in 1924), state treasurer, attorney general, and superintendent of education. (He had no candidate for secretary of state, state auditor, registrar of lands, or commissioner of agriculture.) O. K. Allen was running for the state Senate from Winnfield, and Harley Bozeman was running for state representative.

In the campaign, Huey charged that Wilson and Simpson were both waiters carrying food cooked up by Sanders; friends of Sanders offered to pull Wilson and Simpson out of the race if Huey would allow the Sanders toll bridge to operate without competition; Sanders supported the carbon-black industry that was wasting Louisiana's natural gas and ruining its streams;[60] a Shreveport bank president supporting Wilson had operated a Black dive saloon early in his career; the Conservation Department (or, in Huey's words, the "coonservation" department) was wasting money on useless patronage workers: a doctor had been appointed for $250 per month to ensure that no "coons" got loose on the streets of Shreveport, and later his son was hired for $150 a month to guard the city from "coons" at night.[61] Huey exploited Wilson's congressional votes against a minimum wage, an agricultural bill, and tariffs for rice and sugar.[62]

Huey attacked Simpson supporter Lee Thomas: he "just can't keep from lying. It is in the man."[63] Thomas sued Huey for slander. His lawsuit was dismissed, however, because his lawyer forgot to include the necessary allegation that he was a man of good repute. Thomas cooled off after the dismissal and didn't refile.[64]

Huey was a showman: "watch me Vaudeville 'em," he would say before starting.[65] "He evolved a windmill, or air-flailing arm movement. He screwed up his eyes, tossed off his coat, [and] burlesqued the stuffed-shirt behavior of his opponents." Huey "uttered the once unutterable, then elaborated on it."[66] One man heard Huey's voice blaring from the loudspeaker and the crowd howling its approval: it was excitement, retribution, and entertainment. The orator was jubilant. The listener "tingled with an excitement that was not altogether pleasant."[67] Like a modern rap battle, the quality of the denunciations offered their own visceral pleasure.

Huey provided some classic repartee in the campaign. With respect to Wilson's flood-control record, Huey commented that his record was fourteen feet of higher water than ever before, one for every year he served in Congress. With respect to Wilson's poverty, such as having to go barefoot as a boy, Huey said "that ain't nothin', I got documentary evidence to prove I was born barefoot." When it was charged that all the whiskey drinkers supported him, Huey said "That'd be mighty good news if it was only true. Unfortunately, Simpson and Wilson ain't supporting me." When Huey was stopped for speeding, he said that Simpson had plenty of people in jail cells waiting for room in asylums because there was no money to care for them, but meanwhile they had plenty of money for highway police to follow him all over the state.[68]

Neither Simpson (because he controlled the state government) nor Wilson (backed by the Old Regulars) could effectively campaign against government-spending waste. Newspapers attacking Simpson published exposés about wasteful patronage expenditures in the Highway Department.[69] Huey campaigned against bossism, waste, and bureaucracy and promised to investigate corruption in the Highway Commission. Today, in conventional campaigns, conservatives rail against government bureaucracy and liberals support government services. Huey had it both ways, advocating expanded government services and criticizing excessive government regulations and expenditures.

Simpson appeared with Huey on a platform only once, and he regretted it. Huey said he was glad to confront Simpson so he could tell it to him "good and proper." He then listed Simpson's shortcomings, emphasizing his failure to provide pensions to Confederate veterans and his love of liquor and racetracks. Simpson proposed to tax racetracks and use the money for schools. Huey saw his opening and pounced. He had never been to a horse race, had never bet on a horse race, and had never asked racing interests for a single favor. Whirling around to face the "flabbergasted" Simpson, "How about you?" Huey further prodded Simpson into admitting that he had written to the racetrack asking for free passes.[70]

In other speeches, Huey attacked Simpson for having divorced his first wife and for manufacturing gambling devices, both charges that were unfair or unsupported by the evidence. Simpson's denials were lost among Huey's foghorn blasts.[71] Riley Wilson appeared once with Huey, and an unfriendly newspaper admitted afterward that the crowd favored Huey.[72]

In New Orleans, Huey attacked a man in the audience, who stood up and yelled, "Hold on, you son of a bitch." Huey directed Paul Cyr to "handle him."

Cyr pinned the man's arms back while Huey continued his tirade. In a meeting in Minden, a recently jailed man interrupted Huey's speech (he may have been released to do so), but policeman Louis Jones slugged him so hard his eyebrow fell over his eye. Jones's brother grabbed Louis's gun to hold others at bay. "That's what I call enforcing the law!" Huey exclaimed.[73] J. Y. Sanders found Huey in the lobby of the Roosevelt Hotel and called him a liar. Huey ran out "to collect witnesses" and returned and swung at him but then fled to the elevator. Sanders followed and there was a tussle, with Huey's head buried mostly in Sanders' stomach. The newspapers awarded the victory to the fifty-nine-year-old, corpulent Sanders, and they ridiculed the thirty-four-year-old, 170-pound Huey for running away from the older man.[74] They called him "Hot Foot Huey" and reported that red-blooded men were disavowing their support.[75]

Huey was frightened of physical attack, frequently hearing imaginary prowlers outside his hotel room. He had a limp handshake. Williams concluded that Huey lacked the emotion that makes one want to go for the throat of someone.[76] But he had a temper, which accounted for his vehement and expletive-laced private conversations. Maybe he felt guilty about his verbal attacks and feared reprisals.

As the campaign progressed, Huey discussed voter benefits: roads, bridges, schools, hospitals, mental health facilities, and honest government. Most of the time he discussed free schoolbooks, outlining the experience of other states such as Texas. Texas distributed free books at an average cost per child of $0.90, whereas in Louisiana it was $5.99. With a lawyer's consciousness of the Texas precedent, Huey "diffused" the idea of free schoolbooks to Louisianans:[77]

> [Huey] stacked recently discarded schoolbooks on the table until they were about to fall over and then he lined up a second stack. When he began to call out the names and prices of the discarded textbooks, the applause of the crowd was continuous. He brought the house down when he reached [Congressman] Aswell's spelling book.
>
> "This man Doctor Aswell refused to become the candidate against me, although requested. My enemies painted him a good record of being modern and progressive, but here, they have put his spelling book off the rack because he is out of date when they need to sell some more spellers."
>
> At the conclusion of Mr. Long's address he received a tremendous ovation.[78]

Huey's statistics omitted the cost of the initial purchase of the books. T. H. Harris, the superintendent of education, criticized the omission. Huey replied that he would eliminate waste from government to secure the initial outlay.

He also soft-pedaled how he was going to pay for paved highways. One would think that there would have been a big argument over pay-as-you-go versus bond financing, but there wasn't. Huey said that, while paved roads were more expensive to build, they were less expensive to maintain. The state would recoup the extra cost of paved roads before they wore out in twelve to twenty years by the savings on maintenance.[79]

Paved roads were a very popular issue.[80] A bulletin of the Good Roads Association discussed their advantages: they prevent tire blowouts, double tire mileage, reduce gas consumption, triple the life of a car, reduce maintenance costs, increase the value of adjoining land, and avoid personal injuries and windshield damage from spraying gravel.[81] Those are plain cost-benefit analyses that any fiscal conservative could calculate.

Huey must have known eliminating wasteful government spending was not going to pay for paved highways or free schoolbooks. To say that Huey was going to accomplish these goals some other way is unfair to his critics. To say that Huey made a baseless promise is unfair to him. Politicians often make promises—the ones they intend to keep—with only a hazy or perhaps secret way of accomplishing them. Others oppose worthy reforms, asserting practical difficulties as a smokescreen. Pity the poor voters who must sort through the competing ideas and hidden motives before casting their ballots.

Near the end of his campaign, Huey visited St. Martinsville, where he spoke with poetic idealism under the famous oak tree of Longfellow's poetic heroine, Evangeline:

> And it is here, under this oak where Evangeline waited for her lover, Gabriel, who never came. This oak is an immortal spot, made so by Longfellow's poem, but Evangeline is not the only one who has waited here in disappointment. Where are the schools that you have waited for your children to have, that have never come? Where are the roads and the highways that you send your money to build, that are no nearer now than ever before? Where are the institutions to care for the sick and the disabled? Evangeline wept bitter tears in her disappointment, but it lasted through only one lifetime. Your tears in this country, around this oak, have lasted for generations. Give me the chance to dry the tears of those who still weep here.

> But if you wait here too long an agent from the "coonservation" department will touch you on the shoulder and tell you you are casting for minnows illegally.

He omitted the last sentence from his autobiography, but during the speech itself he could not leave the sentiment alone or linger on it, so instead he ended with a joke.[82] In other speeches, he explained his hopes for progress, saying, "He who falls in this fight falls in the radiance of the future."

There was a practical reason to reduce the attacks. If a runoff were necessary, he might need the votes of the candidate who finished third. His supporters showed the Simpson campaigners that the Wilson camp was denigrating their candidate and vice versa, increasing the chance that the defeated candidate would back him.[83]

Huey's speaking tour covered fifteen thousand miles. He gave six hundred speeches to 300,000 people. Audiences "came from every bottom in the country, by car, wagon, horseback, on foot."[84] Some people followed him from speech to speech. The schedule he kept during the campaign, eighteen- to twenty-hour days, awed observers.[85]

Wilson spoke at Hammond and New Orleans in early January but returned to Washington in the closing weeks of the campaign, either because of his confidence or because his managers knew he was a poor campaigner. Nevertheless, Wilson's managers thought that, between Simpson and themselves, a runoff would be required. Wilson's campaign arranged the defection of Huey's New Orleans Eighth Ward leaders on January 3;[86] Wilson leaders boasted that they had eroded Huey's support even in John Sullivan's home ward. Anti-Long newspapers reported that Huey spoke to small crowds in Morehouse Parish.[87]

On election night, Wilson obtained 38,244 votes in New Orleans; Simpson 22,324; and Huey a dismal third with 17,819.[88] The Old Regulars and Wilson exchanged congratulations. They maintained their optimism when Huey's north Louisiana vote was reported. But when Huey swept the south Louisiana parishes, they realized that disaster had struck. Huey had 126,842, Wilson 81,747, and Simpson 80,326.[89] Even though he lacked a majority, Huey had a bigger lead than any prior candidate in state history.[90]

To prevent a runoff, Huey moved fast, first meeting with Paul Maloney. Maloney agreed to endorse him and get his associates to do likewise. The mayor of Bogalusa and a state senator from Franklinton endorsed Huey.[91] The Simpson New Orleans organization backed Huey on January 20, and this was followed by an editorial in the *Times Picayune,* a Simpson supporter, urging Wilson to withdraw.[92] Wilson's leaders asked for financing for a runoff campaign but obtained promises of only $52,000, when at least one leader thought $500,000 would be required.[93]

The next day, Huey invited O. K. Allen, Harley Bozeman, and O. B. Thompson down to New Orleans to watch "big time" politics. A journalist was appalled at seeing a disheveled and bloodshot-eyed Huey tell his lieutenants to "stick to me. We're just getting started. . . . I'm gonna be President someday." The contrast with the idealistic reformer displayed during campaign speeches was too much for him.[94] Representatives of Wilson and Simpson visited Huey's suite in a constant stream. Sullivan and Ewing stood by Huey's side. Wilson decided to withdraw that day. Huey was elected.

Simpson emerged from the seclusion of a prolonged bender and accepted a minor job with Huey's administration. To help Huey in the bridge controversy, he began operating free ferries parallel to the route of the new toll bridge. Probably as a further concession to Simpson, Huey never prosecuted anyone for corruption or waste in the Highway Commission.[95]

The NEA (Press) Service issued a nice article about Huey after his election, emphasizing his youth, his farm background, his frequent reading of the Bible, his boyhood experience selling books, his job selling Cottolene, the cake-baking contest at which he met Rose McConnell, his false arrest in Shreveport, his defense of Senator S. J. Harper during World War I, and his legal activities against the utility companies. The article included a picture of the Longs on a porch swing and Rose's recipe for the baking contest cake, headlined with variations of "Bible-Reading Governor" or "Romance Caused by Cake."[96] When Huey went home, he celebrated with his extended family by singing songs all night around the piano.[97]

The *New York Times* wrote that Louisiana had elected an amazing personality who would be a colorful governor.[98] But colorful does not equal accomplished. In a revolution, violence often establishes the change of government, which then implements the revolutionary program. Here, while Huey's program of free schoolbooks, natural gas for New Orleans, no-toll highways and bridges was revolutionary for Louisiana, his election alone wouldn't provide those benefits; it was only the start.

History is littered with reformers who won elections and then accomplished nothing. Appealing to the same constituency that elected Huey, Mississippi's Theodore Bilbo won the governorship one year before Huey, but he couldn't pass a highway bond issue and had other disasters: "Scandals rocked the State Tax Commission and other departments . . . ; impeachment proceedings were directed at some of Bilbo's closest political associates; massive dismissals of university presidents and professors had cost the accreditation of the state's only university and most of its colleges; [and] the budget was badly out of balance."[99] Thus, the oligarchy still had strategies and tactics to defeat Huey. While O. K. Allen had been elected to the state Senate and Harley Bozeman was elected as a state representative, Huey's statewide ticket was only partially successful: Paul Cyr had won the lieutenant governor's race, and Huey's candidate won for state treasurer (H. B. Connor). The registrar of state lands (Fred Grace) switched sides and became a supporter soon after the election. Secretary of State James Bailey, Attorney General Percy Saint, Superintendent of Education T. H. Harris, Commissioner of Agriculture Harry D. Wilson, and State Auditor L. B. Baynard opposed Huey or were neutral as of the date of his election. Only eighteen of the one hundred representatives and nine of the thirty-nine senators had been elected as Long supporters.[100] The field of battle now switched from electoral politics to governing.

# Nine

# EARLY LEGISLATIVE SUCCESS

Huey's election prompted a variety of reactions. Corrupt forces offered Huey $250,000 to let the toll bridge be completed without competition. Explaining this to a friend, Huey exploded: "And it was my goddamn city campaign manager that made the proposition. But, no goddamn measly $250,000 can buy Huey Long."[1]

New Orleans's elite tried to make Huey feel loved and accepted. Colonel Ewing presided over a dinner in Huey's honor in February. Eight hundred men attended (no women). Huey's former boss, K. Dawson, came in from Oklahoma City and related the penniless Huey's heroic eighteen-mile walk in the worst of winter.[2] A banker promised the cooperation of the city's business community. Judge Foster now complimented Huey, saying he previously thought Huey was a boy making faces at authority, but now "I think he has grown up." Chief Justice O'Niell of the Supreme Court said the dinner was the equivalent of an "armistice." A big chest of monogrammed silverware was presented to Huey.

Huey was asked to speak, and he outlined his program: attack illiteracy, bring natural gas into New Orleans, build roads and bridges, improve New Orleans's port, and implement fair laws for labor. His ambitions were limited to the governorship. He wanted to be the servant of the people and not the master of the people or any set of people, disclaiming the desire to build up a strong political faction. The crowd applauded. One wonders whether Huey enjoyed comparing this reception with the boos he received at the business dinner after the Galveston rate case.

Not all the hierarchy got the message, however. Mayor O'Keefe, the Old Regulars, and the publisher of the *Times Picayune* boycotted the banquet. The banquet committee snubbed Huey's biggest financial supporter, Robert Maestri, by refusing his tendered donation to the gift of silverware, because he was socially unacceptable. Instead, Maestri bought Huey an emerald-and-diamond stickpin that Huey bragged cost $2,500.[3]

Tradition held that the governor would be invited to one or more of the opulent and decadent parties sponsored by the Krewes during Mardi Gras. But Mardi Gras separates people. Grudges are held. Success in business, politics, arts, or science is no guaranty of entry into New Orleans high society. Huey wasn't invited.[4]

Shortly after the great "armistice," Huey showed that he would not let the edge of his reform drive be blunted by flattery, and he exacted retribution on the Old Regulars.[5] Traditionally, delegates to the Democratic National Convention were elected, allowing every political faction—or at least the New Orleans and aristocratic factions—representation. Huey's statewide organization couldn't dominate such a convention.[6] The Ring sent word to Huey that it was willing to give him "a fair deal, on its terms."[7]

Engaging another lawyer, Harvey Fields, to help him, Huey and Fields researched the law. The state constitution did not *require* a convention, although it set forth rules on how to hold one. Huey decided to have the Democratic State Central Committee (composed of elected members) dispense with the convention and select the delegates. With his patronage, Huey controlled the committee. No one from the Old Regulars or any other opponent was selected. Mayor O'Keefe of New Orleans and former governors Pleasant and Sanders, all excluded, all protested. Pleasant called Huey a "red-mouthed, white-livered, yellow-backboned enemy of our country." Parker's former campaign manager, Harry Gamble, compared Huey to Mussolini. Huey replied that he had "steam rolled" over his opponents because he had promised the voters to eliminate the old "pie eaters" from government. Sanders, Pleasant, and their allies selected their own delegation to seek recognition from the convention.[8]

Leading up to his inauguration, Huey advocated bringing natural gas into New Orleans; suggested a consolidation of state boards governing levees;[9] announced a new head of the National Guard (Raymond Fleming); and supported constitutional amendments to aid victims of the 1927 flood.[10] Unveiled in a speech to the State Bar Association, Huey's judiciary proposals created a "sensation," later modified after conferences with the State Bar Association.[11] Huey selected J. M. Fourmy as highway engineer.[12] The clamor to investigate the Highway Commission continued after revelations that trucks and tractors had been purchased without competitive bidding.[13] Huey predicted legislative success for his program[14] and made plans for the huge crowds expected at his inauguration in May, Justice Brunot to be master of ceremonies.[15]

In February, Governor Simpson asked Huey to attend a New Orleans dinner with Chicago mayor William Hale "Big Bill" Thompson. Thompson had worked with Louisiana leaders on flood control, of interest because of commerce between Chicago and New Orleans on the Mississippi River. Thompson traveled in style, accompanied by 830 Chicagoans, "well stocked with Chicago money, and a brass band,"[16] and made a big impression on Huey.[17]

Before his inauguration, Huey had given a list of legislators categorized as supporters, opponents, and open to persuasion to his Winnfield friends Allen (now state senator) and Bozeman (now state representative) and asked them to meet with the undecideds. They hit the road to line up support for Huey's legislative program, promising patronage and favors: "they all didn't come for free."[18] Swords Lee, Robert Ewing, and John Sullivan supplemented their efforts. Ewing and Sullivan intended to be the powers behind Huey's throne.[19]

Huey arrived in Baton Rouge on May 8, 1928, in advance of the legislative session, setting up headquarters at the Heidelberg Hotel.[20] He kept two secretaries—Alice Lee Grosjean, pretty and efficient, and Miss Anna Fetter, a secretary under Governor Parker—busy answering over a hundred letters a day on the day received, with neither subject to the "reported foibles" (whatever that meant) of women.[21]

For president pro tempore of the Senate, Huey supported Philip H. Gilbert, the running mate of Colonel Stubbs in the gubernatorial race eight years earlier. Cyr supported him, and Gilbert had held the same position under Fuqua and Simpson. For Speaker of the House, Huey settled on a freshman representative, John B. Fournet, a young lawyer from southwest Louisiana. Huey investigated Fournet but didn't at first tell him about his selection. Instead, Huey invited him to Shreveport for a meeting and, when Fournet arrived, introduced him to his other guests as the next Speaker. That was all the conversation they had about it.[22]

Historically, fights over leadership positions in the Louisiana legislature took place behind closed doors in private or semiprivate caucuses. Huey met with opposition leaders, asked them to support his program, and promised them chairmanships of committees in return, but they wanted patronage and the freedom to oppose his legislation. Huey told them they lost patronage "as the spoils of war."[23] His opponents had the unpalatable choice of either agreeing with his selections or openly opposing them. They took this latter option, but their weak showing "exhibited a poor strategy."[24]

The legislature met on May 14, 1928, one week before Huey's inauguration on May 21. Gilbert won the Senate presidency twenty-seven to ten; Fournet won the Speakership seventy-two to twenty-seven.[25] The Long candidates for minor positions (secretary of the Senate and sergeant-at-arms) almost went down to defeat, however. Huey appeared on the floor of the Senate, lobbied fast, and saved them.[26] Simultaneously, the head of the penitentiary resigned by letter to outgoing governor Simpson, and his replacement, Clay Dugas, a close friend of Gilbert, became his successor.[27]

Traditionally, committee memberships were allocated based on the strength of the different factions. Instead, Huey dictated the memberships of the committees to Senate President Gilbert and House Speaker Fournet.

The political philosophy Huey displayed was the opposite of bipartisanship. The election had resolved any objections over his program. Now Huey turned to implement it. A few places were allocated to representatives Huey was trying to entice to his side, and a minority of positions went to opponents, but not in numbers to do any harm. Thirteen of the seats on the committee on New Orleans's affairs went to country adherents of Huey and only two to the Old Regulars. O. K. Allen became floor leader of the Senate and chairman of the Highway Commission. Harley Bozeman was appointed chairman of the House Appropriations Committee.[28]

Nevertheless, J. E. McClanahan became one of Huey's House leaders, notwithstanding that, as sheriff, he had been part of the plot to let Bob Prophit attack Huey in 1926. Elected on the Simpson ticket, House of Representatives member Allen Ellender nevertheless joined McClanahan as one of Huey's leaders.

Once he had organized the legislature, Huey had fun at his inauguration on May 21. The biggest crowd ever to attend a gubernatorial inauguration in Louisiana showed up, coming by trains, automobiles, buckboard wagons, or on foot. Invitations were not required for any event. Water was served in big buckets with dippers. Several bands—including the New Regular Democratic Band, the Standard Oil Band, Robards Serenaders of Ponchatoula, and Sou Generes of Baton Rouge—entertained the crowd. The reception was held in the LSU campus pavilion; ten thousand people attended.[29] Huey was the youngest governor in the United States.[30]

During the inaugural parade, Chicago Mayor "Big Bill" Thompson joined an exultant Huey. Big Bill and Huey spoke, Huey from a three-page typed manuscript, striking a humble ("I am deeply indebted to all of our people for the great honor which they have bestowed") and optimistic tone ("our face is toward the rising, instead of the setting, sun"). He promised to end waste and favoritism.[31] Pictures show Huey and Big Bill wearing Big Bill ribbons.

From his first day in office, May 22, 1928, Huey moved to expand and consolidate his authority and implement his campaign promises. "Huey dashed about and roared orders to assistants" while "beads of sweat dripped from his brow."[32] Seventy-three New Orleans Dock Board employees and between fifty-six and eighty (estimates differ) of the Highway Commission's speed cops were fired on his first day.

From his office window, Huey saw Simpson slowly walking away, lugging his suitcase. A lone speed cop hurried to Simpson, took Simpson's suitcase, and said something that lightened his steps. Huey asked an assistant to investigate the cop's name and whether he was on the termination list. "I'm keeping him on the payroll," Huey said. "I might be going out of office myself one of these days."[33]

Superintendent of Education T. H. Harris had run against a candidate endorsed by Huey and had opposed Huey's free-textbooks proposal. But Harris had his own reform goal: to have the state equalize school funding for poor parishes. Huey promised to help Harris with this, and Harris agreed to support Huey's free-schoolbooks law, if the funds to pay for it were found from a new source.[34]

Huey eventually crafted a unique arrangement with the press. Weary of news reporters following him around, Huey asked a newspaper editor to name a single reporter as a liaison. The editor suggested Charles Frampton. Huey yelled, "put that sonofabitch on the phone." Frampton heard the remark, got on the phone, and told Huey that he didn't want to be spoken to that way. Huey laughed and said, "you'll do." They became friends, with Huey giving Frampton priority access to gubernatorial announcements.[35]

Huey addressed the legislature at the start of the session, and a few days later his floor leaders introduced his bills, drafted by Huey's friend, Winnfield lawyer George Wallace, an excellent lawyer "whose weakness for alcohol had hindered his career."[36] Key measures included providing free schoolbooks, bringing natural gas to New Orleans, a bond issue for highway construction, an increase of severance taxes on oil and other natural resource extractions, and a tax on malt syrups to equalize the school funding of the poor parishes with the rich ones.[37]

Note the political appeal of Huey's program. Every family with children in school would benefit from free schoolbooks. Everyone with a car (to say nothing of road contractors) would benefit from good roads. Every New Orleans consumer would benefit from having natural gas imported into the city. Note, too, that these programs were readily achievable: schoolbooks had been provided in other states, natural gas pipelines were at New Orleans's doorstep, and the plans for highways had been developed under Governor Parker. Much later, Huey said he always let others do the preliminary work. They would get the fry pan and heat the oil; he only plopped in the eggs.[38]

Huey's opponents in the legislature were cohesive, experienced, and conservative, especially in the House, where Cecil Morgan and Harney Bogan of Caddo, Mason Spencer of Madison, Norman Bauer of St. Mary, George K. Perrault of St. Landry, and J. Y. Sanders Jr. of East Baton Rouge met each evening in Sanders's law office to plot strategy. They became known as the "Dynamite Squad" that planned to blow up Huey's program. They cooperated with the Old Regulars.

Williams's interviews superbly revealed the psychology and politics of these opponents, and he quoted several of them:

(1) "We resented being told we had to be with [Huey]."
(2) If the bond issue [for highway construction] were passed, "Huey Long would use the money to corrupt the people of Louisiana."
(3) "The two worst things that ever happened are universal suffrage and universal education."
(4) "I was elected with the support of powerful, wealthy people, and they were against [the free schoolbooks law]. Later I could see Huey was right about some of his bills."
(5) "If [Huey] did it, it would just have to be wrong."[39]

Alex McManus's lengthy study concluded that Huey's original sin was his proposals for expanded government services and a diminished government subsidy for the elite, despite hypocritical efforts by his opponents to conceal the real basis for their opposition. Most of the oligarchy manifested a snobbish sense of entitlement and, even decades later, bemoaned expanded government services and support of civil rights. An exception was anti-Long newspaper publisher Hodding Carter, decades later a civil rights advocate.

But in retrospect he confessed this harsh assessment of Huey's opponents. Their key mistake was to oppose everything Huey proposed, merely because he proposed it.[40]

Huey wrote the bill providing free schoolbooks on a piece of cardboard he had taken from a freshly laundered shirt. Schoolbooks would be distributed free to the schoolchildren of Louisiana. Harris protested. Written that way, he said, the bill would assist Catholic schools, contrary to the freedom of religion guaranty in the U.S. Constitution. Huey brushed this aside. The schools were only distribution centers. The books were provided directly to children. "I am a better lawyer than you are, and books for children attending private schools go in the act." If he hadn't written the law that way, Catholic representatives in south Louisiana would have objected to using tax dollars solely to benefit non-Catholic north Louisiana schools.[41] The measure to provide the books passed almost unanimously.[42] But before then, a Senate amendment to restrict their distribution to the public schools was narrowly defeated, sixteen to twenty-one. This was the key vote. Providing the books to Catholic as well as Protestant children reinforced the loyalty of Catholic voters to Huey.[43]

To pay for the books, Huey proposed on May 25, 1928, a change in the severance tax. While this violated his campaign promise to pay for the books by eliminating waste in government, increasing the severance tax was consistent with the position Huey had taken since 1920. It was opposed by the oil industry.[44] In the 1926 legislative session, the supervisor of public accounts, W. M. McFarland, had proposed changing the tax from a value to a quantity basis because it would be easier to administer (oilmen reported market prices below what was paid at the pump to reduce their taxes). His bill was defeated. Standard Oil and others thought McFarland's proposal would impose the same tax on higher gravity crude (worth more) as lower gravity crude (worth less).

Now, Huey and McFarland proposed a tax of 7.5 cents per barrel on crude and 1.5 cents per thousand cubic feet on natural gas. This would produce enough to fund the free schoolbooks and eliminate the unpopular tobacco tax. The oil industry fiercely criticized this proposal. Huey met with industry spokesmen, listened respectfully, and then compromised. The oil tax would be graduated based on gravity, the natural gas tax would be reduced to 0.2 cents per thousand cubic feet, and a 0.4 cent tax on carbon black would be imposed. Huey compromised his proposed tax rates with the lumber interests, too.

Most of the oil industry still opposed the tax. Huey's supporter, radio station owner Will Henderson, opposed it. Some conservatives who voted for the schoolbook proposal opposed the tax to pay for it. Sidney Herold of Shreveport, representing the Ohio Oil Company, threatened to sue for discrimination because its oil had a uniform gravity whereas oil in southern Louisiana varied.[45]

Before a legislative committee, Herold called the tax's proponents parasites. Huey responded. Shortsighted men like Herold—men who opposed progress—were responsible for Huey's electoral victory. Recounting the Pine Island embargo that cheated him out of $2 million, he gloated that now he was going to make Standard Oil pay a lot more than $2 million. Free schoolbooks, Huey said, would have meant a lot to his family. He and his siblings had sometimes walked to school without shoes.[46]

Huey's bitter denunciation prompted this exchange in the legislature:

> [Anti-Long] SENATOR MCDOWELL: "I want to ask you if you know what the constitution says about the governor of the state influencing legislation?"
>
> HUEY: "I do not know what the constitution says. I think the legislature is composed of a group of intelligent men. Now are there any more questions?"
>
> "Yes, you haven't answered my question," Senator McDowell persisted, walking down the aisle and handing the governor a copy of the Constitution.
>
> The Governor tossed the book aside and repeated: "Are there any more questions?"[47]

Incensed, the wife of former governor Pleasant interrupted to charge that Huey was infringing on the right of the legislature, violating the separation of powers. With feigned sweetness, Huey replied that he knew there were three branches of government, "and I have removed your husband from one of those departments."[48] The committee was "in such an uproar that Committee Chairman Hugo Dore was barely able to restore order."[49]

The severance tax passed in early July. It is one of the most politically appealing taxes, as taxes go, because persons and companies outside the state purchase most of the resources taxed and thus bore the tax burden, and it induced conservation. Huey had also threatened to veto the tobacco tax repeal if the Senate failed to approve it.[50]

When natural gas was discovered in the northeastern gas fields, private companies began building pipelines for it to be piped to them because it was cheaper than artificial gas. By 1928, the pipelines were at New Orleans's back door. New Orleans Public Service, Inc., claimed it could not provide natural gas to New Orleans without suffering a loss, even blaming the warm climate for difficulty in predicting demand.

In an interview to the *New Orleans States* (Colonel Ewing's paper), printed in other newspapers, Huey claimed that New Orleans was being "fought from within"; that a closely interlocked combination was determined to keep natural gas out of New Orleans, even while such gas was piped from Louisiana to Houston, Texas; that when New York banks shouted, "At-ten-shun," New Orleans capital clicked its heels and saluted. "Did it ever occur to you that New York capital wouldn't be any too happy to see this city of New Orleans, with cheap natural gas, grow by leaps and bounds until from its present position of battling to keep its place as the second port in America, it was making New York battle for its place as first port?" Was it "better to go ahead supplying a city of 400,000 population with artificial gas at high prices, or to give the cheap natural gas to homes and industries that will make New Orleans a city of more than a million population before you know it. . . . New Orleans citizens are being defrauded every day that natural gas is kept away . . . [and] if the gentlemen who are banded to keep it from coming here want to rough-house, they want to remember that I can stand more rough-house than they ever saw."[51]

The interview demonstrated Huey's thorough knowledge of the facts (pricing, the diameter of gas pipes, and so forth, not quoted here) and his imaginative vision for New Orleans, battling New York to be the number-one port and growing its population to one million people. Mayor O'Keefe and his heir apparent, T. Semmes Walmsley, said that getting natural gas could not be "hastened," but needed to occur in a "sane, orderly, and scientific manner."[52]

The legislation Huey introduced called for a constitutional amendment authorizing New Orleans to issue bonds to purchase New Orleans Public Service, Inc., with separate statutes that would allow the city to operate the utilities or to sell or lease them to private interests. The bills sped through the Senate and then went to the House.

Now converted to the cause, the city said it wanted natural gas, but Huey's rate was too high, whereas New Orleans Public Service, Inc., also newly converted, insisted on a higher rate of $1.15 per thousand cubic feet and a meter charge of 50 cents. Huey then called a conference of the interested parties on

June 25. Huey said he controlled the legislature like a deck of cards, shuffling and dealing as he pleased. If New Orleans Public Service, Inc., refused his terms, he would pass the Senate bills, leaving it defenseless. If the city refused, he would kill the bills, leaving it defenseless. If both refused, he would introduce a new bill setting up a state agency with the power to grant franchises in any city.

New Orleans Public Service, Inc., refused his terms, but the city accepted them. Huey wanted the company to surrender, so he stalled for time and announced legislative hearings. Huey insisted that the city accept his terms by ordinance. The city's representative at the hearing offered a letter accepting the terms but not an ordinance. Huey whispered to his adherents on the committee and led them in a walkout, yelling, "Blame it all on me! Me! Huey Long!" Then he walked out as well, insisting on an ordinance. The next day, the city passed an ordinance, and this was followed by the news that Huey really wanted to receive, the company's surrender on July 7.

Huey had forced natural gas into New Orleans, but some complained that the rate he forced—90 cents plus 25 cents meter charge ($1.15)—was too high. Artificial gas was less efficient than natural gas and cost $1.35 per thousand cubic feet. The rate agreed on was higher than he originally proposed but lower than what New Orleans Public Service, Inc., originally demanded. Critics have overlooked that the price was cheaper than artificial gas and that Huey had succeeded where other city and state officials had failed. "Huey held their feet to the fire," said a member of the City Council. "If he had used gentler methods, he would not have . . . succeeded dramatically where previous governors failed."[53]

No further agitation on the natural gas rate Huey proposed ever developed.[54] When a compromise was reached on the oil-pipeline bill, Huey continued the fight to make pipelines common carriers. In the severance tax controversy, Parker's 2 percent compromise induced years of agitation until the rate was increased to 3 percent. In the natural gas case, either the rate proposed by Huey was fair or no politician was smart enough to continue to fight for lower rates.

Huey's third major legislative initiative was a highway bond program funded by a gas tax to construct roads. This would have to be enacted as a constitutional amendment: passed by a two-thirds vote in the legislature and then ratified by the people in a statewide vote. Opponents argued that the extra gas taxes were burdensome; gasoline used by boats and farm engines would pay a tax for roads they never used; gravel roads were adequate; and Huey would use the proceeds to create a political machine.[55] The clamor of corruption—the former chairman of the Highway Commission was charged with embezzlement, ultimately dropped—also impeded Huey's efforts.[56]

While one representative proposed a $60 million bond issue,[57] Huey asked for a smaller issue, $30 million, to be secured with an increase in the gasoline tax from 2 cents to 4 cents per gallon, with 1 cent to retire the bonds and the other 3 to go into the general highway fund. The money would also pay the Highway Commission's $5 million debt from prior administrations and its overdrawn bank accounts.[58]

Sixty-seven votes were necessary to pass the bill in the House. On the day of the vote, two of Huey's committed voters failed to show up. Huey had his leaders stall by filibuster and sent the police after them. When the police brought them to the floor to vote, he passed his bill.[59]

The Dynamite Squad were clever parliamentarians. They introduced numerous bills to clog up the legislative process so that Huey's could not come up for a vote. In a response worthy of a judo master, one of Huey's floor leaders suggested that they pass all bills, leaving Huey to veto those sponsored by the Dynamite Squad. Huey implemented this idea, and the calendar was cleared. In the avalanche of so many bills passing, a drunken member of the House of Representatives rose: "Mr. Speaker! A point of order!" Speaker Fournet replied, "That pint is well-taken."[60]

Huey then vetoed numerous bills. Most noteworthy were funding for the Public Service Commission, because it was under the control of his opponents, a ruthless decision; a cattle-tick eradication measure popular with health experts but not with farmers, an understandable political decision; and appropriations for Southeastern Louisiana Colleges at Hammond, without explanation.[61]

While he was pushing these major initiatives, Huey was also acting to control all the patronage he could. On June 1, 1928, Huey appointed his personal physician, frequent expert witness in injury cases, and former head of the Shreveport Medical Society, Dr. E. L. Sanderson, to be superintendent of the State Charity Hospital at Shreveport, and appointed to the board Will Henderson, Ernest Bernstein (his client), and other supporters.[62] Allen of the Highway Commission left the technical employees alone but replaced all lower-level employees with loyal followers.

The Orleans Parish Levee Board supervised the maintenance of the dikes that protected the city. A nine-member board elected to fixed terms ran it. Huey convinced the legislature to pass a law changing the board to a five-member body. Huey appointed four members loyal to him and John Sullivan, keeping only the existing president, Joseph Haspel.

The Board of Health was headed by Dr. Oscar Dowling, who had served under five administrations and had four years left on his term. Seven days after his inauguration, Huey asked Dowling to resign. This was front-page news in the anti-Long newspapers.[63] Huey and Attorney General Saint disagreed over whether the law permitted Huey to remove him. The legislature passed Huey's bill changing Dowling's term of office to end in 1928. Then Huey appointed loyalist Dr. Joseph A. O'Hara to the position. Dowling claimed that the law—stripping him of his full term—was unconstitutional. Because of the controversy, the legislature passed a law allowing the governor to file intrusion-in-office suits against officeholders who overstayed their term without approval from the attorney general.

In August, after the new law passed, a defiant Dowling employed a guard to occupy his office at night to prevent his forcible removal but lost a request for a preliminary injunction to prevent this "by surreptitious surprise" because Huey denied that he would seize the office.[64] Attorney General Saint filed suit to oust Dowling at Huey's request and won the case in January 1929.[65]

Dr. Valentine K. Irion headed the Conservation Commission. Irion had defeated prolonged attempts by Governor Simpson to remove him in 1926. Opposing Irion, legislator Frank Peterman proposed management by a board instead of Irion. Huey opposed this, but anti-Longs thought he supported it, so they scuttled it, to Huey's immense satisfaction.[66]

A thorough analysis by Huey revealed that the statute creating the commission became effective on August 3, 1916, and stipulated a four-year term of office for the commissioner. The Constitution of 1921 continued this office and, therefore, Irion's term ended on August 3, 1928.[67] The court challenge to his removal dragged on into 1929, however.

The Charity Hospital of New Orleans was governed by a nine-member board plus the governor, each one of whom served four-year terms that overlapped, limiting an incoming governor to two immediate appointments and no more than four during his term. The legislature refused Huey's proposal to reorganize the board. Huey's research disclosed that Simpson could have but failed to appoint two members whose terms had expired, so Huey declared them removed. With the four appointments he now had and his own vote, he possessed his majority.

The superintendent of the Charity Hospital's board was Hunter Leake, the son of the Standard Oil attorney who fought Huey in the Public Service Commission cases. After Huey secured control of the board, he removed Leake, replacing him with Dr. Arthur Vidrine, a young surgeon of Ville Platte, a small city in the southern part of the state. Vidrine had graduated from Tulane University's medical school, was a Rhodes Scholar, had studied two years in London, Paris, and Vienna, and was a junior intern at Charity before setting up practice in Ville Platte, from which he earned $25,000 per year, a large sum for the time.[68] Huey exclaimed that the country people could handle big jobs as well as residents of New Orleans.[69]

The legislature also created a Bureau of Criminal Identification. The governor headed it and appointed its board of managers. Some writers describe this as ominous legislation, a harbinger of a police state, because the bureau could make arrests without warrants. The statute stated that bureau personnel were allowed to make arrests anywhere in the state, "without warrants, for all violations of the law *they may witness,* [and] to serve and execute warrants issued by the proper local authorities" (Sec. 11) (emphasis added). Warrants weren't necessary for observed crimes. Its budget was $36,000. Highway patrolmen on motorcycles were the only other enforcement agency with statewide jurisdiction at the time, but they did not carry guns. The Bureau of Criminal Identification was the first statewide police force, yet it consisted of only three people plus supervisors. Their primary duties were to collect information such as fingerprints from local authorities.[70]

Huey's practice of the patronage spoils system gave him control of most government agencies in the executive or quasi-executive branch of Louisiana state government by the end of 1928. The spoils system was first implemented on the national level when Andrew Jackson was elected president of the United States in 1828. Jackson threw out the old Federalist Party officeholders installed by prior administrations and replaced them with loyal Jacksonian Democrats. Significant Federalist corruption was discovered because of the changeover,[71] although Jackson's appointees were also sometimes corrupt.

In the years after President Jackson, however, civil service became an article of faith among reformers. Theodore Roosevelt's biographer wrote that it was difficult for people today to understand reformers' love for civil service. "How, indeed, could one reformer entitle his memoirs *The Romance of the Merit System.*" But civil service sought to "restore the fundamental principles of American democracy: first, that opportunity be made equal to all citizens;

second, that the meritorious only be appointed; third, that no public servants should suffer for their political beliefs."[72]

While civil service was a promise of Governor Parker, he used the spoils system to defeat the Ring.[73] Louisiana conservatives such as J. Y. Sanders were Jacksonian democrats and thus *defended* the spoils system. Left-wing critic Beals also justified Huey's use of the spoils system. Without it, Huey would have been controlled by the oligarchy just like his predecessors.[74]

Huey never felt the romance of the merit system. To maintain control over appointees, he required many to sign undated resignations. In some cases, he returned the resignations when he was satisfied that the appointee was competent and loyal. In other cases, he made all appointees sign them because he was unsure of one man, later returning them to those about whom he was sure but keeping the resignation of someone he had to appoint, say, if he or she were loyal to John Sullivan, believing that he could get rid of such an employee later if necessary. Huey's insistence on loyalty for nontechnical jobs was absolute. And Huey's view of what a nontechnical job was could be blurred. He once asked a college president to rush out to a polling place to see why the vote totals were not coming in as expected. The president was indignant at being asked to participate in the grubby matter of politics.[75]

Huey probably controlled one-third of the state employees within his first two years.[76] Additional supporters got jobs in private industries that did business with the state. Huey filled political jobs with diligent workers. Bob Maestri was appointed to the Conservation Commission, worked hard, turned a $10,000 deficit into a surplus of $288,000, and refused some favors requested by Huey's friend Joe Fisher.[77]

Huey's bar-examination coach, Charles Rivet, never voted for Huey, but Huey appointed him counsel to a tax agency. Rivet asked for a guaranty of noninterference. Bristling, Huey declared that you can't talk to a governor like that but, when Rivet persisted, said, "Look, I know what you're doing. If you hear that I called you a sonofabitch, well, that's all I can do about it."

Between sixteen and twenty legislators obtained deadhead jobs in state agencies. Relatives and friends of legislators also acquired jobs, or already had them and were threatened with removal if the legislator failed to vote right.

Huey investigated state legislators in detail and ruthlessly fulfilled threats of removal. "'He knew everything about you and how to get at you,' recalled a legislator whose father-in-law was one such victim."[78] Another said: "Huey's great talent was to get men on his side. There were men in the legislature that went over to him that I never thought would go. He bought them or got something on them."[79] A legislative ally recalled that "Huey studied and catalogued skeletons in the families of old aristocrats."[80] A brilliant example of the usefulness of oral history and Williams's interviews, nevertheless these assessments lack a time frame: 1928, 1929, 1930, or later years?

Biographical sketches of Huey often condense his legislative relations from 1928 to 1935 into one snapshot. Overlooked is that, in 1928, many members of the legislature voted independently.[81] Huey successfully maneuvered a limited program through the legislature without dominating it: three major initiatives were passed (along with two major tax bills to fund them), and for each he had overwhelming public support. He had to compromise all of his tax rates. The legislature declined to reorganize the boards governing Charity Hospital and the Conservation Department. He failed to expand the number of judges on the appellate court even though court modernization was one of his campaign promises.[82] He failed to persuade the legislature to purchase a gubernatorial car. The number of vetoes is evidence of the legislature's independence.

There was a lot of vote swapping and trading that would be too tedious to relate. Anti-gambling bills distasteful to John Sullivan were killed, but one to hurt dog track racing—competitive with Sullivan's horse racing—was enacted.

Huey was friendly with his opponents, always stopping to talk, and often made continued efforts to persuade individual opponents to his side. With one legislator who was old and bald, Huey would rub his hand on the man's head and say, "What kind of humor you in this morning, old man?" The usual response: "A damn bad one!" and Huey would laugh and laugh.[83]

Huey called frequent conferences of his colleagues, advisors, and supporters. He would hear them all out while he was lounging in a seat, lying on the floor, or pacing. When he had heard enough, he would exclaim, "I got it," and decide, often espousing a combination of the ideas expressed.[84]

Huey also stayed connected with his constituents. Seymour Weiss marveled that occasionally Huey would sit down and begin calling people all over the state just to talk. What kind of feedback they provided, if any, is lost now, but voters contacted must have fondly remembered the calls.[85]

Recognizing that the legislature was the source of his ability to deliver on his campaign promises, Huey gave it his undivided attention. He did not attend the 1928 Democratic National Convention in Houston that year because it took place (June 26–28) while the legislature was in session. The legislators wanted to attend. Huey first asked them not to go, arguing that there was too much work to do, but they defied him, so, in an artful compromise, Huey's wife, Rose (along with Colonel Ewing and Harvey Fields), led the legislators to the convention while Huey stayed in Louisiana, citing the press of work.[86]

The Louisiana delegation met Franklin Delano Roosevelt on the train to the convention. Roosevelt was New York governor Al Smith's campaign manager, and he solicited the support of Huey's delegation. In exchange, Roosevelt promised to support their claim to be seated against the rival delegation headed by Sanders, Pleasant, and their allies, who had objected to Huey's delegation because it was chosen by the state central committee instead of a convention.

Harvey Fields telephoned Huey that it might be good to stand with a possible president. "Damn a President," Huey replied, "I don't care about that. I just want the Huey Long delegation seated. You tell 'em to vote for Smith."[87] The convention seated his delegation and nominated Al Smith for president and Senator Joseph Robinson of Arkansas for vice president. Focused on his twin aims of implementing his program and increasing his power, the former was advanced by staying home to work and the latter was enhanced by the seating of his delegation. The choice of president, having nothing to do with either objective, was unimportant.

Huey's focus on influencing the legislature led to accusations of dictatorship. In some accounts, an opponent threw the Louisiana Constitution at Huey's head, shouting: "Maybe you've heard of this book." Huey reportedly picked it up, glanced at the title, and said "I'm the Constitution just now."[88] Other strong leaders, such as Mayor Frank ("I am the law") Hague of New Jersey, have uttered similar sentiments. It was quoted in the April 10, 1929, edition of the *Nation*, when Huey was impeached. The *Times* referred to it in 1933, saying Huey had smiled when he said it, but meant it.[89] It may be that the quote was a corrupted (or more accurate) version of the exchange with Senator McDowell during the severance tax debate.

In Huey's autobiography, he did not acknowledge the remark, but he discussed a judicial election in which one candidate criticized the other for lack of legal knowledge. The other candidate replied, "It's not the law that makes the Judge, it's the votes," and he was elected.[90] The sardonic humor of the story derives from its description of the reality of power, its actual source. The source of power in Louisiana and in every other state is not the constitution, but the people. Any politician who speaks for them and can gain their consensus can rewrite a constitution and perhaps embody it. Nevertheless, it hardly reflected Huey's circumstances in 1928.

The basis for Mrs. Pleasant's charge that Huey violated the separation-of-powers doctrine was that he appeared on the floor of the House and Senate during their sessions and invaded committee meetings, conferring with the legislators and barking out orders. He organized his own system of runners. At the time, lobbyists and friends of legislators were allowed on the floor, so it was not as unusual as one might think.[91] His supporters chafed at his public domination of legislative proceedings, however, and some preferred not to be identified as his followers. Any legislator could have asked to remove him from the floor of the legislature, but none did.

As governor of New Jersey, Woodrow Wilson asked to appear at a legislative caucus. His "staunchest allies" thought he had "overstepped the boundary that separated powers." A legislator confronted Wilson: "what constitutional right permitted his presence." Wilson pulled a copy of the New Jersey Constitution from his pocket and read that the constitution allowed "the governor [to] communicate by message to the legislature at the opening of each session, and at such other times as he may deem necessary, the condition of the state, and recommend such measures as he may deem expedient." Wilson won his point.[92] Article V, Section 13, of the Louisiana Constitution of 1921 is similar.

Huey said he would rather violate legislative conventions to get his bills passed than to "sit back in my office, all nice and proper, and watch 'em die." One wonders whether, had Huey been absent from the floor when his highway bills were called for a vote and two of his legislators were absent, his floor lieutenants would have filibustered and been able to send the police out to retrieve them. Acting faster than your competitors or opponents is a recognized principle of success in war and business. Being on the spot allowed Huey to act faster than his opponents. It was more than a desire to pass his bills that moved Huey to appear on the legislative floor, however. "There was a compulsion in him to place himself in the center of a scene of strife and excitement—and to try to dominate it."[93]

Ten

# OVERCOMING AN INTRANSIGENT OPPOSITION

The whirlwind of Huey's activity during the legislative session was matched by his work after it concluded. On July 11, the Anti-Gambling Committee of the New Orleans Chamber of Commerce appeared before a special committee of the City Council and complained that the "city was a mecca for gangsters, narcotic peddlers and addicts, gamblers and other denizens of the underworld." Poolrooms were often fronts for gambling operations, open and obvious. Roulette, craps, keno, and poker games operated in New Orleans and in the adjoining parishes of St. Bernard and Jefferson. The operators paid protection money to local law enforcement.

The committee petitioned Huey to stop gambling because wage earners losing their pay at the gambling tables adversely affected business. Huey promised to act in the adjoining parishes only when gambling was shut down in New Orleans and only if local law enforcement failed. On July 26, the sheriff of St. Bernard Parish announced that gambling dives had been closed.[1]

On August 1, 1928, Huey threatened to call out the state National Guard to patrol New Orleans—despite reluctance "to have the state intervene"—unless the city suppressed gambling. The next day the New Orleans police raided a club and closed it.[2] One newspaper said the gamblers were leaving the city: "New Orleans businessmen started it, Governor Huey P. Long gave it impetus, and the local police added the final shove."[3]

Bootleggers, smugglers, and gamblers south of New Orleans, in Jefferson and St. Bernard parishes, described by Huey as a "cesspool of hell,"[4] were told that Huey would not tolerate "open lawlessness." Prior to the push against gambling in 1928, there had been sporadic but ineffectual efforts to stop gambling. Occasionally, local law enforcement had raided the clubs, probably for show, after which operations resumed. In July 1928, Sheriff Dr. Louis A. "Doc" Meraux of St. Bernard Parish shut down some clubs, but his history revealed why gambling was always resurrected.

Well educated, Meraux had been the most powerful politician in St. Bernard for years. Once indicted for trying to bribe a Prohibition agent, Meraux was never prosecuted. Meraux told the court that his sheriff's salary was inadequate, forcing him to moonlight as a lookout for smugglers. Meraux's brother was a bootlegger who once participated in a shootout that left two deputies dead. Indicted for it, Meraux's brother fled to France, but returned to get elected as judge of St. Bernard Parish while the indictment pended. Bootlegging was such an accepted practice that hijackers of bootleggers were prosecuted in the court system. Yes, bootlegging was a crime, the courts reasoned, but hijackers were criminals *and* a menace to business.

No one believed Huey's threats to call out the National Guard, and no one said he shouldn't. On August 12, the gamblers in the Jai Alai and Arabi clubs across the street from each other on the notorious Friscoville Avenue in St. Bernard Parish were thus unprepared when the National Guard raided them. All gambling equipment was confiscated and the money seized. Huey had delivered the secret order to raid the clubs in person to Guard commander Raymond H. Fleming, after a long taxi ride—not trusting a messenger. Eight men raided one club while seven raided the other. Women screamed, and several fainted. A club sentry fired one warning shot. Fifty patrons beat a newspaper photographer—because he was suspected of being an informer and to prevent his report of their attendance—until the Guard rescued him. The Guard bashed in the locked doors, and the gambling equipment was burned in a big bonfire or hacked to pieces with an axe. All the items taken by the Guard—dice tables, slot machines, roulette tables, a keno table, and chips—were inventoried. All the money was deposited into a locked safe brought in by the Guard. The establishment manager was given a signed, itemized receipt for the money taken. The seized cash ($25,000) was deposited into the state treasury.[5]

A club owner was interviewed: "I wanted to open, but I had a hunch something might happen. Finally, I decided to toss a coin. If it came heads I was to open, and if it came tails I was to stay closed. It came heads and now look what has happened."[6] The raids were reported in big stories on page one in small newspapers throughout the South and in a small story on page one of the *New York Times*.[7]

This first raid earned praise from the civic, business, and religious groups. Sheriff Meraux was out of town at the time but "thoroughly approve[d]." The operator of the Jai Alai Club traipsed in to see General Fleming to ask for the return of his property and ask what he could do to prevent a recurrence. Fleming told him to leave Louisiana.[8]

Governor Hall had once used the National Guard to raid gambling dens in 1916. Huey's use of the Guard was nevertheless forceful and terrifying. Preceding its use with warnings and threats, however, was cautious. Huey threatened to call out the Guard again in September, but a few days later changed his mind, because his informants had told him that the gambling houses were closed.[9]

Other crises competed with gambling for Huey's attention. As the schools prepared to open in the fall, free schoolbooks had been ordered, but the severance tax revenue was not yet collected. Several lawsuits were filed to set aside the law and to annul the tax measures to fund it. Typically, Louisiana governors borrowed funds under authorization from the state's Board of Liquidation, which operated in conjunction with a consortium of New Orleans banks. When Huey met the bankers to borrow $500,000 to buy the schoolbooks, however, they informed him that the Board of Liquidation loans were illegal because a suit had been filed challenging the severance tax law. Huey answered that there were loans of $935,000 that the state owed to the banks. The bankers replied that the last legislature had authorized repayment. Huey said: "Yes, but it hasn't been paid yet. And what's more, it ain't going to be paid. Your attorneys ruled those loans illegal, and if it's illegal to make them it's illegal to pay them. We'll keep the $935,000 and buy the books and have $435,000 to spare, under the ruling of your lawyers."

Huey left the meeting "somewhat outdone." He went to his hotel's restaurant and ordered from the waiter a "thin sandwich." Then one of the bankers unexpectedly arrived at Huey's table and said "let's stop this talk where it is. We voted to make you the loan." Huey could have it immediately. Just then the waiter returned, and Huey said, "Take back the sandwich. Fry me a steak!"

Huey said that "[n]o accomplishment of [his] career [gave him] such satisfaction."[10] The free books substantially increased school enrollment.[11]

Huey's home parish of Caddo (Shreveport), however, refused to distribute the books. Mayor Thomas articulated the reason: "this is a rich section of the state" that did not want to be "humiliated" by receiving them.[12] It won a preliminary injunction in a trial court temporarily forbidding book distribution. The state school board appealed, and the appellate court reversed it, a decision affirmed on appeal to the Louisiana Supreme Court by a four-to-three vote.

In the meantime, the Supreme Court justice from Shreveport's district, John Land, came up for reelection. He had supported Huey's position on the free schoolbooks in the preliminary ruling. He faced a formidable candidate backed by conservatives, who hoped to defeat him and then reverse the preliminary ruling when the case came up for final decision. Huey managed Land's campaign, and he was reelected in early September. Huey had preserved his majority on the court.[13]

Enraged over Huey's campaign attacks on his competence, Land's opponent encountered Huey in a building lobby. Huey said, "good morning." The opponent (a lower court judge) tried to hit Huey. Huey ducked, said the opponent was an "old man," "patted him on the shoulder," and suggested that he hold his temper.[14] When the schoolbooks case was heard on the merits, the preliminary ruling allowing distribution was made permanent.[15]

Although the bankers loaned the money to buy the books, the court challenge to the severance tax had to be won. The Ohio Oil Company, represented by Sidney Herold, filed suit on August 6, 1928, and the next day a temporary restraining order against collecting the tax was issued. A hearing on whether to continue this ruling was scheduled for August 16. The day before this hearing, Huey discovered that Attorney General Saint had defaulted on his duty to defend the state, filing no pleadings to oppose the challenge. The case was going to be heard in Shreveport, three hundred miles away, in less than twenty-four hours. Appropriating a young lawyer from Saint's office to help, Huey prepared the necessary pleadings, after which he boarded a train for Shreveport that night and successfully argued the case before the three federal judges the next day. The court denied the injunction, but the company appealed to the U.S. Supreme Court.[16]

The Old Regulars and other conservatives opposed Huey's constitutional amendments authorizing the bond issue for road construction. Opponents charged that there were no safeguards for spending the money. Huey countered by proposing to have an oversight board composed of civic-minded businesspeople, including his opponents, to approve expenditures. The conservatives then argued that this oversight board was not written into the legislation. Huey replied that he would call a special session to enact the safeguard if the conservatives would promise to vote for the measure, as amended. The conservatives shilly-shallied in response, making them look insincere if not ridiculous.[17] Huey pushed his highway bonds agenda at state fairs[18] and even advocated a $30 million road bond measure sponsored by Governor Theodore Bilbo of Mississippi.[19]

Huey took time to attend a football game in Mississippi between Tulane and Mississippi A&M, at which a new football stadium was dedicated,[20] and to campaign for Al Smith to be elected president. Smith was unpopular in the South because he was Catholic, advocated Prohibition repeal, and had a background in the Tammany Hall organization, the corrupt New York City machine. The *Baptist Messenger* opposed free schoolbooks and Al Smith with equal fervor.[21] Some Democratic politicians in southern states supported Republican Herbert Hoover rather than Smith.[22]

Huey denounced religious bigotry forthrightly,[23] which must have pleased Catholic voters and alienated fundamentalists, and he campaigned for Smith with former opponents in a show of unity.[24] But Colonel Ewing and other Smith campaigners including Huey stooped to the stock southern prejudice against African Americans, with Huey accusing Hoover of advocating "negro domination." Huey's racist remarks outraged none of his constituents or his opponents, all of whom were white and shared the same prejudice.[25]

Despicable as these remarks were, Huey did not win his elections by denouncing African Americans, praising Jim Crow laws, or justifying white supremacy. In this, he was a significant improvement over many popular southern mass leaders, and he was far more popular among African Americans than his opponents. Black families received free schoolbooks and traveled on some of the new roads (not always paved in black neighborhoods). But Huey had the standard southern prejudices of his time in 1928 and signed a bill establishing Jim Crow race separation on buses. It duplicated a preexisting law for train travel that led to the reprehensible 1896 U.S. Supreme Court decision permitting the Jim Crow laws in *Plessy v. Ferguson*. He could not have done otherwise and remained governor.[26]

On November 6, 1928, Smith carried Louisiana in the presidential election while he lost several southern states.[27] An overwhelming vote approved Huey's constitutional amendments allowing bonds to construct highways. Despite opposition by the Old Regulars, the amendments passed even in the City of New Orleans, by a majority vote in fifteen out of the seventeen wards. In the two wards in which they were defeated, the margin of defeat was only eight votes.[28] The constitutional amendments had passed by larger majorities than Huey commanded for himself, a pattern that recurred in later years. Neither Huey nor his opponents grasped the significance of that.

Within a week after the election, on November 12, National Guard raids on Beverly Gardens and Fargo's Grocery Store, both gambling houses in Jefferson Parish, yielded cases of dice, all of them crooked, along with $18,000 in cash, with Huey "sitting on the edge of the bed in a hotel room," threatening "with flashing eyes" to raid New Orleans next.[29] Patrons' checks were confiscated. The club owner obtained from the Guard or the state their return in exchange for his check for the entire amount. Five days later, Attorney General Saint announced that the check exchange had destroyed evidence of a crime and that the raids were illegal.[30] Huey replied that, if he had to declare martial law before the raids (as Saint opined), the gamblers would have had a warning to close.

On November 20, 1928, Huey greeted twenty visiting governors for the National Governor's Conference and hosted them in New Orleans and at a reception in Baton Rouge. Interestingly, the governors endorsed (one year before the Depression) President Hoover's plan to create a $3 billion reserve fund for construction projects to be undertaken in slack times to alleviate unemployment.

The man who made the entertainment arrangements later said the governors were on a big drunken spree and sampled some of the illegal entertainment of New Orleans, paid for with a $6,000 Louisiana legislative appropriation. New York governor-elect Franklin Roosevelt didn't attend because his election was still contested.[31]

Riding a wave of power and influence, Huey called for a special session of the legislature for December 1928 to pass road construction laws to implement the constitutional amendments, including an increase in the gasoline taxes necessary to secure the bonds. For an unrelated reason, this session was of compelling interest to Shreveport. The U.S. Army wanted to build an airport adjacent to Shreveport. "It was a fine and needed improvement. . . . By some act of Providence, it developed that the State of Louisiana owned 80 acres of the ground needed for its construction," Huey said. A bill passed during the May legislative session allowed cities to acquire land to donate to the federal government, but a typographical error left the city unable to acquire the eighty acres necessary to win the air base.

Shreveport had refused to distribute the free schoolbooks even after they were delivered, so Huey said, "Whenever you get ready to allow these free schoolbooks to be handed out to the children, then I will be ready to talk to you about the State deeding 80 acres of land to the [federal] government." Huey's self-appointed prime minister, Colonel Ewing, "called [Huey] to New Orleans and stormed." Huey still refused.[32] The state also withdrew road maintenance funds for Shreveport.

A meeting was arranged between Shreveport leaders and Huey. Huey demanded that the Shreveport Chamber of Commerce apologize to him in a newspaper advertisement for excluding him from banquets for Army representatives, that the city and Ewing's newspaper show him more respect, that the parish withdraw its lawsuit opposing distribution of the free schoolbooks, and that the parish's representatives support his legislation in the upcoming legislative session. Outraged at both his manner and his demands, the city leaders refused.

The Army meanwhile announced that Shreveport had won its bid, and the controversy became common knowledge. Huey's radio station supporter, Will Henderson, asked him to change his mind, but Huey declined. Henderson said Huey was a "damned fool."[33]

Twenty-seven legislator opponents of Huey signed a petition asking him to include the air-base matter in a supplemental call. Having vented his feelings and recovered his senses, Huey now functioned as a normal, pragmatic politician and secretly proposed to one of those opponents a face-saving out. If the petitioners changed their petition seeking to include the air base in the supplemental call to also require distribution of the schoolbooks without prejudice to their court challenge, Huey would agree and add the air-base matter to the legislative call. Twenty-five of the twenty-seven legislators who had signed the original petition signed the one designed by Huey. The Shreveport Chamber of Commerce was satisfied. The school board ordered distribution of the books, and Huey added the air-base matter to the agenda for the special session. Later Huey spoke about how he forced Caddo Parish to accept free books. "They said they were coerced. I didn't coerce them. I stomped them into distributing the books."[34]

The legislature approved Huey's highway legislation and the air-base law in three days. The *Times-Picayune* congratulated the people of Louisiana on the success of the special session "and the speed, precision and unanimity" by which it transacted business. It hoped "the example and precedent" would be "followed throughout the future."[35]

Having arranged for funding, Huey turned to constructing the highways.

His plan was clever and careful. Courtesy of the Parker administration, Huey had a map of highways planned to span the state. But Huey decided to scatter the road placements. When the people discovered the pleasure of traveling on concrete, Huey reasoned, they would support more bond issues to connect the separated links. Huey's $30 million bond program was more conservative than in North Carolina, for example, which had authorized two bond issues totaling $115 million.[36] Of all of Huey's plans, none "ever worked better."[37]

Huey sent O. K. Allen and other officials to Missouri, Tennessee, Illinois, Ohio, Pennsylvania, New York, Virginia, North Carolina, and Florida to review road construction programs.[38] On Allen's recommendation, Huey pirated North Carolina's chief engineer, Leslie R. Ames, to work in Louisiana, more than doubling his North Carolina salary of $6,000. In the absence of sufficient Louisiana engineers and draftsmen, Huey hired technical experts from other states. This policy was "new to the state, and strange to all classes, including the aristocracy, whose supposedly cosmopolitan members were its severest critics."[39]

In matters of personal friends and political associates, Huey was, if not cosmopolitan, eclectic and hospitable. The governor's mansion was in the wealthy section of Baton Rouge, three blocks from the capitol. Its architecture was typical of the times, with square pillars in front and wide hallways connecting high ceilinged rooms. Friends and followers from all over the state visited him, sometimes staying for days or weeks. They would sit around the dining room table and talk politics or listen to the radio. On one of these occasions, probably early in 1929, Huey acquired the nickname "Kingfish." The most popular radio show in the country was *Amos 'n Andy*. According to one story, he began calling one of his friends "Brother Crawford," the name of a lodge brother in the Mystic Knights of the Sea, to which Amos and Andy belonged. In response, his friend called him "the Kingfish," the humorously scheming leader of that same fictional lodge.[40] Another was that a discussion among his followers prompted Huey to say, "Shut up, you sonsofbitches, shut up! This is the Kingfish talking." Huey said that the name arose when the Highway Commission was selling bonds and a potential purchaser objected that, technically, the law required the bonds to be sold by the Highway Commission, not the governor. Huey replied that he was participating anyway and that, in the absence of any other title, they could call him "the Kingfish." Having applied that name derisively to opponents, the name now stuck to him. He made no effort to discourage it, believing a little levity never hurt in politics and that it was an easier name than Long to understand over the phone.[41]

At the Roosevelt Hotel, where he stayed when in New Orleans, Huey befriended Seymour Weiss. Weiss had joined the hotel to manage its barbershop and then became assistant manager, manager, and then principal owner. Immaculate in dress and impeccable in manners, with the self-taught vocabulary of a college professor, Weiss saw to Huey's every need at the hotel, improved Huey's sartorial tastes, and became the trusted financial manager of Huey's political organization.[42]

By the time he was elected governor, Huey had developed a psychosis that he was in physical danger. Around crowds, Huey carried a pistol, although he never drew it or fired it. He gave a former prizefighter, Harry "Battling" Bozeman, a job on the payroll of the Highway Commission, which was a cover for his real duties to guard Huey. Slow, amiable, and dimwitted, Bozeman was not a good guard or loyal to Huey, so he was fired. Joe Messina replaced Bozeman. A part-time errand boy and tailor at the Heidelberg Hotel, he was hired as a sort of super-valet who literally lived with Huey. The Highway Commission authorized Messina to carry a pearl-handled revolver, but he had little skill with it. Messina required little sleep, perhaps due to shell shock he had suffered during World War I as an Army truck driver. Other guards were gradually added: Paul Voitier, an ex-prizefighter; Murphy Roden, a combination chauffeur and security guard; Louie Jones, the policeman who clubbed a campaign heckler; Elliott Coleman; George McQuiston; Goldman Grant; and others. Jim Brocato, alias Jimmy Moran, was sometimes identified as a bodyguard, but he was a cook, specializing in Italian dishes (his descendants still manage acclaimed New Orleans restaurants). He was close to Bob Maestri and some members of the Mafia.[43]

The bodyguards deterred some confrontations, and Huey felt more secure during the confrontations that occurred. Once a man in a coffee shop began cursing him. Huey took Jones with him over to the man's table, and when the man jumped up, Jones slugged him. Huey asked Jones to keep quiet about it, not because he feared publicity, but because Huey did not want to disabuse the man of the thought that Huey—not Jones—had hit him.[44]

While his followers, friends, and bodyguards stayed for long periods of time in the mansion, his wife and family, brothers and sisters, and his aged father were conspicuously absent. At some point, Alice Lee Grosjean became more than a secretary. Williams leaves some doubt about the matter. But Huey's boyhood friend Harley Bozeman was contacted by Williams seeking an interview for his book. Bozeman wrote Huey's son, Russell, that the only people still living who knew Huey intimately enough "for a TRUE biographical history. . . . are your mother, Alice Lee Grosjean and myself."[45] Days later, Bozeman wrote that he would not reveal several chapters of Huey's life until he had talked to Russell. Fournet asked Williams's interviewer to turn the tape machine off when this subject arose, and other interviewees were not so circumspect, so I draw the obvious conclusion. Originally, Rose and the children had lived in the mansion but, according to one report, Huey moved Alice Lee Grosjean in as well, installing an aunt of hers in the same room. Rose threatened divorce, and Alice Lee moved out and took a room in the Heidelberg Hotel; Rose moved back to the mansion. After Huey took a room across the hallway from Grosjean, however, Rose moved the family to Shreveport. Huey often stayed in the Heidelberg Hotel when he was in Baton Rouge and the Roosevelt when he was in New Orleans.[46]

If Huey were closer to Alice Lee than to Rose, it was at least in part because he lived a public, political existence, and Alice Lee shared that existence because of her public duties, whereas Rose had to raise their family. Huey's relationship with Alice Lee was long-term, not a meaningless sex-capade. There might have been other affairs, but for the most part Huey "had no time for women"; in fact, "no time for sleep."[47]

Brother Julius wanted Huey to house their father in the mansion, but he refused.[48] Huey gave brother Earl one of the best jobs in the state, attorney for the inheritance tax collector (a position that, during the campaign, he suggested he might abolish).[49] As a private condition of the job, Earl had to support their father and sick sister, Caledonia. Earl's duties were light. On Huey's behalf, Earl organized support in parishes or negotiated with individual legislators. Earl was good at this, but Huey worried that Earl would double-cross him.

Huey had a low opinion of many of his relatives, expressing wonderment when an acquaintance said he was going to move to be closer to his family. The relatives Huey put on the state payroll often had to put up with abuse. His cousin Jess Nugent had to endure a routine in which Huey would say, "Well, look at old Jess. He's the best employee we got in the whole state." When someone asked what he did, Huey always responded "Not a goddamn thing!"[50]

When he spent time with his family, Huey would play with his children or read books to them or discuss the benefits of right living. If he were working at home, however, the noise of their play would occasionally make him explode in a rage that only Rose could assuage. The phone in his office once rang too many times and he smashed it into splinters.[51] At times, he could find a resigned humor in his frustrations. When Alice Lee went on vacation and Huey and his colleagues couldn't locate some important papers, he called her for help: "Nobody can't find nuttin'."[52]

The energy that Huey had often dissipated in his youth was now concentrated on politics, making him intense and nervous. Despite his youthful gambling, he now refused to play any kind of cards, including Rose's favorite card game, bridge. The social events that he attended with Rose were sometimes planned by people with ulterior motives, such as when one dinner host asked Rose to influence Huey to support him for a Senate race. Afterward, Huey sighed that maybe they should curtail such events. Outside the home, Huey single-mindedly inspected the state projects he initiated. He appreciated the spontaneous cheers of schoolchildren more than the company of his wife.[53] Rose would occasionally upbraid him, sometimes sharply, especially if her children were involved, and he bore her occasional wrath without protest.

Huey's intensity showed itself in some peculiar habits. He would commandeer food from companions or a passing waiter and eat it, either unconsciously or deliberately to dominate someone. Once during a campaign, no restaurant was available, so he "lunched on crackers, canned Vienna sausage, sliced raw onion and peanut brittle candy, munching them together quite indiscriminately with every outward evidence of relish and enjoyment."[54] He ate potlikker, turnip greens, cornbread, sweet potatoes, hot biscuits, and watermelon. From New Orleans's restaurants, he enjoyed fried oysters and steaks, but not spicy French food. At one fancy restaurant, he asked, "What's this wood I'm eating?" The waiter replied, "That's not wood. It's bay leaf. You are not supposed to eat it. It is for seasoning." Saying it was too hot, Huey pushed the plate away.[55] In another, he swept a plate of oysters to the floor, claiming they weren't cooked to his liking.

Nervousness made it difficult for Huey to sleep. Customarily, he slept about four hours a night. Every week or so, he would catch up by sleeping eight hours or more. He liked a big bed, eventually having one custom built, seven feet long. He kept a pad of paper and a pen on a nightstand in case he got ideas during the night. Once on a trip with a colleague, he woke up in the middle of the night, turned on the light, and began to write. His roommate asked him where he got the idea. "From the Lord," Huey said.[56]

Huey often drank himself to sleep. Huey told a friend that some of his best ideas came to him when he was sleeping off a debauch. Illegal liquor was ordered in large quantities. He would take a glass of half whiskey and half wine and down it at a gulp. One drink would stimulate him; two would intoxicate him; more than that would get him into trouble.[57] In 1994, the

Mutual Life Insurance Company released its medical records on Huey; the file showed that he was not as heavy a drinker as reported. It "was more that he wanted to be positioned as one of the good old boys." Huey drank "good whiskey," and he had "almost unlimited energy." The report's author said: "it is hard to see how he stands the physical strain, traveling a great deal by train and automobile." Huey weighed 165 pounds with a thirty-six-inch chest and a thirty-four-inch waist, was in excellent health, and had unusual stamina.[58]

Huey would drink in hotel bars or in nightclubs, talking to anyone. Several times in the clubs he mounted the stage to sing to the patrons, gaining the sobriquet from his enemies as the "singing fool" of New Orleans.[59]

The drinking or his urge to talk or both got Huey into trouble. Some say his manner became unbearable. An opponent reported that Huey refused to shake hands with someone, saying "I bought and paid for you; I don't have to shake your hand."[60] One wonders whether his extreme behavior—such as his fiery denunciation of Shreveport leaders—was occasioned not just by their fierce opposition, but by an irritability brought on by fatigue and drinking.

One of the reasons Huey lived in the hotel and his family lived in Shreveport, he claimed, was that the Executive Mansion was dilapidated and full of rats and termites.[61] The legislature had appropriated money to repair it, but when carpenters began work in October 1928, the extent of termite infestation caused them to stop. When Huey asked to tear it down, the Board of Liquidation had the Baton Rouge building inspector examine it. The inspector said it would need to be completely reconditioned but was not as bad as Huey claimed. Expert exterminators could not guaranty a remedy for the termites, however.[62]

Having asked the legislature for nothing for the mansion in December, in January 1929 Huey asked the Board of Liquidation for $150,000 so he could build a new one. They agreed, with the proviso that he would poll the legislators for approval by mail. Conservatives were outraged that he wanted a new mansion. Ewing's papers agreed with the criticism. Some claimed the old mansion was good enough for his predecessors; Huey replied that it was *too* good for them. Huey finally analogized their opposition to a boardinghouse manager who replied to a complaint of dirty towels by saying, "People have been wiping on that towel for a month without complaint; I don't see what's the matter with you."[63]

After getting the $150,000, Huey phoned the warden of the state penitentiary, asking for a gang of convicts. He then supervised their demolition of the old mansion.[64] The new mansion would be a symbol of progress.

After this disagreement with Colonel Ewing, a sensational murder precipitated a split from Lieutenant Governor Paul Cyr. Cyr was loyal to Huey during the legislative sessions of 1928 but had not received word that he would be an endorsed candidate to succeed Huey in 1932. Difficulties between the two men were rumored as early as October 6, 1928.[65]

James LeBoeuf, his good-looking wife, Ada, and their four children lived in Morgan City, on the Gulf Coast, where hunting and fishing were popular. In July 1927, Mr. LeBoeuf was seen paddling a pirogue with Ada on a lake, after which he disappeared. Frog hunters found LeBoeuf's body in the lake. It had been slashed open and weights attached to his head and feet. A slight elevation in the bottom of the lake was the random piece of luck that allowed discovery of the dead body. Ada was having an affair with Dr. Thomas Dreher, a wealthy physician. After the discovery of the body, Ada and Dr. Dreher were arrested. When Dreher was arrested, he grabbed a pistol and moved to commit suicide, and then confessed.

Dreher's hunting guide, Jim Beadle, was taken into custody. Beadle turned state's evidence, pleaded guilty, and was sentenced to life imprisonment. The evidence was that Ada had suggested the trip in the pirogue but rode in a separate boat from the shooter. On the water, they were met by Dreher and Beadle, who shouted, "Is that you, Jim?" When he answered, he was shot. The jury found Ada and Dreher guilty of murder and sentenced them to hang. The trial took place before Huey assumed the governorship, but the Louisiana Supreme Court affirmed the conviction after he took office.[66] The macabre details were discussed throughout the state.[67]

Ada and Dreher asked Louisiana's Board of Pardons to commute their sentence to life imprisonment. The board consisted of Attorney General Percy Saint, the trial judge James Simon, and the lieutenant governor, Paul Cyr. Saint and Simon voted to deny the request; Cyr dissented. Huey signed the death warrants but then extended the date of execution beyond the holidays of December 1928.

The newspapers originally emphasized the grisly murder, but then shifted to focus on the love affair and the precedent-setting event of having a white woman hanged. Ewing's two newspapers urged clemency. Cyr had connections with Dreher's social and political circle. He became the champion of the revisionist sentiment for mercy. Attorney General Saint reversed himself and, at another meeting of the Board of Pardons, commutation was recommended by a two-to-one vote, with trial judge Simon dissenting. Eleven of the twelve jurors recommended mercy. Huey received death threats if he allowed the convicted prisoners to hang. Cyr claimed the execution would equal "judicial murder."

After studying the trial transcript and numerous conferences with friends and advisors, Huey overruled the recommendation of the board and ordered the sentence carried out on January 5. Ada and her lover had committed cold-blooded murder, Huey said, not one mitigating factor existed, and the perpetrators had simply changed their stories from what they said at trial to what they said to the Pardon Board. The only injustice was that Beadle wouldn't be hanged, too. The *Times-Picayune* complimented Huey's decision.[68]

On the night before the hanging, the Louisiana Supreme Court considered a request from the defendants to stay execution to empanel a lunacy commission to determine their sanity, although the trial judge had already heard such evidence. The justices argued for five hours. When they exited their chambers, Justices Brunot and O'Niell were yelling at each other. Attendees separated them just before a fight erupted.[69] Brunot called the Sheriff and told him that, by a four-to-one vote, the sentence should be carried out, but O'Niell wrestled the phone away from Brunot and ordered the sheriff to stay the execution. The sheriff was too confused to do anything. Huey issued a reprieve to allow the court to write an opinion. A week later, it did, overruling O'Niell, authorizing the execution.

Some of Huey's opponents argued that Huey was inconsistent in denying relief to Dreher and LeBoeuf because he had earlier commuted the sentence of one Pleasant Harris, who had killed his wife. Huey said, however, that in the Harris case the trial judge and the Board of Pardons had unanimously recommended commutation, with the trial judge confessing he had overlooked the gun's discharge being accidental, and that the recommendation passed through his office as a matter of form. Author Carleton Beals relates the gruesome facts of the Pleasant Harris case: he was a violent underworld pimp with connections, and the decedent was a prostitute killed after a drunken party led to a fight in which he beat her savagely in the middle of a street. Beals suggests that influence was brought to bear on the Pardon Board or Huey but did not deny that the Pardon Board recommended the commutation or that the recommendation passed through Huey's office as a matter of form.[70]

Huey fired a prison gatekeeper who testified that Beadle told him that he had killed LeBoeuf, because he should have reported that to his superiors or to Huey, and then barred visitors from seeing Beadle. This further outraged Cyr and his allies.[71] Cyr charged that Huey had double-crossed him on a deal by which Huey would travel to Mississippi long enough for Cyr to function as governor and commute the sentence. When a rumor reached him that Huey had been kidnapped, Cyr rushed to Baton Rouge to assume the duties of governor. Disappointed at finding Huey safe and sound, he told a newspaper that, if Huey were kidnapped, he would "not only settle the LeBoeuf-Dreher case," but he "would pardon the kidnappers."[72] Once when Huey was near him on the Senate floor, Cyr growled, "I wish I could get that sonofabitch in the woods with me. Only one of us would come out."[73]

The hanging took place on February 1, after the federal courts denied last-minute relief.[74] Huey warned the local sheriff to fulfill the order, or he would have the National Guard do it.

Cyr's break with Huey in January preceded Huey's break with Ewing and Sullivan in February. Relations were already tense between them because of their disagreements over the Shreveport air base, the governor's mansion, and the Dreher-LeBoeuf case. They had produced only five thousand more votes for Huey than he had obtained in New Orleans four years earlier without their help, yet Ewing presumed to be Huey's prime minister and Sullivan made disproportionate demands for patronage. At various times, open breaches between Ewing and Huey were narrowly averted, and Huey was never friendly with Ewing's son,[75] who ran the Shreveport newspaper. In private conversations, Huey nicknamed Sullivan "Bang Tail" (he liked to attend horse races), Ewing "Colonel Bow Wow" (he looked like a schnauzer), and Ewing's son as "Squirt."[76] Ewing in February 1929 proposed a merger of the Old Regulars with the New Regulars. Huey rejected this.[77]

On February 8, Jefferson Parish sheriff Frank Clancy raided Riverside Inn for illegal gambling. Patrons shouted, "why don't you raid the other places," referring to Rudy O'Dwyer's Original Southport Inn and others. Someone quoted Clancy as saying Huey told him that only three places could open; the rest should be raided or closed. To give the lie to that quote, the next day Rudy O'Dwyer's was raided and several thousand dollars in cash seized. Clancy denied quoting Huey.

Right after Mardi Gras ended, on February 13, Tranchina Night Club, the Suburban Gardens of Jefferson, and the St. Bernard Country Club of St. Bernard were raided. The patrons were searched, and gambling paraphernalia (but not much cash) was recovered. Someone was tipped off. Huey had attended a small party with a supporter, hotelman Alfred Danziger, where

Huey consumed a lot of liquor, flirted with a cabaret singer and hula dancer, and allegedly let slip the planned raids.[78] Huey issued a tough statement after these raids, warning that patrons would henceforth be treated as criminals. The proprietor obtained an injunction to prevent the state from depositing the money into the state treasury.

In a dispute that raged over several days, the issue of whether and how to search women patrons, whether the National Guard had accounted for all cash received, and whether the Guard was authorized to raid gambling joints was debated. Now, Ewing's papers denounced the raids. In one edition, Ewing's papers published a picture of a woman who was subject to the humiliation of a search. Another newspaper, however, proved that she was the wife of a gambler and provided her police record.

Caught in this mistake, Ewing then scorched Huey with an editorial that Huey wasn't fit to tie the shoes of his predecessors, reported Huey's attendance at Danziger's party, and charged that gamblers had contributed to his campaigns. Huey responded that Ewing should stop defending murderers (Dreher and LeBoeuf) and rogues (the gamblers) and then retaliated by accepting the undated resignations of Sullivan's adherents on state agencies and by firing others. Ewing charged that Huey was drunk with power.

The break was complete. Without any support or patronage, the New Regulars had to merge with the Old Regulars. Sullivan was reduced to being a coleader of a single ward. Huey, however, now lacked any New Orleans organization.[79]

Meanwhile, Huey had obtained the Supreme Court's approval to remove Oscar Dowling from the Board of Health at the end of the preceding month, and Dr. Joseph O'Hara, his replacement, took office. Huey appointed Bob Maestri to replace Valentine Irion of the Conservation Commission, but Irion refused to leave when Maestri showed up to take the job. That court battle continued.[80]

Representatives of Caddo Parish, led by Huey's former client Ernest Bernstein, held a meeting with Huey about roads in the parish. Huey again denounced them in harsh, unreasoning terms, cursing them and using racial slurs. He would teach them to get off the sidewalk and bow down damn low when he was in town, he said, and this is the polite version. (See chapter 11, below.)[81]

Huey's actions after his successful legislative session, part of the trajectory of his revolution, have provoked a lot of comment. He had used the National

Guard to conduct warrantless raids on gambling houses, cast aside his family, established himself as the Kingfish among his friends, used convicts to tear down the governor's mansion, vented ugly feelings against leaders of Caddo, and broken with his most prominent supporters.

The gambling-establishment raids have shocked historians, who fail to mention that Huey was asked to act, threatened the raids first, and received no protests ahead of time. Joe Fisher related that Huey was like a rattlesnake: he always warned before he struck. While the image conveyed is lethal, a warning is cautious, acting as a trial balloon.

Considering the compromise that Huey effected, Williams thinks the boast that he stomped the Caddo leaders hid a typically pragmatic politician who liked to appear more terrible and powerful than he was. In contrast, Williams thought demolishing the old mansion was designed to humiliate his critics and to stun his opponents into a state of acquiescence.[82] If he became increasingly brutal between these events, why?

There are examples of people outgrowing their early backers or wanting to reconfigure their support groups. A new king who fires his father's counselors,[83] a musician who leaves his band or replaces his agent are examples. Huey undoubtedly felt confined by Ewing, Sullivan, Cyr, and maybe his wife and family, in somewhat the same way.

There is also the opposition to consider. The bankers' reluctance to make the schoolbooks loan was mild. But Caddo's opposition to free schoolbooks, the Old Regulars' opposition to road bonds, and Attorney General Saint's failure to prepare court papers to support the severance tax were all efforts to sabotage the program that had been endorsed by the people and the legislature.

Caddo leaders must have thought Huey was deranged when he denounced them. Was he overcome with delusions of invincibility from his recent successes or frustrated at their insane opposition to his program? Probably it was everything in combination: his own intensity, drinking, ambition, and carelessness combined with his unyielding and unreasonable opposition.

His opponents must have been frightened of his successful consolidation of power. There was no one to influence him; there were no power brokers to intercede with him, no way to reach him with appeals to reason or fairness, or fear of social ostracism. By selling $10 million of highway bonds on February 26, he had money to spend.[84] Huey's opponents must have feared what an unstoppable Huey would do next.

On March 5, 1929, the U.S. Supreme Court ruled against Huey on a rule of procedure when considering the severance tax.[85] Because no law allowed recovery of tax overcharges paid without consent of the state, the court ruled that the oil companies should pay the lower rate that preceded Huey's increased tax until the case was finally decided. This would deny the state the revenue to repay the loans made by the banks to buy the new schoolbooks. This, to Huey, was alarming. (The bankers who loaned the state the money for the schoolbooks against the advice of their lawyers must have second-guessed themselves.) Huey was "outraged at the persistence with which the big oil companies resisted the payment of taxes and with the political opposition they continued to give."

Huey announced another special legislative session to fix the problem pointed out by the Supreme Court and a few other matters that, for the moment, he concealed. Huey had decided to propose a licensing tax on refined oil of 5 cents per barrel, a "gauge" of his battle to the oil trust. In his autobiography, he said he had secured commitments from most of the legislators to support this proposal.[86]

Motivated to counterattack, the hierarchy was simply looking for the reason, the occasion, and the leader. The Dynamite Squad and the Old Regulars were already out to destroy him. After Huey's success with pipeline regulation, Standard Oil had thoroughly defeated his efforts to prescribe its rates. It was his richest—and maybe smartest—opponent. It employed eight thousand people and directly affected five times that many, more when economic relationships are included.[87] With his proposed tax, Huey selected the most formidable leader to battle him: "The Kingfish had been going from one triumph to another, treading the peaks. Now in the session that was about to meet he would encounter sudden and frightening defeat. He would enter a dark valley that seemed to lead to political oblivion."[88]

# Eleven

# THE OPPOSITION STRIKES BACK

## IMPEACHMENT

Huey announced the special session of the legislature on March 14; it was called on March 16 and scheduled to start on Monday, March 18, to last for six days. The original agenda included only correcting the problem pointed out by the Supreme Court. The official call listed several subjects: (1) an occupational licensing tax on the business of refining crude oil; (2) a revision to the drunk driving law; (3) authorizing New Orleans to pay for rights of way; (4) correcting the severance tax problem pointed out by the Supreme Court; and (5) changes to the inheritance tax laws.[1]

Oblivious to the fear his recent actions caused, Huey assumed his support in the December session would carry over. Overlooked was that the Old Regulars had voted for Huey's bond issue only in obedience to the will of their constituents. The Dynamite Squad "had discussed for months the possibility of bringing charges against Huey and had [begun collecting] incriminating information." Some of Huey's supporters, moreover, opposed the oil tax, believing it was anti business. Harley Bozeman was one of them.[2]

Huey claimed in his autobiography that the oil tax would produce only a "rather insignificant" $1.5 million of "badly needed" revenue.[3] Given Standard Oil's reaction, it must have considered the tax significant or a harbinger of worse things to come. Baton Rouge had been on "fairly amiable" terms with Huey, but it considered the proposed tax "poison."[4]

Standard Oil mobilized to oppose the tax. Its president, Daniel Weller, recruited Jeff Snyder, the popular Madison Parish politician and Klan leader to lobby the legislators. Weller and Snyder reserved a floor of the Heidelberg Hotel as their headquarters. Snyder demanded an unlimited budget. Then he went to work. By the time he was "through paying 'em off, things were pretty hot." Legislators could pick up $15,000 to $20,000 any evening.[5]

The *Baton Rouge State-Times* began a series of unrelenting attacks with a double-columned editorial, with a theme of "grass will grow in the streets" if the tax is passed. Standard Oil's parent had recently approved an expenditure of $8,500,000 to renovate the refinery but would not do so or continue to refine imported oil (90 percent of the oil it refined was imported) if the tax were imposed, and thus at least two thousand employees would be laid off.[6]

On Monday, March 18, Rabbi Walter Peiser refused to offer the legislature an opening prayer, feeling Huey was unworthy of divine favor. The motion to suspend the rules (requiring a two-thirds vote) that had passed easily in December failed, forty to thirty-six.[7] Huey left the legislative floor just ahead of resolutions to expel him, and on occasions the House was in an uproar. Huey still misjudged the opposition, because he thought he had pledges of legislators to support his tax and because he had been successful before in overcoming opposition.[8] Superintendent of Education Harris called a meeting of local school superintendents from all over the state to support the tax because its revenue was devoted to education. The press buried Harris's comments.[9]

The problem of cattle ticks is remote to our time, but they were a big problem for farmers in the South. The federal government and associations of interested parties—doctors, veterinarians, and agricultural leaders—advocated dipping cows in a solution to kill the ticks. Farmers disliked the expense and didn't see the benefits. Huey had vetoed a dipping measure passed in 1928.

Faced with declining support in the legislature for his oil tax, however, Huey now spoke to a tick eradication conference and offered to support its legislation if the conference would support his tax. They refused. Some legislators were in the audience. One of them, J. Y. Sanders Jr., construed this speech as an attempted bribe.

Huey then issued another legislative call to last for eighteen days, starting on Wednesday, March 20, to last until midnight April 6. At a longer session, the rules would not have to be suspended and his bill could pass with a majority vote. Huey also added local measures (paving a road in a parish, for example) to appeal to individual legislators he hoped to win to or keep on his side.[10]

He added a tax on carbon black, however, which backfired, eroding support from legislators representing districts that included this industry, some of whom had supported him and the oil tax.[11] On Wednesday, when he appeared on the legislative floor, he encountered overwhelming hostility. On the objection of one member, approved by a thunderous majority, Huey was ordered off the floor, and he hustled off just ahead of the sergeant-at-arms. Sanders offered a resolution accusing Huey of offering a bribe at the tick eradication conference. A resolution condemning Huey's actions passed the House and, the next day, the Senate.

On Thursday March 21, Lieutenant Governor Cyr addressed the Senate in an emotional but effective speech and accused Huey of allowing the state to be defrauded. A lease of state oil lands was assigned to a Texas company at a huge profit for the lessee but not the state, with Huey's approval. Huey was a tyrant who padded highway commission payrolls and wanted to "dictate every move" of the legislature and "dip" into the court system as well. He asked God's forgiveness for supporting him. Wild applause followed from the legislators and the galleries. Further resolutions extolled the oil industry and denounced Huey for appointing legislators to state jobs.[12]

On the same day, the *Baton Rouge State-Times* carried a front-page editorial titled: "This, Gentlemen, Is the Way Your Governor Fights." Its editor, Charles Manship, had been given a message from Huey telling him to lay off him or he would disclose that Manship's brother was in a state "insane asylum." Admitting that his brother was being treated for mental illness, the editorial closed powerfully: "My brother Douglas, whom Governor Long has brought in the discussion, is about the same age as the Governor. He was in France in 1918, wearing the uniform of a United States soldier, while Governor Long was campaigning for office."[13]

By Friday, floor leader William H. Bennett deserted Huey on the oil tax issue (noting that it was only on this issue). On Saturday, March 23, the *Shreveport Journal* suggested a probe of Huey and impeachment if Cyr's charges proved true,[14] although the *Times-Picayune* suggested immediate adjournment during this "troubled and delirious time."[15] Caddo's state senator called for Cyr to initiate impeachment.[16] Huey responded that Cyr's charges implicated Governors Parker, Fuqua, and Pleasant, which made no impression.

The Senate passed by a vote of seventeen to fifteen a bill to have a committee investigate Huey's claim that state institutions needed more money. Huey had thus lost his majority in the Senate. Huey issued a supplemental agenda asking the legislature to enact any revenue measure to support schools and state institutions. This was a face-saving compromise for all sides, but his opponents smelled blood and wanted the oil tax voted down. To prevent this humiliation, Huey and his remaining leaders decided to adjourn on Monday night. They figured that he still commanded a majority vote in the House. If the House adjourned, the Senate would have to as well. The plan was for House leader Fournet to recognize J. Cleveland Fruge, who would move to adjourn indefinitely. Fournet would then dispatch a committee chairman to notify the Senate, and fast.

But the Dynamite Squad was now talking impeachment, and the *New Orleans Item* wanted to avoid an early adjournment to humiliate Huey. Because the oil tax was dead, Jeff Snyder prepared to leave. When he learned of the impeachment plans, he advised Huey's opponents to impeach him "now," because if they "fooled around" and waited, Huey was so smart that they would lose.[17] The Dynamite Squad wasn't planning on delay. They heard rumors of Huey's plan to adjourn and searched for a reason to stop it.

Representative Harney Bogan of Caddo produced a reason. Huey's ex-bodyguard, Battling Bozeman, claimed that Huey, with the odor of liquor on his breath, had asked Bozeman to kill J. Y. Sanders Jr. Bogan secured an affidavit saying this from Bozeman. Anti-Long Representative Cecil Morgan was selected to present it. Sanders believed that Huey uttered the words while drunk, not intending Bozeman to act on them. Anti-Long Representative Mason Spencer didn't believe a word of the affidavit but used it to impeach Huey anyway.

Rumors of some spectacular move by the Dynamite Squad had reached Huey's forces. When the House convened, therefore, both sides were edgy.[18]

After the roll call, Morgan announced a point of personal privilege and talked without being recognized. Morgan waved the Bozeman affidavit before the legislators and described the murder plot. Fruge shouted his motion to adjourn, Fournet recognized him and ordered Morgan to take his seat, under the direction of the sergeant-at-arms. The Dynamite Squad formed a human barricade so the sergeant couldn't reach Morgan. They escorted him down the center aisle toward the podium. Bedlam erupted. Fruge yelled for his adjournment motion to be put to a vote. Fournet called for the vote. The voting machine showed sixty-seven yeas and thirteen nays. Fournet declared the motion passed, discarded his gavel, and exited.

What had been bedlam now became violent mayhem. Representatives rushed the podium, some climbing over desks, many yelling "No, No, No," the "machine is fixed," or "you goddam crook," because their votes had shown as yes when they had voted no. Believing the vote was faked, they were outraged: "Oh God, please don't let them get away with it."

Fournet returned to the podium but faced a sea of outraged representatives. Huey's supporters Lorris Wimberly and Lester Lautenshlager (who had left to notify the Senate but returned to find a melee) now protected Fournet from anti-Long legislators rushing to attack. Clinton Sayes jumped from desk to desk, vaulted from the clerk's table to the ladder leading to the voting machine, tumbled down, landed on the cedar desk with a crash, leapt to the press table below, hurdled the bullpen to a front-row member's desk, all the while screaming "the machine's wrong." Sayes and Wimberly fought. Sayes's forehead was cut by Wimberly's diamond ring, someone's brass knuckles, or a ceiling fan that hit him while he was standing on a desk. Depending on who tells the story, it either bled a few drops or in a gushing stream. George Perault charged through and carried Sayes to safety. The blood—a little or a lot—gave a name to the evening, "Bloody Monday."

A brawl followed. Inkwells, books, and pastepots were thrown. Grown men wrestled around and threw punches. The sergeant-at-arms and his colleagues tried to separate the combatants. Several anti-Long legislators asked Fournet to put to a vote a motion appealing his ruling of adjournment, but he refused. Representative Williams took the speaker's chair and yelled for all "red blooded" members to stay in session. Mason Spencer then gave a "hog call" and obtained enough silence to conduct an oral poll of the members on whether the House had voted to adjourn. Nine votes to sustain the ruling were far outweighed by the seventy-nine votes to overrule it. Spencer nominated anti-Long Representative George J. Ginsberg—he had pointed out that the vote was a nullity anyway in the absence of a concurrence by the Senate—to be temporary Speaker. He was approved by a voice vote, after which a motion to adjourn only until the next day at 11 a.m. was passed.[19]

In the Senate, meanwhile, a resolution condemning the tax passed. The president of the Senate, Philip Gilbert, then moved to adjourn. They got word from Lautenschlager and Wimberly of the House's adjournment, but then heard the pandemonium and discovered that no adjournment had taken place. Cyr (as lieutenant governor, presiding) ruled Gilbert's motion out of order. On Gilbert's appeal of that ruling, Cyr was sustained, nineteen to seventeen.

Everyone now concedes that the House's voting machine was not fixed,[20] although Fournet should have known something was wrong (did he really think they would adjourn by a vote of sixty-seven to thirteen?) and did nothing about it. The primitive electric machine didn't clear all votes from the earlier roll call. Anti-Long legislators who knew the truth kept silent to foster the impression that the machine was rigged. Huey lost votes from legislators (F. B. Pratt of Morehouse, for example) who believed the voting machine was rigged and therefore switched to opposing Huey "'til Hell freezes over."[21]

That night the Dynamite Squad decided to impeach Huey. They typed up nineteen charges. To avoid the charges being sent to a committee whose chairman would be appointed by Fournet, the House would meet as a committee of the whole, with someone else made chairman. A large, strangely calm crowd milled around the capitol, many armed.[22]

The next day at 11 a.m., Fournet apologized for announcing the adjournment and explained the malfunction of the voting machine. Another motion to adjourn was made but lost with only thirty-nine votes for it. Huey's old majority had dissipated for good. Cecil Morgan asked to investigate (a) the Bozeman charge of murder solicitation, and (b) the spending of $6,000 of state funds to entertain the National Conference of Governors and $10,965 to repair the governor's mansion. These resolutions passed. They were the warm-up.

In serious tones to a hushed House, the Dynamite Squad committee of four asked the House to impeach Huey on nineteen charges:

(1) Using his appointive powers to influence the judiciary and boasting of his control over judges.
(2) Bribing or attempting to bribe legislators.
(3) Requiring undated resignations of appointees.
(4) Misuses of funds allocated to state boards.
(5) Contracting illegal state loans.
(6) Removing school officials for political purposes and intimidating teachers and pupils to suppress free thought.
(7) Illegal use of the militia to pillage private property.
(8) Trying to force parish governments to follow his direction.
(9) Carrying concealed weapons.
(10) Using abusive language.
(11) Acting immorally in a nightclub on February 12, 1929.
(12) Usurping the powers of the legislature and its committees.
(13) Having the state penitentiary install ice machines for $20,000 without bids.

(14) Attempting to intimidate Charles Manship by threatening to disclose his brother's mental illness.
(15) Destroying the executive mansion without authority.
(16) Destroying or disposing of furniture and other property in the mansion and other state offices.
(17) Illegally paroling a convict.
(18) Intruding on the floor of the legislature.
(19) Trying to employ Battling Bozeman to kill J. Y. Sanders Jr.

Baton Rouge was euphoric. Huey had been blocked and now might be overthrown. Ironically forgetting, as Williams notes, that Huey was a native Louisianan and that Standard Oil was a foreign corporation, the celebrants compared their joy to that felt when the carpetbagger Reconstruction governments were overthrown. The *Times* was more restrained: Huey was isolated but was "certain to put on a very good show."[23]

The impeachers scheduled a mass meeting, with special seats reserved for legislators, and six to ten thousand people crowded the Community Club Pavilion on March 26 to attend a rally. The Standard Oil Band furnished music. They tried to disguise their sponsor by changing their normal uniforms for plain blue suits but forgot to rub off "Stanacola Band" from the big bass drum.

Concealed from the crowd, Huey heard some speakers describe him as incompetent and others as a brilliant schemer. The lead resolution adopted at the rally stated that Huey should be impeached because he proposed to tax Standard Oil to satisfy a personal grudge. Further resolutions denounced all taxation that would injure industrial, commercial, or agricultural property. "[I]t appeared that the opposition . . . was about ready to tax nobody but the one-horse farmer and small businessman."[24]

Huey was paralyzed and depressed after the resolution was presented.[25] He looked "as if a threshing machine passed over him," and he "moped about the state house, a perfect picture of dejection and despair."[26] Julius said Huey was in bed, sobbing and suicidal. Huey confessed to two friends, "they've got me."[27] He considered resigning, reasoning that he could run for the Senate in 1930 without having an impeachment conviction on his record and win if the people were still with him.[28] He told his wife he might be impeached. "Money does funny things to people," he told her.[29]

Huey recovered, however, crediting—perhaps apocryphally—O. K. Allen with urging him to fight back legally in the legislature and politically by rallying the voters. Bob Maestri—"the fairest of all friends in foul weather"—pledged $40,000 to help. The money was spent to distribute circulars. The conservative rally and press handed him his theme, that he was being impeached because he proposed to tax Standard Oil.

Huey's circulars featured long headlines and long copy. The first was titled "THE CROSS OF GOLD: STANDARD OIL COMPANY VS. HUEY P. LONG." It suggested that members of the legislature had been bought by Standard Oil "for the purpose of crucifying" him. Here is an excerpt from another:

> THE SAME FIGHT AGAIN!
>
> THE STANDARD OIL COMPANY VS. HUEY P. LONG
>
> Has It Become a Crime for a Governor to Fight for the School Children and the Cause of Suffering and Destitute Humanity? Newspapers of Standard Oil Company Battle to Keep This Nefarious Corporation (Thrown Out of Texas) from Paying Any Reasonable Tax at All
>
> People of Louisiana:
>
> I had rather go down to a thousand impeachments than to admit that I am the Governor of the State that does not dare to call the Standard Oil Company to account so that we can educate our children and care for destitute, sick and afflicted. If this State is still to be ruled by the power of the money of this corporation, I am too weak for its governor. . . .
>
> They've fought me harder this time than ever before. Where they poured out hundreds in other fights, they have poured out ten thousand in this one. They have covered their newspapers, front, inside and out with every imaginable lie and vilification; they have stormed the State House to where the weak-hearted feared even for the life and safety of my supporters and myself. By a process known only to them they have been able to either "take over, to beat over or to buy over" some in whom I had reposed respect and confidence and for whom I yet indulge a charity. . . .
>
> . . . I asked that on a gallon of lubricating oil manufactured in Louisiana and selling for $1.40, that the State be paid 1/7 of 1 cent (out of the $1.40), and that the same tax be paid on the gasoline, benzene, kerosene, etc. The bill which I drew distributed the money thus raised to the school children and to the various hospitals and colleges of the State. . . .

> Why, today we make such things as cotton seed oil mills pay this tax to refine our own cotton seed oil; but the Standard Oil Company is to be allowed to tear the State wide open and to remove the Governor from office who dares to mention that anything can be done with them.[30]

Another one, headlined "THE STANDARD OIL REGULARS," claimed the old "gang" was trying to scuttle his free bridges. Another promised revelations that would split his opponents wide open.[31] State-owned trucks driven by off-duty state policemen delivered these circulars to his followers and state workers. A circular printed in the evening would be distributed all over the state the next day.

On April 1, the House convened as a committee of the whole to decide on the impeachment charges. When the impeachers sought to remove Fournet as speaker, Huey had three supporters suggest three separate opponents for the position, and when that debate concluded, they suggested three more, until a majority was against Fournet's removal, "one of the most brilliant political maneuverings in the face of overwhelming odds ever effected by any political leader."[32]

Nevertheless, the *Times* now predicted the end of Huey's career.[33] Attorney General Saint asked an impeachment expert from Oklahoma—that state had recently impeached several governors—to help. The House and Senate demanded that Huey furnish proof of vote buying but dropped this when Huey asked for a committee investigation and promised to provide it his evidence in confidence.[34]

On April 2, Huey's adherents cited an 1855 law prescribing an impeachment process but lost their motion to use this procedure.[35] One representative denounced the impeachment: "It looks to me like an illegal mess. . . . We are trying to imitate Mexico. We are trying to copy after Oklahoma who has had four governors in seven years. . . . I am not a Long supporter. None of my family is on the payroll, but . . . we should dump this whole thing into the Mississippi River, tuck our tails between our legs and run home."[36] Also attacked was the imported Oklahoma impeachment expert. Saint sent him packing.[37]

Huey called a mass meeting in Baton Rouge on April 4. State workers[38] and his followers across the state attended, and some looked as if they had not stopped to change clothes. Huey sent dozens of telegrams to local leaders telling them to bring their people to the rally. The crowds overflowed the hall and exceeded the size of the impeacher's rally.

John Overton gave a dramatic opening address—either because he believed in Huey or because he was paid—claiming that Huey was the first governor to keep his promises and was throwing out the old clique. Ending, he said:

> He is backed to the wall in his efforts to redeem his campaign pledges.
>
> As I see him there now, with his rapier flashing, fencing off the enemies to the left, to the front and to the right, when this smoke of battle shall have cleared, as in the beginning, I will be standing or lying by the side of Huey P. Long.[39]

Huey spoke for two hours. "That night men and women laughed, wept, shouted, clenched their fists as Huey cried scorn, told country jokes, talked of vindication in phrases from his favorite romantic novelists, and ended... with [the poem] 'Invictus.'"[40] "[P]eople in front of the old capitol [were] on their knees praying for Huey during impeachment."[41]

Earl Long dealt with legislators individually; he "never slept in the impeachment." Earl sent an airplane to fetch one businessman to come to the capitol to lobby a legislator.[42] Leander Perez of Plaquemines Parish, a rising power in his local organization, a shrewd and ruthless lawyer, led the daily caucus of the thirty or more Long legislators. Former governor Simpson helped Huey; he was perhaps the best parliamentarian in the state.[43]

The Dynamite Squad recruited volunteer lawyers, including Esmond Phelps and Edward Rightor, to arrange for witnesses and marshal the legal precedents to justify the impeachment. Cecil Morgan was the floor leader who examined witnesses.

The Louisiana Constitution allowed impeachment for high crimes and misdemeanors, incompetency, corruption, favoritism, extortion, gross misconduct, and habitual drunkenness. Members of the Dynamite Squad believed the legislature could impeach anyone for any reason and, thus, any of the nineteen charges could justify impeachment and removal. Some impeachers, however, conceded that some charges were thrown in for scenery.[44] The *Memphis Commercial Appeal* wrote that Huey had not yet been impeached for the heinous offense of playing the saxophone.[45]

Huey's boyhood pal Harley Bozeman deserted him. In a story Bozeman denies, Bozeman went to see Huey in his hotel room and urged him to resign to save his friends. In the middle of cutting his toenails, Huey snapped: "Bozeman, I wouldn't give the value of that toenail for a sonofabitch like you."[46]

With the battle lines drawn and the procedure decided, testimony began. Huey's wife came down from Shreveport to sit in the gallery, wearing a new white dress. A prominent Baton Rouge woman remarked, "Doesn't Mrs. Long have cheek, wearing white when she should have on black."[47]

Testimony on the Manship charge was taken first. Professor Hair points out that Huey's cruel tactic rightly backfired, but that he "was also telling the publisher that a wealthy family that placed one of its members in a public hospital so crowded that not all persons needing treatment could be admitted, and then opposed taxation to upgrade the institution, was vulnerable to criticism." Huey made speeches to that effect,[48] but he didn't always take this high road. In at least two speeches, Huey said the insanity of Manship's brother resulted from syphilis, not wartime-induced shell shock.[49]

Three legislators next claimed that Huey offered, respectively, help obtaining a loan or repayment of a debt owed to the state, some appointments, and a job. McClanahan said all prior governors have given patronage to their friends, an argument offensive to J. Y. Sanders Jr., the son of one of those governors.[50] Then witnesses related that Huey had bragged that he had bought Senator Bennett like a "sack of potatoes." Huey denied this. Others insisted it was a jesting political brag. One witness, however, said: "I thought he meant it. The Governor said that Mr. Bennett was one of the brainiest men in the lower House and I had to have him."[51] Bennett testified that while he was elected as an anti-Long candidate he voted with Huey when he could and had helped pass several of Huey's bills. After the session, he asked Huey for a job, and Huey gave him one with the Highway Commission.

Bennett did an about-face the next day, however, not as to the facts, but as to Huey. Now convinced that Huey had made the remarks, he described them as contemptible and resigned the job Huey gave him. After this juicy testimony, however, the impeachers dropped the bribery inquiry, probably for the reasons stated by McClanahan and because they might expose their colleagues' misconduct, colleagues whose votes they needed. They also declined to call judges to testify. Cecil Morgan offered a resolution that all judges would, if called to testify, deny that Huey ever influenced them. Nevertheless, on April 11 they charged Huey with attempts to bribe legislators and judges.[52]

When $6,000 was appropriated to entertain the visiting governors, Alice Lee Grosjean took the check and cashed it, receiving $6,000 in twenty-dollar bills. Seymour Weiss arranged the entertainment for the governors. Weiss said the total bill was $6,200 but wouldn't explain what $2,100 of it was for—because it was used for illegal liquor and prostitutes.[53] A legislator called Weiss contemptible, an insect, and decried the use of state money, not for the needy as Huey claimed, but, as he suspected, in a whorehouse.[54] In his autobiography, Huey said he had a receipt for all expenses.[55]

On April 24, Representative McClanahan, always vocal on Huey's behalf, said the money "went where all such money goes for entertaining conventions other than religious ones. The governor had no opportunity to put his witnesses on the stand for this is a grand jury proceeding. But you know that money was spent on champagne and fine whiskies. I challenge you to deny it. Even if it was wrong, you cannot say the money was spent for the governor's personal benefit."[56] The House could have cited Weiss for contempt for failing to answer their questions, but didn't, and never offered him immunity in exchange for his testimony.[57]

The day after Grosjean cashed the $6,000 check, Frank Odom paid for a car for Huey, trading in his own car and paying $1,300 with twenty-dollar bills. The car he bought had painted on the side "Not State Property, Executive Department." Huey was quoted as telling anti-Long legislator Sayes over beers that "You damn suckers wouldn't give me $10,000 for a car but I will get the car just the same."[58] The impeachers thought he must have taken some of the $6,000 allocated to the governor's conference to buy the car.

Further testimony established that Huey had purchased law books by writing a check on the mansion fund. Huey ridiculed the legislators for thinking the governor had no need to consult law books, but this dodged the issue of using money appropriated for one purpose differently. It was a small amount of money ($1,100), but wrong. Whether it deserves removal from office or, say, censure, reprimand, or an order of restitution is open to debate.

Williams writes that Huey treated the books as "his private possession," but how one could distinguish between private use and public use while he was governor is difficult to understand (he was allowed to practice law privately while governor). The books were stored in a Highway Commission office rented from a bank, not at his home or private office. After his death, his family sold his complete collection of law books, including those purchased in 1928, to the state, but this does not establish Huey's intent in 1928.[59]

The impeachers charged that Huey paid for defective highway culverts because a political ally did the work. Huey said the culverts were contracted for by a previous governor, that he negotiated a deduction from further invoices, and that the culverts were still in use.[60]

The impeachers charged Huey with cursing, with testimony from a telephone operator who was caught eavesdropping and heard Huey profanely tell Allen to fire her. Shreveport witnesses testified to Huey's denunciations at the time of the air-base matter: "there is that goddamned n—— loving Andrew Querbes; there is that goddamned Randall sonofabitch Moore . . . and that goddamned shitass Ewing." The ladies in the galleries blushed and clutched their pearls; the Longites excoriated the impeachers for allowing this language in front of ladies. The secretary of state said the epithets would have to be removed from the record or he could not send the journals through the mails because of laws against obscenity.[61]

Hotelman Alfred Danziger explained Huey's attendance at a "studio" party. Held after a hotel dinner celebrating someone's birthday, the party included a piano player and six girls who danced the hula in skimpy island-type costumes. Danziger thought Huey stayed an hour and had one drink. One of the girls tried to sit in his lap, but he pushed her away. One of the entertainers, Helen Clifford, said Huey was drunk and "frisky," and that he had stroked a girl's hair. Several legislators insisted on the record that she give them her telephone number.[62] Clifford's husband (they were separated) testified that she had been offered a job to make her affidavit. The impeachers tried but failed to get evidence that Alice Lee Grosjean was Huey's mistress.[63]

The president of the State Normal School in Natchitoches claimed that Huey forced him to resign after an eighteen-year career because he refused to campaign for a judge, support the referendum on constitutional amendments, or fix a problem at a polling place during an election. "I was incensed. I never heard such a request being made of a college president." Other witnesses said he had an "over-disciplined" policy and pressured faculty and students to buy cars at the president's car dealership, or that he was deeply political and should have been fired.[64]

The last witness called was the impeachers' least favorite: Battling Bozeman. His testimony revealed him as a dim-witted, pathetic person who made his allegations because Huey fired him. In later speeches, Huey joked about this charge: "If J. Y. Sanders Sr. had died twenty years ago I wouldn't be governor. If J. Y. Sanders Jr. lives twenty more years I may be President of the United States. A Sanders is what I need for my political future."[65] That was an incisive comment—not about the murder charge—but about how politically obtuse conservatives made it easier for Huey to win. The House declined to impeach Huey on this charge. They never even brought this charge to a vote.[66]

Huey's supporters claimed that all charges voted on after April 6 were illegal, because that was the last date set by Huey's call for the special session. The impeachers, however, believed the legislature had the constitutional ability to impeach at any time. An article by political scientist Newton Baker[67] explained that at regular legislative sessions, scheduled by the Louisiana Constitution to take place every other year, the legislature can act on anything, including impeachment. Under the Louisiana Constitution of 1921, a special session could not *legislate* on matters outside the governor's call, but legislating is different from impeaching. Special sessions cannot last longer than the shorter of thirty days or the time set by the call, however. The provision's wording can be read to limit the time for the session itself rather than only the time for legislative enactments during a special session (384). If "legislating" is different from "impeaching" and the constitutional time limits only apply to legislating, the legislature could self-convene to impeach. Yet Baker denied this, "although there seems to be some authority which inclines that way." (380). Omitted by Baker was that two-thirds of both houses could force a special session to be convened.[68] One therefore wonders (1) why the legislature should be allowed to self-convene or exceed the time limit on the special session without a two-thirds vote and (2) why the impeachers didn't invoke this provision to schedule their own special session to begin immediately after April 6 (the last day of the special session) to checkmate Huey's timeliness defense.

On April 6, the House voted to impeach Huey on the Manship charge. Huey's forces agreed to allow this charge to be voted on before midnight. This was a weak charge and therefore a bad agreement for the impeachers. Defending Huey, House leader Ellender strangely conceded that the threat might amount to blackmail, but it was made as a private individual and, therefore, was not an impeachable offense. A representative who often criticized Huey's crudeness described this argument as "heifer manure."[69]

Another ally—George Delesdernier—then rose and gave a ridiculous address, comparing Huey to a divine creature trying to relieve suffering and remedy illiteracy, but who was shackled to a cross of paper, one of the uprights manufactured from a saintly piece (whatever that is), the horizontal part from the beams of the moon. Confronted with cries of blasphemy, he shouted: "Take my life but give me my character!" and then fainted.[70]

Huey's leaders offered a compromise that he be reprimanded and apologize to Manship. All of Huey's adherents voted for this, but to no avail. By a vote of fifty-eight to forty, Huey was impeached, and nine members headed by Mason Spencer would present the case for Huey's removal from office to the Senate.

The Senate appointed one committee to escort Chief Justice O'Niell to preside, and another to prepare the rules. That night a drunk O'Niell met a member of the Dynamite Squad in a hotel lobby. Discussing accusations of bias, O'Niell declaimed, "Don't they think that I'll give the thieving sonofabitch a fair trial?"[71]

On April 25, the House added to the Manship charge voted on April 6 and the attempted bribery charges voted on April 11 charges of (a) misappropriation of state money (governor's conference money and automobile purchase); (b) interference with the state training school and the removal of one of its officials by paying him $5,400 to do no work; (c) misappropriation of the mansion maintenance funds (including a payment of $728.25 to Huey's cousin Otho Long); (d) the purchase of law books for $1,112; and (e) payment of a state contractor $4,000 for defective culverts. On April 26 the House voted the final charge: that Huey had forced appointees to sign undated resignations, insulted citizens, discharged a college president, appointed a corrupt parole officer, and demonstrated that he was incompetent and temperamentally unfit for office.[72] One publisher threatened to have a court declare Huey insane. Fournet argued in vain that "you wouldn't convict a . . . chicken thief on such evidence."[73]

The votes and the speeches took place in an atmosphere of tension, danger, and violence. Men on each side armed themselves, ate together, and traveled together. Conservative businessman Oscar Whilden wrote a circular that said hanging, shooting, or knifing would be too good for Huey, that instead he should be nailed by the ears to a blackjack post, stripped naked, and "thoroughly horsewhipped." Opposition leader Harney Bogan and Bob Maestri met in a capital hallway when Earl Long accosted them: Why was Maestri talking to that "sonofabitch?" Bogan then hit Earl, and the two men fought. Earl bit him on his face and neck, scratched him, and tried to pull his cheek off. Earl later bragged that he tore Bogan to pieces. Bogan got a tetanus shot. When Huey was told about the fight, he said, "I bet Earl bit him, didn't he?" Then Huey suggested to state Senator Boone that they go to the capitol. They found a large and hostile crowd. Boone draped a handkerchief over a penknife to pretend he had a gun and coaxed Huey from the site, convinced that, had Huey remained, he would have been shot.[74]

The struggle for votes intensified when the forum shifted to the Senate. The Old Regulars had collected money from businessmen to "get" Huey.[75] Representative Joe Fisher was offered $40,000 to persuade his brother, state Senator Jules Fisher, to vote to convict, and they offered power "unheard of" to Jules directly.[76] Senator William C. Boone was offered $25,000 but refused it, then was offered $50,000, but Boone threatened to kill the offeror.[77]

The unpopularity of Lieutenant Governor Paul Cyr, next in line for the governorship, was a handicap to the impeachers. Impeacher Mason Spencer told three senators he would impeach Cyr if they voted to convict Huey. The president of the Senate, Phillip Gilbert, next in line for the governorship after Cyr, was offered the job but turned the impeachers down.[78]

Earl Long called a man who had opened a new typewriter agency and asked him how many he could assemble. He made thirty-five available. Secretaries and Huey appeared as if by magic. Huey then strode up and down dictating hundreds of telegrams to be sent to people throughout the state—without notes. When Alice Lee Grosjean returned the typewriters and asked for a bill, the man had a defining moment or a revelation that character was destiny. He said the typewriters were free.[79]

Huey's local leaders came to Baton Rouge to meet with senators who might be wavering. Huey's local supporters regularly lobbied Senators Larcade and Barousse to counteract intense pressure exerted on them by Huey's opponents. Printed notices appeared in Larcade's hometown that, if he voted to acquit, he would be tarred and feathered.[80]

Roads for their parishes and jobs for themselves were offered to secure other votes. Ironically, the Constitutional Convention in 1921 changed the Louisiana Constitution to allow an impeached governor to remain in office until and unless convicted. Without that provision, Paul Cyr would have taken over upon impeachment, dismantled Huey's patronage army, and crippled his ability to offer jobs or favors to legislators.[81]

Earl Long and O. K. Allen visited one senator at 11 p.m. one evening and stayed until 4 a.m., offering him a congressional seat, the state treasurer position, or the business of state insurance, which would have yielded $50,000 per year. Baptist preacher and state Senator James L. Anderson was a supporter, but Huey discovered that he was meeting with his opponents and suspected he might defect. Anderson had planned a trip to Shreveport to visit a sick friend who was a fierce enemy of Huey. Huey suggested that Anderson join him on the platform for a speech in Shreveport. Anderson agreed but then was a no-show. Learning that Anderson had traveled to Baton Rouge, Huey drove all night to confront him. They had a violent argument. Huey provided him with a small amount of cash to repay a loan. Before or after this confrontation, Huey's allies either set Anderson up or learned that he had set himself up by having a "drink" with a woman in her hotel room. Huey's men got the key to the room from a cooperative hotel employee and burst in on the pair. "They bought him and we bought him back," one Long leader said. "I don't believe in killing people, but in war I think you have to kill people," said another.[82]

On April 15, Gilbert offered a resolution in the Senate stating that charges voted on by the House after April 6 could not be considered because they were processed in a special session scheduled to end on April 6; anything done after that was illegal. Gilbert's resolution failed by a vote of twenty-three to fifteen. This should have warned the impeachers that Huey had fifteen senators on his side, one more than necessary to acquit him.

Two days later, on April 17, Huey held a news conference to announce a speaking tour and remarked that he had fourteen senators who would stand by him. Huge crowds greeted him. It is a measure of the incompetence of the impeachers that Huey could ridicule or admit so many of the charges:

- [The impeachers] voted for the money to build a new mansion "yet they claim that didn't give me license to tear down the old one. Where'd they expect for us to put the new building?"
- "When I tore down the old mansion I took that silverware that belonged to my wife, and I sent it to her at home in Shreveport—and now they want to throw me out of office for sending that silver to the woman whose name was on the dad-gum spoons."
- [Regarding cursing:] "you bet I did. . . . Those were the people that tried to hold up the free schoolbooks. . . . I'm like a whole lot of other men, when I get that mad I do some cussin'."

Huey made his own accusations: W. H. Cutrer was bought so cheap "they felt like they were stealing him";[83] Senator Labbe received a new car from Standard Oil; J. Y. Sanders wanted the state to buy a bridge for $5.5 million when the one right beside it cost only $1.5 million. About a deaf representative, Huey said: "Deafness sometimes passes for honesty." This representative replied: "No gentleman refers to another's infirmity," but continued by calling Huey "crazy," apparently not an infirmity.

The large crowds gave Huey an enthusiastic reception. He sprinkled promises—more roads for example—into his speeches.[84] Huey was used to receiving flowers and tributes, but now he often received flowers that had never seen a hothouse and were tendered by hands too young to vote.[85]

Either Huey himself or one of his supporters, probably Leander Perez, maybe Simpson, Senator Boone, or his brother Julius, decided to record his supporters on a document that became known as the "Round Robin." It stated that the impeachment proceedings were illegal to the extent that they considered any charge after April 6, and that the Manship charge, the only one timely filed, was not a reason to remove him.

In law, motions to dismiss a complaint are made in many cases. The theory is that, even if everything in an opponent's filed complaint is true, there is no basis for the lawsuit. (Someone could sue on a contract for prostitution, for example, but the case would be dismissed in most states because it was an illegal contract even if made.) A motion to dismiss saves everyone the expense and delay of a trial when it can be determined from the complaint that the lawsuit cannot be won.

It was difficult to get fifteen senators to sign the Round Robin. Many were reluctant because they were committing to vote to acquit regardless of the evidence. Once Huey got the signatures, it would be difficult for the adherents to change their minds. He made phone calls to the likely signers, sent them an automobile, and summoned them to Baton Rouge.

The last signer, Fred Oser, was reluctant. He talked to Huey until dawn, and then wanted to discuss it with his law partner. Huey brought the law partner to Baton Rouge. The partner and Oser talked until breakfast time, when Oser signed. After he signed, Huey said it was the first time he'd been able to eat breakfast in months. He had been subsisting on strawberries and cream.[86] Now that he had his fifteen signers, Alice Lee Grosjean put the document in her brassiere, and then it was transferred to a bank safety-deposit box.[87]

After Mason Spencer presented the final charge, the Senate ordered Huey to answer on May 14. Huey ended his speaking tour on May 13. On the same date, Standard Oil denied in the press that it had "interfere[d] in politics." On May 14, Huey appeared in the Senate, confident, wearing a white suit with a black tie, carrying a cigar. He shook hands with several senators. O'Niell proclaimed the Senate was ready to sit as a court of impeachment. Nine lawyers accompanied Huey: Leander Perez, Caleb Weber, George Wallace, Allen Ellender, Harvey Peltier, his brother Julius, Louis Morgan, John Overton, and Dudley Guilbeau, an array of talent showing geographical and political diversity.[88]

Overton moved to dismiss (a demurrer, according to the terminology of the time) the last seven charges because they were filed too late. The demurrer was over five thousand pages long, and the arguments took all day, after which the Senate recessed. The next morning, a vote was taken on whether charges two through eight were untimely. The demurrer failed, but by a vote of twenty to nineteen. Three senators who opposed Huey and one additional senator agreed that the charges were untimely, four more votes than Gilbert's resolution received and five more votes than the one-third necessary to acquit.

Next, the first charge regarding Manship was considered. Perez argued that the information about Manship was a public record and that Huey had uttered his remarks in a personal capacity. The impeachers argued that Huey tried to influence the legislature by squelching editorials. The motion against this charge was based on its substance—even if true, Huey shouldn't be removed—as opposed to timeliness, a procedural (but constitutionally based) argument. The three anti-Long senators who had voted with Huey on the timeliness motion now rejoined the anti-Long side, voting that the Manship charge was an offense justifying removal. But five senators who had voted against Huey on the timeliness motion voted that the Manship charge was insufficient to remove him. The charge was therefore dismissed by a vote of twenty-one to eighteen.

Conservatives cast some of the twenty-one votes for Huey. The state senator who had been offered by Huey any job he wanted except the governorship joined Huey—not because of any reward; he received nothing—but because he thought the impeachment was doomed to fail and was tearing the state apart. Senator Labbe switched, probably because of Huey's speech accusing him of accepting an automobile from Standard Oil. Another conservative switched in exchange for a promise of a road in his district. (The irony here is rich.)

The impeachers were crestfallen and Huey's supporters jubilant. They decided to end the impeachment the next day, bringing the Round Robin out of the bank box, preparing another version, more condensed, and readying it for May 16. Senator Gilbert presented it, reporting that the signers would not vote to convict on the only remaining charges, two through eight, because they were untimely, and then moved to adjourn indefinitely. One anti-Long senator (oddly, one who agreed that charges two through eight were untimely) insisted that the signers be questioned whether they would vote to acquit "regardless of the testimony." Each answered yes.

The senators took a break. The impeachers offered a resolution deploring the Round Robineers but consented to adjournment. And so, it was over, just like that. Huey left the chamber and went to his office where a group of friends gathered. Rose threw her arms around him and he kissed her, saying she was still the state's First Lady. She left to phone their children. He acknowledged the loyalty of Gilbert. He gave some autographs, signed "Huey P. Long, Governor of Louisiana by the grace of the people."[89]

Huey was still subject to impeachment during a regularly scheduled legislative session or could be subject to a recall election.[90] His supporters had begun a recall election against an anti-Long representative, but one proponent was egged at a public meeting on May 9 and others were threatened. Advisors counseled Huey to "proceed carefully."[91]

# Twelve

# STALEMATE

Some perceptive observers, mostly his family and friends, said the impeachment changed Huey, made him less open and trusting and more calculating and ruthless. Most other observers, generally opponents, deny that there was any change. Williams concludes that it changed him somewhat.[1]

In some court cases one can see when an opposing party has its resources exhausted or the emotional toll of the lawsuit causes it to yield. In watching sporting events, one can occasionally spot a point at which one team wants it more than the other team, even absent a talent differential. In law or a sporting event the price of victory can be willpower, energy, money, effort, or physical or emotional pain, whereas in politics the price can include a moral component, the sacrifice of one principle to gain another.

Huey had brains, talent, and energy, but one secret to his success was a willingness to pay the price to win. Huey said: "If I possess any qualities or if I have acquired any particular learning in law or public affairs, I owe much of it to the opposition which the big interests have furnished and the intense research and exertion which they have at all times required me to make."[2] Huey omitted the moral component to this price, one that the impeachers were also willing to pay.

The impeachment increased the price Huey had to pay to win; he didn't forget the price he had paid and was prepared to pay it again. This forged a more scarred, experienced, hardened, and determined politician.

In later years, Huey spoke wistfully or bitterly about his opponents' efforts to eliminate him from politics, but he turned it into humor in speeches, opening a speech to new audiences with this introduction:

> I was elected Railroad Commissioner in 1918. [short pause] And they tried to impeach me in 1920. [smile from Huey] [audience titters]
>
> When they failed to impeach me in 1920, they indicted me in 1921. [another smile from Huey] [audience chuckles]
>
> And when I wiggled through that I managed to become governor in 1928. [Stanislavsky pause] And they impeached me in 1929! [huge smile from Huey] [explosive laughter from the audience][3]

After the state Senate adjourned without removing him, Huey took the Round Robineers and about twenty-five representatives and other supporters to Grand Isle for a celebration: fishing, hunting, drinking, and feasting on crab, lobster, and shrimp, while Rose returned to Shreveport. Everyone who stood by Huey received jobs or favors. Gilbert was appointed judge; McClanahan became warden of the penitentiary; Anderson was appointed chief enforcement officer of the Highway Commission; Fournet and others were appointed counsel for various state agencies; Simpson was made supervisor of assessments in New Orleans.[4] The man who provided the typewriters got all state business for typewriters, and Huey fended off other connected friends who tried to muscle in for a share of his business, in a story uncannily similar to that of Slade in *All the King's Men.*[5] Years later, one of the Robineers was old and out of work and asked then-governor O. K. Allen for a job. Huey chanced to be with Allen. When the visitor was announced, Allen said he had nothing for him. Huey said, "Who did you say it was?" When told, he replied: "That's one of my old friends who signed the Round Robin to keep them from impeaching me. What do you mean, you haven't got a job?" Allen repeated that he had no job. "Well, find one for him!" The newspapers "never ceased to call attention to any favor I did one of those fifteen men," Huey said, which became a "matter of considerable mirth among" them.[6]

All mirth aside, Huey proceeded to do battle. He refused to call out the militia to break a streetcar-union strike in New Orleans.[7] All disloyal patronage workers were purged. Huey loaded most of his office into a truck and moved his "Government on Wheels" to New Orleans to "perfect an organization to give battle in that City."[8] Starting over, he formed the Louisiana Democratic Association with seventeen ward leaders.

The highway engineer he had lured from North Carolina, Leslie Ames, was a casualty of the purge. A mutual friend tried to reconcile them, and Huey was willing, if Ames promised loyalty. When Ames said he'd have to check with his wife, however, Huey snorted: "Goodbye. Just forget it." But other stories reported that Ames was merely sent to Washington, DC, to coordinate Louisiana's federal highway aid.[9]

The head of the Orleans Levee Board was fired, and the "painfully obsequious" Abraham Shushan took his place. Shushan sold supplies to the state and was a campaign donor. The Orleans Dock Board president resisted Huey's demand for his resignation, but Huey somehow secured the resignation of a different board member, at last obtaining a board majority in October 1929.[10] Patronage appointments were reported in the papers, including personnel changes of the Dock Board,[11] district attorneys (one selected was the lawyer who defended Dr. Dreher),[12] and highway engineers.[13]

Huey organized recall elections against legislative opponents to "grow a new crop" of legislators. Success eluded him. His supporters were sloppy in getting signatures on the petitions; many were thrown out as invalid. Two supporters were arrested for electioneering fraud, though never tried. One of Huey's recall petitioners was threatened with loss of his suppliers and credit at his bank and then arrested; the legislator died before the recall could be held.[14]

Opponents from anti-Long districts resisted removal, and voters disliked the inconvenience of a special election. In the few recall elections that took place, Huey only won one race, defeating a legislator who had decided after "prayer" to vote against the oil tax. Huey said the legislator mistook the identity of the responder to his prayers. Deutsch believed that the margin of victory was supplied by a precinct subject to threats of increased tax assessments.

In a one-day campaign swing on August 9, Huey failed to recall Representative J. S. Bacon of Webster Parish, despite the slogan: "If you want to bring home the bacon, keep Bacon at home." When Bacon won, his supporters wired Huey: "Webster Parish preserves its own Bacon" and "Please quote present market price on Bacon in Baton Rouge."[15] George J. Ginsberg, a leader of the House impeachers, said he had his bank closed by Huey's bank examiners, but another witness denied this. Huey had to wait until 1932 to defeat him, spending a lot of money to do it. In one speech, he called him George Jackass Ginsberg. One day later a bale of hay was delivered to Ginsberg's office.[16]

Thus, Huey's opponents' frontal assault to remove him had failed. Flush with his defensive victory, Huey counterattacked the retreating forces, but they regrouped and held their position. The two sides were like two opposing armies, skirmishing and threatening each other, neither of which could win a decisive victory.

About one month after the impeachment ended, Huey's opponents formed the Constitutional League of Louisiana to oppose Huey in every endeavor. Three hundred persons attended its birth, and they subscribed donations of $100,000 in fifteen minutes.[17] Former governor Parker headed the organization, but W. D. Robinson, Huey's former public relations agent, fired when Huey caught him rifling through Highway Department files, did most of the work.[18] Huey called it the "League of Notions."[19]

The Constitutional League announced that the impeachment charges were still alive and pending. It claimed corruption in the Highway Department. It publicized patronage awarded to Huey's relatives and legislators. There was talk of a recall effort against Huey. Its most significant success was winning a lawsuit to forbid legislators from holding other state jobs. Despite supposedly being dominated by Huey, the Louisiana Supreme Court ruled in favor of the league, forcing sixteen legislators to give up their jobs. Eight Old Regular legislators were holding positions in the city government, so they also had to resign. Huey's only fun was discovering that a brother-in-law of Esmond Phelps of the *Times-Picayune* was holding two state jobs. He discharged him from both, claiming he had caught the spirit of its editorials against dual officeholding.[20]

A group of industrial leaders headed by utilities magnate Harvey Couch, a boyhood resident of Winnfield and friend of Huey despite political differences, perhaps spurred by the news that a company was considering Louisiana as a site for a new $20 million chemical plant, called for a truce to promote industrial development. Their open letter of July 18 prompted private negotiations with Huey that culminated with this agreement:

(1) Recall elections would be halted.
(2) No new occupational taxes would be proposed by Huey.
(3) Business interests would form a Commercial Affairs Committee to survey the state's needs for public improvements and support legislation to construct them.
(4) Standard Oil would build the $8.5 million expansion and improvement to its refinery.

Contemporaneously, the chemical company announced that it would locate its new $20 million plant in Louisiana.[21]

Huey won his suit to oust Irion from the Conservation Commission in early November, personally arguing the case, defeating Irion's lawyers Rightor and Viosca.[22] When he took over, Maestri fired all commission office personnel on the spot.[23]

Huey removed Attorney General Saint's nephew from the Insurance Commission, but Saint had the appointive authority and promptly reappointed him, with Huey calling him incompetent.[24] Huey maintained his right to appoint one judge by refusing to accept the resignation of the incumbent, the first time a governor had done so.[25] He was unsuccessful trying to cancel another judicial election where Hewitt Bouanchaud was the candidate. Backed by sheriffs in three parishes, the election was held in accordance with the opinion of Attorney General Saint, who disagreed with Huey's proclamation to postpone it.[26]

After the compromise, however, mostly Huey threw himself into the details of his job to recover his political standing. Having backed Numa Montet in the Democratic Primary for Congress in the Third District, Huey helped him withstand a Republican challenger—campaigning for tariffs—in the general election. Montet was grateful.[27]

Huey entertained requests from civic groups about the location of roads[28] and other suggested improvements,[29] participated in flood-control meetings,[30] announced savings from intelligent management practices by the state government,[31] promised support for an International Trade Exhibition in New Orleans,[32] and announced a reduction in the charge per bale for handling cotton at the public warehouse in New Orleans to better compete with Houston and Galveston.[33] He appeared at ribbon-cutting ceremonies for new bridges,[34] let contracts for highways and the new governor's mansion,[35] participated in a Mississippi Riverfront festival,[36] and attended football games.[37] Huey dominated a charity baseball game that became a "first-class burlesque show." Huey changed his position every inning, cut up on the sidelines, engaged in a mock fight with Abe Shushan when things got dull, got two hits and struck out a few batters while pitching.[38] Huey replied to periodic attacks made by the Constitutional League about wasteful spending, the number of his relatives on the state payroll,[39] whether legislators could hold state offices,[40] and whether Earl Long collected as much inheritance tax money as his predecessor.[41] Huey tried to conciliate certain opponents. He told Governor Parker that he would remove any corrupt officeholder based on any information Parker provided if Huey failed to convince Parker he was wrong. Parker waved a friendly salute as he left.[42]

Huey defeated the court challenge to the severance tax on oil.[43] The lawsuit had been called for trial during the impeachment. Huey sent a state official to request a continuance over the objections of the oil companies and Attorney General Saint. One of the judges asked Saint if he had witnesses present. When Saint said none, the court postponed the trial. Taking no chances with another Saint default, Huey sat beside him at the counsel table. On August 29, 1929, the federal court approved the tax.[44]

Huey stayed out of the New Orleans mayoralty race in the fall of 1929, claiming he was concentrating on his improvement program.[45] T. Semmes Walmsley of the Old Regulars opposed Francis Williams. Huey wanted Paul Maloney to run, but Maloney declined.[46]

Bob Maestri and Earl Long wanted Huey to endorse Williams, but Huey —probably because of personal hostility to "Frans-Ass"—rejected this advice. On the eve of the election, he told his leaders to show a good result for Walmsley in some wards so he could claim credit for his victory. When he saw that Walmsley only won by nine thousand votes and that a runoff election would be required absent a Williams concession, he realized too late that he could have controlled the outcome, given his five thousand patronage workers in the city. After the election, Huey secretly offered to support Williams in a runoff. Williams's campaign manager, Harry Gamble, advised him to forego Huey's support and the runoff. Williams followed this advice.[47]

With Huey mistakenly rejecting good advice and Williams mistakenly accepting bad advice, Walmsley was elected. At six feet, two inches tall, with a long neck and small head, a former football player and boxer, educated at Tulane, and the heir of an old-line family, he had the appearance of being a gentleman.

Between January and May 1930 (when the legislative session began), Huey was hard at work selling highway bonds or letting construction contracts,[48] announcing progress to pull Louisiana out of the mud,[49] speaking at labor-union conventions[50] and civic celebrations,[51] and making administrative appointments.[52] In one case, he fired a tax commission member who proposed a tax increase to fund education and a new capitol, giving a succinct and clear explanation: "the only way we can convince the public that [a tax increase] is not concurred in by me is to ask your resignation."[53] Senator J. O. ("Bathtub Joe") Fernandez, elected with Old Regular support, defected to Huey.[54]

The Commercial Affairs Committee—a product of the compromise—asked Huey to appoint an advisory committee to oversee expenditures of the

Highway Department. Huey flip-flopped several times on this but, in the end, it was included in the legislation. Huey rejected the committee's suggestion to depoliticize the Dock Board.[55]

Huey also negotiated with toll-bridge companies to build eight bridges at a cost of $6 million. This was $1 million less than the cost estimated by the Highway Commission. The company selected would earn 6 percent on its money from tolls, with any excess deposited into a state fund to purchase the bridges. John Overton was its lawyer. Some said Huey suggested that Overton be hired; others that Overton acted on his own to make a huge fee (about $200,000), and that Huey, despite thinking that Overton was "money mad," entertained the proposal to repay the man who had stood by him since 1918.

The Highway Commission's engineers opposed toll bridges because the federal government would not aid toll-bridge construction and they wanted federal funds. They persuaded O. K. Allen to issue a written statement opposing toll bridges. Allen foresaw a hostile public reaction if Huey, who had fought the Watson-Williams toll syndicate, suddenly proposed toll bridges. (In one speech in Alexandria during his campaign, however, Huey had said he might consider toll bridges, but never for profit.) Allen refused to back down in a meeting with Huey in which they cursed each other. Huey then surrendered. But Huey funneled $5,000 to the bridge company to give to Overton to try and assuage him.

Huey's motive for negotiating with the toll company was speed. The bridge bond legislation was defectively drawn in the 1928 legislative session. No bonds could be sold. The bridge over Lake Pontchartrain had been completed with existing revenues. (The Watson-Williams syndicate filed for receivership as a result.)[56] Regardless of motive, Huey's plan was a potential blunder. It is ironic that Allen, remembered now only for being Huey's flunky, had the guts to stand up to him.

Huey as compulsively planned and supervised construction of the new governor's mansion as he had his first home in Shreveport, going to the site during the day to watch the work and even at night with a friend and a flashlight to ensure the specifications were followed.[57] It was designed to resemble the White House. He wanted it completed before the legislature started its session in May, and he succeeded. Mrs. Long and the children moved into the mansion and thereafter stayed in Baton Rouge on an almost permanent basis. She attended the mansion's opening reception in an ecru lace evening dress. Huey wore a white linen suit and listened to the LSU band.[58]

Also significant are the things Huey did not do after the compromise.

There were no raids of gambling establishments. No singing fool performances. No hula dances. No controversial proposals.

One interesting aspect of Huey's arrangement with his new business allies—about a thousand businessmen attended committee meetings where slide shows displayed relevant statistics—was his request for help surveying the needs of the state. Huey knew the need for roads and bridges but asked the business community to figure out what to build next. High costs of New Orleans's port in comparison to Houston's were a concern, attributed to interest payments on prior port bonds. Weeks were spent conferring with the interested parties. Reporters were eventually excluded from these meetings so the businessmen could discuss civic problems without advertising them. They didn't produce much beyond extending what Huey had already begun, but the program proposed was large and impressive.[59]

By December 1929, Huey advocated legislation to improve the Port of New Orleans (dedicating part of the highway tax to retire its prior bonds), build three thousand miles of roads across the state, construct a bridge across the Mississippi and other bridges throughout the state, and build a new state capitol. The total cost would exceed $100 million. Bonds would fund the plan, but existing taxes were sufficient to secure their repayment, Huey said. (Later he advocated a slight increase in gas taxes.) The public works projects would provide jobs to cushion the Depression that began with the stock market crash in October 1929. Louisiana was making progress, but he wanted to "go faster."[60] The *Baton Rouge State-Times* admitted that Huey's projects were good but denied that Huey should get any credit for proposing them or be allowed to implement them.[61]

An architect drew plans for a new capitol building with funds Huey borrowed from the State Board of Liquidation in January 1930. It would be a skyscraper, the tallest building in the South; would house all state departments; and cost only $1 million. Huey was asked what he planned to do with the old capitol. Huey joked that he would turn it over to an antique collector.[62]

The national press began to notice Huey. A February 1930 visit by former president Calvin Coolidge and his wife was covered only in Louisiana newspapers. When Coolidge asked where Huey was from, he said "Winnfield, way out in the sticks. I'm a hillbilly, more or less, like yourself." At a banquet given in their honor, Huey arrived thirty minutes late in a brown suit and blue shirt but continued an animated conversation with Mrs. Coolidge that moved an aristocrat to say, "If Winn Parish could only see Huey now." When pictures were taken, Huey said it was a picture of past and future presidents. He asked Coolidge about the condition of the White House, mentioning that he might have to tear it down and build another one just as he built the governor's mansion.[63]

But in early March 1930, Huey provoked national press coverage. A ship from Germany, the *Emden,* was on a goodwill tour and docked in New Orleans. On the Sunday set for a courtesy call, the *Emden*'s commander and the consul appeared in full dress uniforms. Seymour Weiss was in uniform as an honorary colonel and aide-de-camp on the governor's staff. Weiss escorted them to Huey's hotel suite. Huey, who had been listening to a radio sermon, greeted them dressed in green pajamas, a red and blue bathrobe, and blue slippers, looking like "an explosion in a paint factory." Huey apologized for his attire, saying he had been working all night. Huey and the commander amiably chatted, but the consul was furious. Thirty minutes after they left, he called Weiss to complain. Weiss suggested to Huey that he apologize. Huey either said "Tell him to go jump in the lake" or "Apologize. What for? I treated them like home folks."[64]

Weiss persuaded Huey to meet with the consul. Huey apologized, saying he had not been well for several weeks and his colonel hadn't warned him against "unbecoming raiment": "You see, I come from Winnfield up in the hills of Winn Parish, in this State. I know little of diplomacy and much less of the international courtesies and exchanges that are indulged in by nations. In fact, I only happened to be governor of the State by accident, anyway. There was no royal heritage but simply by chance I happened to receive more votes than the other men aspiring to the same office." (Huey may have written this newspaper article, not an unusual occurrence.)[65] They agreed to a formal visit the next day on the *Emden.* Weiss and other friends loaned Huey formal clothes. No one had a stovepipe hat, so Alfred Danziger loaned him a fedora, which he wore with striped pants, the swallowtail coat, and a gray tie he borrowed from Weiss.

The commander stated that Huey was an intelligent, interesting, and unusual person. A twenty-one-gun salute was fired at the visit's conclusion.[66] Later the commander said his pajamas were louder than Huey's.

The incident repulsed those who expected a governor to manifest first-class behavior but appealed to those of democratic dispositions in the same way Ben Franklin's refusal to dress in the ostentatious manner of European diplomats reinforced his democratic brand image. Even the cultured few should have appreciated the sly, Franklinesque description that he was only governor "by accident."

A visiting countess from Poland noted that the dictators of Spain and Italy received visitors while wearing intimate garments. Huey said maybe everyone should go back to Noah's time to figure out the "garb complication." But he was "ruined" in Winn Parish now that people knew he slept in pajamas.[67]

In future years Huey often wore pajamas when meeting newsmen. Writer A. J. Liebling stated that Huey kept trying for laughs with an old gag.[68] Huey may have thought it made him more colorful and newsworthy, but his mind was active enough to create new gags. No writer has posited the obvious motive for the practice: a disregard for conventions that did not serve him. He began working when he woke up and got dressed when he needed to. He later greeted a commander of the U.S. Fourth Army in his underwear (the commander only laughed) and the *States-Times* congratulated him on his narrow escape, contending that Huey had earlier met a Baton Rouge delegation in the nude.[69]

To counteract the Louisiana press, Huey started his own weekly newspaper, the *Louisiana Progress,* on March 26, 1930.[70] The night editor of the *Times-Picayune,* John Klorer, was hired to run it. Cartoonist Trist Wood, who had penned hostile cartoons against Huey, accepted a job at an increased salary (from forty-five to one hundred dollars per week) to draw its cartoons. The cost of a subscription was deducted from the wages of state employees, so the newspaper achieved significant circulation in no time.[71]

This was followed by an April 14 announcement that Huey would oppose incumbent Senator Joseph Ransdell for his U.S. Senate seat, *provided* he could conclude his gubernatorial term before taking the seat. He would refuse to leave the state, he said, if Lieutenant Governor Cyr could act as governor.[72]

Huey was optimistic about May's legislative session. The *Times* reported that he had spent a lot of time with "influential and cultured men" and was not making "so many enemies needlessly," noted that the electorate was either violently favorable or violently opposed to him, and opined that he was a "remarkable fellow to observe and talk to."[73] It carried a flattering story about the planned lake-girdling drive around Lake Pontchartrain that would rival Chicago's Lake Shore Drive, and a bridge across the Mississippi from New Orleans to Gretna. The $5 million worth of equipment to begin construction would impress the city's Canal Street visitors, along with a new $2 million coffee terminal and a $2 million steamship terminal, with landscaping to enhance the appearance.[74] Huey's free schoolbooks law and his severance tax on oil had survived their final court challenges. The influential Louisiana Police Jurors Association, including a New Orleans delegation headed by Mayor Walmsley, voted to support Huey's highway and bridge program.

Considering the completion of the governor's mansion, the opening of the new Lake Pontchartrain bridge, the number of contracts let, the number of new highways and bridges opened, the number of highway and other projects announced, the excitement of getting Louisiana out of the mud, the contractors' recognition of the money to be made, the support of the business leaders organized by Harvey Couch, and the number of speeches he had made articulating his vision of three thousand miles of paved roads, Huey might be excused for dreaming of success in the upcoming legislative session.

Instead, when the legislature convened, J. Y. Sanders Sr., John M. Parker, Lieutenant Governor Cyr, Esmond Phelps of the *Times-Picayune,* and publisher James Thomson of the *Item* lobbied the House to remove John Fournet as speaker. If successful, they planned to revive impeachment. Huey was on the scene, however, and saved Fournet in a vote of fifty-five to forty-four. Seventeen of sixty-one pro-impeachment representatives had defected to Huey.[75] But the vote was less than the two-thirds necessary to pass constitutional amendments for the expanded highway and bridge bond program. Huey reshuffled committee assignments, removing Judge Dupre from the Judiciary Committee, for example, but this did not help, and Judge Dupre resigned his other committee assignments in protest.[76]

A similar move was made to install an opponent of Huey as president of the Senate because the prior president, Gilbert, had resigned to accept a judgeship. Huey defeated this, too, but only by supporting an independent candidate who had not signed the Round Robin, Alvin O. King, and only by a vote of twenty-two to fifteen, also less than the two-thirds he would need.[77]

On the day after the two houses were organized, Huey spoke to a joint session about his program, emphasizing roads and bridges, improving New Orleans's port, and asking the legislators to approve a $68 million bond program, dedicating 2 of the 4-cents-a-gallon gasoline tax to retire the bonds. The road bond bill was the only legislation Huey would propose, he said, but a $5 million bond program was soon introduced to build a new capitol.

The *Times* called Huey's proposals "amazing" and thought they would "place Louisiana on a par with more populous states."[78] The New Orleans press, however, claimed that they would help Huey establish his dream of "absolute dictatorship." It was a "sheer broth of dementia" and a piece of "executive hysteria." In proposing projects to benefit New Orleans and Baton Rouge, they thought Huey was making an unprincipled bid for support from the legislators in those areas, political logrolling. The newspapers urged legislators to resist the temptation to benefit their part of the state because the price of that benefit—supporting something Huey proposed—was too great.[79] Baton Rouge legislators lined up behind the conservative press. Capitol or no capitol, they would oppose Huey's program. That was unsurprising. But then New Orleans's Old Regulars and Mayor Walmsley announced their opposition, breaking their word. Open political warfare resulted, as if the compromise of the preceding summer had never occurred.

The state bank examiner had found earlier in March that the city had borrowed more than it would collect in taxes, and now that the Old Regulars opposed Huey's legislative program, Huey had the examiner pressure the banks to call their loans because of the shortfall, leaving the city without money. New Orleans then lost credibility by denying Huey's demand to audit its books. Only its citizens could review them. "The ring plunges the City into the red and then hides the books," Huey said. Huey had a CPA supporter and resident of New Orleans inspect them, but he was ejected after one day because, the city said, he was compiling information for political purposes.

Huey then had the state Tax Commission, empowered to receive and review municipal tax assessments, withhold New Orleans's books. The city couldn't issue tax bills. A court order required their return. The Highway Commission withheld funds it owed the city until a court required them to be paid. During the legislative session, Huey dictated an appeal from that order to a secretary, who put it in final form and filed it. The injunction was overturned as Huey asked the next day.[80]

The *Louisiana Progress* charged that the mainstream press was captive to the interests that bought advertising. Huey proposed a 15 percent tax (later reduced to 5 percent) on newspaper revenues and a law permitting injunctions against pornographic or defamatory writings, but the newspaper publishers lobbied successfully to defeat this.[81] Over Huey's opposition, the legislature voted to investigate corruption in the Highway Commission.[82]

The conservatives announced a mass meeting in Baton Rouge on June 18, and Huey promptly organized a rival rally. Separate trains brought Old Regulars and Huey's adherents to Baton Rouge. Fights broke out between the rival groups whenever they met in the streets. Between four thousand and six thousand people attended the conservative rally, and more than seven thousand people attended Huey's.

Walmsley denounced Huey as insane, an anarchist, a liar, and a brute. He denied that he had broken a promise to support the road bond program. The *Times-Picayune* ran a picture of the crowd at Huey's meeting identified as the crowd at his opponents' rally, but "the Irish countenance of [Huey's leader] of the 11th Ward . . . could not be disfigured," leading to "severe ridicule" of the newspaper.[83]

Colonel Ewing and others compared Huey to a carpetbagger. The heroism of those who drove out the Yankee carpetbaggers would have to be matched by their descendants to rid the state of the "little chineapin-headed misfit." The *Baton Rouge State Times* called Huey a "little sniveling demagogue."

At Huey's rally, he denounced his opponents: Colonel Bow Wow Ewing, Turkey-Head Walmsley, and Esmond Phelps, who never spent a dime for a shoeshine in his life. "He uses Shinola and if he has none rubs his shoes on his pants' legs." Afterward he was known as Shinola Phelps. Huey asked his audience to pressure their legislators to let the road bond amendment be voted on by the people.[84]

Huey's opponents rejoiced when a New York bank loaned New Orleans the necessary funds to avert a financial collapse. Yankees had their benefits.

Allen Ellender led the fight for Huey's road bond amendment. Incredibly, Sack of Potatoes Bennett now supported Huey. Ellender stalled its progress until mid-June while Huey tried to round up sixty-seven votes, but he came up seven short. Anticipating this defeat, about a week earlier, Ellender introduced a bill calling for a constitutional convention, which could be enacted by a majority rather than a two-thirds, vote. The conservatives then jammed the legislative calendar with bills and filibustered them.

On June 21, Huey appeared on the floor of the House to rally his followers to change the rules to allow the constitutional convention bill to be taken out of order, arguing that this required only a majority vote. Fournet allowed the motion. J. Y. Sanders Jr. led a furious backlash and threatened bloodshed: "We are all white men here. . . . [Our race] does not fear danger, . . . does not lay down the sword once it is drawn. . . . [Therefore,] we must respect the rules we have drawn to govern our deliberations. The consequences of failure to do so might be appalling."[85] One member demanded that unauthorized visitors be cleared from the chamber, forcing Huey to exit. When he peeped through the doorway, the door was slammed in his face. At the close of the debate on the appeal of Fournet's ruling, Ellender spoke, saying he would withdraw his motion to take the bill out of order, contingent upon conservatives permitting it to come to a vote. They caved in and, on June 25, the constitutional convention bill passed by a vote of fifty-six to forty-two. Now it was up to the Senate.[86]

Cyr prevented the Senate from considering the measure,[87] recognizing only conservative senators, who filibustered. Among them was Henry Larcade, one of the Round Robin signers, who recently had quarreled with Huey over the award of an insurance contract for highway bonds.[88] One senator held the floor for days, drinking soda pop on the floor and castigating Huey. While Huey had twenty-two votes to select the president of the Senate, he could not get twenty votes—he could not get a majority even from senators who had voted his way—to take the constitutional convention bill out of order and voted on.

The legislature independently voted for an investigation of Angola prison.[89] When Huey appeared before the Senate committee, its members ordered him to leave. Back in January, the prison chaplain was removed by the new warden, McClanahan, but left with a blast that prisoners were being mistreated. McClanahan said that accredited newspaper reporters and any citizen without ulterior motives had a standing invitation to visit because the public had a right to know, and he would welcome any investigation. Huey agreed.[90] In February 1930, McClanahan had to resign when the Louisiana Supreme Court held that legislators could not also hold executive branch jobs. Huey appointed a twenty-seven-year-old LSU law student, A. P. Steckler, to replace him. In August, after the legislative session, it was alleged that convicts were treated as slaves and forced to work illegally on rice farms, and that one of them was shot and killed when he refused.[91]

The legislative session ended on July 10 without enacting any of Huey's program. "I am licked," Huey said. The *Times* wrote that this session was "the beginning of [Huey's] end."[92] For someone who has been consistently called a dictator, thus far he was able to secure only four major pieces of legislation (natural gas for New Orleans, a $30 million bond issue for roads, free textbooks secured by an increase in severance taxes on oil, and a new governor's mansion), had faced impeachment during a special legislative session that about 60 percent of the legislators supported, and had failed to enact any legislation during his second regularly scheduled legislative session in 1930.

After the session, Huey somehow obtained a letter to the attorneys for the Southern Pacific Railway Lines, stating that the legislator they had undertaken to "reach," though previously allied with Huey, opposed him throughout the session.[93] The *Louisiana Progress* reported this, but the mainstream press didn't.

Huey took some measure of revenge by vetoing funds for the Public Service Commission (denying support to Francis Williams), traveling expenses for Lieutenant Governor Cyr, money to probe the Highway Commission, and certain expenses of Attorney General Saint (Huey asserted that Saint only represented the Constitutional League).[94] In the lobby of a train station, Huey ran into L. F. Sherer, a staff member of the "now fundless [Public Service Commission] who knew" Huey well. Sherer "held out his hat, closed his eyes, and pretended to be a blind beggar" as Huey walked by. "Huey flipped a shiny new dime into Sherer's hat" without saying a word.[95] Usually portrayed as bold, Huey straddled the tick eradication issue. He signed the law enacted without his support but vetoed an appropriation to enforce it.

Huey retaliated against a bank that supported his impeachment, as he explained in his autobiography:

> In the impeachment proceedings of 1929, . . . money had to be borrowed to pay the expenses. The Legislature passed a resolution authorizing the Board of Liquidation to borrow $100,000 for that purpose. As a member of the Board I voted against the approval of such loan. I warned the banks against making it [because it was illegal]. . . .
>
> The banks made the loan. The 1930 Regular Session of the Legislature appropriated the $100,000 to repay it.
>
> I vetoed it.[96]

After the conclusion of the legislative session, however, Huey revealed his last, and best, countermove.

# Thirteen

# THERE WAS NO MIDDLE GROUND

Immediately after the unsuccessful legislative session, Huey made unconditional his decision to run for the U.S. Senate against incumbent senator Joseph E. Ransdell. The fear about turning over the state government to Paul Cyr—the reason for his contingent announcement in April—had evaporated. Once elected, Huey would finish his term as governor and join the Senate in May 1932. Ransdell had been inactive and ineffective, according to Huey, so the seat would be no more vacant between January (when the Senate session started) and May than it already had been during Ransdell's thirty-two years.[1] Huey cared too much about his good friend Cyr to visit the burdens of the governorship upon him.

Huey would resign and retire if he lost but, if he won, he expected his highway bond and other programs to be enacted. "There was no middle ground," he said in his autobiography: "In effect, my election will mean that the legislature will submit my plan to the people, or those who refuse to accede to the publicly expressed stand of the voters will be signing their own political death warrant."[2]

Ironically, Ransdell won his seat by portraying his opponent—former governor and incumbent senator Murphy J. Foster—as old and out of date.[3] Now, Huey made the same attack on Ransdell. The goateed senator embodied in appearance and policy government by goatee, a laissez-faire, pro-business conservative. While Ransdell supported the League of Nations, voted for federal flood control, women's suffrage, sugar tariffs, and veteran's legislation, and took a sincere interest in public health, Ransdell was more comfortable with and more apt to be speaking about religious virtues, patriotism, and good citizenship. He sponsored a constitutional amendment forbidding divorce.[4] In defense of the "sacred" marital relationship, he called divorce "the greatest enemy of the nation and the home." The home was a bulwark against anarchy and socialism: a "little state in which our fond parents were the rulers and we, the children, were willing subjects."

Ransdell had no claim on Huey's loyalty by 1930. He kept quiet during the impeachment, notwithstanding Huey's campaign help to him in 1924. Afterward, Ransdell supported the Constitutional League.

Ransdell was unperturbed by the competition. He had money. The Old Regulars and the Constitutional League backed him. Seniority and tradition were on his side. His fellow senators passed a weak but image-enhancing public health bill he sponsored before the election campaign.[5]

The Great Depression is usually considered to have started with the "Black Thursday" (October 24) stock market crash in 1929. In mid-October, a wave of selling had engulfed the market. On October 21, the market had a poor day, but renowned professor Irving Fisher said the decline was only "shaking out . . . the lunatic fringe." Heavy losses occurred on October 23, with Fisher still denying that securities were inflated. Then came Black Thursday. Crowds formed outside brokerage houses in horrified incredulity. But leading brokers and bankers met and agreed to pool resources to support the market. Prices firmed up for a few days. On October 28, however, trading volume was huge and the losses immense. No one stepped up to support the market. Black Tuesday, October 29, 1929, was the most devastating day in the history of the stock market.

The first week had slaughtered the innocents. The second week hit the wealthy. Rumors circulated that, while publicly expressing confidence, banks were selling stocks and calling loans. Margin calls broke many investors. On a few days—based on announcements of industrialists or other events—stocks rebounded, but not for long. Suicides were reported, but their increase during the Depression is a myth. Discovery of embezzlements increased, however, as people scrutinized their holdings.

Industrial production had reached its zenith the preceding June but saw a sharp setback in July. A slow, partial crash of the stock market had been taking place for three years. While the prosperity of the 1920s was real, something was wrong with the economy, not just with the stock market.[6]

By March 1930, four million people were out of work. Breadlines appeared for the first time since 1921. Old cellars were converted into shacks built of loose bricks and metal and inhabited by people who cooked on loose stones.[7] Relief sources were strained. Teachers fainted from hunger in their classrooms. Fifty men in Chicago fought over a barrel of garbage.[8]

By 1930, the effects of the Great Depression had reached Louisiana, although farmers had suffered throughout the 1920s. Cotton and sugar prices declined. Unemployment was spreading. A drought added to the misery.[9]

Ransdell ignored the Depression. Instead, he discussed floods, seniority, and Huey's corrupt administration. At his opening rally, a group of housewives presented him with a fitting symbol of his clean record and the necessity for clean government, a feather duster. Ransdell considered this an "almost sacred" emblem, and that "fine women should entrust it to [him] . . . to clean up Louisiana politics, touche[d him] deeply."[10] Huey seized upon the feather duster's similarity to Ransdell's goatee and called him "Old Feather Duster Ransdell," the first of several examples of Huey's celebrated ability to swiftly turn an attacker's thrust upon the attacker.

Statewide campaign managers were Harvey Peltier of the state Senate and Allen Ellender of the House. They could emphasize the destruction of Huey's program by the legislature. The jobs promised by the roads-and-improvement program Huey proposed would cushion the Depression. In New Orleans, Robert Maestri, Dr. Joseph O'Hara, and Paul Maloney ran Huey's organization. Huey designated Maloney as a congressional candidate. Maloney was dubious about it but was converted when he returned to his office to find a crowd of supporters there to congratulate him and heard newsboys proclaiming his candidacy. Huey had appointed Seymour Weiss as president of the Dock Board, which had a large group of patronage workers mobilized for the campaign.[11]

Patronage employees of the state were assessed 10 percent of their salary for two months to support the campaign. Pick-and-shovel workers were assessed between 2 and 5 percent of their compensation.[12] Additional funds were raised from state contractors. The money Huey spent on the campaign was small by today's standards and was less than he spent to become governor. Huey could have raised more money. He didn't think he would need it.

Trucks outfitted with speakers enabled Huey to speak to large crowds without strain. Circulars listing the town and time of his speeches were distributed ahead of time, and the trucks would precede Huey into a town and announce his imminent arrival. Huey would follow in a car. The tour seems informal and haphazard compared to the scripted political events today. It was a simpler time. Sources of entertainment and novelties were sparse, and politics was a primary interest. The novelty of the trucks helped draw a crowd, Williams said, an effect like Lyndon Johnson's use of helicopters in his Texas senatorial campaign eighteen years later.[13]

Big crowds turned out to hear Huey taunt Ransdell in a light and jesting fashion. One sunrise, Huey mounted a bale of cotton with a Bible in hand and looked out over the crowd for some minutes. Then he suddenly asked, "Is there a single person here who can tell me the name of your United States Senator, my opponent?" Momentarily spellbound, no one in the crowd could think of Ransdell's name. After that moment, Huey announced: "Well, I'll tell you. It's Old Feather Duster Ransdell. But when I get to Washington, you'll know the name of your Senator." Critics and supporters alike noted his magnetism as a speaker. Hostile journalist T. O. Harris could only explain Huey's appeal as an "undefinable something."[14]

The state and national press endorsed Ransdell. The smaller out-of-state papers billed the campaign as a clash of youth versus age.[15] The *Louisiana Progress* counteracted the adverse press and supplemented Huey's jests about Ransdell with more bite. Trist Wood cartoons showed Ransdell as old and decrepit. Sometimes instead of "feather duster" it called him "old trashy-mouth." J. Y. Sanders Sr. was drawn bent over. John Parker's face was drawn wrinkled, and he was labeled "Old Sack of Bones." The three New Orleans newspapers were drawn as a three-headed snake hissing "lies." Marshall Ballard of the *Item* was pictured with hypodermic needles sticking out of his arms. Two million circulars attacked the New Orleans Ring or skewered Ransdell.

The best circular turned Ransdell's claim of seniority into a liability, listing the results of his long years of officeholding:

1. We lost the United States Mint.
2. We lost the Federal Reserve Bank.
3. The United States Navy Yards in New Orleans were closed down.
4. The United States Army abandoned the Military post at Jackson Barracks.
5. We lost a station on the Transcontinental Air Mail Route.

WE HAVE NOT YET LOST THE POST OFFICE.[16]

Huey criticized Ransdell for giving the nephew of United Fruit Company's chief executive a job and, Huey said, for inducing the War Department to intervene in Central America to protect the company's interests. The CEO of United Fruit Company, Samuel Zemurray, was described as a "Banana Peddler."[17] After being criticized for ignoring national issues, Huey advocated tariffs to protect Louisiana's industries (especially sugar); the use of reservoirs in addition to levees to control floods (Ransdell favored only levees); the right of labor to organize; opposed the yellow dog contract by which employees had to sign contracts not to organize a union; and supported the export debenture plan to help farmers (government subsidies to export surplus crops abroad).

Huey sometimes digressed from the sabotage of his road construction program to discuss his manners, how he outraged the aristocracy, or the green pajamas episode. In one speech, Huey claimed he had too much Cajun blood to be dignified. This disgusted conservatives but apparently delighted his audience of Cajuns. One of Huey's speeches in Shreveport—an energetic speech without notes—was allegedly given while he was "dead drunk."[18] However abrupt or rude he was to subordinates or opponents, Huey was cheerful and folksy to ordinary people. Everyone should keep calling him Huey, he said. His great memory for names and faces made people feel important because Huey "knows me, remembers me."[19]

Huey also endorsed candidates for Congress in the First (state Senator Bathtub Joe Fernandez, an Old Regular who had defected to Huey, over incumbent James O'Connor), Second (Paul Maloney), and Third (Representative Numa Montet) districts. Once Huey suggested that, if the crowd could vote for only himself or Montet, they should vote for Montet because Huey didn't need their votes as much as Montet.[20] Williams notes that his relaxed confidence never left him during the campaign.

His opponents were not relaxed or confident. They outdid themselves with insults. Parker said Huey was "devoid of every element of honor and decency." Ex-governor Pleasant said Huey was akin to "Marx, Lenin, and Trotsky." Mrs. Pleasant said Huey was "common beyond words," that he had a "sordid, dirty soul," and that he exemplified the "greed and coarseness of the swine, . . . the venom of the snake, [and] the cruel cowardice of the skulking hyena." A Mrs. May Pilsbury charged that she saw Huey "drunk as a beast" and being taunted by newsboys on Canal Street about a week before the Dreher-LeBoeuf decision.[21] Mayor Walmsley said he was a "cur" and a "madman." John Sullivan said Huey had "the face of a clown, the heart of a petty larceny burglar, and the disposition of a tyrant." A Shreveport conservative said Huey was a "degenerate in mind and morals." Colonel Ewing compared Huey to the worst ruler of New Orleans, Benjamin Butler of the Reconstruction days, who could not match Huey for anarchy and destruction of civilized government. Roland Howell, a veteran of World War I and former head of the Louisiana American Legion, lapsed into a séance-like oration at a Ransdell rally, relaying "the command of . . . comrades speaking from the bivouac of the dead." As Williams drily notes, "The dead spoke clearly and with amazing detail through the voice of Howell: they directed their comrades not to vote for Huey Long, 'a notorious liar, a slinking coward, and a self-acclaimed slacker.'"[22]

The American Federation of Labor and Huey criticized Ransdell for voting to confirm a U.S. Supreme Court nominee who favored the yellow dog contract. In response, Ransdell claimed that he voted for the nominee because the NAACP opposed him. Huey and the AFL must be working with the NAACP, too, and must want racial equality, charged Ransdell.

Huey made this boomerang on Ransdell by resurrecting the letter Ransdell wrote to Black Republican leader Walter Cohen that Shreveport mayor Lee Thomas had criticized him for in the 1924 campaign. Huey had defended Ransdell in 1924, alleging that Thomas must have obtained it from Cohen, but now the *Progress* used it as proof that Ransdell, not Huey, favored racial equality. The letter simply asked Cohen to endorse the application of another African American for a job, but the *Progress* emphasized that he addressed the man as "Dear Mr." If he were going to address him as a schoolmate or buddy, Ransdell should have done so to get a job for a white man. The *Progress* urged a vote for the rights of labor and white supremacy and against Ransdell.[23]

Huey's relaxed confidence might have been shaken on September 3, days before the election on September 9. Alice Lee Grosjean's uncle-in-law, Sam Irby, a drinking companion of her ex-husband, James Terrell, walked into Ransdell's New Orleans headquarters to say he could reveal corruption within the Highway Department, from which he had just been fired. The attorney general took him to Baton Rouge to appear before an anti-Long district judge. Irby returned to New Orleans and then said he was flying to Shreveport and, after the election, would sue Huey for saying he was a drunkard and a wife-beater. In Shreveport, Irby met Terrell, who had traveled from his home in Arkansas. From their hotel room at the Gardner Hotel, one of them called Alice Lee, after which she told Huey that Irby and Terrell were drunk in their room and threatening to ruin him.

A few hours later, Irby phoned the city police and reported that someone was trying to remove him from his room. He opened a window and shouted "help!" When reporters learned this, they descended on the city Police Department, which knew nothing, and the hotel, which reported that Irby and Terrell had checked out on September 4. The men couldn't be found. Where were they?

After Huey was notified by Alice Lee of Irby's threats, Huey called a conference of advisors. Earl Long said the men should be killed. Huey kicked Earl and kicked him out of the meeting, shouting "I don't want to be United States Senator or anything else if I have to murder anybody." Another advisor suggested removing the two men to a remote location until after the election. Huey therefore asked the district attorney of Jefferson Parish, under the control of Huey's legislative allies, the Fisher family, to issue an arrest warrant charging the two men with possession of state documents. Then, officers of the Bureau of Criminal Identification went to Irby's hotel room.

Huey sent his wife's brother, Dave McConnell, along with bodyguard George McQuiston and cousin Wade Long, all members of the Bureau of Criminal Identification, to arrest Terrell and Irby. Irby and Terrell were both drunk when McConnell arrived and knocked on the door. Irby threatened to shoot the first man who entered the room, then called the Shreveport Police Department, and then opened the window to yell for help. Two of the city's officers arrived, but McConnell explained that he was going to take Irby to the parish jail, so they left.

When McConnell entered the room, Irby and Terrell "suddenly became abject." McConnell said that Alice Lee's father was looking for Irby to harm him (Huey worried that if Irby were harmed, he would get blamed). McConnell suggested going to a place of safety. "Let's go," said Irby. (If Irby and Terrell consented to go and were not coerced to consent, there was no kidnapping. If they were coerced without justification under color of state law, today one would conclude that their civil rights were violated.) In separate cars, Irby and Terrell were driven to a town on the Gulf Coast where a waiting boat took Irby to a camp on Grand Isle and Terrell to Barataria Bay, unusual detention centers for arrestees.[24] A telegram from Terrell sent to his mother said he was all right, but because it listed her maiden name, she doubted its authenticity.[25]

Needing to prove his charges of graft and now lacking his witness, and learning of the so-called arrest, Attorney General Saint requested from the federal court a writ charging kidnapping against Huey, the Jefferson Parish district attorney, and six policemen. The U.S. marshal served the writ on Huey at his suite at the Roosevelt Hotel, directing him to appear in court the day before the election, September 8. A reporter from the *Item* slipped in behind to observe. After the marshal exited, Huey demanded to know who he was. Once he identified himself, Huey began a loud, arm-waving denunciation of the newspaper, accused him of impersonating a federal marshal, and called the reporter a "sonofabitch." Outraged, the reporter punched Huey in the mouth. The bodyguards immediately sprang into action, pinning the reporter's arms behind him and, on Huey's excited orders, searching him for weapons. None were found. Huey calmed down. After telling the man he had done a terrible thing by striking the governor, the reporter replied that Huey should not have insulted his mother. Huey slapped his face, apologized for the insult, and said, "Now, we're even." The reporter told the press that Huey's blow caused him to laugh. Huey warned him that with all the armed men in the room he could have been killed.[26]

Having prevented Ransdell from using Irby to hurt him, Huey now used Irby to hurt Ransdell. He prepared a statement for Irby and gave it to McConnell, who had him sign it. Irby didn't read it; he was just fishing and drinking. Next, Joe Fisher took Irby by plane back to Jefferson Parish, and then by car—secretly by backstreets to avoid New Orleans police—to the Roosevelt Hotel. Newspapermen were tipped that there would be a story on September 7. Fisher brought Irby up the freight elevator to Huey's suite, where his leaders, bodyguards, and two privileged reporters (a crowd of reporters milled around in the hallway outside) waited near a radio microphone. Huey announced that Mr. Sam Irby had a message to broadcast to the people of Louisiana.

Irby read the statement that Huey held up before him, introducing himself, calling Huey his best friend, and denying that he was kidnapped. Instead, he had gone to Shreveport to trap Huey's opponent. Lo and behold, he had discovered $2,500 under his pillow, implying that either Cecil Morgan or Harney Bogan put it there. The kidnapping was staged to see who else was in on the payoff. Irby had spent the past few days camping on Grand Isle. Concluding, he asked Huey to protect him from the New Orleans police. Huey then told the newsmen that they had a scoop, and he would pay them $1,000 if it made the front page: "Ha! Ha! Ha!" Joe Fisher and the bodyguards hustled Irby back down the freight elevator, pushing two reporters out, and into a car. They escaped pursuing city police cars until they were safely over the parish line.[27]

On September 8, Huey testified before Judge Borah, denied knowing where the two men were, and explained the telegram to Terrell's mother: he had received handwritten notes at his hotel suite from Deputy Sheriff Sardis of Jefferson Parish and assumed they were written by Irby and Terrell. (Sardis testified that he handed subpoenas to unidentified Bureau of Criminal Identification agents.) Huey copied the substance onto a telegram.[28] In Louisiana the matter was looked upon as a newspaper story or a "good joke."[29]

After the election, Irby told the federal judge that he was on a fishing trip and had always been free to travel. The judge granted his request to drop the charges.[30] Irby got a job with Harvey Couch's utility company.

Irby put his name to a ghostwritten book in which he said he was kidnapped, manacled to a tree, eaten by mosquitos, and threatened with death by gangsters. The correspondence between Irby and his ghostwriter analyzed by Williams reveals that this was fiction. Irby bet money that Huey would win the election and asked to vote for him on Election Day.[31] Over a year later, the *Chicago Tribune* featured Irby's accusation that Huey offered him $50,000 to suppress his book. Two weeks after that, Irby was fined for leaving the hotel without paying his bill. Irby died of pneumonia in Texas Charity Hospital in 1935, unidentified for days.[32]

Under the protection of the police, the Old Regulars interfered with Huey's campaign rallies and arrested his campaign workers. Cyr beat up a Long partisan who had taunted him.[33] Huey sent one hundred state policemen to the city, but the city police arrested them because they were "disturbing the peace." Rumors circulated that members of the National Guard or Bureau of Criminal Identification were going to raid the jail to free their colleagues. The city and Huey instead negotiated a deal: the state police would be released from jail if they left the city.

In this election, the Old Regulars prepared to file eleven dummy candidates. Dummy candidates do not intend to get elected but allow their names to be filed as candidates so their political organization can designate election commissioners to help count votes. The organization with the most dummies will have the most vote counters. Huey turned this common ruse against the Old Regulars. Huey's campaign prepared to file twenty-three dummies.

Huey's campaign manager Allen Ellender called Ulic Burke of the Old Regulars just at the deadline and suggested they play pool. Right before midnight, Ellender asked Burke if he had arranged to file dummy candidates, and Burke, with self-satisfaction, admitted it. Ellender calmly surprised him with his own papers. In shock, Burke left. The next day, Mayor Walmsley called Ellender. They agreed to equal representation.[34]

Election night, September 9, brought conservatives another disaster. Huey won 149,640 votes to 111,451 for Ransdell, 57.3 percent of the vote statewide. He came close in New Orleans: 38,682 to Ransdell's 43,373. He won fifty-three parishes out of sixty-four. His vote total was at least one short: Huey missed his train to Shreveport and therefore was unable to vote for himself. The elderly Ransdell was through in politics but outlived Huey, dying in 1954 at age ninety-five, in good health almost to the end.[35]

Huey's congressional candidates—Fernandez, Maloney, and Montet—were elected, Fernandez barely, and with the aid of fraudulent voters in St. Bernard and Plaquemines parishes. The Plaquemines Parish voter rolls listed Babe Ruth, Jack Dempsey, and Charlie Chaplin. "They had trees registered down there," a bodyguard recalled. A desire for political peace and the promise of a job representing the city of New Orleans in Washington, DC, convinced the defeated congressman O'Connor to cancel a vote-fraud investigation.[36] Harvey Fields won Huey's old spot on the Public Service Commission, defeating Harley Bozeman.[37]

Huey's election effected the surrender of his opposition. The Constitutional League disbanded. Some of the Old Regular ward leaders wanted to defect to Huey. They could not deliver their wards for Ransdell. Huey's popularity was too great. Mayor Walmsley, however, maintained the fight.

The city's business leaders, under the leadership of Rudolph Hecht, president of Hibernia Bank and chairman of New Orleans Public Service Inc. (the public utility monopoly of New Orleans that Huey forced to bring natural gas to the city), intervened. The city had debts contracted for under other governors that were coming due. The municipal loan that had staved off surrender to Huey during the legislative session had to be refinanced or paid. Why not get in line behind a governor who wanted to improve the Port of New Orleans? Hecht told Walmsley to meet with Huey and said that Huey would be generous.[38]

A truce was agreed upon. It contemplated a special legislative session that would approve a $75 million bond issue for roads and bridges, an increase in the gasoline tax from 4 cents to 5 (half of the increase went to schools, the other half to retire debts of the Port of New Orleans), a $5 million bond issue for a new capitol, increased funding for public schools, a modern airport (added at the start of the legislative session), the first bridge over the Mississippi River at New Orleans, a state appropriation of $700,000 for New Orleans streets, and a resolution withdrawing the impeachment charges.[39]

Huey often remarked that his opponents could not see something until after they had been knocked down by it a half-dozen times.[40] Anyone looking at the facts today must wonder what Huey's opponents were thinking. Huey's public improvement program had the support of business leaders. No economic class opposed his program. Huey was the only political leader who proposed a solution to the upcoming maturities of New Orleans government bonds and loans. He wanted to maintain the preeminence of New Orleans's port. The Old Regulars had broken their word to him, disregarded the wishes of conservative business leaders and their constituents, and offered no substitute or alternative.

The legislature was called into a special session to begin September 16. The Long and Old Regular legislators passed Huey's bills by large majorities and expunged the impeachment charges. Judge Dupre, J. Y. Sanders Jr., Mason Spencer, and Cecil Morgan disregarded the election returns to vote against the improvements.[41] Huey drilled a hole in the state capitol roof over Dupre's desk, so it rained on him. When Huey strolled into the chamber during a heavy rain, Dupre railed that the roof should be repaired. Huey wrote on the deaf legislator's pad: "Are you in favor of the new capitol?" "Hell no!" Huey pushed Dupre's chair under the leak and wrote "Die, damn you, in the faith." Dupre was either "much amused" or outraged.[42]

The only legislation Huey had difficulty with was the bond issue for the new capitol. Either to demonstrate his independence or out of some uncontrolled desire to hurt, embarrass, or prank Huey, Earl Long convinced several legislators that Huey secretly wanted it defeated. Huey delayed the vote until he ran around the chamber and convinced the gullible legislators that Earl had double-crossed him.[43]

At the end of the session, legislative leader Lester Hughes's son died of leukemia. Huey went to his home and stayed most of the evening, reading Bible verses with him.[44]

The vote on the constitutional amendments was set for November but was never in doubt. They were approved by margins of twenty and thirty to one. Huey had the election returns sped to the capitol by police escort, a dramatic touch justified by the desperation of the people who wanted the jobs that these projects would provide.[45] Unemployment relief was managed by assessing state and city employees 5 percent of their pay. "Not one word intimating that [Huey] sought to divert this money to political purposes has ever been uttered even by his most implacable enemies."[46]

---

While Huey had permitted an advisory committee to oversee expenditures for the highways to be written into the legislation and appointed several political opponents to it for the express purpose of avoiding corruption, the roads program included graft. Highway contractors kicked back 20 percent of their contracts to Huey's organization. Harley Bozeman claimed that Huey's friends (not Huey) acquired a rock quarry by means of threats of increased tax assessments that then overcharged the state for an inferior grade of crushed stone, although the hardness of the roads exceeded federal government standards. Shell contractors were told to keep their prices reasonable, but to divide up the districts so that each got a fair share of the work, undermining competitive bidding but keeping the peace between rival contractors.[47]

Huey wanted the roads built for $14,000 per mile. This was unrealistic because Louisiana had soft soil and many waterways. The cost was about $26,000 per mile. The roads were built eighteen feet wide instead of twenty-two feet wide pursuant to an agreement with the federal government that the speed limit would be forty-five miles per hour. Illinois highways were eighteen feet wide, and their cost was almost $23,000 per mile, excluding the cost of land. In the early 1920s, Harry Byrd estimated the cost of Virginia's paved roads at $40,000 per mile.[48]

In some places concrete was laid on the ground without roadbeds or back drains or on the gravel roads built by Parker. Some writers conclude this left the roads unsafe or subject to erosion. Deutsch believed to the contrary that Huey might levy political taxes (kickbacks) upon road contractors and the roads might be located to favor supporters, but they "must" be "good road[s]. There will be no shoddy paving work."[49]

Huey wanted the roads built fast. He liked to stop his car on worksites to spur the highway work. He spotlighted defects and unsafe conditions and had them corrected. Huey kept a chart in his office that tracked the number of roads built each day.[50]

In December 1930, the Airline Highway connecting New Orleans and Baton Rouge was completed, two concrete lanes for cars and two gravel lanes for buggies. It was so straight that it cut thirty-eight miles off the trip. Huey's drivers could cover the eighty miles in an hour.[51] In July 1931, with the sale of $15 million of the bonds approved by the voters in November 1930, the construction program accelerated.[52]

Huey's highway engineer told Huey it was impossible to build more than one thousand miles of roads in a year. Huey asked the engineer if he could oversee construction of a thousand miles of roads. When the engineer said yes, Huey then replied that he should build one thousand miles of roads, and Huey and O. K. Allen would operate a second department and build another thousand miles.[53] The engineer saw the point.

When the program reached its maturity, Louisiana employed twenty-two thousand people on its roads program, 10 percent of the entire country's road workforce, and had built over two thousand miles of surfaced roads. This was a record that exceeded all other states; it was more highway workers than New York and Pennsylvania employed, even though they were much larger states.[54] The money spent on the highways cushioned the effect of the Depression in Louisiana in 1931 and 1932. The Depression reduced incomes in some other states by about 50 percent, whereas in Louisiana the decline was 26 percent.[55]

The program was revolutionary for its time, but you can still find on the Internet $5,000 bond notes with Huey's signature on them. It is astonishing how close the governor was to the actual work; how small the scale was compared to state governments today. In December 1930, Huey announced *for the first time* that an appointment would be necessary to see him.[56] Huey negotiated with landowners the right of way over their lands. A lone curve in the Airline Highway resulted when one landowner failed to agree to Huey's price.[57]

While issuing bonds to fund highway construction sounds simple, it was not. Once the voters approved the bond proposals, Huey did not have $75 million to spend. The bonds were sold in tranches, generally $15 million at a time. Huey had planned to offer $15 million for sale in December 1930, but after "consultation with all the leading banking houses," had to delay it.[58] Louisiana law forbade the sale of bonds for less than par, and the Depression hurt the market for bonds.

In October 1930, a month before the vote on the road bond amendments, anti-Long secretary of state James Bailey died. Without warning, Huey appointed Alice Lee Grosjean to the position. When interviewed, the "thrilled" appointee explained her family's patrician credentials but denied plans to run for the seat in 1932. She preferred her politics from the sidelines, and she expected to go to Washington, DC, with Huey as his secretary. One New Orleans paper said that this appointment set "many a gossipy tongue to wagging," but most circumspectly referred to her as pretty, charming, and well-proportioned. The *Louisiana Progress* reported that she was probably the best-posted individual on "state affairs."[59] A $20,000 shortage in the secretary of state's accounts was soon noticed. All of Bailey's relatives, including his widow, were dismissed. Two years later, Grosjean acted as governor for ten days.[60]

In a case of political déjà vu, another great banquet was held during the special legislative session, adjourned temporarily so that the legislators could attend.[61] Huey was praised for his energy and genius. Alfred Danziger, president of the New Orleans Association of Commerce; John Overton; P. M. Milner, an advocate for good roads; U.S. District Judge Rufus Foster; Mayor Walmsley; Rudolph Hecht; W. C. Ermon, another advocate for paved roads; T. H. Harris, the state superintendent of education; and John Klorer, editor of the *Louisiana Progress,* all spoke, with Danziger, Milner, Klorer, and Ermon all praising the public works program.

Mayor Walmsley applauded Huey's work on the problems of New Orleans: "[Y]ou would have thought that he was the mayor."[62] Harris said school appropriations increased by $1,900,000 with an additional $500,000 given for state colleges. Huey had appropriated tax money, and Harris or Huey or both had obtained support from the Julius Rosenwald Foundation to begin a night-school program to educate adult illiterates, both white and Black. Teachers conducted classes three nights a week in churches, school buildings, and private homes. Over 125,000 adults attended the classes and were certified literate at the time of Harris's remarks. From 1920 to 1930, the adult illiteracy rate was reduced from 10 percent to 7 percent for whites and from 38 percent to 23 percent for Blacks.[63] Huey was immensely proud of this achievement.

Huey responded with a story about a funeral in which a man was favorably eulogized but, at various points during it, his mother-in-law got up to peer at the open casket. When finally asked why she did that, she replied, "I just want to stand here, parson, to be sure that that man you're talking about was my son-in-law."[64]

One-half cent of the gasoline tax approved by the voters in November was devoted to the schools. It helped Superintendent of Education Harris to extend state control over local school boards. (The malt syrups tax enacted in 1928 had been evaded because people home-brewed it or bought it from other states.) Harris used the additional revenue to force local boards to improve teacher certification requirements, increase their wages, and lengthen the school year. The program was Harris's, but Huey was the first governor to accept the ramifications of Harris's idea—that through state control he could force the improvement of educational programs throughout Louisiana.[65]

Huey's concentration on secondary education evident in the first two years of his governorship was about to be augmented by his attention to university education. Events had been brewing at the state university. Behind the scenes of his fluffy public relations events and work selling bonds and building highways, Huey had been considering what became a whole new expansion of his proposals for Louisiana.

# Fourteen

# LSU

## A SIGNAL ACHIEVEMENT

Colonel Campbell B. Hodges was a professional soldier from Louisiana and then commandant of the Military Academy of West Point. After the impeachment collapsed in 1929, members of the Louisiana State University Board of Supervisors suggested to Huey that Hodges be selected as president of the university. The current president, Thomas Atkinson, was incapacitated from a heart attack. LSU was established as a military academy, known as the "Old War Skule," had a large ROTC program, and graduated many who chose military careers. Hodges was asked to take the job in 1926 before Atkinson was appointed, but his Army commitments prevented his acceptance.

The Hodgeses were old-line aristocrats and conservative. Hodges's brother was the campaign manager for Riley J. Wilson in the 1928 gubernatorial election and joined the Constitutional League in June 1929. Undoubtedly for these reasons, Huey stated that the new president should be a civilian and vetoed Hodges.

Huey's intervention to veto Hodges was his first significant involvement with LSU. When Huey became governor, LSU was a class C institution—third rate—but it obtained an A rating from the Association of American Universities in November 1928, without Huey's help.[1] There were 1,600 to 1,800 students at the time, with 168 faculty members, and an annual budget of about $800,000. Compared to other American universities, it ranked eighty-eighth in size. In the "psychological retrogression" after the Civil War, the attitude of Louisianans and southerners toward many of their colleges was "resigned":[2] they knew their educational institutions were second- or third-rate and, worse, accepted it.

The campus was located just south of Baton Rouge, a new campus to which the university moved in 1925, after Governor Parker arranged for it to acquire an old plantation, and after he had obtained consistent severance tax revenue for it. New buildings were constructed. Student enrollment as well as the hiring of faculty members increased. In 1924, Huey had criticized Governor Parker's plan to expand LSU, claiming that "our kind" don't need to learn fancy ways to farm. This attack backfired at the time and was not repeated then or during the campaign of 1928. Huey was preoccupied with his legislative program in 1928, with his impeachment defense, post-impeachment recovery, and the campaign against Ransdell in 1929 and 1930, so he gave scant attention to LSU. But Huey did have the band play "Streets of New York" in 1928 in Shreveport before the LSU-Arkansas game: it was a dig at the Klan and support for Al Smith in a bastion of anti-Catholic sentiment.[3]

After winning election as president of the student government at the LSU Law School, Kemble K. Kennedy led a delegation of fifty students to Huey's office to protest the Law School's dean, Robert Lee Tullis, in December 1929. Kennedy had been a law client of Huey[4] and was a political supporter in Union Parish and LSU. Kennedy claimed that Tullis was ineffective. Huey tried to have Tullis removed, but criticism made him back down.[5]

In June 1930, a satirical student newspaper, the *Whangdoodle,* was published, but instead of the lame lampoons of the past, it was now filled with accusations of embezzlement, dirty stories, and juicy gossip about faculty members. The university's business manager was embezzling funds; the wife of a faculty member was having an affair while her husband taught in the classroom; an English professor was a drug addict who slept with prostitutes "of the fifty-seven variety."[6]

The convalescing Atkinson hired a detective to discover the perpetrators. Kennedy's fraternity was identified as the producer, with Kennedy the editor. Atkinson expelled him. The local district attorney in Baton Rouge had Kennedy arrested for criminal libel. The faculty member accused of being a dope addict—John Uhler—was one of the four complaining parties, and the business manager denied embezzlement. While the legislature was still in session, Huey asked Atkinson to allow Kennedy to graduate, but after Atkinson showed him the *Whangdoodle,* Huey retracted his request. In November 1930, Kennedy was convicted and sentenced to one year in jail.

Petitions seeking a reprieve were given to Huey, who complained that Kennedy was being singled out and that everyone who was in on the scurrilous publication—they were all "mean as the dickens"—should serve thirty to sixty days in jail to learn their lesson. After a week, Kennedy got a reprieve from Huey, citing a recent broken arm he suffered in an automobile accident that required medical care.[7]

Huey visited the university in November, unannounced. He asked for President Atkinson, but the secretary told him Atkinson was at home, ill. Huey then asked for the business manager. The secretary ran to a separate building to try to retrieve him, but he was out at the old campus, on an errand. Huey was carrying a gold-headed cane that day and pounded it on the table, demanding that she obtain someone for him to talk to.

In tears now, she brought to him the dean of men, Fred C. Frey. When Frey arrived, Huey said he didn't want to talk to a "damn kid." Frey said he was two years older than Huey. Huey laughed and the two men went to Atkinson's office. At Atkinson's desk, Huey sat down, leaned back, put his feet on it, and asked Frey how he would look as president of the university. Frey thought he had a list of people to fire, most of them old-timers. Frey was friendly and diplomatic.

Huey asked Frey to summon the band director, Pops Gilbeau, so he could fire him. Frey demurred, warning of difficulties with accreditation authorities if Huey interfered, and noting Gilbeau's popularity. Frey suggested that Huey consult with the commandant of cadets, Major Troy H. Middleton, who also urged noninterference with personnel decisions. Huey directed Middleton to expand the band from 28 to 125 pieces. A few days later, Middleton found a new band director, A. W. Wickboldt. Gilbeau had two jobs and kept the other one.

Middleton sensibly asked if President Atkinson had been informed, but Huey said "To Hell with him. You and I are going to have us a real band." Middleton sensibly informed Atkinson, who said to go along up to 75 pieces. Huey followed up. When Middleton reported the 75-piece restriction, Huey blew up, shouting "he has nothing to do with it," ordered him to expand to 125 pieces, and hung up.[8]

Atkinson resigned on November 17, 1930.[9] Earlier in August 1930, Huey had appointed the last members needed to control the Board of Supervisors. Huey investigated potential replacements for Atkinson. Board member George Everett suggested James Monroe Smith. A graduate of LSU, Smith had a background as a country schoolteacher and dean of Southwestern Louisiana Institute, a small state college. Smith had earned a PhD in educational administration from Columbia University. O. K. Allen and Harley Bozeman interviewed him and then recommended him. Huey interviewed him and introduced him to the board, and he was hired.[10] Legend has it that Smith appeared unimpressive. Huey gave him cash and said, "God damn you, go out and buy a new suit. At least try to look like a president."

After Huey's death, Smith disgraced himself by forging and illegally speculating with LSU bonds and was convicted and jailed. While Huey was alive, however, he was an imaginative and skilled administrator and popular with students.[11] The deplorable absence of budgets was remedied. Student aid changed overnight. Huey believed that every child ought to have a chance to attend college.[12]

Smith got as much money as possible to improve education at the university but accepted Huey's direction, as necessary. Huey was savage in supervising Smith, sometimes for Smith's own protection. Smith's wife, for example, let her husband's new position go to her head. She obtained an exotic moon display in New Orleans that cast a romantic glow over her garden during elegant parties[13]—until Huey told her to get rid of it. Mrs. Smith sponsored a riding club with expensive, thoroughbred horses. At one riding event, an LSU coed was injured. On the campaign trail at the time, Huey only had time to send a telegram: "SELL THEM PLUGS." Upset at its peremptory tone, Smith showed the telegram to George Everett. "Why show it to me," Everett exclaimed. "He fires me every other day. But I know what you're going to do—sell them plugs."[14]

Familiar with football, Huey attended a practice. Watching the kicker practicing extra points, Huey asked to try it. The ball only dribbled off his foot. Again, Huey issued a mighty kick and failed once more, telling the boy, "I guess I'm a little off today." When the team gathered around, Huey asked if they were going to defeat their rival Tulane at the next week's game. The boys were optimistic but mentioned a star halfback who played for Tulane. Huey suggested they pirate that player for the game by offering his father a state job. With embarrassment, they schooled him on anti-pirating rules. Nor did Huey understand that a coin flip determined who would receive the first kickoff. He thought it was their turn to receive because Tulane got the first kickoff last year. Huey understood one thing, however: "I don't fool around with losers."[15]

LSU had not been a loser, but its record was mediocre: 6–2–1 in 1928;

6–3 in 1929. Most of the wins were against small schools. In both years, Russ Cohen coached the team. Cohen had played college football at Vanderbilt and had been an assistant coach at Alabama. Tulane was a big rival and had trounced LSU in 1929, 21 to 0. When Huey watched the team practice, LSU had a 6–3 record but was expected to lose big to Tulane in its next game.

What Huey saw in Cohen he did not like. Former players said that Cohen made them nervous, could not inspire them, and issued strange edicts, such as a prohibition on smiling. Smiling meant, he thought, that they did not want to win. But the mediocre record was also due to the inability to recruit top talent. Without waiting for the Tulane game, Huey fired Cohen. Cohen, his assistants, and the sportswriters covering the team were all infuriated.

At the game, Huey arrived with a huge LSU badge. Ignoring the governor's box seat on the Tulane side of the field, he went to the LSU locker room, ran out on the field with the LSU players, and stayed on the LSU bench or roamed the sidelines. At halftime, he blew off a scheduled appointment with Paramount News to have his picture taken, saying, "I'm running my team," returning to the locker room. At the end of the third quarter, Huey left the LSU bench and crossed the field resignedly to the governor's box because LSU was losing 12–7, earning a chorus of boos from the Tulane fans. LSU in the fourth quarter drove down the field and narrowly missed scoring when time ran out. This so-called moral victory thrilled LSU fans and emboldened the reporters in the jubilation after the game: "Are you going to fire that man after a game like that?" one reporter asked, grabbing Huey's suit lapels. The emotion overtook Huey, who thundered above the din that Cohen would stay and be given the resources to recruit more talent. LSU shortly hired an athletic director and additional assistant coaches. Recruiting star high-school players became routine.[16]

Although Huey began with the band and took charge of the football team, he had studied the entire school. Enrollment had doubled despite the Depression, but the school lacked the money for equipment and buildings. A law authorized construction of a medical school, but it was never built. Many qualified premed students could not get admitted to the only medical school in the state, Tulane.

Huey decided that LSU needed to be expanded and the medical school built. But there was no money to build the medical school. Huey told LSU personnel to "dare a bit": develop the plans, let the "people see what we propose, and we will find a way to do it."[17] One anti-Long leader said Huey developed the idea for the medical school years earlier,[18] which seems unlikely, but his plans must have been preceded by detailed study.

A month later, in December, Huey announced that LSU was going to build a new medical school. No one knew where Huey would get the money to fund the expansion, however. Even if the legislature were in session, Huey would have had difficulty persuading it to appropriate money for LSU.[19]

On January 3, 1931, the mysteries were revealed. In describing construction of the new capitol building, Huey declared that more land was required for it, and he authorized the purchase of real estate from LSU's old campus. The first purchase for $350,000 was used to construct the medical school. Shortly after this surprise, the LSU Board of Supervisors and the governing board of Charity Hospital in New Orleans met in a joint session at Huey's suite at the Roosevelt Hotel. They agreed to create a medical school and named Dr. Arthur Vidrine, the superintendent of Charity, as dean.

Conservatives thought Huey created the LSU medical school to spite Tulane for its failure to grant him an honorary degree, but Williams debunks this. In February 1931, however, Huey received an honorary doctor of laws degree from Loyola University in New Orleans.[20] Either George Wallace or Huey had conceived of an idea to compile the eight prior constitutions of Louisiana with extracts of the decided cases under the various provisions, permitting a historical comparison of the decided cases that would be useful to lawyers. In March 1930, it was printed and praised. It listed Huey as compiler. At that time, he said he had worked on it in spare moments while he was governor. In his autobiography, he claimed credit for undertaking "the work of combining [the cases] in substantive order" but admitted that the "credit for the compilation was due as much or more to those working under [his] direction."[21]

Loyola relied on this work to award him a doctor of laws degree, but the citation emphasized his political accomplishments more than the compilation. The Catholic university wanted to record its appreciation to the man who had given free textbooks to Catholic children.[22] After the award, he signed some pronouncements as "Huey P. Long, LL.D., Governor and Senator-Elect."

A *Times-Picayune* editor called Huey to complain about the effect of the new school on Tulane. Huey's response: "Raise all the hell you want to, print what you want to. But we're going to have that medical school and every qualified poor boy can go." A doctor who talked to Huey was "utterly astonished by his knowledge of medical history and what was needed to make a good medical school." Critics charged that it was theft for one state agency to make purchases from another. Afraid to sign the paperwork, agency official Jess Nugent asked Huey to sign it first. Huey demanded the documents and with a flourish signed his approval.[23]

From then on, Huey turned the accusation on its head. Naming himself the "official thief" for LSU, he made additional purchases of land, probably amounting to $9 million over time. LSU built a music and dramatic arts building, a French chateau for the Romance languages department, a fine arts building, dormitories for girls, a gymnasium, an enlarged football stadium, and a student center, the Huey P. Long Field House. By the end of 1935, LSU had constructed sixty-two new buildings out of the ninety-six planned in the early 1920s; in 1934–35, ten new buildings were constructed or extensively remodeled.[24] Huey planned the LSU buildings in detail.[25]

Appropriations from the state budget increased as well so that, by 1935, LSU had the "finest and largest physical plant in the South." The student body more than doubled to 4,300 by 1935, plus another 900 in the medical school. Another 1,000 students were added in 1935 on a work-for-tuition plan. On a newly purchased 664-acre tract near the campus, the students would grow, can, and market farm products. If his organization stayed in power another four years, Huey said, enrollment would increase to 15,000.[26] Tuition was low. Over half the students were on the state payroll. By 1937, LSU ranked twentieth in size among universities and eleventh among state universities. There were 7,000 students and 400 professors.[27]

To save money, dormitories were installed in the space under the football stadium stands. The stadium was expanded several times, along with the dormitories to house the growing enrollment. They were Spartan but occupied until the late 1980s.[28]

When Huey was inspecting construction of the women's dormitories, he saw the workers about to pour concrete for the sidewalks. Stop and wait a year, Huey said, and see where the students walk, and then pour the sidewalks on the paths that they naturally created. "The gently winding sidewalks of LSU still survive as a testimony to his lively and creative mind."[29]

Commandant Middleton and board member Everett showed Huey the design for a pool that would cost $75,000. Huey said he knew more about pools and sketched one that cost $500,000. During construction, he inspected it and asked if it was the biggest in the country. When told that the Naval Academy's pool was slightly longer, he turned to the foreman and told him to put ten more feet on the pool.

The quality of the faculty improved. Growing to 245 members (excluding the medical faculty of 149 members) from 168 when Huey was elected governor, many were recruited from northern schools with impressive reputations. One of Smith's best decisions was to promote Charles Pipkin as dean of the Graduate School, who "blew like a bracing current of arctic air into a campus which for decades had gone its languid way."[30] First-class writers and scholars such as Cleanth Brooks, Robert Penn Warren, and Robert B. Heilman were recruited. Brooks was hired in 1932, Warren in 1934, and Heilman in 1935. Recruited along with Heilman, from Harvard, was Thomas A. Kirby, from Johns Hopkins, and Nate Caffee, from the University of Virginia. Heilman wrote several essays about Huey's influence upon LSU.

LSU was advancing—"the Huey Long way of doing things"—while other universities were retrenching. "Warren had already published a biography and was publishing poems and essays; Brooks was writing essays. Likewise, people in other departments were writing. In some way the university had acquired members who wrote spontaneously, autonomously."[31]

The results "were a first-rate music school, a superior fine arts department, a flock of good appointments in various departments, and at least four new journals ( . . . in history, sociology, and political science), of which the outstanding one was the *Southern Review*. . . . The *Review* grew famous; the English department picked up luster from it and attracted some very good graduate students; and through it the university . . . gained respect in quarters that had hardly known of it before." The influx of talent created among the faculty many contrasts in aims, attitudes, and sensibilities, but they were "energizing differences" during "extraordinary times."[32]

Harold McSween agreed with Heilman and added:

> LSU's graduate school under Charles W. Pipkin, late a professor of political science at the University of Illinois and a Rhodes Scholar, had begun an ambitious doctoral regimen. . . . LSU . . . seemed a model in proliferating courses of study within a boundless curriculum. . . . The university operated a sugar school that attracted students from throughout the Caribbean. It engaged in agricultural research related to all the state's crops. It had begun initiatives in petroleum geology and engineering, aeronautical engineering (in addition to existing staple engineering curricula), speech, music, voice,

> theater, dance, and other fine arts. Its music department produced grand opera accompanied by its own symphony orchestra under directors of international acclaim. . . . [I]t was attracting outstanding young academicians in law, political science, sociology, economics, mathematics, physics, chemistry, astronomy, botany, biology, classical and modern languages (including medieval literature), philosophy, psychology, education, history, English.[33]

In addition to the *Southern Review*, Brooks and Warren coauthored *Understanding Poetry* (1938) and *Understanding Fiction* (1943), which became popular textbooks used in many universities across the country. They fostered a revolution in education.[34] (Warren's masterwork of fiction, *All the King's Men*, was published in 1946, after he had left LSU.) The Southern Historical Association was started in 1934 and began publishing the *Journal of Southern History*.[35] The LSU Press was established in 1935.

While the growth of the number of students, faculty, buildings, and budget can all be quantified, the unquantifiable psychological impact on students and faculty was also "tremendous," said Troy Middleton, and how could it not be, with the plethora of new buildings, faculty members, and students? Huey always mentioned LSU as one of the top universities in the country, along with Harvard, Yale, or Johns Hopkins, setting the standard for the university to live up to.

In 1964, Warren discussed Huey's impact on students: "Among the students there sometimes appeared, too, that awkward boy from the depth of the 'Cajun' country or from some scrabble-farm in North Louisiana, with burning ambition and frightening energy and a thirst for learning; and his presence there . . . was due to Huey, and to Huey alone. . . . For the 'better element' had done next to nothing in fifty years to get the boy out of the grim despair of his ignorance."[36]

The psychological impact extended beyond the school and the students. The *Southern Review*, for example, "won some honor among a laity of whom such reading might not be expected. Once a Baton Rouge printer showed [Heilman] with pride his own seven bound volumes of the *Review*. His sense of it as a regional achievement of national repute was surely not unique."[37]

The *Southern Review*—"one of the best literary magazines anywhere"—usually contained three or four academic discussions of contemporary issues, followed by fiction, criticism, poetry, and book reviews. The index of the *Southern Review* "would be a roll call of the best Southern writers of the century." New criticism by Kenneth Burke, Theodore Spenser, R. P. Blackmur,

Delmore Schwartz, and L. C. Knights all "achieved their reputations" largely through the *Review*. While those with established reputations such as T. S. Eliot, Wallace Stevens, and Aldous Huxley were published there, the early works of Mary McCarthy, Nelson Algren, Peter Taylor, W. H. Auden, John Berryman, and Randall Jarrell were published early in their careers or before they were known.[38]

Some have written that Huey's intense devotion to LSU allowed him to live out a college life as governor that he was denied when he was of college age. Others believed that he was laying the groundwork for future electoral success. Huey often talked to students about politics. Some believed that his football antics were motivated by the desire to get news coverage in the sports pages.

More probable is that after passage of his public improvement programs—the roads, bridges, new capitol, and airport—he was ready with some new ideas. These new ideas show personal growth. The candidate who criticized the idea of a college teaching fancy ways to farm became the foremost proponent of the university that taught fancy ways to farm and a lot of other fancy things, too.

While the medical school was being built, the press treated Huey favorably over the last months of 1930 and the early months of 1931.[39] On February 12, 1931, the assistant secretary of the Navy hosted Huey on the battleship USS *Wyoming*. No pajamas this time, just a blue suit.[40]

Favorable press was also generated—nationwide—from an unlikely source. Potlikker is the broth in the pot left over after cooking greens and salt pork. Usually eaten as soup with corn pone (meal mixed with salt and water baked into a hard patty), it is healthy but an acquired taste. It was a staple food for poor whites and African Americans. No one knows why Huey discussed it. Emphasizing it as a healthful food and cheap and providing further ethical proof of his kinship with rural voters, Huey described a stylish way of eating potlikker—dunking the cornpone instead of crumbling it into the soup broth—and food editor Julian Harris of the *Atlanta Constitution* saw some comedic potential. In a mock serious tone, Harris exclaimed that crumbling, rather than dunking, was the only way to eat it, and accused Huey of crumbling in private.

Huey matched his tone and defended his position—denying that he crumbled in private, for example, saying he had only demonstrated it to show faults in the technique—and the controversy took off. On the *Amos 'n Andy* radio show, Andy crumbled but Amos liked it either way; the St. Regis Hotel in New York added it to their menu; a Paris newspaper commented; Governor William H. (Alfalfa Bill) Murray of Oklahoma advocated crumbling for humans and dunking for dogs; Baptist governor Doyle E. Carleton of Florida recommended dunking on scriptural grounds, preferably "an absolute and complete submerging"; etiquette writer Emily Post refused to take a stand; and New York governor Franklin Roosevelt, seeking to burnish his credentials as a southerner (he vacationed in Warm Springs, Georgia, and said he was an adopted Georgian), wrote that the controversy should be referred to the Platform Committee of the Democratic National Convention.

At various intervals thereafter, Huey would refer to potlikker or serve it, at one point—with what must have been malicious glee—at a dinner with bankers. The publicity lasted for about three weeks, and Huey became friendly with food editor Harris, telling him the controversy was the only fun he had had since becoming governor.[41] Decades later, John Edge wrote his graduate thesis on this potlikker-cornpone debate.[42]

In March, Huey dedicated the Baton Rouge Airport and officiated at the air races.[43] On March 26, he convinced the Cleveland Indians to continue spring training in New Orleans instead of going to the West Coast, getting stock in the club in the process. Huey knew the club officials and players because they often stayed at the Roosevelt Hotel. The stories claimed that once Huey joined the team in Detroit because they were suffering a losing streak, after which they won twelve of their next thirteen games.[44] The papers even gave Huey a fluffy story when he played the "Jew's harp" for mansion visitors."[45]

In the shadow of the favorable press, the medical school was built with astonishing speed. Architects issued their plans in January, contracts were signed in March, construction began in April, and, in October, classes began. Dean Vidrine had recruited an impressive faculty, and the first class included 109 students, but that number doubled the next year and increased every year afterward. By 1935, over 900 students were enrolled. Enrollment at Tulane increased, too, corroborating Huey's belief that there was a need for two schools and that the South needed more doctors.

In comparison to the medical school or the quality of the faculty, the size of the LSU band was unimportant. But Williams perceptively notes that "a consummate politician would instinctively begin with something impressive, something that was also simple—something that anyone with eyes to see or ears to hear could understand."[46] Huey's actions—the band, the football team, and the medical school—were begun in November or December 1930, required advance study, and were rolled out after his smashing triumphs in the senatorial election and legislature. It was a coordinated approach designed to develop public support, give everyone in Louisiana a chance at a college education, and generate major improvements in public health. Exhibited at parades and football games, the big band symbolized to the average man that LSU was now a big-time university.

Critics state that Huey politicized LSU.[47] The new medical school was built in New Orleans. The Charity Hospital, with seventeen hundred beds available, provided the patients and the beds. Charity granted privileges to the doctors who practiced there, those from the new LSU School and from Tulane. Tulane doctors were allocated five hundred of Charity's beds, and the LSU administrators pledged not to disadvantage them. When Huey controlled the Board of Charity Hospital, however, he had control over the privileges of all doctors, including those at Tulane.

One of the best surgeons at Tulane, Dr. Alton Ochsner, famous throughout the South, wrote a letter to a friend stating that Huey was politicizing the hospital. Vidrine pilfered the letter from Ochsner's coat and gave it to Huey, who then ordered Charity to revoke Ochsner's privileges. No historian excuses this act. Criticized by others as being pro-Long, Williams said it revealed "something . . . sinister," a concept of Huey's that any program or institution he sponsored was personal to him. Through a psychological alchemy, an attack on Huey was an attack on his program and produced a self-defense response to remove the offender from any position Huey controlled.

Huey's retribution fed the myth that he created the LSU medical school to spite Tulane and created another myth that he banned all Tulane professors from Charity. Openly anti-Long doctors faced delays and interference, the type of hassle that civil service is designed to prevent but often doesn't. One intelligent Tulane professor asked Huey to write his request for privileges. In his letter on behalf of the professor, Huey noted that anything he did was construed as political. While politics could never be entirely absent from his mind, Huey concluded that political power had built Charity into a great hospital.[48]

Robert Mann comprehensively analyzed Huey's influence over Louisiana's higher education personnel. Figuring most prominently are Huey's selection of Smith, band leaders, and football coaches of LSU, and the ban on Ochsner. Huey also fired the president of Louisiana State Normal College, Victor L. Roy, and one faculty member, on recommendation of his sister, Olive, who taught there (*Kingfish U*, 39), and this was criticized during his impeachment; and he fired the replacement president (third cousin W. W. Tison) years later when he failed to reinstate the rebellious son of a political supporter (165). The reinstated student, William Dodd, later became lieutenant governor of Louisiana. Huey intervened in 1933 with LSU's law school to grant Kemble Kennedy a special degree not signed by the dean of the law school and contrary to the wishes of the faculty, something discovered in 1934, and he caused Dean Tullis's removal, all of which contributed to the law school being put on probation by the American Bar Association (223, 231) and censured by the American Association of Law Schools (244) in 1935. Huey tried but failed to fire President Edwin L. Stephens from Southwestern Industrial Institute at Lafayette (now the University of Louisiana (42)). Smith finessed Huey's early effort to fire more faculty and staff at LSU (97). Huey ousted the prior head of the Surgery Department at the LSU medical school in favor of the more qualified Urban Maes and recruited an outstanding tropical disease specialist (133).[49]

The ban against Dr. Ochsner failed. He was granted privileges at Charity two years after his ban when the accreditation authorities put their foot down. The reinstatement plus the recruitment of the outstanding surgeon, Maes, secured the medical school's accreditation. It received an A ranking.

There is the conundrum in a nutshell. Huey's opponents—in LSU, in the Charity Hospital, and elsewhere in the state—did not share his vision of Louisiana preeminent in education. Without Huey, the entire university would have remained small and second-rate, and every administration making a change is going to make mistakes, reward friends, and punish foes. Based on the condition of LSU, whoever controlled it before deserved to have it taken over and improved. Should opponents of these worthy goals have been permitted to retain their positions of influence to defeat or impede these goals? Should Huey have been able to remove qualified surgeons from a hospital because they criticized him? The answer is no.

Criticism because of the identity of the decision-maker is more problematic than criticism of decisions themselves, however. The ban on Ochsner would have been terrible if it had been made by Vidrine without Huey's input. The recruitment of Maes was not terrible simply because it was engineered by Huey. The appointment of Smith was within the ambit of Huey's duties as governor.

Williams's favorite anecdote about Huey and LSU, the one with which he started his chapter 18, had Huey describing Frederick the Great's decision to attack the city of Vienna. Meeting objections from his nitwit ministers, "Old

Fred" said his soldiers would take Vienna and his professors at Heidelberg would explain why. Closing, Huey said LSU had cost him $15 million, and his professors there would explain "why I do like I do."[50] Huey's belief that LSU belonged to him, if not sinister, was wrong: LSU, the Charity Hospital, indeed, every position in the state government, were public trusts.

The Frederick the Great story was a harmless manifestation of his erroneous belief, and the instances of interference with LSU were few, however. Fred Frey, "Mr. LSU," had experience with many LSU presidents and many Louisiana governors. There was less interference under Huey than under his anti-Long successors, he said.

Frey described a nationwide meeting of deans of colleges, hosted by LSU. At the last minute, Frey asked Huey if he would speak to the group. The legislature was in session so Huey could only spare twenty minutes, but he gave an extemporaneous speech advocating a college education for every qualified person that left the assembled deans spellbound and wishing they had a similar governor.[51]

The question of academic freedom is a twin concern of interference. But all kinds of questions of institutions, ideas, and philosophies took place at LSU. Observers believed there was more academic freedom at LSU than anywhere else in the country. Huey opposed loyalty oaths for colleges, saying radicals in colleges wouldn't do any harm and wishing the country had a few million radicals.[52] Huey said he allowed anti-Long faculty members to remain at LSU to maintain a diversity of opinion. An anonymous faculty survey reported no political interference.[53]

Heilman notes there was a faint "derivative air of quid-pro-quoism" emanating from some campus functionaries tied in with Huey's administration, but on "the other hand, there were campus characters who hated Huey and all his works and methods and successors." There were liberals, conservatives, communists, and Marxists.[54] Professor White quotes a minority opinion that: "I'll bet there wasn't dictatorship mentioned in sociology, government, anything."[55] Warren's lecture on Shakespeare's *Julius Caesar* was packed because of the means-and-ends parallels with Huey. His class paid close attention to it. Huey's daughter, Rose, sat in the back row and earned *A*s.[56]

In 1931, Professor Uhler of *Whangdoodle* fame wrote a novel, *Cane Juice.* Father Gassler, an anti-Long Catholic priest in Baton Rouge, denounced it as slimy animalism and filth in early October 1931. President Smith suspended Uhler. The Executive Committee of the Board of Regents dismissed him. Huey was on this committee, but it is unclear whether he attended the meeting. All university functionaries and legislators criticized the novel; none supported Uhler; none wanted to be seen as endorsing his description that Cajun boys and girls "made love" in "dark corners."[57]

Uhler wrote about these facts to his lawyer in early November without mentioning Huey. Later in November, however, Uhler reported that Huey had called one Mr. Heller and said that, if the archbishop made a gesture, the matter would be dropped. This doesn't establish that Huey had a hand in his termination; it was probably an effort to diffuse and rectify the situation after it came to his attention. Late in November and thereafter, however, Uhler said Huey ordered him fired to curry favor with Catholic voters right before the January 1932 elections.

In other contexts, Huey relished using his opponents against each other, and he might very well have enjoyed using his opponent Father Gassler against Kemble Kennedy's nemesis Uhler. The hesitation in judging this with finality results from Uhler's reliance on a political motive during the 1932 election that was never in doubt, although two of Huey's secondary candidates had French Catholic opponents; the natural desire for his defenders or groups like the ACLU, which backed Uhler, to select Huey as a big target to gain maximum publicity and engage someone who could reverse the decision; and the position of Thomas W. Cutrer, who had plenty of criticism of Huey, that it could not be shown that Huey ordered the suspension or termination. Russell Long denied that Huey had anything to do with it.[58] Assuming nevertheless that Huey caused the suspension or termination, he did so because of Father Gassler's denunciation, reflecting more conservative times. This was something any administrator sensitive to retaining public support would have done. While all administrators and politicians denounced the novel, academicians nationwide supported Uhler, and no public outcry took place. Uhler was reinstated in April 1932, after the January 1932 elections.[59]

Misplaced priorities are another criticism. Professor White points out that, in 1931, $14,345 were allocated for LSU's band while $837 were allocated to its law school and $493 to its graduate school.[60] No law school could run on $837, and no graduate school could exist on $493. Perhaps the law school and graduate schools only needed a small state subsidy, with tuition payments covering most costs.

By promoting the band and the football team, Huey developed fans of the school throughout the state, assuring its support. In 2014, *Forbes* magazine pointed out that even an exorbitant salary spent to recruit a great football coach was a sound investment. A good football team would improve the entire university, including its academic reputation.[61]

Two authors reported that the LSU pool was installed without drains.[62] Huey had engaged architects for the state capitol, the airport, the governor's mansion, and other structures, all of which were acclaimed. The missing drains cannot fairly be attributed to him.

Huey loved LSU and its students and was sincerely committed to their advancement. Professor Williams must have enjoyed interviewing former band members, football players, and coaches of the LSU football team. The stories he collected have a certain humorous pathos.

Huey often attended band practice and was popular with its members. Listening quietly at first, he would suggest changes of tempo or tone, and then wind up directing. Huey's favorite songs included "Harvest Moon," "Smoke Gets in Your Eyes," and "That Lonesome Road." The band was expanded to 250 pieces, the largest marching band in the nation.[63] Its uniforms of purple and gold were designed with Huey's approval into a flamboyant pattern. Huey once asked to hear a saxophone solo, but the band member who played that instrument was too nervous to perform. A clarinet player was secretly induced to play instead. Unaware of the deception, Huey characteristically pronounced the solo the best he had ever heard.[64]

In 1935, Castro Carazo from the Roosevelt Hotel was made bandleader. He and Huey composed two songs still played today: "Touchdown for LSU" and "Darling of LSU." The drum majors were equipped with huge shakos, and tall students were recruited for the job; the height combination was freakishly impressive. Huey sometimes conducted the band and led it at parades and football games, marching at the head between the drum majors. Once during Mardi Gras, he led the band in a parade and a policeman signaled him to stop. Raising his baton, Huey shouted, "Stand back! This is the Kingfish!"[65]

Huey recruited football players. One high-school star was brought to the governor's mansion and there said he was considering Centenary College instead of LSU. With disdain, Huey said Centenary only had one old teacher there who taught the Bible. Huey knew "a hell of a lot more about the Bible than he does" and assured the boy that, if he attended LSU, he would teach him the Bible. The boy chose LSU.

Huey would help injured players at halftime, wrapping bandages or holding ice packs. Three injured team members were invited to the mansion to recuperate, where he fed them steaks, turnip greens, cornbread, and pineapple upside-down cake. Once they had finished one steak, he would put another on their plate. They learned to eat slowly. One fullback gained fifty pounds and, when he returned to a game, collapsed after five plays.

The players who stayed in the mansion were sometimes woken up at 2 a.m. by Huey to talk football or give advice. Huey told one player, "For every crime there's a loophole if you know which book to grab. You're looking at a man who knows which book to grab."[66]

Huey prescribed a Winn Parish Epsom salt remedy for a player who had a boil between his legs. Drinking it induced nausea. The vomiting player was exiled from the LSU huddle, confusing the opposite team and some observers, who thought Huey had invented the new formation of the lonesome end.

Sometimes Huey set up chairs in the mansion ballroom and ran between them to demonstrate plays he designed. At halftime in a game against Arkansas, Huey gave the pep talk while Coach Cohen stood there speechless and at other times walked on the field to tell Cohen what plays to call. Once, when Cohen told his players how he would signal them the plays to run, Huey said, "And when I grab the coach around the neck, it means a forward pass." Huey called so many passes that Cohen got a stiff neck. At another game, when LSU was losing at halftime, he promised every player a job on the Highway Commission if they won (and they did).[67] Before another game, Huey told the team that it had to win, so he wanted no drinking: "not even two or three."[68]

If these stories induce a kind of wonderment at a grown man and governor bandaging college football players at halftime and giving them pep talks and leading a band, nevertheless his unrestrained authenticity also induces a grudging admiration. He didn't hold back. He did what he wanted to do. He followed his instincts.

A large gong was assembled at the university. When it rang, the students were to assemble so that Huey could announce and discuss the latest developments or plans for the university. It rang often as the changes and the construction accelerated. Note the huge amount of time and energy Huey spent communicating with the students and administration. He carried them along with him.

When LSU students came to his hotel room one year with a copy of the yearbook (the *Gumbo*) dedicated to him, he sat on his bed and cried. Professor White wrote that "deep down he loved his university and its student body.

. . . [H]e looked upon the students at LSU as his own."[69] Heilman wrote that the "remarkable influx" of talent "had its ultimate roots in the imaginativeness evident in [Huey's] very complex makeup."

"It was an imaginativeness which could grasp ends beyond profit and power," one that "gave him visions of excellence in LSU, an excellence beyond band and football fame."[70] Harold McSween wrote from a perspective of decades that, "while it would challenge any scholar . . . to allocate academic credit between Huey, who fostered the university environment, and the scholars who actually did the work," nevertheless, "In retrospect, [the] burgeoning LSU of the depression years seems one of [the] strong man's signal achievements."[71]

About seven years after Huey's death, his opponents were in power, and James Monroe Smith was in disgrace. Fred Frey was asked to become president, but when he bridled at interference from the new "reform" governor, the offer was withdrawn, and someone else was selected.

The *Southern Review* was terminated (revived only in 1964), notwithstanding that the June 10, 1940, issue of *Time* magazine hailed it as the best journal in the English language and at the center of America's efforts to maintain precious traditions of art, scholarship, and culture. LSU's Board of Supervisors declined to renew sponsorship of the *Journal of Southern History* and the *National Mathematics Magazine.* Robert Penn Warren left for Minnesota because LSU would not match its salary offer that would have required a $200 raise.[72] Later Warren transferred to Yale and became the first poet laureate of the United States. Heilman left for the University of Washington. Cleanth Brooks left for Yale. The pool Huey designed is now a lawn.

Heilman denies that the anti-Longs burst the bubble on the energy and accomplishments of LSU. Professor Williams arrived in 1942.[73] But no leader in Louisiana thereafter spoke of LSU in the same sentence as Yale and Harvard. The band and the football team remain among the best in the nation. Later Louisiana leaders missed the whole point. Huey's showmanship was a means to an end, not an end in itself.

Cleanth Brooks, Heilman, and others opposed the presidential choice of Huey's opponents, the reformers who won election in Louisiana in 1940. Heilman commemorated their visit to a member of the board to lobby for their choice. Not only were they overruled, with the board member insisting that "he had the best interests of the university at heart," but

> he took a tack that was devastating in effect, though I am unsure whether he just fell into it, made honest use of a good thing, or took a deadpan demonic revenge for our bothering him. Having found that we professed literature, he took on the air of a kindly benefactor. . . . Then he revealed to us a manuscript or privately printed pamphlet, the poetry of his wife, and introduced us to the maker herself. . . . On the scene I limped in clichés while Cleanth managed benign words, in which the chilly critical spirit was somewhat muffled in the folds of courtesy.

One observer said the new appointment was fortunate, however. If he had not been appointed to head LSU, he would have been sent to Europe and set back the World War II effort of the Allies by two years. The appointee who presided over the budget cuts and loss of faculty talent? Colonel Campbell B. Hodges.[74]

# Fifteen

# THE VISION THING

Occasionally political matters interrupted Huey's LSU and public relations activities. When James Aswell died, Huey backed John Overton for Aswell's congressional seat, and Overton won the election in April.[1] Huey had a political discussion with Mayor Walmsley, but no agreement was reached.[2] Walmsley was frustrated: "[Huey] will be the whole show or none." Equally harsh, Huey denied a suggested merger with the Ring: "I won't have it."[3]

In April, because of the legislative investigation into dreadful conditions at Angola prison, Huey appointed LSU's business manager, R. L. "Tighty" Himes, to run it, accepting Clay Dugas's resignation for reasons of "private business." Huey had prearranged the private sector job for Dugas.[4] Huey generally found replacements before any resignation to preempt job seekers ("Oh, I didn't know you were interested in that job; I've already promised it to ——.").[5] Huey "directed Mr. Himes to operate the penitentiary 100 per cent on the basis of efficiency. . . . He can fire and hire anybody he chooses, and I will help him [do] it. I have appointed him [because] . . . he guarded every fund and property [of] the university for 33 years. His careful manner . . . has given him the name of 'Tighty' on the campus, and that is the kind of a man we need at the penitentiary."[6]

Under Himes, private companies contracted for prison labor. Nondangerous inmates were released early. The number of escapes declined because, contrary to the ideas of reformers, prisoners again wore stripes rather than street clothes. Some barbarous practices were eliminated, some services improved, and a few prisoner education and training programs began. Flogging and inadequate training of guards continued. Huey's supporter Abe Shushan disliked Himes and tried to get him fired, but Huey insulated Himes from politics. After losing money for years, Angola almost became self-sustaining.[7]

In June 1931, with Walmsley's support, the state Democratic Committee elected Huey to replace Colonel Robert Ewing, who had died.[8] By July 2, 1931, after four straight days of talks with Walmsley, Huey got the right to name three of the seven state Senate candidates, eight of the seventeen Louisiana House of Representative candidates from the city, and the right to name the statewide Democratic ticket. Huey contended that, because the Old Regulars carried the city against him, they should name most of the representatives and senators unless they were trying to destroy him. Later, Huey found several of the Ring's candidates objectionable on this ground, and they realized "they had been euchred."[9] Huey was a graceless winner, saying the Old Regulars had to give in because their own people would have exterminated them, whereas Walmsley refused to comment because it was too hot to talk politics. Huey also agreed to keep his hands off the mayoral election of 1934.[10]

The biggest leverage Huey used was the expected continuation of the previous year's state financial benefits extended to New Orleans. Huey's popularity, the positive press he was receiving, and the absence of controversies also contributed to his leverage. Eugene Stanley, the district attorney, had indicted Walmsley for misallocating funds, and that may have helped, although nothing came of it.[11] Naming the city's representatives to the legislature improved Huey's control of it *independent* of the Old Regulars. It may have been the single most important negotiation he ever won.[12]

The peace and unity in Louisiana allowed Huey to expand his influence beyond the state. In early August, he intervened behind the scenes on behalf of Mike Conner, a candidate for governor of Mississippi. Robert Brothers and Frank Odom were sent into the state to help Conner develop local organizations, and Huey called Mississippi leaders, urging them to support Conner. Seymour Weiss traveled to Jackson, Mississippi, to help Conner's headquarters operation. Conner's opponent, Hugh L. White, a wealthy lumberman, attacked Huey. Huey "answered in kind to attacks made and at times made statements about them without waiting for them to attack [him] further." White led Conner in the primary but lost to him in the runoff election.[13]

---

Later in August, Huey extended his influence throughout the South when he intervened to protect cotton farmers, significant because "[m]ore people in the South owed their daily existence to cotton than to any other enterprise." Large crops, rising costs, and foreign competition diminished profits even during the prosperous 1920s, and the boll weevil infestation drove the costs of raising cotton up and the yield and quality of the cotton down. The Great Depression diminished income from cotton lint and seed, for example, from $1.5 billion to $826 million.[14] In 1931, cotton prices dropped to a new low, about 6.3 cents per pound for middling-grade lint cotton, down from 20 cents in 1930, and 40 cents in 1920. Six cents per pound was below the cost of growing it.[15]

Then on August 8, the U.S. Department of Agriculture forecast a yield of 15.5 million bales for 1931. There were already 8 million bales of surplus cotton on hand. This mere prediction drove cotton option prices down and some cotton-state senators crazy. Many criticized the *forecast,* and many threatened investigations because of it, but the crop came in at 17 million bales. Brokers "expressed fears the decline might reach 2 cents a pound." In New Orleans cotton prices closed down 104 to 111 points, "or from $5.29 to $5.55 a bale less." The anticipated loss was $150,000,000 in cotton and another $100,000,000 to dependent businesses.[16]

President Hoover's federal Farm Board suggested that farmers *voluntarily* plow up every third row of cotton. This would cost farmers uncompensated time, money, and effort—after plowing and cultivating—and it could not be policed. One writer said that only a "nitwit would destroy every third row of cotton" while people needed clothes.[17]

Huey was out of step, temporarily: he was damned if he knew what to do about the problem; the Farm Board proposal was "pretty good." Most cotton-state governors opposed it. Bilbo wanted to leave every third row in the fields; Murray wanted to prevent one-third from being ginned; and Carleton wanted to provide storage. South Carolina's Blackwood, however, suggested a prohibition on planting any cotton for a year.[18]

Coincidentally, north Louisiana planters proposed this to their congressman, John Sandlin. The surplus would disappear, and prices would rise, they thought, if cotton planting were prohibited for a year. Studying the plan for twenty-four hours, Huey decided to back it and, once he backed it, he backed it all the way. On August 16 he invited cotton-state officials to New Orleans to consider the plan.[19] Huey's argument: farmers still had this year's crop, and they should keep it until the results of the meeting were known. A surplus of

15 million bales would exist after this year, so that with a year off there would still be enough cotton for the whole world to use. The "Lord told us to lay off raising these crops one year out of every seven." The cotton industry was financed through New Orleans, making it a fit site for the meeting.[20]

Huey gave radio speeches on Will Henderson's station, and James Thomson of the *New Orleans Item* wrote favorable stories and editorials. Thomson, a former opponent, saw this along with Huey's advocacy of flood-control legislation as evidence that he was progressive.[21]

The governors of Arkansas and South Carolina, Georgia commissioner of agriculture Eugene Talmadge, and the legal advisor of Governor Murray of Oklahoma attended. Huey sent an airplane to Austin to bring Texas lieutenant governor Edgar E. Witt. Arkansas senator Caraway telegrammed Huey that he liked the idea but doubted that all the necessary states would support it.[22]

At the meeting, Louisiana political foes sat side by side to support the plan. The attendees endorsed it if states that produced 75 percent of the cotton agreed. A competing resolution for acreage reduction was voted down after Huey as chairman announced, "We are going to vote that down."[23]

The 75 percent proviso was directed at Texas, which produced about 33 percent of the cotton in the United States. Texas governor Ross Sterling secretly opposed the plan but declined to attend the meeting, using noncommittal political boilerplate extolling the "great cotton industry."[24] Sterling declined to introduce the first law. It was Huey's baby, and he should "wash it first." Huey responded: "All right old boy we are getting ready to . . . wash the baby and dress it. It will be on your desk and yell Da Da before the week's out."[25]

Huey called the legislature into session. To demonstrate bi-factional support, Huey's opponents introduced the bill. It passed unanimously[26] in both houses. Wakened in the governor's mansion after midnight, Huey signed the bill while wearing a cotton nightshirt in a bed with cotton sheets. After the photographers left, he said, "Now I can take this damn thing off," and changed into silk pajamas. As a cotton "super patriot," he ordered cotton stationery for Louisiana's government. O. K. Allen, Seymour Weiss, and Huey's son Russell then flew in a chartered plane to present the bill to Sterling in Texas. Chasing Sterling from Austin to Houston, Allen gave him Huey's baby "all washed, powdered, and wrapped in a cotton dress."[27] Sterling responded that the plan lacked legislative support.[28]

Huey spoke over the radio nightly, reaching audiences throughout the South. Listeners expressed support and sent donations, which Huey returned.

Enough interest developed to force Sterling to call the Texas legislature into session. Sterling stood about six feet tall and weighed 250 pounds. A successful oilman, in 1930 he also owned a Houston newspaper and interests in banks, railroads, and real estate. The farmers had reason to think he might help. When oil prices had declined, the Texas legislature passed oil production controls and Sterling enforced them by declaring martial law. Cotton-dependent businesses in Texas (cotton ginners, banks, railroads) disliked the holiday idea, however. Huey asked Sterling to listen to downtrodden farmers.[29]

A crowd of twelve thousand Texans descended on the capitol in Austin and invited Huey to speak. Huey wouldn't let Cyr function as governor, so he sent a radio technician to erect amplifiers and other speaking equipment, including a direct phone line to Louisiana. Huey drove five hours to Shreveport to speak in an auditorium to five hundred people, with his remarks broadcast to the crowd, including Governor Sterling, in Texas. Arriving, Huey shook hands, took off his collar and necktie, and scattered notes about the table. In Texas, Gene Talmadge warmed up the crowd. Huey began at 8 p.m. While he was talking, Huey held a phone to his ear while Seymour Weiss, present with the Texas crowd, reported its reaction.[30] Huey was cheered repeatedly. Huey asked those who favored the plan to stand and, when told by phone that they all stood, said: "that's the spirit. You all stood." The intimate interplay between Huey and the audience despite the separation of three hundred miles was an "awesome display of intelligence and ability."[31]

Sterling was now forced into the open. He said the government should not tell farmers what they could plant and grow. Sterling invoked the memories of Texas independence heroes Sam Houston and Stephen Austin to repel the interference of the governor of Louisiana and blamed President Hoover for the difficulties.[32] The audience would have none of it. Sterling was booed and hissed. Accusatory shouts and cheers of "Hurrah for Long" and threats to egg him caused him to sit down, "a thoroughly defeated and dejected man."[33]

Huey plunged ahead with his campaign, hindered by his inability to leave the state. North Carolina's governor wanted foreign nations included.[34] Georgia's governor Russell favored it if Texas would. Mississippi governor Bilbo favored acreage reduction.[35] Alabama's governor was dubious, but other officials favored it. Nightly radio broadcasts during the first week of September earned Huey front-page press notice throughout the South. Mass meetings were scheduled in Arkansas, Georgia, and other states at which overwhelming support was voiced.[36] Telegrams and letters, sixteen hundred in all, poured in, two-thirds from outside Louisiana.[37]

By September 7, Huey thought Mississippi, Alabama, South Carolina, North Carolina, and Arkansas would back his plan.[38] South Carolina adopted it.[39] It all depended on Texas. "We are at the threshold of victory and of relief . . . if Texas does not spoil the whole problem by [passing] a half and half measure, which will be less than no act at all."[40]

A swarm of lobbyists descended on Austin. Huey charged that they blandished legislators with wine, women, and money. Unlike his accusations against the Louisiana legislature in 1916, these charges neither prompted nor accompanied a turnabout. Texas legislators were outraged. They called Huey a liar, a jackass, a coward, an ignoramus, a buffoon, a meddler, and poor white trash. On September 16, the Texas legislature killed the bill and passed resolutions denouncing Huey.[41] Huey conceded defeat.

Huey's plan was popular, better than acreage reduction, and bold. Some critics wonder how his plan would have helped the tenant farmer or thought that tenant farmers would have formed groups of roving brigands, but this assumes that no crop at all would be raised if cotton were not. Senator Harry Byrd of Virginia later stated that land suitable to grow tobacco and cotton would grow peanuts.[42] Substitute crops would have a collateral benefit of diversification. One farmer wrote Huey that tenant farmers would benefit:

> I . . . have about 3,000 acres of land leased. . . . On this farm, I have about 340 negroes. At the present price of cotton and seed my negroes cannot pay their debts, not to mention the purchasing of clothes which they are badly in need of. If your plan goes through . . . it will mean a better price for this year's crop. . . . [E]very family on it will live better than they ever have before. All of them have hogs and cows and chickens. They can raise an acre of Irish potatoes and five acres of sweet potatoes and five acres of peas and as much pumpkins and squash and other vegetables as they can put away.[43]

Acreage reduction with a continued decline in prices hurt the tenant farmer more.[44]

Other critics said the holiday would open U.S. markets to foreign cotton.[45] If foreign supplies were the threat, however, then acreage reduction made no sense either. If there were 8 million bales of surplus cotton already and 17 million bales on the way, there was enough stock in the United States to supply consumers for two years without any imports. It is true that the price would not rise as much if imports were offered at a lower price, but considering the supply available, the farmers would work for one year, not two, to supply the demand at whatever the price in the United States ended up being.

The arguments hostile to the plan seem to clothe a more instinctive or reflexive hostility to the government telling property holders what to do. Huey's justification for the legislation was to exterminate the boll weevil, "Anthonomus grandis, bohemian," to eradicate cotton root rot, "phymatatrichum omnivorum duggar," as well as to aid the cotton industry.[46] Later in the New Deal, legislation provided that portions of crops were to be obtained by the government pursuant to set aside programs without direct compensation in order to reduce supply and maintain prices, a program recently ruled unconstitutional.[47] Under Huey's plan, the farmers always owned their crops, and it would be difficult to deny the government's police power to exterminate hazards to property. The extermination of the boll weevil would have reduced costs to farmers by 25 to 40 percent.[48]

Without Huey's plan, the price declined to 4.6 cents per pound.[49] Huey's stature improved all over the South, except perhaps in Texas, where even a supporter asked Huey to apologize to allay the bitterness from his charges. Huey declined.[50]

In the words of Pete Daniel, Huey's plan represented a "tantalizing what-might-have-been in Southern history." It was "the last chance that farmers had to solve the overproduction crisis before the federal government became their landlord."[51] Huey said that it was "pretty well known that I have suffered almost every reverse that a living human could endure and survive. But . . . I have never been struck to the heart as I have been in the last twenty-four hours when . . . I saw the veil of doom and distress maliciously forced upon the families of two million Southern farmers." The partial acreage reduction law of Texas was "a mere faked delusion through which they hope to escape the wrath of an afflicted people."[52]

The national press noticed,[53] but Huey denied national ambitions because no one who advocated wealth redistribution could be nominated by either political party, and therefore he was "nothing" beyond Louisiana.[54] Humorist Will Rogers wrote that, if Huey's comments about the Texas legislature were false, they would have laughed it off instead of attacking him. Huey had "the only real cotton idea that's been suggested." In Louisiana, some former opponents in the river parishes now saw him as crusading, gutsy, and progressive. Grateful for the *Item*'s approval, Huey deducted the cost of the *Item*'s subscription from state employees' paychecks so they could read the paper every day.[55]

---

The man who kept Huey prisoner within Louisiana, Paul Cyr, cramped opportunities for Huey to reach regional and national audiences and prevented him getting sworn in on time with other newly elected senators in January 1932. Huey had to send a representative to a regional flood-control conference in Chicago hosted by Mayor Big Bill Thompson.[56] In May 1931, Huey couldn't attend a bridge dedication connecting Louisiana with Mississippi at Vicksburg.[57]

Cyr ruined Huey's plan to publicize LSU in New York, coincident with a football game between LSU and West Point. The *Louisiana Progress* announced in August 1931 that three thousand LSU students would travel by special train through St. Louis, Cleveland, Niagara Falls, and New York City, with the band parading in each city. In New York, the students would attend a Broadway play.

Alas, Cyr refused to renounce his right to function as governor if Huey stepped out of the state, despite students who begged him to relent. Instead, Huey's wife, three children, and Alice Lee Grosjean led the students on a more limited journey. The band was overwhelmed in New York City, and the team lost the game to West Point on November 7, twenty to nothing.[58]

When LSU lost the last game of the season to Tulane, thirty-four to seven, Huey again fired Cohen, this time for good, and searched for a big-name coach.[59] Meanwhile, Tulane went to the Rose Bowl, where they played a great game but lost to the University of Southern California. They received a hero's welcome from Huey and other officials upon their return.[60]

When Huey was elected to the Senate in 1930, he sent his certificate of election to Washington. In October 1931, Cyr filed suit claiming that Huey had thereby vacated the governorship. Other anti-Long leaders thought the same thing,[61] and there was no harm in asking a court to decide the question. Before obtaining a court ruling, however, Cyr took the oath of governor and proclaimed that he was governor. Thereafter he failed to perform any duties or to accept a paycheck as lieutenant governor.

Conscious of rumors that Cyr was recruiting an army, when Huey learned of Cyr's proclamation he panicked. Grabbing a pistol and his favorite reporter, Chick Frampton, Huey drove like a maniac to Baton Rouge, narrowly avoiding several collisions and scaring Frampton. General Fleming summoned the National Guard to protect the capitol, but when Huey arrived he said it wasn't needed. Instead, the state police added machine guns at the capitol doors.[62]

The humor of Cyr's unilateral decision to swear himself in as governor dawned on unemployed bill collector Walter Aldrich. He appeared before a notary public and took the gubernatorial oath. And his idea was contagious. In cities across the state, men appeared before notaries to take the oath. Louisianans merrily greeted each other on the street over the next few days with "Hello Governor."[63]

The national press soon discovered this "opera bouffe."[64] Their stories prompted men throughout the country to swear themselves in as governor of Louisiana.[65] Louisianans were amused, but the controversy imperiled the sale of highway bonds. Huey had to cancel the sale of $12 million in bonds on October 29, blaming Cyr.[66]

Beyond seeing the humor of what Cyr had done, Huey considered its legality. Hadn't Cyr abandoned his position as lieutenant governor? Huey had Alvin O. King, president of the State Senate, sworn in as lieutenant governor because he was next in line for that job. This set off another swearing-in craze, this time for lieutenant governor. A Mr. E. H. Reed asked to take the oath as lieutenant governor because, if the state were to have three governors, each one should have a lieutenant governor.[67]

Huey then countersued Cyr. Cyr had failed to perform any duties as lieutenant governor or collect his pay and had acquiesced from Election Day in 1930 until 1931 in Huey's retention of the governorship. The U.S. Senate, not the courts, was charged with evaluating the qualifications of its members, and Huey cited historical examples of governors who had delayed taking office as senator.[68] Arguing the case himself on November 3, Huey won dismissal of Cyr's suit.[69] On appeal in December, again argued by Huey, the Louisiana Supreme Court reserved ruling until after the January election.

The last impediment to taking the national stage was thus the January 1932 election. After an agonizing consideration of his options, Huey named O. K. Allen as his gubernatorial candidate and John B. Fournet for lieutenant governor.[70] Allen was weak in mind and character, dominated by Huey at work and his wife at home. He could not remember names and faces. He was awkward meeting people. At a rally, Allen circulated among the people saying "Hello," and when he met a younger boy he said in a friendly way, "How's your father?" The boy said he had died. Allen moved on but somehow in circulating among the crowd came upon the boy again. "How's your father?" Allen asked. "He's still dead," replied the boy.

Allen would do what Huey wanted, however. Huey could go to Washington as a senator without relinquishing his authority in Louisiana. Earl Long later said that a leaf blew in the window of the governor's office; Allen signed it. Anti-Long Mason Spencer once joked that he had less influence with the administration than Allen.[71] It was unusual but not unprecedented for a U.S. senator to remain leader of a state political organization. The LaFollettes in Wisconsin and the Byrds in Virginia did it.

Earl Long decided that, with Huey on his way to Washington, he could begin an elective office career. Earl asked Huey to support him for lieutenant governor or, alternatively, not to oppose him. Huey refused, telling him he was already criticized for having too many relatives on the payroll and could not afford to have two candidates from Winn Parish. This was not the real reason. The LaFollette brothers, Phil and Bob, dominated Wisconsin politics at the same time, one as governor and one as senator. The real reason for the refusal—understood by both men—was that Earl in Louisiana, not Huey in Washington, would dominate Allen. Huey didn't trust Earl either, with good reason, if only the example of Earl's secret opposition to the new capitol is considered.

Overcome by ambition, jealousy, or pride, Earl ran anyway, claiming that Huey's alliance with the Old Regulars was the reason.[72] Julius and his sisters backed him: "Brothers and sisters, first aggravated at [Huey's] failure to support [Earl], later became angry until finally well-defined and displayed articles of the press fanned their anger into flame and then to a madness," in Huey's view, such that the "distracted and almost annihilated opposition took heart."[73] One sister later conceded they were "premature" in backing Earl: "We had growing pains."[74]

The "almost annihilated" opposition had two candidates for governor, however: Dudley J. LeBlanc, still on the Public Service Commission, and George Guion, a New Orleans lawyer. Paul Cyr announced for the office, won the endorsement of Senator Broussard, but then dropped out. In November, the Old Regulars endorsed Huey's slate, dooming his opponents.

In December, one of Huey's campaign trips was interrupted by an early morning visit from a group of distressed New Orleans bankers. A bank in Jackson, Mississippi, was about to fail. Mississippi was planning to declare a bank holiday. This would precipitate a run on Louisiana banks. Cursing, Huey asked if "you insane men" had "done anything about this yet?" They hadn't. Some of the bankers turned to exit. "Oh, no, you ain't! You crazy men ain't going nowhere! When a man goes crazy, regardless of how big he is, he's got to be protected from doing harm to himself and others." Ordering Joe Messina to stand guard, Huey retreated to his bedroom. Remembering New York City banker Charles McCain, whom he had met during a courtesy call at the governor's mansion weeks earlier, Huey called him, and McCain called the head of the National Credit Corporation (NCC). Huey asked Seymour Weiss to send up food to the bankers to "help Joe Messina hold up the gold standard." When the NCC official called, Huey convinced him to rescue the Mississippi banks.

On another occasion, Huey learned that a bank in Lafayette was in trouble. Huey drove all night and sat behind the desk of the bank's president the next morning. A line of customers had formed, and the first man asked to withdraw $18,000. Huey waved a state check for $265,000 and said he was there first, and the state had priority, but he would leave the state's money in if the customers would. They did. The bank was saved when other banks helped it. Healthy banks often helped their weaker brethren or took them over[75]—with Huey's supporters sometimes given an inside track—because, if they didn't, they feared that Huey's state bank examiner would close them. Sometimes Huey would send funds to shore up a bank by police escort with sirens blazing.[76] Louisiana had fewer bank failures than almost any other state in the country.[77]

The theme of Huey's campaign was to "complete the work." Allen spoke on their tour, but Huey spoke last and longest and didn't hesitate to interrupt Allen's speeches to suggest new themes. Earl and Julius claimed credit for all of Huey's successes and called him an ungrateful coward. Sister Lucille compared Huey to Judas Iscariot. Huey was the "better brother" by not returning criticism but couldn't resist a story. Many years ago, at an all-day church picnic, the babies were put under a tree while dinner was served. A violent storm erupted, causing everyone to clear the table and grab their babies. One baby wasn't claimed, an ugly baby that wouldn't stop bawling. Huey's mother felt sorry for it, retrieved it, and adopted it. That was Earl.

LeBlanc was a good speaker in English or French. He lacked a record to run on during his tenure on the Public Service Commission, hampered by Huey's veto of its appropriations. Although Huey was confident that he could beat LeBlanc for governor, he was a foe that he would later want to defeat as commissioner on the Public Service Commission. LeBlanc had formed a mutual aid society to manage funeral and burial expenses. Huey planted a spy in the company. When a member died, the living members would be assessed a fee, and LeBlanc's company arranged the burial. *Louisiana Progress* cartoons disclosed that the burial society interred Black people and that LeBlanc divided the profits with Black partners.[78] The shrouds were recycled, moreover, horrifying many of his Black members. LeBlanc's newspaper showed cartoons of Huey distributing free schoolbooks to Black people, pictured in demeaning caricatures.

In Bunkie, the two rivals set up their sound trucks about seventy yards apart, turned up the amplifiers, and for two hours exchanged insults. It was entertaining but not edifying. The most quoted remark from that night was Huey's: "You pronounce LeBlanc's name by trying to grunt like a hog and changing your mind when you're half-way through."

LeBlanc's main issue was that he had served in World War I, whereas Huey had not. He attacked Allen Ellender for selling the state penitentiary "inferior" potatoes at "superior" prices. LeBlanc promised state pensions and to rid the state of Huey and his blood-sucking, tax-eating, bribe-giving, and bribe-taking crowd. LeBlanc gave over five hundred speeches during the campaign and nine on the day before the election. Huey responded that LeBlanc had only served a brief time in the Army, did not serve overseas, or even get kicked by a mule or bit by a horsefly.[79]

Candidate Guion, Earl's running mate, accused Huey's administration of corruption and promised honest government, but nothing else. The cotton holiday plan, he stressed, was unconstitutional.

On January 19, 1932, Huey's ticket crushed its opponents, 215,000 votes to just 110,000 for LeBlanc and 54,000 for Guion. Huey's slate ran better in New Orleans (70.6 percent) than in the rest of the state (51.5 percent). LeBlanc reduced Huey's margin in French-speaking parishes.

The votes of two parishes illustrate opposite points. St. Bernard Parish voted unanimously, all 3,152 votes, for Huey's ticket, whereas the census takers had found only 2,510 eligible (that is, white) voters. Huey said some voters were in houseboats deep in the swamps and thus not discovered by census takers, but many were fraudulent. Before the election, the sheriff told Huey that the opposition would get two votes. When the returns arrived, Huey said, "What the hell happened to those two fellows?" The sheriff replied, "They changed their minds at the last minute."[80]

In Grant Parish, previously a Long stronghold, LeBlanc outpolled Huey's ticket. Sindler attributed this to the Old Regular alliance,[81] but Hair dug deeper to discover why. In spring 1931, LeBlanc's brother and a campaign aide, Joe Boudreaux, were beaten up by Robert and O. R. Brothers, working for Huey. The pro-Long judge and sheriff had the LeBlanc partisans jailed. A grand jury, empaneled to indict them, refused. The repudiation of Huey's ticket, knowing LeBlanc would lose and that their parish might lose state benefits, was courageous, but also belies that election fraud permeated all election results.

Twenty-eight of the House incumbents were defeated, most of them anti-Long. Other anti-Long legislators declined to run. Oilman James Noe defeated a candidate who had voted to impeach Huey. Noe became a Long leader in the state Senate.[82]

Two days after the election, the Louisiana Supreme Court dismissed Cyr's suit as moot by a four-to-three vote.[83] Huey said he was going to remain as governor, however, because of the pending sale of highway bonds.[84] Then Huey suddenly left for Washington on January 23, 1932, with his wife, friends, and politicians. As soon as Huey was sworn in as junior U.S. senator from Louisiana, word was relayed to an open phone in Baton Rouge so that Alvin King, now the lieutenant governor, could immediately take the oath as governor. The secretary of state refused Cyr's subsequent tender of the oath of office because Alvin King's oath was already on file. Traveling to Baton Rouge, Cyr again took the oath of governor, set up in the Heidelberg hotel, and proclaimed that King was usurping the office and headed a rebel government.[85]

In response, guards were doubled around all state offices and Huey rushed back to New Orleans from Washington, arriving on January 29.[86] He needed to deal with Cyr, met with bankers about road construction bonds, and said he had to move his family out of the mansion in Baton Rouge.[87] The bankers were worried about issuing $35,000,000 more bonds while Cyr was contesting the governorship. Huey called the Heidelberg's owner and had Cyr kicked out.[88] Cyr moved to a dilapidated hotel and proclaimed that the people should call him there. No one did. Forlorn now, he filed a new lawsuit against Governor King that dragged on until his plea was denied.[89]

The highway bonds were offered for sale. Observers were confident that Huey would find a way to continue the program, given that the "easy sledding" Louisiana experienced during the Great Depression was attributed to the expansive highway program.[90]

On Saturday, January 30, in a lightning-fast sequence of events, Huey scanned a list of residences for sale sent over by a New Orleans politician, selected one, summoned Mrs. Long to join him from Baton Rouge to look at it and, when she approved, had the lawyers draft the purchase paperwork on Sunday, January 31, before he returned to Washington that night. Maestri financed the home, a spacious one on Audubon Boulevard in the upscale Garden District. Rumors were that it was acquired from an unlucky gambler.[91]

After ridding himself of Cyr, Huey sped back to Washington, but returned to Louisiana and missed Senate sessions between February 5 and 24. Some have suggested that Huey was homesick. Huey's wife and Alice Lee Grosjean stayed in Louisiana. Grosjean had expected to accompany him to Washington,[92] but Huey was told he should not give Washington gossipers a female secretary to discuss.[93] Given his travels throughout the South while he was a salesman and his frequent trips to New York as a lawyer, it is doubtful that homesickness caused his return. But some of his activities gave that impression.[94]

He led the LSU band in a Mardi Gras parade in New Orleans on February 10 and stole the spotlight at a New Orleans charity golf tournament on February 11.[95] When his partner, the great Walter Hagen, gave him some advice, Huey said don't you think you better let me play this ball? Hagen doubled over with laughter that spread in a roar through the gallery.[96] That evening, he "electrified" an LSU banquet at Baton Rouge with an unexpected appearance.[97] On February 22, he traveled to Oklahoma and regaled an audience of Young Democrats with a twenty-minute speech recounting stories from his semester at the University of Oklahoma.[98]

Huey addressed some serious business during this time, however. He had the state Central Committee elect the delegates to the upcoming Democratic National Convention. The same procedure as in 1928 was used. Some selections were revealed on Friday, February 12,[99] but forty-eight delegates and alternates, ten presidential electors, and at-large committeemen were chosen on Saturday, February 13. A proposal to hold a convention on June 1 to elect delegates was voted down.[100] Huey controlled the delegation, still uncommitted. Ex-governors J. Y. Sanders Sr., Ruffin Pleasant, and John M. Parker were again omitted. Some of the selected delegates later resigned, asserting that a convention should have been held.[101]

As Huey lingered in Louisiana, his success there, especially compared to Governor Parker, is worth lingering over. Consider their vision, personalities, knowledge, opposition, and tactics.

*Vision.* Parker deserves credit for finding a new, more spacious campus for LSU, assuring it a source of revenue from the severance tax, and for raising consciousness about the value of education. But his vision for LSU was a maximum enrollment of three thousand students. Parker's gravel road construction program exceeded other southern states, but he envisioned only gradual progress—no bonds—and few paved roads were built.

Parker awakened the desire for reform, but Huey had the greater, more politically appealing vision: New Orleans doubling in population and battling to become the number-one U.S. port; LSU becoming one of the best universities in the nation; Louisiana citizens getting educated, transacting business on modern roads, with access to health care. Cheap natural gas and the inexpensive rail and phone service implemented by Huey on the Public Service Commission benefited businesses as well as consumers. A new mansion and capitol were symbols, to be sure, but the hospital, the medical school, the port facilities, a stable banking system, free schoolbooks, and the development of LSU supported business by providing a healthy, trained workforce, extended opportunity to those previously denied it, and enhanced the quality of life.

A critic said the Airline Highway that Huey built between Baton Rouge and New Orleans was "smooth, hard and satisfying to a motorist who has recently jolted over the Virginia mountains, dodged chuck holes in Tennessee and breathed Alabama and Mississippi gravel dust. It is a jewel of a road, urgently contemporary."[102] Huey had the key insight—missed by Parker and the oligarchy—into the power of bond financing.[103] The rising power of money killed feudalism in France in the 1400s.[104] Bond financing—and the contracts and contributions derived from it—helped kill political feudalism in Louisiana.

*Personalities.* Parker reflected some of the problems of progressives in general: they could be elitist and paternalistic, prejudiced against immigrants and ethnic minorities, and humorless. Parker sought to restrict voting and to make government more efficient by eliminating elective positions and concentrating authority.[105] Huey also believed in concentrating power and responsibility, but his humor, inclusiveness, and dislike of class distinctions differentiated him from many progressives. Huey's New Orleans leaders included Jewish and Italian businessmen, ethnic groups historically ostracized and excluded.[106]

Parker couldn't match Huey's energy, diligence, or conception of his responsibilities.[107] Acting as the state's lawyer to save his tax program, for example, while Huey was engaged in other administrative and political activities, shows enormous energy, legal skill, and dedication to victory. The attention to political patronage approached micromanagement. Huey accepted responsibility for rescuing shaky banks.

*Knowledge.* Despite campaign promises, Parker failed to get a pipeline bill that protected independent oil drillers and failed to bring natural gas into New Orleans. Parker lacked knowledge of the oil and gas industries and may have been blinded by upper-class sympathies. Because of his private-practice legal work and public duties on the Public Service Commission, Huey knew a lot about the oil and gas industries. This might be termed lucky, but Huey's study of problems has been underappreciated. After his compromise with business leaders in July 1929 until May 1930, most of Huey's reported activities were routine and most biographers omit them. That he researched the issues of education and medical care during this liminal time is a fair inference.

*Opposition.* Sindler noted that many of Huey's opponents made Parker the "symbol of the glory that was pre-Huey Louisiana. There is more irony than accuracy in that view," however. "Conservative interests that were later to attack Huey Long and to enshrine John Parker fought Parker in his own day on the issues of severance taxation and larger appropriations to state institutions."[108]

In some ways, Huey and Parker had similar reactions to their opponents. Parker increased the severance tax on oil but compromised when opposed. Industrial opposition prevented him from taxing carbon black. After the contest over the severance tax, Parker agreed not to increase it again during the rest of his administration. Huey proposed a higher tax on oil and carbon black and then compromised. When Huey tried to tax Standard Oil, he got impeached. After the impeachment, Huey agreed to enact no further tax increases.

Huey, however, used deficit financing to the extent that the state had never seen before, and those who believed that governments should balance their budgets and reduce their expenditures held these beliefs intensely. The intensity of these beliefs is the only way to reconcile the good intentions of most politicians of the time with their failure to ameliorate the widespread suffering in the Depression. Senator Walsh of Massachusetts, an Al Smith Democrat, said he had "heartfelt sympathy" for those in distress, but federal relief was a "dangerous proposition." Senator Gore of Oklahoma, a populist who was one of the earliest supporters of Woodrow Wilson, compared relief to free grain offered by despotic Roman emperors, which destroyed the character of the recipients.[109] Senator Logan of Kentucky said if a farmer were broke, no one would advise him to get a loan to tear down his barn and build a new one and hire more people, and yet that is what the relief bills prescribed for the country.[110]

This thinking can explain the origin of an economic policy mistake, but not the psychological fury of those who objected to the government's failure to economize and to proposals to relieve distress. Limited government, self-reliance, balanced budgets, and economy were an ingrained, fundamental, unshakable dogma. The questioning of or breach of this dogma was blasphemous.

The idea that increased government spending would help end a Depression was held by only a minority in 1930–32, and Huey was one of them. The debt financing he obtained cushioned the effect of the Depression in Louisiana.

The resource-extraction taxes were fought by the affected industries but caused no apparent damage to their ability to compete. Davis reported that gas prices, for example, were lower in Louisiana than they were in other states. Combining all taxes (state, parish, and municipal) in Louisiana, it had the third lowest tax burden of the twenty-four states that kept records.[111]

To minimize Huey's achievements, one critic pointed out that other states offered free schoolbooks and constructed roads and public improvements funded with bonds.[112] That makes Huey less radical, but not less accomplished. Harry Byrd defeated highway bond programs in Virginia for all time. Governor Floyd Olsen's free schoolbooks proposal failed in the Minnesota legislature in 1935.[113] When Mississippi Governor Paul Johnson proposed a free schoolbooks law ten years after Huey had done so, the strain of the opposition—which claimed that the law would "socializ[e] the state"—ruined his health.[114] Moreover, if this criticism of Huey makes him less radical and more reasonable, then his opponents must be considered proportionately more reactionary and less reasonable.

*Tactics.* Sindler thinks that "[f]rom Parker's experiences Huey Long drew lessons which . . . were not without logic. Liberal economic policies could be effected only through a concentration of gubernatorial employment of the same kind of tactics customarily used by professional politicians. If political ruthlessness resulted, it could be excused as a precondition for the defeat of Parker's foes, the Choctaws and the unenlightened conservative interests."

Parker tried to destroy the Ring and elected a reform candidate over its opposition but failed to subdue it. Petty factionalism, apathy, blindness to vice and gambling, and the failure to adopt a merit or civil service system allowed the Ring to return. Huey warred with the Ring, too, but allied with it once it supported his program, benefiting from its vote-getting power. The political blunder of allowing Standard Oil to draft the severance tax law and his underestimation of support for a higher severance tax rate lessened Parker's influence. Parker's war with the Klan and support of Bouanchaud was part heroic and part quixotic.

Huey recognized that his ability to accomplish his goals resided in the legislature. Probably only Woodrow Wilson collaborated more closely with legislators as governor. Knowing that it was the votes that made the judges and that the judges then made the law, he worked to elect sympathetic judges. In contrast, Parker stayed out of judicial elections.[115]

Huey's program benefited a huge majority of the voters. He did not pick Mother Hubbard programs that benefited a few people here and there.[116] In his autobiography, Huey listed these accomplishments:

(1) Doubling the capacity of two charity hospitals while reducing their death rate and their per capita costs;
(2) Founding the LSU medical school and expanding LSU;
(3) Increasing primary school enrollment by 20 percent because of the free schoolbooks and educating 100,000 adult illiterates;
(4) Obtaining natural gas for New Orleans, noting it was now available throughout the state;
(5) Improving the ports of New Orleans and St. Charles and reducing their charges;
(6) Preventing bank failures;
(7) Building two thousand miles of concrete roads, one thousand miles of asphalt roads, numerous bridges, an airport, and a new state capitol.[117]

Most of these improvements were visible to and benefited everyone in the state.

The enormity of what he accomplished belies the extremely focused program with which he started. Whether by instinct or lack of education in a broader array of issues, Huey focused on only a few popular initiatives. Huey's 1928 success gave voters a glimpse of what was possible: natural gas, roads, free schoolbooks; 1929 saw the reaction; in 1930 the reaction continued and then collapsed with Huey's senatorial victory. The free schoolbooks, natural gas, and the patchwork of roads spread throughout the state, built with the first, small bond program, won public support. Once Huey had whetted the people's appetite, they expected more from their government. Huey overwhelmed his organized, well-financed opposition in the senatorial race against Senator Ransdell in 1930. This opened the floodgates to Huey's new ideas for LSU and the new medical school. Huey delivered results despite huge obstacles. Voter participation increased. The elections meant something.

Williams credits Huey with reducing barbarism at Angola prison, and

Carleton denies it. The key is that Huey kept the voting majority in mind: no escapes and efficient administration. Huey's reforms were not meant to appeal to the few prison reformers. But he implemented the majority's concern for efficiency—civil service as a matter of policy—*rather than* his own interest in patronage.

The concrete benefits created a class of people loyal to Huey's faction and a class of people that disliked him. This bi-factionalism (pro-Long vs anti-Long) approximated the two-party system that exists in the United States at large. Creating a class of beneficiaries must be one of the secrets of a successful revolution. Huey's beneficiaries, a majority of the voters, felt—correctly[118]—that they had something to lose if he were defeated.

Although more people supported his program than supported him, Huey's followers were committed to him and unified. No matter what Huey did from then on, he had a huge base of loyal support.

Long left home at the age of sixteen to become a traveling salesman, an experience that proved invaluable to his career in politics.

Photograph reprinted with permission from the Long Family.

Rose McConnell met Long at a cake-baking contest that he organized. He then asked her for a date to "prove" that she had actually baked the contest-winning confectionary. They married two years later.

Louisiana Political Museum and Hall of Fame, Winnfield, Louisiana.

J. K. Skipwith, an Exalted Cyclops of the Ku Klux Klan, was an eighty-year-old veteran of the Confederate Army. He orchestrated the kidnapping of five white men, two of whom were murdered, causing then-governor John M. Parker of Louisiana to request federal assistance. The newly established FBI provided little help, and local law enforcement was dominated by Klan members. When Skipwith was finally convicted of a minor offense, he was incredulous and asked, "What's this world coming to?"
Courtesy *St. Louis Post-Dispatch*, Sunday edition, p. 45, December 31, 1922.

Long lost the 1924 gubernatorial race, in part, because the Ku Klux Klan endorsed one of his opponents. Pictured here is Hiram Evans, the Grand Wizard of the Klan, which was at the peak of its influence in the 1920s. In 1934, when Evans threatened to visit Louisiana, Long said if he did, he would leave with "his toes turned up." Evans stayed away.
Sueddeutsche Zeitung Photo/ Alamy Stock Photo.

Mayor of Chicago William Hale ("Big Bill") Thompson visited Louisiana in 1928 to discuss flood control, accompanied by a large band and many other Chicagoans. He made a lasting impression on Long, who had just been elected governor, and Long invited him to his inauguration. He is pictured here, *third from left,* hat in hand.

Leon Trice Photographic Negative Collection. Louisiana Secretary of State. Archives Division. Baton Rouge, Louisiana.

This picture of Long and his family was widely circulated after he won the governorship in 1928. It was frequently featured alongside a story referencing his Bible-reading habits or the recipe used by his wife to win the cake-baking contest where the two first met.

Leon Trice Photographic Negative Collection. Louisiana Secretary of State. Archives Division. Baton Rouge, Louisiana.

An animated Long speaking to Louisiana legislators.

Leon Trice Photographic Negative Collection. Louisiana Secretary of State. Archives Division. Baton Rouge, Louisiana.

At the time of his impeachment, Long was roundly criticized for threatening to disclose that a newspaper editor's brother was being treated at a state mental hospital.

Louisiana Research Collection, Howard-Tilton Memorial Library, Tulane University, New Orleans, Louisiana.

Long with his lawyers at his impeachment trial. By the time the trial started, he felt certain he would be exonerated because he had secured the signatures of enough senators (more than one-third) who pledged they would not remove him from office.

Leon Trice Photographic Negative Collection. Louisiana Secretary of State. Archives Division. Baton Rouge, Louisiana.

Long's younger brother Earl (*right*) was invaluable as a liaison to legislators and other local political leaders, especially during the impeachment trial. After Huey's death, Earl enjoyed a remarkable political career of his own in Louisiana.

Leon Trice Photographic Negative Collection. Louisiana Secretary of State. Archives Division. Baton Rouge, Louisiana.

Long was fond of potlikker, the soup broth left over from cooking greens, and was often pictured eating it or, as seen here, posing with chefs preparing it.

Leon Trice Photographic Negative Collection. Louisiana Secretary of State. Archives Division. Baton Rouge, Louisiana.

Long with Seymour Weiss (*second from left*), the treasurer of the Long organization.

Leon Trice Photographic Negative Collection. Louisiana Secretary of State. Archives Division. Baton Rouge, Louisiana.

Bogalusa to Sun Road before Long Administration.

Same Bogalusa to Sun Road Built by Long Administration.

BEFORE LONG
The Kind of Recreation and Mind Relief Furnished Patients in the Central Hospital for the Insane; note the Barbarous Locked Chairs of the Dark Ages.

UNDER LONG ADMINISTRATION
Occupational Therapy for the Patients; Their Mardi Gras Ball, Showing Accomplishment in Patients' Operated Amusements, Beauty Parlors, etc.

A Crossing on Dixie-Overland Highway (Bayou Mason) Before Long Days.

Same Crossing at Bayou Mason Built by Long Administration.

In his autobiography, Long interspersed about a dozen before-and-after pictures depicting the accomplishments of his administration. Pictured here are three examples. They show both the dramatic progress the state experienced during his tenure as well as Long's penchant for continuing salesmanship.

Reprinted with permission from the Long Family.

Hattie Caraway was projected to finish sixth in the race for the Arkansas U.S. Senate seat in 1932. In a one-week campaign described as a "circus hitched to a tornado," Long helped Caraway vanquish her opponents, and she became the first woman elected to a full six-year term in the U.S. Senate. Long and Caraway are pictured here on a ferry.

Huey P. Long Photograph Album (Mss. 4495), Louisiana and Lower Mississippi Valley Collections, LSU Libraries, Baton Rouge, Louisiana.

Long speaking in support of Hattie Caraway's 1932 senate bid in Arkansas.

Huey P. Long Photograph Album (Mss. 4495), Louisiana and Lower Mississippi Valley Collections, LSU Libraries, Baton Rouge, Louisiana.

In 1932, Long helped elect his friend and supporter O. K. Allen (seated to Long's *right*) as governor of Louisiana. Thereafter, Long continued to run the state government as the de facto governor. Allen was so subservient to Huey that Earl Long claimed that "a leaf blew into the window of the governor's office . . . [and] Allen signed it."

Leon Trice Photographic Negative Collection. Louisiana Secretary of State. Archives Division. Baton Rouge, Louisiana.

Long addressed the 1932 Democratic National Convention in support of the seating of his state's delegation, impressing many commentators and famed lawyer Clarence Darrow. Without Long's support, Franklin Roosevelt would not have been nominated. Here, Long is photographed arriving to the convention.

Reprinted with permission from the Long Family.

In 1933, Long attended a charity event at the Sands Point Club, a ritzy establishment just outside of New York. He was overserved and got socked in the eye in the bathroom after inadvertently urinating on another man. *Collier's* magazine commemorated the event with this medal, amusing many but convincing others that the rich had too much spare time and too little common sense. The event marked a severe downturn in Long's prestige and influence.

YA/BOT/Alamy Stock Photo.

After Long attacked the conservative leadership of the Democratic Party, it questioned the legitimacy of the election of one of his allies in 1932, engaging Samuel Ansell, pictured here (*second from right*) talking to Long, to lead the U.S. Senate investigation. Long publicly denounced Ansell, who sued him for defamation.

Leon Trice Photographic Negative Collection. Louisiana Secretary of State. Archives Division. Baton Rouge, Louisiana.

Long is pictured here with Mississippi governor Mike Conner (*third from left*) and two members of the LSU band. In 1934, Long led the band and students to football games in Tennessee and Mississippi, which was witnessed by tremendous crowds. By the end of 1934, he regained much of his popularity.

Underwood Archives, Inc./Alamy Stock Photo.

Over Long's objections, congress backed Franklin Roosevelt's reduction of veterans' benefits. This cartoon was one of many bemoaning the treatment of veterans by the administration.

Reprinted with permission from *VFW* magazine, July 1933.

Franklin Roosevelt was unpopular with veterans early in the 1930s because he cut their benefits and vetoed payment of the soldiers' bonus. Here, Long, flanked by his two sons, Palmer Reid (*fourth from left*) and Russell (*third from right*), lead a march protesting the veto. Russell became a U.S. senator representing Louisiana in 1948.

Huey P. Long Photograph Album (Mss. 4495), Louisiana and Lower Mississippi Valley Collections, LSU Libraries, Baton Rouge, Louisiana.

Long's speech in Philadelphia attracted an overflow crowd. A worried supporter of Roosevelt who attended wrote the president about Long's surging popularity: "something must be done."
LSU Libraries Special Collection, Baton Rouge, Louisiana.

Long spoke to an enthusiastic Georgia legislature in 1935 before posing for a photograph with the state's governor, Eugene Talmadge. Talmadge presented him with a pair of red suspenders, a symbol of his support for farmers.
Photograph courtesy Associated Press.

Fred Parker, a former East Baton Rouge deputy sheriff, was implicated in a plot to kill Long and subsequently given a job by the Roosevelt administration to, apparently, intimidate his supposed target.

HUM Images, Universal Images Group Collection, Getty Images.

Long's assassin, Dr. Carl Austin Weiss, lived just several blocks from the state capitol, where the tragedy occurred.

## *Sixteen*

# MAGNIFICENT DEFIANCE

When Huey went to Washington, the national press was on alert, the conservative *Chicago Tribune* editorializing about "King Hooey" on January 22.[1] The train stopped in Atlanta on the way, and Huey stepped outside to talk to a reporter. He expected to get an "education" in Washington, and his blood pressure was normal for the first time in five years. No longer was he sleeping with four telephones in his bedroom. Life as a senator would be more restful.[2]

It took over a day to reach Washington, DC, from New Orleans by train.[3] At 4 a.m. on January 25, Huey arrived. At 6:00 a.m., wearing lavender pajamas, he met reporters, acknowledging that while he was called the "Kingfish" in Louisiana, he was just a "little fish" in Washington. Huey opined that several southern politicians (Senators Harrison and Robinson; House Speaker Jack Garner) or 1928 nominee Al Smith would make good presidential candidates. Franklin D. Roosevelt had just announced his candidacy, but he had run too poorly with Cox in 1920, Huey thought. Tradition required a state's senior senator to escort the junior senator to take the oath of office, but Huey provoked an argument with Senator Broussard that morning. Broussard stomped off angry. Senator Joseph Robinson (D-Arkansas), the minority leader, escorted him to take the oath instead. Huey carried a lit cigar down the aisle, disobeying a Senate rule, putting it on Robinson's desk to take the oath. The *Chicago Tribune* wrote: "Long Shatters Traditions of August Senate."[4]

After he was sworn in, Huey fidgeted at his back-row desk for a few minutes, expecting other senators to greet him, but when they didn't, he swaggered around the chamber, waving to his wife and friends in the gallery, and introduced himself to the senators. The galleries were "astonished" and asked the ushers the name of this "dynamic" and "pleasing" personality, who walked as fast as other senators ran, whose whole athletic body was brought into action when he talked, and who had a "commanding presence." Republican Senator Watson (R-Indiana) received a hard blow to the chest as Huey announced, "Jim, I want to get acquainted with you." Huey made sure to meet progressive Senators George Norris (R-Nebraska), Hiram Johnson (R-California), and William E. Borah (R-Idaho), putting his arm around Borah and telling him he was the ideal senator.[5]

A newsreel clip of February 1 shows a relaxed Huey and Senator Robinson greeting each other. Louisianans were better off than people in other states, Huey said, and the economic difficulties were not related to tariff policy or Prohibition, but rather to the "overconcentration of wealth," against which Moses had warned in the Bible.[6]

Huey's first votes related to the Reconstruction Finance Corporation, which provided bailout financing to industries and banks.[7] Senator Hugo Black (D-Alabama) proposed to limit the salaries of executives of companies bailed out by the corporation. Huey voted for it. Progressives such as John Blaine (R-Wisconsin), Bronson Cutting (R–New Mexico), George Norris, and Burton Wheeler (D-Montana) and populist conservatives such as Kenneth McKellar (D-Tennessee) and Thomas Gore (D-Oklahoma) voted for it, but it failed, twenty-five to forty-seven. Progressives Robert LaFollette (R-Wisconsin) and James J. Couzens (R-Michigan) voted against it.[8] An amendment to protect the wage levels of those bailed out by the corporation also failed, twenty to forty-nine, with Huey voting with the minority of progressives. Black, Alben Barkley (D-Kentucky), Carter Glass (D-Virginia), and Robert Wagner (D–New York) voted with the majority.[9]

On February 27, Huey made his maiden speech, opposing the nomination of William E. Humphrey to the Federal Trade Commission. The *Chicago Tribune* said he was "[u]nabashed by the Senate tradition that new members should be seen and not heard." Huey "sided with Senate radicals . . . who opposed Commissioner Humphrey on the ground that he favored 'big business.'" The *New York Times* decided that Huey was a "frontier senator" in the tradition of Pitchfork Ben Tillman.[10] Huey's speech was brief and followed those of three other senators with whom he agreed. Humphrey was confirmed, fifty-three to twenty-eight.[11]

After he dispatched the Cyr threat in Louisiana at the end of January, he returned to Washington, arriving on February 2. On February 3, a bill authored by Senators LaFollette and Copeland (D–New York) proposed relief and highway funds to be administered by the federal government. Conservatives opposed this, contending that local charities and governments could manage the problem, even though local governments and charities had run out of funds, and because they were appalled at the prospect of increased government debt.

Equally sad is that those who favored relief split between those who wanted the federal government to administer the program and those who backed Senator Black's plan to loan money to the states. There were legitimate concerns against Black's plan because some state constitutions prohibited borrowing money, but it only required the states' governors to use their best efforts to repay the funds.

Huey said that people were starving and the bill as drafted was not going to pass, so why not accept the amendment as better than no relief at all? The governors could certify that they would try to get it repaid, such as by asking their legislators to support a constitutional amendment to permit it. Wheeler protested that this was subterfuge.[12]

Progressives such as Borah, Costigan, Couzens, LaFollette, Norris, and Thomas (D-Oklahoma) helped defeat the Black amendment, thirty-one to forty-eight. The LaFollette-Costigan bill then failed, thirty-five to forty-eight.[13] In an editorial, "Delicate Consolences," the *Times* criticized LaFollette. It said that Huey had "strip[ped] off the metaphysical flesh and [came] to the bone. Suppose the people don't pay the money back. 'In the meantime, the hungry have been fed.'"[14]

Huey had returned to New Orleans by the time these votes were taken on February 15 and 16 but was paired (absent senators on opposite sides of a bill would be paired in order to count their votes) for both versions. Convinced by Huey's comments, Wheeler voted the same way.

Huey measured the Senate and was disgusted:

- "A Democratic senator seems a whipped rooster, standing quiet and bleeding while the victor pecks him on the head. They suffer from political paralysis. . . ."
- "Washington [is] the farthest place from the United States I've seen."
- "The world is disgusted with Hoover . . . and now, with the country anxiously awaiting the Democrats to deliver the knockout blow, there

> seems to be plenty of Democrats ready to . . . support everything that Hoover . . . want[s]."[15]

Huey must have recognized, then, that he could not get an *education* from whipped roosters. But if he were not going to accept pecks to his head, he also realized that he knew too little to teach them.

*Times* reporter Raymond Daniell recommended books about economics and history that Huey read. John Truslow Adams's *The Epic of America* impressed him. The American Dream is a cliché now,[16] but a book tracing it as an idea begins with this one.[17] Adams emphasized the "colossal power" in the hands of a few, argued that wealth should be "more equitably controlled and distributed in the interests of society," and decried the current "wasteful and unjust system" that was "inimical" to the "American Dream." Twelve men controlled the business of the United States and, while a few distributed charity "upon the public in ways chosen wholly by themselves. . . . [,] the system [is] at fault. Nor is it likely to be voluntarily altered. . . . No ruling class has ever willingly abdicated."[18] Huey also studied Senator Underwood's Senate career[19] and ordered a twenty-volume set of the *Messages and Papers of the President.* A receipt of March 6, 1932, lists purchases of Balzac, Greek and Roman classics, oriental tales, Stevenson, and Talleyrand.[20]

The *Congressional Record* reads as if Huey got the cold shoulder from the Senate. His remarks about the relief bills were more favorably received by the *Times* than by other senators. On his return from Louisiana on February 25, 1932, Huey spoke in favor of the bill prohibiting injunctions against labor unions, describing a case from his law career. But he was ignored, as if he had butted into someone else's conversation. Interjecting again, he scornfully asked Senator King whether he had ever heard of a case in which an injunction was entered in favor of a laboring man. King couldn't answer. Senator Wagner answered, but not in the way Huey expected, because Wagner was aware of a few such cases. Huey got into a brief argument with Senator Tom Connally (D-Texas) in which Connally first cross-examined and then bested Huey in a short argument.[21]

Huey abruptly left the Senate again, absent from Tuesday, March 1, in midafternoon[22] to March 12 (a Saturday session), after it was apparent that the anti-injunction bill would pass. Huey faced a crisis because of difficulty selling Louisiana highway bonds. Fifteen million dollars' worth of bonds had been sold in June 1931. After those proceeds were spent, the work continued because the Highway Commission issued promises (certificates of indebtedness) to contractors against future bonds yet to be sold. In addition to withdrawing the sale of $12 million of bonds in October 1931, $5 million of the bonds were offered for sale separately thereafter, but no one bid on them.[23] Highway workers were asked to take a 10 percent pay cut.[24] Construction had then stopped, leaving many highway gaps. Road bonds worth $35 million had been advertised for sale since January 30.

Huey was in New York on March 3. It is probable that he met with the law firm that represented Louisiana with respect to bond sales, Thomson, Wood, and Hoffman. Huey also arranged a meeting with presidential candidate Al Smith.[25] The meeting with Smith went badly, however.[26]

Huey ate at the Waldorf Astoria Hotel and told the maître d' that they were using the wrong recipe for the Waldorf sandwich. The *New York Herald Tribune* criticized Huey's recipe but said, "There is something of magnificent defiance in the gesture of Huey Long, who came to the Waldorf and instructed Oscar himself in the art of making a Waldorf sandwich."[27]

Huey returned to Louisiana on Thursday morning (March 10) for "important business."[28] A newspaper reported that the whole bond issue of $35 million had to be sold. From the bond proceeds, $12 million would pay off the certificates of indebtedness and another $12 million would go for outstanding contracts to construct more roads.[29] Huey returned to Washington over that weekend. The bonds were offered for sale on Monday, March 14. On March 16, $15 million out of the $35 million bonds offered for sale had been purchased, but the lawyers said this was legal.

A combination of cash ($12 million) and stock ($3 million) was used to buy the bonds. Pyramid Securities Company (one wonders whether Huey chose the name), a principal of which was Seymour Weiss, issued the securities and bought the bonds. The plan was to pay highway contractors 80 percent of their outstanding bills and use Pyramid Securities for the balance. The $12 million was borrowed by Pyramid from New Orleans banks. The *Times* viewed this arrangement "as another mark of [Huey's] genius."[30]

The *Times* congratulated him too soon. On March 23, road material men balked, and it was thought they might be given bonds directly as payment (later determined as illegal).[31] Huey returned to Louisiana to meet with creditors and bankers on Wednesday, March 23, and he was absent from the Senate until March 30. A creditors' meeting was held in Louisiana on March 24.[32] The next day, highway creditors were reconsidering the bond plan and another meeting was scheduled. Huey told two to three hundred creditors that he had devoted four weeks to accomplish what others said couldn't be done, he wasn't responsible for the poor condition of the market, he had tried other schemes, and this was the best he could do. Concluding, Huey invited questions. There was silence for one minute. Someone finally spoke up that they could probably work it out.[33] On March 26 the newspapers carried Huey's letter to the creditors explaining the plan. It would not be put in operation without a consensus.[34] By Tuesday, March 29, his plan was accepted.[35]

When Huey returned to the Senate on Monday, March 14, 1932, he spoke sardonically for a few minutes, joking that an appropriation for Howard University was only designed to get votes. He got a few laughs. After the appropriation to Howard was approved, Huey proposed a similar allocation of $200,000 to Louisiana for a night-school literacy program. The amendment was ruled out of order. Huey appealed the decision of the chair. Senator Ashurst of Arizona "begged" him not to force a vote on the chair's ruling because he was sure to lose. Huey withdrew it.[36] He still had a lot to learn. But the following days evidenced Huey's plan to increase his influence and push for higher taxes on the wealthy.

In the House of Representatives, progressive congressmen of both parties had rebelled against President Hoover's proposed national sales tax. Contemporaneously, the *Washington Post* criticized Huey for ousting Paul Cyr. On Monday, March 21, Huey rebutted the *Post*'s article and segued into a two-hour speech against the sales tax. According to the *Tribune,* he flung "himself about excitedly" and waved his arms near the face of his Senate neighbor, Senator Hattie Caraway, who had been elected to serve the rest of her husband's term after he died. "She scrootched up in the corner of her chair to dodge his gestures." Senator Carter Glass of Virginia walked up and down in the back of the Senate, "furious, but futile." All eight Louisiana congressmen attended the speech. Having been received coolly by senators, Huey imported a friendly audience. They nodded in agreement when he said they would oppose a sales tax and applauded when he concluded.[37]

In the following days, Huey supported legislative positions of Senators Robinson,[38] McKellar,[39] and Thomas,[40] complained about the selective enforcement of Prohibition laws, and supported an oil tariff, but still made little impression.[41]

On Monday, April 4, he used John Truslow Adams's phrase and delivered a speech entitled "The Doom of America's Dream." The *Saturday Evening Post*'s 1916 article was updated with statistics from an FTC report of 1926 showing that 1 percent of the people owned 59 percent of the wealth. Middle-class opportunity—the corner grocery store—was gone. When threatened with starvation and the need to support a family, the country couldn't expect adherence to its laws against theft. Philosopher John Dewey, the dean of the Harvard Business School, labor leaders, and others recognized the problem. The economy crashed because no one had the money to buy goods and services. The only remedy was high taxes on the holders of concentrated wealth. That would permit the fruits of the economy to be enjoyed by all people. The galleries applauded.[42]

The speech excited only one syndicated columnist, Frank Kent of the *Baltimore Sun*. It was "extraordinary," delivered with a "vehemence hard to describe," and catapulted Huey as the most advanced thinker of Senate progressives.[43] Harrison responded that Huey's suggested tax rates were confiscatory and contrary to the American spirit, unjustified when no one was making money. The *Tribune* extolled Harrison and omitted Huey's remarks. Other progressive senators jumped into the debate and supported Huey, however.[44]

On April 6, Harrison and McKellar worried about the budget and a deficit. Huey asked whether the Senate was spending excessive time on small expenditure reductions that would not mean much to the people.[45]

On April 7, Huey had the steward of the Senate dining room add potlikker to the menu. The ingredients were purchased from the African American section of the grocery store. Huey supervised its preparation for senators, who gathered as a group for lunch to eat it, with Huey sitting next to Robinson. This made the papers and may have broken the ice.[46] In the Senate, Huey supported Senator Black's bill for disaster relief in Alabama. Black appreciated Huey's comment.[47]

On April 8, Senator Cordell Hull (D-Tennessee) acknowledged that Huey had some strong facts for his view that concentrated wealth caused the economy to shrivel.[48] On April 11, Senator Arthur Capper (R-Kansas) cited an editorial by Republican newspaper editor William Allen White favoring a tax of 100 percent on inheritances over $10 or $15 million because it gives "a man his liberty and preserves to society the sense of opportunity and equality for all its members." Young people should be taken "back to the toe mark when they start." If they could not be successful with that much money to start, society should not entrust them with more.[49] On April 21, Huey introduced a resolution to tax at the rate of 100 percent incomes over $1 million and inheritances over $5 million.[50] On April 13, Huey attacked corruption in the administration. A Republican senator asked to rule him out of order. Harrison defended Huey.[51] By April 17, a veteran Capitol guide said that sightseers lately had given him more requests to point out Huey.[52] On April 22, Huey exposed a railroad's lobbying efforts with support by Senators Norris and Shipstead.[53]

Invited to Cleveland, Huey gave a "stirring speech" to a civic group and shivered with Governor Allen at a Cleveland Indians baseball game.[54] One wonders whether he met Newton Baker, an undeclared presidential candidate and attorney for the Indians, while he was there. On his return, Huey voted against Senator Thomas Heflin's challenge of his electoral defeat by Senator Bankhead of Alabama, supporting Senator Black.[55]

If Huey thought he was ingratiating himself with colleagues (the newspapers and the *Record* suggest he was), his hopes were dashed on April 29. At a Democratic caucus that morning, Huey thought that, based on a "splendid" speech by Walsh of Montana, the caucus was unified in favor of higher tax rates on the wealthy. Robinson told Huey that he could call up his tax resolution, but Robinson would not support it. Furious, Huey asserted on the Senate floor that there was a coalition of both parties to protect the wealthy, with Robinson traipsing to the White House to cooperate with Hoover. The Democrats needed to offer relief to the starving, the naked, and the homeless with a redistribution of wealth, and not cooperate with the disastrous policies of Hoover. Dramatically, he resigned all committee memberships to which Robinson had appointed him because he disagreed with Robinson's leadership.[56]

Robinson was autocratic, arrogant, and sarcastic, with a powerful and terrifying open-air voice that could visibly shake the Senate chamber.[57] Hattie Caraway said Robinson was "cooler than a cucumber and sourer than a pickle."[58] Robinson controlled committee assignments, which maintained his power. No Democrat had openly opposed Robinson, and no conservative Republican needed to.

Robinson was prepared for Huey's outburst from their confrontation in the morning. He got laughs when he described Huey as handsome and intelligent. Confiscating inheritances or income was un-American even though they were products of the law. Any time another senator wanted to test his views, they could ask the caucus to replace him. Leadership required responsibility, not class warfare. Courtesy was owed to the president regardless of his party affiliation. He had told Huey in the morning to vote as he pleased and keep his assignments. Huey's insistence on resigning was therefore "a comic-opera performance."[59]

In reply, Huey said that Robinson had conceded the philosophical basis for his tax resolution when he admitted that income and inheritances were the product of laws. The Declaration of Independence supported the Democratic Party and his proposals. Huey got laughs when he noted that in 1928 he had given more votes to Robinson in Louisiana (when Robinson ran for vice president with Smith) than Robinson had obtained in his own state, and that he campaigned for Robinson in Arkansas and had not needed Robinson to campaign in Louisiana to carry that state for him.

It was not the trips to the White House that irked Huey; it was that the Democrats were not offering the voters a choice. He was not declaring war on the rich, but rather was saving them from a time when they would be "awakened some morning . . . surrounded by a crowd of men" and forced to give up everything. "[W]hen they have been divested of all their properties it will be too late to cry out for what I now advocate, for the abyss is yawning for all."[60]

This was no mere defiance of the Waldorf's maître d'. It was a high-risk attack, contrary to Senate custom and thus shocking. The *Times* reported that Huey had whirled about, waved his hands, clenched his fists, and mopped his flushed face with a bright pink handkerchief.[61] Some viewed Huey's resignations as petulant: things weren't going his way, so he refused to play. The *Washington Post* said Huey was shirking his duties and should resign.[62] Others just thought he was interesting, different, and colorful.[63]

Part of Huey's rationale was warped. The committee memberships were public trusts, not the private possession of Robinson. But what better way to neutralize Robinson's ironclad control than by taking what he valued—and was using to keep senators in line—and declaring them worthless? Robinson had excellent points to make against letting partisanship paralyze the government and the need to treat the president, whatever party he belonged to, with courtesy and respect.

But Robinson's views were little different from Hoover's. Huey proposed a new, issue-oriented or ideological politics. Huey had no plans to run for president at the time.[64] The Democrats should draw a contrast with Hoover, Huey thought, propose legislation, and make Hoover's party accept it or not. The voters would then choose in November who was right.

Many Democrats attacked Hoover for the Great Depression, and a few had attacked the big financiers, but they had not proposed much antithetical to their interests. Harrison and Robinson often attacked Hoover and the Republicans on tangential issues, such as whether they were claiming credit for something the Democrats had done, or denying Democrats credit for cooperation, or trying to outdo Republicans on the issue of economy in government.[65] Democrats were vague on what they would do about the Depression, but knew enough to blame Hoover. Huey criticized this as dishonest:

> It is time for this political humbugging to stop. . . . I have sat here . . . and listened to speeches condemning the president . . . in the most vicious and caustic terms . . . and when those who make the speeches formulate a plan . . . the administration supporters . . . send one of Hoover's disciples down there, and they rewrite the bill, and the Democrats come in here with it just as they say, and then they go out and tell the country that we ought to make a swap between the parties! [*Laughter.*][66]

The newspapers missed this key point. Historians have missed a related key point. All emphasize Huey's ambition or compulsion to lead, but in a separate lengthy, droll, and self-effacing speech, Huey stated that he believed in the principle of organization and leadership and wanted Norris to be his leader.[67] Huey didn't have to be the leader if he could find one who believed in the principles he believed in.

Huey's reply evidenced some quick thinking. He could not defeat Robinson in a Senate caucus vote, so to respond to Robinson's challenge of a test, he shifted the frame of reference to election tests ("the only kind of test that matters"). Included was a vague threat that he might engage Robinson in some future test in front of the people in Arkansas.

Huey continued his attack on May 1 in the press when he suggested that Democrats nominate Republican George Norris for president and that Robinson be replaced as minority leader and run as Hoover's running mate. They "work together for the same things, with the same ideas, and with the same results." Confronted with his January statements favoring Robinson for president, Huey admitted that he "met himself coming back rather quickly on that one" and that he was "very much discouraged." He felt as if he were "in a kind of a maze."[68]

Huey told the Senate on May 3 that he expected the Democratic caucus, now that it knew where he stood, to give him committee assignments in place of those he had resigned. But Robinson had accepted the resignations and assigned other senators to those spots. Huey sarcastically "reciprocate[d]" the "compliments" Robinson paid him and sent to the chair an extract from the legal directory of Little Rock listing forty-three giant corporations that Robinson's law firm represented as proof of Robinson's "great standing" in the South—as a captive to big corporate interests. The *Times* printed the list of corporate clients.[69] Huey's brother Julius got more space in the *Tribune*, however, by labeling him selfish.[70]

In the dispute with Robinson, Huey said Robinson's similarity to Hoover gave the people no place to go, no choice at the ballot box. Now, because of his dispute with Robinson, Huey had no place to go, no presidential candidate to support. The only third party available, the Farmer-Labor Party, was too weak to be credible. Thus, he was caught in a "maze."

Franklin Delano Roosevelt was now the front-running presidential candidate. A cousin of President Theodore Roosevelt, although in the opposite political party, he was born into politics and into a wealthy and aristocratic family. Marrying his distant cousin, Eleanor, the new couple was upstaged at their own wedding by the president.

Opposed to the corrupt city machine of New York, Tammany Hall, Roosevelt was an independent, if dilettantish, New York state senator, elected in 1911. He failed to organize a new Democratic Party coalition in 1912. Appointed assistant secretary of the Navy in 1913 before World War I (cousin Theodore had been assistant secretary of the Navy before he became president), he was an effective advocate of an expanded Navy and a good administrator. A 1914 run as an independent for the U.S. Senate failed. Within Wilson's administration, a secret cabal of advocates including Roosevelt wanted the United States to enter World War I, but this disloyalty was mooted when Wilson declared war.[71] After Roosevelt reversed himself to compliment Tammany Hall, Tammany Hall helped nominate him for vice president in 1920.

Running with James Cox, governor of Ohio, their ticket was trounced by Warren G. Harding. After World War I, the public wanted a "return to normalcy." Wilson's dream of the League of Nations had been defeated in the U.S. Senate. The paralyzed, wheelchair-bound president, in halting but heartfelt words, urged the candidates to run the campaign as a referendum on the League of Nations. This advice was taken but wrong.

Roosevelt contracted polio in 1921 and lost the use of his legs. An iron determination forged his rehabilitation efforts. He spent hours trying to move a toe. Exercise built up muscular arms, chest, and back, necessary to manipulate his useless legs, kept stiffened with braces. Crutches, the arms of his sons or aides, or a wheelchair were necessary for him to move, although this was concealed from the public.

At the Democratic Convention of 1924, Roosevelt nominated New York governor Al Smith, a Roman Catholic, for the presidency, marking his return to politics. Smith's rival for the nomination was William Gibbs McAdoo of California. Smith and McAdoo both lost the nomination after more than one hundred ballots, bitterly dividing the party. Corporate lawyer John Davis won the nomination as a compromise candidate but lost in a landslide to Republican Calvin Coolidge.

In 1928, Roosevelt again nominated Smith. Smith won the nomination (with Robinson as his running mate) but was clobbered in the general election by Herbert Hoover. Smith was a progressive governor of New York, a good speaker, with excellent timing and a comedic touch. Newsmen liked him. The loss was blamed on his Catholicism, his New York City accent, his association with Tammany Hall, his opposition to Prohibition, and the booming economy. Roosevelt ran for governor of New York at Smith's request only to help him in the general election. Roosevelt won the governorship by 25,000 votes, while Smith was defeated in New York—his home state—by over 100,000 votes.

Roosevelt was reelected governor in 1930, nominated at the state convention by Smith, and stepped up his presidential candidacy, which had begun just after the 1928 election. In New York, Roosevelt advocated public power, developed parks, and set up state agencies to aid the unemployed. But his relationship with Al Smith soured.

James A. Farley, head of the state athletic commission, headed Roosevelt's campaign. Academics were among his policy advisors. In 1931, Farley visited eighteen states and met with 1,100 Democratic Party leaders, winning friends everywhere, and storing names and faces in a memory as prodigious as Huey's. Roosevelt personally managed southern politicians, hosting leaders from Alabama, Georgia, Mississippi (Harrison), South Carolina (Byrnes), and Tennessee (Hull) at his Georgia home in October 1931. Roosevelt announced for the presidency on January 22, 1932. Al Smith declared on February 6.[72]

By early May 1932, Roosevelt's major rivals were Al Smith and speaker of the U.S. House John Nance Garner. Garner was well liked by both parties, known for playing poker and drinking whiskey. His platform called for a one-third reduction in government expenditures, relief supported by a sales tax, and the repeal of Prohibition.[73]

Newton Baker was an undeclared candidate from Ohio. A wealthy corporate lawyer, he was a protégé of Woodrow Wilson and had been his secretary of war. Columnist Walter Lippmann promoted his candidacy and, during this time, wrote his often-quoted assessment of Roosevelt: he had "no firm grasp on public affairs," was "no enemy of the privileged," and was "a very pleasant man who, without any important qualifications for the office, would very much like to be President." Preceding that opinion was an analysis of how Roosevelt straddled the issues.[74]

Governors of Virginia (Harry Byrd),[75] Maryland (Albert Ritchie),[76] and Oklahoma (William "Alfalfa Bill" Murray),[77] were favorite-son candidates. Most of the domestic policy debate revolved around Prohibition and tariff policy. The League of Nations was the big foreign policy issue. No one had a philosophy by which the government could end the Depression. Economizing was advocated by every candidate and was a chief accomplishment of the governors.

Roosevelt first favored a national referendum on Prohibition (writing to dries that they would win and to wets that the dries wouldn't) and then mildly favored repeal (promising to support the law if it weren't repealed). Under pressure from isolationist newspaper publisher William Randolph Hearst, Roosevelt reversed himself on the League of Nations and said that "in its present form" it should not be joined.

When Huey arrived in Washington, he had favored Smith, Garner, Robinson, or Harrison. On February 5, Huey eliminated Robinson and Harrison because they voted for Hoover appointees and he criticized Roosevelt for "weather-vaning" on the issues of Prohibition and the League of Nations.[78]

Senator Wheeler asked Huey to reconsider. In one speech, Roosevelt said the government had to remember the man at the bottom of the economic pyramid, the "forgotten man."[79] After Wheeler's request, Huey told reporter Clark Howell of the *Atlanta Constitution* that he was inclined toward Roosevelt. Howell passed this on. Roosevelt then wrote Huey that they were alike in their devotion to the common man.[80]

Huey hesitated. But in late April, Smith overwhelmed Roosevelt in the Massachusetts primary. On May 3, Roosevelt lost the California primary to Garner. Huey decided to endorse Roosevelt. It would counteract Roosevelt's recent defeats. Huey returned by train to Louisiana on May 5 to attend the dedication ceremonies of the LSU medical school. On the way to New Orleans from Washington, he stopped in Atlanta, met Clark Howell, and gave him a written endorsement of Roosevelt, emphasizing Norris's role in persuading him. Norris confirmed Huey's statement. It secured wide news coverage.[81]

Supporting Roosevelt and tying it to Norris allowed Huey to escape his "maze." It was consistent with his compliments of Norris and his criticisms of Robinson. It secured his acceptance among the progressives in the Senate and counteracted his threat to bolt the party. Roosevelt was best able to help Huey's delegation get seated if challenged and thus aid him in his civil war with other Louisiana Democrats. Endorsing the leading nominee and probable president gave him leverage to continue his war with Robinson or to leapfrog him into a position of leadership in the Senate or influence at the White House.

Huey did not ask Roosevelt to endorse his tax plan. A Roosevelt speech in Atlanta on May 23, however, included a sentence that must have been designed to satisfy Huey: the "basic trouble with the economy was not an insufficiency of capital; it was an insufficient distribution of buying power coupled with an over-sufficient speculation in production." Huey inserted an article about that speech into the *Congressional Record* the day it was published.[82]

Huey's ideas affected Robinson, not with respect to taxes, but with respect to the need to differentiate the Democrats from Hoover. On May 11, while Huey was returning from the medical school dedication, Robinson proposed his own plan to combat the Depression: a balanced budget, maintenance of credit, a fair tax plan, $300 million in federal government bonds to be given to the states for relief, a $2 billion construction program (roads, slum clearance) to stimulate employment, a thirty-hour work week, and Reconstruction Finance Corporation loans to help farmers refinance their debts. Robinson had opposed LaFollette's relief bill in February, although he voted for Black's substitute. In a Jefferson Day dinner speech in April, Robinson advocated only cessation of loans to bankrupt foreign nationals, denial of foreign war debt readjustment proposals, repeal of tariffs, curbs on monopolies, economy in government, and, vaguely, disposal of farm surpluses and a controlled increase of money supply. It is a fair inference that Robinson's new positions were caused by Huey's complaints that the Democrats lacked a differentiating program from Hoover.[83]

Theoretically, Robinson's change could have fostered their reconciliation. But the *Tribune* ran a cartoon on May 5 showing Robinson as a patriotic American standing by the American flag and Huey as a Senate radical carrying a Russian flag. The cartoon was widely circulated in Louisiana, in part because, coincidentally, the LSU band was scheduled to play "The Chicago Tribune March" at the medical school dedication. Huey scotched playing that song. This made the papers.[84]

Returning to the Senate after the dedication, Huey exhibited the cartoon and described it on May 12. The U.S. flag carried by Robinson in the cartoon had only stripes; it was missing the stars. Huey pulled out the Little Rock legal directory again and said the listed corporations consisted of forty-three stars, some of the most nefarious interests in the country, and the remaining five stars he supplied included one for pestilence, misery, and similar terms. Robinson had few law clients when he arrived in the Senate. Now he had forty-three of the biggest and most powerful corporate clients in the country. Resolutions passed at a mass meeting in Robinson's own state of Arkansas on May 2 and by the Chicago American Federation of Labor, representing 300,000 labor-union members, approved his stand.[85] Citing the *Saturday Evening Post* article on "Lost Leaders," Huey said Robinson could be great if he would exhibit more courage.

Huey was now comfortable in the Senate. Sarcastically he said that, if a lawyer represented chain stores, "that will not affect him . . . ; oh, no; not a bit." Senator Reed objected:

> MR. REED: "[Huey's remarks] were capable of no interpretation but that [Robinson] would be influenced in his vote by the fact that his firm had been retained by the companies the Senator mentioned."
>
> MR. LONG: I said, "Oh, no." [*Laughter in the galleries.*]

Senators Blaine, Walsh, Trammell, and Dill supported Huey's right to speak. When Reed later got up to leave, Huey paused and impishly asked him to stay to ensure that he obeyed the rules.

Huey called prominent businessman Bernard Baruch "Barney" and said he operated a "certain investment stock marketing racketeering enterprise . . . [*laughter*]." Democrats should renounce Baruchism and beware of the influence of big corporations, but "I want now to disclaim that I have the slightest motive of saying, or that in my heart I believe, that such a man could to the slightest degree be influenced in any vote which he casts in this body by the fact that that association might mean hundreds of thousands and millions of dollars in the way of lucrative fees [*laughter*]."[86]

The *Tribune* called Huey's speech "almost incoherent." The paper either grossly mischaracterized it or the Senate reporters cleaned it up.[87] The *Times* said Huey violently assailed Robinson and emphasized the confrontation with Reed. Huey "denied that he had impugned Mr. Robinson . . . but, with a grin on his face, proceeded to drive his points home."[88] Robinson was angered but declined to answer.[89] Louisianans approved.[90]

Historian Brinkley asserted that Robinson did not share the law firm's revenues from the corporate clients and therefore Huey's attack was unfair,[91] but a law firm's power is augmented by its association with a U.S. senator and minority leader, and by its ability to list major corporations as clients. Robinson's law firm partner Hamilton Moses was the attorney for Arkansas Power & Light Co. Moses provided Robinson (unspecified) "campaign aid." A case Robinson tried for the firm gave him a big fee of $25,000 that allowed him to buy a "showplace" house and relieved him of the awkwardness of living with relatives. The most Robinson had earned from his prior firm trying cases (in 1923) was $3,400.[92]

The Senate Finance Committee studied the tax code for three weeks. They had agreed on a 55 percent rate for the wealthy, but Hoover's treasury secretary, Ogden Mills, appeared before the committee, opposed this, and the committee dropped the 55 percent rate and added sales taxes in accordance with his wishes and proposed this legislation to the Senate. On May 13, Senator Couzens, voted down in the committee, proposed an amendment requiring higher taxes on the wealthy.[93]

The actions of the committee—studying a matter for three weeks and then changing its mind in twenty minutes—were mistakes made to order for Huey. During a three-hour domination of the Senate on May 16, he complimented the committee members as intelligent, wise, and just; he wanted to follow the judgment of the committee. But should he follow their mature, considered judgment rendered after three weeks of hearings or its hasty judgment after Mills's objections? Which recommendation should he follow? An old man had died, and he put a little poem on his tombstone:

Remember, man, as you pass by,
So as you are so once was I,
So as I am, so you must be.
Prepare to die and follow me.

His wife who put up the tombstone did not want to be bound by what was on it, so as a saving grace to herself, wrote two more lines:

To follow you I'm not content,
Until I know which way you went.[94]

This convulsed the audience. The laughter was so loud the proceedings almost came to a halt.[95] Harrison was peeved and left the Senate floor, but Huey "waxed more eloquent as time wore on, rolling out platitudes, poetic and biblical references and homespun sayings of the Southwest" until at 10 p.m. he "dropped exhausted into his seat."[96]

In the following days, Huey was as active as Norris or Connally or Robinson or Couzens in the debates. They didn't give him the cold shoulder now; he had shouldered his way into the club. Huey gave tactical advice to Norris on the floor.[97] There were about thirty-one progressives, a respectable minority. Robinson and Harrison doggedly supported the Republican line to keep high taxes off the wealthy but balance the budget, if necessary, with taxes that hit the poor man—taxes on automobiles, radios, and theater tickets, for example.[98]

Huey's speaking style helped him get publicity: the ditties, descriptive words (critiquing senators trying to "scalp" the wages of government employees), and a gift for bringing the exalted down to earth ("Who is this Barney Baruch anyway?"). The show was good—attacks and jokes on behalf of the people—and the galleries filled up to listen. Huey mimicked Senator Smoot's method of speech and manner of pounding the table, which left the galleries in stitches. The intensity of his speeches—the "hammer and bang" and the "fire and force"[99]—was balanced by a sense of humor. On May 16, he promised to outdress Sen. J. Hamilton Lewis (D-Illinois), known for his spats and wavy pink toupees. On the appointed day, Huey looked Lewis over but conceded sartorial defeat.[100]

The Couzens amendment and his own amendment of the Couzens amendment were defeated. But a 55 percent rate was passed later in the session, a compromise victory.[101]

The tax bill included four excise taxes (tariffs) on imported oil, coal, lumber, and copper. The Democratic Party in the South and Republicans from farm states opposed tariffs because they purchased manufactured goods and exported their wheat, corn, and cotton. Conventional wisdom is that tariffs add to the cost of manufactured goods, diminish exports because foreign nations retaliate, and foster monopolies, decreasing competition.[102] Needing to protect Louisiana's sugar industry, however, Huey was out of step from his party's articulated position on tariffs.

The argument on the oil tax deconstructed traditional tariff debate.[103] Huey recounted the Pine Island freeze-out and said that Standard Oil told him it would import oil after it lost the court case challenging Louisiana's severance tax. An excise tax on imports would force Standard Oil to accept oil from independent drillers in Louisiana, preserve severance tax revenues that supported Louisiana schools, and give Standard Oil competition from independent drillers.

Senator Tydings of Maryland admitted that Standard Oil was a monopoly but argued that made it more certain that the tax would be passed on to consumers. Tydings calculated the amount that prices would be increased for each state's citizens. Other Democrats spoke against tariffs, giving traditional arguments. Senator Johnson of California asked: If the tax were going to be passed on, why was Standard Oil fighting it?[104] Senator Gore suggested that Tydings was acting on behalf of Standard Oil because it had a huge refinery in Tydings's state and had won concessions from Venezuela, from which it was importing oil.

The difference in labor wages came into the discussion. Foreign countries used "slave labor," and American workers ought not to have to compete with it. American consumers ought to get the benefit of low prices for goods produced by foreign labor, the opponents of the excise taxes argued. During the debate on the lumber tax, Huey asked: "On the theory of a homeowner having the right to build his home at the very best price, what would be the Senator's objection to letting Chinese labor come in without immigration restriction to build the houses?"[105] Allowing cheap foreign labor to immigrate or to manufacture goods that American consumers buy will depress consumer prices and American labor wages.[106]

There was a lot of tariff hypocrisy within the Democratic Party,[107] and Huey looked up the record of anti-tariff senators. Senator LaFollette had voted for a tariff on casein, used to make margarine, which competed with Wisconsin dairy farmers' butter. Confronted with this vote, LaFollette exclaimed that the tariff was only based on differences between foreign and domestic costs of production. Huey pounced. The oil tax was less than the difference in the cost of foreign oil production.[108] Discrimination between the oil industry and the dairy industry couldn't be justified.[109]

In a terrible lapse of courtesy, however, Huey interrupted Tydings and then objected to his routine request for the clerk to read a document. The Senate overruled Huey's objection. Later, Tydings refused to yield the floor to Huey because Huey did not "understand what the definition of courtesy is." Tydings lost his head, too, threatening to tie up the Senate with five hundred amendments to defeat the four excise taxes.[110]

Huey also read several of Senator George's votes to increase tariffs or against a decrease. As he had in February, Senator Ashurst begged Huey to stop. Huey declined to listen. After Huey finished, George delivered a stinging rebuke. He had never voted in accordance with anything other than his duty; Huey had used the record without decency. When Huey asked with false innocence what was wrong with reading George's record, George responded that, if Huey were "unconscious of what he had done," he was "utterly lacking in the sensibilities which usually characterize the intercourse between men in this body."[111] Huey did not reply. The *Tribune* reported that Huey had been verbally spanked.[112]

In the end, Norris and the anti-tariff senators adhered to their views and voted against the excise taxes. Senators from oil, coal, lumber, and copper producing states outvoted them, however, and the excise taxes passed.

Huey left the Senate on May 26 (he cast his tax votes by telegram or as paired) and returned to Louisiana. Meeting his son Russell at the train station, Huey said he needed "a rest," after seeing he couldn't do any more in Washington.[113] Actually, he returned because the Louisiana legislature was in session. The road bond compromise of March had only paid the highway contractors. The state treasury faced a critical shortfall. Huey had to solve this problem fast, before he left for the Chicago Democratic Convention to help choose a presidential nominee.

# Seventeen

# NOMINATING A PRESIDENT

While Huey was in Washington, O. K. Allen had been sworn in as governor of Louisiana to "Complete the Work" on Huey's program. Allen gave the shortest inaugural speech in Louisiana history. The legislature gathered in the old capitol and then continued its session at the new one, just completed and dedicated on May 16. At thirty-four stories, it was the tallest capitol in the nation and the tallest building in the South. Anti-Long journalist T. O. Harris "doubted whether even Pericles ever achieved anything half as magnificent and imposing."[1] In a style the *Times* called a "restrained modern interpretation of classical motifs," it had Alabama limestone, Vermont marble, Minnesota granite, and stone and marble from Italy, Spain, France, and Germany. Fifty-foot portals led to Memorial Hall, where murals by Jules Guérin in the style of early Mayan color panels, bronze plaques by the Piccirilli Brothers, and a "ceiling of rare beauty by Louis J. Borgo" were among the attractions. Forty-eight steps, one for every state at the time, led to the entrance. Around the doors were reliefs featuring Louisiana's resources and economy, carvings of historical significance, a frieze at the base of the building, statues, flags, and murals. One-ton bronze doors that led into the Senate and House chambers pictured scenes of Louisiana history. Outside were gardens with native trees. The fifth floor included a lounge for women different in style from the rest of the building. The temple surmounting the tower was "topped by a 23-foot lantern symbolizing the higher aspirations of Louisiana." Huey received credit for the visualization of the new capitol, although one legislator called it "Huey's silo."[2] It received thousands of visitors each month.

After his return on May 26, Huey confronted the crisis caused by the $4–5 million revenue shortfall.[3] The state was close to insolvency.[4] Huey could have but did not point out that state payrolls had been trimmed. Instead, Huey opposed calls for economy and proposed new taxes: on cigarettes and cigars, life insurance premiums, electricity, freight trucks, pay telephones, firearms, vehicles for hire, corporate franchises, and bottled drinks.[5]

Huey told LSU graduates that, if they wanted to get anything done, they would have to knock down the person in their way to get it.[6] Huey demonstrated this as he fought for his tax bills. They were referred to the House Ways and Means Committee, where lobbyists gathered to object. Huey denied hearings: "You can't have it. We know what we're doing and we're going to do it." The Chamber of Commerce protested, but Huey said: "The Assassination of Commerce didn't amount to much during my administration and ain't going to amount to even that much now." The Manufacturer's Association objected, but Huey said: "Why didn't all you lovin', kindly manufacturers, with your hearts bursting with human sympathy, do something to help us feed the hungry and aid the unemployed?"[7]

Huey dominated Governor Allen, too. Before the Ways and Means Committee, Huey asked for copies of bills under consideration. When they weren't at hand, he told Allen to go to the clerk of the House and get them. Allen pretended not to hear. Huey exploded: he could "break him" as easily as he had "made him." Allen "hot footed back, placing the desired papers in the hands of the 'Kingfish.'" Huey ignored protests demanding that he return to Washington, DC,[8] but taxpayer outrage caused him to allow testimony before a Senate committee.[9]

When that meeting started, no one showed up at first. Feigning indignation, Huey said he had worked all night on a speech and now "there's no audience." Huey had spoken too soon. Protesters arrived in a steady stream until there was a crowd of unhappy taxpayers. The critics demanded government economy measures and asked what Huey was doing there, given that Allen was the governor.

Huey imported jobholders from New Orleans to counteract the taxpayer protests. In argument, Huey said that, because the state subsidized local governments, a refusal to enact his tax proposals would require local governments to raise theirs; that the corporate tax was copied from North Carolina, a state friendly to corporations, and was only half as much as the tax in Ohio;

and that the reductions of expenditures advocated by critics amounted to $200,000, a drop in the bucket to what was needed.[10] Huey said he neutralized the oil industry by threatening to reintroduce the occupational license tax if it opposed his tax program, so it decided not to, and that because he neutralized the powerful industries in this way, the other (weaker) opponents couldn't mount an effective protest.[11] But in the Senate the tax rates and the number of taxes were reduced. The carbon black tax was eliminated to keep that industry in the state. The bottlers' association met with Huey and Allen and achieved a compromise.[12] The Kingfish was thus cited for his domination of the legislative process but also twitted when the representatives "made a tremendous slash" in taxes,[13] a compromise characteristic of functioning democracies.

Democracy didn't satisfy everyone. Wealthy planter John Wartell, giving a speech to a tax protest delegation he led to Baton Rouge, said, "How many of you men have Springfields? Well, it's about time to use them. When peaceable methods fail, then it is time to use something else. . . . A bunch of red-blooded Americans can show the Kingfish a piece of rope and tell him to go back to Washington."[14]

Williams said that Dudley LeBlanc's bodyguard, Joseph Boudreaux, had a reputation as a tough, had been prosecuted fifteen times for assault, and had once put Huey's friend Bob Brothers in the hospital. If this latter reference was to the Grant Parish incident, Williams was mistaken. Boudreaux had threatened to blacken both of Huey's eyes, however, so when he appeared at the capitol, Huey's bodyguard Louie Jones hustled him outside. Jones claimed that Boudreaux reached for a weapon and Jones beat him to it, pistol-whipping him, but the papers reported that Boudreaux was slugged from behind as he went to investigate the expulsion of his chauffeur from the capitol at the point of Joe Messina's gun. Jones was indicted in Baton Rouge, convicted of assault and battery, and sentenced to six months in prison. Reprieved by Governor Allen after serving two months, he was welcomed back into Huey's service.[15]

After more than three weeks of hard work, Huey's revenue bills—as reduced—passed.[16] A *Times* reporter wrote that, "There is no such thing as precedent, . . . delay, . . . [or] lack of money. Huey Long always finds a way. . . . The remainder of the United States must expect to be startled by the tactics of this roaring, rushing, ruthless enemy of custom and caution. His success lies in his ability to make the matter an accomplished fact while his opponents are still discussing it. . . . What could be stranger than that the people of a state in

1932 are fairly well content with new taxes and an increased budget."[17] Ironically, some taxes were like the sales tax that he had denounced in Washington, but Huey claimed they were not passed on to consumers.[18]

At the last moment in June, ex-governors Parker, Pleasant, and J. Y. Sanders Sr. convened a convention of sorts to select a rival delegation to the Democratic National Convention.[19] It lacked representatives from each parish, but it met and elected delegates to challenge Huey's delegation. There is something funny about a bunch of ex-officeholders getting together to declare themselves delegates, especially after the Paul Cyr farce.

Huey decided to make a farce of their convention by arranging for a third group to declare themselves delegates, named the Unterrified Democrats.[20] They announced their devotion to Senator Jules Fisher for president and Representative George Delesdernier (he of the ridiculous speech comparing Huey to Jesus) for vice president. This mocking burlesque proceeded with a parade into the legislature. Banners proclaimed: "Democracy Needs Delesdernier" and "Delesdernier, Democracy's Darling." The legislature went along and selected a delegate from each parish to vote for the slate. Their platform endorsed the gin fizz cocktail. All three groups traveled to Chicago for the Democratic National Convention while the legislature was still in session, but after all revenue bills were passed.[21] Huey drafted an appropriation bill to be enacted while he was gone and then left to attend the convention.[22]

A big detour delayed Huey's arrival in Chicago. While in Washington earlier in the session, Huey had objected to the appointment of Ernest A. Burguieres as commissioner of immigration in New Orleans.[23] When Huey was in Louisiana, however, Broussard got a favorable committee vote and tried to call up a confirmation vote. Senator Reed denounced Huey's prolonged absence from the Senate and supported Broussard. The committee chairman and others unsupportive of Huey's politics prevented the confirmation vote in Huey's absence, however.[24]

Senators with no ideological affinity whatsoever often supported each other on matters of personnel or elections. Thus, although Huey lacked any political kinship with Senator Bailey of North Carolina, one of the most conservative senators, he supported Bailey's objection to a U.S. attorney nominee for North Carolina because the candidate was personally obnoxious to him. Expecting to be backed on his personnel objections, Huey had reciprocated in advance and, on the matter of Burguieres, Republican Senator Bingham of Connecticut likewise supported Huey blindly.

When Huey arrived in Washington on June 20, anxious to get to Chicago for the convention, he denounced Reed. Previously Reed was absent because of private law business, whereas Huey's absence was caused by his devotion to the education of 650,000 Louisiana school children. Norris and others agreed that, because the committee chairman told Huey that no vote would be taken while he was absent, the vote should be postponed until Huey had a chance to present evidence against Burguieres. On June 21, Huey opposed appointing Marcel Garsaud to the Federal Power Commission.[25] Throughout the debate, Huey proclaimed his impatience to get to Chicago because in the upcoming election the chickens were coming home to roost on Hoover and his party.[26]

Vowing to outdress that "pink whiskered [Senator J. Hamilton Lewis of Illinois] old man" in his own state, Huey arrived in Chicago with a trunkful of new suits. As he exited the train, newsmen asked if he would accept the nomination of the Farmer-Labor Party as president. No, Huey replied, there was no use being nominated if there was no one to rule. What about the vice-presidential nomination of the Democratic Party? "Huey Long ain't vice to anybody or anything"; he would rather be the biggest man in a small town than the second biggest man in a big town. What about the challenge to his delegation? The antis' optimism reminded Huey of the drunken Irishman who woke up the next morning in a graveyard and, after looking around, decided that it was resurrection day, and he was the first to rise. What about the Republican platform? It was like Mother Hubbard's cupboard, it covered everything and touched nothing.

Huey's bodyguards were made honorary Chicago policemen. One was assigned to shadow Mrs. Pleasant, a member of the rump delegation. Victor Thorssen, Huey's first traveling salesman boss, then an accountant living in Indiana, got free passes to the convention.[27]

A "Stop Roosevelt" coalition had developed but had not united behind anyone. Many states' delegates were pledged to favorite sons, politicians of their states with no chance to win absent a deadlock that required deals to secure a majority. Of the noncandidates, Mayor Cermak of Chicago, Mayor Frank Hague of New Jersey, and John F. Curry, the head of the Tammany Hall organization, controlled many delegates. At the convention, Smith and McAdoo met and agreed to stop Roosevelt, appearing to smooth over their rivalry from 1924.[28]

Roosevelt's inner circle of advisors was not familiar with Huey. Farley was puzzled when he received Huey's reply to his question about whether Louisiana followed the "unit rule," whereby a majority of a state's delegation bound the entire delegation's votes: "We vote as a unit on everything." The statement was colorful but not true. When prohibition repeal was proposed, Walmsley joined the wet parade while Huey stayed seated, and the Louisiana delegates voted for repeal seventeen to three.[29]

In early June, Roosevelt had a preconvention meeting at his home in Hyde Park, New York, with Burton Wheeler, Cordell Hull, Thomas Walsh, Josephus Daniels, and other supporters. They were hostile to the two-thirds rule, which required the nominee to obtain two-thirds of the convention votes. Roosevelt left it up to Farley whether to do anything about it.

On June 23, 1932, Huey attended a preconvention meeting in Chicago of a wider group of Roosevelt leaders led by Farley. They discussed asking the convention to abolish the two-thirds rule. Huey gave a rousing speech in favor of abolition that took the hardened politicians present "by storm." They voted overwhelmingly to propose its abolition. It was the "most sensational development" of the convention.

Farley wrote later that Huey's move hit him "like a blow on the nose,"[30] but other leaders such as Senators Hull, Dill, and Wheeler also spoke in its favor. The two-thirds rule gave the southern states veto power over the nomination. Thus, even some Roosevelt delegates in the South rebelled. All other candidates—hoping Roosevelt would fail to get the two-thirds vote to win—objected, arguing that the rules should not be changed in the middle of the convention. Farley backed off.

This is often portrayed as an example of Huey the loose cannon, acting on his own and boxing the Roosevelt forces into a disadvantageous position. Years later, however, Farley said Roosevelt wanted to abolish the rule but lacked the courage to propose it. By having Farley appear to lose control over the meeting, Huey would take the brunt of any backlash and Farley could deny responsibility for it if it failed, and this is what he did. The progression of articles about it shows the successful effort to spin it this way, as opposed to what really happened.[31]

In Roosevelt's concession on the two-thirds rule, he suggested that some mechanism be put in place to prevent a convention deadlock, such as had occurred in 1924. Huey appeared before a subcommittee of the Rules Committee and urged that the two-thirds rule be abolished after a certain number of ballots if a nominee had not been selected. The subcommittee voted in favor of this change, but reaction again was fierce, and the Roosevelt forces again retreated.[32] The Roosevelt campaign used Huey as a kind of political Jeb Stuart, who probed and prodded and pressed the opposition, looking for weaknesses and seeking advantages. It showed a microcosm of their contrasting styles: Roosevelt working in the shadows, subtle and devious; Huey open, bold, and aggressive.

Before the convention, Roosevelt had agreed that long-time Democratic leader Jouett Shouse would become chairman of the convention. He began acting like one. Shouse could influence the contest over whether to seat Huey's delegation. Roosevelt decided to repudiate his deal and Huey, not part of the original deal, could help upend it.

The contest over seating Huey's delegation, along with contests about delegates from Puerto Rico and Minnesota, were no mere fights about correct procedure, state law, or national party policy. Anti-Roosevelt forces knew that Huey had endorsed Roosevelt and therefore wanted to seat the rival delegation led by Parker, Pleasant, and Sanders.

Shouse had appointed a subcommittee of the credentials committee to hear contests challenging the legitimacy of state delegations. Huey believed that the appointment of the subcommittee was illegal in the absence of a vote by the convention itself and that appearing before one appointed by Shouse portended defeat. The other contested delegations joined him and refused to appear before it. "The boycott worked," with the subcommittee declining to make any recommendation in the absence of evidence, and the Democratic National Committee then heard the controversy.[33]

Here, Huey blundered. Sanders gave a magnolia-and-molasses speech, arguing that his delegation was filled with "clean" Democrats who had been "elected" in contrast to Huey's delegation that was "selected." The Unterrified Democrats argued next. Their spokesman said, "There are three kinds of fishes here. The Kingfish on one side, the ex-fishes on the other, and I am the little fish"; joked about graft; promoted gin fizzes; and withdrew Delesdernier's candidacy for vice president because no one could "pronounce his name."

The *Times* story made funny reading, but the delegates had no time to waste on a burlesque by a delegation that was obviously a front for Huey. Huey spoke last, gave a vitriolic attack on his opponents, and was booed and heckled. The Roosevelt loyalists, a majority, voted to seat Huey's delegation, many of them doing so reluctantly, and some southern Roosevelt supporters voted against him.[34]

When the credentials committee accepted the appeal, the hearing room was jammed. Walmsley spoke first and led off, foolishly, with the statement that he was not Huey's "henchman"—basing it on his opposition to Huey during the Senate race—which provoked only a roar of laughter and ridicule. The audience cheered and jeered Huey, and again he gave an arm-waving, emotional performance. The committee argued until 3 a.m. before voting to seat Huey's delegation with another divided vote, thirty-four to seventeen. It more narrowly defeated a proposal to give each delegation a one-half vote.[35] The committee minority appealed to the entire convention.

Roosevelt's floor leader, Arthur Mullen, told Huey the Roosevelt forces would back him, but only if he quit clowning. Ordinarily credentials decisions have little impact, H. L. Mencken wrote, but the contest between "Huey Long and his enemies in Louisiana" had "stirred the convention."[36]

Huey was everywhere at once, "wild-eyed, gesticulating," but also "one of the most outstanding figures in the Roosevelt clan."[37] Author Oulahan said Huey was indefatigable in his efforts for Roosevelt, whom he *had not* met, but only because he *had met* the other candidates. Al Smith described Huey and Wheeler as the two new generals, with Huey "breezing" through the hotel in an "ice cream colored suit."[38] At one strategy meeting, Huey joked about stuffing ballot boxes, disgusting Roosevelt fundraiser Frank Walker.[39] A chance, cordial meeting with McAdoo was reported.[40] Huey barged into Garner headquarters and bet someone $1,000 with two-to-one odds that Roosevelt would take Texas by 100,000 votes.[41] He met William Jennings Bryan's son, who gave him a pen that had belonged to his father. Huey said he was carrying on Bryan's work.[42] Huey was photographed with Honey Fitzgerald, former mayor of Boston. Huey tried to recruit Alfalfa Bill Murray to Roosevelt's cause, waking him up at daybreak ("You're the farmer's candidate, aren't you; farmers are up by this time of day"). Murray tried to convince him to run for president. When Murray went into the bathroom to shave, Huey ate Murray's room-service breakfast—proper punishment for Murray's effort to "exuberate" him—and left. Murray said the two had used some cuss words, but all in good fun.[43] Governor Ritchie gave Huey a cigar; in response Huey promised him the Louisiana delegation on the ninety-ninth ballot.[44] When Huey wanted to relax, he joined boyhood friend and singing star Gene Austin at his apartment where, with Austin's friends, they held jam sessions. Huey composed a campaign song, but the feedback was harsh. Huey snarled that the critic could work on it. The critic, Harry Woods, did, turning it into a hit, "We Just Couldn't Say Goodbye," one week later.[45]

One of the themes of the press was the role of women in politics, and some of Huey's opponents were aristocratic women, such as Mrs. Pleasant, who said that Huey was a "gibbering monkey" and lacked respect for women. Stella Hamlin quoted Huey as saying if you were going to tell a story, tell a tall one, but the article noted that Huey had a letter of hers that supported what he said against her.[46] To rebut the critics, Huey cited the women leaders in his delegation[47] and brought Rose up to Chicago to show people that he knew how to treat a "skirt." Newsmen asked Rose how long she had been married. She replied, "I don't even remember."[48]

The boss of the Tennessee delegation, Mayor Ed Crump of Memphis, was reminded by Huey of his services in the election eve brawl when he was a salesman sixteen years earlier. Crump remembered and told Huey that he would "go to the bridge" for him.[49] Incensed to learn that Senator Byrd's Virginia delegation was going to oppose his slate, Huey yelled in the middle of a hotel lobby that he was "going to kill" Byrd, frightening Byrd's seventeen-year-old son. Later, Huey invited Byrd to his suite. Byrd told his associates that, if they hadn't heard from him in ten minutes, to come over with a gun and rescue him. Huey only wanted to urge Byrd to run for vice president. "I got used to the vagaries of politics," said his son.[50]

The seating of Huey's delegation would be the first convention-wide test of Roosevelt's support. Arguing against Huey was Illinois senator Scott Lucas, a former prosecutor and a capable senator. Roosevelt floor leader Arthur Mullen and Huey would speak for Huey's delegation. Lucas argued that Huey was warned in 1928 to hold a convention but had vetoed a bill to require it. The Sanders group was selected by a convention and therefore should be seated.

Wearing a white linen suit and a royal purple tie, Huey was booed, especially by the Texas delegation, when he stood up to respond. The proceedings were broadcast by radio. Huey leaned into the microphone and shouted, "Don't applaud me! Don't applaud me! My time is limited, and I don't want applause!" Huey expected that radio listeners would accept his word that he was applauded.[51] Huey then gave a well-reasoned speech, citing Louisiana statutes and Democratic Party rules showing that his delegation was legal. Gone was the clowning and boorishness. The expected southern demagogue was absent. Present was a lawyer summarizing the law and the facts.

During his speech, he would have an assistant (some say this was Mayor Walmsley) hand him different law books, and Huey would open them to a marked page but then quote from statutes or case decisions, without reading them, sometimes for several paragraphs. The Louisiana State Central Committee that elected the delegates was itself elected. The current leader of the rump convention (Frank Looney) was a member of that committee and had acquiesced in its action. The Sanders delegation held its meeting shortly before the convention, because if they had held it soon after Huey's delegation was selected in February, there would have been time to get an injunction to stop it as contrary to Louisiana law. Illinois's at-large delegates were selected by the exact same procedure (by its state central committee), a circumstance serviceably close for Huey to argue that Lucas was inconsistent. Huey closed with one rhetorical flourish: his delegation represented the living Democratic Party of Louisiana. Its delegates included the eight congressmen, the two U.S. senators, the sitting governor, and the immediately preceding governor.

The delegates first quieted down, then listened respectfully, and finally applauded genuinely. Clarence Darrow told Huey that it was one of the greatest summaries of fact and evidence that he had ever heard. Will Rogers wrote that Huey had won his own game. The *Times* said Huey "spoke eloquently of his cause." Its columnist Arthur Krock said Huey "impressed the convention with his high abilities as a persuasive advocate."[52] The *Chicago Tribune*, characteristically biased, said many delegates were disappointed at the absence of rhetorical fireworks.[53]

The vote to seat Huey's delegation was a decisive victory for Roosevelt: 638 to 514. A shift of 63 votes would have reversed the outcome. Farley said this was the most vital moment of the convention. As the vote was announced, Huey "grabbed the Louisiana standard, jumped on a chair, and waived his arms in triumph."[54]

The Roosevelt forces also prevailed in the following delegate contests, but never by the magic two-thirds vote. A few historians note that the other contested delegations received larger votes, because Huey's politics and manners repelled some southern Roosevelt delegates. But Roosevelt supported Montana senator Thomas Walsh, a hero of the Teapot Dome scandal and a fair chairman during the exhausting 1924 convention, to be convention chairman instead of Shouse. Huey received more votes than the squeaky clean and respectable Walsh, who defeated Shouse by the narrower margin of 626 to 528.[55]

Now the presidential candidate voting began. On the first ballot, Roosevelt took the lead, but not the nomination. The unknown was how long the delegations would remain loyal, whether to Roosevelt or favorite sons. Senator Harrison of Mississippi, a Roosevelt supporter, left the convention after two ballots, thinking it would adjourn. Instead, the third roll call began. Alarmed at the possible defection of the Mississippi and Arkansas delegations, the Roosevelt command asked Huey for help. Huey stormed onto the floor, sweat streamed down his face; his pongee suit wilted. He shook his fist in Governor Mike Conner's face, and said if he broke the unit rule, he would invade Mississippi and break him, calling him a sonofabitch. Harrison made it back to the convention, not fully dressed, having received a panicked phone call. Huey cajoled and reinforced individual delegates from those two states and others, if they were wavering.[56] With Huey's crucial help, Roosevelt's forces held during the third and fourth ballots.[57]

When Roosevelt agreed to take John Nance Garner of Texas as vice president, he broke the deadlock. Delegates from Texas and California switched to Roosevelt, after which Mayor Cermak led a general stampede to Roosevelt, nominating him. Huey was not involved in this deal or any of these negotiations. Joseph Kennedy, the biggest of Roosevelt's preconvention fundraisers; William Randolph Hearst; Sam Rayburn; John Nance Garner; William McAdoo; and the Roosevelt forces did the negotiating and the dealing. The key fear of Hearst was that, if Roosevelt failed, the convention would turn to Newton Baker, the internationalist protégé of Woodrow Wilson, whom Hearst hated. Kennedy called Hearst to scare him with the prospect of Baker; Hearst called Garner's people about Roosevelt; and then Farley negotiated with Garner's confidant, Congressman Sam Rayburn, and, separately, McAdoo. McAdoo enjoyed thwarting Al Smith's chances because of their rivalry since the epic 1924 convention. The vice-presidential deal with Garner omitted Huey's friend Senator Wheeler, who wanted the nomination and who had been the first senator to endorse Roosevelt. Wheeler was disappointed.[58]

Roosevelt leaders conceded that Huey helped nominate Roosevelt. Had he fumbled the argument over seating his delegation or failed to hold for Roosevelt the southern delegations on the third and fourth ballot, the convention would have nominated someone else.

A harbinger of trouble between Huey and Roosevelt occurred at some point during the balloting. In 1924, World War I veterans had been voted a bonus to add to their low wages during the war. These adjusted service certificates came due in 1945. The severity of the Depression caused veterans to ask that they be paid now instead of in 1945. In the spring and summer of 1932, they descended on Washington, DC, to urge legislation to pay the bonus. Conservatives thought this would unbalance the budget; progressives supported it to help the veterans and add consumer spending to the economy.[59] When it looked as if the Roosevelt coalition would splinter, Huey called Roosevelt and urged him to endorse the soldiers' bonus. When Roosevelt declined, Huey said he was a "gone goose" and hung up.

After his big speech, Huey continued in an active role. When seconding speeches of the presidential candidates dragged on interminably, Huey moved to cut them off, drawing laughter and applause. When Alfalfa Bill Murray was nominated, Huey from the speaker's stand motioned for Louisiana's delegates to join his parade, even though they were not voting for him. Huey joined the Ritchie parade "all in fun" after a lady "blew him a kiss."[60] One of the thirty-seven speakers to second the nomination of John Nance Garner for vice president, "the irrepressible [Huey] brought a laugh by shouting: "we sent soldiers to Texas in 1836 and we'll help 'em again."[61] Ross Sterling must have enjoyed that. Will Rogers wrote that "Huey Long, the Louisiana porcupine, is still the hero of the whole convention."[62]

Roosevelt announced that he would break precedent and appear in person to accept the nomination, a bold symbolic move, and would travel to Chicago by plane, to boost the developing airline industry. Roosevelt's acceptance speech offered a "New Deal" for the American people. Roosevelt warned "nominal" Democrats who were "out of step" with the party because the people wanted a "genuine choice." Roosevelt asserted "the right of all people to a more equitable opportunity to share in the national wealth."[63] Huey said it was arduous work getting him nominated, but now Roosevelt would win in a landslide.[64]

Huey didn't drink during the convention, but after Roosevelt won the nomination, he got plastered.[65] He left Chicago before Roosevelt's acceptance speech was delivered to return to Louisiana.

While Huey was in Chicago, his legislative supporters had split over a bill Huey proposed before he left. It added regulations designed to drive the burial society Dudley LeBlanc owned out of Louisiana. Two of Huey's legislators had a fistfight about it. The House voted it down.[66] After Huey returned, the legislature passed the bill. If the legislature's action on taxes shows a functioning democracy, the legislation to put a political rival out of business shows a democratic, that is, a majoritarian tyranny. Or does it? Republican Ed Talbot, a lawyer in the U.S. Attorney's Office, told Huey that LeBlanc's burial society was fraudulent, with LeBlanc skimming money that the members contributed. Talbot had obtained a warrant to seize records from LeBlanc's office to indict him for mail fraud, but that night a fire destroyed them. He couldn't prove his case without the records. Talbot's statement may be true, but it isn't corroborated. Whether the legislation was justified or not, it took LeBlanc only a brief time to move his business over the state line, where it continued.[67]

In this session, the legislature often acted independently of Huey, who concentrated on the vital revenue measures. They voted for a tax on chain stores,[68] passed a tick eradication measure,[69] a tax on nightclubs,[70] and defeated a bill to allow former governors privileges to appear on the floor of the legislature.[71] Allen vetoed several bills.[72]

Two days before the Louisiana legislative session ended, Huey dashed up to Washington, DC, to help pass a relief bill and legislation to aid farmers. Senator Norris introduced a resolution to publicize Reconstruction Finance Corporation loans, and Huey spoke for it more than Norris. Huey decried secrecy. The corporation was just a back door for the House of Morgan or people with connections to borrow money, shoveled out by the "wheelbarrow."[73]

On July 7, Huey urged passage of the relief bill and relief for farmers, regardless of the threat of veto by Hoover. It passed. He voted for the conference report on the public works bill, which passed forty-three to thirty-one. On Saturday, July 9, just to get some laughs, Huey criticized Senator Bingham for withdrawing his own beer amendment: "in the thirst that has come, with lips just waiting for it. . . . But now, behold, the leader . . . has fled, and there is no beer here, and no beer near here, nor any beer that can be near here . . . [*laughter*]."[74]

Huey renewed his fight against the appointment of Marcel Garsaud to the Federal Power Commission. Norris submitted an editorial from the *Washington Herald* opposing him.[75] Huey said he had witnesses ready to be heard. Senator Couzens argued in vain that the evidentiary record was closed.[76] Huey was allowed to cross-examine Garsaud in committee and bragged that he blew him out of the water. Neither Garsaud nor Bergeruires was confirmed.[77]

Huey supported Norris's lengthy attack on utility company misconduct and intervened on behalf of the relief bill, which was subject to disagreement between the conferees of the House and Senate. Now Huey was less willing to provoke a veto; he wanted to get the bill passed.[78] Conscious of the upcoming campaign, Huey confronted Senator Smoot about his claim that World War I caused the Depression, questioning him about the absurdity of blaming the war after nine years of intervening prosperity. Smoot quit the debate, saying: "I want to get through. I do not want all of this nonsense in my remarks."[79]

In 1937, M. S. Cushman wrote that Huey was absent for eighty-one Senate sessions after he arrived in 1932 and present for only fifty-six days. Cushman drew no adverse inferences from these statistics and did not purport to explain what Huey was doing when he was absent. Later historians have quoted him to criticize Huey's Senate career. Considered a favorable biographer, Williams nevertheless wrote that Huey used the Senate as a forum to advertise himself. Brinkley was the harshest: Huey lacked any "serious interest" in the work of the Senate, "shamelessly" pursued publicity, and "flagrantly" and "consistently" neglected his duties. The Senate was a "casual plaything—a toy to be used" when he wanted publicity.[80]

The first four months of Huey's Senate career are a microcosm of how he approached politics. There was a maldistribution of wealth. The defining issue to remedy it was taxation. A tax proposal would smoke out everyone who didn't believe that there was a maldistribution or who didn't want to do anything about it. Huey measured the Senate and learned that the men in power there wouldn't do anything about it. He realized that he didn't know enough, so he studied authorities. The March sales tax and the April "Doom" speeches show that he had done significant homework between them. Huey cited more authorities in the "Doom" speech. Huey's April 29 speech included quotations of Lord Francis Bacon, and the May 12 speech cited Talleyrand and others in addition to John Truslow Adams.

Huey's tax and "Doom" speeches and the potlikker publicity stunt all evidence a plan and advanced the tax issue he championed. He ignored the cold shoulders—explicit or implicit reprimands—and persisted. Huey refused to play it safe. When opposed, he dramatically confronted his biggest opponent. By the end of May, he had broken through to the national consciousness. Some senators never break through. It had taken four months.

A holistic view of his schedule, moreover, explains his Senate absences. The extended absences in February and part of early March were prompted by personal and political Louisiana business, particularly relating to the highway bond sale crisis and the selection of delegates to the Democratic National Convention A collapse of state finances or the road bond program might have derailed his career as well as the state.

After breaking through to the national consciousness, Huey stayed in Louisiana from the end of May through mid-June, missing twenty-one Senate sessions. Huey was lobbying the state legislature to impose controversial new taxes to replenish the depleted state treasury. He was present in the Senate on June 20 and 21 but then missed eleven more Senate days attending the Democratic National Convention. He returned for nine days in July, missing only the last Saturday session.

During the extended absence of twenty-one days, Huey could have advertised himself and chased publicity if he had stayed in the Senate while new public works and relief bills were debated. Huey missed an opportunity to gain experience about the bills under discussion and to get to know his colleagues. He could have contributed to the banking and highway construction debates that occurred during these absences. Most of the skipped sessions involved tedious discussions of appropriations, however, about which Huey knew little.

Theoretically, Huey should have left Louisiana state business to the state officials for whom he had campaigned. But one doubts that they could have saved the road bond program or passed the tax increases to cover the state revenue shortfall. No other politician in the country was then advocating tax increases to maintain government spending. Huey needed to safeguard his base in Louisiana. He didn't want the state to run out of money, cut spending, or reduce his patronage.

Huey left Louisiana in February to return to the Senate during its debate on labor-union injunctions, important to his union constituency and an issue with which he was familiar from his labor-union work as a lawyer. In March, he returned to the Senate to participate in the debate over tariffs, important to Louisiana's sugar and oil industries. The other periodic absences in April and May involved less significant Senate debates or matters over which he could exert no influence. Huey left Louisiana and skipped an event that he would have liked to attend and at which he was scheduled to speak—the dedication of the new state capitol in May—to participate in the Senate debate over taxes.

Before Huey returned to Louisiana at the end of May, he caused Minority Leader Robinson to propose a new relief program to combat the Great Depression, helped obtain a higher tax rate on the wealthy and an excise tax on oil, and decided—based on Senate and House votes on the issues—to reverse himself and support Franklin Roosevelt for president. Relief bills were passed late in the same Senate session that had rejected them in February.

Huey's first four months in the Senate also evidence in a small way Huey's characteristic mistake of overreaching. After the success he had dramatizing the need for taxes on the wealthy, Huey enraged Tydings and George and the Senate during the excise tax debate. Some in the Senate viewed Huey as a publicity hound, a gasbag, or as someone who was willing to delay Senate business to get his way.[81] The senators from the lumber, coal, copper, and oil producing states could not have disliked him very much.[82] And the outnumbered progressives could use all the help they could get. Huey helped them get the compromise victory on the tax rates for the wealthy. Norris and Wheeler liked Huey and cooperated with him. Senator Lewis—opposed to Huey's tax views—joked with Huey.[83] One of the most conservative senators (Bailey of

North Carolina) didn't hesitate to borrow a pair of cufflinks from Huey.[84] Roosevelt supporters such as Walsh of Montana or Wagner of New York were courteous to him, perhaps because he supported Roosevelt.[85]

The evidence thus contradicts the idea that Huey lacked friends in the Senate, that he viewed it in 1932 only as a platform for publicity, or that he was irresponsible. Senators with an ideological affinity often differed on details, means, and tactics. In the next Senate session, Huey thanked George for suggesting a change to an amendment of Huey's that gave no hint of prior bitterness by either man.

Huey also perceived that the best way to change the power dynamics in the Senate and the country depended on the presidential election. The February selection of his state delegation to the Democratic National Convention—accomplished in Louisiana—was essential to cement his influence at the convention. Huey's early March meeting with Al Smith was a responsible effort to vet one of the candidates. Huey analyzed the contenders, changed his initial view, and supported the candidate at the convention who professed to be the most progressive of the candidates.

Having helped nominate a candidate who warned "nominal" Democrats that the people wanted a "genuine choice" and a more equitable distribution of the national wealth, the two elements of Huey's quarrel with Robinson, Huey had seemingly leapfrogged Robinson in influence and prestige. And he wasn't through demonstrating his ascendancy over Robinson. Huey's final speech of this session was to help a fellow senator get reelected. The campaign that followed was made on behalf of the person who sat beside him in the Senate. It made Huey famous.

# Eighteen

# AN OVER-THE-BORDER RAID

Senator Hattie Caraway of Arkansas was a mousy little woman who looked as if she should be sitting in a rocking chair darning socks, said the *Times*.[1] Instead she sat next to Huey in the Senate. She considered Huey a radical and thought his more vitriolic speeches ill-advised. But she had voted in favor of his tax resolutions, and they were friends. Huey would ask how his "pardner" was doing. When he returned after some absence, Huey would ask if she had remained "true" to the Kingfish.

Hattie's husband, Arkansas senator Thad Caraway, had died three days before the time that would have allowed his successor to be appointed to fill the remainder of his term. Although an election was therefore required, the state politicians could not unite on a candidate. Rather than bear the expense and time of two campaigns (one for the remaining term and another for the full term), they united behind his widow. They could either resolve their differences before the next campaign started or fight it out in one campaign. No one thought Hattie would run when her husband's term ended or, that if she ran, she could win.

Six candidates announced for the full-term seat. They were prominent: a former two-term governor, a national commander of the American Legion, a Democratic National Committeeman, a sheriff of Pulaski County (Little Rock), an attorney, and a former U.S. senator and current Arkansas Supreme Court justice.

After significant indecision, Hattie filed to be a candidate on May 9, the day before the deadline.[2] She asked Huey if she had any chance. Huey checked. After a few days, Huey told her she had no chance and shouldn't run. She wept. Journalist Deutsch wrote that Huey had a sentimental streak. When Huey discovered that she had voted with him while her home was being foreclosed upon, that "settled matters." On May 21, Huey bounced into her office and told her she should run, and he would help her campaign. Huey also saw the campaign as a "glorious opportunity to show Joe Robinson who was who."[3]

They would make her campaign in one week, Huey said, just before the election on August 9, which would not let their opponents overcome their surprise. She thought about it, then accepted, if he wouldn't try to control her vote or attack Joe Robinson.[4]

Hattie had no chance to win without him. Her journals include entries such as "Guess my political life is nearly over." Out of 250,000 votes expected, it was thought that she would finish last, with 3,000 votes from resolute feminists, personal friends, and devotees of her late husband. No woman had ever won a contested election to a full term in the U.S. Senate from Arkansas—or any other state.

At Huey's suggestion, Hattie left the Senate to start her campaign in July, a few weeks before the election. She sounded a feminist theme. "The time has passed when a woman should be placed in a position and kept there only while someone else is being groomed for the job."[5]

On July 13, 1932, Huey read Hattie's statement that she was returning to Arkansas to campaign, and then gave his last Senate speech of the session, recounting her progressive record, noting that she had not voted with Senator Robinson, even though he was the leader of her party. She had a humanitarian record, as shown by her votes for tariffs on oil and lumber and for higher taxes on the wealthy.[6] Questioned on July 15 whether he were going to campaign for her, Huey denied plans but said he might, if asked. Huey then left for Louisiana.[7]

In Arkansas, rumors circulated that Hattie might withdraw. Few responded to her announcement. None responded to her requests for contributions.[8] Many people who might have supported her had signed on with someone else, believing she would not run. Seymour Weiss investigated her organization but found nothing, no mailing list, no supporters, no fundraisers or contributors.[9]

Days after Hattie arrived in Arkansas, she selected Marshall Purvis as her campaign manager. Purvis was a lawyer. He had represented a prostitute who fled a whorehouse brawl in such haste that she was struck by a streetcar. Suing the streetcar company, Purvis brought her to court in a dress from neck to toe, covering her numerous tattoos. Huey guessed her occupation, and he and Purvis became friends on the date Purvis celebrated a favorable settlement. Senator Robinson had once asked a grand jury to investigate Purvis for telling a witness to lie. Purvis hadn't, but from then on, he disliked Robinson and relished the chance to embarrass him.[10]

Hattie made a few radio speeches stressing her service to her constituents, her apprenticeship under her late husband, and her opposition to the Reconstruction Finance Corporation. It was a big spongy funnel that poured its money to big financial interests, socialism for the wealthy.[11]

Contemporaneously, Huey's Louisiana leaders had planned the campaign for John Overton for the Senate against Edwin Broussard. Meeting in Huey's dining room, most objected to a Caraway campaign, stating Huey was needed in Louisiana. Huey turned to Purvis, who told the group that Huey could elect Hattie; the victory would show his national appeal and set him on the road to the presidency. Huey then issued some orders relating to the Caraway campaign and "bam," the matter was decided. Huey told Louisiana leaders Weiss and Peltier that he could elect her, and it would help his prestige.[12]

On July 19, Huey revealed that he would campaign for Hattie: five speeches on August 1, six on the 2nd, four on the 3rd, three on the 4th, three on the 5th, and five on the 6th. It was a grueling schedule, but Huey complained that additional stops should have been added.[13]

About 125,000 reprints of Huey's Senate speech supporting Mrs. Caraway were mailed into Arkansas in late July. Huey wrote three circulars for her, one entitled "Wall Street Versus the People," another "A Letter from Uncle Trusty," and a third, "What the Re-election of Senator (Mrs.) Caraway Means to the People of America." Two had a cartoon in the middle.[14]

At night, Huey woke up his favorite printer, Joe David, and told him to get his crew and meet him at the shop to print the circulars: 'We're going to invade Arkansas!" David had no idea who Hattie Caraway was.[15] David also reprinted the American Federation of Labor newspaper endorsement of Hattie and Huey's "Doom of America's Dream" speech.[16] Bundles of circulars were shipped by railroad to Arkansas and given to individuals (students, for example, earning money for school) instructed to distribute them door to door and in general stores in towns of less than three thousand people.[17]

Everything was done in haste. Mrs. Caraway's name was misspelled in Huey's letter to the people of Arkansas, as was one of the towns that was the site of a planned speech in the circular announcing it.[18] Two tons of Caraway campaign literature were loaded onto trucks. Some of them were state government vehicles. When the *Times-Picayune* questioned using them for a private campaign, Huey, implementing his advice to always stay on the offensive because the defensive wasn't worth a damn, turned on the *Times-Picayune*. It was raising a "dust cloud" about the circular distribution without challenging the accuracy of the information in the circulars or the need of the people to be informed of the facts they contained.[19]

While Huey prepared for this campaign, the United States Army routed the camps in Washington, DC, where World War I veterans had gathered to urge payment of their soldiers' bonus. Unable to afford hotels, they had set up ramshackle shelters, called "Hoovervilles." Oblivious to the political and moral implications, President Hoover ordered General Douglas MacArthur to restore order there. Using tanks and tear gas, their ramshackle dwellings were torched.[20] MacArthur reflected a class-based dislike of the veterans: they were communists or bums. While governor of New York, Franklin Roosevelt, displaying the same distaste, offered the veterans a free train ticket to leave his state.[21]

On the way to Arkansas, Huey's party stopped in Winnfield, and he visited his father. Old Hu asked him if it weren't a mistake to campaign for Mrs. Caraway. Huey replied: "it wouldn't be the first mistake I've made. I don't think I am. She's as fine a person as there is in the Senate, and I don't like the gang that's fighting her." Huey borrowed a Bible from an elderly neighbor, and she told reporters how Huey used to help her make soap "right out there in the yard." Reminded that he was caught slipping a watermelon into a cotton bag, Huey pointed out the watermelon patch from which he "hook[ed]" the watermelon. A picture shows Huey in a shirt with cufflinks, eating watermelon, with a pensive expression.[22]

Hattie's Arkansas campaign team (a doctor, a druggist, and Purvis, all from Little Rock) had difficulty lining up speakers to introduce the campaigners. Anticipation had built for the campaign, however, because of the antipathy between Huey and Joe Robinson. The *Times* thought Huey was campaigning to take over Senate leadership. When Robinson returned to Arkansas from Washington, however, he announced that he would remain neutral. The newspapers nevertheless expected the Kingfish to attack him.[23]

Local writers wore themselves out using descriptive words for Huey: "pyrotechnic," "fiery," "stormy," "colorful," "dynamic," and "pugnacious" were just a few. He was expected to put on a "political circus," a "medicine show," a "first class show," a "spectacular," a "road show," and the greatest political rally ever. By July 31, Huey had put the finishing touches on his caravan: a Cadillac limousine, one advance small truck, two sound trucks, and four larger literature trucks. He would come with a Bible in one hand and a throat atomizer in the other.[24]

The sound trucks had four amplifier horns, two on each side. Inside were loudspeaker panels, phonograph-record playing equipment, a folding table and chairs, an electric fan to cool the operator, and pitchers and glasses for water. The roof was slatted. A portable stairway permitted access to it for use as a speaker's platform. It had retractable railings and lights around the edges for night speeches. While one truck was in use during the speech, the small advance truck and the other sound truck would proceed to the next town, select the location for the speech, hook up electrical connections, pass out handbills, play music, and attract a crowd.[25]

Wearing a tailored grey suit, white shirt, and flaming red tie, Huey began his tour before daylight on August 1. Farmers stood at their lot lines by the streets along which Huey drove, waving and cheering. People arrived before daybreak at his first scheduled stop in Magnolia at 9 a.m.

Huey's speeches were extemporaneous, and the absence of an advance copy of the speech reduced the size of newspaper articles reporting them. Huey preferred not to provide advance word of what he was going to say: "I never write out my sermon or make any notes. The devil would look over my shoulder and tell the congregation the answers before I could ask the questions." The speeches used similar ideas but were presented in different language, in a different order, or with different emphases at each location, until gradually, over the course of the week, it developed into an almost set speech, much as a play gets refined before it hits Broadway, or a comic hits the road and perfects material for each audience until she is ready for a television special.[26]

The "printed reproduction of fragmentary excerpts cannot convey the whole picture, the unhalting rush of words, the quick, haphazard gestures, and above all the rural intonation—'cain't' for 'can't,' 'pore' for 'poor,' the Southerner's easy slurring of consonants." Huey was not a political silver tongue and didn't use sonorous rhetoric, but rather was a gospel shouter, a revivalist, someone who could transmute ponderous abstractions into the idiom of the people with an uncanny plausibility. Many came to scoff but remained as prey.[27] Deutsch engaged a stenographer to write down one speech, and a copy of it [or part of it] is contained in his papers at Tulane although, unfortunately, it omits the crowd's reactions.[28]

Huey started with a disclaimer about Robinson. Because "Senator Robinson has announced he is taking no hand in this campaign," he wouldn't discuss their differences, which will be "thrashed out" in the Senate. "Not that I am taking back anything. Oh no. Don't get that idea." Then he explained why he was making the campaign when he could have "stayed at my quiet home" rather than "making hard, long trips over these hot and dusty roads." The reason was to save those senators who were standing by the people and defeat those who stood against them. Hattie had stood by the people.

About five minutes into the speech, Huey lauded Hattie's record with a story. Huey had an uncle, he said, who was forty years old, a gambler, a man they thought would die without being saved, but who heard a hellfire sermon that scared him into a baptism. Taken to Dugdemona Creek at 3 p.m. that Sunday, as he was dunked in the water, the ace of spades floated out of his pocket, face up, then the King, Queen, Jack, and ten of spades. His wife cried, "Don't baptize him, parson. He's lost; my husband's lost!" But the man's son said, "He ain't lost. If he can't win with that hand . . . , he can't win at all!" If Hattie couldn't win with her record of standing by the people, she couldn't win at all. Huey had originally planned to be the brilliant Thad Caraway's lieutenant in a fight to redistribute wealth. When Thad died, Huey had to take over the fight. Why was this fight necessary?

> We have more cotton and wool and silk and mohair and calico and gingham and leather than 120,000,000 people can wear out in two years and a half if we never raise another boll of cotton or sheer another sheep, and yet people are going around without clothes. We have got more houses empty and for rent and for sale than at any other time since this got to be a country, and yet people have no shelter where they can lie their head. Why is it? Why? Too much to eat and more people hungry than during the drought years; too much to wear and more people naked; too many houses and more people homeless than ever before. Why? This is a land of super-abundance and super-plenty. Then why is it also a land of starvation and nakedness and homelessness?

The answer was first found in the *McGuffey Reader:* the Aesop fable of the dog in the manger, where the dog would not let the cow eat the hay even though the dog could not eat it. Statistics backed this up. In the bad year of

1930, there was $70 billion in income, enough for $3,000 for every family, not that he was contending for an equal division. If Wall Street took half of it, there would still be enough for $1,500 for every family. One percent of the people owned 59 percent of the wealth, however, and "540 men . . . made more money than all the cotton farmers and all the wheat farmers and all the cane farmers by $100,000,000."

When Huey got to the Senate, he consulted with Senators Norris and Caraway and proposed his resolution to tax at 100 percent all incomes over $1,000,000. The newspapers then "printed cartoons of me carrying the red flag of communism, and some of them were kind enough to say that there had been other demagogues in the Senate that was as low-down as me, but that I was the most dangerous one because I was smart." Democratic and Republican leaders "hollered holy murder" when he sought to limit someone's wealth to $5 million. "Why that meant that if he stopped under a fan to cool himself off he wouldn't be making but about four dollars a minute while he was doin' it. . . . And the other part of it meant that a poor boy wouldn't be able to start out in this life with but five million sorry dollars to start him out." Mrs. Caraway's record in the Senate on the tax bills proved that she had stood by the people. (In other speeches there was the repetition of "Mrs. Caraway voted for it," or, as the case might be, "Mrs. Caraway voted against it.")[29]

There were Republican waiters on one side and another set of waiters on the Democratic side, "but back in the kitchen is only Wall Street, and no matter which set of waiters brings you the dish, it's Wall Street that has cooked it up." It reminded him of

> a patent-medicine man that used to come around my country selling two bottles of medicine. One of them he called High Popalorum and the other he called Low Popahirum. We asked him one time what was the difference between them, and he said the High Popalorum you made by skinning the bark off the tree from the bottom up, and the other one by skinning the bark from the top down. And all I can see is that the Republicans are skinning the people from the ankle up, and the Democratic leadership is taking the hide off them by starting at the ear and coming down. Now I am a Democrat and I hope I can always be one. But we have got to drive the money changers out of the temple of Democracy and return this great party of Jefferson and Jackson to the people.

The guinea hen story was revised: Wall Street took eggs and put half in the Democratic incubator and the other half in the Republican incubator, but the hatched chickens had the Wall Street cackle, cluck, and strut. This was the only time in his speech that he told three stories or analogies in succession.

Progress was being made against Wall Street, however. Senator Thomas had been reelected in Oklahoma, and Senator Clark had been elected in Missouri. Senator Broussard, one of Wall Street's own, would be defeated shortly.

> He'll be like the revenue agent that in the old days saw a boy and said where's your pa, and the boy said, up over the mountain, making whiskey. And the agent says, where's your ma, and the boy says she's there helping him. So the agent says if you take me to where they're at, I'll give you a dollar. And the boy said, gimme the dollar, and I'll take you. The agent says, I'll give you the dollar when I come back, and the boy says, no, give it to me now, because if you go up there, you ain't coming back. He ain't coming back either, Mr. Broussard ain't.

Mrs. Caraway voted right on the power trust tax when her circumstances should have induced her to vote the other way. This provided a dramatic fulcrum—story appeal—for Huey's speech. Hattie's house had been foreclosed upon.

> That was the test, my friends. With all the big-bellied politicians in Arkansas campaigning against this one little woman, she stood by you in spite of the fact that the sheriff was selling her home. . . . And don't you ever forget that she wouldn't have had to have this home sold. There was an easy road for her to take too. Wall Street takes care of its own. But this brave little woman senator stood by you in spite of it, and in spite of the fact that the big men politicians of her own state had their feet on her throat. Oh, we've pried a few of those birds loose already, and they'll all show you how to get their big feet off her neck before we're through with them in the state of Arkansas![30]

Rebutting critics of him invading the state, Huey said one of the candidates had spoken in Louisiana against him when he was being impeached. "[T]hey sent to Oklahoma for one lawyer and to Florida for another and to New York and got two. Why they came from the east, and they came from the west and they came from over the cuckoo's nest." There was no record of any Arkansas candidate coming to Louisiana when he was impeached, but what could be gained by arguing about it?

After lightly critiquing the other candidates, Huey explained that he had traveled in Arkansas as a "drummer and a printer and a sawmill hand" twenty or twenty-two years ago, "going around in wagons and on horse-back and by ankle express," a long time ago "before any of you ladies in this crowd was born," and he didn't think Arkansas people had changed in the interim. The opponents blamed him for coming into Arkansas when the problem was with them. They were like Davy Crockett, who went out to hunt a raccoon in the moonlight. He saw one, shot, but missed. He saw it again, shot, and missed again. Finally, he realized it was not a raccoon, but rather a louse in his own eyebrow. "These birds" have "got a louse in their own eyebrow that's a-bothering them."[31]

The Bible supported Huey. "Don't take my word for it. Go home and read your Bible, in Leviticus Chapters 24, 25, 26 and 27, and Chapter 5 of Nehemiah and Chapter 5 of James in the New Testament." Wall Street said he was socialistic and that "the Lord didn't know we were going to have conditions like this." The Lord "did know we were going to have birds like that to fight" and if you review the record, the countries that broke the Lord's commandment went to pieces: "Rome and Assyria and Greece and Carthage and Babylon."

Huey lacked any selfish, personal interest. He could make ten times as much money practicing law, and no one in Arkansas could vote for him in Louisiana. But he was raising children and worried how they were going to make a living. You couldn't make it farming or as a laboring man. Merchants were all broke "flatter than a pancake" because nobody had anything to buy with.

With conditions like that, were they going to turn out of office the woman with the only perfect record in the U.S. Senate? Huey fell for one scheme by which it was said if they poured $2 billion into the big men at the top, it would trickle down to the little men at the bottom. "But the trouble with that dad-blamed percolator, my friends, is that it just won't percolate." When they proposed to percolate from the bottom up, "oh no, they said, that would be socialism." It wasn't socialism to aid the wealthy, but it was socialism to aid the farmer.

Huey didn't want to go to World War I but, if they had forced him to, he would have said, "Give me a flag. Hurray!" The country promised everything to the soldiers who went: "we're going to kill the fatted calf for you, and we'll take the purple robe and put it on your shoulders, and there'll be jobs in plenty when you get back. . . . That's what we said, and they believed us." Given that Wall Street got two billion of government money, why not pay their soldiers' bonus note in this time of starvation, the veterans asked. "But no! They were shot down and driven out with fire and gas from the capitol of the nation for asking for what that nation promised to give them." When Wall Street knocked at Hoover's door, they were invited in. When the veterans knocked, saying their wives and children were starving, they were told that Hoover was out.

"Oh, they tell you they don't want a woman in the Senate. That ain't it, my friends. They don't want this woman. If she had voted with them, they would have had her picture on every front page in the press. . . . You wouldn't dare turn out a man senator that stood by you and your cause like she has. Why would you want to turn on her just because she's a woman? If you're going to be fair to a man that fights your battles for you, you've got to be at least that fair to a woman."

While the categories are somewhat arbitrary, there were twelve humorous stories or analogies, one Aesop fable, one extended reliance on the Bible, three statistical analyses, six Senate votes explained, rebuttal of his reasons for traveling into Arkansas, and two rebuttals of her being a woman candidate. The stories included authentic details: his uncle's baptism took place at 3 p.m. at Dugdemona Creek. The word pictures—quiet home versus the hot and dusty roads and use of Biblical descriptions that showed familiarity with it—existed throughout the speech. Demeaning those birds who opposed him. Disclaiming any personal interest. Ingratiating himself with the audience by praising Thad Caraway and referring to his prior time in the state. Building himself up by quoting opponents who said he was smart. Holding out hope as he recounted favorable electoral results contrasted with the fear that the cause would be lost if they didn't help Hattie.

The speech started with humor, audience ingratiation, and demonstration of personally pure motives, followed by posing the problem, statistical references explaining its cause, and Senate votes to prove his contentions. But he never went long without citing a humorous analogy or story, until more than halfway through his speech. After citing the Bible, he acted as if the Bible were being questioned and named examples of countries that disregarded it and paid the price, using historical examples that sounded legitimate. As he progressed, he got more pointed, definite, and indignant. Opposition to Hattie as a woman was just a smokescreen. Socialism was just an epithet when they wanted to turn the starving and homeless away. They shot down veterans after lying to them.

Huey echoed prior appeals of former Arkansas U.S. senator Jefferson Davis. In 1910, Davis had attacked concentrated wealth in the Senate in order to sweep the cobwebs out of that chamber, known as the "Cobwebs Speech."[32] Arkansas voters in the past had favored the exact appeal Huey made.

By this time, Huey was a practiced platform performer. When a railroad train whistle interrupted his remarks, he said, "Those fellows operating that train are all right: they're going to vote for Mrs. Caraway."[33] When a train whistle made a dog bark, Huey said it reminded him of the dog that howled when the boardinghouse dinner bell rang: one of the guests exclaimed: "what are you howling for; you don't have to eat it." Huey's crew managed crying babies: they would give the baby a drink of water or change a diaper while Huey commented that, based on his experience of raising three children and campaigning, most of the time a crying baby only needed a drink of water. One of his crew took a yelping dog to the park and played with it. It quieted down.[34]

Several times locations had to be changed at the last minute to accommodate huge crowds or avoid inconveniencing local businesses. Other events were sometimes canceled so that people could attend the speech, or additional events were scheduled to take advantage of the crowds. In one town, a murder trial was adjourned so that the lawyers, the jury, and the spectators could attend.[35]

Huey's drivers blew out six sets of tires racing from one location to another at speeds of seventy to eighty miles an hour on gravel roads, and several times had to replace windshields that were shattered from spraying gravel.[36] They depended on residents for directions, and there were a few close calls when the drivers got temporarily lost. Once Huey awoke from a nap just as the driver hit a dead end. Huey asked the driver if he could find his way back to Louisiana on foot. The driver found the right town and mused about whether he would have enough time to return and throttle the man who misled him.[37] It was so hot in El Dorado that Huey had to keep stepping around the microphone to keep his rubber shoe heels from being vulcanized to the wood platform on top of the truck. The Arkansas Power and Light Company once demanded a twenty-five-dollar deposit to hook into the electrical system. When Huey arrived, he said he would talk longer and louder about the power trusts and would make them pay more than twenty-five dollars if he lived long enough. Once during a speech, an electrical connection in the truck failed, and one of Huey's attendants held the wires together, nearly getting thrown through the windshield from the electric shock, but he maintained the connection for another forty minutes.[38]

In Fort Smith, Huey said that the interests were going to try to buy the big labor vote there. "I'm for you boys. Take all the money you can get. And then go to the polls and vote as you damned please."[39]

In Hot Springs, the speeches were broadcast over the radio. The mayor of Hot Springs gave the introduction, extolling his city's virtues. Huey said that the mayor was a smart boy: the radio time was costing him two dollars a minute, and the mayor had used about $20 of time to get $20,000 worth of advertising for his city, but that was OK. This tickled listeners all over the South.[40]

In Helena, Huey mimicked President Hoover's pronunciation of budget. Criticized was the "boodget" balancing efforts of "Herbert Hoover of London." The cheers almost broke up the meeting.[41]

Huey had promised Hattie not to attack Joe Robinson. Early on, Huey said he could get along without politics and didn't have to get into the Senate to get a law practice. This implied that Robinson lacked law clients before he went to the Senate. In another speech, Huey said Hattie was the only representative you have "who can be depended on to vote the rights of the common people."

As the tour progressed, Huey stepped up the references to Robinson. When he arrived in Fort Smith on Thursday, August 4, he claimed that Hattie's opponent was employed by the power trusts "when the Insulls [Insull was an owner of a power trust but was under indictment and a fugitive living in Greece] were in power."

> He can't serve two masters. The Lord says you can't. But maybe he's smarter than the Lord. They tell us he has resigned. That's for us to eat up. All who believe that bring me a half dollar. . . .
>
> You've already got one from Arkansas in the Senate who is on the power trusts' pay roll and if you think he is lonesome, maybe you want to elect this other bird to keep him company.

On the last day, he said in the morning speech:

> If you want to know how rough the road is for those who stand by the people against the interests, and how smooth the road is made for those who drift with the tide and stand by the interests against the people, all you've got to do is to examine the records of your two Arkansas senators who draw the deadly parallel.

At the end of the last day, he made his most explicit attack on Robinson:

> The honorable Joseph Robinson don't vote with us. The Democratic leaders and the Republican leaders are really not different. One skins from the toes up, and the other skins from the ears down.
>
> But Joe Robinson ain't running this time. It's Mrs. Caraway that's running. Oh, ain't you glad the other senator isn't running? It's just too bad, too bad.[42]

Hattie's opponents were helpless. One complained of outside interference. The others tried to ignore Huey. After one newspaper noted that Huey had denied his opponents access to his loudspeakers (citing the need to proceed to the other engagements), in the hometown of one opponent, he graciously made them available to the man.[43]

Observers marveled at Huey's vehicles. His long, low, rakish, and speedy blue Cadillac limousine seemed to stretch for a city block. The sound trucks, too, attracted a crowd. Dozens of men and boys crowded around the vehicles and questioned the drivers, who answered courteously.

The military precision of the tour impressed, with some observers believing there was an irony in Huey preaching old-time values while using the most modern campaign techniques. Others noted the duality of Huey's friendliness but determination. Huey shook very few hands and elbowed his way through the crowd in a manner that "might be considered rudeness and unwarranted brusqueness" to ensure that the schedule was kept.[44] Yet at Pine Bluff, he stopped at the Pines Hotel, the headquarters for the tour group, shook hands with many guests, and recognized an old acquaintance, C. E. Philpot, a highway contractor in several southern states, and a man Huey had represented as a lawyer. Philpot invited him home. Huey asked if he had a sleeping porch, and when the man said yes, Huey said let's go, pushing through the crowd to leave. In Prescott, Huey spotted an attorney acquaintance from years ago and invited him to sit on the platform. In Helena, an old teacher who was now a local official introduced Huey.[45]

From the first day, the campaign was a huge success. One observer wired his colleagues: "A cyclone just went through here and is headed your way. Very few trees left standing and even these are badly scarred up." Another observer called the campaign a circus hitched to a tornado.[46]

Early in the campaign, a local sheriff helped set up the meeting out of courtesy but asked not to be mentioned for fear of offending Robinson. Ten minutes into Huey's speech, seeing the crowd hypnotized and frozen in its tracks, he told a deputy: "pull Huey's coat tail and tell him if he wants to mention my name it will be all right with me." In many cases, audience members attended out of curiosity, expecting a vitriolic demagogue, but found instead a speaker who was humorous but seemed reasonable, rational, smart, and sincere, as opposed to emotional and irrelevantly entertaining.[47] Speeches were added at the last minute at the request of cities or towns.[48] The crowds were of record proportions, culminating in a Pine Bluff crowd of twenty thousand and a Little Rock audience of thirty thousand, the largest political gathering in the history of the state.[49] Cheers, rebel yells, and shouts of "pour it on 'em!" or "give it to 'em, Kingfish," punctuated his remarks.[50]

At the beginning, Hattie made only a few awkward remarks, followed by Huey as the main event. She improved, however, and began to draw applause. Government appointees of Hoover claimed to be dirt farmers, but they seemed to be well manicured, she said. When Wilson was president, she owned a farm; when Coolidge was president, she owned some equity in the farm; but now that Hoover was president, she only owned an echo. Hattie learned by copying Huey's techniques.[51]

The Arkansas towns went out of their way to make Huey feel welcome. Pine Bluff restaurants added potlikker to their menus.[52] In Little Rock, a dinner of potlikker was prepared and served by waiters dressed in green pajamas. All dunked their cornpone. A Rotary Club (men only) luncheon was held in Russellville, but Huey was told that no controversial issues could be mentioned. Huey was speechless, for once. But Huey was asked if he would ever stop advocating for those things in which he believed. Huey responded that he wouldn't and then quoted poetry:

> I burn the candle at both ends,
> It will not last the night,
> But oh my foes, and oh my friends,
> It sheds a lovely light.

While Huey was there, Hattie met with the women of Russellville. Many women's groups throughout the state enthusiastically supported her.

Reporters from national publications covered the campaign, and Huey joshed and joked with them.[53] Asked how Mrs. Caraway was standing the rigors of the campaign, he gave a characteristically overstated compliment: "She's standing it even better than I. She's the greatest little woman I ever saw!" Actually, she and most of the campaign party, excepting Huey, suffered fevers, diarrhea, and other travel ailments.[54] Hattie marveled at Huey's stamina, giving several hour-long speeches each day, perspiring through his clothes, speaking in the sunshine, and gesturing without inhibitions except where a necessary microphone limited his freedom to move. Sleeping soundly in the car while traveling between engagements helped maintain his energy.[55]

Huey had planned to end his tour on August 6, after which he was too tired to dunk his cornpone. A delegation from Mississippi River counties asked him to remain over the weekend, however, and speak in their cities on Monday, the 8th. He agreed.[56] Resting at a hotel on Sunday, reporter Deutsch asked him where he was going to church. "Me go to church? Why I haven't been to a church in so many years I don't know when." "But you're always quoting the Bible," Deutsch said. Huey replied: "Bible's the greatest book ever written but I sure don't need anybody I can buy for six bits and a chew of tobacco to explain it to me. When I need preachers I buy 'em cheap." Deutsch kept that remark secret for twenty-five years.[57]

By the end of the speeches on Monday, Huey had traveled twenty-one hundred miles, given either thirty-seven or thirty-nine speeches (it is hard to determine how many speeches Huey added), and had spoken to 200,000 people. His bodyguards drove him to Memphis, where an exhausted Huey caught a train to New Orleans. On Tuesday, August 9, he learned that Hattie had won a smashing victory.

Huey had accomplished a miracle. Hattie was the first woman elected to a full term in the U.S. Senate. He had aroused "into full fury [the] resentment vaguely felt by the farmers" of Arkansas and welded it "into a genuine class protest."[58] Hattie's vote was much larger where Huey had spoken. She had a reservoir of credibility from her husband's popularity, and her opponents lacked strong organizations,[59] but Huey was responsible for her victory.

Afterwards, Roosevelt's vice-presidential running mate, John Nance Garner, was eating breakfast at a New Orleans restaurant. Suddenly Huey appeared, beaming. "Hello Jack. Thought you might want to touch my garment to bring you luck," Huey said. "Judging by what you did for Senator Caraway, I think I ought to," said Garner, patting Huey's lapel three times.[60] In addition to several brief stories about it,[61] the *Times* recounted Huey's career, emphasizing his audacity, persistence, ability to surprise, grandiloquence, capacity for hard work, craving for the spotlight, and inability to get discouraged or shamed.[62] Deutsch wrote a big article about the campaign that ran in the *Saturday Evening Post* on October 15, 1932.[63] Twenty-eight years later, Theodore White described Connecticut politician John Bailey's recruitment of New York delegates for John F. Kennedy an "over the border political raid unmatched in domestic politics since Huey Long's raid of Arkansas from Louisiana."[64]

After his return from Arkansas, Huey rested a few days and then joined the Overton campaign, where Overton had been regaling audiences with the main speech. When Huey arrived, he gave Overton ten minutes and Governor Allen five minutes, cut them off on schedule, and then talked as long as he wanted on the plight the country faced because of concentrated wealth. Sometimes he criticized Broussard for voting for a tariff on cement, which increased the cost of the roads that Huey had built in Louisiana. If neither Overton nor Allen was discussing the issues he deemed important, he interrupted them to suggest new themes. Once Overton begged the pardon of the crowd because he had laryngitis. Huey kicked him from behind. "What do you mean giving a sore throat such a fancy name? They might think it's catching." Huey's early speeches lacked the benefit of his sound trucks because the campaign for Hattie had worn them out. After a few days on tour, Huey confessed he had a sore throat, but said it would clear up after he gave another twenty-five speeches.[65]

Overton had been a congressman since 1931. He had wanted to be governor, but Huey thought he was unsuited for the job: he knew a lot about government but little about politics. Overton worried too much, Huey thought, and told him so, bluntly. But when he decided to support Allen for the governorship, Huey told Overton that he would back him for the Senate against Broussard. Overton could make speeches, something he was good at, but wouldn't have administrative responsibility. This placated Overton and satisfied Huey.

Huey also backed seven of the eight incumbent congressmen, some of whom were opposed, and campaigned for Wade Martin against Dudley LeBlanc for the Public Service Commission. Given that Broussard and LeBlanc were both popular in the French parishes, Huey spent a lot of untraceable cash to defeat them. Over 1.4 million circulars were issued for Overton, Martin, and congressional candidates.

Huey's dummy candidates proliferated. In New Orleans, which was safe for Overton—the Old Regulars had voted to endorse him—he arranged to have 1,119 commissioners to only 61 for Broussard. Huey was building up his own organization separate from the Old Regulars in case they ever parted ways.

In the French parishes, Judge Benjamin F. Pavy enjoined the selection of commissioners nominated by dummy candidates. But Huey's ally, Attorney General Gaston Porterie, instructed the Democratic parish committees to certify the names anyway. Pavy sent five of the committee members to jail for contempt. Governor Allen issued telegraphic reprieves suspending their sentences until after the election. When the Broussard supporters appealed to the Louisiana Supreme Court, it held by a four-to-three vote that it lacked the authority to interfere with the actions of parish committees.[66]

Whereas Huey discussed the concentration of wealth, a national issue, and attacked Broussard for his votes in the Senate, Broussard criticized Overton's recent conversion to Prohibition repeal and Louisiana's state government, characterized by "corruption, extravagance, tyranny."[67]

Overton won a comfortable victory in September: 181,464 to 124,935. Broussard and LeBlanc ran well in the southwestern French parishes, however. LeBlanc was defeated by only 3,000 votes. St. Bernard and Plaquemines parishes voted almost 100 percent for Overton and Martin, again with the help of fraudulent votes. Huey had called Sheriff Meraux during the evening, who said they were still voting. "We have already won," Huey exclaimed, "For God's sake, stop counting."

At a victory banquet after the election, Huey resigned as president of the Louisiana Democratic Association. He had done all he could for Louisiana, and now it was time to help the rest of the country. In the same speech, Huey said he would ensure that all "dad gummed maligners" were driven from office. Francis Williams was going to be deposed as chairman of the Public Service Commission as soon as Wade Martin replaced Dudley LeBlanc.

Having elected both a senator in Arkansas and one in Louisiana, Huey earned a spot on the October 3, 1932, cover of *Time* magazine. The editors predicted that Huey would be the Southern Democrat closest to Roosevelt if Roosevelt won the presidency.[68]

Freed from the confines of Louisiana since the Paul Cyr denouement, Huey now could advertise himself to other states besides Arkansas. In early October 1932, he traveled to Houston to see LSU play Rice accompanied by the LSU band and four hundred students. Huey led a parade to the stadium and conducted the band when it played songs for the crowd. A huge crowd of Houston citizens and dignitaries turned out to greet him. LSU lost to Rice but ended the season with a respectable record of six wins, three losses, and one tie.[69] A new coach had improved the team.

After firing Coach Cohen in 1931, Huey searched for a replacement. President Smith found Lawrence M. "Biff" Jones, a former standout player and then coach at West Point. Initially Jones demurred, fearing Huey's interference. Reassured by LSU administrators and then by Cohen, who had found a job as an assistant coach at Vanderbilt and thought Huey would be too busy in Washington to interfere, Jones accepted.

When Huey met Jones, he asked him if he had everything he needed, and Jones, serious, told him he would like to hire a public relations director. Huey chuckled and said, "I'll get you all the publicity you need." Jones insisted that Huey stay out of the locker room and sit no closer to the bench than the thirty-five-yard line. Huey still managed to interfere, once telling a referee that he knew he had to call some penalties but asking him to call them on LSU only at midfield, not when they were close to the goal line.

To get Jones, Smith had to beg permission from General Douglas MacArthur, who controlled his assignment in the Army. After an uncomfortable interview, MacArthur asked about Jones's compensation and was told he would make $7,500 a year. Staring out the window smoking a cigarette in a holder, MacArthur said, "I like Biff Jones. If a poor army captain can make that much in addition to his salary, I'll let you have him." Then he whirled around. "But don't you ever come back to this office and ask for a single thing."[70]

Senator Connally cited the press of the campaign to avoid greeting Huey at the Rice game. But he had been appointed to investigate Senator Broussard's postelection complaint that his defeat was the product of vote fraud. The first Senate subcommittee meeting to investigate this was scheduled for October 5.[71]

Shortly after the Rice game, Huey visited Hyde Park, New York, to meet Franklin Roosevelt. It had taken Roosevelt a long time to invite him. After the national convention, Roosevelt's academic advisor, Rexford Tugwell, overheard a phone call between Roosevelt and Huey in which Huey complained that Roosevelt's parade of visiting industrialists such as Owen Young provided the wrong perception to the rest of the country, that Roosevelt could lose the election, and requested an invitation to his home and money to campaign: "turn me loose." Upon hanging up, Roosevelt told Tugwell—in a remark widely quoted—that Huey was one of the two most dangerous men in the country.[72]

In mid-1932, Huey was a political boss, but less so than Cermak of Chicago, Pendergast of Kansas City, Crump of Memphis, Hague of New Jersey, or John F. Curry of Tammany Hall. In votes obtained or delegate or electoral votes controlled, Huey was less significant than all of them (see table below). Huey lacked the ironclad control that those bosses had, moreover. The New Orleans organization was independent of Huey. It made an autonomous decision to cooperate with him in the election of 1932. Walmsley had flirted with the idea of opposing Broussard himself.

Table 1. Relative Influence of Certain Powerful Democratic Leaders in 1932

| | Votes at Democratic Convention | Electoral Votes | Votes for Roosevelt in 1932 election |
|---|---|---|---|
| New York (Curry) | 94 | 47 | 2,534,959 |
| Illinois (Cermak) | 58 | 29 | 1,882,304 |
| Missouri (Pendergast) | 36 | 15 | 1,025,406 |
| New Jersey (Hague) | 32 | 16 | 806,630 |
| Tennessee (Crump) | 24 | 11 | 259,473 |
| Louisiana (Long) | 20 | 10 | 249,418 |

*Source:* American Presidency Project, "1932 Presidential Election."

*Note:* Louisiana had two-thirds of the electoral votes of Missouri with only one-fourth or less of the votes cast, showing the effect of the poll tax and disenfranchisement of Black voters.

Nothing in Huey's political views should have alarmed Roosevelt. In the Senate, Huey acted on behalf of progressive causes with which Roosevelt professed an affinity. Huey may have been more obstreperous, but he voted with about thirty-one other senators. None of them were dangerous. While Huey was an effective speaker, there were many first-rate orators in the country and in Roosevelt's campaign. Several were sent on the campaign trail for Roosevelt.

A problem with memoirs is that they often are recollections shaped by later events and condensed in retrospective evaluation. Maybe the remark was made later, after Huey became a serious threat to Roosevelt's reelection. If Roosevelt did make the remark in 1932, based only on phone calls between the two men and whatever his friends and advisors told him, and Tugwell always insisted that his recollection was correct, it might show Roosevelt's sagacity in judging a potential political rival. More probably, Roosevelt was only adding a touch of melodrama for the benefit of an academic, not a political, advisor. Had Roosevelt made the remark to any experienced politician in 1932, they would have scoffed.

After that phone call, Huey visited Jim Farley in New York and suggested that he barnstorm the country by train. Farley declined because such a campaign would overshadow Roosevelt. In a second meeting, Farley asked Huey to campaign in North and South Dakota, Nebraska, and Kansas, states safe for Roosevelt or hopelessly lost. Huey jumped up and said Roosevelt was going to get licked if his campaign advice weren't followed and threatened not to campaign at all. Farley pressed him to acquiesce, and Roosevelt thereafter invited him to Hyde Park on October 9.[73]

In truth, Huey had no doubt that Roosevelt would beat Hoover. He told newsmen that the Democrats should offer to sell a million votes to Hoover for a million dollars. "We can spare the votes and we can use the money."[74]

Roosevelt chose to win the election rather than attempt to gain a consensus for progressive change. Republicans attacked the alleged radicalism of "Senator Norris, Senator LaFollette, Senator Cutting, Senator Huey Long, Senator Wheeler, William R. Hearst, and other exponents of a social philosophy different from the traditional philosophies of the American people."[75]

Outside Roosevelt's home, Huey waited for his host, talking to newsmen. He would campaign for Roosevelt, he said, but not in the South, where Roosevelt was already strong. Huey wore a loud suit, an orchid shirt, and a pink tie, flamboyant even for him. Huey wanted Rose to accompany him, but she declined.[76]

When Roosevelt arrived, Huey ate lunch with the rest of Roosevelt's family, with Huey sitting on Roosevelt's right, and they conducted an animated conversation. Huey distressed Sarah Roosevelt, Franklin's mother. She audibly whispered either "Who is that awful man on my son's right," or, later, "Frankie, you're not going to let Huey Long tell you what to do, are you?" The genial Roosevelt charm masked his intentions and fooled Huey.[77] Huey told his friends that Roosevelt meant well but was not a strong man and had more sonsofbitches in his family than Huey had in his own.[78]

Seymour Weiss arranged the tour that Farley wanted, meeting Huey in Bismarck, North Dakota. Huey spoke in twenty- six cities over nine days.[79] Arriving in Bismarck, North Dakota, on Thursday, October 20,[80] Huey then spoke in Fargo, North Dakota, where "the crowd overflowed the auditorium, and hundreds of people stood in the streets outside, listening to his voice over his sound truck's amplifiers that had been attached in the building."[81] On October 22, Huey returned to Bismarck to speak to yet another overflowed auditorium. The *Bismarck Tribune* described it as a "glorified Huey Long political rally."[82] On the morning of October 23, Huey spoke to a crowd of about a thousand in Sioux Falls, South Dakota, including a young but impressed Hubert Humphrey,[83] before continuing to Lincoln, Nebraska, to speak that night. Huge crowds greeted them everywhere.[84] On October 24 he spoke in

Pittsburg, Kansas, and on the 25th in Columbus, Kansas.[85] On the 27th he canceled a speech in Hutchinson, Kansas, because his voice failed.[86] That evening, he had recovered enough to speak in Parsons, Kansas.[87] Huey told reporters that cornpone and potlikker were no longer his favorite dish. His "new loves" were chili and tamales.[88]

Throughout this tour, Huey accused Hoover of giving tax rebates to large corporations in exchange for campaign contributions.[89] Recognizing the strength of the Republican Party, he asked for support of Roosevelt the man rather than for the Democratic Party. The *Sioux Falls Argus-Leader* was astonished to hear the Kingfish "give an address, for him, of singular conservativeness."[90] Yet Huey's speeches advocated his tax program, the issue that gave him his radical reputation. It may be that he started his speeches with the attack on tax rebates, an issue appealing in these farm states as an attack on profligacy, waste, and favoritism, and then segued into his tax plan, it may be that his jokes and stories removed the appearance of radicalism, or it may be that his style was calmer and more rational than expected. As a Mena, Arkansas, newspaper put it: "Instead of putting on a show the much-publicized Kingfish talked more good, plain common sense than was expected."[91]

Contradicting its own news story, an editorial in the *Argus Leader* denied that Huey's speech was well received. "South Dakota laughed at, instead of with, Huey P. Long." The only reason Huey had been elected to the Senate in Louisiana was its illiteracy rate of 13.5 percent compared to South Dakota's 1.5 percent.[92] The newspaper lied or was whistling in the dark. The Democratic chairmen for the states Huey visited wired the Roosevelt campaign that they should send Huey to any doubtful state.

Huey knew it: "We would have lost North Dakota if I hadn't gone there and straightened things out. I have been in South Dakota, and we will carry that state."[93] After the tour he stopped in Chicago and met Rose.[94] Farley later ruefully wished that he had sent Huey into Pennsylvania, a state they lost and could have won. Roosevelt carried all four of the states Huey visited. Farley never again underestimated him.[95]

# Nineteen

# THE SENATE STRIKES BACK

By the November election, the Great Depression was a disaster. The Gross National Product had fallen from $181.8 billion in 1929 to $126.6 billion in 1933:

| 1929 | 1930 | 1931 | 1932 | 1933 |
|---|---|---|---|---|
| $181.8 | $164.5 | $153.0 | $130.1 | $126.6 |

*Source*: Chandler, *America's Greatest Depression*, 21.

From 1929 to 1933, national income fell from $88 billion to $40 billion; wages and salaries from $50 billion to $29 billion.[1]

At least 12 million people nationwide were unemployed, and many more could find only part-time work. In Philadelphia in April 1931, 25.5 percent of the workforce were unemployed and 13.8 percent were employed only part-time. By early 1933 in Chicago, 624,000 people—40 percent of its workforce—were unemployed.[2]

Farm revenue declined from $14 billion in 1929 to $7 billion in 1933:

| 1929 | 1930 | 1931 | 1932 | 1933 |
|---|---|---|---|---|
| $13,985 | $11,432 | $8,385 | $6,371 | $7,081 |

Net farm income declined from $7 billion in 1929 to $3 billion in 1933.[3]

Behind the statistics was human misery of a type difficult to conceive today. Now, unemployment insurance tides over someone who gets laid off. In the Depression, they were dependent on private charity. By 1933, the resources of family and friends, relief agencies and churches, were exhausted. "Starvation" and "homelessness" were not rhetorical hyperbole. Millions of people were starving and homeless—and without hope.

Orphaned by age ten, President Herbert Hoover had made his fortune as a self-made mining engineer, more comfortable with numbers than language, and his name as a relief administrator after World War I, as Commerce Department secretary during the 1920s, and as a flood relief administrator in 1927. The tragedy of Hoover's career is that his worldview—that unregulated or only lightly regulated capitalism would spontaneously correct itself after a recession—collapsed and he just couldn't believe it or react to it.[4] Ironically, Hoover's proposal a year before the crash in 1928—to create a $3 billion public works fund to cushion unemployment if it ever occurred—was never implemented. Even from the cold *Congressional Record,* one can feel Senator Cutting's frustration with Hoover's pigheadedness in opposing his own idea.[5] Had he supported the public works or relief legislation and then administered it with the skill with which he attacked relief in Europe after World War I, how would history have regarded him? Hoover's dour personal style complemented his dogmatic rigidity. In a speech to Congress in May 1932, Hoover had the "smile of a dying man" and spoke in a "tense monotone" that could not be heard beyond the front row.[6]

Roosevelt was the opposite of Hoover. His optimism, infectious smile, ease with crowds, and sympathy for the unemployed—giving the people hope—accompanied an aversion to fixed principles. Roosevelt's 1932 campaign speeches consisted of "painfully discordant themes" and "oscillations on fiscal policy."[7] During the campaign, Roosevelt was given two different speeches on tariff policy, one reductionist and the other protectionist, so Roosevelt airily asked the two writers to go "weave the two together."[8] Roosevelt recognized relief as a federal issue, however. For that reason, Republican Senators Johnson, LaFollette, Norris, Cutting, and others deserted their party and endorsed him.

The result of Roosevelt's studied ambiguity and varied electoral appeals was an incongruous group of supporters. A week before the election, syndicated columnist Mark Sullivan discussed Roosevelt supporters Bernard M. Baruch, Owen D. Young, John W. Davis, Huey, and Senators Burton K. Wheeler, George W. Norris, and Robert LaFollette. Davis would never agree with Huey's plan to limit incomes. Baruch would never agree with Wheeler's inflation proposals. Young would never agree with Norris about public ownership of utilities.

If Roosevelt displeased wealthy industrialist Young, thought Sullivan, it might not disturb anything but his lunch. But,

> if Mr. Roosevelt displeases Senator Huey Long, something quite different happens. First of all, Senator Huey will "bawl out" the President. He literally will—let no one doubt that. The White House will ring with his sulphurous expletives. Senator Huey will remind Mr. Roosevelt that he, Huey, was instrumental in nominating Mr. Roosevelt, having delivered the Louisiana delegation to him. . . .
>
> Thereafter he will go on the Senate floor, where in language that will be little short of profanity, he will again and publicly "bawl out" the President and declare that henceforth he proposes to fight every measure proposed by the President. Finally, Senator Huey will go on the stump, with his radio equipped fleet of automobiles, and do everything he can, which is a good deal, to prevent Mr. Roosevelt from being re-nominated.[9]

That forecast didn't influence the election.

Roosevelt won in a landslide. Prominent Senate leaders of the Republican Party—Majority Leader Moses of New Hampshire, Majority Whip Watson of Indiana, tariff author Smoot of Utah—were defeated in their home states. The *Times* speculated that Huey might lead a coalition of liberal Democrats and Republicans to hold the balance of power in the Senate.[10]

Roosevelt invited Huey to Warm Springs, Georgia, where he was vacationing and meeting with political and industrial leaders before his inauguration. Huey spent "considerable time" with Roosevelt, joking and pressing his tax views, and talked to patronage chief Farley.

Something must have bothered Huey about Roosevelt or other Democratic leaders, however.[11] On December 6, the second day of the lame-duck Senate session, Huey broke an unwritten rule (prohibiting speeches until the fourth day) to argue that the Senate should implement the mandate of the election: to scale up income and inheritance taxes, limit the working day, put farm surpluses under federal control, and inflate the currency. Quoted were several Roosevelt campaign speeches advocating these principles. The Democrats talked harmony, but this should not divert them from helping the people: The talk is to "tread easily"; to be quiet; "Don't wake up the baby"; "nothing but harmony." What kind of harmony? Starvation harmony? Nakedness harmony? Homeless harmony?[12] Huey expected Robinson's cooperation and, if his leadership "is in accord with the wishes of the American people, let's keep it; but if it ain't, then let's throw it out." Progressives could unite under Senator Norris, but he denied press reports that there was any factional block of senators.[13]

On December 8, the *Times* reported that Huey was absent from a Democratic Party caucus because of his feud with Robinson. Huey first and then Robinson denied it.[14] Huey in the caucus had argued in favor of his tax plan, and the caucus issued a compromise statement favoring taxation in accordance with party principles.[15]

In the lame-duck session, the first legislation considered was independence for the Philippines. The Philippines' production of sugar made this bill important to Huey. Several times he grabbed the Senate floor and yielded it piecemeal to other senators, thereby acting as a floor leader to effect an agreement, with the implicit threat of a filibuster hanging over everyone's head. Huey won some concessions.[16] The House-Senate conference weakened the provisions for which he had fought, but he voted for the compromise bill.[17]

One of Huey's speeches was compared to a "vaudeville show which kept more of the Senators in their seats than usual during such proceedings." Huey said he didn't care whether President Hoover vetoed the Philippines bill. It reminded him of a poem:

> When I asked to wed, go to father, she said.
> And she knew that I knew that her father was dead,
> And she knew that I knew what a life he had led.
> And she knew that I knew what she meant when she said:
> Go to father.[18]

Hoover did tell the Senate to "go to father."

On January 3, Huey heard Senator Arthur Robinson (R-Indiana) defend veterans.[19] On January 4, Senator Hiram Johnson discussed foreign war debts[20] and Senator Borah spoke on economic conditions.[21] Huey had something planned for the New Year, too.

On January 5, Carter Glass proposed a banking reform bill. Its main features were to separate commercial and investment banking, to prevent speculation, and to increase the regulatory powers of the Federal Reserve Board.[22] Seventy-five years old in 1933, Glass was short, slim, and "prickly, with large scornful eyes, an aggressive brush of white hair shooting back from his forehead, and the defiant, contemptuous bearing of a man who feared nobody. His habit of talking out of the left corner of his mouth gave his face a peculiar twisted expression well adapted to his snarls and snorts. . . . He was intensely vain and intensely honest."[23] And intensely conservative. Glass could recall passing the Federal Reserve Act in 1913.[24] He was still conservative in 1933, but knowledgeable, and he took a proprietary interest in banking legislation.

Glass's bill allowed large banks to establish branches. Larger, healthy banks could therefore take over the undercapitalized small banks that Glass thought were nothing more than pawnshops. Glass knew that the branch-banking feature might be controversial and was prepared to water it down. Given the 5,096 bank failures between 1930 and 1932,[25] most accepted the necessity for reform. Robinson loyally supported the bill.[26]

Huey had exhaustively questioned Louisiana and New York bankers about it.[27] Before Glass explained his bill (Glass considered this discourteous), Huey offered an amendment on January 5 to prohibit branch banking except in municipalities where the bank was already located. Otherwise, the big banks would drive out the small ones, Huey claimed. Huey quoted a Roosevelt statement years earlier that was hostile to branch banking.[28]

The next full legislative day, Monday, January 9, Glass explained the bill and asserted that Roosevelt favored it. Huey asked him how he knew that. There was no satisfactory answer.

Senator Elmer Thomas of Oklahoma and Senator Wheeler joined Huey in what became a filibuster against branch banking. It went on for days, paralyzed the Senate, and grabbed the attention of the country. On January 11, Huey advocated government insurance for bank deposits, one of the first politicians to do so.[29]

Glass sneered and snarled at Thomas and denied Huey's request to have documents read by the clerk—a routine courtesy usually extended to filibusterers—to provide a short rest.[30] Huey read the document slowly, pausing to ask with feigned innocence whether he was "going too fast." Neither interruptions nor insults bothered Huey. He became more cheerful in inverse proportion to their nastiness. Huey was weary on January 12, however, and had to be rescued by Wheeler and Thomas. Glass demanded that the Senate sit in longer sessions, and this was done. But Huey, Thomas, and Wheeler continued the filibuster.[31]

The filibuster became the issue. Will Rogers said that ninety-five senators couldn't outtalk Huey, they couldn't even "get him warmed up," and Huey was getting near the truth in his criticisms of Wall Street.[32] The *Times*, however, was appalled at the "sickening" spectacle of the "impotent" Senate and lamented the obstruction of the bill by a man with a front of brass and leather lungs.[33] Yet its reporter wrote that Huey put on a good show and, unlike other obstructionists, had "uncommon forensic ability and a definite legislative philosophy." Long lines of spectators waited for a chance to see the Kingfish in action.[34] Republicans enjoyed the spectacle of a divided Democratic Party, and this further inflamed party leaders.[35]

Glass was the type of politician Huey had steamrolled in Louisiana: an older, conservative man past his prime. Glass had shaped the Federal Reserve Act in 1913 to be sure, but had Glass litigated complex cases against banks, issued and sold highway bonds in a down market, supervised a state bank examiner, obtained loans from the Reconstruction Finance Corporation, and saved his state's banks from depositor runs and failure? Huey never said this, but it must explain why he never deferred to Glass. Huey did coordinate his views with Representative Steagall, chairman of the Banking and Currency Committee in the House.

Note again Huey's skill at drawing an issue. There were more independent bankers than Wall Street bankers. Like independent oil drillers fighting Standard Oil, they were the underdogs, but they were capitalists, leaders in their communities, and connected with other businesses. A Chicago banker whose several small banks had failed, John A. Carroll, testified in Congress against branch banking and supported Huey.[36]

On January 17, Glass exploited minor inaccuracies ("rhetorical rubbish") in some of Huey's arguments, claiming that Huey had conducted a "circus" for the galleries and was secretly doing the bidding of big bankers who disliked other provisions of his bill.[37] Huey submitted a resolution to investigate Glass's charge, so it is doubtful that it was true, and Glass never proposed to strike the branch-banking provision so that the rest of the bill could be enacted, which would have been the easiest way to test his suspicion.[38] Wheeler said that had Roosevelt favored branch banking he never would have been nominated.[39]

Twenty-nine more conservative Senators, however, including Robinson, signed a petition asking for cloture, a vote to limit debate and stop the filibuster.[40] On January 18, after negotiating off-the-record for hours, Huey and Robinson agreed to have cloture withdrawn and then a compromise branch-banking amendment voted upon. Huey playfully punched Robinson and slapped him on the back. Alleging that the outgoing Republican leaders were supporting the filibuster, however, Couzens opposed this compromise (one objection was enough to kill it) and insisted on a vote on the record. It failed by one vote. Senator George denounced southerners who voted for cloture. Robinson rebuked George. Huey defended the filibuster and George and contended that branch banking had to be opposed by the leaders of the people. Robinson interrupted to demand by whom those leaders were chosen. Huey exclaimed "by the election returns!" to thunderous applause.[41] The limitation of debate was agreed to, fulfilling the terms of the agreement negotiated by Huey and Robinson. The filibuster ended.[42]

The next day, Huey asked to meet Roosevelt in Washington before his inauguration in March. Arriving a half-hour late, he pounded on the door and said he was going to talk turkey, to ask Roosevelt if he meant it. Emerging smiling, he said Roosevelt would be a great president. Newsmen would just have to watch his actions to see what was decided; he was too ignorant to explain things. Roosevelt favored county branch banking but not state branch banking. Complete loyalty was professed: "He don't want to crack down on me. He told me 'Huey, you're going to do just as I tell you,' and that is just what I'm a-going to do."[43]

Privately, however, he said: "When I talk to him, he says 'Fine! Fine! Fine!' But Joe Robinson goes to see him the next day and again he says 'Fine! Fine! Fine!' Maybe he says 'Fine!' to everybody."[44] Huey did not really understand what Roosevelt said (you're going to do just what I tell you). By the end of the month, Huey wrote Roosevelt that he figured "all the time you wanted men like me to advise you." After Glass declined the treasury job, Huey urged supporters to ask Roosevelt to appoint Henry Steagall.[45]

A compromise limitation of branch banking was added to the bill. Senator Black's motion to eliminate it was defeated, but indicated widespread hostility to it among southern, midwestern, and western progressives. Minor amendments Huey proposed failed. The most interesting was that the secretary of the treasury should remain a member of the Federal Reserve Board. Glass wanted to insulate the board from treasury influence. Huey thus tried to preserve Roosevelt's influence over the board, evidencing a sincere belief in focusing authority and responsibility over government boards with the elected executive, even if he were not that executive. Roosevelt should have appreciated this.[46]

Only one article in the *Times* explained the controversy, rather than the conflict of Huey versus Glass.[47] Banks with branches should be stronger and better run, with economies of scale in administration and increased capitalization. Opponents believed that the local banks would be destroyed, that local businesses would be denied credit or subjected to national policies irrelevant to local conditions, and that, therefore, the communities they served would suffer. The banks would become more powerful than the regulators or, if one member of the chain failed, they all might fail, requiring a huge bailout because it would be too big to allow to fail.

Branch banking was opposed by many as a reaction to modernity, for the same reasons that some at the time tried to prevent chain stores[48] or, today, oppose allowing Walmart into the neighborhood. Rural progressives—Huey's allies in this fight—opposed the establishment of the Reconstruction Finance Corporation because it propped up the interests that had caused the Depression and was socialism for big financiers. Huey was invited by his ally Wheeler to join the criticism of the corporation. Huey declined. It had helped rescue some small Louisiana banks, perhaps because he was on intimate terms with its personnel (Harvey Couch, Rudolph Hecht). Separately, he acknowledged modernity, saying good roads had killed some country banks; they couldn't stand the competition once people could drive a little way to find another bank.[49]

Huey thus stood up for the local banks but conceived of a national support system. That would have had a similar effect to the one envisioned by branch banking proponents, but with more diverse ownership, more competition, more local control, and greater governmental regulatory power.

In his filibuster, not only did Huey advocate the new idea of insurance of bank deposits, tentatively at first, then forcefully, but also gave an insight into his January 1933 ideas for solving the Depression:[50] crop holidays, $10 billion in public works secured by high inheritance taxes, shorter labor hours, and the soldiers' bonus. It might soon become necessary, he said, to enact a tax on capital to secure mass purchasing power. With Huey's support, Senators Thomas and Wheeler tried but failed to amend Glass's bill to increase the money supply by coining silver.[51]

The strange thing about this spectacle is Roosevelt's silence.[52] Huey had Robinson and Glass just where he wanted them: they were supporting branch banking, something Roosevelt had opposed. An overwhelming number of small bankers and their small-business allies agreed with him. Robinson and Glass should never have taken on the fight or should have had to capitulate. One wonders whether Huey had the filibuster in mind when he started; maybe he thought that, once he read Roosevelt's prior statements against branch banking, Glass would back down, or Roosevelt would speak up. Roosevelt refused to back him up or tell him to shut up. He did nothing to stop the filibuster or effect a compromise. Roosevelt told Huey everything was fine, fine, fine, but denounced him privately to Senator Johnson two days later.[53]

Hofstadter details Roosevelt's "signal failure . . . in the realm of financial policy" as governor of New York. A state investigatory commission suggested banking reforms, citing the Bank of the United States for abuses. Roosevelt ignored it and appointed another investigative commission, with a director of the Bank of the United States among its members. This commission rejected the earlier recommendations. Shortly thereafter, the Bank of the United States failed, after which Roosevelt, "self-assured, unabashed, impenitent," hectored the legislature to rectify abuses.[54] Hofstadter's essay is entitled "The Patrician as Opportunist."

Huey traveled to New York after the banking controversy concluded. He planned to see reporters at 2 p.m. and then go to a show at 2:15 p.m. At 2 p.m. Huey opened his door "an inch and let out a gust of radio music" and said that an important conference delayed his plans. At 6 p.m. he met reporters. Huey was in a manic or mystic mood. If his economic ideas were adopted, golf links would replace farmland, and everyone would have time to read *The Count of Monte Cristo*. Newsmen asked how he got the name "Kingfish." "He grinned . . . and walked up and down the room. 'As the mist rises in an October field, as the cotton boll opens in the sun . . . (and so on) . . . so the name of Kingfish came.'"[55]

The Sunday *Times* on January 29 traced his career and described his mannerisms: he was always in action; centrifugal force impelled his body and mind; as a speaker his mind ran ahead of his words, leading to some erratic speech transitions; but he could be "as coldly logical as a corporation lawyer." In the Senate he wandered around, sitting in any unoccupied seat, then bounded up again like a jumping jack. Huey's jerky movements reminded the author of early motion-picture films that were always flickering. When interested, Huey would sit near a speaker and stare at him. "Nothing daunts him and no ridicule or contempt can pierce the armor of his self-esteem. His hair may stand on end, his arms wave like a windmill, his clothing may become ruffled, but behind all his explosive force is a keen and resourceful mind, which acknowledges no master."[56] Westbrook Pegler separately noted Huey's impudence and intelligence.[57] Journalists observed that, instead of the Senate hazing Huey, Huey had been hazing the Senate since he arrived.[58]

But Barkley argued Huey to a draw over whether the secretary of the treasury should remain on the Federal Reserve Board. Other senators debated Huey and sometimes had the last and best retort. What is extraordinary is Huey's energy, resilience, and confidence despite a retort or adverse vote.

In January 1933, while Huey was proclaiming his banking expertise, the Union Indemnity Bond Group, tied in with his highway construction program, failed. Louisiana took the news calmly, in part because there had been so few bank failures. As the *Times*'s editors excoriated Huey for filibustering, its reporter wrote: "It is unanimously agreed that this record [of few bank failures] is due to the activities of Huey Long as Governor and Senator. . . . Whatever may be said about his oft-assailed dictatorship, it has operated for the good of the state in the hard years since 1929. . . . Louisiana banks were just about as heavily loaded with farm mortgages [and cotton loans] as any other banks. . . . But the immediate and sometimes drastic intervention of Huey Long brought aid whenever it appeared the day could be saved."[59]

On January 25, the Glass bill was passed, but it was sent to the House of Representatives and killed. In the meantime, Huey had packed the membership of the National Rivers and Harbors Congress, an influential group lobbying for public works. Assisting him was Frank Reid, a Republican congressman from Chicago, ally of former Mayor Big Bill Thompson, and advocate for flood control.[60]

The year 1933 thus promised to be as triumphal as 1932, when he had confronted the Senate, made his views and himself known, helped nominate and elect a president and two senators, and was considered influential with Roosevelt. Now the subject of feature articles, he fostered the idea that he was big. When he went out to eat, he mixed his own salad dressing in restaurants. "It was quite a rite," with the dumping of ice, and the mixing of cheeses and oil and vinegar. "Neighboring patrons regard[ed] a glimpse of the ceremony as justification for a cover charge."[61]

The hallowed customs of the Senate could not be overcome so easily. Joe Robinson was not charmed or awed by Huey's expertise in mixing salad dressings. Robinson could not deny Huey's influence with the voters of his home state or overcome him in an open Senate debate.

Open debate or electoral defeat are not the only weapons to silence an upstart, however. We always have a wild man, one senator observed; we let him blow off steam and then tame him.[62] One way to defeat a charging politician, like a charging army, is to attack his home base.

When Overton defeated Broussard in September 1932, Broussard asked the Senate to refuse Overton his seat.[63] The appropriate Senate committee sent researchers to Louisiana. They talked to Allen Ellender and Harvey Peltier, Overton's campaign managers, who admitted spending about $13,000, based on Seymour Weiss's records. Overton had spent $400 or $500. The initial hearing was held on October 5 under Senator Connally.

Edward Rightor was Broussard's attorney. Rightor's propensity to pass gas caused Huey to nickname him "Whistle Britches." Rightor conceded that he could not prove fraud, that Broussard got more votes, or that Broussard should be the nominee. The chairman of the Honest Election League, Burt W. Henry, asked the committee to infer fraud based on the use of dummy candidates and the amount of campaign money spent. They both wanted Overton to be denied his seat, however, forcing a new election.

Huey responded for Overton that the New Orleans results—where most of the dummy candidates were—had been attested to by a special arbitration committee set up between Overton and Broussard. Broussard's representatives—headed by Rene Viosca, a law partner of J. Y. Sanders—signed its report. The arbitration committee never asked for a recount. There the matter stood in October before Roosevelt's election, and there Huey expected it to end.[64]

After the election in November, nothing was done, but Huey either didn't get the implied threat or chose to ignore it. During the filibuster over the banking bill, Connally asked to extend the deadline for his report. Startled, Huey asked why, but Connally finessed his inquiry. On January 27, 1933, days after Roosevelt's visit to Washington, DC, the committee announced resumed hearings. "Interest [was] heightened by Senator Long's recent activities . . . in which he has vehemently opposed the leadership of his own party." Engaged as the committee's counsel was Samuel T. Ansell, a former judge advocate general in the Army. In early February, the committee resumed its inquiry under Senator Howell of Nebraska, an ineffectual senator who never practiced law.[65] Huey left for Louisiana to represent Overton. It is difficult to lead or filibuster in Washington when you are defending your ally in Louisiana.

Huey and Ansell clashed. On the first day, Huey said Ansell was taking so long he must need a job. Ansell retorted that Huey always had a job. Huey jibed that he could be elected, whereas Ansell could not. Ansell beat Huey by saying he had not run for office and would not do so under Huey's circumstances. Ansell threw away his victory, however, by then asking if Huey should be referred to as "the Kingfish." Huey acknowledged the title and the scope of his powers: he was Kingfish of the (Louisiana) lodge.

Weiss had destroyed supporting expenditure records but reconstructed them.[66] Ansell charged that he was dealing with a deliberate, evil design. Huey replied so angrily that Ansell invited him to step outside. Huey said he would walk outside and whip hell out of him, and Ansell responded with a sneer: would he walk out alone or with a lot of armed guards? Huey replied that he would supply a guard for Ansell if he needed one.

Huey was then allowed to instruct Weiss to avoid naming banks that held campaign money because of a new banking crisis in Louisiana. Congressman Hamilton Fish of New York accused Rudolph Hecht, chairman of Hibernia Bank in New Orleans and director of the Regional Reconstruction Finance Authority, with arranging a loan from the Reconstruction Finance Corporation to a bonding company that owed Hibernia money. The bonding company used that money to repay a loan it had with Hibernia, and then failed.

A run on Hibernia ensued that afternoon. The bank president told Huey that night. Huey called New Orleans bankers into conference, summoned Governor Allen from Baton Rouge, and told him to bring the official seal of Louisiana. Huey's plan was to declare a bank holiday on February 4 to stop the run while he arranged with the Reconstruction Finance Corporation to infuse $20 million in cash on the following Monday. But no one could discover anything noteworthy that occurred on February 4. After a frantic search by librarians and others, a publisher phoned to say that Woodrow Wilson had severed diplomatic relations with Germany on February 3. Huey decided that must have taken "two nights at least." Allen made the proclamation for February 3 and 4.

The members of the conference had sworn themselves to secrecy. A *Times-Picayune* editor—also a bank director—had been present. The paper's morning edition contained some details of the conference. When Huey learned this, in a towering and perhaps inebriated rage, he ordered General Fleming of the National Guard to seize its office. The paper recalled the edition, and Huey's order was revoked.[67]

With the holiday declared and the Hibernia run averted on Saturday the 4th, Huey wrangled with the Reconstruction Finance Corporation all weekend, not having slept on Friday, and made radio announcements that no one would lose "so much as one slick, slivery dime." Late Sunday afternoon, the corporation agreed to send $20 million, and Huey departed for a supper party, where he was treated as the conquering hero. Then the phone rang, and Huey was heard to say, "No, you can keep your damn fifteen million dollars. It'll be twenty million dollars or nothing. . . . I don't care if they did change their minds. If you send me any fifteen million or seventeen million or anything else but twenty million, I won't take it, and we'll all go to hell together." Twenty million was wired to Hibernia. On Monday, Huey deposited $12,000 into Hibernia, money borrowed from his life insurance, declaring that he couldn't think of a safer place to put his money. Days later, the state deposited several hundred thousand dollars into Hibernia.[68] The *Times* wrote: "When speed and an idea or two are needed, the Kingfish will pop them out as rapidly as a machine gun. Even those who do not like him are willing enough to admit that his services in this crisis were extremely beneficial."[69]

This crisis, very real, provided cover for Weiss to refuse to answer some of the Overton Committee's questions, and Huey didn't want many questions answered. Inquiries into campaign finances met a dead end because of the absence of recordkeeping, sloppy recordkeeping, or uncommunicative witnesses.[70] Robert Maestri testified that he had been asked to donate to a relief fund and had done so, but, when asked if he had been requested to make a campaign contribution, Maestri said, "No; for the relief fund to be put in the expenses of the campaign." Dr. Joseph O'Hara, who had replaced Maestri as the head of the Louisiana Democratic Association, testified that patronage workers were not forced to contribute to the campaign: they "had to pay that ten per cent voluntarily."[71]

Ansell had an easy time demonstrating what Huey's leaders conceded. They paid filing fees for "dummy" candidates who were going to drop out solely so they could appoint loyal election commissioners. The candidates lacking a sincere intent to run were committing perjury. But the Old Regulars had used dummies for decades, defeating court challenges to the practice, establishing the precedent.

Charles Suer, a part-time painter, restaurant proprietor, and exterminator, was asked why he decided to run for Congress. Suer just thought he was qualified. The highly educated Ansell moved in to humiliate the uneducated witness, asking him if he could convince others that he was qualified. Suer conceded that he "couldn't convince anybody, because the facts are I never spoke to anybody about my being a candidate." Ansell pretended shock: "Nobody?" That was correct, Suer replied, not even his wife. Did he announce his candidacy to the press or put up campaign posters? Again, no. Ansell bored in for the kill but asked one question too many: How did you expect to be elected? Suer paused: "That is the chance you take."[72]

Inquiry into coerced payments of campaign contributions by government workers and the use of dummy candidates was a legitimate inquiry into the conduct of elections. A good chairman, however, would not have permitted the relentless, cumulative questioning of lay witnesses when the points about which they were testifying were conceded.

The committee's inquiry, however, had little to do with the 1932 election but instead explored Huey's entire career, a fishing expedition. Judges in civil cases try to prevent fishing expeditions—nonspecific searches for information—because they waste time, invade privacy, and distract from the relevant issues.[73] The hearing lasted from February 3 to February 17 and provided a platform to all of Huey's opponents.

Easily the most vicious and irrelevant witnesses were Huey's brothers Julius and Earl. They testified that Huey accepted cash contributions from public utility companies in the 1928 campaign. Huey interrupted, stood up, and shouted that this was a "goddamn lie" but then apologized for his language, muttering to Overton within earshot of newsmen that he would put Earl in jail if he repeated the charge outside the hearing room (testimony in hearing is privileged).[74] Bozeman testified that, when he was chairman of the Louisiana Tax Commission, Huey asked him to raise tax assessments on some opposition businesses and newspapers. Huey yelled that he was a "lying thief."

The toll bridge plan was aired, with allegations that Overton stood to gain $200,000 if the toll bridge went through and that Huey collected $5,000 to give to Overton to assuage him when the plan was scrapped.[75] One witness testified that the state overpaid cement dealers to build roads. Huey objected. "What has that got to do with the Overton seat in the United States Senate? Why not try us on whether the hens laid more eggs in June than they did in January?"[76]

Gamesmanship livened the inquiry. Huey showed an assistant U.S. attorney a copy of a case in which the U.S. Supreme Court had ruled that a witness at a congressional hearing did not have to answer irrelevant questions. The lawyer acknowledged the ruling. Huey then told the committee that he had secured a "ruling" from the assistant U.S. attorney that the witness did not have to answer irrelevant questions. Letting Huey start a row in the opposition camp, Ansell summoned the assistant U.S. attorney, who sheepishly explained that he was only opining as a matter of general principle.

On the last day, Huey called several witnesses who testified to the absence of fraud in the election. Chief of police Reyer said it was the quietest election in the city's history. The day afterward, Ansell said the inquiry was not half finished. The committee disclaimed Ansell's remarks, and an early report was anticipated.[77]

The national press emphasized the ugly charges from the Overton hearings: Huey's brother testifying that he was bribed, testimony that campaign contributions were extorted from state workers, that graft riddled the Highway Department, that dummy candidates could choose election commissioners, and the attempted retaliation of raising tax assessments on opponents. The papers also reported Huey's denials, countercharges, and threats to jail perjurers, and the raucous, unruly conditions of the hearing.[78] The *Tribune* opined that, when cornered, demagogues like Huey turn to irrelevant derelictions. It failed to see that the Senate leadership was doing this to Huey.[79]

Chairman Howell was worn out and did not care to return to Louisiana. Some blamed Huey's circular, "The Kangaroo Court," issued to protest the committee's investigation,[80] for Howell's death in March. On the night of February 17, when the hearing concluded, Huey's New Orleans home was set on fire.[81]

Almost in conjunction with the Overton hearings, Huey's Louisiana's opponents investigated election fraud related to the vote on seventeen constitutional amendments. Only two were controversial: to issue bonds to refinance Board of Liquidation debts and to permit New Orleans to purchase a ferry. These amendments were defeated in the rural parishes but passed in New Orleans by such big margins that Huey's opponents suspected fraud. The district attorney, Eugene Stanley, somewhat independent of the Old Regulars and Huey, agreed to investigate and asked the court to turn over four ballot boxes to the grand jury. The court granted this request on November 23.

The following day, Attorney General Porterie asked Stanley to end the investigation to avoid imperiling the sale of the bonds, but Stanley refused. Porterie then supplanted Stanley, as permitted by law, but unwise. Porterie met with the grand jury on November 29. It took no action, which increased demands for an independent review. The Louisiana Bar Association, the New Orleans Bar Association, and the Young Men's Business Club of New Orleans joined the Honest Election League to ask Porterie to step aside for Stanley. Porterie declined. The grand jury adjourned without counting the ballots. This outraged the judge and the bar association. It probed whether Porterie should be expelled for exerting improper influence on the grand jury.[82]

A third attack on Huey was led by the IRS. After Long's Senate activities in April and May 1932, Hoover's IRS began an inquiry into Huey's taxes.

In charge was agent Elmer Irey, who had obtained the facts used to convict Chicago mobster Al Capone for income tax evasion.

Senator Wheeler was sitting in a restaurant in Shreveport traveling to visit Roosevelt, just at the start of Stanley's investigation. As a courtesy, he called Huey. Minutes later, two state policemen appeared and told him that Huey wanted them to drive him to New Orleans to meet. Wheeler demurred, but the policemen, grim and insistent, convinced him. They drove Wheeler to the capitol but arrived after midnight and Huey had gone to bed. They met the next morning. Told about the grand jury machinations, Huey suggested, as a pretense because of Wheeler's presence, that the officials should be forced to brave the investigation. Huey asked Wheeler to talk to Roosevelt about the Treasury Department probe (Huey didn't ask him to intervene in the Overton investigation, which shows that he didn't think it would be resumed). Wheeler said nothing to Roosevelt.[83] In January 1933, an article about the IRS probe appeared in a Memphis newspaper. It reported that Huey's bank accounts were scrutinized, that he was shadowed by government agents during the Christmas holidays, his telephone was tapped, and his every movement watched.[84]

The psychological effect on Huey of the Overton, Stanley, and IRS investigations and the arson at his home can be guessed. When Huey returned to the Senate on February 21, he gave an address, "surpassing in violence all his previous outbursts," denouncing Ansell. Huey accused Ansell of letting a criminal escape while he was in the Army to split a pot of gold with him, called him a dog-faced son of a wolf, a liar, a crook, a scoundrel, a Benedict Arnold, a burglar, and thief of the deepest dye. Most of Huey's biographers report his speech only to that extent. The allegations about splitting a pot of gold seem surreal.

But "throughout his violent speech Senator Long was seconded by Senator Bennett C. Clark." Even Senator Broussard, who denounced Huey in the Senate, said that he would "hold no brief for Gen. Ansell."[85] Why? A House committee had investigated Ansell a decade earlier. After resigning from the Army, Ansell became the attorney for Grover Cleveland Bergdoll, a draft dodger. Ansell obtained permission for Bergdoll to be released from prison so that he could locate $150,000 in gold that he said was buried in a Maryland hillside. Bergdoll then escaped to Germany. The House Committee wrote that Ansell was out of the Army and therefore "beyond the jurisdiction of court martial proceedings, but provision should be made against his future practice before any of the departments, before any court martial or in the courts of the District of Columbia, or the nation above whose safety and integrity he has placed gold."[86]

Shocked at Huey's speech, Senator Bailey asked him if he claimed the senatorial privilege from libel. Huey said he did not, but when Bailey persisted, he qualified his answer by saying Ansell could sue him in any court of competent jurisdiction, meaning Louisiana. The next day Ansell sued in Washington, DC.[87] Huey asserted immunity and was upheld. But Huey had excerpted the speech in circulars, and such publications are not privileged, so Ansell amended his complaint. In a series of stories about Ansell's lawsuit between March and May, the papers emphasized that Huey asserted immunity after he told the Senate that he wouldn't.[88] They disregarded Ansell's misconduct.

Before Roosevelt's inauguration, Huey recovered his cheerfulness. He flashed a million-dollar smile as he circulated among senators during the last day of the lame-duck Senate session.[89] Huey got the IRS investigation killed by having his bank examiner force a bank to call a $250,000 loan of Hoover's assistant secretary of the Navy, E. L. Jahncke of New Orleans. Huey's friend Harvey Couch, a director of the Reconstruction Finance Corporation, called Huey to protest. Huey denied doing anything to call the loan: "I don't have anything more to do with that bank examiner than the Assistant Secretary of the Navy has to do with the Treasury Department." "Oh, is that it?" "That's exactly it." Embittered, Jahnke became an FBI informant. Inside the IRS, Irey was told to stop investigating so that the incoming administration could decide what to do with Huey.[90]

Also with the aid of Harvey Couch, Huey reached a truce with Joe Robinson. It was not revealed in the press, and the exact time of it is unknown. In March, the Overton Committee denied that it would tighten the "lax rules regarding admissibility" of evidence, but by June it revealed that testimony would be "confine[d]" to the defeat of Broussard.[91] Huey's attacks on Robinson ended. Robinson became the majority leader. Huey applied for committee memberships and received assignments.

Huey thought he would have influence with the Roosevelt administration and let it show, sometimes in ways that did not enhance his reputation. At a Roosevelt advisor Raymond Moley dinner party, Huey crashed in, took a vicious bite out of an apple he plucked from a fruit bowl, tapped J. P. Morgan banker Norman Davis with it, and said, "I don't like you and your goddamn banker friends." Huey left as suddenly as he arrived. One guest was found cowering in the bathroom.[92]

Huey was not invited and didn't crash a February 18 dinner hosted by the Inner Circle, a group of newspaper reporters. Roosevelt attended. The reporters lampooned the politicians and "told what they thought was on the minds of the party men." One of the humorous songs was sung to the tune of "Fit as a Fiddle (and Ready for Love)." An excerpt:

> We have a mandate we must carry out,
> None of us knows what the hell it's about,
> Hungry for office and thirsty for beer,
> Now with Johnson, and George Norris,
> Huey Long and Cactus Jack,
> We can run this gosh-darned country
> With a hey-nonny-nonny and a hot-cha-cha.
> Hey diddle diddle, they helped us to win,
> But we'll throw 'em overboard now that we're in.[93]

# Twenty

# A RIGHT TO COMPLAIN

On the eve of Roosevelt's inauguration, banks across the country collapsed. In thirty-two states (including Louisiana), they closed. In another ten states withdrawals were limited to 5 percent of customer deposits.[1] In New Orleans, even the Hibernia shut down.

Inaugurated on March 4, 1933, in the midst of this crisis, Roosevelt electrified the nation with his speech that the country had nothing to fear but fear itself.[2] Huey ran up to speak to Roosevelt just before he was sworn in but, changing his mind, did an about-face.[3] Despite advocacy by advisors,[4] Roosevelt said nothing in favor of wealth redistribution, but pledged to throw out the money changers from the temple. Upon taking office, Roosevelt declared a bank holiday. The White House received over 500,000 supportive letters in the next few days.[5]

The promise to throw out the money changers was crowd-pleasing rhetoric, nothing more. Roosevelt nominated industrialist William Woodin to be secretary of the treasury, over the worries of Senators Couzens, Norris, and Steiwer that he would be subject to conflicts of interest. Other money changers were now "swarming through the corridors of the Treasury."[6] A group of academics, nicknamed the Brains Trust or the Brain Trust, also advised Roosevelt. Its most prominent member was Raymond Moley, a professor from Columbia University.

Moley and Woodin worked with Hoover's outgoing treasury secretary Ogden Mills and a group of big bankers to craft emergency banking-relief legislation. The bankers quarreled like children, were often bereft of ideas, and one had a series of nervous breakdowns. Ogden Mills wrote most of the plan.[7]

Conceived as a temporary measure until more detailed legislation could be drafted, it confirmed Roosevelt's bank holiday orders, allowed impaired banks to operate under conservators, authorized the Reconstruction Finance Corporation to purchase stock of banks to give them liquidity, permitted $200 million of Federal Reserve notes to be issued to prop up shaky banks, embargoed gold and silver, forbade the purchase of foreign currency, and provided that federal banks would reopen as fast as the government could determine their soundness.[8]

Roosevelt didn't participate in the deliberations and was not interested in the advice of progressives. Huey overlooked a "No Admittance" sign and tried to crash the Senate Banking Committee meeting considering the bill but was expelled.[9] On the Senate floor, he complained that he had been trying to discover the bill's terms all day. Robinson refused to explain it, saying he would have to wait for the committee's (meaning Glass's) report.[10] Senators LaFollette and Costigan personally begged Roosevelt at the White House for comprehensive banking reform, unsuccessfully.[11]

The banking bill passed the House by acclamation, but in the Senate, Huey complained that it lacked aid for state banks and that it would help 5,100 federally chartered banks reopen but would leave 14,900 others closed. It would help the big banks but ruin the small state banks. Their depositors needed their own money. LaFollette gave a two-hour speech opposing the bill.[12]

Unlike LaFollette, who proposed nothing, Huey suggested an amendment empowering the president to make state banks members of the Federal Reserve System so that they would be entitled to the same benefits. Roosevelt was yet a great president, Huey said, but he wanted him to get more advice than he had been getting but "lacked the time" to take. Glass, Robinson, and Barkley defended the bill.

Senator George helped Huey craft his amendment to add the state banks, and Senators Tydings, Thomas, Gore, Reynolds, and Goldsborough voiced support. But it was defeated on a voice vote and Huey's request for a record vote was denied. Administration spokesmen promised that the banks would open the next day if the legislation were passed. Senators suggested they needed to "subordinate" their convictions or to pass the bill now and "fix it later."[13] LaFollette, Borah, Costigan, and others voted against it. Huey voted for it as better than nothing, and it passed on March 9.

On March 10, New York's legislature called for the banking provisions

Huey advocated.[14] Other senators realized that reopening only 25 percent of the banks wouldn't solve the problem and, if the other 75 percent of the banks failed, the system might collapse anyway. The banks weren't opened on Friday, either, leaving some legislators feeling duped as Roosevelt extended the holiday. Because of this, Huey again suggested an amendment.[15]

By Saturday, March 11, backed by hundreds of telegrams and letters, Huey charged that, without protection for state banks and a guaranty of bank deposits, fire and destruction would spread across the country. Robinson defended the bill, pleaded for support of Roosevelt, and attacked the big banks that opposed reform. Huey agreed with Robinson's "justified tirade" against the big banks but asked why the bill only saved the big banks Robinson criticized. Even if the bailout cost $12 billion, Huey said, it was worth it. Europe owed the United States $20 billion from World War I that it hadn't repaid, and the United States was still standing.

Roosevelt's administration presented a confused legal analysis. Could the president legally close the state banks? Glass thought he couldn't; Woodin thought he could. Administration leaders had difficulty reconciling the authority to close state banks without helping them reopen. Senator Pittman, perhaps tipsy, confessed that Huey's idea was included in the administration's bill but dropped in the House, leaving a stench that big financial interests caused its removal.[16] Huey didn't criticize Roosevelt, but he pilloried Glass: "As a fitting and glorious climax to his career, the sun rose, for the first time since Columbus discovered America, on this country with every bank closed on the same day!"[17] Huey's new resolution to aid state banks was referred to the Banking and Currency Committee.

As he was leaving this Saturday session, Glass snapped, whirled, and called Huey a sonofabitch. Huey returned the insult, and senators separated the two men. Joe Robinson hustled off Glass.[18] Huey got into a taxi and went to the White House. Afterward, he told Louisiana reporters that everything would be fine if the administration could escape the influence of big bankers.[19]

Roosevelt then changed course. He gave his first and best fireside chat on Sunday night, March 12, to explain how he would reopen banks. One paragraph emphasized that state authorities in conjunction with federal officials would protect the state banks,[20] foretelling adoption of Huey's amendment. Sixty million people crowded around twenty million radios to hear it. Public confidence was restored. In the following days, money flowed back into banks and the stock market rebounded.

The next day, Monday the 13th, Robinson proposed an amendment embodying Huey's thinking.[21] Roosevelt had it read to Huey from the White House.[22] When Huey was out of the Senate chamber on March 14, Robinson suddenly called it up for a hearing out of order and it was passed, with Robinson—flip-flopping to keep up with the administration's flip-flopping—stating that it put state banks "nearer on parity with [Federal Reserve] member banks."[23]

Moley wrote that "Capitalism was saved in eight days."[24] But many banks remained closed, and the inability of their depositors to get their own money stunted economic recovery.[25] Until the end of the session, Huey engaged in a constant struggle with Roosevelt's conservative Treasury Department to get a progressive banking bill and a liberal administration of it.

After the Long-Robinson amendment was adopted on March 14, for example, Glass secretly held up the bill rather than transfer it to the House. Couzens said this was "reprehensible." Huey gave "advice to my friend, the President," that he "better get that set" in the Treasury Department removed.[26] The delay allowed the House to pass its own bill that aided state banks after inspection, which was omitted from the Robinson amendment. The Senate thus had to debate the House bill. The subtext that aid to state banks would proceed more slowly or not at all could not overcome the seeming reasonableness of requiring inspections. The Treasury Department thus kept control, what it and Glass wanted.[27]

Historians often state that Roosevelt tried to work with Huey, but that Huey was too ambitious or unruly to cooperate.[28] This is wrong. Early on, for example, Huey, intending to be a team player and at the request of Moley, allowed Roosevelt to appoint a relative of a political opponent to a position.[29] Considering the controversy over the Glass banking bill two months earlier, Roosevelt's failure to solicit Huey's support before the Emergency Banking Act was proposed must have been deliberate. The hostility toward Huey that Roosevelt expressed to Senator Johnson in January persisted, and he threw Huey overboard.

Historians also write that Roosevelt's administration lacked philosophical coherence. This is correct. The zigzags between conservatives and progressives continued for the rest of the hundred-day session.

Roosevelt's second bill was the Economy Act. Introduced on March 10, the day after the Emergency Banking Act was passed, it proposed to cut $400 million from veteran benefits, government salaries, and scientific research. Budget director Lewis Douglas, a swaggering, wealthy cowboy from Arizona, then in the middle of a bromance with Roosevelt, was a strong advocate, as was the National Economy League chaired by retired admiral Byrd. Roosevelt believed it fulfilled the budget-balancing provision of the Democratic Party platform, but neither the platform nor Roosevelt during the campaign had suggested cuts to veterans.[30]

In the House, Democratic majority leader Joseph Byrns refused to sponsor it, but a rival maneuvered it through with Republican votes despite defections of ninety-two Democrats. Thousands of letters and telegrams arrived in Congress from veterans' groups protesting the cuts. Senator Harry Byrd saw the political dangers. In letters to his brother, Admiral Byrd, he asked him *not* to emphasize cutting payments to veterans, but to promote giving Roosevelt discretion to cut government spending and then *resign* from the Economy League before Roosevelt decided what to cut![31]

Huey opposed the Economy Act on Monday, March 13. Discussing the banking bill, he criticized Glass rather than Roosevelt. Discussing the Economy Act, he attacked its sponsor, the Economy League, not Roosevelt. Huey read to the Senate a list of its wealthy contributors. Cutting the benefits of those in need would have "disastrous consequences."[32]

On March 14, Senators Clark, Borah, Trammell, Steiwer, Copeland, and Couzens denounced the bill. Huey said nothing. Senator Couzens called it an "iniquitous measure" that House Democrats were forced to swallow because of threats that they would lose patronage. Did we have a government of moneylenders or a government of the people? "I know my friend the Senator from Louisiana is condemned because he makes these unhappy comparisons; but notwithstanding what you may think of him, notwithstanding the ridicule the great press of the country may heap on him, nevertheless the comparisons he makes from day to day and which I have the honor to make today, are odious."[33]

Huey voted against the bill and for several amendments to limit the cuts. He did not filibuster it, dominate the debates, criticize Roosevelt, or obstruct its passage. Roosevelt called Huey on the Senate floor to ask for support, but Huey refused, saying the government couldn't retract its promises to veterans.[34] On Wednesday, the Act passed sixty-two to thirteen.[35] The Volstead Act, allowing the manufacture and sale of nonintoxicating beer, was proposed right after the Economy Act was proposed (Roosevelt hoping that, in their haste to pass this act, Congress would speed consideration of the Economy Act) and passed right after the Economy Act passed.[36]

Immediately thereafter, Huey went to New York with Illinois Representative Reid on unspecified flood-control business and proved that, if nothing else, he was good copy. America's favorite pastime, he said, was jumping on dead lions (such as utilities tycoon Insull).[37] "The only ones we pull out of the den are the dead ones. First we prod them, kick them, poke them, and make sure they're dead. Then, once we're sure of that, we all shout together, 'let's go after them,' and we do."

Huey would support Roosevelt even if he were wrong, but he had to vote against the Economy Act because we had promised "the earth" to veterans. Huey advocated taxes on the income, capital, and inheritances of the wealthy so that the government could be supported without taxes from anyone else and spend $11 billion on public works.[38] Days later, the *Times* reviewed the first biography about Huey, *The Kingfish, a Biography of Huey P. Long*, by Webster Smith (a pseudonym). It told an "astounding story" of a man with an "active, agile and resourceful brain as well as persistence and determination." It would move the reader to "gusty laughter" and "amazed wonder."[39]

Five days after Roosevelt's first fireside chat, Huey gave a thirty-minute radio address in support of his resolutions to redistribute wealth. Citing philosophers, statesmen, and Roosevelt, he urged listeners to write or wire their representatives to endorse the Long plan.[40] Thousands wrote in approval.[41] For Huey, this was no different from purchasing a newspaper ad to urge passage of an oil pipeline bill in 1922. Other senators gave radio speeches, but Huey did so more often: on April 4, in a low-energy, meandering, ad-libbed talk, promoting his tax bills and government funding of college educations, and on April 21, advocating an increase in the money supply.[42]

On the same day the Economy Act passed, Roosevelt admitted that the government needed to employ people and reduce crops to increase farm prices.[43] On March 21, Roosevelt proposed the Civilian Conservation Corps (CCC). Single men would plant trees and conserve natural resources. Its cost was $500 million. Labor initially opposed it because the wages were only $30 per month and because of the military-style organization, but the bill passed on a voice vote in the Senate on March 28, and Robert Fechner, a union leader, was appointed to head it.[44] LaFollette wrote that Roosevelt thought the "bank bill and dramatic gesture of a few thousand men in the reforestation group are all that is needed to start the United States back on the road to prosperity. . . . To my mind this is pure bunk."[45]

Roosevelt also proposed the Federal Relief Administration to provide $500 million to the states for relief. Drafted by Senators LaFollette, Wagner, and Costigan, it duplicated their 1932 measure but provided for the states to administer it. On March 30, Huey backed it because it was "out of harmony" with the administration's prior proposals. He hoped it marked a turn to decentralize wealth "and overcome the great suffering that is already in sight as a result of the administration of the banking bill and the so-called Economy Act." The bill passed on April 7.[46]

Secretary of agriculture Henry Wallace was a remarkable plant geneticist and editor of *Wallace's Farmer*. He had a mind in which the "concrete and the utilitarian mingled . . . with much that was vague and dreamy." For farmers, he proposed a domestic allotment plan by which the amount of crops raised would be controlled and surplus crops would be sent abroad, all financed by a processing tax.[47] Henry Morgenthau Jr., Roosevelt's neighbor and friend, proposed government leasing of marginally productive land, mortgage relief, government loans on crops stored under seal, and licensing to support compliance with government directives. Roosevelt convinced Cotton Ed Smith to sponsor a bill combining these ideas. Bernard Baruch's associate, George Peek, would oversee the program.[48]

On April 7 in the Senate, Smith and Robinson were peppered with questions that they had trouble answering, and Smith's heart wasn't in it.[49] On Monday, April 10, many conceded that it probably wouldn't work but that it ought to be given a chance.[50]

Smith labored on and finally lost his composure. On the 11th he launched a tirade advocating the redistribution of wealth. Equally frustrated, Huey was incited to a tirade of his own. The administration's program had closed half the banks, deflated the currency, diminished payments to veterans, and reduced government spending. More people were out of work than when Roosevelt was inaugurated, and he was listening to J. P. Morgan instead of keeping his campaign promises. Planting saplings was not going to solve the Depression; it should be called the sapsucker's bill. Huey would "eat" every sapling planted in Louisiana.[51] Of his proposals, Roosevelt took the most personal interest in the CCC bill.[52] Huey's acidly expressed disdain for it must have stung.

Robinson now had Huey just where he wanted him. While feuding with Robinson in the Senate, Huey endorsed Roosevelt to outflank Robinson. Now Robinson defended Roosevelt to isolate Huey. Huey replied that he was only repeating the remarks of Smith and had no beef with Robinson.[53]

Huey expressed the covert dissatisfaction of progressives with Roosevelt. LaFollette privately complained on April 3 that the "whole policy of the administration is deflationary."[54] John Simpson of the Farmers Union, Milo Reno of the Farmer's Holiday Association, and farm state progressives opposed the farm bill, reasoning that the problem was not overproduction, but underconsumption. Simpson said: "What we have overproduction of is empty stomachs and bare backs."[55] They proposed a government guarantee that farmers receive the cost of production and that the currency be inflated to give consumers more purchasing power.

Defeating Roosevelt and Robinson, Norris added a cost of production amendment on April 13, forty-seven to forty-one. Huey voted for it.[56] Following up that victory, Huey, Wheeler, and Thomas proposed amendments calling for an increase in the money supply. Huey's proposal was based on a bill introduced in the House. He had a *Saturday Evening Post* article endorsing inflation reprinted and placed on the desk of each senator. Roosevelt viewed this with alarm.[57]

Wheeler spoke at length for inflation. Thousands of banks were still closed and industry depressed. Neither the banking bill, economy act, nor the beer legislation would cure the depression. The CCC would only employ one out of every fifty-two unemployed people. Wheeler wanted inflation, a farm-mortgage breathing spell, bond issues to relieve homeowners and the unemployed, and $500 million for relief. Wheeler thus made the same points Huey had made about Roosevelt's program, albeit more diplomatically. The Wheeler amendment was defeated, thirty-three to forty-three, but was supported by two-thirds of the Democratic senators.[58] Huey withdrew his amendment.[59]

Roosevelt convinced Thomas to support an amendment giving Roosevelt *discretion* to inflate the currency.[60] Robinson announced Roosevelt's partial flip-flop on April 21. Connally had voted against Wheeler's amendment but now favored this bill, because $6 billion more would just regain the ground lost because $6 billion of deposits was frozen in closed banks.[61] Huey supported the Thomas amendment while stating that he had not been consulted about Roosevelt's plans and was not offended by his exclusion. Huey congratulated "our great President" for supporting inflation as quickly as he got "other tremendously important matters out of the way."[62]

Some newspapers favored inflation, and at least one applauded Huey's April 11 tirade.[63] Huey upped the ante on the 26th and pushed for payment of the soldiers' bonus, an effective expedient to get $2 billion of purchasing power into the hands of soldiers' families without any discretionary holdups. Robinson said that Roosevelt opposed the measure. Huey rejoined that Roosevelt rejected inflation until two-thirds of the Democrats in the Senate voted for the Wheeler amendment. Roosevelt just needed more time to change his mind. Robinson snapped: "The senator has a habit of getting smart here on the floor, and he has a habit of quoting scripture. 'How long will thou speak these things, and how long shall the words of thy mouth be like a strong wind' [*laughter*].'"[64]

The bonus was defeated, twenty-eight to sixty. The Thomas inflation compromise passed sixty-four to twenty-one, and the farm bill passed sixty-four to twenty on April 28. The previous day a mob of Iowa farmers had taken a foreclosure judge out to the countryside, stripped his pants off, smeared him with grease and dirt, and put a noose around his neck, before letting him go. Farm Holiday Association leader Milo Reno called for a farmers' strike to start May 13.[65]

The House-Senate conference removed the cost-of-production amendment and a sugar-protection provision that had been added by Huey. Norris and Wheeler accepted these deletions because of the inflation feature. Huey followed their lead as he had throughout the debate, without any big speeches. One day before Reno's threatened farm strike, the Agricultural Adjustment Act was signed.[66]

Most conservatives were horrified by inflation. In sensational news, Carter Glass voted against the administration.[67] A respectable minority of businessmen, however, feared a violent farmer revolt and believed that the government needed to control the currency, including by removal of the gold standard. Leaders of J. P. Morgan supported the farm bill and inflation.[68] In December, however, Roosevelt explained privately that he had no intention of issuing the additional currency.[69]

Senate dissatisfaction with Roosevelt's program or at least a willingness to proceed independently was further manifested by its adoption of the thirty-hour workweek. Senator Black proposed this bill to combat child labor, inhuman hours of work, and unemployment.

Black believed his bill would "share the work" and that capital was overpaid while labor was underpaid. Why have 12 million unemployed, he said, just so that another 12 million or more could work from ten to sixteen hours a day? The Judiciary Committee, of which Huey was a member, reported it favorably, eleven to three. A similar bill in the House passed with a provision to embargo foreign goods exported to the United States by companies that made their employees work more than thirty hours a week.

Robinson doubted the bill's constitutionality. This parroted Roosevelt's opinion and was a flip-flop from Robinson's endorsement of the idea in 1932. Roosevelt opposed the bill, believing it would depress wages as working hours were reduced. Black omitted minimum wages only because the courts had ruled such legislation unconstitutional. Black contended that public opinion and an improved ability of labor to bargain if most people were employed would prevent or limit wage reductions.

Without any long speeches, Huey supported Black, sometimes with pithy summaries of Black's more laborious arguments.[70] Huey fought efforts to exempt industries, such as the canning industry, even though it was important to his supporter Jules Fisher. Huey opposed an exemption for cotton gins when even Black allowed it. In opposing the bill, Reed rhetorically exclaimed that laborers would not want to drop their tools and go home after only six hours of work; why would they? Huey piped up: "Does the Senator from Pennsylvania ever play golf? [*laughter*]"[71]

On Roosevelt's behalf, Robinson proposed a thirty-six-hour week, but this was defeated, forty-one to forty-three. Black's bill then passed, fifty-three to thirty.[72] Roosevelt had it scuttled,[73] however, in favor of what became the National Industrial Recovery Act, administered by the National Recovery Administration (NRA).[74]

Huey called up his tax resolutions—to prohibit ownership or inheritance of more than $5 million per person and an income of more than $1 million per person—on May 12. Huey used charts showing how the middle class—33 percent of the people who possessed about 35 percent of the wealth two decades ago—was squeezed. Some had made it to the top 1 percent; most joined the 99 percent of people who had nothing.

Huey had not coordinated his proposals with Roosevelt but took him at his word. Senator Borah asked how the taxed wealth would get redistributed. It would relieve the bottom 99 percent of paying taxes, Huey said, allow the restoration of veteran benefits, and permit relief. Huey dropped the capital tax bill before the vote yet lost eighteen to fifty-four.[75]

On May 17, Roosevelt introduced the National Industrial Recovery Act.[76] Many wanted $6 billion in public works,[77] but budget director Lewis Douglas scaled this back to $3.3 billion, authorized in Section II. Section I required industrial planning. Largely the brainchild of Brain Truster Rexford Tugwell and Bernard Baruch, it created government boards of industry, labor, and consumers to set prices, wages, hours of work, and output for each industry, suspending the antitrust laws. The theory was that, left to their own judgment and competitive pressures, industrial concerns would overbuild capacity, and some of them would thereafter go broke, laying off workers in the process, and disrupting the economy.

Woodrow Wilson used government planning administered by a War Industries Board to win World War I. Baruch and his employee, retired general Hugh S. Johnson, both had experience on this board, and both were Roosevelt advisors. Johnson was fond of Italy's corporate state that had revived the Italian economy under fascist dictator Benito Mussolini. Roosevelt selected Johnson to manage the NRA planning, whereas Interior secretary Harold Ickes, a former Chicago social worker, was appointed to administer the $3.3 billion of public works.

Big businesses backed this legislation because it eliminated the antitrust laws and permitted them to fix prices and control output. Labor appreciated its seat at the planning table, where it could advocate for higher wages, shorter hours, and better working conditions. On June 7, the Senate Finance Committee favorably reported the bill. That day, Senator Borah opposed loosening the anti-monopoly provisions as a sell-out to big business and denounced the bill.

Huey followed Borah. His speech was lengthy, but its best quote was short, incisive, and prescient: "Every fault of socialism is found in this bill, without one of its virtues." Baruch would control the agency on behalf of big business. Standard Oil, General Motors, and General Electric executives were going to run the NRA. Huey objected to numerous codes to be written by a soviet-style council, administered by the same kind of bureaucrats cutting veteran benefits, unknown to small businessmen, and to the jail terms for violations; opposed price fixing; and criticized Congress for pretending it was legislating when all it was doing was delegating power to the "President, to the Secretary to the President, to the secretary of the secretary, to supervisors, assistant supervisors, secretaries to supervisors and to supervisors of secretaries [*laughter*]." The bill was "infernal," "tyrannical," "detestable," and "reprehensible."[78]

Senator Wagner of New York, the bill's sponsor, denied that it would increase wealth concentration because the boards would provide adequate wages. Wagner frankly admitted the theory of the bill. Industry would never be in order without a nationally planned economy. This was the first step toward it.[79] Senators Barkley and Robinson defended Baruch (he funded their campaigns). Robinson shouted that Huey would never stand in Baruch's class.[80]

In a lengthy extemporaneous reply, Huey attacked Baruch, who could advise Hoover on one day and Roosevelt the next. While he was speaking, he had a page fetch his anti-Baruch remarks from May 12, 1932, so he could quote them. Huey was accepted in the party councils after he made his anti-Baruch remarks in 1932. Why was he criticized for saying the same things now?

> I come here now and I complain. I complain in the name of the people of my country, of the sovereign state I represent. . . .
>
> I complain [that Baruch associate Hugh Johnson is going to be put in charge of the NRA]. . . .
>
> I complain [that Baruch associate George Peek is in charge of the farm program]. . . .
>
> I complain [that Baruch associate Mr. Brown is working in the Budget Department]. . . .
>
> I complain because, on the 12th day of May 1932, before we went to Chicago to nominate a President . . . I stood in this very place on this floor and told the people of this country that we were not going to have the Baruch influence, at that time so potent with Hoover, manipulating the Democratic Party. . . .
>
> I have a right to complain. The Senator from Arkansas might not have that right because he has not uttered such words. . . . the Senator from Kentucky might not have such right, but I have that right because within the hearing . . . of 120,000,000 people my voice went up that the new deal meant an end of "Baruchism" in America.[81]

Robinson answered that Huey was "mad because Roosevelt will not let him run the administration. [*Laughter in the galleries.*]" Huey replied, "That may be so [*Laughter*]," but Robinson wasn't running the country either. He was merely a soldier making column right and column left. "I have only asked [Roosevelt] to carry out the promises he made the American people." Robinson threatened to campaign against Huey in Louisiana. Showing the effect of their truce, Huey replied that he was "sorry" Robinson was coming to Louisiana:

> MR. ROBINSON: When the Senator comes into Arkansas.
> MR. LONG: Well, I may not have time to go into Arkansas.
> MR. ROBINSON: And I may not have time to go into Louisiana. [*Laughter.*]

MR. LONG: All right. So I think, Mr. President, we will just "call it a day" for the present. [*Laughter.*][82]

"[L]ater they both laughed about the threats."[83]

Huey thereafter supported progressive amendments and fought regressive amendments to the NRA. One of his own, to prevent the codes from ensnaring simple housewives or farmers who bartered, was adopted by a voice vote. But it was dropped in conference and was absent from the enacted bill.[84]

Roosevelt recovered his standing with some progressives upset at his initial conservatism (LaFollette and Couzens, for example) because they wanted a planned economy. Norris, Wheeler, LaFollette, Couzens, and administration Democrats voted against Clark's amendment to strike Part I, the planning section, from the bill, which failed thirty-one to forty-nine. Clark was supported by Huey and a strange assortment of conservative Democrats (for example, Byrd, Bailey, Tydings) and Republicans (for example, Reed, Fess, Vandenberg), southern populists (for example, Black, Bankhead, Connally), old midwestern and western populists (for example, Gore, Schall), and Western progressives (for example, Borah, Dill).[85]

An amendment to prohibit combinations in restraint of trade proposed by Borah and two minor amendments by Clark and LaFollette were adopted, with Huey's support. While Huey disliked the planning section (Part I), he liked the public works feature in Part II. At the time of the vote, he asked the chair how a senator should vote if he were half in favor of the bill. Vice President Garner replied that he should cut himself in two. Amid jeers, Huey changed his vote from no to yes, and the bill passed, fifty-eight to twenty-four, with Democrats Bailey, Clark, Connally, Tydings, and Gore among the minority.[86]

The conference committee eliminated or weakened the three amendments.[87] The vote to pass the last version of the NRA was closer, forty-six to thirty-nine, because many liberals—including Huey—who had voted for the bill when it had the three amendments, on June 9 voted against it.[88]

On May 19, 1933, Glass proposed a permanent banking bill. Glass's original bill removed the secretary of the treasury from the Federal Reserve Board. Now Glass kept him as a member. The original provision that Huey had opposed was eliminated at the request of the person Huey opposed. Barkley said nothing.

Branch banking was limited; commercial banking was divorced from home-mortgage banking; state banks were aided; and bank deposits were insured. Roosevelt opposed bank-deposit insurance, but acquiesced.[89] Having won the substantive policy battle against Glass, Huey defended the bill at length against the suggestions of his friends Wheeler and Norris that aid for postal savings banks should be included. The Banking Committee of the Senate, with its counsel Ferdinand Pecora, was then exposing banking misdeeds, such as the issuance of stock to politically influential people at below-market prices. This increased sentiment for reform. The bill passed on May 25, 1933.[90]

One of those exposed favored insiders was William Woodin, Roosevelt's treasury secretary. On May 26, Huey denounced Woodin in a speech entitled "Our Constant Rulers," as "mired in the mud of the House of Morgan." While it was humiliating to see the money changers still in control of the temple, it was unfair to blame Roosevelt, Huey said, since it would have been impossible to find a treasury secretary who had not dealt with Morgan. Huey read press reports that Woodin would soon resign and predicted that Roosevelt would soon issue progressives more encouragement.[91] Resisting Huey's pressure and newspaper speculation to dump Woodin, Roosevelt publicized a river cruise with him and his wife.[92]

Huey's attack resulted from the policies Woodin followed. The bank bailout was slow. The frozen deposits—estimated variously at $4 billion or $6 billion—in closed banks kept the economy deflated. Huey blamed this on the continued malignant dominance of Morgan associates in the Treasury Department.[93]

Under the most generous measure, the stock of money in the United States was about $32 billion in December 1933, compared to almost $50 billion at the time of the stock market crash in 1929. The Reconstruction Finance Corporation's loans to banks rehabilitated some of them, but bankers remained reluctant to lend.[94]

On June 2, Huey attacked rumored treasury influences to get the House-Senate conferees to drop deposit insurance for state banks.[95] Vandenberg said on June 5 that the Treasury Department had recommended to the conferees the rejection of bank deposit guaranties, an action "utterly inconsistent" with the Senate bill.[96] On June 6, again in response to reports of Roosevelt's hostility to deposit insurance, Huey forcefully advocated it. Huey did not care what kind of "pronunciamento" or "ipsi dixit" came from "the other end of Pennsylvania Avenue." He had helped elect the occupant of the White House on the promise of protecting the American people, and he was going to fulfill that promise.[97]

There was also a personal reason for his attacks on Morgan. *Collier's* magazine published a favorable article about Huey in 1930 but a hatchet job on him in 1933. It mailed an advance copy of the latter article to every member of the Senate. Moreover, the same man wrote the two articles! During its investigation, the Senate Banking Committee called a Morgan representative, Thomas Lamont, to testify. Given permission to question him, Huey established that Morgan owned or controlled *Collier's*. Lamont denied knowledge of the two inconsistent articles, but only after Huey criticized Morgan did its magazine discover that he was a demagogue.[98]

On June 16, the banking bill was passed by acclamation, and it included the provisions that Glass and Huey wanted.[99] The bank-deposits guaranty was the most successful of the early New Deal legislation because it improved confidence in the banking system. Hofstadter wrote that Roosevelt opposed deposit insurance, but its adoption would "add lustre to [his] name." Confirming Hofstadter's prediction, Schlesinger minimized Roosevelt's opposition, but said its final passage was "one of the most brilliant and successful accomplishments of the Hundred Days."[100]

On May 4, a railroad reform bill was passed by a voice vote, with Huey constructively offering several amendments—based on his experience as public service commissioner—that were accepted on the floor.[101] On May 8, the Senate passed legislation to regulate securities by a voice vote, the precursor to the current Securities and Exchange Commission.[102] Legislation to create the Tennessee Valley Authority and build the great Tennessee Valley Dam, long the dream of Senator Norris, but stymied by successive Republican administrations and the utility lobby, passed in the Senate by a vote of sixty-three to twenty (Huey voting for it), and was signed by Roosevelt on May 18.[103]

Forgotten now are the many bitter letters veterans directed to Roosevelt in 1933. They complained of a "raw deal" instead of a "new deal." They preferred being merely the "forgotten" men to being remembered and "knocked down." "The new regulations [of Budget Director Douglas pursuant to the Economy Act] removed 501,777 veterans and their dependents from the pension roll, including approximately 100,000 veterans suffering from tuberculosis who were unable to prove that they contracted the disease during their time in the service. . . . Even more galling to veterans, members who retained disability benefits—those with documented service-connected injuries—shouldered anywhere from 25 to 88 percent reductions in their benefits."[104]

Mistreatment of veterans was a constant feature of Senate proceedings from April through the end of the session. When a group of veterans descended on Washington in May 1933 to protest the benefit cuts, Louis Howe sent Roosevelt's wife, Eleanor, to bring them food and coffee. Many were directed to work for the CCC. Hoover had routed similar protestors with the Army; Roosevelt routed them with kindness, an example of Roosevelt's superior political acumen.[105]

On May 10 some regulations were revoked. But the CCC couldn't employ veterans who were disabled or hospitalized. Veterans despondent over the cuts committed suicide. State charity hospitals were overloaded with veterans while federal hospital rooms were empty. One veteran had returned his government-issued clothes and left the government office in his underwear. Another veteran sent Huey a package with his pension-cut protest letter. Inside were his false teeth. He had no use for them, he said. A month later a different veteran wrote to Huey asking for the used teeth. He couldn't afford dental work, and he would file them down and make them fit.[106]

Roosevelt obstinately fought efforts to repeal the economy bill or limit his authority to cut benefits. Senators bickered: they were misled, said some, while others denied it, given that the bill's purpose was to cut $400 million from the budget. Barkley said the unemployed had lost 100 percent of their benefits, as if that justified cutting veteran benefits. Louis Howe gave a paid speech on the radio against restoration, despite the dubious propriety of him being paid by a radio station while he drew a White House salary.[107]

Before Senate votes, preemptive announcements of planned liberalizing regulations were made, and some senators latched onto them to vote against liberalized legislation. Others said that, because of what had happened thus far, Roosevelt's people couldn't be trusted to make adjustments. Huey attacked the "squint-eyed experts, fumbling around . . . parceling out rules and regulations. Even if they would take the gum out of their mouths . . . half of them could not be sold into slavery for their lifetime for $500. [*Laughter.*]"[108] Supporting the regulation revision process, Tydings said they would be retroactive. Cutting interrupted:

> MR. CUTTING: That will do a great deal of good to the veteran when he is already dead.
>
> MR. LONG: Yes; that will help him some—to give him a tombstone![109]

The speeches consisted of a good deal of politician doublespeak. They all loved the veterans. The speeches "were almost tearful," Huey said. But "let us not send them the fine speeches that have been made here today. Let us send them some grub. Let us send them some medicine. Let us put them back in the hospitals. Let us put clothes on their backs."[110]

Senator Cutting wanted to restore 154,000 veterans removed by Douglas's regulations to the benefit rolls. Roosevelt asked him to compromise, limiting the cuts to 25 percent of their benefits until review of the individual veterans' files could be made. Cutting refused. Having attended Groton and Harvard, Cutting's background was as privileged as Roosevelt's, and having survived near death by tuberculosis (the reason he moved to New Mexico), he was as internally hardened.

Cutting's principled tenacity provoked Roosevelt to a "cold fury frightening to witness."[111] On Monday, June 12, Cutting gave a detailed speech in favor of his proposal that kicked off a three-day debate. Connally, Byrnes, and Robinson threatened a presidential veto. Huey held the floor to try to effectuate a compromise but failed.[112] The Senate passed Cutting's amendment on June 14, fifty-one to thirty-nine.[113]

The amendment, however, was written out of the conference report. Huey urged the Senate to reject it: "Here is a photograph of a man cut all over the back, operated on eight times, and his compensation is cut from $67 to $8 a month." Asking Senator Copeland, a surgeon, to examine the picture, Copeland replied, "it is indeed very cruel to have this man's compensation reduced in the way it has been." Congress should stay in session, Huey said, until the kind-hearted president recognized the true facts from someone "besides the chief executioners of the Veterans' Administration." Huey wanted to prevent his party from making a mistake. Partisanship could not compel him to drive "out upon the streets of the country the orphans of the World War veterans, their widows, nor any of the blind or disabled men who fought the battles of this great country of ours. . . . It is above Democracy. It is above party." How could someone reason, "I know that we ought to take care of the blind and suffering veterans, but the President will not let me?" Roosevelt's fierce pressure overcame Huey's eloquence. Black, Caraway, Reynolds, and Walsh, among others, surrendered and switched sides to approve the conference report, forty-five to thirty-six, on June 16, the last day of the session.[114]

Huey voted with Cutting but knew that he would lose and that his party would claim victory. He had participated in many Democratic Party victories, Huey said, but they were against "the giants of finance. We have grappled with them and won; but I do not care for my share in a victory that means that the poor and downtrodden, the blind, the helpless, the orphaned, the bleeding, the wounded, the hungry, and the distressed, will be the victims."[115]

# Twenty-One

# INEVITABLE CONFLICT

Ironically, ancestors of businessmen who today believe that Roosevelt was capitalism's enemy supported his National Recovery Administration (NRA) at the time because of the appeal of controlling prices; and historians who today believe that Roosevelt was capitalism's savior overlook that the NRA tried to kill it. Huey's biographer Richard White erroneously states that "[Huey opposed] even the most progressive of Roosevelt's proposals . . . including the Emergency Banking Act, Economy Act, Civilian Conservation Corps, National Industrial Recovery Act, and Agricultural Adjustment Act,"[1] ironic because Huey supported all progressive measures and because all these measures are described as progressive.

At the time, few knew what caused or had good solutions for the Depression. Schlesinger quoted the mistaken advice of Bernard Baruch in Senate hearings: "Balance budgets . . . stop spending money we haven't got. Sacrifice for frugality and revenue. Cut government spending—cut it as rations are cut in a siege. Tax—tax everybody for everything." Business, banking, and government leaders came "in a melancholy parade" with either the same advice or none.[2] Economists Friedman and Schwartz wrote that contemporary economic comment on the Great Depression was "depressing,"[3] and Galbraith stated that it was "uniquely perverse."[4] Today, there are several opinions about it.

To curb stock market speculation in 1928 and 1929, the Federal Reserve Board made money more expensive to borrow. When the stock market crashed in 1929, the board further restricted the supply of money or failed to expand the supply and thereby made the Depression worse from 1929 to 1933. Consumption declined because of the stock market crash. Those who lost money in the stock market cut their investments and spending;[5] those without stock market investments worried about the economy and eliminated discretionary purchases of durable goods such as cars and washing machines.[6]

The banking system was weak without government guarantees of bank deposits or diversification. Farmers were hurt by their own productivity improvements and by shrinking foreign markets for their commodities after European farmers recovered from the devastation of World War I. Commodity prices therefore declined, and many had borrowed to buy farms or farm machinery when commodity prices were high and had more difficulty making their loan payments when prices declined.[7] Undiversified rural community banks dependent on farmers' loans failed in increasing numbers as farmer loan defaults increased. Other banks had loaned money to businesses and, as consumption fell and the stock market crashed, many of them failed. When banks failed, depositors lost their money. This further reduced the money supply and consumption.[8]

Profits from productivity increases in the 1920s flowed to the wealthy rather than to wage earners. The top 1.19 percent of American families earned in total as much ($17,915,191) as the bottom 59.525 percent of American families ($18,264,000).[9] Between 1923 and 1929, manufacturing output per person increased 32 percent, but wages increased only 8 percent. The uneven distribution gave more money than was required for investment and less money than was necessary for consumption,[10] even though America had become the richest country in the world per capita.[11]

Consumption was impeded because long-term contracts for labor made prices for products rigid when they should have declined so that more people could buy them.[12] An increase of tariffs raised the price of imported goods and reduced the market for exports, but foreign trade was not a big enough percentage of the economy for the tariffs to have contributed to the Depression on a net basis. Farmers were hurt, however, because they paid higher prices for goods protected by tariffs and, when foreign countries retaliated, their market for exports was reduced. Consumption was also reduced because in 1932 Congress increased taxes.

It is possible that lax regulation led to moral hazards that got out of control. There was significant fraud—defining that term broadly—among bankers, stock market brokers, and other business speculators, but it is difficult to quantify the frauds to predict when too many will cause a crash.

The cause of the stock market crash is considered as an instance of "animal spirits" getting out of control or as a singularity. Hyman Minsky asserted that prosperity sows the seeds of its own crash because in good times entrepreneurs will inevitably seek more speculative investments. Any significant asset decline or external (exogenous) economic shock afterward will cause a crash, a "Minsky moment."[13] Had the wealthy avoided "speculative" investments, in the absence of adequate consumption, nonspeculative asset prices would have increased, causing a decline in investment returns. A Minsky moment might be likely then but is not axiomatic.

Monetary theorists believe that the decline of the supply of money was the key and that its increase was the remedy. The necessity of sound and trustworthy banks either accompanies this prescription or is separately asserted as the cure. Fiscal theorists believe that government deficit financing would restore consumption and therefore spur recovery.

Critics of the monetary supply remedy point to how the supply of money gets into circulation as a reason it might not work: interest rates by the Federal Reserve Bank are lowered, inducing people to borrow for plants, equipment, durable goods, and so forth. The critics say this is pushing on a string because, if people are shocked and scared, for example, because of a stock market crash, they won't borrow regardless of low rates. It thus takes time for a decline of interest rates to increase the money supply, although perceptions of an impending increase or decrease have an impact.

Government spending—fiscal policy—depends on government contracts to build something—say, a warship, a dam, or a park—and thus forces money and consumption into the economy. Such contracts should be of the quick-hit variety, such as highway spending, rather than long-term investments.[14]

Fiscal policy pushes money into the economy by issuing contracts for what the government wants built whereas monetary policy depends on the voluntary actions of entrepreneurs to borrow money, and they decide how to invest it. In each case, however, the government should create more money. Otherwise, government borrowing could cannibalize private borrowing, yielding either a smaller benefit or none.[15]

Economists or historians have not considered one aspect of the debate. If the economy had continued to grow as in the 1920s, say, by ensuring an adequate supply of money and a strong banking system, what effect would the increasing disparity between rich and poor have had on Huey's appeal? Revolutions have occurred in times of rising expectations when a segment of the population is left behind. Huey's rise in Louisiana occurred during the 1920s.

How do the policies of Roosevelt and Huey during the first hundred days stack up against these theories? The Glass-Steagall Banking Act that Huey improved remained in place for years until it was finally fully repealed in 1999. Within ten years of its full repeal, the banks again got themselves into a crisis, requiring the huge bailout of 2009 and new remedial legislation. The deposit-insurance features insisted upon by Huey and maintained after the repeal of the rest of the act prevented the number of banking panics characteristic of the Great Depression.[16]

Professor Christina Romer states that Roosevelt prompted economic growth of 10 percent per year from 1933 forward because he untethered the dollar from the prior gold standard. An increase in the supply of money resulted partially by this policy and partially by accident as Europeans, worried about Hitler and Mussolini, sent their gold to the United States, an uncanny parallel to the accidental increase in the gold supply that vindicated William Jennings Bryan. While this growth was spectacular, she says, the economy didn't reach the trend line of the 1920s until 1942. In other words, taking 1933 as the starting point, the economy looks as if it grew spectacularly after 1933 (see chart below). The trend line from the 1920s, however, shows that the economy failed to recover until 1942 (see chart on next page).[17] Economist Telser opines that there was a great expansion of the money supply from 1933 to 1939, "but no Great Recovery ensued."[18]

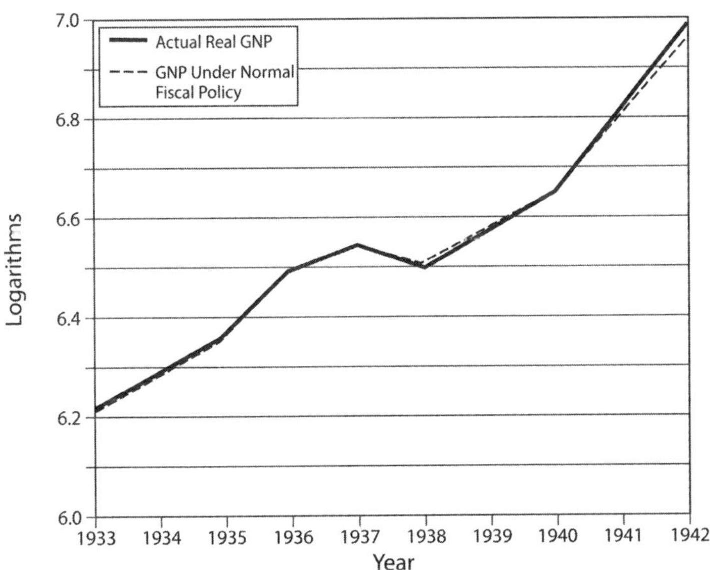


Gross National Product from 1933 to 1942, Showing Actual Growth Compared to Expected Growth under Normal Fiscal Policy.

From Romer, "What Ended the Great Depression?"

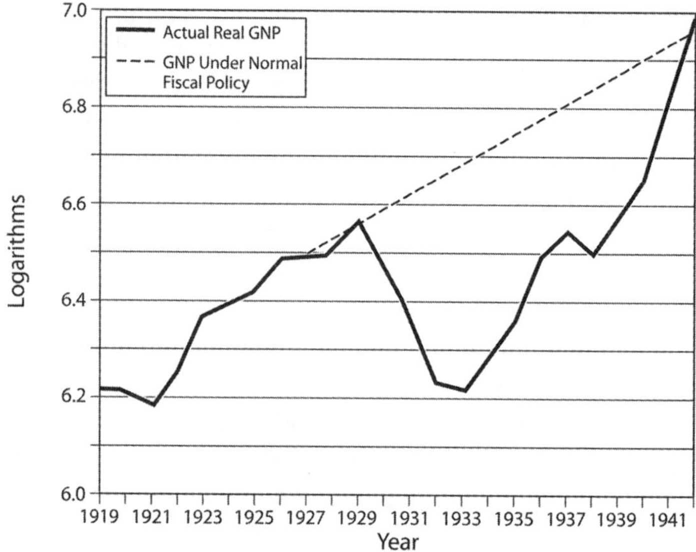


Gross National Product from 1919 to 1942, Showing Actual Growth Compared to Expected Growth under Normal Fiscal Policy. (The economy didn't recover to the expected trend line from the 1920s until 1942.)
From Romer, "What Ended the Great Depression?"

No one considering the banking record of Huey in Louisiana, of Roosevelt in New York, and of both men at the national level can deny that, had Huey had his way, he would have increased the supply of money as Friedman advocated, strengthened the banks as Telser recommended, and spent more money in public works, as fiscal theorists urged. A larger and more enduring recovery would have been stimulated in 1933.

Acknowledging the government's responsibility for the unemployed, as Roosevelt did, was a big advance over Hoover's policy of neglect. But Roosevelt fought Huey, Wheeler, and Thomas, who wanted to increase the money supply. Roosevelt also failed to request enough public works money. There was wide agitation for $6 billion of public works; Huey advocated $11 billion. Roosevelt chose $3.3 billion. This, plus the Civilian Conservation Corps and Federal Relief Administration programs, was too small a stimulus to induce economic recovery. "'Fiscal policy [was] an unsuccessful recovery device in the thirties—not because it did not work, but because it was not tried.'"[19]

Roosevelt's NRA was taken over by big business, and its codes allowed businesses to control prices and production costs. This was not capitalism, and it stunted recovery. Industrial production improved between March and July 1933, but this was artificial. Businesses had advanced production of goods and services to evade the anticipated inflation and new regulations.

"[F]rom its very inception as an administrative agency, the NRA proceeded along the lines that had been predicted for it, not by its proponents but by its opponents, during the Senate debate," says Roosevelt biographer Davis.[20] Professor Brinkley states, "The codes [Huey] predicted (correctly, as it turned out), would be written largely by the leaders of the industries involved and would become an excuse for price-fixing, for cartelization, for large interests driving small ones out of business."[21] One Roosevelt biographer, Conrad Black, agrees that Roosevelt's economic policies were all wrong but claims that the NRA was worthwhile because it lifted spirits and saved capitalism.[22]

Schlesinger believed the NRA always contained the possibility of becoming an organized profit-wage conspiracy of big business and big labor against the consumer and that it promoted scarcity and retarded recovery. But the "problem here was not the level of price but the gross failure of demand, and this was something that NRA by itself could not cure" (*Age of Roosevelt: The Coming of the New Deal*, 172). Remedying the gross failure of demand was Huey's goal.

Nevertheless, Schlesinger believed the NRA stopped further depression of prices ("It represented a holding pattern" [174]), established the principle of maximum hours and minimum wages, abolished child labor and sweatshops and, by allowing collective bargaining, transformed the position of organized labor. But legislation on these matters could have been adopted without the planning features of the NRA.

Under the leadership of General Hugh S. Johnson, the NRA was ballyhooed with parades and distribution of the Blue Eagle medallion. Patriotic and optimistic spirits were engendered. Johnson became a folk hero, temporarily, until the NRA disadvantaged businesses and consumers. Tugwell then recommended price controls, but no one agreed with him. Dissatisfaction with the NRA steadily increased after 1933.[23]

The Agricultural Adjustment Act plowed up crops of wheat, corn, and cotton and killed hogs and piglets. Wealthy farmers dominated the planning agencies.[24] Destroying crops and slaughtering animals while people were starving and lacked money to buy clothes "struck a great many who watched it as both insane and obscene."[25] Agriculture Secretary Wallace denied that there was reason to be upset because the animals were going to get slaughtered eventually anyway.

Schlesinger writes that Wallace didn't like crop destruction, but his critics never suggested that factories continue production *ad infinitum* regardless of demand and notwithstanding such goods might have "fed, clothed, and housed cold and hungry Americans. . . . How could anyone who granted industry the right to control its production deny the same right to agriculture?. . . . The logic was unanswerable" (63). These premises are wrong. Huey and other progressives wanted to provide for people to buy food and clothes. It was inhumane to destroy them—food, clothes, whatever—while people suffered.

Schlesinger's account of the Agricultural Adjustment Act (indeed, his complete set of books) is so well written—you feel as if you are in the middle of this fabulous cocktail party with all these remarkable people—that the implications of policy choices are often lost. The advocates of cost of production and promoters of full consumption are treated as political problems (which they were, but only from Roosevelt's point of view) (64–66). This receded when the Act's programs increased farm prices and incomes (71). Later this achievement "was beginning to play out" (82). Then in 1935, "Wallace and his associates started to think about programs which would promote and subsidize consumption. . . . If the American people, particularly low-income groups, were to eat all they needed, the Department estimated, the agricultural surplus would largely disappear" (83).[26] They "started to think" about this in 1935? They should have thought of it in 1933. Huey did.

Acreage reductions decimated tenant farmer employment. It was a "social calamity of major proportions," driving them off the land to slums in the city or onto the road west, "their few pitiful belongings strapped to their running boards, the tops, the rear trunks of battered jalopies." Reformers administering the Agricultural Adjustment Act lost a bureaucratic war and got fired en masse on February 4, 1935. "By and large, the New Deal's attacks on rural poverty must be counted a failure."[27]

Huey disliked the Act but voted for it because of its inflation feature. Yet Roosevelt never implemented the inflation feature that Huey liked.

Roosevelt gets the credit for the insurance of bank deposits added to the Banking Act because of Vandenburg and Huey. The Economy Act and mistreatment of veterans is generally ignored or minimized. Veterans' issues dominated the entire congressional session about which Schlesinger wrote. Yet he devoted less than one total page to the Economy Act out of a book of 588 pages, and part of that was a laudatory reference to Roosevelt's success defeating the veterans' lobby. No mention is made of veteran suicides or suffering.[28] Professor Stephen Ortiz's book, *Beyond the Bonus March,* is a welcome corrective.[29]

Roosevelt's business-regulatory measures were overdue but not controversial. The Senate adopted the Securities and Exchange Commission Act by a voice vote without debate. The railroad bill was non-controversial, and Huey submitted amendments to it adopted by voice vote. The Senate voted for the TVA project by a huge majority, including Huey. It has proved to be a valuable source of cheap electric power.

If it is wrong to judge Roosevelt too harshly because of the uniquely perverse or depressing status of economic thought in 1933, Huey should be judged more favorably for his superior economic insights against this same backdrop. He improved the Banking Act, advocated an increase in the money supply, and wanted to increase public works spending. Huey said the NRA, the Agricultural Adjustment Act, the Economy Act, and a grudging administration of the Banking Act were going to aggravate the Depression, and he was right. He opposed the hardship on the veterans created by the Economy Act, artificial scarcity, regressive taxes, and business cartels. If Huey's tax proposals were extreme (Keynes but not Friedman would have approved of something similar), nevertheless they would have permitted more public works with less deficit spending.

To keep senators in line, Roosevelt withheld patronage decisions—he had 100,000 jobs to award, a little more than 2,000 per state—until the end of the legislative session in June 1933.[30] In July 1933, Roosevelt awarded two Louisiana positions without Huey's endorsement. Huey traveled to Washington to investigate why. Farley set up a showdown conference with Roosevelt for July 25, 1933. Huey breezed in wearing a straw hat and kept it on his head (a breach of etiquette) except to tap Roosevelt's knee with it. (Midway through the conversation, Huey took his hat off.) Huey argued that his support before and during the Chicago convention entitled him to patronage. Roosevelt took a "rope a dope" approach, saying he would appoint well-qualified people to positions. As he was leaving, Huey told Farley that there was no use coming to see Roosevelt, referring to Roosevelt's refusal to give straight answers.[31] Publicly, Huey said that there were no good people to appoint to federal positions in Louisiana outside of the Long organization and that he would be "satisfied whichever way matters go."[32] Privately, Senator Byrnes congratulated Roosevelt on the "magnificent" appointments because it showed that "woe" would result to those "who fail to cooperate."[33]

Williams writes that "It was Roosevelt's choice of method [denial of patronage] that revealed the . . . reason for the break: two great politicians had come into inevitable conflict. Each was so constituted that he had to dominate other and lesser men. Neither could yield to the other without submerging himself and dimming his destiny. And instinctively each recognized the other's greatness, and feared it."[34]

Louisiana leaders dominated by Huey such as Richard Leche said that Huey couldn't follow; he had to lead. Williams accepted this evaluation. But Huey's personal secretary in Washington (Earle Christenberry) believed that Huey had no plans to run for president immediately. This dovetails with his public statements in 1932 that he planned to get an "education" in Washington. Huey apparently thought that he and Roosevelt were still on the road toward the same goal, with Huey just ahead of him on that road.[35]

Thus, Huey's criticism of Roosevelt policies was ideological. He supported the administration more than many other senators given patronage. Bailey had a strategy for dealing with Roosevelt. He voted against all progressive measures but gave a speech in June cheering the progress made under Roosevelt.[36]

If Roosevelt's motivation were not ideological, what explains it? It might have been hubris. Roosevelt must have felt that he was politically impregnable after the first hundred days. He passed an extraordinary number of bills. His fireside chats captivated the country. The NRA ballyhoo was beginning, and everyone was caught up in a patriotic fervor.

After taking an informal survey, journalist George Coad, who had followed Huey since 1928, wrote that Louisianans knew that Huey's highways cost more than he promised and that maybe somebody got something by way of graft, but they enjoyed the roads and liked and supported Huey. But Coad found unanimity among all segments of the population, including Huey's supporters, in their dislike of Huey's denunciations of Roosevelt programs.[37]

Roosevelt might have made a political judgment that Huey would self-destruct, politically or personally, and cut him off to preempt any fallout. While Huey was busy fighting for progressive legislation, John M. Parker visited Washington, DC, in April to present a petition to remove him. Parker claimed that Huey was a corrupt and dangerous paranoiac and, to save him from probable killing, the Senate should have him committed to an insane asylum. Two upper-class women from New Orleans, Hilda Phelps Hammond and Mrs. Ruffin Pleasant, on behalf of a women's auxiliary, asked the Senate to expel Huey.[38] Counterpetitions were filed supporting Huey.[39] At the end of May, Mrs. Pleasant sued Huey for defamation.[40] In mid-June, Huey's Louisiana enemies hired lawyer Samuel Ansell, who filed a petition to the Senate demanding that it renew the Overton investigation.[41] The articles about Huey's controversies with his Louisiana opponents outnumbered those covering his policy speeches.

There are stories, hard to date and verify, but all before or during 1933, about Huey's drinking. It could have been commented on more, but it lacked the stigma it has today.[42] In 1932, Republican leader Watson took Huey to Senate backrooms to drink, hoping he would embarrass himself, but Wheeler warned him. After stopping, Huey said, "I'm so sober now I'm ashamed of myself."[43] At the end of the Caraway campaign in August 1932, a defeated opponent charged that Huey was "maudlin drunk" in a hotel on the Sunday before the election.[44] Wheeler's wife confronted Huey about a news story that he was inebriated and tried to direct a band; Huey confirmed the story, and she urged him to set a better example.[45] *Times* reporter Raymond Daniell spent an evening in 1933 in the Roosevelt Hotel with Huey, Alice Lee Grosjean, and Grosjean's aunt, drinking and plunking on a tiny guitar.[46]

Republican Ed Talbot, about to leave the U.S. Attorney's Office in New Orleans, wangled a trip to Washington, DC, in 1933 before he left and went to Huey's office, lined with people as always, to arrange a meeting with Seth Richardson, a Washington, DC, lawyer. Mrs. Richardson despised Huey but came to the dinner, and they met another businessman and Congressman Reid. They were all drinking.

When the businessman and Reid left, Huey mixed drinks and denounced whatever came into his mind. Mrs. Richardson asked him the secret of his success, and he said coordination of government: when the rich planters inflated the value of their land when Huey wanted to purchase the right of way to build roads, he had the tax assessors follow immediately and change their lands' assessed value for future tax years. "That's what I call coordination in government." When asked what he would do if he were not in politics, he said he would go on stage and clown or act. Mrs. Richardson asked, "What does your wife think of all this?" Huey replied, "She was my first convert." The first half of the evening she thought he was rude and crude, but then she sat back and decided to enjoy the personality display, and she did.[47]

The circumstances in 1933 may have provided the catalyst for an increase in this habit: the Overton and Stanley investigations; the bad press; the arson at his home; the attempts to unseat him by John M. Parker, Hilda Phelps Hammond, and Mrs. Pleasant; the controversy with Roosevelt's Treasury Department; and the sheer excitement of new political realities. One wonders if a contributing cause was the absence of his family or Alice Lee Grosjean. One wonders how he was able to be so active in the Senate while running the state of Louisiana, drinking, and defending himself from efforts to expel him.

Roosevelt might have felt that it was politically unsafe to keep Huey. Huey was developing personal support through advocacy of his more radical tax program, which Roosevelt opposed. A senator from France predicted that Huey might succeed Roosevelt. A Harvard Business School professor, Georges Doriot, asked, "Do we really want a change from . . . Roosevelt to Huey Long?"[48] If Roosevelt feared Huey, it was not as potential dictator—although that was a devastatingly effective brand—it was Huey the political rival.

Huey's inability to weld the senators into a united force for change belies any threat to democracy. Huey agreed with LaFollette on tax and banking policy but opposed his efforts to ratify the St. Lawrence Seaway project. Huey disagreed with Lewis about everything except the St. Lawrence Seaway. Huey agreed with Connally about oil and, in general, about inflating the money supply, but not much of anything else. Huey loved and respected Norris but disagreed with him on tariff policy. He agreed with Copeland about relief and the seaway, but not about tax policy or the NRA.

Senators were subject to local and regional political pressures that made consensus building an issue-by-issue proposition. Much of the Roosevelt legislation gave him discretion, with conservatives believing it would be administered conservatively and liberals believing it would be administered liberally. Roosevelt could choose either course depending on the pressures prevailing or his desire to reward supporters or punish opponents.

Roosevelt may have wanted to make an example of Huey, as Senator Byrnes noted, to warn other senators not to imitate his independence. On April 15, 1933, it was reported anew that Huey's taxes were being investigated, perhaps in retaliation for his April 11 speech.[49] This wasn't yet true but was perhaps a warning. Huey wanted to be on good terms with Roosevelt but was not going to curb his opinions for patronage.[50]

While Huey was never committed to Roosevelt personally, he was committed to a program. Unlike others who accused Roosevelt of asking for dictatorial powers or other failings, Huey avoided personal critiques of Roosevelt even though he used extreme language in denouncing proposals or Roosevelt advisors—who deserved it—in the Treasury Department. Had Roosevelt followed a progressive course and made Carter Glass and conservative

Republicans the opponents, Huey would have been one of his most formidable Senate leaders. If Roosevelt had listened to Huey on the Banking Act (as he eventually did), the Economy Act, and Section I of the NRA, and if he had, for example, increased taxes on the wealthy, or inflated the money supply and increased relief expenditures, how could Huey have rebelled? Enactment of Huey's 1933 ideas wouldn't have established or contributed to a revolution or dictatorship, furthermore, and would have cemented the loyalties of Huey's potential constituency to Roosevelt, increasing his power and diminishing Huey's.

The Economy Act provided the litmus test. In October, the *Times* reported that many congressmen feared reprisals if they opposed Roosevelt.

> Any complainant within the party would risk being laughed to scorn by a public that has been worked up to unquestioning support of the "Blue Eagle" campaigns, "Buy Now" drives and the general "stand by the President" appeal which they themselves have helped to put over throughout the country.
>
> But there are quite a few Democrats of a more regular stripe who get a secret satisfaction out of the mouthings of Senator Huey Long. There are several who, after seeing that the door is locked and that no one is in the closet or under the desk, will tell a friend that they feel exactly like the "Kingfish."[51]

In a society that values principles and pragmatism, the fight over the veterans presented a conflict between these two values. Roosevelt valued personal loyalty at the expense of or subordinate to principles, although he sometimes let senators vote against him if they did so quietly or, like Bailey, while praising him. Progressives who voted against the veterans forfeited their principles but preserved their relationship with Roosevelt. Huey voted for the veterans in accordance with his principles, and Roosevelt cut him off.

While Roosevelt was fiercely committed to remaining president, he was not committed to a program of wealth redistribution. Huey was. When Roosevelt announced that he wanted a more equitable distribution of the nation's wealth, when he warned "nominal Democrats" that the country wanted a choice, and when he promised to remove the money changers from the temple, he didn't really mean it, in the same way people will tell someone they meet on the street, "let's do lunch."[52]

---

Williams's suggestion of a psychological conflict warrants further consideration, however. Roosevelt was an only child born to a New York aristocratic family of inherited wealth, earned from the opium trade in China. Huey was the seventh of nine surviving children, born in a small, poor southern town. Roosevelt was regulated, conventional, dutiful, conformist, secure, and pampered in his youth, traveling to Europe, sailing, and enjoying high society. Huey was rebellious from birth. No sailing. Huey hopped trains to run away from home or to sell books in other southern towns. Roosevelt received a formal college and law school education. Huey mostly educated himself.

Roosevelt relied on his mother to organize his social life in college and hesitated to take an unguided step. She arranged his first rented marital home and then purchased two houses for the couple. Roosevelt obtained through family connections cushy jobs on or near Wall Street. When Roosevelt cheated on his wife and she threatened to leave him, Roosevelt buckled to his mother's threat to disinherit him if he divorced. Huey's family helped him, too, but on a much smaller scale, and he had to work hard for everything he got. By the time he was an adult and cheated on his wife, his mother was dead.

Roosevelt never knew the desperation of sleeping on a park bench or walking for miles in the cold without any money. Huey never knew the desperation of trying for hours to move a toe that you could not feel.

Four more factors offer clues to their clash: brains, personal growth, how they dealt with conflicts, and courage.

*Brains.* There is a myth that, after Roosevelt called on Justice Oliver Wendell Holmes, then ninety-two, just after his inauguration, Holmes sighed that Roosevelt had a second-class intellect but a first-class temperament.[53] The unkind sentiment about Roosevelt's brains was widespread among politicians of his time and remains a consensus. Roosevelt suffers in comparison to Lincoln's mastery of Euclidian geometry, Theodore Roosevelt's authorship of a two-volume classic on the Navy, and Woodrow Wilson's writing of acclaimed history and government textbooks.

Nevertheless, consider Roosevelt's experience. He met his first president at age five in the White House. When in college, Roosevelt shared a speaker's platform with Theodore Roosevelt and Woodrow Wilson. As President Theodore Roosevelt's nephew, he joined him at his inauguration in 1904 when he was twenty-two and watched the parade with him and attended the inaugural ball. He was a two-term state senator in New York. He was assistant secretary of the Navy, including service during World War I, for one of our most talented presidents. He perceptively observed that Theodore Roosevelt had an ability to stir enthusiasm about issues or legislation, but not the larger moral fundamentals, whereas Wilson could dramatize the larger moral issues but not particular pieces of legislation.[54] At age thirty-eight, Roosevelt was a candidate for vice president and traveled all over the country to campaign. He attended four Democratic National Conventions. Elected twice to be governor of New York, he had obtained executive experience in the most populous state in the country. Even a mediocre intellect absorbing this experience would be formidable. On political matters, Roosevelt seldom delegated, confident in his own judgment.

Roosevelt often assigned multiple people the same or similar tasks. Giving assignments can have purposes other than the one the assignee is told: to test drafting ability, political judgment, or capacity to recruit allies, for example. The multiple authorizations created a kind of planetary system that revolved around Roosevelt, keeping supporters jealous of each other and competing for his continued favor, but with his gravity keeping them in orbit around him.[55]

Much later, Huey humorously noted why he remained outside Roosevelt's orbit. His grandfather had a farm, Huey said, and hired a man who picked twice as much cotton as the other workers. Naturally, the man was fired. His grandfather reasoned that, if the worker were that smart, his grandfather might end up working for him.[56] On another occasion, Huey said that Hoover was a hoot owl and Roosevelt was a scrootch owl. A hoot owl just "bangs into the roost and knocks the hen clean off, and catches her as she's falling," whereas a scrootch owl "slips into the roost and talks softly to her. And the hen just falls in love with him, and the first thing you know, there ain't no hen."[57]

In contrast, Huey had a powerful, fast, and analytical mind, coupled with an excellent memory and abnormal energy. He could think fast based on a superficial review of the facts, and he could study a problem—such as the Bernstein litigation—in depth. Moley was contemptuous of Roosevelt's brains but said that Huey had a mind such as was given to few men.[58] Newspaperman Marquis Childs said Huey had "great intellectual capacity" plus a "tremendous emotional and psychological drive."[59] Contemporary critic T. O. Harris and hostile historian Jeansonne both credited Huey's brainpower. Senators Vandenberg and Russell separately said Huey was the smartest man they ever met.[60]

Huey would stare continuously at someone talking, whereas a normal person would glance away to digest what the speaker is saying or to think of a reply. Huey got extra credit for his brains because people expected a southern demagogue. His brainpower was extended because of his energy; he could work longer than others. His memory allowed him to talk for hours without many notes, and his speeches often displayed a gift for effective organization.

Huey had a novelist's vocabulary, eye for the telling detail, and talent for word pictures. His quick wit and memory made him formidable in debate. His knowledge of farm life gave him a source of metaphors and analogies.[61] His years on the road gave him an appreciation for yarns, humorous stories, and proverbs. His experience as a trial lawyer taught him to analyze and organize the scattered facts of a case quickly and then present them in a compelling way.

Huey had little experience in national politics, however, having been trapped in Louisiana because of Paul Cyr's enmity. Entering the Senate only in 1932, he later attended his one and only national convention, and had appeared at only one of the annual National Governor's Conferences because, except for 1928 when it was held in New Orleans, they were held in other states. This lack of experience caused him to think he could clown at the 1932 convention and that Roosevelt would replace Joe Robinson as majority leader. Like Roosevelt, he believed in divided lines of authority so that none of his leaders could develop too much power.

Roosevelt compensated for his second-class brains by assembling first-rate advisors, aided by his much lengthier tenure in government and by the advantage of his family name. These advisors, lawyer Sam Rosenman, Professors Moley and Tugwell, and others, wrote his speeches, subject to his editing, and they advised him on policy, often conflicting with each other, and Roosevelt would fall in and out of love with them.

Huey wrote his own speeches. After he entered the Senate, however, he began his self-education program and tapped governmental analysts for research. Williams's book can be as misleading as Huey's critics insofar as it portrays him as a Harrison Bergeron figure with amazing brains, energy, and confidence, who dominated the Senate. Huey engaged with issues about which he had experience or political instincts and sympathy for the underdog. On matters he had encountered as public service commissioner or governor, his knowledge was deep. Huey knew a lot about banking from his gubernatorial experience of selling state bonds, state bank crises, and from the DeLoach and Bernstein litigation. Even with that knowledge, he exhaustively questioned bankers about Glass's bill before it was debated.

There are many days of Senate proceedings, however, during which Huey was present but said little, and many occasions when he was obviously following someone else's speech and interjected, generally with incisive questions or comments or pithy summaries of the point being made, and often with remarks intended to be humorous, sometimes welcome and sometimes annoying. Someone once wrote that Lincoln's absences from his family and his travels on the road gave him the time to remedy educational defects. With his family in Louisiana, Huey was similarly unencumbered and used much of that time to read and debrief people.[62]

Huey compensated for his lack of experience on other issues by relying on others, just as Roosevelt did. Initially he respected George Norris above other senators and visited him informally to discuss policies and strategy. Some of Huey's Senate remarks read as slightly embarrassing efforts to prove himself to Norris. Huey became friendly with Wheeler and visited his family. Wheeler said that LaFollette liked Huey,[63] something the *Congressional Record* would not suggest. Huey deferred to Norris on the farm bill, Borah on the NRA, Wheeler and Thomas on money supply issues, Black on the thirty-hour week, and Cutting for the details on veterans' regulations. Sometimes, as with Black's thirty-hour workweek proposal, he fought more consistently for the sponsor's idea than the sponsor. On the veterans' bills, Cutting knew the regulations inside and out; Huey knew the hardship that would be felt by veterans and their families. Cutting's speeches were more detailed and factual, Huey's more emotional and powerful.

*Personal growth.* Having inherited the most politically potent name in the country, Roosevelt could afford to be vague on the issues at the start of his career. Originally, he was only against "bossism" and Tammany Hall's New York City machine, a "matter of publicity and power, not policy or substance," the "silly conceits of a political prig."[64] Roosevelt biographers then discuss his growth from a privileged snob and dilettante to someone who triumphed over polio and his own background to defeat the Depression and then the Axis powers in World War II.

In contrast, Huey was self-made politically and concentrated on realistic economic issues from the start. Huey's growth from salesman to lawyer to politician, from schoolbooks and highways to the university and medical school and then to the cotton holiday plan, is also apparent and, in truth, more pronounced. In one year in the Senate, he broadened his knowledge from the single issue of taxation in 1932 into major opinions and proposals about banking, money supply, labor hours, public works, and veteran benefits. Huey did a lot of reading.[65] By 1935, a journalist wrote that Huey made observations impossible without an understanding of the formal literature on the subject.[66]

*Dealing with conflicts.* Roosevelt had learned to evade and lie and dissemble to deal with his domineering mother, often ignoring disagreements, hoping the matter would pass, whereas Huey was loud, confrontational, crude, and bullied people who would take it. Huey's insolence got on Roosevelt's nerves.[67]

*Times* reporter Arthur Krock was asked to introduce Huey to two women diplomats. The champagne flowed and then Huey asked for a phone, called someone, and made bloodcurdling threats to the person on the other end of the line such as had never been witnessed by Huey's guests, or Krock. When he hung up, Huey told them he had just spoken to the governor of Louisiana, O. K. Allen, and the women were spellbound.[68] Riding with Allen in a limousine, the driver hit a bump, causing Huey's head to hit the interior roof. Huey ordered the driver to get out and walk home. Allen protested: "Don't put my driver out." Huey replied, "Shut up or I'll put you out."[69] Huey always "walked" his drivers if they bumped his head and periodically rudely treated Allen.[70]

Huey didn't bully Seymour Weiss, Bob Maestri, Harvey Couch, Chick Frampton, or Earle Christenberry, however. When Allen once fired an employee in Huey's presence, the man hotly explained in detail that he was happy to go because he was surrounded by incompetents. When he left, Huey told Allen to rehire him, that he was the kind of man they needed.[71] If the Morgan banker accosted by Huey at Moley's dinner party had tapped Huey on the chest and said he didn't like Huey either, they would have had a good laugh and toasted each other, one sonofabitch to another, just as General Patton reportedly did with a Russian general after World War II. Huey's ruthlessness generally meant more efficient service. When he told LSU president Smith to "sell them plugs," them plugs were sold.

Huey had no trouble firing people. If someone were fired in a moment of Huey's temper, however, they could ignore it.[72] Huey wooed certain rivals such as Paul Maloney and Bathtub Joe Fernandez, and he collaborated smoothly with some senators on some issues while violently disagreeing with them on others. While a few policy confrontations were so brutal that friendship despite differences became impossible, in both Louisiana and Washington, Huey spoke civilly and regularly to opponents, who often gathered in the large law library Huey maintained in his Senate offices.[73]

The stories of Huey's mean streak—a defect of temperament and character—can be misleading. By most accounts, O. K. Allen and Huey genuinely liked each other,[74] notwithstanding instances of humiliating treatment. Reporter Deutsch said Huey was subject to sudden and ungovernable rages but "in a few instants" the "tempest" would blow out and the incident forgotten.[75] Often, but not always,[76] he was apt to joke or praise associates moments after being furious with them. Many other bosses in business or politics, such as Steve Jobs, Bill Gates, Lyndon Johnson, and Richard Nixon, had famous episodes of rudeness.[77] Yet these men attracted loyal aides. How remarkable it was that a mean streak was absent from Lincoln and Washington.

While some newsmen wrote that Huey lacked friends and was surrounded by sycophants, this is wrong. A flood of individuals maintained a friendship with Huey and visited him for long periods of time in Washington: Bob Brothers, Jimmie O'Connor, and Melvin Purvis, to name only three. Huey's flood-control ally, Illinois Republican congressman Frank Reid, retired in 1934 and moved to Louisiana, where his daughter attended LSU and roomed with Huey's daughter, Rose, and was a bridesmaid in the marriage of one of O. K. Allen's children.[78]

Roosevelt's reputation for having a first-class temperament is based on his sunny disposition, his equanimity, and his displayed empathy for people, but this should not be confused with a first-class character. Lincoln was rarely petty, but Roosevelt was. Roosevelt lacked Lincoln's ability to collaborate with rivals. Rivals were excluded from Roosevelt's gubernatorial appointments in 1928 and 1930 and from his presidential ones in 1932. Roosevelt was sensitive—revealing an intellectual insecurity or an extraordinary vigilance over his political reputation—to any story that described any advisor as the power behind the throne. Lincoln was honest; Roosevelt lied.[79]

Roosevelt was also ruthless. He enjoyed tormenting people, teasing them or forcing them to listen to him extol a position they abhorred. Roosevelt must have enjoyed causing Black, Connally, Clark, and the others to yield on the Cutting amendment to the Economy Act, knowing they wanted to vote for it.

Historian Davis explains that Roosevelt had a sadistic streak, the flip side of his empathy. Schlesinger says Roosevelt had a thin sadistic streak and was often remorseful afterward. This sadistic streak, Davis said, was employed against those who threatened his political power or who made him feel small. It kept aides insecure. Roosevelt disliked the confrontation of firing someone but enjoyed deviously arranging an enemy's downfall.[80] Jeansonne perceptively wrote that "Both [Long and Roosevelt] were strong, decisive, and vindictive. . . . Roosevelt's revenge was silent, steely, and cold, masked with social amenities. Long was more direct and brutal."[81]

*Courage.* Roosevelt exhibited fearlessness with respect to his physical safety during World War I when he went to Europe and again when an assassin tried to kill him right before his inauguration. The assassin killed Mayor Anton Cermak of Chicago—standing next to his car—instead. During the 1924 Democratic Convention, Roosevelt made an agonizing walk on crutches to get to the convention podium, the audience silent as he slowly made his way across the stage, bursting into applause when he made it. Yet Roosevelt lacked political courage. Theodore Roosevelt's widow said he was 90 percent mush and 10 percent Eleanor.[82]

Huey was the reverse. He lacked physical courage, but had political courage, and accepted responsibility for his policy and personnel choices. Opponent Frank Peterman said Huey would say what he believed even if he got repeatedly knocked down. Opponent R. Norman Bauer said Huey was a physical coward but fearless intellectually.[83]

*Leadership.* The differences between Huey and Roosevelt make their career and style similarities more surprising. Both Roosevelt and Huey liked people and could talk to them for hours. They could tell jokes and stories and would appreciate humor related by others. Each was adept at debriefing people and absorbing what they knew about a topic. Both were positive people, optimistic, and confident. Both had a religious faith but spent little time meditating about it. Huey would often praise his associates, guests, or colleagues in extravagant terms. Roosevelt had the capacity to inspire subordinates and colleagues.

They both defied convention to campaign among farmers in automobiles in their first political campaigns. Both compulsively planned the construction of their homes. Huey designed his sound trucks; Roosevelt designed his car with hand controls that he could operate after his legs were paralyzed. Both had early newspaper careers, Roosevelt with the Harvard University newspaper and Huey with his town's paper. Both believed that they would become president.

Huey was more decisive, intentional, and hands-on than Roosevelt. One cannot imagine Huey taking the hands-off role of Roosevelt during the banking crisis. Huey would have been right in the middle of the discussions and would have directed his colleagues to save all banks, save all the depositors' money, and keep all banks open for business. But it is a mistake to overstate this. While governor and senator, he changed his mind in response to comments of others. It is a mild shock to read many instances in the *Congressional Record* and newspapers in which he was modest, couldn't find documents, confessed mistakes or ignorance, complained that the proceedings were happening too fast, and took a supporting role to other senators.

Huey's confidence was greater than Roosevelt's, so he was more consistent, more willing to scale a proposal to increase its beneficiaries, and more likely to attack someone who had a different point of view. Roosevelt was more apt to compromise and keep the scale of his proposals small or experimental.

In his biography of Roosevelt, James MacGregor Burns described eventful (or role taking) and event-making (or creative) leaders: "[A role-taking leader] mirrors society rather than transforms it. The creative leader, on the other hand, stands somewhat apart from society and . . . in the long run seeks to broaden the environmental limits in which he operates. Far from being a slave to a role system, the great leader . . . may actually smash it and set up another system." Roosevelt was an eventful or role-taking leader, he said.[84] Roosevelt led public opinion from behind. He was a genius at political positioning, as was Lincoln. Huey was an event-making or creative leader. If events failed to occur naturally, he produced them.[85] Huey smashed the environmental limits in which he operated in Louisiana and was forming public opinion to do so nationwide.

The banking bill provided one model of how Huey and Roosevelt could have worked together. A good bill resulted from their undeclared confrontation even in the absence of collaboration. Roosevelt gave in reluctantly, only in the face of the determined advocacy of Huey and Vandenberg, and because of political pressure, not the merits. Had Roosevelt talked to Huey, the better bill that resulted would have been proposed, passed, and implemented from the start.

There are three interesting comparisons to Roosevelt's decision to cut Huey off. When Roosevelt became governor, succeeding Al Smith, Smith thought he would remain a power behind the throne. After Roosevelt failed to choose any of Smith's recommended candidates for governmental positions, Smith was slowly and with increasing irritation disabused of that notion, leading to open political warfare.[86]

Brain Truster Moley had garnered publicity as the man with brains telling Roosevelt what to do, and a certain disdain for Roosevelt's intellect and presumptuousness with his advice crept into his personality. An international monetary conference was set for London after the congressional session ended to consider the gold standard and currency exchange rates. Roosevelt gave inconsistent instructions to the delegation, headed by secretary of state Cordell Hull. Roosevelt sent Moley over to join Hull. Joseph Kennedy warned Moley not to go, that Roosevelt was setting him up. Moley went anyway. Roosevelt then torpedoed the conference and Moley. When Moley returned, he was sent to another federal agency for two months before he resigned to edit *Newsweek* magazine.[87]

The uncompromising Bronson Cutting, a Republican senator who had endorsed Roosevelt in 1932 but had stood up for the veterans against him, was also marked for destruction. Roosevelt waited until Cutting's next election to oppose him and had Senate leaders contest the close election that Cutting won. While he was plotting against Cutting, Roosevelt pretended to be his friend. This distressed but didn't fool Cutting.[88] On one of Cutting's trips necessitated by this contest, he was killed in a plane crash in 1935. Cutting's friends in the Senate burst into tears upon hearing the news. Many of them walked out when his successor, Roosevelt's choice, was sworn in.[89]

Huey was fooled like Smith, principled like Cutting, and more intelligent than Moley. Roosevelt wasn't smart enough to see through the economic orthodoxy of the day and wasn't psychologically or politically secure enough to defer to someone who was. Huey made him feel small. Roosevelt had to cast him off.

# Twenty-Two

# THE KINGFISH GETS A BLACK EYE

Even though Huey was "the first Southern populist to transcend state lines," Roosevelt filled the "public eye to the exclusion of everyone else in Washington," making Huey "a diminished figure."[1] The good federal jobs went to opponents because Roosevelt was "disciplining" Huey.[2] J. P. Morgan's publicity machine hired a public relations firm for $25,000 to make sure that, when Huey received any press, it was bad.[3] The Stanley investigation into voter fraud provided substance for the stories. The bonds for the ferry had been sold. After supplanting Stanley in November 1932, Attorney General Porterie met with the grand jury twice. It didn't recount the ballots, though, and then adjourned. A new judge, Frank T. Echezabal, empaneled a new grand jury, but on May 17, 1933, it also declined to charge anyone. Judge Echezabal refused to accept its oral report and ordered it to be thorough. Instead it was deliberate. They failed to meet again until June 30. Just before then, Porterie was disbarred for unethical conduct because he supplanted Stanley and interfered with the grand jury. Blaming politics, Porterie resigned, but the bar refused his resignation and expelled him. On June 30, the grand jury told a substitute judge, Alexander O'Donnell, that it had decided nine-to-three to decline indictments.[4]

Under the influence of the *Times-Picayune*, Huey claimed, O'Donnell then allowed the sheriff (ally of John Sullivan) to eject the grand jurors and remove the ballot boxes. On July 30, Huey (through Allen) declared partial martial law, at the request of eleven of the twelve jurors, who said that Judge

O'Donnell had ejected them. Anti-Long leaders complained that this was an attempt at intimidation, but no one was scared, and the order was revoked. Judge O'Donnell ordered the ballots counted in open court on August 1, under the supervision of Stanley, not Porterie. A separate judge dissolved the grand jury.[5] The recount found that the vote in favor of the ferry was reduced and against the ferry was increased, but not enough to change the outcome.

The commissioners were otherwise unemployed and needed a day's pay, Huey said. They never expected that they would have to work past midnight counting ballots. At 9:00 p.m., the news broke of Roosevelt's election, the first Democratic president in sixteen years. The commissioners wanted to join the city celebrations, a November Mardi Gras. They averaged the vote results on the first few constitutional amendments and applied them to all of them.[6] The ferry was the fourteenth proposition. Some voters favored the other amendments but voted against the ferry, leading to discrepancies.

Angry at the incorrect counts, "some who have been neutral or even lukewarm for [Huey were now] in the opposition." By September 1, Stanley had indicted 512 officials.[7] Three were tried as test cases, and they were convicted in October and December.[8] Huey promised to protect them with new legislation that would be passed the following year.

To counteract the negative press, Huey started another newspaper. The *Louisiana Progress* had ceased publication in 1932. Huey recruited the same men to publish what he now called the *American Progress.* Estimates of its circulation ranged from 100,000 to 400,000 copies, printed monthly although, on occasion, 1.5 million copies were distributed. It was printed in Mississippi because Huey thought the hostile Louisiana newspapers would have an accidentally-on-purpose breakdown of their presses on the *Progress*'s publication days.[9] Using red headlines, the newspaper carried stories about the wealthy underemphasized by the mainstream press and gave Huey's viewpoint—often rehashed Senate speeches—without an independent editorial filter. Some nonpolitical stories were included.[10]

Huey also added one full-time and one part-time press agent. Publisher William Randolph Hearst sent George Maines to research Huey during the Overton hearings. To keep his mission secret, he posed as a press agent for Huey's singing-star friend, Gene Austin. Impressed with Louisiana's progress, he visited Huey's hotel room. Mistaking him for an Overton investigator, Huey vehemently cursed Maines. Shouting, "Goddamn it, I'm a friendly reporter," he left but sent a telegram stating his purpose, after which he met Huey. Because of his many contacts among reporters and editors, Huey hired him. He worked to persuade editors and reporters to write favorable stories, while attempting to convince the White House to reconcile with Huey. George Allen was a second public relations man who worked for Huey on specific projects. To satisfy one editor, he authored an anti-Long story first and then a pro-Long piece that "knock[ed] into a cocked hat" his previous day's work.[11]

Allen also helped Huey with his autobiography. Beginning in 1932, in spare moments, Huey stood up and performed each incident as he dictated. Harvey Peltier assisted with citations to newspaper articles or legal cases. From memory, Huey would give him the date and page number of the stories, and he was never wrong. It took about five drafts to get it right. Allen edited it and negotiated a contract to get it published.[12] After the plates for printing were readied, the publisher backed out, thinking the book defamatory. Huey incorporated his own book company and published it in October 1933, distributing it himself, at the price of $1 per copy.

The autobiography described some of Huey's clever political stratagems and included descriptive details, funny stories, and ironic asides. Interspersed were before-and-after photographs showing the dramatic differences between pre-Long dirt roads and post-Long paved highways; pre-Long and post-Long ferries and bridges; and pre-Long and post-Long medical facilities. He specified a gold book cover and that no picture should be printed on the reverse side of his picture.

Huey couldn't think of a title. Discussing it with Peltier one night, Peltier recalled the William Jennings Bryan quote that Huey used in his 1928 campaign, "every man a king, but no man wears a crown." Huey stood up in his bed: "By God, that's it!" *Every Man A King* it became.[13]

The *Tribune* quoted the last paragraphs of the book, Huey's description of the Valhalla that would exist if wealth were redistributed: no tears of poverty, hunger, nakedness, homelessness, or greed.[14] It was the most favorable story he ever received from that newspaper. Allan Nevins thought Huey was brilliant but unbalanced, a dangerous political type. The *Times* panned the book because of bad grammar, egotism, and bias. The Women's Committee boycotted the book.[15] Darrell St. Claire, however, said that every senator and representative in Congress got a copy and considered it essential reading.[16]

When he was a public service commissioner, Huey often traveled to New Orleans, the state's largest city, to initiate contact with press, political, union, and business leaders there and to enjoy its recreation. As a U.S. senator, Huey visited New York, the country's largest city, for the same purposes. The New Yorker Hotel gave him free rooms. At times that are impossible to date, he visited banker Charles McCain, who had helped Huey avert a banking crisis and whose bank had purchased Louisiana highway bonds. Huey displayed his curious combination of charm and gall. He played with McCain's children, stayed for dinner without invitation or a tuxedo, used McCain's telephone to make calls all over the world, and urged that his bank invest in Louisiana.[17]

With his bodyguards, Huey dropped in uninvited on newspaper columnist Walter Lippmann, who was not impressed.[18] A. J. Liebling interviewed him twice, but nothing Huey said interested him.[19] *Times* reporter Arthur Krock used Huey as a source and, after Huey proclaimed his friendship in the Senate, was asked to introduce people to him.[20] Huey dropped in on newsreel services. Music composer and president of ASCAP Gene Buck ("Tulip Time") and producer Lou Irwin—known for representing Ethel Merman—became friends.[21] Will Rogers often sought him out.

On August 21, 1933, Huey visited New York. He denied regret for supporting Roosevelt in 1932 and said the NRA would help "some" but "not enough." Huey distributed pictures of Louisiana public works projects, explained his night-school program to educate adult illiterates, and submitted algebra problems that no newspaperman could solve. "Earnestly shaking his fingers at the silent assembly," he recommended a school sabbatical every seven years.[22]

*New Yorker* humorist James Thurber was surprised to get an interview. Huey was in "rooms 2643-4-5-6." "He needs a lot of space." Huey was "a bit tuckered" from a walk around the city. It was not his legs that were tired, Huey said, but his eyes, from seeing too little grass and trees on Broadway. New Yorkers were the most courteous people "in the north." They tried for a few minutes to discuss light topics such as diet but soon—after "possibly seven minutes"—the talk turned to politics, and Huey denounced his opponents as rats and lice. Returning from answering phone calls, Huey would jump into bed, so his feet and his shoulders hit at the same time. Someone knocked on the door. "Open it," Huey commanded. They did, getting a message and handing it over.

A New York mayoral election was underway between Democratic machine candidate John O'Brien and reformer (Republican-Fusion Party) Fiorello LaGuardia. Huey liked both men but thought, if he could, he would vote for LaGuardia. When asked how he liked New York, Huey answered with characteristic exuberance that "the port here is the best-managed port there is, the traffic system is wonderful, and the waterworks system is the goddam marvel of the world!"[23] Huey's extravagant comments would have ingratiated himself with New Yorkers, and even Louisianans reading the story could conclude that Huey visited New York to study its port and roads.

That Saturday night, August 26, Gene Buck invited Huey to a charity dinner at a Sands Point, New York, country club. Sands Point is a wealthy village on Long Island's north shore, an hour outside of New York City. Meeting at Buck's home before dinner, Huey mixed Sazerac cocktails—a New Orleans specialty—for the group, which included Mrs. Buck; Edward P. Mulrooney (former New York police commissioner) and his wife and daughter; Alford J. Williams, a former Navy pilot and oil industry executive; and Williams's wife.

At the club, Huey got drunk and, according to various reports, hopped from table to table, danced with unwilling partners, tried to force a young lady to take a drink, told a plump woman she was too fat to eat the asparagus on her plate which he proceeded to grab, and insulted a Black musician. During a bathroom break at about 4:00 a.m. Sunday the 27th, Huey "swung it too far" and urinated on the man next to him. Some later reported that he tried to pee between the man's legs. The man, probably Alford J. Williams, slugged him, opening a cut over his eye. Huey used a handkerchief to stop the bleeding, returned to Buck, and said he was "on the spot." Wrestling promoter Jack Curley drove them to Buck's home. Buck called a taxi to take Huey back to New York City. The incident was front-page news.[24]

Unfortunately, Huey had promised to give a speech to ten thousand veterans at the national convention of the Veterans of Foreign Wars. He took a train to Milwaukee but remained in seclusion until it was time to speak. Also speaking was Major General Smedley Butler, the highest ranking and most decorated war hero in Marine Corps history. Butler was radicalized, believing that the armed forces had been used to enrich Wall Street businesses.[25] Senators Thomas and Arthur Robinson attacked the cuts to veteran benefits.[26]

When Huey spoke, a bandage over his eye was visible. Newspapers couldn't be trusted, he said, and then bellowed: "We've had an exodus of polecats in Louisiana, but when I picked up your Milwaukee newspapers I knew where all the polecats had gone." When the photographers crowded to take his picture, Huey said: "Fellows, do I have to put up with this?" Thrown into an uproar, the delegates responded by surging toward and threatening the reporters.

After order was restored, Huey gave a ninety-minute speech on the need to redistribute wealth, pay the soldiers' bonus, and avoid domination by Wall Street. The audience handed questions to the stage and "begged him to continue with cries of 'go ahead!'" His speech was vociferously applauded, and his wit and droll anecdotes elicited long laughter. Afterward, the convention passed a resolution apologizing for the abuse of newsmen—a rebuke to Huey—but also endorsed wealth redistribution. The *Times*'s headline was "Long Amid Bedlam Denounces Foes." The *Washington Post*'s headline was "Kingfish Fans VFW Frenzy." They omitted the redistribution-of-wealth resolution.

Roosevelt's opposition to the bonus and his reduction of their benefits radicalized the veterans and spurred the VFW's explosive growth. Roosevelt chose the more conservative American Legion to defend his opposition to the bonus on October 2, 1933, where he said: "The fact of wearing a uniform does not mean that [the veteran] can demand and receive from his government a benefit which no other citizen receives." This remark infuriated most veterans.[27]

Huey was cantankerous as he returned from Milwaukee to New Orleans. During the train ride, he pushed past a man so violently that he fell into the laps of two nuns. Upon his arrival in New Orleans, he said "bust 'em up boys; don't let them take my picture," and the bodyguards elbowed photographers out of the way. One camera was smashed. A newsman yelled a question whether he would accept $1,000 to "appear as a freak at Coney Island."

When he finally issued a statement, Huey said he was "ganged" by three or four men and something sharp opened a cut above his eye. This, plus the unknown identity of the assailant, prolonged the story. Witnesses denied seeing any rowdies, criminals, or gang at Sands Point. Will Rogers said that Huey's assailant was wearing a dress suit and Huey failed to recognize him in this "disguise"; in Louisiana, dress suits were only worn by dead politicians. Huey had been taking boxing lessons, but his trainers were disappointed; he had good footwork but a "maiden's heart." The Women's Committee added this to Huey's list of sins. Displaying bruised knuckles, Alford Williams was asked if he did it but grinned as he said his hand got caught. A theater actor announced that he was not the assailant. Someone offered to stage a rematch with proceeds going to charity. A sportswriter suggested that baseball hitters emulate Huey and stand on home plate to get hit with a pitch. Someone said that a herring would have put up a better fight. The country club announced that he would not be allowed back.[28] Some Louisiana papers referred to him as "Huey Pee Long." A *Collier's* editor commissioned a medal showing a fish with Huey's head getting punched.[29] This amused Huey's opponents but convinced others that they had too much time on their hands and too little ordinary brains.[30] Huey wrote an open letter to imprisoned mobster Al Capone and promised him a release from jail and a reward from the House of Morgan if he acknowledged his involvement in the attack.

Huey never apologized or acknowledged any shame, but the reputational harm lasted a long time. As late as August 1934, Gene Buck said that Huey had done nothing wrong.[31] Two years afterward, sociologists interviewing people in Muncie, Indiana, unsurprisingly discovered that people still resented Huey's behavior at Sands Point.[32]

The Sands Point black eye added to the Stanley and Overton investigations, charges of graft, and Ansell's libel lawsuit and Huey's claim of immunity induced a widespread open revolt against Huey in Louisiana.[33] By September, these facts plus Roosevelt's patronage ban pressured Huey's alliance with the Old Regulars. In mid-September, Huey issued a circular denouncing the Old Regulars, headlined "The Course of the City Campaign" and "No Combination with Lice and Rats." Some speculated that Huey denounced the Old Regulars so that they would get federal patronage and then he would patch things up with them.[34] Three weeks later, no one knew whether the alliance would hold.[35]

Meanwhile a state Tax Reform Commission, appointed to review state taxes, recommended in early October some additional taxes, property tax relief for home and farm owners, and elimination of some government jobs to save money.[36] Despite holding no state-government position, Huey intervened. He liked the new taxes coupled with relief for property owners but didn't like the proposed job cuts. One proposal was to abolish Alice Lee Grosjean's position as supervisor of public accounts. Eventually the commission scrapped the plan to reduce jobs, and Huey announced in October that he would tour the state to speak on behalf of its recommendations.

The tour was an opportunity to demonstrate his popularity before negotiations with the Old Regulars about the city election in January. Instead, it was a nightmare. In Donaldsonville on October 15, he expected a crowd of twenty thousand people, but only eight hundred showed up, several of whom heckled him about Sands Point. Huey lost his cool and threatened to man-to-man it with a spectator, a threat made empty by the numerous bodyguards who protected him. He criticized the NRA. When Huey claimed that President Roosevelt wouldn't have been nominated without him, he provoked scornful laughter. Allen audibly pleaded with him not to lose his temper.[37]

After the speech, Huey decided to curtail—but did not end—his tour.[38]

The New Orleans Stock Exchange objected to Huey's speech describing it as a "gambling house."[39] In Franklinton, local leaders told him to curb his attacks on Roosevelt. He was jeered about dodging World War I. His stock defense was that he wasn't mad at anyone over there, but he added a stupid comment here, saying that most of the soldiers were dragged into the war by the hair on their heads. The American Legion was furious. A Hammond newspaper urged its readers to egg Huey when he spoke there, so Huey canceled his speech. This was gleefully reported to Roosevelt's political advisor, Louis Howe.[40]

At Monroe, Huey attacked Judge Harmon Drew for defrauding a bank of $3,000, enraging Drew and his friends. They threatened to kill Huey if he repeated his remarks in Minden. Word of their plans leaked to Colonel E. P. Roy, superintendent of the state Highway Patrol. Roy asked Huey to cancel his speech, but Huey refused. Huey eventually agreed to speak without mentioning Drew. Drew paced in front of the platform during Huey's remarks, backed by his armed and ready friends. Huey's bodyguard Louie Jones told Drew that if he put one foot on the platform he would be killed. Murphy Roden said all of Huey's bodyguards had Drew's gunmen "covered." "Goddamn I was scared," Huey said afterward. When Huey left, Drew mounted the stage and taunted him for lacking the courage to repeat his remarks.[41]

On October 20, Huey dedicated a new bridge over the Red River near Shreveport and watched LSU's football team play Arkansas. The fans booed him and threw things at him, with one bottle just missing his head. Sixteen persons tore his name off the bridge on the night of November 1, 1933.[42] A week later at Ruston he described himself as a "rooster with a broken wing."[43]

On November 10, he ended his tour at Alexandria, speaking to the largest crowd (fifteen thousand) of the trip. The vast majority raised their hands and applauded when he asked if they supported him, but he was pelted with rotten eggs and vegetables. Huey paused uncertainly after one egg was thrown, glared at the crowd and then at the buildings nearby and said, "Whoever done it, you got to hide, you low-down, polecat scoundrel." Huey's guards prevented any direct hits, but an elderly Confederate veteran invited to sit on the platform was hit. He pulled out a knife to scrape it off his suit, saying: "if I could catch the dirty little rat that threw this, I'd scrape his ass just like I'm scraping this off." State troopers located the source of the egging, the second floor of a bank, and rushed there to stop it. The Alexandria chief of police, Clint O'Malley, barred the door to prevent an "illegal entry" onto "private property."

It is an unusual politician who will talk for two hours while getting egged.

His enemies were trying to put ants on him to prevent his return to the Senate in January, Huey said, but he vowed to keep up the fight to redistribute wealth. Hundreds of supporters escorted him to his hotel for fear that he would be attacked.[44]

The anger of Huey's opponents infected the Overton hearings, which resumed in November. The Women's Committee charged that Huey had boasted that the Overton committee had been instructed to lay off him.[45] The Senate committee attributed such statements to inexperience or ignorance, but this further inflamed them.[46] They could not supply evidence to expose Huey and were infuriated that the full might of a federal investigation was not forthcoming.[47]

Broussard's attorney, "Whistle Britches" Rightor, declared that he had lost all confidence in the committee, whereupon Vice Chair Logan shouted, "Get out from before this bench and stay out" and threatened to hold him in contempt. Broussard stated that the proceedings were a farce and withdrew, as did the Honest Election League. The committee's own investigator, John Holland, turned on it, and charged that the hearings were held only to exonerate Overton. He called Chairman Connally yellow. Connally replied that Holland's charges were vile, scurrilous, and untrue. The only persons afraid of this investigation, he said, were "you cowards in Louisiana."[48] The spectators shouted, booed, and hissed.

On the third day, the excitement attracted a crowd so large that Connally had to enter the room through a fire escape, while he was mocked with yells of "Sands Point" and "don't get socked." Holland again gave an arm-waving, fist-shaking tirade against his own committee. Connally criticized both Holland ("blinded by headlines") and Hammond (the committee was not a "sounding board to advertise" herself).[49]

Witnesses said ballots were destroyed, voters pressured or "slugged unconscious,"[50] salary deductions taken for campaign contributions, patronage workers dismissed for nonsupport, whiskey given for votes, and a ballot cast by a dead man.[51] On November 21, Overton pounded the table, saying the committee was unfair, and the audience cheered him. Mayor Walmsley defended the necessity of dummy candidates, harmless enough, but then admitted that his organization was like Tammany Hall in New York, and that seventy-five men were available on election day to use strong-arm methods.[52]

Huey "electrified the hearing" and denied that he tried to extort a $5,000 campaign contribution on threat of sending an oilman to jail. The man who made the charge admitted that he contributed $75,000 to LeBlanc to get the severance tax amended, which would have deprived Louisiana of $2.5 million of revenue. Broussard declined yet another chance to present evidence. Huey got his best headline when he produced a voter that his opponents said was dead. Connally joked that the "committee has the power to raise the dead."[53] The hearings concluded, and Connally returned to Washington to write a report.[54]

At the Gridiron dinner, at which newsmen satirized politicians, there was a skit about a Louisiana lottery. Someone tried to stuff the prize-drawing box but was told professionals had already done it.[55] A *Tribune* editorial criticized the committee.[56] A *Times* editorial defended it, noting that Broussard and the Honest Election League dropped out of the inquiry, that the committee was not there "to investigate the politics" of Louisiana, that Huey's opponents "seem content with being a Noise Society," and that Louisianans must live on a "diet of roast pelican stuffed with firecrackers."[57]

As bad as his situation was, Huey now made it worse. The congressman for the district that included Baton Rouge was Bolivar Kemp. Huey had backed Kemp, but he was semi-independent. Kemp died in June. Anti-Longs in the district pressed Allen to call an election, but he delayed it, allegedly to save the state money, but probably because any candidate Huey backed would lose.[58]

In late November, Allen announced that a general election would be held on December 5. Normally a primary would be set at least thirty days before the general election, but the tardy announcement left insufficient time to hold one, so the Democratic Central Committee certified the Democratic Party nominee as Mrs. Bolivar Kemp, widow of the deceased. Anti-Long forces in mass meetings opposed her designation[59] and got a judge to enjoin the printing of ballots.[60] The Long forces then revealed that they were already printed; they were printed before the announcement. On December 2, 1933, 200 men forced their way into the office of the clerk of court and burned 11,000 ballots, the entire parish allotment. Thousands cheered.[61] On December 4, shots were fired to stop a truck believed to be carrying a new supply of ballots. "Long Island Huey Long" was hung in effigy in Hammond. Roland Howell warned of "bloodshed" and "revolution." A parish judge swore in 150 men to enforce his injunction. Included among the deputies was his eighty-year-old father.[62]

Armed anti-Long forces kept people from voting, conducted armed raids on polls, and displayed placards that said, "In effigy now, in person next."[63] Huey declined to call out the militia to overwhelm the armed anti-Long forces. Only 5,000 votes were recorded. Three parishes falling under the court's injunction cast no votes. The anti-Long forces then scheduled their own unauthorized election. Mrs. Kemp offered to resign as nominee if the anti-Long election were canceled.[64] When this idea was rejected, she was declared the nominee.[65] The anti-Longs held their election on December 27, using ballots printed by private citizens. About 19,500 votes were submitted for J. Y. Sanders Jr. Both sides pressed their claims to the congressional seat in 1934. Both claims were denied, and a new election scheduled.[66]

Following the congressional election fiasco, Huey and the Old Regulars negotiated about the January 1934 city elections. On December 14, Francis Williams became a mayoral candidate, pledged to the "elimination of Huey" from Louisiana politics and the end of "the tyranny under which we live."[67] Huey asked for more influence over the selection of candidates, outraging Walmsley. Huey dropped most demands, asking only to name the district attorney to replace Stanley, who had prosecuted the commissioners who miscounted the constitutional amendment ballots. The Old Regulars should have agreed, given that they helped miscount them.

Instead, in mid-December 1933, they voted twelve-to-five to break with Huey. "We will have a new deal," said Walmsley. The police protection for Huey's home, installed after it was arsoned, was removed. The city police arrested Huey's workers who were "distributing circulars without a permit."[68] Although the IRS inquiry into Huey's taxes had been stopped, it received press as if it were ongoing, a portent.[69]

In December 1932, Huey had been on top of the world. Every move he made succeeded. Now by December 1933, every move he made backfired. Newspapers wrote that he was finished. Several of the reasons were self-inflicted: Sands Point was the grossest, clearest, most publicized example. Rural supporters who laughed when he greeted a foreign dignitary in his pajamas could not condone drunkenness, rudeness, and cowardice at a ritzy country club. The cynical manipulation of the date of the congressional election and the disclosed voter fraud produced disgust.

Attacking Roosevelt didn't play well considering that in 1933, 325,611 Louisianans got federal welfare or jobs, and it still appeared that the NRA might work. The Overton and Stanley investigations; the Senate petitions to oust Huey; the facts that prompted them; the attempt to burn his house down; the cries to overthrow Huey without waiting for an election put him under a strain.[70] The mistakes he made while under this strain increased the fury of his opposition in a nasty self-reinforcing loop.

There were, finally, defects in Huey's program. There had not been much new and beneficial for Louisiana since the December special legislative session in 1930. The high expenditures for highway construction had alleviated the Depression in 1931 and 1932 but were reduced with the program's substantial completion in 1933. Compared to 1929, the real income of Louisianans dropped only 26 percent in 1932; in 1933 it dropped to about half of 1929's figure.[71]

By mid-December, Huey could at least display a sense of humor. In a satirical letter, Huey refused a social register listing because no one in society could grasp the art of eating potlikker. While Washington had taken up drinking soup out of cup-shaped plates with handles, he had been drinking soup off the plate for twenty years, "and without having any handles on the plate, either."[72] The *Times* featured this on page one, distressing a reader in New Orleans, who complained that it was "trying to entertain the public with his jokes," making Huey harder to defeat.[73]

On December 8, banker McCain was called before a Senate committee investigating corruption between bankers and politicians. McCain admitted that he had done Huey some (unspecified) favors and that they had shared a meal. A newsman called Huey for comment. This was a good occasion for a big fib, and the Kingfish was up to it:

> I know these Wall Street bankers and just what to expect of them. Their first custom, when they're supposed to be giving you something, is to take back half of what they're giving you before you ever get it.
>
> So when Charley offered to buy breakfast—and for me it was dinner, because it was nearly 12 o'clock—I ordered plenty, knowing the chances were that McCain would take most of it. He said he wasn't hungry and ordered only a cup of coffee or something.
>
> But I knew what to expect. And the facts are he ate one dozen of the oysters, all the French-fried potatoes and half of the ice cream. Then he remembered a pressing engagement and left before the waiter could get back with the check, so I paid.
>
> You rarely get the best of those birds, but it so happened that I got back the amount I was out, because he sold some highway bonds at one price and they fell off a few points in the next day or so.[74]

On January 3, 1934, Huey was in Washington, DC, for the start of the Senate session. On the 4th, he reintroduced his tax resolutions along with one to overrule Supreme Court precedent relating to the antitrust laws.[75]

William Woodin had finally resigned from the Treasury Department for reasons of health, and Roosevelt chose Henry Morgenthau Jr. to replace him. Huey hoped he was better than the "disaster," Woodin.[76] After an Executive Committee session, Huey announced that Morgenthau may have made some unwise decisions, but he would learn from his experience, and he would vote to confirm him.[77]

Huey saw Roosevelt in the White House on January 8,[78] saying he requested a copy of an October speech by Roosevelt favoring wealth redistribution. It is easy to speculate what else Huey wanted: thanks for his vote to confirm Morgenthau, rapprochement in advance of the New Orleans mayoral election, patronage, or a commitment to tax reform, so he could resume support for Roosevelt while saving face. Huey said that, given the departure of Woodin, he asked Roosevelt whether there was any room in the boardinghouse for him.[79]

Roosevelt must have loved their meeting. He told his secretary to allow Huey ten minutes. Huey lasted twelve. Huey had nothing to offer. In the aftermath of Sands Point and his criticisms of Roosevelt, Huey's followers were in revolt, the Old Regulars had deserted him, investigations revealed election misconduct, and he was about to put the IRS on his trail. Did Roosevelt offer rapprochement? Think Huey was finished? He let Huey talk. Was Huey brash or subdued? No one knows. It was probably after this meeting that Huey told his friends that Roosevelt was as smart as he was, that he couldn't travel with him, and that he had lied to him.[80] He never saw Roosevelt again.

Huey proposed an old-age pension bill that called for payment of $30 per month to those over sixty who had less than $1,000 annual income and a net worth of less than $10,000.[81] Referring to Senator Robinson of Indiana and Senator Robinson of Arkansas, bitter opponents regarding Roosevelt's policies against veterans, Huey urged that both support his tax plan so the veterans could be taken care of without breaking the budget, citing Roosevelt's October speech.[82] The press wasn't listening.

They were listening to his opponents. The Women's Committee held a banquet at which they sipped sherry and listened to the *Collier's* editor of Sands Point medal fame recite a poem about it: "and I lift a glass of legal booze, and toast the happy guy, who sent the fish back to his mud, with beefsteak on his eye." The ladies enjoyed this more "than they did the filet de sole bonne femme."[83]

Just as Seymour Weiss had counseled Huey not to criticize Roosevelt, he now advised him to stay out of the New Orleans mayoral election of January 1934.

Huey agreed on December 20 and proclaimed neutrality. This didn't last. Huey called Weiss from Washington, DC, and said he had recruited a ticket that was sure to win, headed by John Klorer Sr., and reproached Weiss for recommending that he sell his birthright.[84]

On January 10, Huey entrained to New Orleans to lead Klorer's campaign.[85] Although a colorless speaker and personality, Klorer had impeccable reform credentials. Businessman Alfred Danziger, the incumbent coroner, Nicholas Carbajal (a former ally turned opponent, now ally again), and, most unusually, Gus Williams, Huey's candidate for district attorney, joined him on Huey's ticket. Gus said: "you don't like me and I despise you, but I'll run on your goddamn ticket."[86]

Huey supported Klorer with speeches to large and enthusiastic crowds and for hours over the radio. The crowds howled as he described Walmsley as a poor, downtrodden thing who came to him on bended knee,[87] explained how much he had done for Turkey Head in the past and forecasted an execution of Turkey Head on Election Day. In radio speeches, he would stop and sing a song he made up. One, about Walmsley's nepotism, was sung to the tune of "The Whole Dam Family." The other, "Anti-Long Little Bogey," was sung to the tune of "Git Along, Little Doggie."[88]

Walmsley's mother had promised a printer that he would get city business if he supported her son. Weiss talked Huey out of featuring this in an attack circular. Weiss said everyone has a mother. The chief of police said he would arrest Huey for libel if he wrote it, also because everyone has a mother. When Walmsley heard about it, he snapped. Waving his fist, he vowed to follow Huey to Washington to beat him up. Huey never did criticize his mother. Properly sardonic, Huey noted that Walmsley threatened to "mess him around," and the crowd cheered as he said he hoped Walmsley changed his mind. Walmsley proclaimed that Huey had "betrayed" Roosevelt.[89] Roosevelt gave the Old Regulars a disproportionate share of relief and public works expenditures during the campaign.[90]

Huey or his organization gave Walmsley a great issue about a week before the election. A judge had enjoined tampering with the voter registration books. But a week before the election and in the middle of the night, the registrar of voters (a state employee), C. S. Barnes, with armed men, was caught in the registrar's office marking off allegedly fraudulent names. An alert Old Regular noticed the light on in the middle of the night and called the police. Barnes was arrested.[91] Rumors that state police would stage an armed rescue of Barnes were squelched by a negotiated agreement governing election-day proceedings. Weapons imported in case of conflict remained unused.[92]

The Old Regulars went all out to win this election. And they did. Klorer got only 29 percent of the vote, about 32,000 votes; Williams only 28,000. Klorer's vote was a little less than Huey's strength before he allied with the Old Regulars, but they had increased their votes from about 42,000 to 48,000, probably with the aid of dead voters, but also because Huey's prestige had declined, Roosevelt's coattails were strong, and extra money for relief was spent. Francis Williams refused to back Klorer in a runoff, so Klorer conceded, and Walmsley won.[93]

Dumbfounded at his defeat, Huey blamed it on fraudulent voters, padded payrolls, and large campaign contributions by the utilities and gamblers. Huey (through Allen) authorized a state investigation into New Orleans voter rolls.[94] The crowds had turned out to hear him and laughed at his jokes, but the votes weren't there.[95] Again, the newspapers wrote Huey's political obituary.

Huey's resolve to speak for two hours in Alexandria while getting egged was matched by his resolve to recover from this reverse. Huey vowed vengeance on Walmsley, without quarter.[96] The *American Progress* wrote "God Pity New Orleans."[97] Upset at Huey's attacks on him, Old Regular Ulic Burke demanded an apology or challenged Huey to a duel.[98]

While Huey was in Louisiana, Senator Connally had issued the final Senate report on the Overton election. It concluded that dummy candidates and shaking down state workers for campaign contributions were deplorable and fraudulent but conceded that the evidence was conflicting and that partisan crowds made their job difficult, as did the misconduct of the committee's investigator, John Holland, and Broussard's failure to contest the election. Overton thanked the committee for stating that his reputation was intact. Connally interrupted to say that was not its conclusion.[99]

When Huey returned to the Senate, he responded to the report. Dummy candidates were used in other states, and he and his allies had gone to court three times in the 1920s to stop the practice. When those efforts failed, he simply beat his opponents at their own game.[100] No credible, uncontested evidence was given that anyone lost their job for failing to contribute to the campaign. Huey had defeated the "feudal lords" of Louisiana, who raised stupendous sums to defeat him, while he obtained only nickels and dimes. Williams states that Huey was grim and wistful in commenting that he had "never held a public office in my life during which I was not under . . . threat of removal or impeachment. . . . I have tried for about sixteen years to have it some other way, and it has never been any other way, so now I have stopped trying to have it any other way." Big companies had engaged John D. Rockefeller's former public relations expert at a huge expense to direct a publicity campaign against him. A letter from the IRS collector of revenue, Lawrence Merrigan, disclosed efforts to investigate Huey's taxes and to leak word of it but confessed that Huey was innocent. If the government would just give him unlimited ink, paper, and stamps, Huey would never raise another dime for a campaign.

Connally couldn't say much in reply because Huey agreed with the committee that dummies were a bad system that he had tried to stop. Robinson commended the committee for a good job in difficult conditions.[101] The press ignored Huey's speech.

Walmsley followed Huey to Washington to beat him up. The press didn't ignore this. They stalked him in the hotel lobby, hoping to witness the confrontation. Huey couldn't be located. Walmsley decided to visit the Capitol and other tourist sites and meet with administration officials. Needing to return for Mardi Gras, he finally announced that he would be leaving. The day before he was to go, he got an urgent call. All relief allotments to the South were going to be canceled! He was needed to meet at once with the president! A few minutes after Walmsley left, Huey strutted into the hotel in front of the newsmen. Where was Walmsley? Wasn't Walmsley looking for him? Later, Walmsley couldn't suppress a smile when he realized Huey's trick.[102]

Tricks alone wouldn't rehabilitate Huey's standing. The feedback from his constituents from Sands Point through the mayoral election was unpleasant, but Huey heard it. He quit drinking. He cut out tobacco because it contributed to his hay fever. He resolved to lose weight. At two hundred pounds on a five-foot ten-inch frame, he was then pudgy. Huey renounced banquets, ate only two meals a day, and fasted on a liquids-only diet on Wednesdays, losing twenty-five pounds.[103] A Shreveport preacher, Gerald L. K. Smith, accompanied Huey to Washington. One wonders whether, beset by problems, he had a foxhole religious reconversion.

There were political problems to solve. Huey's enemies could support Roosevelt against Huey and wrap themselves in his popularity and get his patronage. The state of Louisiana lacked the money to compete with federal benefits.

Huey also must have considered Senator Borah's question about how his tax resolutions would redistribute wealth. And when he was backing the inflation bills, he was too smart not to see that, while cheaper money made it easier to pay old debts and represented a worthwhile tax on hoarded money, as conservatives now acknowledge, it depended on voluntary borrowing to work, and consumers might not be able to afford the inflated price of goods.

Instinctively, Huey supported the soldiers' bonus. It was a defining issue. James Truslow Adams, who decried the concentration of wealth in his history book, opposed the soldiers' bonus as a giveaway that would debase the currency.[104] Roosevelt's conservative advisors Moley and Morganthau thought it was essential that Roosevelt oppose it.[105] Huey correctly believed that the veterans were owed the money and adding $2 billion of purchasing power through the bonus would stimulate the economy.[106]

The soldiers' bonus was a one-time payment, however. Huey lacked a proposal to distribute fortunes taxed, something akin to the soldiers' bonus, something that would improve the economy and benefit the people rather than just punish the wealthy.

When the answer to Huey's problems—the political and the economic—came to him, it came to him in the middle of the night. He didn't wait for dawn to act on it.

## Twenty-Three

# THE COMMAND OF THE LORD

At 3 a.m., Huey summoned his secretary, Earle Christenberry, to his hotel room. There Huey explained the solutions to his political problem and the country's economic problem: he would organize societies called "Share-Our-Wealth" (SOW); the motto: "Every Man a King."[1] On February 5, 1934, one month after the *Tribune* wrote that Huey was in "decline" and one day after the *Times* wrote that his star was "setting,"[2] Huey published an open letter to the people of America requesting them to join SOW to "Carry Out the Command of the Lord." Under SOW, every deserving family would have a homestead of one-third the national average ($5,000), a new idea. Old-age pensions would be paid as he had proposed. Hours of work would be limited if and as necessary to give everyone employment and a fair share of leisure time, a modified version of Black's share-the-work proposal. Agricultural production would be balanced according to his cotton-holiday plan. Public works projects would employ anyone not raising substitute crops during holiday years. The cuts to veteran benefits would be restored. Taxes to pay for this would come from the top incomes and fortune holders.[3]

Months later, Huey added a new element to his plan: education. The right to college, professional, or vocational education would depend on the mental capacity and energy of students rather than the financial ability of their parents. Removal of students from the workforce would also reduce unemployment.

To differentiate SOW from socialism, on March 2, 1934, Huey debated

Norman Thomas, the Socialist Party candidate for president in 1932, in New York.[4] Thomas thought that government boards should plan the economy and own the resources and means of production. Huey's plan was inadequate, he said, because it would require periodic surgical operations to keep wealth distribution in balance and lacked a provision for worker incomes.

Huey adopted one of his characteristic poses, the southern rustic. He didn't understand what Thomas said, Huey drawled, but when he did, he would write him a letter. He believed that all debts should be ipso facto remitted. Maybe the audience didn't know what "ipso facto" meant. (*Pause.*) He didn't neither. The audience erupted. Then Huey dropped the drawl and grammatical errors and explained his views. The *Times* portrayed Huey as a kind of southern rube.[5] The audience was too pretentious to take his biblical references seriously and was predisposed to Thomas and socialism. When the debate concluded, however, autograph seekers mobbed Huey.[6]

Thomas might have had some impact on Huey's thinking. At some further date, Huey supplemented his ideas again, suggesting a minimum national income between $2,000 and $2,500 per year for each deserving family, one-third the average family income.

Huey created a thirty-two-page booklet to explain SOW. There was nothing "wrong" with the United States, but conditions presented only three alternative futures:

(1) A monarchy ruled by financial masters—"a modern feudalism";
(2) Communism; and
(3) Sharing the wealth.

In a dig at Roosevelt's "bold, persistent experimentation," Huey's letter said that his own plan was "simple and concrete—not an experiment." It provided both a floor and a ceiling for wealth, but "from the worst to the best there would be no limit to opportunity." The booklet contained pages of quotations from Huey's 1932 "Doom" speech, historians, politicians, religious leaders, the Bible, and Plato, all stating that concentrated wealth was bad.

The homestead and minimum family income ensured that the taxed wealth would be redistributed and thus answered Borah's question from 1933. The plan was less bureaucratic at the consumer level than food stamps, welfare, Section 8 housing vouchers, and the other myriad government programs that now benefit the poor. Unlike inflation alone, it ensured that purchasing power permanently reached consumers.

Compared to the NRA and unlike socialism, SOW was capitalistic. It set no codes for prices, wages, or production targets, although it contemplated keeping track of aggregate production and demand. Incentives to earn or accumulate wealth disappeared after the confiscatory tax levels were reached, but that would affect only the super-rich, a few people, Huey thought, and everyone else would still have the incentive to work and save. Supply and demand and competition would govern pricing and resource allocation.

Schlesinger described the ideas of David Cushman Coyle, who "crystalized" the intellectual reaction to the New Deal. Coyle called for high taxes on the rich, old-age pensions, public works of $10–15 billion with "indirect rather than direct" planning to "put money in the hands of the many." Coyle would not "impose precise rules as to how people should make specific economic decisions; rather [he would use] the powers of government to bring about desired general results."[7] This would not be planning for control but planning for freedom. The similarity to Huey's ideas is plain even though Coyle's scope was limited.[8]

Huey used populist themes to describe the economic problem. Opportunity (before chain stores, for example) used to be more widely available, the Bible was the word of God, and the man at the end of a plow was as capable as a lawyer or accountant. Whereas some populists idealized the economy before the advent of large companies, Huey only wanted their ownership more widely dispersed. Technological advances would be encouraged. If labor-saving devices allowed all to work for only fifteen hours a week, let the Lord be praised, Huey said.

Huey provided organizing advice. It was better to have a live society of ten people than a sleeping one with a hundred members. Outreach to other communities should occur. Circulars and lapel buttons would be provided at cost. A whole paragraph prohibited dues; otherwise "the thieves of Wall Street and their newspapers and radio liars would immediately say" that he "had a scheme to get money. . . . Keep money raising as far away from this society as you can."

Criticism was preempted. As SOW membership increased, the interests would abuse Huey in the media. Because they controlled the newspapers, they did not tell the truth and, therefore, some of the persons who read the most were the most ignorant of the relevant facts.[9] Members should beware of "slurs and snickers" of some "high-ups." If a "smart-aleck tool of the interests" asked questions, Huey would answer them.[10]

The letter's call to action said: "let us get to work quick, quick, quick to put an end by law to people starving and going naked in this land of too much to eat and too much to wear. . . . The Gideons had but two men when they organized. Three tailors of Tooley Street drew the Magna Carta of England. The Lord says: 'For where two or three are gathered together in My name, there am I in the midst of them.'"

On February 23, 1934, Huey announced his brainchild in a nationwide radio speech: the Depression would be solved if the superrich gave up some of their wealth so it could be scattered among the people, he said. Then each citizen would have an equal opportunity for success as the Declaration of Independence, God, Moses, Jesus, and Greek philosophers advocated. (He quoted the scriptures not to convince anyone he was a good man; that was between him and his maker.) It was not a "fair shake of the dice" for one child to be born inheriting $10 million while another child was born with nothing. (In doing God's work, gambling analogies are permitted.) The alphabetical agencies of the Roosevelt administration required the ordinary man to read complex codes to do business: "You can have the NRA and PWA and CWA and the UUG and GIN, and any other kind of dad-gummed letter code. . . . Why hide? Why quibble? You know what the trouble is. The man that says he does not know what the trouble is just hiding his face to keep from seeing the sunlight." The people viewed their government almost as a religion, the kind in which parents would throw their babies into the all-consuming fire in days gone by. Now their children went hungry. If he were in their place, he wondered whether he would have their fortitude to keep a good government alive even as it let them starve, just so that a handful of men could accumulate more than they need. As a closing touch, he assured his wife and children that he was entirely well and would see them in a few days.

*American Rhetoric* ranks this speech as Huey's best and number twenty-six of the top hundred speeches of the twentieth century. A severely edited version is included in William Safire's book of the best American speeches.[11] The radio station thought it prudent to explain to the White House why it gave Huey the radio time.[12]

Listening to it will surprise those who have seen the Ken Burns documentary about Huey. Burns excerpted the dynamic parts of Huey's speeches. This speech, in contrast, had a slow start and a low-key delivery, with hesitations and ad-libbed phrases that turned back on themselves, although there were very few "ums" or other fillers. The organization was redundant and circular. But it had some vivid metaphors, effective ridicule, and interesting ways to phrase his ideas.

SOW out-promised Roosevelt. Roosevelt was a phony whose mother wouldn't let him go too far, he told a *Times* reporter.[13] It included something for farmers, labor, students, retirees, veterans, and the great mass of American families, with a controversial proposal to pay for it all: confiscatory taxes on the wealthy. Professor Sindler wrote that a master political craftsman put SOW together.[14] If promise, large promise, is the soul of an advertisement,[15] then Huey had crafted a powerful appeal.

While Huey's proposal echoed principles of Theodore Roosevelt and Woodrow Wilson, Huey was the first—and only—politician to propose a plan to remedy inequality while preserving capitalism. Even historians critical of Huey and SOW concede that he had focused on the real, relevant problem of wealth inequality.[16] Eventually, there was criticism of the plan's mechanics and calculations. Initially, however, because Huey's opponents failed to take his organizing seriously, the Depression's misery was great, and Roosevelt's actions conservative, SOW spread fast, like a virus.

Huey wrote to his Louisiana supporters, asking them to form societies. Within a month, 200,000 members were enrolled.[17] In April, he asked the Senate for a larger stenographer allowance.[18] By May 1934, Huey was flooding Georgia with circulars.[19] By mid-1934, Huey's mail exceeded that of all other senators, combined. Huey enlarged his secretarial staff from four to eighteen and at times added a night shift.[20] Correspondents received doughnut letters from Huey, a standard opening and closing in blue ink with a customized middle in red ink.[21]

To spur the growth of the SOW societies, to test the appeal of the plan, and to regain the support of Louisianans while he was in Washington, Huey hired an organizer. Gerald L. K. Smith grew up in a small town thirty miles north of Madison, Wisconsin. His grandfather and father were part-time, fundamentalist, circuit-riding preachers. His father sold patent medicines, not very successfully. Populism influenced his family, and his father was a fan of progressive Senator Robert LaFollette Sr.

Going into the ministry, Gerald preached in Wisconsin, Illinois, and Indiana in progressively larger and more prestigious churches, but his wife's tuberculosis necessitated a move from Indianapolis to a warmer climate. A doctor recommended Shreveport, and in due course he received a call to the First Christian Church.

A dynamic preacher, about six feet tall, and brawny, with wavy brown hair and an attractive smile, he attended Shreveport labor-union meetings, and his sermons sometimes included political themes about bad working conditions, corruption, or high utility rates. When some of his parishioners faced foreclosure, Smith tried to stop it but failed. Philip Leiber, the head of the foreclosing bank, told him to mind his own business and implied that his church's mortgage was at risk. Labor leaders introduced Smith to Huey. Huey threatened to close Leiber's bank. Leiber canceled all the mortgages. After that, Smith periodically traveled to Washington or New Orleans to consult with Huey. Favorable mention of him crept into his sermons, irritating his conservative parishioners.

After the New Orleans mayoral election in January 1934, Smith was erroneously identified in a newspaper picture as one of Huey's bodyguards.[22] His identification with Huey necessitated his resignation from the church in February 1934. Huey hired him for $6,500 per year. At the time, he displayed standard rural progressive ideas. Smith denied flirting with fascist William Dudley Pelley and concealed his nascent anti-Semitic ideas.[23]

Smith idolized—Williams says "worshipped"—Huey. He wore Huey's old suits, slept on the floor of Huey's bedroom, and later wrote an article in *New Republic* magazine extolling him as a superman.[24] He thought that a mass movement had to be superficial for quick appeal, fundamental for permanence, dogmatic for certainty, and practical for workability. Some actions would be akin to a locomotive engine that belches smoke and soot but pulls the pretty parlor car, which would be helpless without it. Smith reveled in meeting Huey's celebrity friends such as Will Rogers. Many of Huey's other colleagues resented him.[25]

With a booming voice and a good vocal flow, Smith could stretch out vowel sounds in a dramatic crescendo.[26] Smith, like Huey, would sometimes ask how many in the audience had four suits, then three suits, then two suits, then one suit. Most had one suit or less, and Huey or Smith would then cry out that J. P. Morgan had hundreds of suits, each one stolen from the working man. One of his perorations said, "Let's pull down these huge piles of gold until there shall be a real job, not a little old sow-belly, black-eyed pea job but a real spending money, beefsteak and gravy, Chevrolet, Ford in the garage, new suit, Thomas Jefferson, Jesus Christ, red, white, and blue job for every man!"[27] He closed with a prayer: "Lift us out of this wretchedness, O Lord, out of this poverty, lift us who stand here in slavery tonight. Rally us under this young man who came out of the woods of north Louisiana, who leads us like a Moses out of the land of bondage into the land of milk and honey where every man is a king but no man wears a crown. Amen."[28] H. L.

Mencken thought Smith was better than William Jennings Bryan, the "gustiest and goriest, the deadliest and the damndest orator ever heard on this or any other earth—the champion boob-bumper of all epochs."[29] Huey thought he was the greatest rabble-rouser in the country, "next to me."[30] Huey kept Smith out of the newspapers, off the radio, and away from major population centers, however.[31]

From April to September 1934, Smith toured Louisiana and spoke to between 100,000 and 200,000 people at 143 rallies in small towns.[32] Opponents disrupted some of his speeches, but he soldiered forward. SOW helped transform three contiguous parishes in southwest Louisiana into a Long stronghold.[33] Smith traveled into other southern states later in 1934, and the response and episodic disruptions were as great. By February 1935, SOW claimed 4.5 million members.[34]

SOW provided Huey no immediate influence in the Senate, but he threw himself into Senate business, just as he threw himself into the details of being governor after his impeachment. Along with Senator Nye, he fought to force disclosure of data about employees of the NRA, to expose big business domination, but Robinson buried the bill.[35] Along with Cutting, Norris, and LaFollette, Huey tried to increase public works appropriations, but they lost.[36] Huey supported an amendment to require Senate advice and consent over public works jobs, in the new Civil Works Administration, but it failed.[37] He disclosed that an article by columnist Arthur Brisbane that contained several complimentary paragraphs in the midnight edition of the *Washington Herald* were cut from the morning edition.[38] This was ignored.

More successful was Huey's effort to restore the cuts to veterans' benefits. That bill passed.[39] Roosevelt vetoed it, including in his message the odious sentence that veterans could not count on more benefits than anyone else.[40] With Cutting and Huey's advocacy, the Senate overrode the veto.[41]

Huey's opponents were determined to keep him on the defensive, however.[42] John M. Parker's April 1933 petition to have Huey expelled was given preliminary consideration by a judiciary subcommittee in January, but in March it found the allegations defamatory.[43]

The St. Lawrence Seaway Treaty proposed to construct a system of canals and channels through parts of Canada and the United States to allow ocean-bound vessels to travel from the Great Lakes to the Atlantic Ocean through the Gulf of St. Laurence. Huey's normal allies—Norris, Wheeler, and LaFollette—supported the treaty, as did Roosevelt, believing that it would make transporting midwestern crops to the East Coast cheaper.[44]

Illinois Senators Lewis and Dieterich, protecting Chicago-to-New Orleans shipping from Lake Michigan, other senators whose states bordered the Mississippi, and Huey and Overton from Louisiana led the opposition.[45] Midwestern railroad labor unions opposed it as a threat to their jobs.[46]

Usually a loyal administration Democrat, Senator Wagner opposed the treaty and rebutted LaFollette's data.[47] Huey later implied that he helped gather the data used by Wagner,[48] shrewd if true because Wagner was respected within the party. After weeks of debate, the treaty was defeated on March 14, 1934, and this potential blow to New Orleans was averted.[49]

Patronage matters also kept Huey on the defensive. Roosevelt nominated Rene Viosca to be U.S. attorney in Louisiana. The nomination was referred to the Judiciary Committee and, within the committee, to a subcommittee headed by Huey. Relying on Viosca's activities related to the Watson-Williams Pontchartrain Bridge, he secured an unfavorable recommendation.[50]

A more prolonged fight arose over Roosevelt's nominee for Louisiana's collector of revenue, Daniel D. Moore, who was affiliated with Huey's enemy John Sullivan. Huey said that Moore was personally objectionable to him, but Roosevelt tried to force confirmation. A subcommittee headed by Barkley reported the nomination favorably over the objections of Gerald L. K. Smith, who introduced letters from labor unions denouncing Moore. Huey made a brief appearance at the end of this hearing and ineffectively cross-examined Moore. Barkley was upset at Huey's absence, claiming that the meeting had been scheduled to accommodate him; Huey cited a schedule conflict.[51]

On the Senate floor, Huey argued that gambler John L. Sullivan, an affiliate or business partner of E. R. Bradley, a Florida gambler and Kentucky horse breeder, sponsored Moore. These charges infuriated Senators Harrison, Barkley, and Clark because they weren't brought before their subcommittee, where they could have overruled them. Wheeler defended Huey. Couzens suggested that personal dislike of Huey or his delay in providing the information should not cause the charges to be ignored. Huey said he would take responsibility for objecting on grounds of personal obnoxiousness, or he would prove his charges, whatever the committee preferred. The Senate returned the nomination to the committee. Huey said in ten days he would run Moore "out of here."[52]

A group of Bradley supporters in Kentucky burned Huey in effigy.[53] On April 3, Huey told the Senate that Bradley and Sullivan had a business relationship with New Orleans's racetrack and, based on a laudatory article in *Collier's* magazine, Bradley ran a gambling house in Miami. From the head of the IRS, Guy Helvering, Huey had obtained a list of people that Moore—

already working for the IRS pursuant to a temporary appointment—had hired to work for him. Using their own application forms or New Orleans phone books, Huey showed that Sullivan was their sponsor and prior employer and, in some cases, still their part-time employer.

Lawyers and dramatists build up to a point. In discussing Bradley, Huey showed this ability:

> [*Collier's* magazine,] in order to show his great charity . . . [quotes Bradley, who explains that,] "when a man dies owing me any money, I tear up the slips and forget it."
>
> That is very remarkable. This great big gambling-house man tears up the slips when a man dies—and that is charity of the first order. . . .
>
> Why the charity? Here is where the heart of the man is seen in its best and truest light: "The law doesn't recognize a gambling debt." And so the good, true, honest, righteous Kentucky sportsman tears up the slips, because the law does not recognize the debt! [*Laughter.*][54]

Sullivan, Rightor, and Bradley attended the hearings. When Huey spoke, Sullivan bit through his cigar, rose in anger, and had to be restrained, muttering "You couldn't prove that in a thousand years. You dirty, rotten ——. You dirty rotten ——, ——, —— ——. You Sands Point ——." According to the *Tribune,* Huey paled but, according to the *Times,* he was "unruffled," and his questions forced Bradley to invoke the Fifth Amendment against self-incrimination.[55] The next day, Huey and Rightor challenged each other to fight, Harrison and Huey clashed over how to react to Sullivan's outburst, and Huey called Bradley a liar when Bradley claimed he had contributed to Huey's campaign in 1928.[56]

Contemporaneously with these explosive developments, Harrison's Finance Committee reported out its tax bill. LaFollette asked for higher taxes on the wealthy and gave a good speech on April 4, citing experts and tracing the increased concentration of wealth. Senators Bone and Borah followed with good speeches. Huey followed Borah at the end of the day.

The Moore committee hearing was the equivalent of a small trial; it is a rare person who can prepare for and conduct a trial for several days and then make a major speech on a separate topic. Huey gave one of his poorer speeches, a very long one, as if he knew he were out of sync and thought, if he kept talking, he would find his groove. He repeated his frequent contention that Roosevelt had failed to offer a difference from Hoover.[57] This and the preceding days' controversies on Moore, however, provoked Harrison, much as an aggrieved spouse will say, "It's not last night; it's the last ten years." Harrison exclaimed that Huey's opinions were less respected by the Senate and the country than any other senator's.[58]

Incensed, Huey unloaded a vicious attack. Harrison had been a protégé of Senator Vardaman, winning election to Congress as a Vardaman ally. When Vardaman opposed World War I, however, Harrison defeated Vardaman for the Senate. Huey contrasted that with his defense of S. J. Harper, who had the same criticisms of the war and was indicted for it: just the difference in people; in one case, find your friend in trouble, stab him in the back and drink his blood, and in the other case stand by your friend and heal his wounds.

Clark called Huey out of order, but Harrison asked that Huey continue. Huey then blamed Harrison for holding a promissory note from Union Indemnity Company. Huey was criticized when it failed while Harrison's note, obtained from a man Harrison had gotten appointed to the Federal Home Loan Bank Board, was among the failed company's assets.

Harrison responded that his reputation would not suffer from Huey's "wild and rambling" utterances, that no other senator would have brought up "the personal affairs" of another senator, and that he held Vardaman in high regard despite political differences. As a loyal Democrat, he owed support to President Wilson, his party leader, on the war, just as he owed Roosevelt his support now.

Harrison referred to Bradley's contribution of $5,000 to Huey in 1928. Huey exclaimed that Bradley couldn't be believed; he had taken the Fifth Amendment. In a surreal moment, Clark jumped up and yelled that eight senators at the hearing asserted the Fifth Amendment for Bradley before his own counsel had done so, as if that somehow made Bradley credible.[59]

Huey resumed his attack on Harrison, exhibiting mainly his unwillingness to cede the last word and his energy to outtalk an opponent. It was a good rule not to touch a porcupine, "unless you expect to get some quills in you." He recounted his support for Roosevelt at the Democratic Convention. Several times he claimed that Harrison opposed Roosevelt's interests on procedural votes, but Harrison accurately contradicted him.

Without contradiction, Huey declared that he was denied patronage because of his vote against the Economy Act last year, yet this year two-thirds of Congress voted to overturn it. He was right last year. Now everyone admitted it was a mistake.[60]

Clark again defended Harrison, and he and Huey tangled with a hostility reminiscent of Huey's attack on Ansell (then, ironically, supported by Clark). Among other things, Huey accused him of not paying for use of a sound truck he had provided for Clark's Missouri campaign. When the day ended, Clark was mid-tirade against Huey.[61]

On Friday, April 6, the crowded galleries expected a continuation of their battle. Clark then shocked everyone. Yesterday's remarks were made "in hot blood" and violated the Senate rules, so he asked that they be stricken from the record. Surprised, Huey agreed to remove his own unparliamentary remarks. The record thus omits what they said about each other.[62] Clark sent a check to Huey for the sound truck.[63]

This was Huey's lowest point in the Senate, and he had started at a low point. Senators avoided him like the smallpox, columnist Drew Pearson wrote.[64] Columnist Rodney Dutcher said that, in the Senate, Huey was disliked but feared.[65] Other senators told Arthur Krock that Huey was not a member of the Senate "club" by which senators agree to live and let live. He fought "without regard to any set of rules, and [was] resourceful, intelligent, and cunning."[66] The *Times* wrote that Huey was a "rowdy" who was always "beginning or keeping up rows."[67]

Huey tried to gain the offensive, but Sands Point and his electoral defeats left a long political hangover. LaFollette's amendment to increase taxes on the wealthy lost thirty-six to forty-seven.[68] Couzens, with Huey's support, lost a similar effort.[69]

Huey exposed corruption in the New Orleans office of the Home Loan Bank Board. Connected firms affiliated with his opponents raked off fees at the expense of consumers refinancing their mortgages. This made no impression.[70] Huey favored the new SEC legislation, which, unlike the 1933 bill, provoked some opposition. The stock exchanges and the cotton exchanges stole money from the common man, Huey said, and had less ethics than a "colored crap game."[71] This received no press.

Huey attacked Standard Oil for dominating the NRA oil codes and for funding Bolivia in a war against Paraguay for oil lands, the Chaco War.[72] In Paraguay, Huey became a hero, but the press in the United States noticed only when the Bolivian diplomat denied that Huey knew the facts.[73] Huey rebutted the diplomat, citing the facts, getting favorable press throughout South America as a "beautiful spirit" who "openly goes into the arena to fight for justice and truth." Until Paraguay named a fort it captured from Bolivia the Huey P. Long Fort, American newspapers again ignored the issue.[74]

Huey suffered another defeat in mid-April. J. Y. Sanders Jr. beat Huey's new candidate, Harry D. Wilson (Mrs. Kemp declined to make the race), the former Louisiana commissioner of agriculture, in the Sixth Congressional District, which included Baton Rouge. Sanders won by 2,376 votes out of about 30,000 cast. Sanders led a celebratory parade through Baton Rouge after the election, with a hearse bearing the sign: "The Crawfish Is Hunting for His Hole."[75]

This defeat encouraged Huey's opponents to plot to unseat Louisiana House Speaker Ellender in the legislative session in May. Old Regular George K. Perrault would replace him and, after that, Lieutenant Governor Fournet and then Governor Allen would be impeached and removed on charges to be decided later. Perrault would then be governor. They had forty-seven written and five verbal pledges (for a majority of fifty-two out of a hundred) for their cause, and crowds—many of the men armed[76]—invaded Baton Rouge to witness the coup, to support it, or to effectuate it by violence. Word of the plot reached Huey. He left Washington, DC, for Louisiana at once.

Through Allen, Huey mobilized the National Guard to counter the armed force, but Ellender thought this would give them a reason to remove him, so the order was revoked. Some of the legislators had warned him to stay in Washington,[77] but Huey worked all night to cajole, intimidate, or award favors to the legislators. After some duplicitous maneuvering, brother Earl Long, convinced by Robert Brothers to reconcile with Huey, helped stave off the reorganization.[78] The anti-Long forces were beaten, and they never brought up their removal motion for a vote. Armed men considered storming Huey's hotel suite but instead dispersed in disillusionment. Huey left the statehouse smiling.[79]

Huey devised additional legislation for his leaders to enact during the rest of the session and then rushed back to Washington where, albeit with some ups and downs, he improved his standing. Having been rebuffed by the Judiciary Committee in March, Parker, Hammond, and Pleasant pressed a new case against Huey before the Elections Committee. On May 3, Senator Overton asked to bar Ansell in an impressive oratorical performance.[80] The *Tribune* reported on a late May hearing. Its article evidences the sexism of the times, Mrs. Pleasant's incompetence, and Huey as ruthless trial lawyer:

> Mrs. Ruffin G. Pleasant, head of the Louisiana New Deal organizations, . . . [said] that . . . "The Senate will not have to eject Long from his seat,"

> she shrilled. "He will be attended to by others as soon as he gets rid of his bodyguard and machine guns. . . ."
>
> With many minor embellishments she told how she had gone to the office of Miss Alice Grosjean, supervisor of public accounts, to get some information concerning state employees. . . .
>
> "Then came Senator Long with that cakewalk of his. You all know the way he walks. . . . In a few minutes he rushed out of [Grosjean's office] and said 'Seize that woman. . . . I can't afford to have a drunken, cursing woman in the statehouse.' . . . [and challenged her to repeat her denials of drunkenness to his face].
>
> The witness' voice shook with earnestness. The sides of the audience shook with suppressed laughter. "I turned to him and put my finger just as close to his red clubbed nose as I could and shook it just as hard as I could."
>
> The audience let its laughter go then, much to the witness' indignation. But the merriment subsided when Senator Long interrupted, wanting to know whether it was true that Mrs. Pleasant had once attempted to have her husband arrested in Shreveport.
>
> White-faced with anger, the woman leaped toward the hulking senator. "That is the most contemptible falsehood that ever passed the lips of any man . . . and no one but an unspeakable coward like you would make a false statement like that."
>
> From anger the witness went off into hysteric tears when Long asked her whether she had not once been treated for a mental disorder. Barely able to speak, she gasped out that the insinuation was a lie. . . . [S]he had once been treated for a "general rundown condition" at Asheville, N.C. and that physicians there had pronounced her mental condition excellent.
>
> "You'll hear from this," she sobbed in Long's direction. "I expected the worse kind of treatment from him, but I couldn't believe he would fall so low."
>
> She had continually to be interrupted by Chairman Walter F. George and other committee members, who sought to confine her testimony to the facts.[81]

The Senate took no action. The charges were scurrilous and remain under seal.[82] For a while, the Women's Committee got maudlin press for their efforts to raise funds for their work by having a "sacrifice week" and selling personal family heirlooms,[83] but they were finished in the Senate because the Senate was finished with them.

A vote on the confirmation of D. D. Moore, Roosevelt's nominee for IRS collector, was deferred. Either the Senate lacked time to consider it or was leery of confirming a tool of John L. Sullivan.[84] Roosevelt had given the disapproved Rene Viosca an interim appointment as U.S. attorney. Roosevelt now gave Moore an interim appointment. All postmasters in Louisiana were interim appointments.

Anti-tariff Democrats backed Roosevelt's request to reduce tariffs by up to 50 percent upon negotiations with foreign countries. In opposing this, Huey displayed two cans of beef he bought in the local grocery store, both prepared in South America, notwithstanding the unlimited supply of beef in America.[85] The bill passed, however. It relieved senators of the responsibility of protecting their home state's products.[86]

Roosevelt also defeated efforts to inflate the currency, selling silver senators on a compromise that kept his discretion. Huey denounced the compromise as an all-day sucker or baby rattle.[87]

Roosevelt nominated NRA architect Rexford G. Tugwell to be assistant secretary of agriculture. His writings struck several senators as socialistic. Senator "Cotton Ed" Smith of the Agriculture Committee, perhaps upset at rumors that Roosevelt was going to purge him from the Democratic Party,[88] refused to hold hearings. Robinson moved to discharge the nomination from the committee so the Senate could vote on it. At the end of an angry argument, the Senate let Smith hold hearings, something Huey suggested.[89] In the committee hearing, Tugwell backpedaled on his prior writings, deceiving no one.

Huey voted to confirm Tugwell. A few days earlier, he had introduced a May 29, 1934, *Philadelphia Record* article criticizing Roosevelt: the administration "must go even further to the left—not in theory but in practice—unless the new pace of concentration of riches is to land us in the mire."[90] Huey said now that whenever the administration had gone "left" he had voted with it and whenever it had gone "right" he had voted against it, listing key legislative initiatives and how he voted. He hoped Tugwell's nomination signaled that the administration would go left and redistribute wealth.[91]

Trial lawyers are taught principles of primacy and recency. A jury remembers the first thing they hear and the last thing they hear. Lawyers want to open strong and close strong, each day and on the first and last day of a trial. In this session, Huey introduced his tax and pension bills in the first week. Immediately after the mayoral election defeat, he introduced SOW in February.

Now he closed the session with a dramatic fight. A bankruptcy bill for farmers was proposed in the Senate by Lynn Frazier, a progressive Republican from North Dakota, and by William Lemke, a North Dakota congressman, in the House.[92] Before Huey had returned to Louisiana to rescue Ellender, he gave a two-day speech for it, getting support from Senators Wheeler, Frazier, Thomas, and Smith. The Bible was the original source of law, and he quoted passages requiring the cancelation of debts every seven years and outlawing usury. The bill failed.[93]

It failed for reasons that are unclear. While Borah told constituents that Roosevelt and congressional leaders opposed it,[94] the Judiciary Committee had vetted its constitutionality[95] and the House passed the bill. Conservatives feared devastating effects on the financial community, but even Robinson rebutted some of their arguments.[96]

The Senate was scheduled to adjourn on Saturday, June 16, at midnight. Huey and his allies planned to move the Senate to concur with the House bill when it arrived, but the House leaders failed to transmit it. At 7 p.m., Huey demanded action, saying he had been waiting for hours, not daring to leave the floor to eat. He threatened a filibuster if the bill never arrived and enlisted Norris's support.[97]

When the bill arrived, Senator Bankhead argued that, because the bill applied to future mortgages, it would cause credit to dry up for farmers, so Huey compromised with a handshake agreement to have the House-Senate Conference Committee amend the bill to apply only to existing mortgages. The bill was then agreed to, referred to the Conference Committee, and Huey (not Frazier) was appointed to it.[98] Robinson moved to extend the Senate session until Monday, June 18.[99] During the first recess, Huey stood up the two House members and one senator in a hallway, a majority of the conference committee, and agreed to recommend the House bill with the Bankhead amendment.[100]

On Monday, June 18, however, the conference report was lost in the House. Huey again threatened filibuster. Robinson located the report ("Glory be!" said Huey), but Huey threatened to keep talking, not blaming Robinson ("the trouble is [not] between the Senator from Arkansas and myself. . . . I refuse to have it appear in that way"),[101] but rather the House leadership. Robinson promised to allow a vote on the bill when it arrived. Huey dropped his filibuster.[102] The measure passed.

The *Times* said, "Nobody would have bet a nickel on the chances of the . . . bill as late as six o'clock Saturday afternoon," but Huey's "endurance, gall and indifference to being considered a nuisance" put it through.[103] Lemke told the House that he now had "confidence" because the country was headed toward the "grandeur of this Nation, where every man is a King."[104]

Huey recovered from the debacles of 1933 and early 1934 because of: (1) a trial lawyer's skill and resiliency, combined with corrupt and incompetent opponents; (2) an existential fatalism strengthened by the ordeal of impeachment; (3) his capacity for work, reinforced by his decision to go on the wagon; and (4) his truce with Joe Robinson.

Every trial lawyer has experienced the rollercoaster of a trial: one day you do well; the next day, poorly, and so on. Huey as a trial lawyer experienced the lows of the Senate session but persisted. He investigated Moore and found dirt. He reduced Mrs. Pleasant to a discredited, gasping, and sobbing impotence.

Huey's attack on Harrison was over the top, and his denial that state patronage workers lost their jobs if they failed to make campaign contributions was a lie. But his incisive commentary about Roosevelt's betrayal of the veterans without warning in the campaign that elected him, a mistake recognized by the Senate when it overrode Roosevelt's veto, was truthful and relevant. Paradoxically, in his fights with opponents he could be wild and mistaken, but on policy, he was honest.

Huey's existential fatalism was manifest as he described his career:

> I have had the people throw roses in my path, and I have had them throw brickbats in my window. [*Laughter.*] . . .
>
> I have had them vote to impeach me one month and banquet me the next month, then vote to impeach me the next month and then give me $100,000,000 to spend the next month. I know the vicissitudes of public and private life.[105]

Huey's capacity for work was evidenced by his extensive participation in the Senate in 1934, and his trial work involving Moore. Harrison acknowledged this in a revealing exchange:

> Mr. Harrison [after he discussed the Ansell lawsuit against Huey]. I think if people should sue the senator anywhere they would have a pretty hard time getting anything out of him, because they simply could not beat him. I say that by way of paying a tribute to the Senator. Anyone who has to suffer as the Finance Committee has suffered

> every morning now from 10 to 12, if he had a cause of action against the Senator, would never enter it, knowing what he would have to go through.

Mr. Long. Well, that is not so bad. Go ahead.[106]

Professor Heilman noted that Huey's biography has elements of melodrama: Huey as the hero who battles against evil enemies; as a melodramatic villain; as a melodramatic figure who is both just and unjust. "In melodrama the chief figure may be defeated because he is actually evil or because he is the victim of evil men; or he may triumph." A more complex possible outcome is compromise. Compromise "eventuates when the intensest emotions possible in melodrama do not finally undercut a sensible worldliness."[107]

The Robinson-Huey truce reflected a sensible worldliness after Huey's attack on Robinson in 1932 and Robinson's Overton investigation counterattack. Huey was a pariah to Roosevelt, had disgraced himself at Sands Point, and was apparently politically sinking in his own state. Nevertheless, the idea that he lacked influence in the Senate or that senators refused to collaborate with him is false.

In opposition to Roosevelt, the Senate refused to confirm Roosevelt's appointments and denied the petition to remove Huey or unseat Overton. Huey helped to defeat the St. Lawrence Seaway Treaty despite Roosevelt's support of it, restore the veterans' benefits over Roosevelt's veto, and pass the Frazier-Lemke bill. While the hostility between Huey and Tydings, Clark, and Harrison was evident, mainly Huey was a progressive and most senators were not. No progressive could pass legislation except as Roosevelt allowed or directed. Huey's victories while Roosevelt was at the height of his power and Huey at his nadir are remarkable.

The truce with Robinson is the only explanation for Robinson's appointment of Huey to the Frazier-Lemke conference committee. Acknowledging this truce makes Huey more accessible, pragmatic, and reasonable, and less Herculean, mythic, and dangerous.

In Louisiana, there was no sensible worldliness. While he was in Washington getting the Frazier-Lemke bill passed, his lieutenants had lost control of the legislature. The Kingfish's organization couldn't function without him. As soon as the Senate session in Washington ended, Huey raced back to Louisiana. He hoped to recover his standing there, as well.

# Twenty-Four

# NO QUARTER FOR THE FRENCH QUARTER

After saving Ellender and before returning to Washington, Huey proposed additional legislation: (1) new taxes on incomes, the cotton exchange, utilities, chain stores, liquor, sulfur, and on advertising revenues of newspapers with a circulation of more than 20,000 per week; (2) the elimination of the poll tax, the automobile tax, and property taxes on the first $2,000 of a home's assessed value; (3) a cost reduction of automobile licenses, which would deprive New Orleans of the $700,000 state subsidy it had received; (4) new powers for the Bureau of Criminal Identification; (5) state control, supplanting local control, over liquor licenses; and (6) the placement of the New Orleans police department under a nonpolitical state board.[1]

Rich state legislators opposed the income tax even though the top rate was only 6 percent on incomes over $50,000. Conservatives opposed the abolition of the poll tax, accusing Huey of trying to give Black people the right to vote. Huey's impeachment ally Leander Perez opposed the effort to supplant local self-government.[2]

On June 7, 1934, over one thousand people in New Orleans's Municipal Auditorium cheered two elderly veterans of the 1874 White League gun battle. Walmsley urged the people to throw off the yoke of the state administration by action such "as was taken by Orleanians on the famous September 14 [1874]." Offering free train rides and liquor, Huey's opponents staged a bigger rally on June 12, but they attracted an unruly, drunken crowd that irritated many and impressed few. While some of the participants wanted an armed coup, not speeches, a lot of speeches were made. While swinging a rope, Shreveport Mayor G. W. Hardy said the legislature had been *warned* and *notice* had been given. "If it is necessary for us to teach them fairness and justice at the end of a hempen rope I for one am ready to swing that rope!"[3]

Busy in Washington, Huey couldn't hold the legislators in line. Governor Allen caved in and withdrew several measures.

On June 21, Huey returned from Washington fresh from his victory for the Frazier-Lemke bill. Opposing appropriation reductions, Huey said, "We want all the money circulated that we can get."[4] Over the next few days one could hear the "disjoined members of [Huey's] machine click back into place, one by one." On June 26, 1934, New Orleans closed gambling houses to forestall raids by the National Guard.[5]

Blaming his legislative leaders for the rebellion, Huey replaced them, but thereafter ran from the House to the Senate, from committee meetings to the legislative floor, taking charge of the bills and shouting out commands:

> COMMITTEE CHAIRMAN: Does anyone desire information on this bill?
> HUEY: None!
> COMMITTEE CHAIRMAN: If not, the bill will be reported favorably.

Or, in a Senate committee:

> HUEY: Senator Haywood moves an unfavorable report on this bill.
> SENATOR HAYWOOD: I move an unfavorable report on the bill.
> CHAIRMAN: The bill is reported unfavorably.[6]

Legislator incompetence necessitated Huey's leadership. Members of the Appropriations Committee had argued for thirty minutes about how to divide $78,000 among three schools: $8,000 for one, $20,000 for another, and $50,000 for a third? The schools objected. Senator Dore told Huey. Huey said: "Just reduce the $78,000 to $75,000 and give each school $25,000," and this was done.[7] When legislators complained about working on Sunday, Huey said, "The Bible says if the ox gets stuck in the ditch to work Sunday to get him out." Professor White described Huey's new floor leader Isom Guillory as a "comical little Frenchman." who "pranc[ed] around the floor demanding 'De Governor wants dis bill, de Governor wants dis bill.'" When an anti-Long legislator asked Guillory if the tax on newspapers would be passed on to the people, Guillory responded: "Aren't all taxes passed on to the consumer?" Huey shouted, "Sit down, Isom!" Isom sat down.[8]

Plans to increase funding of schools by the state, expand Charity Hospital, and aid the parishes in paying their bonded indebtedness for roads were included, although some of these plans, but not the taxes, were scaled back after the session.[9] The election law bill was changed as promised, and Stanley dismissed the prosecutions against the vote counters he had charged from the 1932 election.[10] A state liquor control system was passed. Local interests protested. "Yes, we may have one big machine, but we'll bust up these little machines throughout the state," Huey said.[11]

One legislator was promised the patronage in his district to get his vote on the income tax law. To abolish the poll tax, Huey backed a legislative pardon to a bank president (brother of a legislator) who had accepted deposits after his bank was declared insolvent.[12] Another key vote was Old Regular Gilbert Fortier, later appointed curator of the Louisiana State Museum at an annual salary of $5,000.[13]

Some of the bills Huey sponsored had already been voted down or withdrawn. In resurrecting them, Huey was creative. Opponents proposed a bill to forbid state officials from taking voter-registration books when a court forbade it, but Huey's amendment denied the courts authority over the registration books. An Old Regular legislator had proposed a bill regulating New Orleans boathouses. Huey amended it to take over the New Orleans city police force.

During a controversy over newspapermen taking flash pictures, the legislature ordered photographers out of the chamber, with one of Huey's followers leaving the floor in disgust. Huey ordered him to return, but he left.[14] Huey was unable to overcome opposition to expanding the power of the Bureau of Criminal Identification.[15] The newspaper tax passed the Senate by only one vote, with opponents arguing it was punitive, spiteful legislation.[16]

Huey's majorities improved as the session continued, however. This amazed and disgusted his critics. Four reasons explained this:

(1) Huey's opponents "had shown no sign of having learned anything from [their] many defeats."

(2) They couldn't complain about Huey's electioneering tactics given that they were practitioners of the same arts.[17]

(3) Huey coupled tax increases with tax deductions that shifted the burden to those better able to pay.

(4) Huey's control over the legislature—not absolute, however—that was secured from the negotiations with Walmsley and the election in 1932.

Huey's influence in the legislature and his skill in using it to bestow benefits and punish foes were key to his political rehabilitation in Louisiana.

Federal relief administrator Harry Early had argued for months that Louisiana's contribution to relief was inadequate (Huey said his highway expenditures should be counted). Early appealed to Huey on humanitarian grounds during this session and was elated that Huey contributed toward relief. Huey stipulated that the federal government operate the program; he wanted neither his opponents nor his own crowd in charge. By October 1934, Louisiana had the lowest percentage of its population on relief.[18]

To rebut vicious critics of the poll tax abolition, Huey explained that the white primary—not the poll tax—prevented Black people from voting. Huey had Representative Lucas, a railroad engineer, dress in greasy overalls and a smoke smeared cap, holding an oil can, "the uniform of the people," plead to abolish it. It passed by a two-thirds vote.[19]

On July 4, someone lit firecrackers in the legislature. Huey jumped a foot in the air when they exploded, and then laughed and raised his arms in mock surrender.[20] On the last day of the session (July 12), anti-Long leader Rupert Peyton wore a gilt paper crown, a lavender bathrobe with simulated ermine collar, and a putty nose to resemble Huey's, strutting up and down the aisles as legislators blew horns and shot squirt guns. Peyton mounted the rostrum: "Newspapers, consider yourselves glared at. I'm here a-fightin' for the common people. I'm for the redistribution of potlikker, now controlled by J. P. Morgan and Standard Oil. I'm for the Share the Swag Society." He proposed to confer the title of "Your Majesty" on everyone in the state and to give every man a pair of green pajamas, a castle, a hotel suite, a queen, and an income of $90,000. Observing Guillory talking, Peyton roared "Sit down, Isom!" Huey was amused.[21] It is hard to imagine Hitler, Mussolini, Stalin, or Putin allowing such a farce or being amused by it themselves.

Now Huey focused on New Orleans. An election was scheduled in early September for its two congressional seats, public service commissioner, and Supreme Court justice.

On July 20, 1934, Huey had Allen warn Walmsley that something was "going to be done about the cesspool of iniquity in New Orleans."[22] On

July 30, the National Guard marched into New Orleans at midnight pursuant to a proclamation of partial martial law and occupied the Registrar of Voters Office to purge fraudulent voters. The guardsmen allowed voters to freely register, although each registrant had to be able to interpret any part of the Constitution (applied usually to keep Black people from voting). One white Rhodes Scholar was denied registration.[23] The martial law was then expanded to encompass an investigation of vice.

Williams says Huey was trying to awe his opposition with a crude display of force, given that Huey had no legitimate fear of the removal of registration books by a court or the city and the state registrar could remove fraudulent voters' names. White says Huey wanted to embarrass Walmsley by showing he was weak.[24] The *Times* said Huey lost strength in the rural areas and therefore wanted to improve his position in New Orleans.[25] Boulard noted that city police would have long memories and punish Huey's supporters after the guard departed.[26]

More likely, it was a lawyer's analysis of the realities of power and a reaction to violent threats made by his opponents. Huey kept closely guarded in his hotel.[27] A superior armed force might convince these would-be revolutionaries of the futility of a rebellion. Related is the expression that possession is nine-tenths of the law. While the state registrar had a right to supervise the registration of voters, if that right were frustrated or denied by city police, armed vigilantes, or judges sympathetic to Walmsley, as a practical matter the registrar might not get the books until after registration closed.

The city leaders were thrown into an impotent frenzy. Walmsley called Huey a political degenerate, a moral leper, a cringing coward, a gangster, and a madman comparable to Caligula, Nero, Attila, Henry the Eighth, and Louis the Eleventh.[28] Huey replied that, when Walmsley heard the news, he sent his police down to the red-light district to warn the inmates to hide.[29]

Relying on thirty lawyers led by Rightor, Walmsley got a city court to order the National Guard troops removed because the reasons cited for the proclamation were inadequate under state law. The sheriff couldn't find General Fleming to serve the injunction papers, but easily found Huey.[30] The city hadn't thought through the legalities. Huey lacked any position in state government.[31] When Huey got served, he explained that he had no power over state officials but offered to go to Baton Rouge to ask Governor Allen to disband the troops. When he got there, Huey emerged from Allen's office pretending that Allen defied him, so now he would return to New Orleans as a mere observer. Then he announced that he was going fishing.[32] The Old Regulars' futile efforts to serve Fleming entertained or outraged newspaper readers—depending on their points of view—for several days.

Walmsley swore in four hundred special deputies armed with machine guns and tear gas. The National Guard and the deputies faced off against each other, neither being stupid enough to attack, but neither knowing what, exactly, they were doing. Business and civic groups issued periodic neutral statements that business was being conducted normally, requested an end to the controversy, and proposed a compromise rejected by both sides on August 11.[33] Huey said that "there would be no compromise in this fight until one of us is knocked down and dragged out." New Orleans's board of tax assessors retaliated by refusing to recognize two replacement appointees of Governor Allen. Because the city tax commission reported to the state tax commission, Huey announced that the city commission could close because the state commission would perform its functions. Both sides refused to recognize the others' assessments.[34]

The Old Regulars also brought an emergency suit to declare the reorganization of the New Orleans Police Department unconstitutional. Judge Nat Bond, the son-in-law of the late Mayor Behrman and a former secretary to Senator Ransdell, obliged. Huey's lawyers appealed, but "the wily Kingfish" was undecided what to do next.[35] Usually portrayed as decisive, Huey actually changed his mind quite a bit on tactics, often confusing his followers, who said "the only time they can't count on him is when he says he won't do a certain thing."[36] The *Times* opined that he was too erratic to ever be a serious—or dangerous—candidate for president.[37]

On August 13, Huey called another special session of the legislature to propose what Williams calls "power laws, blunt, blatant, and unashamed."[38] Aimed at New Orleans, one law allowed the governor to call out the militia at his discretion, without the state-law limiting principle of only doing so to suppress a riot or insurrection, and deprived the courts of the power to overrule his decision. Others allowed state boards to appoint unlimited commissioners and deputies to preserve order on election days, permitted the governor to grant reprieves without any limitation, increased the size of the Bureau of Criminal Identification, and enabled the attorney general to supersede any local district attorney and stop any court from preventing it.

These laws counteracted the recent efforts to require Huey to send the National Guard home and eliminated the need to field dummy candidates to secure election officials loyal to him. They were power laws, part of the chess match that began when the prior legislative session ended. One wonders whether similar laws would have been denounced if Governor Parker had obtained them to fight the Old Regulars in 1920. Professor Sindler for one was matter-of-fact about the necessity for a sustained, ruthless attack on the Old Regulars to drive them from power.[39]

Williams wrote that contemporary newsmen were fascinated and repelled by Huey's domination of the Louisiana legislature and that later writers noted the special sessions' "malign charm." Careful planning preceded most sessions. Often the bills were drafted weeks ahead of time. Huey explained the bills at his caucuses, which included most of the legislators. Give and take occurred, but mostly he "mesmerized" his supporters with explanations that made it impossible for them to see any imperfections: "he carried you along with him," one said; another that "others had power in their organization, but he had power in himself, and he brought them all to their knees." "Power in Himself" was the title of Williams's superb chapter 26, collecting the candid discussions of the mechanics of the special sessions and the retrospective assessments of Huey by contemporaries.[40]

The caucuses were not visible to the public.[41] Modern ideas of constitutional due process are grounded on notice and the opportunity to be heard. Anti-Long members of the legislature got notice of the special sessions later than Long members and did not receive the proposed bills or explanations on a timely basis. These are weak concepts, however, because they afford no remedy. If a decision-maker is ordered to listen to a critic, he or she can still make the same decision. Minority legislators still had a right to be heard on the floor of the legislature.

Not privy to caucus discussions, the public and the press only saw Huey's domination of the legislature in session, with apparently supine legislators bowing to his will, passing his bills in record time, as if there were an emergency. All were referred to the Ways and Means Committee, and the hearings were attended only by Huey. The bills were read to the legislators as required by law, with the clerk speed talking. Even this dissatisfied Huey: "Tell him to hurry up. They don't have to hear the damn thing. All they've got to do is vote."[42]

When Huey was asked about a potential Louisiana visit by the Imperial Wizard of the Klan, he dictated a formal statement that manifested a similar ruthlessness: the Wizard was a son of a bitch, and he was not swearing but was referring to the circumstances of his birth. The *Times* said he uttered "unprintable descriptions" of the Wizard and said, if he arrived in Louisiana, he would leave with "his toes turned up."[43] The Wizard stayed away.

All twenty-seven bills were passed in record time, in what the *Times* called "eighty minutes of boisterous hilarity" in "Huey's Political Wonderland," that made him a "political dictator."[44] The most important bill, however, was a resolution that authorized a committee to investigate vice in New Orleans, like the Seabury Commission in New York that probed Tammany Hall in 1931–32.[45]

Louisiana's political war was now in the national papers almost every day. The warring themes pitted New Orleans's right to political independence versus Huey's allegations about the city's vice, fraudulent voting, and bankruptcy.[46] Walmsley included social commentary in one gibe: "Huey never goes anywhere in New Orleans, you know. Nobody invites him anywhere. He knows he doesn't belong and he can't take it. Decent people don't want a dinner guest who has to take bodyguards along to protect him from the wrath of the public." Walmsley came in for his share of abuse. New Orleans had taxed awnings, unfair to the "little fellow," said Huey's *American Progress,* and the ordinance also called for a tax on "sniper" signs. Walmsley confessed that he didn't know what sniper signs were because he had copied a Baltimore ordinance without understanding it. The *Progress* suggested he tax other things about which he was totally ignorant:

> Ring-tailed golliwogs
> Bloogers
> Stregomakinaces
> Gurgolines (including naxdus also)
> Mallibasiwitches
> Loggerwoggeranians.[47]

The city claimed that 85 percent of the voters removed as fraudulent were reinstated. Reporter Daniell described Huey's followers as sullen sycophants and the laws passed during the special session as dictatorial.[48] Accompanying several of these articles were reports of violence by Huey's partisans or bodyguards, explicit comparisons to Hitler and his secret police, and suggestions that militant opponents would resort to violence.[49]

The grand jury investigations into income taxes of Huey's political leaders were also in the news. Mike Moss of the failed Union Indemnity Company returned from Arizona to testify. Gone was his swagger.[50] State Senator Jules Fisher's sister-in-law testified: they had "questions a plenty."[51] A deputy sheriff of St. Charles Parish was indicted for perjury.[52]

Huey roared into New Orleans with a caravan of cars, stopping at his home (a photographer who took a picture of his home was detained and then released, without his film), and then rushing to the Roosevelt Hotel. Its lobby became a "maelstrom of rushing bellboys, politicians, and newspaper reporters and cameramen."[53] House leader Allen Ellender had said that the investigation of New Orleans would begin after the election to be deemed nonpolitical,[54] blind to Huey's entirely political purpose. The probe would begin on September 1 and be broadcast over the radio at state expense.[55] The election was scheduled for September 11.

The hearings were secluded on the eighteenth floor of the Canal Bank Building. Fifty guardsmen prowled the corridor to enforce privacy. Huey was tense, yelling at two electrical technicians that they "should have had that damn thing ready. You had all night." Some witnesses used pseudonyms to prevent reprisals. They arrived by back entrances, were given immunity and therefore not permitted counsel, and were faced by Huey—counsel to the committee—and the committee members. The radio broadcasting the proceedings would introduce the listeners to the investigation, the chairman would bring the session to order, and then turn the hearing over to its counsel, Huey, who promised "Turkey-Head" Walmsley sensational disclosures of vice.

Witnesses gave names, addresses, and activities of gambling dens, whorehouses, and handbook shops.[56] The police extorted payoffs. A rooming house owner in the French Quarter said he slipped protection money earned by prostitutes to the police in unmarked envelopes. A madam said that, if she failed to give the police money, they would stand in front of her establishment, making it impossible for her girls to make money. Another witness assessed prostitutes five dollars each in case of arrest; the money would pay off a receptive attaché of the city's night court, who would then convince the judge that the girls should be released.[57] Illegal lotteries above Canal Street were whites-only and operated out of unmarked stores; below Canal Street, Black lotteries operated with street vendors. The betting slips littered the streets, even while the police said the gambling shops could not be located. Some claimed that police chief George Reyer and Mayor Walmsley received payoff money. The witnesses were coached (Huey once slipped and said he was going to cut his testimony short).

Suspense was supplied by speculation over whether Mayor Walmsley would be called.[58] He wasn't, but the testimony brought "graft close to the Mayor," and that related to prostitutes was "too raw" to read to the public.[59] Reyer and chief of detectives John Grosch were called. Huey showed them records indicating payments made to "R" and "G." Did those initials stand for Reyer and Grosch? Others showed they had acquired more assets and properties than they could have afforded on their salaries. Huey at one point said, "Take off your coat, Chief. You look like it's getting hot in here." Decades later, Reyer denied that Huey had proved anything but conceded that he was doing all right with the people.[60] The probe intimidated many who worked in the exposed establishments, an estimated seven thousand persons. Not everyone, however. Shots were fired into Huey's house.[61]

Walmsley had city detectives stake out the Canal Bank Building. They charged some of the witnesses with petty crimes in retaliation. An early witness was arrested for drunkenness and stated that she didn't remember testifying to the committee. The committee recalled one of the harassed witnesses for a second round of testimony about graft and his post-testimony "frame-up" by city police. He was even more damning in the second round. The Old Regulars had better luck with U.S. district judge Wayne Borah. He enjoined the removal of more voter names by the registrar, on a petition alleging that relief was impossible from the state court system under the recent legislation.[62]

Generally, however, Walmsley was reduced to issuing nightly denials of the charges, disclaiming knowledge of payoffs, prostitution, and gambling. A visiting congressman, Martin Dies from Texas, said, "What's going on in there seems to me to be the best politics in the world." The streets were empty except where people were clustered around radios listening to the proceedings, including at every downtown bar, café, and shoeshine stand.[63]

The Old Regulars then imported Colonel Guy "Machine Gun" Molony, a mercenary, and a good one. Molony had fought with the British in the Boer War and had the bullet and bayonet wounds to prove it, with the U.S. Cavalry in the Philippines, and as a tail gunner in the 1910 revolution in Nicaragua. In Honduras, he led a military insurgency on behalf of Samuel Zemurray and deposed its president. The new president granted tax concessions, railway lines, and slave-wage labor to Zemurray's United Fruit Company. Appointed by reform mayor McShane, oddly enough, Molony was police chief of New Orleans between 1920 and 1925. Claims that he was corrupt and a secret member of the Klan caused his resignation. Molony's daughter had no doubt that he would have engineered a coup against Huey if asked.[64] Molony arrived in New Orleans on September 6, the eve of the election. Meeting with Mayor Walmsley, Molony emerged saying his services were at the disposal of the city. Walmsley said the city was under attack by a madman.

Huey's investigative committee issued a subpoena for Molony to testify but, when it was served, Molony contemptuously tore it up. On the advice of his lawyer, he later voluntarily appeared. Huey peppered him with questions. Molony was evasive and unresponsive but cool. Huey accused him of having visited the city the preceding January at election time to organize a militia. Molony, unfazed, said he had men at the St. Charles Hotel, but they were not armed. Molony denied doing the same thing now, but said he'd be "glad to try it." This threw Huey into turmoil: "Try and do it! Try and do it!" Unperturbed, Molony replied, "Just watch us." Molony left the Canal Bank Building confident, strutting, smirking.[65]

Molony's return gave Huey the justification on September 7 to move another two thousand guardsmen into New Orleans in the middle of the night.[66] Enraged that Huey would push things this far, a father of one of the guardsmen publicly threatened to kill Huey if any harm came to his son.[67]

The tension between the rival armed forces increased the risk of ugly incidents or deaths. The newsreels showed the guard and the city police facing off and the competing statements from Huey and Walmsley.[68] Business leaders were horrified at the bad press. They pressured Huey and Walmsley to knock it off.

Fleming called Reyer and they agreed that neither the police nor the guard appear near the polling places. An arbitration committee was suggested and both sides approved. It was empowered to appoint three hundred special deputies to bear arms and handle polling place difficulties. The headquarters was an auditorium with fifty telephones to stay connected with the deputies who were scattered throughout the city.[69]

Meanwhile, Huey's voice and health gave out. The committee took Saturday off to rest.[70] Recovering on election day, Huey set up a radio studio in his Roosevelt Hotel suite, and he spoke several times a day: "Ladies and Gentlemen, it's Huey P. Long again, telling you how we're going to clean out this rotten bunch of grafters."

The Old Regulars were organized and motivated. With four days to go, they held a rally with six thousand people, with fireworks, jazz bands, a bonfire, and a speech by Walmsley. A Huey Long dummy with a placard pinned to his rear end reading "der Kaiserfish" was hung in effigy. Another placard announced that the Crayfish should get ready to crawl back in his hole. A rival rally organized by Huey had three thousand people. Molony sat at the ready in the St. Charles hotel, where Walmsley and the Old Regulars prepared for a celebration.[71]

On Election Day, Huey woke up and, while still in peach pajamas, nibbled on sandwiches and went into his adjoining room to make hourly broadcasts urging people to vote. Late in the afternoon, Huey and Rose voted and then returned to the hotel, joined by the journalist Daniell, who thought Huey looked tired.[72] Despite Daniell's harsh articles, Huey kept talking to him.

The voting was amazingly peaceful. Long lines of people waited to vote without incident. The national media must have prematurely indicated Huey's defeat. A young Lyndon Johnson wrote a love letter to his future wife, saying he was as sad to leave her as Huey Long must have been with the election returns, an unusual metaphor in a matter of love.[73]

Huey knew better and earlier than Johnson that he had won. His ticket won the hometown ward of the Old Regulars' chieftain. He won the labor wards. He won the small-craftsman wards: engineers, carpenters, tailors, millwrights. Late in the day, a Long leader called headquarters to report a theft of some votes, but Fleming told him he should forget about it; "Huey has won his election. Let 'em steal them."[74]

Daniell reported front-page news for the *Times:* "Huey P. Long appeared tonight to have won the most spectacular battle of his political career." Maloney and Fernandez (for Congress), Higgins (for the Supreme Court), and O'Connor (for the Public Service Commission, defeating Francis Williams) all won.[75] The Old Regulars' loss was humiliating: 141,000 to 100,000. The vote margin of 40,000 was the same as when Huey won the governorship in 1928 but was achieved in just two of the eight congressional districts that included the New Orleans stronghold of his opponents.

Walmsley attributed his defeat to election-day fraud. But Judge Echezebal—one of the judges in the voter-fraud complaints of 1932—threw out the complaint two months later because the evidence consisted of "fairy tales."[76] Rumors that Walmsley would resign or get impeached continued, but the troops were sent home, Walmsley denied any intent to resign, and he started his own crackdown on vice.[77]

Huey continued the vice inquiry and brought the trail of corruption to Judge Nat Bond, who had borrowed money pledging inadequate capital to secure it at a time he worked for a bank that later crashed. Huey's health again failed. At one session it was difficult to follow his reasoning or to tell the difference between competent testimony and hearsay or Huey's opinions.[78]

The hand of fate spoiled Huey's celebration. A Supreme Court seat for southwestern Louisiana was being decided during the same primary. Huey endorsed Winston Overton, the incumbent, and brother of Senator John Overton. Opposing him was lawyer Thomas F. Porter, whom Huey detested, once saying that, if he owned a whorehouse, he wouldn't let Porter pimp for him.[79]

Two days before the primary, Winston Overton died. Under the election law, because Overton died within seven days of the election, his opponent was the automatic nominee.[80] The chairman of the Democratic Executive Committee of the district therefore announced a meeting for September 15 to certify Porter. Huey's leaders fumed. Before the election, Huey wondered whether a dead man could be elected, but this was illegal and impractical, even though Overton got a tribute vote of about half of Porter's total. Huey charged that Porter betrayed Overton, who died "broken-hearted." He requested Porter to "be a man" and stand for election, asking "You wouldn't rob a grave, would you." This appeal failed.[81] Huey therefore formulated a plan to thwart the hand of fate.

On September 15, Huey, Lieutenant Governor Fournet, and Attorney General Porterie barged into the Democratic committee meeting. A member moved that J. Cleveland Fruge, loyal to Huey, replace the current chairman. This carried, eleven to four. Porterie announced that certifying Porter as the nominee would be illegal, ignoring the plain language of the statute. A member then moved to hold a new primary on October 9. Porter jumped on a chair to shout that he was the lawful nominee and would fight the committee in court. Huey hadn't said anything up to then. But now he emphasized that Porter was afraid to face the people.

Porter went to court and obtained an injunction forbidding another primary and declaring himself the nominee. Fruge's committee appealed to the three Long justices on the Louisiana Supreme Court. They suspended the injunction until a hearing could be held but scheduled it for November 26, *after* the new election on October 9. Because the court was divided three to three, strictly on political grounds, the suspension order could not be overturned. Porter campaigned while protesting that he should not have to.[82]

Knowing he needed a popular candidate to oppose Porter, Huey selected Lieutenant Governor Fournet to make the race, and moved four sound trucks into the district for a whirlwind campaign. Worried about Fournet's appearance, Huey told him to buy some new clothes so at least he would "look like a judge." After witnessing Fournet speak, Huey told him that without improvement he was a "beat potato" and to "stay up all night practicing."[83] Fournet improved. Huey's brother Earl spoke for Fournet in many of the small towns, whereas his brother Julius spoke for Porter. In one town they almost had a fistfight.[84]

Elected by four thousand votes, carrying ten of the eleven parishes in the southwest Louisiana district, Fournet defeated Porter.[85] The deposed chairman of the committee said he would no longer support Huey's ticket, but this was based on politics, not morality. He came from a parish that, after voting Huey's way for six years, had turned against him. Fruge, however, admitted that Huey was "going pretty far."[86] Winston Overton's death also spoiled Huey's plans to take his sound trucks to the west and northwest to recruit SOW members.[87] That would have to wait.

It is easier to get away with going too far when the ends appear to be justifiable or popular. Denying Porter the nomination preserved the right of the people to choose their Supreme Court justice. Huey went pretty far thereafter in the service of purely popular objectives.

In a story that is revealing but may be apocryphal, the second game of the LSU football season was scheduled against Southern Methodist for October 6. LSU's athletic director had promised Southern Methodist a minimum of $10,000 for its share of ticket sales to induce the school to travel to LSU for the game. Huey had also predicted that LSU would set a new attendance record at the recently enlarged LSU stadium. The advance ticket sales were off, however, and, worried about his ten-thousand-dollar guarantee, the director notified Huey. An investigation revealed why. The Ringling Brothers and Barnum & Bailey Circus was scheduled for Baton Rouge the same day.

Huey asked some law students at LSU to research the tick eradication law passed in 1930. Then he telephoned either the owner of the circus, John Ringling North, or its advance agent, to politely ask if the circus could change its scheduled date in Baton Rouge. Upon receiving a haughty refusal, Huey politely reviewed the tick eradication law with them: an animal crossing state lines into Louisiana would have to be dipped to eradicate ticks and then quarantined for three weeks. "Did you ever dip a tiger? How about an elephant?" The circus decided to visit Baton Rouge on October 8.[88]

Although LSU opened the season with two ties (Rice on September 29 and Southern Methodist on October 6), it began a winning streak thereafter. After electing Fournet to the Supreme Court, Huey resumed his role as the team's biggest fan.

Scheduled to play Vanderbilt in Nashville, Tennessee, on October 27, Huey decided to attend the game. Vanderbilt played LSU in Baton Rouge the previous season. Huey had promised it a good turnout this year. Russ Cohen had become an assistant coach there after Huey fired him. Then the ghosts of the failed trip to West Point in 1931 convinced Huey to enlarge his plans, first to take the band, then to take the cadet corps, and finally to take the entire student body.[89]

Special trains could take everyone. LSU officials discouraged him because of the expense of railroad tickets. The railroad quoted a price of nineteen dollars per student. Huey protested that six dollars was a fair rate. Calling the president of the railroad in Chicago, he again asked for a cheap rate and mentioned that the railroad's bridges in Louisiana were then assessed at less than their value, that the Louisiana Tax Commission might decide to assess them at their true value, and that a Tax Commission meeting was already scheduled to review the matter. A Tax Commission member protested that bridges had never been assessed. Huey replied, "We're going to assess 'em now and everything they own." The railroad agreed to his requested rate.

Huey rushed out to the university to announce his plans, directed the cancelation of classes, and convoked a meeting at the Greek Theater to explain the trip. He laid down some rules: no drinking or rowdyism. State policemen would accompany them to ensure order. They would have to sit up one night to get there and two nights during the return trip. The cadet corps and band would be taken all expenses paid. Huey would loan the rest of them money to make the trip: six dollars for the railroad fare and one dollar to eat.

The students mobbed Huey to get their loans. He ran out of cash, made his associates empty their wallets, sent a courier to his hotel to retrieve more cash, and was followed to his hotel room by more students. Many got multiple loans under aliases; few repaid them. Between four and five thousand students made the trip.[90]

The Tennessee attorney general denied Huey's request to have his policemen carry guns to Tennessee. Its game warden came to the rescue and displayed some humor. He issued Tennessee game warden licenses and special purple and gold badges to let them carry sidearms, so they could guard whatever "wildlife you may see fit."[91] Huey secured permission to lead a parade of LSU's band to a park, to conduct a concert.

Having agreed to Huey's rate demands, the railroad made the best of it. They painted the railroad cars with bright colors and signs that said, "Hurrah for Huey." Huey rode in a car attached to the cadet section and had "more fun than any of the students." He called for a personal orchestra of specially picked members of the LSU band and added a banjo and fiddle players.[92] Crowds of people waited just to see the trains, many standing near the tracks until midnight.

In Nashville, at the beginning of the week the sports pages reported on the upcoming game, a contest between two unbeaten teams, with LSU favored. Then they described the cheap railroad rate and how Huey negotiated it, saying he could do more in Louisiana than Hitler could in Germany. On Wednesday they disclosed the student loans, the denied gun permits, and then the solution and wit of the game warden. At first, they expected that Huey would bring fifteen hundred to the game, then three thousand, then five thousand, and then seven thousand. Game attendance was now expected to break records. By Friday, Huey's plan had caught on like "wildfire" in Louisiana, the "greatest peacetime excursion in the history of America." By game day, Huey's invasion of Nashville was front-page news.[93]

A crowd of eighty thousand people cheered Huey during the parade. The *Tennessean* said Tennessee wanted to see Senator Long with his "hobby," LSU. The idea of five trainloads of students attending a game had "captured the imagination of this section." Huey was "ecstatic, experiencing an almost mystic sense of unity with the crowd."[94] A Nashville paper headlined: "Nashville Surrenders to Huey Long."

After the concert, he led the band to the stadium. The *Tennessean* put his picture on the front page and wrote that he was "full of the stuff it takes to draw crowds. People hung on his every word. People shook hands, people grabbed him by the coat, people did everything but tear his clothes off." The gathered crowd shouted "Heil, Kingfish! Viva, Long! Some guy, Huey!"[95] He drew the biggest crowd since President McKinley's visit in 1903. It was easy to get an interview because Huey "dearly loves to talk" and "his principal topic—naturally—is himself." Huey's wife and son sat behind the bench. He passed notes and smiled or nodded to Rose periodically. At halftime, Huey presented floral wreaths to Vanderbilt coaches McGugin and Cohen and thanked the crowd from a sound truck he had sent up the day before.[96] UCLA's film library has clips from the game, the parade, and some of Huey's remarks. The parade clips show a very tall drum major with a huge shako pumping a baton and marching in a snakelike pattern in front of the band. Later clips show

Huey and his son, Russell, then fifteen, sitting in the stands. Huey and Castro Carazo wrote a song the following year, dedicated to Vanderbilt coeds. The Tigers won twenty-nine to nothing.[97]

On the return trip they stopped in Vicksburg, Mississippi. In the middle of another parade, two mules pulling an ice wagon reared and the wagon suddenly stopped, dumping a ten-pound block of ice that skidded between Huey's feet. "He grabbed it up and, much like a halfback going around end, pitched the ice back in the wagon as the crowd howled with glee."[98]

Huey petulantly called off a planned excursion to Knoxville to see LSU play Tennessee because a Knoxville newspaper criticized his plans as ballyhoo,[99] but he accompanied the team to Mississippi, where LSU played Ole Miss. Huey's band and cadets "burst in on Jackson," "astonished the populace," and "awed the politicians." Mississippi governor Mike Conner joined the parade.[100] Huey led the Mississippi crowd and the bands of LSU and Ole Miss in singing songs at the game. Senators Harrison and Bilbo attended the game but not the parade or concert. LSU won.[101] There was talk of a Rose Bowl bid.

On November 6, 1934, Louisiana voters overwhelmingly approved the constitutional amendments necessitated by the special session. Huey was most proud of the income tax law, which shifted the burden of taxation off the average family. He had worked hard for the poll tax elimination, too.

As the results came in, Huey "slapped his followers on the back and shouted: 'There's never been anything like this in the history of the world. Have you ever seen a slaughter like this?'"[102] Maybe Louisiana should secede from the United States to defeat the Depression. Huey would create a "real Utopia" away from the "damn bureaucrats, hobocrats, autocrats and all those other 'crats" in Washington. If left alone, Louisiana's population would increase from two million to forty-five million in "five or six years," he predicted. He challenged the other top-ranked football teams (Minnesota and Alabama) to play LSU in the same week. "[H]is enthusiasm mounting," he suggested LSU would play them both the same day. Finally, "his faith . . . reached an all-time high," and he exclaimed that LSU would play them "both at the same time—and if they're still afraid we'll let 'em pick any eleven men they want out of our squad and we'll beat 'em with what's left."[103]

# Twenty-Five

# STRANGE, RUTHLESS, AND CYNICAL THINGS

Huey's manic exuberance in November obscured real, continuing threats. Right before the Vanderbilt game, the IRS indicted Abe Shushan for taking $500,000 in kickbacks without reporting them as income. A close ally of Huey, known as a collector, Shushan was head of the patronage-heavy Dock Board. After the indictment, Huey had grabbed him by the lapels of his suit coat and shouted, "Goddamn you, I've got the notion to put you in jail myself." Shushan swore on the soul of his dead grandmother that the charges were false.[1]

After Huey got the IRS called off of him at the time of Roosevelt's inauguration, his opponents kept asking for action. In August 1933, Carter Glass asked Elmer Irey about it and W. D. Robinson pressured IRS commissioner Helvering and Roosevelt advisor Louis Howe. A meeting between John M. Parker and Roosevelt took place on September 7. Helvering declined to say that Huey was guilty of any crime and refused to reopen the investigation without an order from Roosevelt.

Three days after Morgenthau was confirmed as treasury secretary, he ordered Irey to reopen the investigation. Irey's undercover operatives moved into the Roosevelt Hotel to get close to Seymour Weiss; forensic accountants and bookkeepers traced cash and checks. Anti-Long politicians and others gave the IRS tips.[2]

IRS agents interviewed Huey in November 1934. Huey's answers were evasive and lengthy, like a filibuster. Boiled down, the evidence was that Huey deposited currency in bank accounts in amounts more than or separate from what he reported as income, such as in the following years:

| Year | Reported income | Cash deposits |
|---|---|---|
| 1931 | $9,100 | $21,336 |
| 1932 | $18,000 | $28,000 |
| 1933 | $16,000 | $15,000 |

Huey explained that he spent money for campaigns, had borrowed money from Seymour Weiss, Bob Maestri, or Jimmy Noe, and had mortgaged both his Shreveport and New Orleans homes. In discussing 1929 figures, Huey bored in on the agents:

*You don't believe it now that there was any income in 1929. You are convinced now.*

Q: We think there is.

A: *No you don't. I can look at you. I have examined too many men on their voir dire [jury selection in trials]. You know there was more money spent in 1929 on political campaigns than this indicates. . . .*

Q: . . . but if you consider them all, it will mount up.

A: *No it does not.*

Q: Not this particular year, but take other years.

The stenographer admitted that she was "not getting half of what [Huey] said" because "he talks too fast."[3]

Given these facts, Irey's report in his memoir and a separate statement by treasury agent Frank Wilson that Dan Moody agreed to indict Huey on September 7, 1935, must be critically evaluated. Irey was an adroit and shady bureaucrat that Senator Barkley had accused of trying to discredit Helvering before Helvering's nomination as his boss. Irey's asserted reason for the imminent indictment was a secret dividend Huey received from the Win or Lose Company, an oil company Huey and Jimmy Noe set up, paid in 1935.[4] Huey hadn't submitted his tax returns for 1934 yet. They were due on September 15, 1935.[5] No payment received in 1935 would have to be reported until 1936. Professor Field searched Morganthau's papers and diary and found no hint that anyone contemplated an indictment against Huey in 1935.[6]

If, as Irey stated, he had enough evidence to indict Huey in September 1935, it had to be based on Huey's tax returns of 1933 or earlier. The November 1934 statement given by Huey must have given them pause. Justice Department lawyer Robert Jackson, later Nuremberg prosecutor and Supreme Court justice, wrote to the attorney general that "unexplained balances or increases in net worth plus living expenses for which the inference is to be drawn that income was received in excess of that reported" is "a most unsatisfactory basis for proof."[7] Prosecutor Rene Viosca said there was no income tax case against Huey because the kickbacks stopped at his lieutenants.[8] If Irey's indictment was a hallucination, nevertheless the threat of one—at a time most opportune for Roosevelt—was real.

Roosevelt also had the FBI monitor Huey. In August and September 1934, an FBI field agent sent daily reports for a month to Roosevelt's secretary, Marvin McIntyre. The agent didn't report much that was useful, however: a fight among legislators, an assault on a photographer, and the control over the election process that Huey obtained.[9]

Roosevelt's patronage ban was tightened. In August 1934, at the Democratic Central Committee's office, the man in charge shouted to the crowd of office seekers that a recommendation was required from any Democratic senator or congressman, except Huey Long.[10] Several Louisiana congressmen broke with Huey so that they could get patronage. In District Three, Congressman Numa Montet was "weaned" away from Huey by means of federal patronage yet had been reelected in 1934 without opposition. Montet's son said that, in a confrontation in the library of LSU, Montet chased Huey around a table.[11]

District Four's congressman John Sandlin had been allied with Huey in 1932 but opposed him now. As a result, he helped coordinate all federal patronage in the state. Longtime opponent Riley Joe Wilson was congressman from the Fifth District (including Shreveport). In the Sixth District, the hostile J. Y. Sanders Jr. had replaced the neutral Bolivar Kemp. From the Eighth District, J. Cleveland Dear had replaced John Overton in 1932. In 1934, J. W. Ethridge, a state legislator who supported Huey, opposed Dear. Dear won 13,524 to 8,475 and backed Roosevelt.[12]

The Roosevelt administration distributed public works money on a political basis.[13] In New Mexico in 1934, Roosevelt's relief personnel told relief recipients that they had to vote for Dennis Chavez, not Bronson Cutting, for senator.[14] New Orleans got extra relief money at the time of its mayoral election to help reelect Walmsley.[15]

The defection of Montet and the new hostility of Sandlin, the replacement of Overton by Dear and his defeat of Ethridge, and the replacement of Kemp with J. Y. Sanders Jr., all of whom now openly backed Roosevelt and opposed Huey, evidenced the popularity and power of Roosevelt and the decline of Huey's prestige and influence in 1933–34, which was not rectified by his spectacular victory over the Old Regulars.

It is doubtful that Huey had a developed plan to defend himself from the Roosevelt threats in November 1934. It evolved. November 1934 to September 1935 is the time, however, that caused Sindler to say that Huey swallowed the Pelican State whole, Boulard to write that Huey descended into the stuff of dictatorship,[16] and Williams to conclude he did "strange, ruthless, and cynical things," unjustified because his adversaries were enfeebled. The opposition of five out of eight congressmen was acknowledged only briefly by Williams.[17] He lacked the benefit of Field's thesis showing that seventy-two thousand federal workers in addition to the FBI and IRS tax indictments, were marshaled against Huey.[18]

In the events that follow, one can see Huey the idealist, Huey the artist in the manufacture and use of power, Huey the comedian or showman, and Huey the tyrant. The strange, ruthless, and cynical things included Huey's request of one friend to take his list of the hundred richest men in Louisiana and ask each one how far he would go for Huey if he granted some wish he had. The friend receiving the "stark, pragmatic request" refused to do it. Tax assessment threats were used by the Old Regulars to coerce support for their organization or to reward friends, and Huey was said to have used this same weapon.[19] Through the state bank examiner and the Bureau of Criminal Identification, Huey was able to investigate his opponents in detail and pressure those with criminal ties or problematic bank loans.

The political machine Huey built included professional politicians and officeholders, vendors to the state, personal associates, business and labor leaders, church leaders, and policy wonks that he would call on or not as the occasions dictated. Local leaders administered parish and municipal government functions and distributed Huey's circulars. Informants wrote to Huey, so he often knew things that his local leaders didn't. They could get ambushed by telephone calls from him if they were making mistakes or defying him. At other times, Huey encouraged them to solve their own problems. Huey attracted political technicians who respected only his success and believed it would continue.

The money was handled by Seymour Weiss, who kept a safe filled with campaign contributions in a vault at the Roosevelt Hotel. It also contained records and affidavits Huey had regarding his enemies or followers that he might need if they defected. Various persons collected the "deducts," the assessments levied against patronage workers, including doctors, and state contractors, based on the value of their contracts with the state.

One of his local leaders believed that Huey made a deal with his opponents behind his back so that they kept winning the local offices while Huey's allies won the legislative seats.[20] Huey tried to show only a small increase in votes over the prior election so his victories would not get too large. A smaller victory margin would let his opponents say he was slipping.

These ideas manifested, thought Williams, an objectivity that was unique.[21] It extended to covering up misconduct by opponents. Two who embezzled had their shortages covered from Huey's campaign funds. They were removed from their positions but given other jobs, purchasing their future loyalty.[22]

Stuffing ballot boxes took place in the St. Bernard and Plaquemines parishes and cemented the power of Sheriff Meraux and Leander Perez. Perez was a racist, greedy, and authoritarian politician,[23] subordinated to Huey while Huey lived. Meraux was tied in with gambling interests. In New Orleans, the Old Regulars stole votes until the clean election of September 1934. Huey benefited from the crooked votes when he was allied with them but suffered from them when they opposed him in 1928 and January 1934. It is difficult to know whether votes were stolen in other parishes. Anti-Long leaders such as Cecil Morgan, J. Y. Sanders Jr., Cleveland Dear, John Sandlin, Mason Spencer, and others defeated Huey's determined efforts to beat them.

The approximately twenty-five thousand patronage jobs Huey controlled were worth, according to conventional wisdom, five votes each. In the Depression, with jobs scarce, they were even more valuable than they are today. Contractors of the state employed additional people who had the incentive to vote for Huey's ticket. This would give Huey a big lead at the start of any campaign.[24] There were fewer state jobs than the seventy-two thousand people on relief or working in federal government programs, however. This Huey decided to counteract.

Huey always called a special legislative session after an electoral success, while his appeal was fresh in the minds of the legislators. When Huey called one to start on November 12, he proposed forty-four bills. There were no major tax increases, indicating either that state finances were now in good shape or that he wanted to minimize opposition.[25] Two bills had voter appeal: the Public Service Commission would regulate all utilities, preempting municipal regulation, the promise being that it could lower utility costs in New Orleans. A mini–Frazier-Lemke bill, a moratorium on debt payments until 1936, increased Huey's appeal to farmers.[26]

Many more bills were designed to increase his patronage and power: creating a civil service commission (the governor, lieutenant governor, secretary of state, and four other officials) that could discharge unelected local officials, such as police chiefs and fire chiefs, for incompetence, selecting a successor from a list provided by the municipality; authorizing the governor to appoint replacement municipal officials in the event of their death or other vacancy until the next regularly scheduled election; adding state appointees to a variety of New Orleans boards and commissions; creating a new bar association set up by congressional district election (popular vote) to regulate the conduct of lawyers and admit them to practice; making Gaston Porterie, expelled from the Louisiana Bar Association, the new association's president; changing the dates of state primaries, so that Huey's reelection campaign would take place in January 1936 and allow him to participate unencumbered in other state and national elections later in the year; and repealing a law passed at a prior session that required disclosure of sources of campaign contributions.

The House passed the bills in one hour and forty-two minutes; the Senate only took one hour and twenty-one minutes. The two chambers deliberated for a total of only twelve hours.[27] Huey's majorities were secure, so he explained the bills in cynical good humor, except when asked if any municipal police chiefs were going to be removed. Huey expected charges to remove the chief of the Alexandria police because he had permitted a riot to occur when a U.S. senator was speaking in 1933. The debt moratorium law got the most substantive press, but daily stories during the session emphasized Huey's control over the legislature and new patronage and power to supplant local government and wondered if this showed his plans for "a conquest of the nation."[28]

Huey's favorite LSU football player was star quarterback Abe Mickal. Recruited from Mississippi, he was also a good student and president of the Student Council. He wanted to become a doctor. Trying to honor him and enjoying the LSU victories and electoral successes, Huey called a special meeting of the student body and had it vote to make Mickal a state senator to fill the recent vacancy of J. Y. Sanders Jr., who went to Congress, a mocking burlesque of the citizens' meetings that Sanders had organized to hold the rump election for Congress. The students had a good laugh.

Some newspapers failed to indicate the burlesque, and Huey muddied the water by saying he expected Mickal to get sworn in and receive a legislator's pay for one day. Victimized by his reputation for getting things done, many believed that Huey intended to make Mississippi resident Mickal a state senator of Louisiana. One likened it to Caligula having his horse appointed as consul in ancient Rome. Mickal was out of town for a game and was mortified. Each time the ball carrier got tackled (Mickal, ironically, was out with an injury), he'd be asked "How do you like that, Senator!" Coach Jones interceded with Huey to end the gag, so Mickal didn't appear for the mock ceremony at the capitol. The disappointed spectators were told that Mickal was given a leave of absence.[29] Will Rogers wrote that Huey should be "trying to make something out of Senators. I don't blame that boy for not wanting to be demoted."[30]

An LSU student wrote a letter to the student newspaper, the *Reveille*, criticizing the student body meeting as a "mockery" of constitutional government. Its editor, Jesse Cutrer, was a nephew of the state senator that voted against Huey during the impeachment for corrupt reasons, Huey believed. Huey had been told that he was secretly working with J. Y. Sanders Jr. and he had declined to sign the "call" for the student body meeting, despite a personal request from Huey.[31]

Cutrer decided to print the letter; the student assigned to read the proofs showed it to journalism student David McGuire, who was working at the capitol; and McGuire showed it to Helen Gilkinson, a reporter and new member of the LSU faculty. Huey coincidentally came up, grabbed the proofs, read them, and flew into a rage, cursing Cutrer's uncle: "that lying uncle of his sold me out for forty dollars. That's my university and I'm not going to stand for any criticism from anybody out there! Get me Jim Smith on the phone!"[32] The offending letter was pulled from the newspaper without protest from the student reporters or Cutrer. Huey dispatched two policemen to stop the presses and destroy whatever copies had been printed.[33] LSU president Smith suggested that Cutrer explain his thinking to Huey. Cutrer did and thought Huey was mollified, but he wasn't.

Summoned to Smith's office the next day, Cutrer was told that Helen Gilkinson would supervise the paper. Smith and other administrators told them that, when they matured, they would realize that principles didn't matter much, that Huey was virtual dictator of the university, that Smith would not jeopardize the university by offending Huey, and that it was best to submit to those in authority.[34] The *Reveille* staff rebelled.

They stated that, if Gilkinson reviewed the proofs, they would place a boxed note on the front page exposing her. Called to meet at Smith's office, the editors said it was a matter of principle to refuse censorship. Smith said that Gilkinson's supervision would only extend to Huey. The *Reveille*'s editorial staff retaliated with a mass resignation and gave affidavits to the anti-Long press outlining the controversy and their rebellion. Forty journalism students, nearly the entire department, went on strike. Twenty-six of them petitioned Smith to reinstate the *Reveille* editors.

Smith suspended the twenty-six students who signed the petition and the *Reveille* staff members who provided the affidavits to the press for gross disrespect, stating that the petition should have been given to him rather than the newspapers. Twenty-two of the journalism students and four of the staff members who resigned expressed regret and were reinstated. Three *Reveille* staff members, including Jesse Cutrer, and four of the striking students, including David McGuire, remained defiant and were expelled.[35] Cutrer was given a dishonorable discharge from the Cadet Corps. Major Troy Middleton told him he didn't want to, but had no choice.[36] Smith was twice hung in effigy on the campus with signs calling him "Jimmy Stooge" or "Jimmy Moron." The University of Missouri gave those expelled "Freedom of the Press Scholarships" for their tuition and local anti-Long benefactors loaned them money for living expenses.[37]

Senator Elbert Thomas of Utah, who had been on the faculty of the University of Utah, said: "this marks a definite turn in Long's political career. When a man suppresses speech and the press, even if it be only a student publication, he marks himself as a non-believer in the great fundamentals of the American Constitution. Huey wants to be president. In his record until yesterday, there was nothing [that] might bar him if public sentiment should turn his way. But no man can gain the confidence of the American people who will openly suppress thought and break up printing presses."[38]

Combined with the tax on the press passed in 1934, many historians conclude, as Senator Thomas did, that Huey was opposed to the First Amendment. In arguing for the newspaper tax, Huey undermined its justification:

> The newspapers . . . don't pay any tax on anything. . . . They're the only outfit that pays no licenses.
>
> If they call a man a thief, and he comes around to get it corrected, they say that this correction is political advertising and charge him an ungodly rate to print his side of the issue in controversy. I believe in freedom of

speech, but it's got to be truthful speech, and lying newspapers should have to pay for their lying.[39]

A circular he wrote called it a tax of two cents per lie. The tax was challenged, and the Supreme Court ruled after Huey's death that it violated the First Amendment.

Those who challenged the tax thought their strongest argument was that it violated the Equal Protection Clause of the Constitution because it discriminated between newspapers with circulations of twenty thousand and those with less. In campaigning for the tax, Huey noted that one out of the twenty newspapers affected by the tax supported him, but it couldn't be helped: he taxed this newspaper along with the others because they were in the same business classification.[40]

The Supreme Court held instead that this was a tax on knowledge that would restrict the circulation of newspapers, as problematic as a prior restraint on publication, reminiscent of the odious practices of the King of England that suppressed free speech in colonial days. Because of this "history" and the tax's "present setting," the First Amendment was violated.[41]

At the time, one could be indicted and jailed for publishing a lie as well as sued for money damages. Huey was indicted and faced jail time on complaint of Governor Parker in 1921; no one has accused Governor Parker of hostility to the First Amendment, yet that more closely evidences what we would now consider to be a threat to free speech.

It was not until 1964 that the Supreme Court of the United States ruled that a lie told about a public figure would be protected under the First Amendment unless a mental state of actual malice were shown.[42] Very few defamation cases against public figures have been won afterward. The Supreme Court envisioned a robust national debate and a free marketplace of ideas.

The Louisiana press conducted a robust debate—all critical—about Huey. Had Huey been hostile to free speech, he could have prosecuted his opponents for defamation and, if he had dominated the court system as his critics claim, he could have put them in jail, all according to law.

Interestingly, Roosevelt was criticized because the NRA proposed a newspaper code that might stifle a free press. Roosevelt's appointees allowed "spraying" (radio interference) of Huey's speeches.[43] The *Tribune* editorialized against censorship, "whether it be by making government a party to libel actions, as Chicago Mayor William Hale Thompson sought unsuccessfully to do; by censorship, as was tried in the unconstitutional Minnesota gag law; by bureaucratic censorship, as the Roosevelt administration sought to do with its NRA newspaper code, or by misuse of the power of taxation, Long's weapon."[44]

In 1984, Thomas W. Cutrer wrote: "Unlike many of his contemporaries, Long never held higher education in contempt. . . . [He] had an almost reverent faith in it, and certainly cheaper and better public schooling was one of his central objectives. However impetuously he stamped out criticism of himself in the student newspaper at LSU, he also saw to it that the state employed good professors and that they enjoyed academic freedom."[45] Cutrer thought it a paradox that LSU students pursued their studies without hindrance and its professional schools flourished while faculty members were fired (Uhler), students were expelled (the *Reveille* students), and felons (Kennedy) were granted special degrees. Calling Kennedy a felon is accurate but seems ridiculous today, and Uhler's short-lived firing should be blamed on the more conservative times. But while other college administrators have asserted the right to control the expression of student opinion, by aggregating to himself the job of politician and school administrator, and by overreacting to criticism, Huey was deservedly condemned for the expulsions.

Raymond Gram Swing thought Huey was one of several forerunners of American fascism. Yet he said that Huey lacked a philosophic hostility to free speech; his actions in the *Reveille* incident were motivated by trying to prevent his opponents from using LSU against him.[46] Forrest Davis thought Huey was a dictator but wrote that civil liberties were safer in Louisiana than in Georgia, Alabama, and many other states; that he never tried to coordinate the press; and that he was always being attacked in the newspapers.[47]

In 1935, the *Times* reported that Louisiana had a board, as did many other states, to censor motion pictures.[48] But it also reported the "amazing" first issue of LSU's *Southern Review*. Its "contributors include Kenneth Burke, who has Communist leanings; Donald Davidson, one of the Tennessee agrarians; Aldous Huxley, the nihilistic pessimist; and Herbert Agar, who leads off the issue with a ringing defense of American democracy and a ringing denunciation of all forms of dictatorship." Huey "evidently permits free controversy in the new quarterly published by 'his' university."[49]

Success was often Huey's worst enemy. After his victory over Cumberland Telephone, he overreached against Standard Oil. After his success as governor in his first year, Huey broke with his allies and caused his impeachment. The opposite phenomenon was equally true: Huey learned from reverses. From criticizing LSU for teaching fancy ways of farming in 1924 he became its champion in 1930. When drinking got him in trouble in 1933, he quit in 1934. LSU official Troy Middleton believes that, if he had been in town, he would have talked Huey out of the *Reveille* expulsions in the first place.[50] Associates of Huey told Davis that Huey "was sorry he'd messed with" the *Reveille*. At a national convention of student governments, a resolution condemning Huey was tabled; an LSU student was elected president.[51] LSU student reaction to the firings was phlegmatic. They thought Huey had made LSU a good place to go, and if he weren't running it, someone else would be, but perhaps students who had or wanted state jobs censored themselves.[52]

New controversies or events often buried Huey's missteps. By the time the *Reveille* dispute made the national press, Harold Ickes, secretary of the interior, was threatening to withhold PWA money because of Huey's debt moratorium and power laws.[53] Taking his wife to Arkansas for a belated honeymoon, Huey joked that he was "King of the Ozarks" because this area was "Long territory." The mayor of Springfield, Missouri, said Huey "has a wheel loose." Theodore Bilbo pointed out that the last man proclaimed "King of the Ozarks" was bank robber "Pretty Boy" Floyd, gunned down by the FBI the previous month.[54] The honeymoon didn't last long, but he did get some fluffy press when it was reported that Huey and Rose went for a hike, met Mayor McLaughlin of Hot Springs, friendly since the Caraway campaign, and lunched on potlikker. Newsreels showed him chopping wood.

There was a new equilibrium with Rose after he quit drinking. Alice Lee Grosjean had married William Tharpe three months earlier, in August 1934. Before their Arkansas honeymoon, Rose attended the Nashville football game with Huey, and in 1934 she visited him in Washington or New York, often with her daughter, Rose. Secretary Don Devol or publicist George Maines would take them sightseeing while Huey worked. It was not a normal marriage, but Rose thereafter gave interviews that reflected favorably on them. Daughter Rose attended LSU, was well behaved, and obtained high marks from her professors.[55]

Edwin P. Embree, president of the Rosenwald Fund, visited LSU in 1934 and said, "Louisiana has no finer chance for a 'place in the sun' than through LSU." He thought great universities would improve development in regions, and LSU might become the leading university in the Mississippi River Valley. LSU was the most "promising," it had "grown very fast," and it had "good leaders and professors." If "the state will stand by, LSU has every right to come to be included in the first 12 or 15 universities in the United States [and] in the first 20 universities in the world." Embree later denied that southern universities ranked with the top twelve northern universities and denied that LSU was among the best southern universities: Virginia, Texas, North Carolina, Vanderbilt, Tulane, Duke, and Emory ranked better than LSU.[56]

Another blow to Huey's ego occurred in early December. LSU's football team had its six-game win streak snapped with a loss to Tulane. It was one of the most "thrilling games" ever played, and LSU lost because a knee injury—he was too injured to even play in the first quarter—caused Abe Mickal to miss two extra-point kicks. Tulane's final score came with only three minutes left in the game. Mickal had been carried off on a stretcher. Tulane returned a punt sixty yards for a touchdown. The punt returner's mother fainted. An LSU fan died of a heart attack.[57] After the game, Huey was philosophical; he smiled and said, "they just beat us, that's all."[58]

The following week, Tennessee unexpectedly beat LSU in Knoxville and the Tigers' hope for a lustrous season evaporated.[59] No Rose Bowl. No post-season play of any kind. Meanwhile, a group of New Orleans businessmen including James Thomson had sponsored a new post-season bowl game, the Sugar Bowl. In the first Sugar Bowl, on January 1, 1935, Tulane defeated Temple, ending their season at ten wins and one loss, tied for first place in the Southeastern Conference.[60]

When LSU played Oregon on Saturday, December 15, 1934, Huey was quiet. At halftime, with LSU losing thirteen to nothing, Huey attempted to invade the locker room—in violation of his agreement with Coach Jones—to give a pep talk, but Jones blocked him. Huey demanded to talk to the team, but Jones refused. Huey backed off but snarled "All right, but you better win this one." Jones replied that he didn't have to win this game, "win, lose or draw," he would resign. "That's a deal," Huey said.

His voice shaky and his cheeks quivering, Jones then told the team he wanted to win this game more than anything in the world. And they did, fourteen to thirteen, coming back in the second half to score two touchdowns while holding Oregon scoreless. It wasn't enough to salvage the season, however, and Jones resigned. The press reported several days' efforts to reconcile the two men. Privately, Huey said he would rehire someone he had fired but was uninterested in working with a man who quit on him. Publicly, he suggested that Jones was a fair coach, better than some but worse than others.

Because he was a "big man, too," he wanted Jones to ask him to extend his Army tenure so he could remain. Jones never asked and never commented.[61] They apparently met once afterward and parted on friendly terms.[62]

Huey searched for a new coach. He contacted Clark Shaughnessy, at the University of Chicago, and Dan McGugin, now the new athletic director of Vanderbilt. The undefeated coach of Alabama was offered $12,000 a year but declined because he had just signed a five-year contract at Alabama for $7,000 per year.[63] Many candidates demurred because of Huey's propensity to interfere. LSU hired Bernie Moore, one of Jones's assistants. Moore had coached the champion LSU track team and Jones complimented him.[64]

The 1934 controversies, beginning with the mobilization of the National Guard on July 31, provided drama to Louisianans and the rest of the nation. The events must have riveted the attention of Robert Penn Warren, in 1934 a new professor at LSU. *All the King's Men* is not a story about Huey Long, but Warren wouldn't have written it had he not witnessed Huey operate. Huey's exposure of Judge Nat Bond's outstanding mortgage after he had ruled Huey's legislation unconstitutional probably inspired or informed the Judge Irwin character. Abe Mickal's football heroics and dramatic injury in the Tulane game likely inspired or informed the Tom Stark character. Huey's honeymoon with Rose paralleled Willie Stark's moral turnabout near the end of the novel.

The following year Warren saw Huey at the seventy-fifth anniversary of LSU:

> At the high table were seats for the president of the university, ambassadors of countries . . . , various academics of stature. . . . Suddenly, . . . Huey appeared at one end. He strode along behind the table. . . . When he reached a location near the middle of the table, he leaned slightly forward, swept some cutlery and such aside, giving the impression that he was just making a place for himself, wherever the hell his place card was, and sat down, all as calmly as though coming into his own kitchen late at night for a snack.

Speaking at this banquet, Huey said he didn't have anything to do with the first seventy years of LSU, but that he would stack up his five years against the preceding seventy. Warren paraphrased another remark: "People say I steal. Well, all politicians steal. I steal. But a lot of what I stole has spilled over in no-toll bridges, hospitals—and to build this university."[65]

Huey called another special legislative session for December 16, 1934, shortly before he had to return to Washington, DC, to resume his Senate duties. Huey proposed thirty-three bills.[66] The Old Regular defiance of the preceding summer had focused his attention on local government. Each session now reflected refinements in his takeover of local government in the state, cannibalizing local jobs, giving him more patronage without adding to the total expense to the state.

Popular proposals required employers dismissing employees to pay them a pro rata (proportional) share of pension benefits regardless of their termination date and established an LSU School of Dentistry and Pharmacy at New Orleans. Only one new tax was proposed: the corporate capital tax was doubled to qualify for a federal loan to modernize Charity Hospital.

Power bills provided that the state Tax Commission control property tax assessments in New Orleans, retroactive for three years; denied sheriffs the right to hire more than five deputies; denied district attorneys the right to name more than three assistants; required all police and firemen to obtain commissions from the state; allowed a monopoly to be created by Leander Perez, the Fisher family, and others over the fur-trapping trade near Barataria Bay; doubled the number of police jurors in Baton Rouge, the new members to be appointed by the governor and thereby gain control over it; and granted the state police the power to choose all police deputies for Baton Rouge.[67] The takeover of Baton Rouge was unpopular there, but its representatives were isolated, surrounded, and overwhelmed by legislators loyal to Huey. Every bill passed.

Huey's usurpation of local government jobs is usually pointed to as evidence that he was a dictator. Municipalities at that time were by Dillon's Rule "creatures" of the state government, Dillon the name of the judge who decided the principle in 1868. It means that the legislature is the source of whatever power the municipality possesses and can expand or limit it at its discretion.[68] Only Home Rule provisions added to state constitutions overruled Dillon (Huey's opponents argued that certain Louisiana constitutional provisions authorized Home Rule). "Home Rule" was also a phrase used by southern politicians during Reconstruction. Chafing under the rule of the (northern) U.S. Army, they advocated that the states rule themselves.[69]

Whether state preemption of municipal rule was unwise even if legal depends on one's point of view. Senator Harry Byrd headed a political machine that ruled Virginia. V. O. Key wrote that a state compensation board fixed the compensation of the principal county officials and allocated the expenses of their offices; it "punished local officials who declined to accept the orders of the high command." Local judges appointed the electoral board, giving the machine "control over the machinery of elections" and the "school boards." The circuit judges were elected by the state's general assembly. And the state government "perform[ed] directly functions that many states leave to local governments." In the same paragraph, Key asserted two contradictory ideas: (1) that the machine was not dictatorial but (2) that "[l]ocal leaders . . . do not risk their necks by public endorsements of aspirants for nomination for state-wide office until the high command gives 'the word.'" Because of suffrage restrictions, this high command was elected by only 11.5 percent of those over age twenty-one.[70] Byrd's machine never drew the criticism that Huey's machine attracted despite an almost identical subordination of local government.

One can argue that local citizens should elect local officials, placing responsibility on those voters who must bear the consequences. No one denies, however, that New Orleans's police were under the control of the Old Regulars and were used to intimidate voters and corruptly protect the vice interests, and that dead people voted for the Old Regular ticket. Why wouldn't the state have the duty to clean it up? The police bill established a nonpolitical Board of Commissioners composed of persons chosen by the Young Men's Business Club, New Orleans Athletic Club, Loyola and Tulane university faculties, the Chamber of Commerce, the Property Owners Association, and the Central Trades and Labor Council.[71]

Pursuant to Home Rule or legislative enactments, a proliferation of local bodies and authorities with power to tax can make it difficult for the voters to apportion accountability. Progressives often supported making government more efficient by concentrating authority and accountability. Huey's laws made him—clearly and willingly—accountable.

New Deal programs similarly subordinated state authorities to its policies and, in Huey's case, for partisan political reasons. Because Huey recognized exactly what Roosevelt was doing to the states—he was doing the same thing to Louisiana municipalities—he was one of Roosevelt's most perceptive critics on the curtailment of state power by the New Deal.

The real purpose of the December special session, however, concealed from its start, was to settle an old score. Huey was not confident enough in his legislative majorities to openly do so, resorting to secrecy and deception. Only his most trusted leaders were briefed on his plans.

An innocuous bill called for the codification of existing licensing laws. It passed the House and Senate committees and was approved by the House. After observing Standard Oil's lobbyist, Louis LeSage, leave the Senate chamber to report that everything was okay, one of Huey's lieutenants offered a last-second amendment, a bulky one of over a hundred pages that imposed the five-cents-per-barrel tax on oil. The clerk didn't read enough of it to allow every legislator to understand what it was, there were shouted cries of "Question!" and the amendment was approved by the Senate. Then it was sped to the House and—while one legislator shouted, "Isn't that the 1929 oil tax all over again?"—after cries of "Question!" and per direction of the Long leaders, it was adopted.[72]

Just after New Year's Day, 1935, Standard Oil announced a thousand layoffs, blaming the tax.[73] Huey professed to be unconcerned, telling Standard Oil's emissary Pete Couch that he might have the state government expropriate the refinery and run it, using the money for education.[74] But Huey was ready with reasonable terms: if it would agree to accept 80 percent of its oil from Louisiana, instead of foreign, sources, he would repeal 80 percent of the tax he had imposed, impose no new ones, and would make the same offer to any other companies subject to the tax. This would increase the severance tax revenue from oil pumped from Louisiana wells, his consistent goal. Standard Oil also had to rehire the discharged employees and its lobbyist, whom it had fired. After negotiations concluded, Huey left for Washington.

The discharged employees and others, however, not knowing of the negotiations, called a mass meeting to protest.[75] The group's leader, electrical engineer Ernest Bourgeois, had worked as a strikebreaker for Standard Oil in other states. The mass meeting was held on January 6. While they were angrily discussing the oil tax and refinery layoffs, someone announced the compromise. One James MeHaffey, not an employee of Standard Oil, nevertheless gave the crowd an emotional exhortation to hang all the legislators and the governor. This stimulated his audience to form a Square Deal Association. Originally the group was going to wear blue shirts but decided on buttons. MeHaffey said he would wear a button and a six-shooter. Organized along military lines, with an auxiliary women's division, the meeting ended with a demand that the governor call a special legislative session to repeal all "dictator" laws. One member promised that, if the organization were stopped, bloodshed would follow.[76]

In manufacturing power—more patronage and control over local government—Huey had displayed the political arts of dividing, isolating, and overwhelming his legislative opposition in New Orleans and Baton Rouge. In defeating Standard Oil, he relied on deception and surprise, but then the art of compromise.

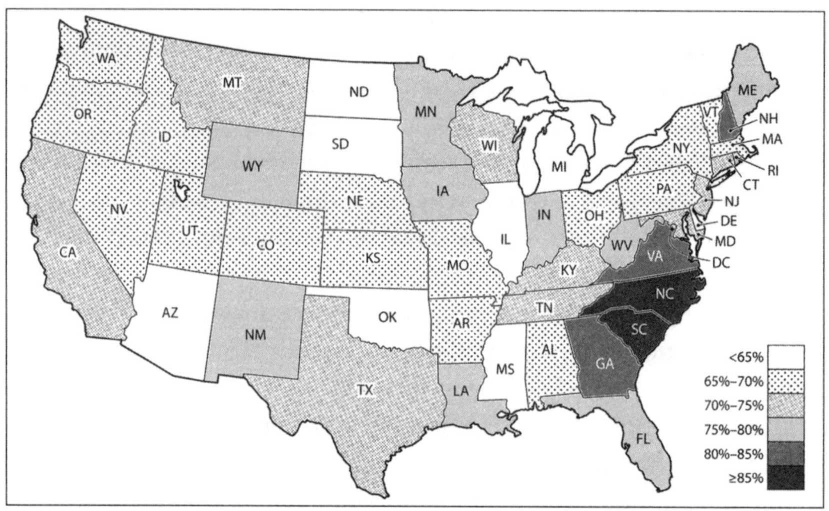


Income received by state as percentage of 1929 income.
From John A. Slaughter, *Income Received in the Various States 1929–1935*.

Compromise became more evident as Huey's control over Louisiana increased. He wanted a unified Louisiana so he could get on with organizing the rest of the country. Merchants helped write his debt moratorium law and defended it as a device to take poor credit out of circulation. The utility reductions benefited manufacturers by reducing their costs. After his Standard Oil compromise, few new taxes were imposed. Huey had increased his support from 20 percent to 50 percent among members of the Chamber of Commerce. More businesses now thought Huey had the public's support and would keep his promises.[77]

Studies showed that by 1935 Louisiana had recovered more than other states from the Depression (see map above).[78] The opposition consisted of malcontents apt to rebel against any kind of authority, anti-Long job holders who were fired or defeated for office, good-government types who objected to the kickbacks, and conservative ideologues who believed Huey was going to ruin the state's credit, corrupt the citizenry by his tax-and-benefit policies, or destroy local government.

Huey had mellowed, too, by 1935.[79] His most fearsome comments—"I'm the constitution just now"; "I can frighten or buy 99 out of every 100 men"—were allegedly made, if at all, before 1934. He was sure of himself, sober, leery of getting into stupid quarrels like the *Reveille* incident, and more conscious of the need to reach the nationwide audience.

Whereas Huey's most successful negotiation was with Walmsley in 1932, his most consequential negotiation failure was with Walmsley in 1935. Huey sent two emissaries to him in February. These men were not fond of Huey but recognized that he was a great tactician. They were close to the Old Regulars and to Walmsley and could explain the facts of political life.

Huey could wreck the city administration because of his power in the state legislature, but he preferred that Walmsley and the Old Regulars remain in office but support him. Walmsley rejected their offer and ripped the emissaries for lacking guts. This failure led to the special legislative sessions that followed, more laws to take over local government, and the reaction to those laws.[80]

In December 1934, the IRS indicted Seymour Weiss, Representative Joe Fisher, and his uncle, state Senator Jules Fisher. They were alleged to have obtained kickbacks from state contractors and not to have paid taxes on them. This was the last straw.[81]

Delayed because of the Standard Oil negotiations, on January 4, 1935, Huey sent a telegram that Senator Wheeler read to the Senate announcing his plans to speak when he arrived, the first time someone claimed the floor of the Senate by telegram. The galleries were thrilled.[82] The day after Huey's telegram, the Roosevelt administration released the public works money it had threatened to withhold because of the debt moratorium laws.[83]

Huey was in a race against time and Roosevelt. Could he expand the number of jobs he controlled to insulate himself from Roosevelt's use of New Deal money to influence Louisiana voters? Could he topple Roosevelt before the IRS indicted or convicted him or his allies? Before the Square Dealers overthrew or assassinated him? Opposed by the IRS, the FBI, billions of public works money, Roosevelt's cabinet and allies in the Senate, and Roosevelt himself, Huey returned to Washington. He intended to open with an attack. He prepared with a vengeance. He had no other choice.

# *Twenty-Six*

# THE PIED PIPER

Huey gained the floor of the U.S. Senate on January 7, 1935. The galleries were packed. In a two-hour speech, Huey proved that New Orleans leaders who controlled Roosevelt's patronage oversaw the vice district. "Whistle Britches" Rightor owned a brothel that Huey's National Guard had closed. Roosevelt's relief administrator, Harry Early, wrote that Huey had "cooperated fully" and "complied with every request," yet Roosevelt had unleashed the IRS on a political persecution of Huey, and had selectively indicted the IRS collector, Lawrence Merrigan, who had written that Huey was innocent of any tax law violations. The grand jury was composed of Huey's political enemies (giving names and affiliations). IRS agents boasted that Huey and his allies were all going away, but he wasn't afraid. Wheeler whispered an objection, but Huey's bitterness was reflected in his speech's title: "A Policy of Ingratitude and Death."

Senator Bronson Cutting of New Mexico had endorsed Roosevelt in 1932, Huey said, even though he was a Republican, risking everything he had by that choice, only to be opposed by Roosevelt—working through Farley—in the election of 1934. Both Wheeler and Norris had asked Huey to support Roosevelt, and he pointedly inquired how they felt about Roosevelt's betrayal of Cutting.[1] Neither Wheeler nor Norris spoke up to disagree or defend Roosevelt; they both disliked Farley.

After this blast, Huey announced for the first time over the radio on January 9 a complete break with Roosevelt. Roosevelt's plans had failed. The nation had "shuddered in its boots" when its debt was $26 billion at the end of World War I, but it would shortly increase to $34 billion, not bad if there were something to show for it, but "at the end of this rainbow of the greatest national debt in all history," more were unemployed, the rich were getting richer, "and the President of the United States quoted as saying: 'Don't touch the rich!'"

No longer did he cast himself in the role of trying to help Roosevelt carry out his promises or prevent him from making mistakes, as any friend would. The only worthwhile legislation, such as the insurance of bank deposits and the Frazier-Lemke Act, was "forced down the throat of the national administration," and Huey had "helped to pass" both laws by holding the floor in "the Senate for days."

> [Roosevelt] has promised and promised, smiled and bowed, and he looks well, I like his smile and I like his bow—looks nice, just as nice as I ever saw. He has read some fine speeches. . . .
>
> What has that meant? We've got to get awake sometime. We have to realize the truth, and now and then speak the truth. There's no use to wait three more years to find out what we're going to have under Roosevelt. . . . [S]ome of them say it's Roosevelt or ruin. I deny that. It's Roosevelt's ruin.

He closed with a poem he had composed, also quoted in the *Times:*

> Why weep or slumber America?
> Land of brave and true
> With castles, and clothing, and food for all
> All belongs to you
> Ev'ry man a king, ev'ry man a king
> For you can be a millionaire
> But there's something belonging to others
> There's enough for all people to share
> When it's sunny June and December too,
> Or in the winter time, or spring
> There'll be peace without end
> Every neighbor a friend
> With ev'ry man a king.[2]

Whereas Arthur Krock had written Huey off in 1934, now he quoted an experienced and conservative Democratic senator: Huey was "brilliant," "dangerous," and "industrious"; the "Depression has increased radicalism in this country—nobody knows how much"; and we "are obliged to propose and accept many things in this New Deal that otherwise we would not because we must prevent a union of discontent around him." Krock warned scoffers to consider that Huey was getting as many as 50,000 favorable letters per week.[3]

Huey traveled to New York and revealed that his poem consisted of lyrics for which Castro Carazo had written music. Agent Lou Irwin would find a publisher.[4] On January 11 and 16, more radio speeches were given.[5] "There is one sure way to avoid Huey Long for President, and only one if I live," he said, "and that is by adopting God's laws."[6]

On January 19, Huey outlined his pension proposal on the radio and attacked Roosevelt's. Those over sixty who lacked $10,000 of property and $1,000 of income should receive $30 per month, at a cost of $3 billion. Roosevelt's plan, in contrast, required the states to contribute, and the $125 million federal portion was to be funded by "taxing the same people who have nothing, on the pretense that you are going to give it back to them." But "it all never does get back, . . . much of it would remain in the hands of these Washington bureaucrats and politicians." Included was Huey's analysis that the government's statistics undercounted the unemployed: 50 percent were unemployed, he contended, and the *employed* were earning 43 percent less than the minimum for a decent standard of living.[7]

Huey closed with a newspaper story that Victor Hugo could have written about a mother seeking help for her sick baby:

> Hear me now read you a report from our newspapers. [He read several paragraphs of the story to set up its conclusion:]
>
> The baby's cries grew more frequent but weaker. She refused the warm water offered as a substitute for milk. Paroxysms purpled her tiny face and the older children, from 3 to 12, whimpered in sympathy and fear. Mrs. Martindale paced the floor, wrung her hands.
>
> A strangling cough wracked the infant girl. The mother acted in desperation. Whirling blankets around the baby and a ragged coat around her own shoulders, she ordered the oldest girl to watch the other children. She raced from the room, carrying the sick child.
>
> At an infant welfare station two blocks away she sobbed out her troubles. The women on duty were sorry, but no doctor would be present for hours. They advised her to go to St. Joseph's Hospital.
>
> Mrs. Martindale had no carfare but she went. She walked—six blocks—

> with the thermometer at 16 above zero. She stumbled on the steps into the hospital.
>
> "My baby," she sobbed to a nurse, "she's sick." The nurse peered into the blankets, then took the little bundle.
>
> "She's dead," she said.

The conservative press viewed Huey's pension plan as utopian or insincere, as based on class taxation, but as a potent threat that required support of Roosevelt's proposal.[8]

Huey impressed *Times* reporter Russell Owen as sincere, however, stating: "I believe in capitalism, but you cannot stimulate it unless there is buying power. . . . [The plan] provides opportunities for more men to become millionaires. They all won't get that far, but persons like you and me might get up into the $100,000 class. . . . It would increase . . . the income of the middle class, enable the government to take care of those who cannot rise by their own initiative, and make this a better country to live in." Dictators had no place in American life, and the laws passed by Congress granted Roosevelt more power than the dictators in Europe. In contrast, Louisiana was government by initiative and referendum, demonstrated by the voters' approval of his constitutional amendments.

Huey was a strange man, Owen wrote, given his pacing and his darting eyes, but he would put his hand on Owen's shoulder, smile, and look directly at him when making some points. If one met him for the first time without preconceived ideas, one would "probably" like him. Huey was insecure and belligerent in 1934 but secure and confident now. Other senators brought their constituents over to shake hands with him. Huey had given up drinking because it made him soft and caused him to bawl out his opponents, which got him into trouble. Huey did not miss it and felt better. Mrs. Long was with him more often in Washington. Huey traveled without bodyguards in Washington, in contrast with Louisiana, where his bodyguards gave people the impression of a Hitler approaching the Reichstag. When asked if there would be a third-party ticket in 1936, Huey said there was sure to be, "and I think we will sweep the country."[9]

Huey's pension speech was given in the middle of the Senate fight to ratify a treaty requiring U.S. participation in the World Court. Robinson supported it.[10] Huey opposed it, accusing the League of Nations of favoring Bolivia over Paraguay because of Standard Oil. At first, Huey emptied the floor but, undeterred, excited the crowded galleries and goaded Robinson into a white rage.[11] Over that weekend, Secretary of State Hull sent a State Department official to tutor Robinson on how to respond. On January 18, Huey proposed reaffirming the Monroe Doctrine as a reservation to the World Court treaty. It failed thirty-five to forty-six on the 28th, but many Democrats supported Huey. On the 29th, the treaty failed, fifty-two to thirty-six. Robinson was "no match for Huey with his documents, maps, and quoted statements."[12]

The isolationist Hearst press and Father Charles Coughlin, a Detroit radio priest, caused an avalanche of 50,000 letters, wires, and telegrams against it, and its Senate support disappeared despite a radio appeal of Mrs. Roosevelt, lobbying phone calls by the president, and personal appeals in the Senate by Secretary Hull. A majority voted for it, but not the two-thirds required,[13] a "decisive defeat of the Administration." Roosevelt wrote Robinson that opponents of the treaty would have to apologize in Heaven for their votes, but he told Johnson that he didn't care about the issue.[14]

The Square Dealers were a regular feature in the press in January,[15] and Huey returned to Louisiana to deal with them in the middle of the World Court fight, from the 21st to the 25th.[16] Pursuant to the laws passed the preceding December, thirteen additional police jurors (the local term for town council members) were added to the existing ones in Baton Rouge, and the reconstituted group fired 225 employees of the parish and District Attorney Odom and appointed an ally to run the courthouse.[17]

Then it was reported that a Square Dealer, Sydney Songy, had been arrested. They panicked. Three hundred of them grabbed their guns, some of them supplied by the sheriff, and took over the Baton Rouge courthouse, physically expelling Huey's appointee. The women's auxiliary brought coffee and sandwiches to support the occupation. At 9 p.m., Songy was released. The mob disbanded.

Their armed coup, as ineffectual and purposeless as it was, along with some secret information Huey was about to reveal, spurred him (actually Governor Allen) to declare martial law in Baton Rouge. A short proclamation was replaced by a more stringent one that forbade carrying, selling, or distributing firearms; commentary that reflected on the state government or its officers; or the gathering of two or more people. Eight hundred troops assembled on the capitol grounds on Saturday, January 26, but this "made little difference" to the average citizen. Working, shopping, and social activities were unaffected.[18] A letter to the *Tribune* from a visitor to New Orleans "marveled" at the freedom of the inhabitants under the reported "dictatorship." Huey was a "regular fellow" and had the "wholehearted support" of the people.[19]

Huey announced a hearing to prove that his opponents planned violence, blamed Standard Oil for it, and threatened to rescind the Standard Oil compromise.[20] Songy, a former Prohibition informant,[21] had infiltrated the Square Deal Association for Huey. Songy testified that Fred Parker, a former deputy sheriff of Baton Rouge; John Fred Odom, the district attorney; Fred LeBlanc, Odom's assistant; Dallas Gross, the manager of Congressman Sanders's local office; Powers Higginbotham, a city official just fired; Fred O'Rourke; and Roland Kizer, an attorney; with the knowledge and cooperation of the sheriffs of two neighboring parishes, had plotted to kill Huey. The news of Songy's arrest—pretextual—had frightened the association.

Songy was unnerved when Kizer paid his bail. Kizer told Songy to keep his mouth shut and promised money to escape. The group considered overpowering Huey at his Heidelberg Hotel suite, but Songy talked them out of it. The Square Dealers planned an ambush at Dead Man's Curve on the road to New Orleans the next evening. Huey decided not to drive there, but some of his colleagues did, finding no one.

Powers Higginbotham was brought in, questioned, and responded to every question, "I don't remember." Huey then asked to adjourn the hearing until the remaining witnesses could be questioned. Decades later, Higginbotham told Professor Williams that Songy's story was false.[22]

But there were people planning to kill Huey. If Huey knew Songy's tale was false, he would not have sent men to Dead Man's Curve. A legislative opponent, Mason Spencer, was invited to a meeting that he thought was political but left when the leader announced that its purpose was to discuss "ways and means" of killing the Kingfish. Huey refused a bulletproof vest suggested by his friends. Huey told Senator Byrd that there were so many plotters that he was "not going to live through it." To others he said, "If somebody's going to shoot me, he's going to shoot me. I'm not going to worry about it."[23]

To rout the Square Dealers, Huey used a similar ruse to the one that fooled Walmsley in Washington, DC. Songy had supplied the names of its leaders and members. A call went out to them to meet at once at the airport with their guns! About a hundred people rushed out there, where the National Guard under General Fleming and Colonel E. P. Roy of the highway police ambushed them. The guard asked the Square Dealers to throw down their weapons and surrender. Some did; others ran. Tear gas routed the runners, and most of the ringleaders were arrested. Bourgeois escaped. A Square

Dealer was wounded by one of his fellow members, whose gun accidentally discharged. One state employee suspected of spying was beaten, but no one died.[24] It was an "opera bouffe skirmish."[25]

Square Dealers asked the federal government to intervene because they were "driven to revolt" by Huey's "intolerable tyranny."[26] One went to Washington and claimed that plainclothes police, Huey's "imperial cossacks," followed him to Mississippi.[27] Bourgeois wrote J. Edgar Hoover requesting protection; he feared he would be killed, but he returned to the capitol, was arrested and released, and then resigned.[28] Meanwhile a kindly looking old German woman visited the "splendors" of the capitol for the first time and told a reporter that Huey was "the only man that was ever good to the poor," as she "lovingly patted his head sculptured in the wall."[29]

Huey rushed back to Washington, traveling with his wife and daughter, who posed for pictures during a stop in Atlanta, while he slept. On Monday, January 28, he proposed his Monroe Doctrine resolution and voted against the World Court on the 29th. Huey's wife and daughter traveled on to New York, the trip a reward for daughter Rose's straight-A report card at LSU. They told the press that Huey had started to write a new book, a satire on manners.[30]

After the World Court vote, Huey dashed back from Washington, his bodyguards striking a photographer and smashing his camera when he took Huey's picture as he alighted from the train. The murder-plot hearing was resumed. Witnesses identified plotters as affiliated with J. Y. Sanders Jr. and Standard Oil. Bourgeois was ridiculed for fleeing. On provoking guffaws from the audience, one plotter stated: "Don't make a joke of everything I say; some of it's the truth."[31] A former East Baton Rouge deputy sheriff testified that Fred Parker had offered him $10,000 to shoot Huey. He tried but couldn't get close enough. The witnesses examined by Huey displayed no fear, and many defiantly opposed Huey's takeover of Baton Rouge.[32] Parker and O'Rourke asserted the Fifth Amendment, yet Parker was afterward given a job by Roosevelt as a guard at the Capitol in Washington, DC.[33]

Huey adjourned the hearing. No one was prosecuted. Standard Oil fired fifty employees active in the Square Deal Association and rehired its hapless lobbyist, Louis LeSage, at Huey's insistence. After meeting with Huey, Baton Rouge's mayor called for calm so that martial law would be lifted. The guardsmen left the city. Utility rates for Baton Rouge consumers were reduced from between 22 and 37 percent by order of the Public Service Commission, represented by its lawyer, Huey. Detecting public hostility to Huey, his rural leaders opposed an immediate special legislative session.[34]

Huey returned to Washington by way of Atlanta to address the Georgia House of Representatives. Huey must have relished this opportunity. Georgia was Roosevelt's adopted second home. Georgia's governor, Eugene Talmadge, identified with farmers and lived on a farm, but was conservative and criticized the New Deal as a combination of wet-nursing and dictatorship.

The state Senate didn't join in the invitation, and two of its members wrote Roosevelt apologizing for it. But Huey was greeted enthusiastically in Atlanta, people stormed the doors of the House of Representatives to hear him, and he spoke for an hour to cheers and shouts of "pour it on, Huey," and "Don't stop now, Kingfish." Huey privately thought Talmadge's organization was "bush league." But at lunch he accepted a pair of red suspenders from him, a Talmadge trademark symbolizing his identification with farmers. Afterward, other state legislatures debated whether to invite Huey, deciding against it.[35]

In Washington, Huey gave two mediocre radio speeches in February. The second one introduced his song, "Every Man a King." The lyrics were the poem Huey recited in his January speech, and the music was written by LSU band leader Castro Carazo. Harry Link, a pleasing tenor singer, composer, and publisher, sang it and played it on the piano during the broadcast.

Roosevelt felt Huey's threat. On February 4, he snapped at a meeting of the National Emergency Council: "don't put anybody in [any federal agency] and don't keep anybody that is working for Huey Long or his crowd! That is a hundred percent!"[36] Every week the White House got copies of speeches Huey made in the *Congressional Record* and every month got the *American Progress*.[37] A *Tribune* reader reminded the paper of its 1934 report that Huey's political sun was setting. Huey "certainly knows how to stage and prolong a really grand finale."[38] The *Times* of February 10 contained a Raymond Daniell summary of Huey's "authoritarian" laws and benefits to the state, an editorial stating it was "small wonder" the opposition armed themselves considering the dictatorial laws, and Russell Owen's profile.[39] Someone sent a bomb to Huey's office, but it broke in transit.[40]

In 1934, postmaster general James A. Farley was exposed in the Air Mail investigation as accepting free plane rides, meals, and a hat during political trips. Newspapers called Farley a menace to clean politics.[41]

On February 11, Huey submitted a resolution to investigate Farley, claiming that he had given away free stamps, was connected to gamblers, solicited campaign contributions from undesirable people, and was financially interested in construction companies doing work for the Public Works Administration (PWA). Sources differ as to how he obtained the damaging information about Farley. One said it was Senator Borah.[42] Another identified enemies of Farley in New York.[43]

If Huey could get rid of Farley, he would impress progressives nationwide and eliminate the general of Roosevelt's patronage army. It allowed Huey to say Roosevelt was corrupt, valuable as an offensive weapon or, defensively, to blunt any charges from Roosevelt that he or members of his machine were corrupt. It was a high-risk and high-reward strategy. In charge of patronage, Farley had friends all over the country and had done plenty of political favors. By taking him on, Huey took on the entire Democratic Party, outraging those who had a vested stake in its continuance.

On February 13, administration senators moved to refer the matter to the Committee on Post Offices, a move Huey and Wheeler opposed unsuccessfully because it was composed of Farley's friends.[44] Huey added charges that Farley required West Virginia's governor to endorse an administration senatorial candidate to get a $50 million Reconstruction Finance Corporation loan. On February 14, Huey asked the interior secretary, Harold L. Ickes, to transmit a file prepared by Ickes's assistant, Louis Glavis, to the committee. Either someone had stolen the file from Ickes's office, or it had been leaked. On the 15th the Senate agreed.[45]

Roosevelt wanted to allow Huey's resolution unless there was something "'seriously reflecting upon Farley' (or so Ickes, who kept a diary, unblushingly recorded his words)."[46] Ickes's Interior Department was responsible for disbursing PWA funds, supervised by the Treasury Department, whose division of procurement was headed by Lawrence W. Roberts, a Farley friend. In bidding for a New York post office contract, the Post Office Department asked Roberts by letter to award the bid to James Stewart Company, despite its noncompliance with federal financial regulations until after it submitted its bid, mentioning an association with Farley. Roberts complied and destroyed the letter, and another official destroyed the carbon copy of it, both actions crimes. Stewart bought supplies from the company of which Farley had been president and in which he still held stock, and of which his brother-in-law was then president. Morgenthau re-advertised for bids.

Ickes learned this. He asked Glavis to investigate without telling Morgenthau or Farley. Glavis learned the facts, but then blabbed the information to Senator Tydings, who told Morgenthau. Enraged at Ickes's secret investigation, Morgenthau and Ickes had it out at a cabinet meeting until Roosevelt pounded the table and shouted that he would not put up with bickering. Roosevelt asked Farley to appear before the Senate committee, but Farley was afraid. Instead, he answered written questions and provided the files. Ickes prepared a report that was reviewed at the White House with Morgenthau and Senators Robinson, Connally, O'Mahoney (a former Farley associate in the Post Office Department), Bailey, Byrnes, and McCarran. Ickes afterward thought that Farley had nothing to worry about, but that "procurement may come in for some rough sledding." Morgenthau was "quite unhappy."[47]

The Farley inquiry dominated the news as Huey added information or charges each day or every other day: Farley postponed a criminal case in exchange for a campaign contribution, interfered with an investigation of organized crime in Kansas City, and had stopped an inquiry into illegal banking practices in Tennessee. Known as "Honest Harold," Ickes denied that his department had investigated "Farley" (it investigated "procurement").[48]

At about the same time, Roosevelt proposed a $5 billion work relief bill. Senator McCarran offered an amendment requiring the government to pay prevailing wages. Progressives and organized labor supported it. Roosevelt opposed it.[49]

As an amendment leader, Huey had a list of absent senators who were paired for and against the bill during the tense roll call. The initial vote showed a forty-three to forty-three tie, but Huey recalled that Dickinson, the Republican leader, was paired with Senator Frazier, who just seconds before the vote was announced appeared and voted. Huey "rushed across the chamber" and had Dickinson transfer his pair to the absent Mrs. Caraway. Robinson challenged this, but Huey said he had called her secretary "and had been assured she would vote for the amendment." "[R]ed-faced and obviously annoyed," Robinson "dropped into his seat" as the vote was announced.[50] Huey had "shown his strength" by inflicting two defeats in a row on the administration.[51] Huey next suggested spending $2.5 billion for highways, but that proposal—a good one—went nowhere.[52]

National muckraking columnist Drew Pearson had written Huey off in 1934. Now he noted Huey's acceptance among progressive senators, attributed to his speech supporting Cutting, persistence in working for progressive causes, courage, and superior intelligence when sober.[53]

Huey darted back to Louisiana to direct a special legislative session to implement the Standard Oil compromise on February 26. On the last day of the session, a concurrent resolution authorized the governor to suspend any portion of the oil tax. Afterward, Governor Allen suspended four cents of the tax to fulfill the agreement. If Standard Oil misbehaved, Huey (through Allen) could reimpose it. Ebullient, Huey said Louisiana was such a great state that he might run for governor.[54]

The effect of Huey's resurgence on Robinson can be guessed. After routing his opponents in Louisiana, Huey had inflicted two defeats on Robinson already, had set his sights on Roosevelt, and now was gunning for Farley, the leader of the Democratic Party, in the Senate, Robinson's domain. In early February they joked on the floor. On his way to speak to the Georgia legislature, however, Huey was quoted in the *Times* as saying he was going to beat Harrison and Robinson in next year's elections. In the Senate on February 21, Huey critiqued an advance copy of a Farley speech, "making gibes that brought laughter from the galleries" as he "swaggered from one chair to another."[55]

It could not be a coincidence that, on February 24, former Texas governor Dan Moody agreed to be a special prosecutor in the income tax cases against Huey's leaders. Roosevelt personally requested it.[56] On the 26th, newspapers said Roosevelt and Farley were planning to defeat Huey in Louisiana in 1936.[57]

Huey claimed the Senate floor on March 4, asking why the Farley report was missing. Robinson took offense at Huey's "very foul insinuation" and acidly observed that the Senate had to wait for the Kingfish to finish ruling his state by martial law. Huey replied that only the Standard Oil domicile was subject to martial law, the only province with which Robinson would be familiar. Huey predicted that Farley was about to resign. Robinson rushed to phone the White House and then confirmed this was false. When Huey asked the source of his information, Robinson banged the desk with his fist and boomed, the president of the United States! Huey said the White House was often mistaken. Robinson's patience snapped, his fists clenched, and he had to be restrained from an assault. Huey suggested that he not get so excited.[58]

Under criticism for his performance and that of the NRA, Hugh Johnson resigned. Johnson wrote memoirs (*The Blue Eagle from Egg to Earth*) and they were going to be excerpted by *Redbook* magazine. It sponsored a banquet at which Johnson would speak, with a radio simulcast.[59] Johnson decided to denounce Huey and Father Charles Coughlin, a nationally prominent radio priest, who had criticized the World Court treaty and Roosevelt's failure to increase the money supply or pay the soldiers' bonus.

Most say Johnson acted on his own.[60] Maybe he told the White House, heard no objection, and assumed it agreed with him, or was trying to ingratiate himself with Roosevelt or generate publicity to sell his book. Johnson was just separate enough from the administration, however, that Roosevelt could deny responsibility for what he said while gauging its impact. Johnson was speaking to a pro-administration audience: Senators Wagner, Harrison, Pittman; Louis Howe; Bernard Baruch; George Peek; Raymond Moley; and Rexford Tugwell.[61] The timing is also telling. An attack on Huey would overwhelm press coverage of the upcoming release of the Farley report.[62] And it took place days after disclosure of White House plans to defeat Huey in 1936.

Johnson let Huey and Coughlin have it. They were pied pipers. Their hope was to see an American Hitler ride into Washington, DC, at the head of troops, and Huey knew what part of the horse he could be. Huey was an able little devil that he liked, but he sarcastically imitated Huey's southern drawl and called him a demagogue, a Punchinello, and a menace offering false promises of economic salvation. Coughlin provided "musical blatant bunk"; he was the political padre, one of two Catilines. The country had eighty million suffering "babies"—two-thirds of the population, an embarrassing admission of widespread misery two years after Roosevelt's inauguration—ready to follow anyone who promised relief, but the sole hope was Roosevelt.[63] Johnson received ecstatic praise for his speech. It was like the ice was broken after a long winter. It was "epochal."[64]

In the Senate the next morning, Huey responded. While languishing in the arms of Morpheus, he heard his name mentioned, and then listened to Johnson's talk. Johnson was the hired hand of Bernard Baruch, whose motto was "Presidents: you make 'em, we break 'em. [*laughter*]." Quoting a magazine article, he proved that Baruch conceptualized the NRA while advising Hoover, before the Depression, and contended that the country hadn't swapped Hoover for Roosevelt, but rather Baruch for Baruch. Johnson was Baruch's man selected to run the NRA, but had failed, and now the administration depended for a defense on one whom it had itself rebuked. One was always warned before taking a first drink, gambling, or other sins, and now Huey warned Robinson—who was "white with rage"—and the Democratic Party: beware, beware, if things go on as they have been going on, you will not be here next year. He then "nonchalantly" left the chamber.[65] Robinson snapped.

Violating the Senate rules with a vengeance never displayed by Huey, incensed and unhinged, Robinson described Huey as egotistical, arrogant, and ignorant. The Senate was disgusted. Its manhood was at stake. Huey and Johnson should go outside and settle their differences the old-fashioned way. Robinson apologized for paying any attention to the ravings of a "madman." As he sat down, about a dozen Democratic and Republican senators crowded around to congratulate him.

Huey returned at the end of Robinson's rant and was informed of what he had said. Taking the floor, Huey noted Robinson's violation of the Senate rules and their 1933 truce. Huey would defeat Robinson when he came up for election next year because the Democratic Party was now in the ascendancy, and it did not get there on his doctrines. "The senator suggests that General Johnson and I have a fist fight. That's bad advice. The senator settled a claim like that at the Chevy Chase Club, and I don't want to settle it that way, because it might be a disaster like he had." Huey "laughed" and "Robinson winced" because it "was not pleasant to sit in the United States Senate, beneath press and public galleries jammed and packed to hear a colleague laughingly tell of a fist fight at a golf tee where you blackened a fellow club member's eye," requiring resignation from the club. Twice Senator Clark interrupted Huey only "to return red-faced and gulping to his chair when Long treated him with contempt as he might a wayward child."[66] Enlivening the debate was a dramatic confrontation over whether Huey brought armed bodyguards into the Senate gallery (Robert Brothers was patted down but unarmed, as always, and an armed bodyguard ran down the stairs so fast that he escaped detection).[67]

Included in the debates was Huey's oratorical eloquence:

> I am not undertaking to answer the charge that I am ignorant. It is true. I am an ignorant man. I have had no college education. I have not even had a high school education. But the thing that takes me far in politics is that I do not have to color what comes into my mind and into my heart. I say it unvarnished. I say it without veneer. I have not the learning to do otherwise, and therefore my ignorance is often not detected.
>
> I know the hearts of people, because I have not colored my own. I know when I am right in my own conscience. I do not talk one way in this cloakroom and another way out here. I do not talk one way back there in the hills of Louisiana and another way here in the Senate. I have one language.

> Ignorant as it is, it is a universal language within the sphere in which I operate. Its simplicity gains pardon for my lack of letters and education. . . .
>
> I have suffered much from a little write-up which I saw in a Chicago paper about a little 4-year old boy who was out at 5 o'clock in the morning with an axe on his shoulder hunting for wood to cut because his mother was freezing. . . . oh, yes; I see you smile! It tickles you. That is what makes it so hellish to me. . . . That is what makes it so disgusting. Where is the honor, the sincerity, the humanity left that a man can smile at such conditions! . . .
>
> We do not know half the misery going on in this country because 80 percent of it is still shielded beneath the pride of people who hate to admit . . . the destitution into which they have fallen.
>
> Let the Senator from Arkansas insult everybody who dares to come here and point out that the wreckage of Baruchism under Hoover is the wreckage of Baruchism under Roosevelt. . . . None the less my voice will be the same as it has been. Patronage will not change it. Fear will not change it. Persecution will not change it. It cannot be changed while people suffer. The only way it can be changed is to make the lives of these people decent and respectable. No one will ever hear political opposition out of me when that is done.[68]

Huey got the best of Robinson that day.[69]

On March 6, Huey's renewed attack on Farley alleged that his witnesses were harassed and wiretapped. Huey threatened to call New York parks commissioner Robert Moses—a Roosevelt enemy—to supply evidence against Farley. Roosevelt was asked about Johnson's speech and only smiled.[70]

After obtaining two days of front-page publicity, Huey wasn't done. He asked for radio time to answer Johnson, getting forty-five minutes on the night of March 7.[71] Huey began: "Ladies and gentlemen: It has been publicly announced that the White House orders of the Roosevelt administration have declared a war." Johnson was "the pampered ex-crown prince," one of those "satellites loaned by Wall Street to run the government, and who at the end of his control over and dismissal from the ill-fated NRA, and who pronounced it as dead as a dodo," was asked to lead the "White House charge." Johnson's status with the Roosevelt administration was akin to the first favorite of a queen in a faraway island: when she died, her first favorite was "done the honor of being buried alive with her."

Then Huey disclaimed any interest in calling Johnson more bitter names than he had called him. The trouble was that the administration had failed to take his advice or implement its own promises. Huey used the Davy Crockett louse in the eyebrow and the two sets of waiters serving the same food analogies. Roosevelt's plans to plow up crops, for example, were the original ideas of Hoover that Roosevelt had criticized.

In an abrupt transition, Huey analyzed the NRA, beginning with a comparison that was easy to understand: the NRA had parades and signs, just like Hitler and Mussolini. It set up the dictatorship to regiment business much more than in Germany or Italy. The only difference was the sign. In Italy the sign of the fascist was the black shirt. In Germany it was the swastika. "So in America they sidetracked the stars and stripes and the sign of the Blue Eagle was used instead for the NRA."

Everyone from a peanut stand to a powerhouse was subject to a book of rules, Huey said, with jail time for noncompliance. A man who charged five cents below the rulebook price for pressing a pair of pants was sent to jail (a true story). The nine hundred codes set up by the NRA were as thick as an unabridged dictionary and as confusing as a study of the stars. It would take forty lawyers to tell a shoeshine merchant how to operate to ensure he wouldn't go to jail.

The NRA became such a disaster that Roosevelt had to let Johnson go as a scapegoat. Johnson was going to blister the administration but was talked out of it in case Baruch needed to loan him to another president in the future. The NRA no longer called for parades because it wouldn't get enough participants to conduct a funeral march.

Roosevelt had only himself to blame for these troubles because he had his way with Congress for two years, yet conditions got worse instead of better. Roosevelt had promised a redistribution of wealth but hadn't followed through, saddening Huey's heart and blighting his ambition.

Huey transitioned again to analyze the cause of the Depression. In 1916, 2 percent of the people owned 60 percent of the wealth, but now 1 percent of the people owned 59 percent of the wealth. The middle class that existed in 1916 had been squeezed out. "Concentrated chain-merchandise and chain banking systems have laid waste to all middle opportunity." The wealth of America, provided by the Lord and Creator, was like a barbecue, except that the financial masters had taken off the table 90 percent of the food. The rest was now "in the hands of the Morgans, the Rockefellers, the Mellons, the Baruchs, the Bakers, the Astors, and the Vanderbilts—600 families at the most—either possessing or controlling the entire 90 percent of all that is in America." Because they couldn't consume it all, they destroyed it to let humanity suffer and to satisfy their vanity and greed.

Many authorities favored redistributing wealth, Huey continued. Only General Johnson "deigned" to disagree with these great men, Johnson the lawyer who had never tried a lawsuit and Johnson the soldier who had never heard a cap snap. Citing campaign statements of Roosevelt and quoting Hoover, they both "swallowed the Huey Long doctrine and never made one single complaint about it before the election of 1932."

Huey then explained his plan "taken from these leaders of all times and from the Bible, for the sponsoring of which I am labeled America's menace, madman, pied piper, and demagogue." Emphasizing first the capital levy tax that would result in the confiscation of $165 billion, he coupled that with providing $5,000 homesteads for every family, enough for a home, an automobile, and a radio, at an estimated cost of $100 billion. Then free college and vocational training would be provided for all who had the energy and capacity to learn.

> Now, Gen. Hugh Johnson says I am indeed a very smart demagogue, a wise and dangerous menace. But I am one of those who didn't have the opportunity to secure a college education or training. We propose that the right to education and the extent of education shall be determined and gauged not so much by the financial ability of the parents but by the mental ability and energy of a child to absorb the learning at a college. This should appeal to General Johnson, who says I am a smart man, and I oughtn't to be made to deny that, since, had I enjoyed the learning and college training which my plan would provide for others, I might not have fallen into the path of the dangerous menace and demagogue that he has now found me to be.

Under his plan college enrollments would multiply by 1,000 percent and the construction program to expand colleges would start a fusillade of employment.

> And how happy the youth of this land would be tomorrow morning if they knew instantly their right . . . to complete college and professional training and education were assured! I know how happy they would be because I know how I would have felt, had such a message been delivered to my door.
>
> I cannot deliver that promise to the youth of this land tonight, but I am

> doing my part. I am standing the blows; I am hearing the charges hurled at me from the four quarters of the country. It is the same fight which was made against me in Louisiana. . . . When the youth of this land realizes what is meant and what is contemplated[, criticism won't] . . . prevent the light of truth from hurling itself in understandable letters against the dark canopy of the sky.[72]

His other proposals—to shorten the hours of labor, provide a minimum family income, arrange crop holidays, pay old-age pensions and the soldiers' bonus were explained briefly, and he rebutted his critics, calling out newspaperman Arthur Brisbane ("Why make that untrue statement, Mr. Brisbane? You know that is not so.") and Hugh Johnson ("Must you be a false witness to argue your point?") for misquoting the benefits he promised. He closed with a call to organize SOW societies and quoted heartrending letters he had received from people desperate for a job.

Much as the Hot Wells speech helped make Huey a statewide name in Louisiana, his reply to General Johnson transformed him, in the words of a critic, from a clown into a real political menace. But the speeches were of opposite types. In Hot Wells, he issued a violent speech to attract more attention. Here, he had the nation's attention from the venomous attacks on him in the Senate, so he transcended the attack with a serious speech promoting his program.

The "consensus" was that Huey's approach was a "sagacious political move." The critics admitted he had "brains" and a "certain genius" for government. The *Times* compared the Senate turbulence to that preceding the Civil War.[73] At first, Johnson won plaudits; now, author Raymond Gram Swing wrote that Johnson's attack was a "demonstration of political feeblemindedness."[74]

Columnist Walter Lippman reported that Huey's critique of the NRA was nothing Senator Borah and others hadn't said before but conceded that Huey used more picturesque language. Lippman suggested, however, that if the government took most of the Ford Motor Company stock as Huey proposed, Ford would tell the government to run the company itself.[75] This isn't true. Managers who get a salary and lack a majority or even a significant minority of stock, then and today run most public corporations.[76]

On March 9, the *Times* asked Huey how the wealth he taxed would be redistributed. Huey responded that he needed first to run the crooks (Farley) out of government and then deal with the mechanics of his plan; he would call in some great minds to assist. Some of the wealth could be distributed in the form of goods, he said, an unworkable, even ridiculous, notion, although it bore some resemblance to production-for-use theories. Other ideas were more reasonable. Wealth would not have to be liquidated for cash to be redistributed.[77] Stock could be submitted by those taxed directly to the government, where it could be converted into nonvoting (but dividend-paying) stock. The mechanics at this point were hazy, however, because Huey had not worked them out.[78]

In the aftermath of Huey's speech, interest in Huey skyrocketed. Letters poured in by the thousands to his office. Invited to Philadelphia on March 15, Huey was dubious, thinking he would not draw a crowd. Arriving thirty minutes ahead of time to find the doors locked, Huey said, "see, I told you they couldn't draw a crowd." But they had locked the doors because the place was jammed with fifteen thousand people. Not even Roosevelt had filled the location during his 1932 campaign. The man who denied ever experiencing stage fright now took a moment to compose himself. The *Times* reported that only a small portion of the crowd cheered Huey's hint that he would lead a third party, but its columnist Krock said thousands cheered him and thousands more fought to gain admission. Roosevelt received two letters about it: one said the speech was a flop and the other said the sponsoring organization was weak and unknown and the promotion nonexistent, yet the place was packed; it was a "serious situation" and "something must be done." A former mayor told Huey that he would get 250,000 votes in the city if he ran for president.[79]

The speech didn't influence the Senate, however. The Committee on Post Offices rejected Huey's plea to investigate Farley by a vote of ten to five, a whitewash. The rumors that Farley might resign periodically resurfaced, however. If he resigned after Congress adjourned, it would not appear that Huey had forced him out.[80]

Meanwhile, the House-Senate Conference Committee watered down the McCarran amendment to the relief bill. The committee increased the wages but not as much as prevailing wages, disappointing labor leaders. By threatening a filibuster, Huey won a delay to allow Coughlin to give a radio speech to mobilize public sentiment for a prevailing wage.[81] Roosevelt countered by offering public works money to senators to defeat the amendment. Huey lampooned this: He was "unbribable" but "I ain't had no $100 million offered to me yet. . . . I might be just as strong" *against* the amendment. This entertained the galleries, but neither Huey's lampoons nor the priest's speech could muster enough pressure to win. Administration senators ruthlessly denied the courtesy of "pairs" for Senators Overton and Caraway, who were ill and absent but supported the amendment. Huey complained, putting Robinson—flushed and clenching the arm of his chair—on the spot "for his loyalty to the administration forced him to sit there and stand accused of discourtesy to a lady senator from his own state."[82] Huey offered one amendment to appropriate $1 billion for college education that failed five to seventy-five and another one to allocate $100 million for college education, but it was defeated, twenty-seven to fifty-eight.[83] After the vote, Huey sat dejected and Robinson and Byrnes glowed.[84] In one sense, Huey should not have been discouraged. Each time he lost he picked up another issue to use against Roosevelt in 1936. With each victory he gained political credibility.

Later in March, on his return from a quick trip to Baton Rouge, Huey addressed students at the University of South Carolina in Columbia, which his LSU student leaders had arranged. Changing trains at Charlotte, a thousand people followed him to his hotel. Huey met with a former senator and parents of LSU students, shocking them by identifying their children by name, and telling one pair the instrument their son played in the band. He praised South Carolina governor Olin Johnston as liberal but planned to campaign against North Carolina senator Bailey.

Faculty members at the university protested his visit, so Huey canceled it but met informally with two hundred students at the campus cafeteria, where they signed up for SOW. Governor Johnston gave Huey permission to speak at the capitol grounds. The newspapers reported an unfriendly crowd,[85] but other witnesses reported that a big crowd was won over.[86] Governor Johnston had been told by telephone that if he showed Huey any favor the White House would cancel all state public works projects.[87]

While he was in South Carolina, Huey learned that the work relief bill was hurriedly passed with an inflation amendment once it was rumored that he might fly to Washington from Columbia: he had filibustered by "remote control."[88] Huey or Gerald L. K. Smith spoke in several other places in South Carolina, and postcards returned by 140,000 people promised to vote for Huey for president. South Carolina was the strongest state for Roosevelt, Huey said (accurately),[89] so if he could sell himself there, he could sell himself anywhere.

Huey again spoke over the radio on March 31, denouncing Roosevelt as "Prince Charming" and the NRA as "blue buzzard government."[90] Huey had presented his plan to the nation. Now conservatives in and out of the administration counterattacked.

# Twenty-Seven

# FDR DRIFTS ON THE *NOURMAHAL*

The counterattack included Roosevelt initiatives, criticism by Roosevelt allies and the conservative media, politicization of relief and public works projects, court and federal action to negate Huey's state legislation, and tax prosecutions. On March 14, 1935, Roosevelt sent a vigorous message to Congress attacking utility holding companies, which elbowed Huey from the news for a day and pleased progressives.[1] In April, Roosevelt and Senator Harrison devised a compromise soldiers' bonus bill—front-page news in some newspapers—a "sudden offensive" designed to counter Huey.[2]

Echoing conservatives in Louisiana a decade earlier, Robinson declaimed that free college educations would destroy the incentive to work hard and that SOW was communistic;[3] and Barkley said that wealth redistribution had to occur in an orderly fashion.[4] Ickes held in contempt the "crooked intellect" (Huey) and the radio poet (Coughlin).[5] Farley criticized "the charlatan, the shallow purveyor of cure-alls, and even the zealot of political upheaval" who seeks to spread suspicion and misunderstanding in a time of hardship.[6] Governor George H. Earle of Pennsylvania denounced radicals who would destroy individual effort.[7] New York Supreme Court Justice Ferdinand Pecora excoriated those who pit class against class.[8]

*Time* magazine put Huey on its cover along with his statement that SOW would "sweep the country"—on April Fools' Day. The *March of Time* newsreel service distributed a venomous attack, reenacting with a stand-in actor his

Sands Point beating and his reception of the German envoy in his pajamas. It took film clips of a speech he gave and rearranged them kaleidoscopically with discordant music that made him appear to be a menace. The director intended no objectivity. He deliberately used an outtake to make fun of Alice Lee Grosjean. The newsreel was never played in Louisiana, but it was in other states.[9]

The newsreel nevertheless made some political mistakes. It said that many bridges were necessary in Louisiana because of its numerous waterways; hence all the farmers cheered when Huey announced the building of the Mississippi River Bridge. "*They* didn't have to pay for it," intoned the narrator. Farmers watching it might conclude that Huey was their friend, and that the narrator was a snob. The broadcast included a video clip of Roosevelt accepting the nomination for president in which he advocated a more equitable distribution of the national wealth.[10] An observer might wonder what was wrong with Huey's proposals if Roosevelt advocated them.

The attacks and counterattacks prompted all kinds of discussion of the programs of Huey, Coughlin, Roosevelt, Johnson, and others by local civic groups and churches; newspaper stories are too numerous to cite. Some considered Huey, Coughlin, and Roosevelt as fascistic,[11] others that Huey was dangerous and undemocratic with Roosevelt as the sane reformer.[12] Republicans criticized Huey, Coughlin, and Roosevelt for promising people something for nothing.[13]

Given the number of negative stories, one wonders how Huey had any support at all. But an average voter who had accepted conventional wisdom and now found himself without a job or with a diminished income could be excused for rejecting establishment judgments.

More than most politicians of the day, Huey depended on direct mail, if he could just get people on his mailing list. The radio gave Huey and others a means of reaching the people without the mediating—actually censoring—effect of newspapers. His use of radio makes it difficult to gauge his impact. The newspapers did not discuss his radio talks in detail.

A speech instructor claimed that Roosevelt had the best radio voice, that Huey was occasionally good but inconsistent, and that Coughlin used an unnatural "pulpit voice." The *Times* responded, "few people will deny Huey Long's effectiveness on the air, which is the thing that counts. . . . I care not who gets the medal for elocutionary technique."[14]

In the Senate, Huey dared anyone to stand up and defend the NRA. No one stood. He had the galleries in stiches when he said the NRA should stand for "National Ruin Administration," "Nuts Running America," or "Never Roosevelt Again."[15]

Senator Wheeler gave a radio speech in which he urged listeners not to reject SOW too quickly. Today's radicalism was tomorrow's conservatism, he said.[16]

The new politicization of relief began with Harry Hopkins replacing the nonpartisan Early—whose complimentary letter Huey had cited in January—with anti-Long state senator Frank Peterman. The anti-Longs thought Peterman was a grafter while he supported Huey, but now he filled every available federal position for them "to win an election." Roosevelt awarded every federal job in Louisiana to an anti-Long man.[17] "Don't give [Huey's] people in New Orleans $1.00," snapped Vice President Garner. Let them "starve to death."[18]

Ickes "rescinded" a Mississippi River bridge project that he had never approved. Ickes threatened an investigation, but the only correspondence he would have found were demands from Rightor to hire a connected man as a "consulting" engineer. Previously in 1934, Ickes had announced the exhaustion of Louisiana's quota for PWA funds. The PWA lacked quotas! Roosevelt withheld the Charity Hospital improvement loan despite Huey's dedication of the corporate franchise tax to its repayment.

New Deal legislation permitting municipalities to apply for debt readjustment temporarily defeated Huey's lawsuit to put New Orleans into receivership.[19] On April 14, Huey left the Senate, in which an anti-lynching bill was about to be filibustered by Senators Black and Borah,[20] and arrived in Baton Rouge to call a special legislative session.[21]

Just before the special session, the Louisiana Supreme Court approved the constitutionality of the bill taking over the New Orleans Police and Fire departments.[22] Excitement was supplied when Huey discussed impeaching the three anti-Long Louisiana Supreme Court justices because they had flip-flopped on their decisions regarding dummy candidates, but the idea was dropped in his caucus.[23]

Huey's new bills proposed that the consent of the governor and the attorney general were required before a city could apply to the federal government for debt adjustment; established a new agency, a Bond and Tax Board, whose members were the governor and four other officials, to approve the issuance of any bonds or debt contracts executed by any political subdivision in the state; made it a crime for the new federal relief administrator to disburse relief money without state administration approval; and allowed the governor to appoint boards of election supervisors in each parish, eliminating the prior system by which election clerks, commissioners, and watchers were selected from nominees of the candidates.

Anti-Long Mason Spencer spoke against the election board bill: "When this ugly thing is boiled down in its own juices, it disfranchises the white people of Louisiana. I am not gifted with second sight, nor did I see a spot of blood on the moon last night, but I can see blood on the polished marble of this capitol, for if you ride this thing through, you will travel with the white horse of death. White men have ever made poor slaves."[24] The galleries cheered, but this bill and the others passed.[25]

Ickes then objected to state control over any spending of federal money and threatened to cancel all public works spending in Louisiana. Huey retorted that he would beat Ickes's ears back when he returned to Washington,[26] that Louisiana was a sovereign state, and that Ickes could go "slap damn to hell."[27] Ickes had a newsworthy reply: "Emperor Long" had "halitosis of the intellect." Roosevelt loved Ickes's quip.[28] Ickes blasted Georgia, too.[29]

Huey and Senator Reynolds separately announced that Huey would show up "this alphabet gang" in the Senate on April 22. The controversy brought to the nation the dispute between Huey's critics, who said his public improvements cost too much to cover graft, whereas Huey's friends "and some not allied with him" were proud of the "greatest highway system in America," free schoolbooks, one of the "finest universities physically" in the country, and a "magnificent medical center and dental school."[30]

A huge crowd lined up for blocks two hours early for seats in the Senate on April 22. When Huey arrived wearing a silk ice-cream suit, checked lavender shirt, red and green tie, and white and tan shoes ("a sartorial aurora borealis"), the galleries let loose a roar of "ahs." Huey disclosed nicknames for Roosevelt cabinet members. Ickes was the "Chinchbug of Chicago." Roosevelt was the "Knight of the *Nourmahal*," *Nourmahal* being Vincent Astor's yacht on which Roosevelt cruised. Roosevelt made states liable for debts incurred by agreement with the federal government without allowing them to ensure that the debts were validly incurred or that the money was properly spent. This subordination of state power might cause a Boston Tea Party revolt, Huey said. The crowd laughed when Huey said he was in bad with Hoover and now was in bad with "this one," meaning Roosevelt.[31]

Huey's friend Joe Fisher was in bad with the IRS and the Justice Department. In late April, after twenty-two days of trial testimony and sixteen hours of deliberations, the jury convicted him on two of seven counts in his income tax prosecution conducted by prosecutors Rene Viosca and Dan Moody. Fisher had earned more than $80,000 over several years from Highway Commission contracts to supply shells under the name of E. R. Scheiffler, who was either a distant relative or an alias. Gambling losses dwarfed any income he made, such that no extra taxes were owed, Fisher contended.

Fisher was convicted of a false filing on a tax assessment protest in 1930, a felony, and of the willful failure to file any return at all in 1932, a misdemeanor. He got an eighteen-month sentence for the felony and a twelve-month concurrent sentence for the misdemeanor.[32] Asked for a statement, Huey said, "He's a good friend of mine, but I've got too many friends in the pen to make any comment about it."[33] I suspect that the prosecutors were disappointed at losing the other five counts, which paralleled the cases pending against other Long leaders. Before the next prosecution and citing the press of other business, Dan Moody resigned.

The next trial was Shushan, the strongest of the remaining cases. It was scheduled first for June and then November 1934 but was postponed, and Judge Borah was unavailable to preside over it. According to a former assistant district attorney, Huey's agents had uncovered evidence of Borah's illicit sexual escapades.[34] Roosevelt took all precautions to keep the new trial date, October 1935, hoping for a conviction right before the January 1936 Louisiana elections. A substitute judge was obtained. Colonel Enos W. W. Woodcock, a former national director of prohibition, replaced Moody as prosecutor.

In the trial (after Huey's death), Shushan's lawyer, Hugh Wilkinson, made some embarrassing admissions related to kickbacks of 2 percent on all purchases: they might ground a prosecution for defrauding the state of the honest services of a state official, but the kickback money was held as agent for a political organization, not personally, and therefore he owed no personal income taxes for its receipt. The government knew as of November 1934 that this defense was available. Woodcock thought the kickback-paying company's testimony that Shushan received the money was enough. At the end of the trial, the judge congratulated Woodcock. The jury deliberated for four hours. Then it shocked the judge. Shushan was innocent.

Some attribute the defeat to Woodcock, allegedly unfamiliar with southern juries, or to Shushan's association with the recently martyred Huey. The FBI heard rumors—but got no proof—that four members of the jury were bribed.[35] Wilkinson argued that the prosecution was politically motivated.[36]

The prosecutions were political. Anti-Long district attorney Rene Viosca confidentially told the administration that two of the cases were weak: one was based on testimony of Mike Moss, who was unreliable and had changed his stories several times, and the other was a ridiculous conspiracy theory in which the government alleged only that Weiss told another man not to pay his taxes.[37] The government proceeded, nevertheless.

Mixed with these controversies was speculation that Huey would form a third party or challenge Roosevelt in Democratic primaries. Huey said he would carry the entire South if he ran for president[38] and that in 1936 he would speak for SOW candidates.[39] Syndicated columnist Mark Sullivan thought Huey would win several southern states' primaries, cause a ruckus at the Democratic Convention, form a third party, and take five million votes away from Roosevelt unless economic conditions improved.[40] Huey offered to support Borah or another progressive if the Republicans would nominate him.[41]

Milo Reno of the Farm Holiday Association dreamed of forming a third party.[42] His national meeting in 1934 had attracted Governor Floyd Olson of Minnesota and Father Coughlin. The gathering had lustily booed Agriculture Secretary Wallace. In 1935, Reno invited to Des Moines, Iowa, in late April Huey and others who might form a third party: Father Coughlin, Olson, and Dr. Francis Townsend, the proponent of $200 per month old-age pensions. Only Huey accepted the invitation, so he was the center of attention.[43] Huey planned to speak in Minneapolis and California in June. Commentators expected Huey to receive a "thunderously enthusiastic" reception.[44] Reno praised Huey's Louisiana record.[45]

On his way to Des Moines, Huey stopped in Chicago, greeting newsmen and bystanders with a swagger. Since Roosevelt's acceptance speech, in which he favored SOW, "I've never heard him talk about sharing the wealth since. He's been destroying wealth ever since."[46]

Republicans in the Iowa state legislature invited Huey to speak, a trap—several legislators had called him a clown—that he declined. The convention was taking place at the same time as the Drake Relays, a premier nationwide track-and-field event, hosted in Des Moines. Huey decided to breakfast with the Drake Relays beauty queens. One said Huey was "sociable and friendly. But I would have known he was a politician even if I hadn't known who he is. He talked about politics mostly—and himself."[47] Huey addressed ten thousand of Reno's farmers at 2:30 in the afternoon. He sang a few bars of "Every Man a King."[48] He used the High Popalorum / Low Popahirum analogy to describe the difference between Republican and Democratic leaders; the crowd laughed.[49] The difference between a radical and a conservative was that a conservative could say it, "but be damn sure you don't intend to do it." There was loud cheering and shouts of "Amen." Author Robert Morss Lovett was captivated by Huey's performance (Huey was Tom Sawyer in a toga) and so reported in *New Republic* magazine. Huey claimed he could take Iowa like a whirlwind.[50]

Later in the afternoon Huey appeared at the Drake Relays, impressed with the youthful crowd and the facilities. He appeared on the field and got cheered and booed. The national press omitted what the local paper reported: people stood up to see him and blocked others' views of the events, upsetting them; people didn't want the events delayed; autograph seekers mobbed Huey; some booed just to razz someone; some had no idea why they were either cheering or booing; some said the cheers outweighed the boos and others the reverse.[51] Huey "loved it all."[52] Sixteen pictures of Huey were taken by the local newspaper: giving autographs, talking to children, and speaking in various poses. His bodyguards were criticized for paying low tips; he showed wide knowledge on many subjects but didn't know the name of Iowa's governor or his politics; in his autographs he barely wrote the Y; the guards were tolerant of autograph hunters; he made a brief visit to a veteran's hospital; talked mostly in the first person; and bodyguards anticipated his every need. "Staccato, swagger, certain, sharp and smart; every minute it's like that with Huey Long." It was hard to keep up as "he shouldered through the crowd before his hotel room door, through the fairgrounds speech, the veteran's hospital visit, the Drake Relays, the brief conferences in the hotel room, everything clicked."[53] The *Des Moines Register* editorialized after the speech that Huey's figures still were incomprehensible,[54] but Reno's association voted to form a third party.[55]

Roosevelt gave a fireside chat the day after Huey's Des Moines speech, hardly a coincidence, responding to unnamed critics who were trying to "confuse" people. The *St. Louis Post Dispatch* editorialized that Huey, as a rustic, southern evangelist, must have appeared strange to Iowans, but Roosevelt's speech after the "impassioned oratory in Des Moines was refreshing. It carried reassurance. It induced calm. We do not need a third party to solve the problems of the nation."[56] Wishful thinking; the farmers voted to form one.

On May 2, Huey responded on the radio to Roosevelt's fireside chat, attacking him for joining Vincent Astor on his $5 million yacht, the *Nourmahal,* which sailed into the "briny British waters" with the Duke and Duchess of Kent.[57] Astor did a lot of "ship subsidy business with the government, where they get as much as $1,000 to carry one three cent letter." Perhaps the country should have Roosevelt remain at sea and trust to luck it would find its way back to prosperity.

In his speech, he read an article in the *New York Daily News.* It had sent one of its most competent reporters, Lowell Limpus, to examine the figures Huey provided in his radio reply to General Johnson but discovered that Huey told the truth. The newspaper hesitated to report this but, finally, in Huey's words, "it decided to tell the truth in spite of itself." The Limpus article rebutted Roosevelt's criticism that he was confusing people. As an aside, he dealt with critics who claimed that wealth, as a practical matter, could not be redistributed: "Now my friends let no one tell you that it is difficult to redistribute the wealth of this land. It matters not how rich or how great one may be. When he dies his wealth must be distributed anyway. If Rockefeller died today, they'd have to redistribute his wealth to his heirs."[58]

Huey's speeches of 1935 reflected his conception of leadership. The leader should explain his program slowly and patiently. Then when it is understood and he is voted into office, he should put it through against all obstacles.[59]

A cardinal advertising rule is that "[e]very advertisement must tell the whole sales story because the public does not read advertisements in series."[60] Huey's speeches in 1935 used the same statistics, explained the cause of the Depression, and described his plan. He shuffled the order of proofs, sometimes starting with the Bible[61] and sometimes ending with it; sometimes citing Greek philosophers; always chastising Roosevelt for betraying his campaign promises; changing the focus of the opening attack (Johnson in the March speech; Roosevelt in this one); adding recent news items such as the Limpus article as appropriate; always rebutted his critics near the end; included poignant stories of distress; and focused on the central insanity of reducing production and piling up big fortunes in the midst of starvation, homelessness, and unemployment. Huey always called for action: to join SOW.

Roosevelt had anti-Long congressmen invite Agriculture Secretary Wallace to Louisiana.[62] On May 11, Wallace spoke to a pro–New Deal audience of three hundred in Alexandria. The five anti-Long congressmen, Mayor Walmsley, and a contingent from Baton Rouge attended.[63] On May 15, 1935, Roosevelt called to the White House lawn four thousand farmers grateful for Agricultural Adjustment Act crop-reduction checks to hear him again charge that critics were misleading the people.[64] Joe Robinson claimed that old-line Republicans were financing all radicals to split Roosevelt's vote.[65]

The Johnson attack should have driven Father Coughlin and Huey together. Coughlin had a huge audience, eight million or more listeners each week. Huey's SOW booklet included a long quotation from him. Coughlin called Huey before his early 1935 weekly radio addresses. In February, Coughlin said Huey was misunderstood, that he was an "honest to God" devotee of social justice.[66]

Coughlin had a weak mind, however. He veered between proposals and between praising and denouncing Roosevelt. He sympathized with the mass of people and denounced the wealthy captains of finance, but he was primarily a sonorous radio voice, occasionally strident. Coughlin's most specific principles were that the government should control the banking system and increase the supply of money by coining silver. Roosevelt officials listened to him, and one infers from reading the correspondence that Coughlin was pleased if not intoxicated by this access. Morgenthau in 1934, however, had leaked an investigatory finding that Coughlin's secretary had invested in silver mines, which undermined him.[67]

Coughlin had first opposed the soldiers' bonus but reversed course in February 1934 and gave an effective Armistice Day address in 1934 supporting it and announcing his National Union for Social Justice. Huey's advocacy of inflation and the soldiers' bonus allied him with Coughlin before they cooperated in defeating the World Court treaty.

In response to Johnson's speech, Coughlin attacked Johnson as a tool of Bernard Baruch, misstating Baruch's middle name as "Manasses," which was false and probably anti-Semitic. Coughlin stated that his opinion was still Roosevelt or ruin, however. Huey called Coughlin's response a "a masterly defense" and complimented his description of "the way Baruch has controlled this man Roosevelt."[68]

Later in March, Huey and Coughlin met for several hours with Senator Wheeler. Louisiana public service commissioner James O'Connor was visiting. After several hours of discussions, Coughlin agreed to support Huey for president and in other conferences deferred to Huey.[69]

By the time of the Des Moines conference, however, Coughlin was skittish about a third party and Huey.[70] It would necessitate an irrevocable break from Roosevelt, and he was feeling independently influential. His bishop had just backed him. A huge rally in Detroit that he sponsored featured Senators Thomas and Nye, Representative Lemke, and other congressmen. Coughlin sent representatives to Reno's meeting in Des Moines but in their "private capacities." Huey unsuccessfully tried to call him from Iowa. Coughlin said he favored the Farmers Union over Reno's Farm Holiday Association.[71] The Farmers Union had resolved that 5 percent of the people owned 90 percent of the wealth and called for limiting inheritances to $500,000.[72] The differences with the Holiday Association were minuscule.

Coughlin on May 15 said he didn't support SOW. Disgusted, Huey told a reporter that Coughlin was just a political Kate Smith on the air; the people would get tired of him. On May 22, Coughlin, smiling dismissively, said he couldn't understand SOW.[73] Coughlin may have thought he did not need Huey. Or he was responding to the percentage of his followers who disliked explicit criticism of Roosevelt.[74]

Having advocated old-age pensions in January and the McCarran amendment for organized labor in February, and recruited students in March and farmers in April, in May Huey led the fight for the soldiers' bonus. Its defeat in 1934 had only intensified support for it. Vowing to get more politically active, the VFW added 340 new posts in one year. Their September 30, 1934, encampment called for conscripting wealth to support future wars, payment of the bonus, and an increase in inheritance taxes. They repudiated Roosevelt's message to view the "welfare of the country" ahead of "lesser things" like the bonus. The American Legion, more conservative than the VFW, was alienated by Roosevelt's remarks to its convention and voted 987 to 183 to support the bonus in late 1934.

A secret meeting between American Legion leaders and Roosevelt in October 1934 resulted in a contrived legion letter asking for Roosevelt's reasons for opposing the bonus. Roosevelt delayed answering until December 27, 1934; then he said it would not help economic recovery. The VFW rebutted Roosevelt's letter, and it failed to convince the American Legion.[75]

Under the sponsorship of Wright Patman of Texas, the bonus again passed the House of Representatives in 1935. In the Senate, three versions of the bonus were propounded. The Patman bill was more inflationary; the Harrison-Roosevelt bill the least costly; a bill sponsored by Senator Vinson lacked an appropriation to pay for it.[76]

Huey argued that the law of political self-preservation would force Roosevelt to sign the bill. Huey thus prepared "a situation from which Roosevelt could not escape with much credit. If he signed the bill, he would seem to do so for completely political reasons; if he vetoed it, he would seem to be opposing a popular measure that embodied the just aspirations of the veterans."[77] As the "field marshal" for the Patman forces, Huey was "all over the floor at once," directing strategy, buttonholing senators, and making parliamentary inquiries. When Huey discussed Roosevelt's war record and defended his own, Senator Tydings went white with rage and advanced with his fists clenched; Huey turned back from Tydings and continued. A veto would be a "political monstrosity that . . . no man can defend, either in his own conscience or in a political campaign." Roosevelt was "leading the Democratic Party to slaughter."[78] Jesse Jones, the conservative head of the Reconstruction Finance Corporation, undercut the administration; he admitted it would not be inflationary.[79]

The Patman bill passed on May 7, fifty-five to thirty-three. The vote disguised some Machiavellian maneuvers: ten administration senators backed the Patman bill because it was more radical than Vinson's, and because they believed that a presidential veto of that bill—now considered likely—would be upheld.[80]

On May 10, 1935, Huey gave a three-hour speech in the Senate that "brought cheers and roars of laughter from the veterans and lobbyists who packed the galleries."[81] Having road-tested his remarks, he condensed them and on May 12, 1935, gave his best radio speech. The effective opening claimed that the bonus was not a bonus at all, used word pictures, and engaged the senses:

> Ladies and Gentlemen:
>
> The Congress of the United States by an overwhelming majority in both houses has voted to pay in full what is generally called the soldiers' bonus, but what in reality is not a soldiers' bonus at all, but the adjusted service wages, and very poor wages at that, which the government allowed to the soldiers for the days that they served in the World War.
>
> We have generally referred to this proposition as a "soldiers' bonus," but here is what it was. When the boys came back from the war in 1918 and 1919 and some as late as 1920, the government said that since all common labor had been paid from three dollars to four dollars per day during the war without taking any chance of being shot down, or of having their legs shot off, or their eyes shot out, that they would pay the soldiers for the time that they worked, fought, and risked their lives and bodies, the same amount per day as the commonest kind of laborer was paid for the same days worked during the war.
>
> Now since they figured that the soldier had already been paid around 30 dollars to 40 dollars per month while he was in the war, they deducted the one dollar or dollar and a quarter per day and gave the soldier a certificate for the balance. . . .

> Now I think you or I or most any other person would say that as a general rule, the man who worked and fought, who slept in the trenches on the ground, in the rain, and in the mud, and who took a chance of never coming back, was entitled to get a little bit more money for that kind of service, than the man who lived in comfort in his home and took no such chance of being maimed or killed.
>
> But we did not regard it that way when we gave the soldiers our certificates for service. We took the view that they were not entitled to any more money than the sorriest kind of field hand or workhand. And that is the certificate which they hold today and which is called the soldiers' bonus.

The legislation to pay for it had passed and would become law notwithstanding a veto if two-thirds of the senators vote to override it, but Roosevelt was the obstacle.

> Now the President tells us that he was a veteran of the World War too, and that he understands it somewhat better than we may think. Well it is true that Mr. Roosevelt was a veteran of the World War, and an honorable veteran. He was Assistant Secretary of the Navy. He stayed up here on Pennsylvania Avenue in the daytime and in a very fine home during the nighttime and he drew 10 thousand dollars a year for his services and he was worth every cent of it. He was three thousand miles away from gunfire. . . .
>
> But the man that he does not seem to have learned about is the man that did not stay on Pennsylvania Avenue and who did not stay in any luxurious home, but the man who scoured the seas, who walked and slept in the rain, who stood in the mud waist deep in the trenches, who went over the top and faced the German guns, who breathed the poisonous gases, and who not only went through 14 kinds of carnage worse than the fires of hell itself, but who, when he came back, found his occupation destroyed and the job which he had held gone.

He indignantly confronted critics: "Someone said to me that some soldiers they knew of ought not to be paid the bonus because they turned out to be bums. Who was it that made them bums? The government sent them into the fires of death, and I wonder that as many came out as well as they did. That's no argument against paying the bonus."

The Patman bill would allow the soldiers to cash their bonus certificates to get circulating money in their face amount, compared to numerous bills that had allowed bankers to draw face value in money on the government obligations which they held.

> Now what's the justification in these senators who have voted to let the bankers put up the bonds and get 100 cents on the dollar and draw the interest just the same and yet turn around here and not let the soldier put up his bond and draw the money without drawing the interest? I want somebody to tell me how they make fish out of one and fowl out of another.[82]

> Oh yeah, [the big bankers] sounded the drum. They played the bands and said everything would be good when the boys came back home. Now these very same men who made millions out of the flesh and blood of the men who fought their battles are the very men who are fighting against these men being paid the bonus after 17 years.
>
> The soldier is entitled to be paid this bonus. He has done his work. He has made his fight. He has taken his chance. He has made the sacrifice. He's kept the faith. And he is the only man, the only one who never was paid the daily wage for the days he worked during the war.

Huey hoped Roosevelt would pay as much attention to the letters he was getting from the American people rather than those views of the "high aristocracy" he surrounded himself with on the *Nourmahal*. "Great good would be done to this country if we paid this two and a quarter billions of dollars into the channels of our commerce. It would stimulate business everywhere." Huey's listeners should write and wire their senators to override any veto.[83]

Emerging from the conference committee, the bonus was again passed and sent to Roosevelt on May 14. Coughlin spoke for it over the radio on May 5 and to 24,500 people in Cleveland on May 8.[84] Farley and Vice President Garner urged Roosevelt to sign it or veto it with a wink and let it be overridden because it would either stimulate the economy or allow him to equally blame Republicans for voting for it.[85]

The day after his radio speech, Huey called up his resolution to investigate Farley. Dramatically he provided two more affidavits from ex-employees of the company affiliated with Farley, only copies, he said, because his office lockbox had been rifled and his telephone tapped. As dramatic were the circumstances by which they had been obtained. Huey got a call at 11:50 p.m.; he rushed to catch the last (midnight) train for New York. The railroad delayed the train for ten minutes for him. One ex-employee had been ordered to remove all letters from Farley after the federal investigation was begun, and she was then fired because "her memory was too good."[86]

Wheeler, Norris, LaFollette, and Republicans other than Borah and Johnson voted for it, but Huey lost the vote, twenty to sixty-two. Huey shouted, "Go ahead and whitewash Old Jim! You can no more make this a pure man than you can make a rotten egg edible."[87] There was enough evidence to investigate, but the Democrats protected their patronage chief.[88]

The attacks on Huey failed to counter the impression that Roosevelt was drifting.[89] Garner said that little was done to satisfy the people's desire for liberal government.[90] Huey's movement was growing. At the end of April, there were 7,682,768 members of 27,431 Share Our Wealth clubs. They were concentrated in the South, but with significant membership in the West and Midwest. In the history books, these were the final membership figures reported, but this assumes no one joined in May, June, July, or August, even after Huey's two powerful radio speeches in May. Estimates in September put the membership at 330,000 members in Louisiana, 60,000 members in Mississippi, and 9,000,000 throughout the country.[91] There was at least one SOW member in every county in the United States.[92] Townsend had 450,000 dues-paying members in his clubs in February 1935, concentrated in the West, even though he had incorporated his organization one month before Huey. Coughlin's audience was mostly in the Midwest and industrial Northeast.[93]

Concerned, Farley commissioned a poll by Emil Hurja to secretly measure Huey's strength if he ran as a third-party presidential candidate. As of April 30, it showed that Huey would get between three and six million votes, that his strength was not confined to the South, and that he could tip the scales of the election to the Republican candidate.[94] He would get 7.8 percent of the vote from those not on relief and 10.9 percent of the overall vote. Drew Pearson wrote that on a Hurja transcontinental trip he found "widespread Huey Longism in the south and west and much Father Coughlinism in northern industrial centers."[95]

The poll understated Huey's strength. Hurja's method was to mail a letter with a prepaid postcard ballot from a fictional magazine to 100,000 telephone owners and almost 50,000 more ballots to relief recipients. One-fifth (31,000) of these ballots were returned. Hurja reported that Roosevelt would defeat Huey 50 percent to 30 percent in Louisiana. That is possible but not probable.

Huey got 140,000 postcards signed by South Carolinians who said they would vote for him for president in 1936 and added 60,000 enrollees in SOW. Only 104,000 people voted there in 1932.[96] Yet Hurja's poll predicted that Huey would get 6.4 percent there and Roosevelt would get 90.2 percent.

It is problematic to reconcile 6 million votes with 7.6 million SOW members in April. But Brinkley proved that not all SOW members would vote for Huey.[97] It is impossible to imagine those *members* who would have voted for Huey not carrying any *nonmembers* to the polling place with them, however. Is anyone prepared to say that *all* of Huey's supporters signed up for SOW—that is, that Huey had no fans who failed to write him?

Farley was "plainly worried" and told Ickes he detected a "decided shift" against the administration. Louis Howe "kept needling the President by sending him letters demonstrating the spread of Long's influence." Big business leaders bitterly criticized Roosevelt, hypocritically with respect to the NRA and without justification for his banking, SEC, and public works programs. A recent attack by the Chamber of Commerce particularly—and justifiably—rankled.[98]

On May 14, Roosevelt called an evening meeting with liberals: Senators Wheeler, Norris, Costigan, LaFollette, and Nye; cabinet members Wallace and Ickes; and informal advisor Frankfurter. Wheeler and LaFollette did most of the talking. Wheeler denounced Roosevelt's conservative course, although he conceded that Roosevelt had gotten a lot out of Robinson. LaFollette said the best way to defeat Huey was to advance the legislative program in progress. Several thought he would never attract big business support and might as well capitalize on its opposition.[99] Ickes was heartened that Roosevelt was now going to adhere to a more progressive course.[100]

But he didn't. Treasury secretary Morgenthau opposed the soldiers' bonus, and the veto-with-a-wink idea was leaked. If it were implemented, Roosevelt would look weak. Roosevelt resolved to veto the bonus in person: "If I win, I'll be on the crest of the wave," he thought.[101] Roosevelt asked Congress to allow him to address it in joint session to explain his reasons.[102]

Huey filibustered against this invitation ("[he is] coming here to be known, coming here to be embellished, coming here to be fawned over"), but the motion was allowed.[103] The administration waited him out to see, in Robinson's opinion, "just how long he intends to make an ass of himself."

Senator McKellar sputtered that Huey couldn't get the Lord's Prayer adopted in the Senate. When the galleries laughed and the chair rebuked the visitors, Barkley asked the chair not to be too harsh on the galleries because, obviously referring to Huey, "'when people go to the circus they like to laugh at the monkey.' 'I resent that,' said [Huey], with a laugh. 'I don't want the Senator from Kentucky to characterize my friend from Tennessee as a monkey.'"[104] The laughter drowned out McKellar's flailing efforts at a reply.

Roosevelt's appearance was covered as a grand, dramatic occasion by the newsreels of the day. Thomas sat with arms folded in disapproval throughout it. People crowded around their radios to hear him. Roosevelt argued that veterans had benefited disproportionately from New Deal relief and public works programs, that the bonus would provide no stimulus to the economy, that inflating the currency would hurt veterans living on fixed pensions, and that wealth would be neither created nor redistributed by paying the bonus.[105]

The same newsreels covered Huey's reaction:

> These three million soldiers, their wives and their children had already figured just what each of them would do with a few hundred dollars that each one of them were to get. No doubt each of them had calculated to pay some debts, to buy some food, and to buy some clothes, and maybe to send a boy or girl to school. . . . And it is especially cruel to have it vetoed in such a grand spectacle and thereby putting the dagger in the heart of these three million soldiers, their wives and their families.[106]

The House voted to override the veto as soon as Roosevelt left the chamber. Coughlin spoke to twenty-three thousand people in Madison Square Garden opposing the veto with other congressional leaders, not Huey. The audience booed New Deal Senator Wagner.[107]

By this veto, Roosevelt created a core constituency that despised him, not the entire group of three million veterans and their families, but a large proportion of them. Many VFW posts doubled as SOW headquarters. Many told Roosevelt that Huey had his number. Bitter cartoons pilloried Roosevelt. The newspapers applauding the veto failed to reflect this overwhelming sentiment.[108]

Huey returned to Louisiana late in May to resume a fight for lower utility bills. Bonus sympathizers joined him in a veto protest parade. Huey marched with his two sons in the parade, pictured in newspapers nationwide.[109]

Added to the pressure from Huey, the attacks of big business, and protests from veterans after the veto came two decisions of the U.S. Supreme Court on

May 27. The court ruled nine-to-zero that the NRA and the Frazier-Lemke debt moratorium bills were unconstitutional.[110] The NRA decision was a disguised gift to Roosevelt, who had said the NRA was a "mess."[111] Rather than let the NRA collapse because of its defects, the court killed it, allowing Roosevelt to blame it as a scapegoat. Roosevelt gave a long disquisition arguing that the Supreme Court was applying principles from the horse-and-buggy days, widely quoted.[112]

But Roosevelt's initiatives of his first hundred days, his first two years really, had now run their course. The economy was still in shambles, and the Supreme Court had just eliminated Roosevelt's plan to rejuvenate it. Roosevelt had no other plan. Huey the pied piper was leading Democrats away from him. Big business was hostile. The bonus veto backfired.

The Knight of the *Nourmahal* now had to figure out how to end his administration's drift. He needed to answer the country's economic problems and his own political problems. An answer didn't come to him all at once, but he had instinctively been working toward one; it finally came to him with clarity, and he acted on it.

## *Twenty-Eight*

# STEALING HUEY'S THUNDER

During the spring, Roosevelt said that to combat Huey's crackpot ideas he might have to throw the forty-six persons who made more than one million dollars a year to the wolves; that the people seemed to be turning to strange gods; that he was fighting Townsendism, Huey Longism, and so on; and that he might have to steal Huey's thunder.[1] Over cocktails at Joseph Kennedy's house, he wished someone would handle Huey "physically," but the senators were afraid of him.[2] Roosevelt had been "down cast."[3] Men close to him thought he would be defeated in 1936.[4]

Having appealed to conservatives with his veto of the soldiers' bonus, Roosevelt now zig-zagged left to regulate utility holding companies. Huey went to Louisiana at the end of May while Senator Wheeler led the two-week debate. Returning to Washington on June 10, Huey complained that the bill was too weak—Wheeler admitted this—because it omitted the gas and oil industries.[5]

Illinois senator William Dieterich led a key fight to gut the "death sentence" for holding companies. Huey confronted Dieterich with an inconsistent vote he cast as a congressman. Dieterich's amendment failed on a close vote, forty-four to forty-five, on Monday, June 11.[6] After the amendment was defeated, the bill passed fifty-six to thirty-two.[7]

Roosevelt then turned to the NRA, set to expire on June 16. Senator Gore proposed an amendment requiring Senate confirmation of NRA appointees. Huey and the conservative Senator Tydings—an odd couple—cavorted about the chamber urging colleagues to vote for it, while Senator Harrison sent aides to the cloakrooms and corridors to recruit senators to oppose it. The count stood at thirty-four to thirty-four when a group of Republicans arrived and voted for it. It passed forty-three to thirty-eight.

Huey hugged Senator King of Utah, looking like a "mischievous boy." Even "pro-administration senators chuckled openly at the hot spot" on which this placed Roosevelt.[8] Huey dashed across the aisle to ask Gore to move to reconsider and then table it, to lock in the amendment. Shouting frantically, Barkley moved for a recess, a privileged motion, and got the votes for it. Huey said he would vote to recess and, if they "want to filibuster," he would "help them."[9]

When the Senate convened the next day, the administration defeated the motion to lay the Gore amendment on the table, thirty-six to forty-four. With his son, Russell, visiting from Louisiana,[10] Huey filibustered the reconsideration of the Gore amendment, which would also delay the vote on the motion to extend the NRA. McCarran, Schall, and Gore helped with friendly questions. Huey wanted an agreement on when to take a vote before he gave up the floor, whereas Senate freshmen—led by Senators Black and Schwellenbach—insisted he relinquish it without an agreement and refused all courtesies.

Visitors from a Shriners' convention filled the galleries. As the galleries emptied, new visitors took the vacated seats. Huey read the U.S. Constitution article by article, explaining its meaning; read from a Victor Hugo novel; took requests from newsmen about subjects on which to speak; gave lectures about historical figures such as Judah P. Benjamin; told jokes; and instructed how to fry oysters, cook potlikker, and make Roquefort salad dressing. At 4 a.m. he finally had to answer the call of nature and gave up the floor.[11]

In page-one headlines, the *Tribune* said it was one of the "most extraordinary exhibitions of buffoonery, personal invective and physical endurance on record." Even when physically exhausted, "mentally [Huey] was a match for the freshest of adversaries, or all of them combined." The filibuster record was held by Robert LaFollette Sr., lasting eighteen hours opposing a currency bill, but he had much more help (quorum calls, having the clerk read a document, requiring unanimous consent by senators, usually given as a courtesy), making Huey's "far more remarkable." What "most amazed the spectators was Long's sense of humor, which his adversaries lacked, and his even tempered, if often affected, urbanity under the hottest fire. Huey laughed good naturedly at the most vicious thrusts, and when he turned them into boomerangs for his foes the galleries laughed with him."[12] Stories noted his recipe for frying oysters, the cost to taxpayers,[13] Garner's quip that forcing senators to listen to Huey's speech would be cruel and unusual punishment,[14] and that the galleries sent down messages suggesting stories for him to tell.[15] Will Rogers joked that when Huey explained the Constitution, many senators thought he was reading a new book.[16]

The *Times*, in contrast, emphasized that Huey was defeated by the freshmen senators, although it gave Huey the last sardonic word ("Just say that I view with alarm the uprising of the young Turks"). Krock thought that breaking the filibuster ended Huey's mastery of the Senate and that he was "frantically jocose" and often boring, but the *Congressional Record* reveals laughter at regular intervals. Turner Catledge contended that the filibuster "ended in no credit" for Huey.[17]

Roosevelt, however, had had enough. On June 13, the next day, Roosevelt convened a meeting of House and Senate leaders and pressed for immediate passage of administration bills, giving a forceful, table-pounding performance.[18] Originally lukewarm about Wagner's social security bill, and especially its old-age pension provisions, Roosevelt supported it now. Tugwell gave Huey the credit for this.[19]

In the Social Security debate that followed, Huey argued against administration by the states: "[W]ho in the South is the most needful of pension assistance? . . . [T]he colored man. How many colored people do you think would get on one of these select lists? Let's be frank about this business. I am possibly the only Southern Senator here who can be frank about it."

Clark proposed to exempt private companies that had their own pension plans. Ironically, liberals who wanted the government to set up a yardstick for private industry in the utilities field opposed this yardstick for the government in the pension field. The amendment passed fifty-one to thirty-five, Huey and many conservatives voting for it, while Overton, Wheeler, Norris, Wagner, and administration senators voted against it.[20] The bill then passed seventy-seven to six. The conference committee later dropped Clark's amendment, and the bill passed. Funded by a regressive tax on workers themselves, Social Security was irresistibly conservative and supported by a consensus.

While Huey was unfazed by the defeat of his filibuster, many senators were now trying to crush him. Huey used the Senate in 1935 primarily as a platform to denounce Roosevelt and explain his program to the country.[21] Darrell St. Claire overstated it only slightly when he said that Huey gave the same speech—a good one, but the same one—every day.[22]

Thus, when Huey criticized Farley during an inconsequential debate about parole policy on Saturday, June 15, Ashurst pulled a clever speech from his desk to ambush him. Accusing Huey of exalting himself, erratic behavior, and an absence of self-awareness, he attributed it to the times, analogized to a storm at sea that washed up various unusual creatures in its wake: crawfish, jellyfish, starfish, and kingfish.

Ashurst forgot to mention tadpoles, Huey replied, a creature far too numerous in the Depression. The tadpole promises one thing and does something else. Wealth redistribution was promised by the current president and by the ex-president, and they were all going to be "exes" until the promise was kept.[23]

Roosevelt wasn't going to wait for the Senate to crush Huey. After the Social Security victory, Roosevelt made explicit what had been an implicit or instinctive strategy to counter Huey: he would coopt him. Hugh Johnson had written that Roosevelt would move to the left as far as necessary to defeat Huey or other radicals, not as a leftist, but rather to avoid "giving up the ship."[24]

On June 19, Roosevelt sent Congress a message about taxes. In December 1934 and January 1935, Roosevelt stated that no new tax legislation would be advocated, the pronouncements Huey had denounced between January and May. No revenue shortfall justified new taxes.[25]

Roosevelt decried the concentration of wealth and advocated increased taxes on high incomes, undistributed corporate profits, and inheritances. Wealthy newspaper publisher William Randolph Hearst, whom Roosevelt despised, was in Roosevelt's mind during the drafting process, and he sadistically enjoyed the prospect of outraging Senator Pat Harrison: he would "have kittens" on the spot. In the House the message was read to cheers culminating in a standing ovation, but in the Senate, it was read in cold silence. Only Huey enjoyed it. He strutted around pointing at his chest and at the conclusion said, "I just want to say, 'Amen.'"[26]

Will Rogers wrote that he would have liked to see Huey's face in his bed when Roosevelt came up and said, "Lay over, Huey, I want to get in bed with you."[27] In stories too numerous to cite, newspapers commented that Roosevelt's program was balanced, unlike Huey's; expedient, not sound, his message designed only to attract Huey's followers; or radical, like Huey's plan.

In the short term, Roosevelt's move negated the Senate's efforts to squelch Huey. Huey chided Ashurst that Roosevelt must be one of those creatures thrown up by the storm of the Depression that he had mentioned, because Roosevelt now endorsed his program. Ashurst went silent.[28] Huey spent a day citing editorials that said Roosevelt was stealing his thunder. Huey sent an open letter to Roosevelt posing questions to test his sincerity. Appealing to the opposite audience, Vandenberg read editorials and stories comparing Roosevelt's tax message with Huey's proposals.[29]

One week after the tax message, Roosevelt struck again, announcing a National Youth Administration to provide money for vocational and college training. This was also "stole[n] thunder from the left from Senator Huey Long."[30] But only $50 million was appropriated.

When the text of the tax bill was received, Krock thought it would neither raise revenue nor redistribute wealth. It was "neither fish nor fowl, but perhaps a good red herring."[31] Huey labeled it a fraud.[32] In a radio speech from New Orleans on July 8, he called Roosevelt a liar and a faker and defied anyone to indict him for saying that. After quoting Roosevelt's Chicago convention acceptance speech, Huey noted that Roosevelt opposed every effort he made to implement an old-age pension plan; pay the soldiers' bonus; and provide college educations, a home, and incomes to the people. The public was roused from coast to coast for SOW, but Roosevelt only made gestures.

> They say that Mr. Roosevelt has only done this so as to steal my political thunder, or to take the wind out of my sails. Call it a mere imitation of my talk, if you will; call Mr. Roosevelt's gesture for the share-our-wealth plan a counterfeit, if you desire; the fact remains that no one imitates another imitation, and no one counterfeits another counterfeit. If Mr. Roosevelt considers that either HUEY LONG or his share-our-wealth plan is so popular or so good that he must either imitate or counterfeit it for his own sake, then he knows that the genuine plan is considered sound enough, good enough, and popular enough to justify his imitation or counterfeit. In all events, you who would take the word or gesture of Roosevelt, must do honor and add prestige and dignity to the share-our-wealth cause, however insincere Mr. Roosevelt may be.[33]

*Barron's* wrote that Roosevelt's tax bill would raise not $340 million as advertised, but $118 million, mostly from corporations, that only $7 million would be collected from inheritance taxes, and only $5.1 million from higher income taxes: "That noise you hear is Huey Long, down in Louisiana, laughing."[34]

Taxing the wealthy was dislodged as the primary political story only by a controversy over seating Senator Holt of West Virginia,[35] by a bill to amend the Interstate Commerce Commission, and by a fist swung at Huey by General Ansell's son on the Shoreham Hotel's dance floor.[36] Huey asked to amend the Interstate Commerce Commission bill and, in a lengthy speech over two days exhibiting a deep knowledge of port regulations, persuaded Borah and was supported by Clark, but was voted down.[37]

Roosevelt now backed all liberal bills. He was unsure about Senator Wagner's bill giving labor the right to organize, but now supported it,[38] plus a modest banking reform proposal to ease credit,[39] and Senator Guffey's bill to regulate the coal industry, improving working conditions and setting a minimum wage.[40] All passed.

There is debate about whether this Roosevelt legislative push, described as a turn to the left or a second New Deal, was caused by Huey on the left, the Supreme Court's NRA decision, or, as suggested by Professor James MacGregor Burns, by abusive criticism from businessmen on the right. The need to coopt Huey was noted by newspaper stories in January before the extreme abuse by businessmen in May and before the Supreme Court killed the NRA. Social scientists advised by Professor Burns concluded that SOW induced Roosevelt to break his pattern of regressive taxation, adopt instead progressive tax policies, and influenced relief spending. Roosevelt's administration spent more relief money where it believed that Huey's third-party candidacy might split Roosevelt's vote and tip a state to the Republicans.[41]

There is a minor debate about the differences between the first New Deal and the second New Deal. The first New Deal intended to manage the economy in the manner of state capitalism or state socialism. It wanted to foster social cohesion, now seen as utopian, naive, and contradictory to the culture of capitalism and individualism, but advocated then by Tugwell, Hugh Johnson, Robert Wagner, and Bernard Baruch.

The second New Deal sought to restore the economy of smaller businesses. It was realistic about the motives and capacity of big business to dominate any regime of regulation and about the prospects of achieving or maintaining social cohesion. Pragmatic men such as Thomas Corcoran and Harry Hopkins spearheaded the second New Deal.

The reluctance to draw the distinction too sharply occurs because (1) the first New Deal contained or proposed elements of the second New Deal (Wagner Act, minimum wages, Holding Company Act, and the Guffey Coal Act), (2) while Corcoran and Hopkins were new, many of Roosevelt's other leaders (Ickes, Frances Perkins, and Tugwell) remained,[42] and (3) even after 1936 Roosevelt proposed NRA-type approaches to economic problems.[43]

To defeat Huey in 1936, Roosevelt wandered toward a conception of the government's role to (a) counteract the loss of purchasing power caused by unemployment and (b) force savings to plan for everyone's retirement or disability. This constitutes an economic safety net.

Did the second New Deal solve Roosevelt's political problems? Opinions varied. Some said it successfully coopted Huey; others, like *Barron's,* that it would backfire because the tax bill was weak. Roosevelt suggested to one friend that he had matters well in hand: he would let Huey and Coughlin have their moments of fame, their one-note radical rhetoric would get tiresome, and then he would reclaim the limelight.[44] While perceptive, these remarks could be a rationalization for indecision. After Huey's death, Roosevelt drifted again when the recession of 1937 occurred, in the absence of any concern about Huey or Coughlin. Leading from behind public opinion required standing back to see which way the wind was blowing.

Huey was not a one-note politician, moreover. His publicity stunts, humorous controversies (green pajamas, potlikker), writing music, conducting the LSU band, and so forth, sustained interest apart from politics. Huey's song, for example, was sung over the radio in 1934 and then played in newsreels by another piano-playing singer. A newsreel stunt showed him breaking a violin over someone's head on a Broadway stage.[45] Huey arranged for it to be played by Ina Ray Hutton and Her Melodears. Some YouTube clips show only the performance by the stunning Ina Ray Hutton, with Huey sitting there a bit weirdly with his eyes half-closed and his hand keeping time with the song. A few of the clips still existing reveal a more elaborate public relations event: Ina Ray Hutton visited his office complaining that Huey's song only mentioned men; what about the sixty-two million women? Huey says "Okay lil lady" and then takes a pen and changes the song so it reads "every man a king and every girl a queen."[46] She then plays the revised song. While the phrase "lil lady" is dated, there was no offense taken. Ina Ray Hutton headed the first all-female band, and her band put on special shows for Huey at the Shoreham Hotel.[47]

The other Roosevelt comment ignores that Huey sometimes ceded the spotlight. After the battle for the veterans in May, Huey returned to Louisiana for more than two weeks while Wheeler led the fight for the Utilities Holding Company Act. In July and August, Huey was often absent from the Senate, although he obtained publicity from his legislative actions in Louisiana. Roosevelt bore Huey's fusillade of blows from January to May while he contemplated his moves, and then dominated the national news from June to August, leaving Huey to plot his next moves.

Huey returned to Louisiana by plane July 3. New Orleans couldn't meet its payroll. Garbagemen, not paid for two months, went on strike, and the garbage piled up in the hot weather on the streets and stank. On June 24, Long leaders in New Orleans asked the union to prolong the strike. This backfired. The union revealed the overture and apologized to Walmsley.[48]

Huey arrived in New Orleans at 9:20 p.m. and, with bodyguards and policemen and a *Times* reporter, was whisked to the Roosevelt Hotel, where he summoned two or three secretaries and legislative counsel George Wallace. A special legislative session was called. He and Wallace worked late drafting bills. At dawn, he left for Baton Rouge.

Roosevelt had stated that WPA money wouldn't be issued to Louisiana because he didn't want it disbursed for political purposes. Huey turned this against him, dictating a telegram to Roosevelt that the Louisiana legislature was ready to pass a bill prohibiting the disbursement of federal funds for political purposes and asking if that would please him.

Bills to remove more patronage from New Orleans were proposed, passed, and enacted. Twenty-six were offered and considered in record time, in front of a relaxed Huey, with only five negative votes. Huey changed his mind about the last bill, shouting, "I don't want that bill passed." Huey was called a crook but yawned. The last vestiges of martial law in Baton Rouge ended.[49] All unelected parish and municipal officials—including those of New Orleans—were now controlled by the Civil Service Commission; sheriffs were denied the ability to fire their own deputies; teachers' employment was put under a budget committee, consisting of the governor, superintendent of education Harris, and other officials; New Orleans's district attorney's assistants would now be appointed by the Louisiana attorney general; and New Orleans was denied the right to levy taxes that had provided it with two-thirds of its revenue. Mason Spencer delivered another warning, not as dramatic as his April prophecy, predicting that the federal government would declare that these bills denied Louisiana a republican form of government.

"I believe in democracies," Huey told the reporter. The people would throw him out if he failed to take care of the weak and suffering. Between running from the House to the Senate, from the floor to committee meetings, Huey wrote LSU songs with Castro Carazo. "Miss Vandy," "Hello, Tennessee," and "Darling of LSU" were just "sweet ditties. Before I'm through I intend to write an opera . . . and a song typical of Louisiana, its beauties, its hopes, its achievements." Someday, "there will only be a few people who will think that I have acted against the best interests of my state. . . . [S]omeday I am coming back here to stay, away from . . . politics . . . to rest and read and sing and dance and play. I am coming to what I hope will be a happy and a contented people." Afterward, he was driven to New Orleans, where he gave a three-hour radio speech. Early in the morning and late at night he was talking to employees, friends, and politicians. "He is restless, nervous and unlimited in energy."[50]

His legislation coerced the surrender of the Old Regulars. On July 10 the ward leaders voted thirteen to four to surrender and demand Walmsley's resignation. Two of the five-person City Council members defected to Huey. Two days later the thirteen ward leaders met with Huey to ask for his terms. After telling them he didn't need them, Huey said he would leave most jobs alone, but wanted petitions circulated block-by-block calling for Walmsley to resign, with the signatures to be delivered the next day. The ward leaders viewed this as magnanimous. Walmsley refused to resign because the Old Regulars had signed a pledge in 1934 to never "do business" with Huey again. After a third member of the council and the remaining ward leaders defected, they excluded Walmsley from their meetings. Some precinct leaders rebelled against the leaders; others advocated a return to the Klan or decided to join "Roosevelt for President" clubs. Huey returned to Washington, promising to call another special session in September to provide relief. Walmsley remained in office, but helpless.[51] The federal court dismissed a challenge to the state law taking over the New Orleans sewage-and-water department. A state court judge ruled Huey's takeover of East Baton Rouge unconstitutional, but Huey planned to appeal.[52]

After Huey left, the five anti-Long congressmen—Wilson, Sandlin, Montet, Dear, and Sanders—conferred at the DeSoto Hotel to plan Huey's defeat, describing him as a "traitor" to the Democratic Party. Twenty-seven men formed the Minute Men of Louisiana, quoting the Declaration of Independence to justify their aims. Ten thousand armed men joined, either to overthrow the government by force or to ensure free elections, depending on the source interviewed. A forty-person remnant of the Square Dealers met in late August to draw lots to determine who would kill Huey.

In Washington on July 19, Huey denounced to a crowded gallery the withdrawal of WPA funds from Louisiana.[53] On Monday the 22nd, after the farm bill had been debated for two weeks without him, he spoke in favor of tariffs[54] and against restricting crop production, after which he voted for the farm bill anyway even though he was "ashamed" of it.[55] Neither speech received notice. Robinson charged that Huey, the Republican Party, and the Liberty League had conspired to obtain control of the government.[56]

The Senate was still in session, but Huey met his wife and two of his children in New York on July 24. Huey flew up a Roosevelt Hotel bartender to teach New Yorkers how to make a Ramos gin fizz. Before a crowd of newsmen and onlookers and after posing for pictures with a shaker, Huey sipped his first drink in eighteen months, saying "I think that's alright, I think that's alright. [*Pause.*] Best be sure about it," and then sipped it again as the crowd laughed. Huey quipped that his grandfather had taught a Louisianan how to mix drinks and had to hand five drinks back to the bartender to ensure he got it right. A newsman asked the cue question, "He handed the drinks back?" "Well," Huey replied, "he handed the *glasses* back." In his hotel suite, Huey talked politics with newsmen. He agreed with what Father Coughlin stood for but didn't know if Coughlin agreed with him.[57]

On August 5, Huey challenged Roosevelt to a debate and promised court action to prevent federal government control over his state: "Defy this kind of autocracy!! Defy this kind of tyranny!" The galleries erupted. Vice President Garner shouted: "The show is over. You can get out."[58] On August 14, Huey said he probably would be a candidate for president in 1936 and chided the administration for a recent loss in Rhode Island of a New Deal candidate, and for Ohio Governor Davies's delay of an election for a congressional vacancy for fear that a New Deal candidate would lose.[59] On the 16th he reiterated his potential candidacy in New York;[60] on the 18th his Louisiana leaders denied it.[61] On the 21st he criticized White House lobbying[62] and asked supportive questions on a munitions bill.[63]

Not even a murder plot made the *Times*. On August 9, Huey read to the Senate from a transcript of the DeSoto conference. Huey's agents eavesdropped by holding a Dictaphone microphone up next to a conference room window, extended at the end of a long pole from an adjoining room window. Oscar Whilden was "out to murder, bulldoze, steal, or anything to win this election." Unidentified voices discussed political possibilities—that federal patronage would be available; that federal troops might safeguard election voting; but one chimed in that it would take "only one man, one gun, one bullet" to do the job. Another suggested that Roosevelt would pardon an assassin.

Surviving attendees denied that the transcript was legitimate but conceded that someone might have said "the only way we could get rid of him was with a bullet." Minute Man Dave Haas's voice was not recorded, but he claimed he attended the conference and was one of five men in a different room who drew straws to see who would assassinate Huey. "We would all have killed him," he said with "relish." Huey was a "dictator just like the Kennedys."[64]

Roosevelt never believed that the people would get tired of Huey. He planned Huey's defeat with anti-Long congressmen that month. Paul Christian would be given a federal position to coordinate efforts across all federal agencies. The seventy-two thousand Works Progress Administration workers would be mobilized to vote. The number of Civilian Conservation Corp camps in Louisiana would be increased and politicized. Having already replaced nonpartisan relief administrator Harry Early with the partisan Peterman, nonpartisan resettlement chief Pete Hudgens was also sidelined.[65]

Roosevelt also asked the Justice Department to determine whether the constitutional guaranty of a republican form of government could compel Huey's removal. The lawyers told him in April that a lawsuit would fail because the courts wouldn't get involved in political questions.[66] If Congress acted, however, there would be no oversight by the courts for the same reason. A bill was passed late in the congressional session to investigate whether Louisiana had a republican form of government.[67]

Now that Huey was supreme in Louisiana, did his appetite for power increase such that, as Williams says, he was unable to distinguish between the power and the goals, the means and the ends?[68]

Huey's goal was to take the offensive against Roosevelt. If Louisiana were secure, he could organize the rest of the country.[69] Beyond his ideas, power consisted of patronage and the money required to mobilize. Controlling every unelected job in the state, including teachers, firemen, and policemen, he had more patronage than any other state leader of any time.

What remains is the topic of money, the mother's milk of politics. In Huey's time and afterward, political parties all over the country raised money from officeholders and state contractors.[70] Huey was more blatant—and transparent—than other politicians about his deduct system, and it had never been applied on the scale that Huey employed it because state spending had never been as great, he methodically enforced it, and the Depression made other employment options scarce. Machine politicians often justified their methods because it made them independent of the wealthy,[71] and the wealthy in Louisiana opposed Huey's policies.

The money Huey needed to mobilize for a nationwide campaign was more than he could command from his customary sources. In 1935, Huey obtained more money. Or did he? Newspapers reported that he was rich from fees earned as the state's lawyer securing utility-rate reductions and collecting delinquent taxes.[72] The money remained in various bank accounts, however, as if, Williams asserts, Huey thought he might have to disgorge it.[73]

Gambling was another source of money. Huey announced at the end of May 1935 that he would allow gambling in St. Bernard and Jefferson parishes. He was a failure as a reformer and had done his best to stop it. There was nothing more to do, Huey said, except to move insane asylums next door to the gambling joints for people crazy enough to gamble. The *Times* reported that leaders in those parishes told Huey that they would desert him unless he permitted gambling and that assessments to Huey's organization would total $125,000 per month.[74] There is no corroboration for this figure. On June 4, Huey explained that gambling had to remain limited and discreet.[75]

This provoked little criticism. One of the secrets to Huey's success was his transparency. Huey admitted things other politicians would try to conceal, and he always had an explanation.

The most tantalizing aspect of Huey's ties with gamblers related to Frank Costello, a New York mobster. Costello moved with ease among legitimate businessmen, a gentleman mobster resembling the underworld character in *The Count of Monte Cristo*. Joseph Kennedy was allegedly his bootlegging partner in the 1920s.[76] Costello attended the 1932 Democratic National Convention. Show business promoter Lou Irwin was a friend.

Slot machines in New York City provided income for his organization. But Mayor Fiorello LaGuardia confiscated them in June and July 1935.[77] Having been introduced by Lou Irwin earlier that year,[78] Huey asked Costello to survey potential locations for slot machines in New Orleans. Huey was considering a plan to license them to support a new pension plan. Or so Costello testified under oath in 1939 when he was indicted for tax fraud. Costello reiterated this to the Kefauver Senate Committee in the 1950s. Costello forcefully denied that Huey broke the law or asked him to break the law:

> [Huey] did it, just like you have a race track up in New Hampshire and if you went there and passed legislation, you are doing it practically for the state.
>
> QUESTION: Well, you put the machines in, didn't you?
>
> COSTELLO: Then I broke the law! [Huey] never broke it.[79]

Russell Long told Professor Williams that Costello was covering for a deal he made later with Robert Maestri and that a deal with Huey was impossible because he couldn't provide "protection" in New Orleans. One of Huey's leaders told Williams that Huey never would have concluded a deal with Costello personally; he would have sent someone. Bodyguard Louis Jones told Williams that Huey several times received gamblers politely, but always turned them down. Williams accepted these reasons.[80]

Huey had control over New Orleans by July 1935, however, and Costello's introduction by Lou Irwin six months earlier rings true, given Huey's relationship with Irwin. Whether Costello truthfully related their conversation is open to debate. It may be that he was attributing the deal to Huey to conceal a deal made with Maestri.[81]

Huey typically investigated people before doing business with them.[82] But Costello's associate Phil Kastel knew Seymour Weiss and Jimmy Brocato/Moran. The *Times Picayune* reported that the slot machines were installed in New Orleans after Huey left for Washington in July and were not removed, unlike competing machines, despite denials from police chief Reyer.[83] The machines were installed, then disappeared, then reappeared.[84] On September 5, the head of the Bureau of Criminal Identification, Louis Guerre, ordered all slot machines in the state confiscated. On September 7, the machines had been removed, but the *Times Picayune* speculated that they were removed because Huey was in town and that they would be reinstalled later: it was "au revoir, not goodbye."[85] To Williams, Guerre denied getting any instructions from Huey except to avoid hiring his enemies, but he was not asked about slot machines.[86]

Hostile biographers assert that Huey allowed the slot machines into New Orleans. They ignore without reason whether Costello was a credible witness, his testimony—if credible—that he was only authorized to do a survey and that Huey planned to make any installations legal, and that the machines were confiscated.[87] It would be naive to deny that Weiss, Maestri, Kastel, and Moran wanted to install slot machines, but unfair to conclude that Huey had approved a deal.

After Huey's death, a rumored meeting in Arkansas in 1936 between Weiss, Maestri, Kastel, and mobsters resulted in slot machine installations in 1936 at a big profit to shareholders Kastel and Costello. Hostile public reaction in 1937 caused their removal once more.[88]

The most controversial source of money, however, was oil.[89] James A. Noe, a state senator elected on Huey's ticket in 1932, was a wealthy oil man.

He knew the oil and gas fields in and around Monroe. There were about 1,250 wells on private land. The field had been producing for over fifteen years. About half of the oil or gas in the field was depleted. Much of the drilling was conducted by United Gas Public Service Company and Interstate Natural Gas Company. Noe knew that state land in this oil field (including waterways) was not drilled. Noe and two associates (D. J. Simmons and M. S. Rhoads) agreed on a joint venture to secure leases on this state land. Noe wanted the lease in his name so he would get credit for it. The state would get royalties and severance tax revenues from land previously undeveloped and before the field was depleted by the drilling on private land. The men had the same joint venture with respect to oil and gas on private land.

After public competitive bidding, Noe secured a lease for five hundred acres of this state land on October 23, 1934. Governor Allen certified that this bid was the most advantageous to the state. There were no other bids. The lease, number 309, required fifty wells to be drilled. Noe sold these fifty tract leases to his colleagues plus one other individual—J. E. Farrell, who was putting up the money to drill—for $27,500 and a reserved one-fourth royalty. At the last minute, Huey and Noe negotiated to keep twenty tracts and only transferred thirty. Rhoads was relieved that they would now only have to drill about thirty wells. His lawyer was upset about the removal of the twenty tracts at the time, but not later, after they successfully drilled thirty wells. Noe told Farrell that they wanted to be sure his group could bear the expense of drilling, pipeline construction, and marketing the oil and gas produced. If the group proved itself, it might get the remaining twenty tracts later, Huey told them.

In November, Huey and Noe formed the Win or Lose Company. Huey drew the charter. Noe (98 percent), Christenberry (1 percent), and Seymour Weiss (1 percent), were its original shareholders. Noe paid for his ninety-eight shares in Win or Lose by contributing the twenty reserved tracts of lease 309 to the corporation. But his ninety-eight shares were endorsed in blank and in odd lots: there were two certificates for thirty-one shares, for example, endorsed but blank. Out of these odd lots one share was given to Alice Lee Grosjean Tharpe, one to Lucille May Grace, twelve to O.K. Allen, and twenty-four to Weiss.

On August 21, 1935, Win or Lose transferred ten of the twenty tracts to the United Gas Public Service Company and the other ten to Interstate Natural Gas Company, each company paying $160,000. The lease with the state was amended contemporaneously so that only thirty wells had to be drilled. Because the companies had other producing wells in the same field, albeit not on state land, they were interested in securing the tracts so that no one else would drill on them. Noe handled these negotiations, and Governor Allen approved the amendment. From the $320,000, on August 27, Win or Lose purchased three cashier's checks, all made payable to cash, for $62,000, $50,000, and $24,000. Allen got $24,000.

When Huey died, thirty-one blank stock shares of Win or Lose were found among his effects, without identifying a shareholder. Christenberry testified that Huey was not a shareholder. Noe told IRS agents in 1937 that Huey was not a shareholder and had not received a nickel from Win or Lose.[90] When it filed its tax returns in 1936, Win or Lose reported that salaries and commissions, not dividends, were paid. The tax returns reported that these salaries and commissions were paid to Noe and Weiss, no one else. Weiss and Noe were indicted in 1941 for filing false tax returns because the checks issued were dividends and paid to them and others. Weiss pleaded guilty and was sentenced to five years of probation. Noe was found not guilty after a trial. In the trial, Noe testified that he and Huey were in the deal 50/50 from the start and that he gave thirty-one blank shares of stock earmarked for Huey and $62,000 in cash (the dividend proportionate to the thirty-one shares) to Seymour Weiss at Huey's direction on September 6, 1935; and that he kept Huey's ownership of stock secret so that the newspapers would not criticize him. Because the blank stock certificates were among Huey's effects, they were listed in his succession filed in 1937. In 1937, Noe said the Long family lawyers made an error.

Huge royalties were earned by the heirs of Huey, Allen, and Noe from Win or Lose for decades after lease 309 was executed, outraging people. Most of this revenue was earned from other, larger (250,000 acres in one case) leases obtained by Win or Lose after Huey died. The leases were publicly bid according to law. Various lawsuits were filed and settled over the years contesting the bidding, drilling, or royalties. Some of the outrage occurred because the market price for oil and the value of leases increased after World War II in ways not foreseen by anyone in 1935.[91]

Having criticized the Win or Lose transactions in the 1940 campaign, reform governor Sam Jones and reform attorney general Eugene Stanley studied Win or Lose but struggled to find a violation of the law. The controversy persisted. As late as 2013, the State Mineral Board of Louisiana prepared a massive report (MBR). It concluded that no law was violated at the time that Noe obtained lease 309 or when he transferred it to Win or Lose. Other Win or Lose leases obtained after Huey's death were similarly within the law at the time.

Lease 309 was only a part of the study. The MBR's analysis accurately asserted that it was too late to undo the leases in 2013: many were no longer producing, the state had accepted benefits under the leases, and settlements in prior years foreclosed new lawsuits. The leases were bid publicly according to law and market prices, and the statutory minimum royalties were obtained. On a revenue-per-acre basis, the state had not suffered any monetary loss. Lease 309 lacked any upfront cash payment, unlike every other lease obtained from the state, but there were no competing bids for it, so it was in the best interest of the state to accept it.

The law granted discretion to the governor. If someone asked to bid for a lease, the governor did not have to advertise it.[92] This incentivized use of politically connected persons to ask for the leases. Because it was often difficult to determine what the best bid was when different upfront payments, royalty rates, wells to be drilled, and the length of time for the lease were proposed, the governor also had discretion to decide on the winning bid, another incentive to use a politically connected bidder. Because the law allowed the winning bidder to then assign the lease, the system developed that someone politically connected would propose a lease, the governor would advertise it, the connected person would win the bid and then assign it for a large profit (a profit denied to the state) to a company that would drill.

What are potential remedies? The voters could elect someone able to negotiate more favorable leases. The law could require sliding scales for minimum royalties, to charge for assignment approvals, or to forbid assignments. The state did not want to drill the wells itself. That would have given the state all the profit—and all the risk.

A policy to prevent state officials from profiting from state leases sweeps very broadly if it forbids part-time legislators from earning a living in their industry just because state leases are required. If they are allowed to have *any* outside business interests, business transactions can disguise influence peddling, *whether or not* those deals relate to state licenses or leases. Mayor Richard J. Daley advised politicians to avoid bribes: "just hand them your business card."[93]

The state's interest was to induce drilling for the positive effect on the economy and the severance tax and royalty revenues. Assigning the thirty tracts fulfilled the benefits of lease 309. The customary royalty was paid, the wells were drilled, and the state received several hundred thousand dollars of royalty and severance tax revenues from lease 309.

The price paid to Win or Lose for the assignments of the reserved twenty acres, however, was due in part to the interest of the purchasers to *prevent* draining the oil field with more drilling. This was a common business practice: to safeguard the production of a well already drilled, nearby locations are purchased so that a competitor would not deplete the field. That was not in the state's best interest, however. The state officials who approved the *amendment* of the lease to reduce the number of wells to be drilled and received money from the assignment had a conflict of interest in approving this amendment. It is not the royalty rate that is at issue. Rather, the reduction in the number of wells that would be drilled, contrary to the terms of the publicly bid lease 309, with payment to state officials who approved the amendment, is the problem. Applying principles of fiduciary duty, those subject to the conflict or conspiring with them should have had to forfeit all compensation received and be liable for money damages for the wells that were not drilled, or the lease should have been recovered for the state.[94]

MBR's finding that no profits were lost was based on a revenue-per-acre comparison to all leases, a large sample size. Lease 309's revenue, to the extent it conformed to the average, showed no losses. But this requires believing that thirty wells produced the same revenue as fifty wells would have produced had they been drilled. That doesn't make sense and is belied by the payment of $320,000 to prevent the drilling.

In one of the cases litigated to settlement in 1945, lease 309 was recovered for the state, along with a payment of $10,000. Russell Long said Noe wanted to fight but his mother lacked the money to pay lawyers and didn't want the lawsuit's headache.[95] The terms of the settlement, however, indicated that the lawyers for Win or Lose understood only too well the potential civil and criminal exposure. Under the settlement, the state ratified the lease *and the amendment* before recovering it, thus preventing any further criminal or civil exposure.

On the assumption that Huey was a shareholder and concealed it, the secrecy of that relationship also indicts it. As a lawyer, Huey was quick to reject retainers, a listing as a bank lawyer, free tickets to the cotton exchange and, while governor and senator, offers of money. When Richard Leche, then a judge on the Appellate Court, had to hear a case involving one of Huey's supporters, Huey told him to decide the case on the merits because a crooked judge was no credit to him. The FBI reported that Huey kicked out of his hotel suite men who offered him $50,000.[96] Huey hated petty grafters. He declined fees to give speeches in Cleveland and New York to industry or civic groups.[97] Huey was indifferent to or contemptuous of money. He was confident that at any time—say if he were defeated in politics—he could earn a lot of money, as he had in 1926.[98] Anti-Long Mason Spencer said Huey kept corruption in reasonable bounds. Long leaders Christenberry, Fields, Ellender, and Lorio believe that Huey didn't know the extent of Shushan's kickbacks and had determined to clean up his organization after the elections of 1936.[99]

In 1935, Huey obtained legal fees for representing the state but left them untouched in state bank accounts. The slot machines were installed, removed, installed, and ordered confiscated. The stock certificates found among his effects were blank. If the deal became public, he could deny that he was a shareholder and return them, or he had not decided whether to accept them. Unless Huey kept the stock, the $62,000 was a campaign contribution, not a taxable dividend. If he kept the stock, he would have had to report the $62,000 dividend when he filed his 1935 tax returns in 1936. Huey's family never found the $62,000, missed a deadline to appeal the tax determination on grounds that it was lost or stolen, and kept the stock and paid the tax on the money it never received. To pay the taxes, the family sold its New Orleans home and, separately, Huey's law book collection to the state.[100]

Progressive Governor Philip LaFollette of Wisconsin described a $100 million works project he proposed: Roosevelt agreed to it, Ickes came to Wisconsin and supported it, and Phil barnstormed the state advocating it. But Phil refused to use any "underhanded" means of getting legislative support. His bill lost by one vote. If he had it to do over again, Phil wrote later, he would not have been so "squeamish."[101]

In politics today, one must either advocate programs that appeal to people who have money to donate to a campaign or make or inherit a lot of money first before running for office. Illinois's 2018 gubernatorial race featured two billionaires running for office. Neither had held office before running for governor. They outspent a Kennedy running against them. Politics: the sport of kings.

In *All the King's Men,* protagonist Jack Burden considers someone who does wrong things to accomplish the right result:

> All change costs something. You have to write off the costs against the gain. . . . The theory of the moral neutrality of history, you might put it. Process as process is neither morally good nor morally bad. We may judge results but not process. The morally bad agent may perform the deed which is good. . . . Maybe a man has to sell his soul to get the power to do good. . . .
>
> All that was a high historical view from a chilly pinnacle. Maybe it took a genius to see it. To really see it. . . . Maybe it took a hero to act on it. (548)

A typical hero pays for the sins of others by dying, as in the New Testament or *A Separate Peace.* The hero is too perfect to survive the broken world. Warren's quote articulates the opposite: sinning for the benefit of others. Is there something of the hero in someone who would choose to do evil to accomplish good? Christian martyr Dietrich Bonhoeffer and the hero of Stephen King's novel *The Dead Zone* come to mind.

In *All the King's Men,* Jack Burden ultimately rejects the choice of evil to accomplish good and goes to work for Hugh Miller, the attorney general who refused to use immoral means for worthwhile ends. "History is blind, but man is not," he says.[102] Confronted by different facts but the same dilemma, the pacifist preacher Dietrich Bonhoeffer conspired to assassinate Hitler.[103] In *All the King's Men,* the novel does not reveal whether Hugh Miller was successful. It ends. In real life, Bonhoeffer was caught and jailed. Just before the Allies liberated Germany from the Nazis, he was executed in a final, petty act of evil. Neither history nor man is blind to Bonhoeffer's choice—or the Nazis'.

Huey warned his associates several times that, if he were to die, they must not attempt to use his powers, or they would go to prison.[104] The comment at first blush seems to be only an eerie premonition. But it also impeaches Williams's idea that Huey had lost sight of his goals and was raising money and obtaining power for its own sake. He could see what he was doing and why, debated his options, and knew that his followers lacked the same vision. It doesn't mean he was right. About several matters, what he had decided, if anything, remains a mystery.

While Roosevelt was stealing his thunder during summer 1935, Huey was working behind the scenes, meeting people who could help him, reaching out to potential allies, and working on a project to present in the fall. Huey worked on another book while Roosevelt dominated the news. Set in the future, it imagined that Huey was elected president and explained what he would do and how he would do it. Its title was *My First Days in the White House.*

## Twenty-Nine

# CONCEIVING HUEY'S FIRST DAYS IN THE WHITE HOUSE

Williams speculates that Huey's plan to capture the White House was complete by August 1935. Huey or a candidate he supported would enter Democratic primaries, win some delegates and, when he lost the nomination at the convention, would bolt, form a new party, split the liberal vote with Roosevelt, and elect a Republican. No Republican would redistribute wealth, the Depression would get worse, and Huey would run and win in 1940, when he was forty-six.[1] This would replicate his Louisiana gubernatorial 1924 (loss)–1928 (victory) experience. In boneheaded comments, Republicans crowed that a third party made their prospects brighter. Huey saw this blunder and denied that he would run to deprive anyone of the office; he would only run if he wanted to win it for himself.[2]

More likely Huey was undecided: considering alternatives, keeping people guessing, and keeping himself in the news. Allen Ellender denied that Huey would have run as a third-party candidate because of the legal impediments to getting a third party on the ballot.[3] Christenberry said Huey intended to stump the country sounding out sentiment before deciding,[4] and it may be that he would have backed someone like Wheeler instead of running himself. The issues Huey framed appealed to families who wanted a home, an automobile, and a radio; farmers; labor; the elderly; veterans; and students. For each group, he had promised more than Roosevelt.

Mobilization centered on SOW societies. Huey's Washington office distributed circulars, newspapers, records (the song "Every Man a King" on one side, a speech on the other), and buttons. The societies organized speakers and meetings. Many SOW leaders and members were of the middle class, or formerly of the middle class: for example, a city cabinetmaker, a Montana bank president, the two-time president of the Atlanta School Board, a University of Illinois engineering professor, a Cleveland attorney, a Chicago Municipal Court Traffic referee, a justice in Pennsylvania, a Texas state senator, a Jacksonville City Council member.[5] A former congressman bankrolled Huey's Philadelphia speech.[6] Former Chicago mayor Big Bill Thompson prepared to back him. Former Oklahoma presidential candidate Alfalfa Bill Murray predicted that Huey would win the presidency in 1936.[7]

A sound plane with loudspeakers and new and improved sound trucks were ordered.[8] The plane would circle a town and announce that he would speak. The airport would be the speech site. A campaign would be expensive, but Huey had the money for it. Huey's associates asserted that Andrew Mellon (believing Huey would split the Democratic vote),[9] Henry Ford,[10] Al Neiman,[11] and others[12] gave Huey money or pledged an estimated $5–10 million (a lot of money in 1935) for his campaign. Huey accepted their pledges but "would not promise to lose."[13]

Much organizing didn't make the newspapers. One Otis Marshburn heard Huey on the radio, contacted him, and was sent to North Carolina to organize that state.[14] A deli owner in the Bronx had a picture of Huey and an "Every Man a King" banner on his wall as late as 1964. When the owner fixed Huey a huge pastrami sandwich in 1935, another customer protested, but he said, "he's my brother; he just come over from Poland."[15] In Chicago, SOW rented a downtown office, a former Indiana state senator made weekly radio broadcasts, and the group raised money and mailed circulars.[16] In California, Robert Noble packed every house he talked to for SOW.[17]

There was resistance. The mayor of Stamford, Connecticut, disallowed an SOW speech.[18] In Chicago, Coughlin couldn't get a permit to hold a rally at Soldier Field. A local SOW member, two years out of law school, intervened in court to support him.[19] The delay caused Coughlin to postpone his rally—fearing winter weather—after winning the right to hold it.

In Mississippi, the gubernatorial primary took place in August. Huey proclaimed neutrality.[20] Paul Johnson came in first by a plurality. The other defeated candidates endorsed Hugh White.[21] Having won his Senate seat stating he was more radical than Huey, Bilbo campaigned all over Mississippi for the conservative White, denouncing Huey and praising Roosevelt, and then claimed credit for his win. Huey nevertheless had an organization in Mississippi, through Mike Conner, the outgoing governor who disliked Roosevelt, and an estimated sixty thousand SOW members. In Florida[22] and Kentucky,[23] Huey participated in gubernatorial maneuverings.

Professor Brinkley argues that SOW didn't take on local power structures, ignoring that Huey opposed Louisiana's local power structure when he ran for state offices. He also said that SOW insinuated itself into local farm, church, labor, or veteran organizations that discussed local matters; that they failed to form cooperatives; and that some organizers used the clubs to make money or caused divisions with other members.[24] Neither the Republican nor Democratic parties form cooperatives or other businesses. They get coopted and attract con men. Insinuating your organization into other established organizations such as a VFW, moreover, makes mobilization easier.

Brinkley writes persuasively, however, about the difficulties of an alliance among progressives. Roosevelt also counted on this. Progressives agreed that the wealthy should pay more taxes, that public works should be expanded, that credit should be made easier, that the soldiers' bonus should be paid, and that the economy was still not benefiting farmers and laborers. Progressives were furious at Farley in general and at Roosevelt for opposing Cutting. One wondered whether Roosevelt's 1935 tax legislation was just a "creampuff."[25] But there were ideological differences between Huey and those who advocated a planned economy. A meeting of leftists after Huey returned from Des Moines omitted him.[26] There was a certain intellectual snobbishness that made it difficult for them to embrace Huey.

LaFollette's weekly newspaper, the *Progressive,* is a good barometer of Huey's mobilization among progressives.[27] The paper featured Phil and Bob LaFollette at the center, but in concentric circles outward, there were first Cutting, Norris, Wheeler, Nye, and LaGuardia, then Congressmen Lemke, Amlie, Maverick, and Lundeen, and then Coughlin, Townsend, and others. Its themes were the same as Huey's *American Progress,* and it reprinted some of the stories from Huey's paper. Huey was ignored in 1934, but in February 1935, because of "inquiries," the paper reprinted two abridged articles from the *Nation* side by side, one by anti-Long journalist Hodding Carter and the other from Gerald L. K. Smith.[28] In March, it reported Huey's controversy with Hugh Johnson: Huey was vague and crude, and they didn't always agree with him, the paper said, but he had accomplished things in Louisiana and dramatized the key issue.[29] In May, it reported Reno's third-party plans and the "tremendous ovation" Huey received at Reno's conference. (Huey's reception in Iowa dumbfounded Senator Johnson.)[30]

Phil LaFollette wanted a third party built state-by-state.[31] Norris was against it.[32] Some hoped that Roosevelt would lead a third party. Ickes was an old Bull Moose progressive, so there were the competing ideas of working with Roosevelt through Ickes to accomplish something, versus working separately from Roosevelt to try to accomplish more. Bob and Phil LaFollette had many cordial meetings with Roosevelt. Bob was helped by Roosevelt in his 1934 reelection campaign, while Farley assisted Phil's Democratic opponent.

Conferences of progressives held in many states gave the illusion of action. One in Chicago was cheered in LaFollette's paper when privately Nye regarded the group as crackpots.[33] While the progressives were conferencing, Huey was raising money, speaking on the radio, and signing people up.

Women were active SOW leaders.[34] Appealing was Huey's record as governor—he had appointed two women to his cabinet (Alice Lee Grosjean and Lucille May Grace)—and his efforts on behalf of Hattie Caraway.

In June, Huey met with Francis Townsend and his political director, Robert Clements. The Townsend Plan (to give the elderly $200 per month on condition that they spend it) spread fast among the elderly and is often mentioned in the same context as SOW, as an unworkable scheme to end the Depression. Huey bluntly told the two men that he doubted the workability of their plan, but he was out to "bust" Roosevelt. They planned to cooperate.[35]

A Black SOW leader in New York said he and Huey would take New York like an "epidemic." Critic Forrest Davis was convinced that Huey, unlike other southern leaders, lacked hatred of Black people.[36]

Roy Wilkins of NAACP's magazine, the *Crisis,* scored an interview with Huey in New York in February 1935. Huey shook his hand (unusual for a southern politician) but used racial slurs to his face, unconscious of giving offense. Huey opposed a federal anti-lynching bill, saying that only an "occasional n——" was lynched and that some white people were lynched. (Roosevelt hadn't supported the anti-lynching bill either.) Huey told Wilkins not to say that he was working for Black people, but rather that he was working for all people who needed a job, a home, and an education and that he had insisted on providing education to Black people so that the planters couldn't cheat them out of their pay. Wilkins thought that Huey would help Black people only insofar as it would not hurt him politically. Huey would have admitted this. He told Wilkins that a delegation of Black nurses asked for jobs in a hospital. Huey went into the hospital and pretended shock that white nurses were treating Black patients, declared that an outrage, and therefore secured jobs for Black nurses. Wilkins's boss edited another story he wrote to remove a harsh characterization of Huey.[37]

At the end of his March 1935 speech replying to Hugh Johnson, Huey read affecting letters from poverty-stricken citizens. One of them was from an African American with whom Huey sympathized but described as a "poor n——." Huey's use of the slur was printed in the *Times* without adverse comment. Black newspapers denounced the slur. Huey then apologized to a Black newspaper for use of the term, saying Black people in Louisiana didn't take offense and used the term themselves, but it was a slip of the tongue, and, in the future, he would be more tactful. SOW was for all people, he said, and he needed Black voters in the North were he to run for President.[38] A *Chicago Defender* columnist concluded that, because Huey's plan would increase wealth held by Black people from $1 billion to $5 billion, and because this economic improvement would render the slur obsolete, they should give Huey serious consideration.[39] One writer suggested that pre–civil rights leaders could be categorized between those seeking integration ("status") and those seeking economic betterment ("welfare"). While the terms are not mutually exclusive, Huey appealed to the latter category.[40]

In the South, Black SOW members were kept segregated in meetings and Christenberry tried to determine which SOW applicants were Black to ensure that southern conventions were maintained. SOW members in Georgia told him they would only solicit white voters to join SOW for fear that otherwise racism would impede their efforts.[41]

Black people in Louisiana preferred Huey to his opponents.[42] They got an education (substandard, but more than before), free schoolbooks, bus rides to school, exemption of property taxes of the first $2,000 of their land's value, and were able to drive on some of his modern highways. Huey's organization registered some Black voters in New Orleans, a right they treasured. Black newspapers reported the victory of a non-racist candidate supported by Huey over a racist candidate backed by Walmsley.[43] Walmsley tried to exclude Blacks from jobs on the New Orleans docks.[44] A letter to the editor of the *Bunkie Record* (June 19, 1935) claimed that Huey planned to register Black voters and that Oscar DePriest, a Black former congressman from Chicago, visited New Orleans and said Huey was the best friend Black people had."[45]

Deutsch wrote about the slip-of-the-tongue apology and that anti-Long newspapers thought the apology disgraceful. Huey's abolition of the poll tax was a prelude to giving Black people the right to vote, he said, and Huey would announce this at a national convention planned for St. Louis or Detroit in 1936.[46] Deutsch cited no sources for these latter statements, however, and his papers at Tulane are silent about them.

Mobilization was facilitated by Huey's personality. Working people in Washington liked him because he was down to earth.[47] On long train rides, Huey sought out people who looked lonely to talk to.[48] A train waiter said Huey taught him how to cook mustard greens.[49] A Senate reporter had an autographed picture of Huey hanging in his office. On the streets of New York, passersby shouted friendly greetings.[50]

Inroads among the elite and academics were made. In his bathrobe he met Cissy Patterson, publisher of the *Washington Herald,* a Hearst paper, dressed to the nines ("Well, sister, you are dressed up"). Arthur Brisbane now reported he agreed with Huey that production was inadequate for consumption[51] and told George Maines that Huey was misunderstood.[52]

Assigned by Hearst to investigate Huey, reporter Adela Rogers St. Johns brought him to a dinner party at Cissy Patterson's opulent estate and described Huey's monologue: "I watched [Richard E.] Berlin, who had no use for Huey Long personally or politically. . . . Out of courtesy to his hostess, his handsome Irish face was expressionless, then it began to break up in humor, in interest, in excitement as Huey shifted into a plan he had. . . . I saw [Huey] carry all before him. The blazing triumph on his face as he ended was indecent." At dinner, the table displayed crystal, linens, flowers, and silverware inherited from George Washington. With "gusto," Huey said "'I don't know what all these are for. Where I come from we use one knife and fork to eat all our vittles with,' and put everything else in [St. Johns's] lap. . . . It was impossible not to laugh." Huey told Cissy that she should let him teach her cook how to make salad dressing and Cissy said, why not now? Huey ordered the ingredients and mixed them, all while discoursing on the "origin of salad, on hot-and-sweet, sour and spiced from the Pharaohs to Escoffier." Huey dunked a leaf into the dressing and put it into Cissy's mouth, which was "wide open and had been for some time." She said, "Another of your miracles, Senator."[53]

Following up on his visit to America, where he described Huey as an "institution" and "200 percent American,"[54] H. G. Wells, a socialist with impeccable establishment credentials, wrote in the conservative *Collier's* magazine that Huey was crude, a Winston Churchill who had never attended Harrow, but credited his focus on education. Sherwood Anderson thought Huey had a real feeling for the underdog. Gertrude Stein preferred Huey because, unlike Harding, Coolidge, and Roosevelt, he was not boring and had a real sense of people.

Ezra Pound urged Senator Cutting to form a new party with Huey. British author Rebecca West visited Washington, called the Roosevelt administration the most hopeful in the world today, and wrote three paragraphs about Huey. She was told he was a grotesque "clown," but she viewed him as odd only in that he was a skilled dancer. Behind the Mardi Gras mask of his conversation was a steely intelligence, a "shrewdness, coherence and even a little genius, wearing a disguise." They discussed an intimate breast operation she had so he could try to recruit to LSU the London surgeon knowledgeable about it.[55]

If Saul Bellow were the alter ego of his narrator in *Ravelstein,* he collected Huey's humorous sayings.[56] Gore Vidal recounted Huey's comedic monologue to a meek young desk clerk: "Why, when I was your age I would spend what little idle time I had with an instructive book not that racing form I see that you're now trying to hide. Of course I was not given to late-night dissipation in the fleshpots of the District of Columbia! Oh, you can't hide your ruinous habits from me! I can see by the trembling of your hands what demon rum is doing to you."[57] Ivy Leaguer Philip Johnson, later a famous architect, first announcing his intentions to the press, stalked Huey or Christenberry to a meeting. Huey rejected his speeches but sent him to organize Ohio, and he did.[58]

Inventor and author Lester Barlow wrote *What Would Lincoln Do? A Call for Political Revolution Through the Ballot,* advocating a $2 billion four-lane interstate highway system to eliminate unemployment. One he suggested is currently Interstate 80. He mailed Huey's circulars all over New England.[59] In late summer, George Maines finished a vacation swing through New England with Rose and the children and wrote his mother that everyone supported Huey and disliked Roosevelt.[60]

Someone (unidentified) from the Brookings Institution advised Huey about public works projects, including plans to irrigate the West, prevent dust storms, eliminate floods, and build cities along new highways. The reporter believed that Huey wanted to be prepared to be president.[61] Recruiting experts was also good politics.

Harry Truman insulted Huey, who never spoke to him again, according to Truman,[62] but his chief of staff, Edgar Faris, "struck up quite a friendship." Huey gave him an autographed picture and told Truman that he was "'going to take [Faris] away from you.'" Faris "was very flattered."[63] A Norris secretary had effusive praise for Huey.[64]

*New Yorker* columnists motoring in May 1935 got stuck in Mississippi mud but were rescued, towed, and driven to their destination by polite Louisiana policemen. They said Huey liked them to call him by his first name.

They thought Huey could accomplish anything in about a week. They contributed to Huey's campaigns to help, not viewing it as extorted.[65]

Alice Roosevelt Longworth wrote that Huey was not perturbed by Roosevelt's effort to steal his thunder; his imperviousness to actions that his opponents thought would ruin him was so strong that the public disregarded them. She saw Senator Glass joke with Huey about Roosevelt's effort to steal his thunder, provoking Huey to laugh and give him a bear hug. In the Senate galleries, all heads turned Huey's way when he walked in, a "veritable hum" became audible. As he moved across the floor in his "curious, rolling, loose-jointed gait," all eyes followed him, as children pored over comic strips describing the adventures of mischievous kids. He was "able, crafty, resourceful, humorous and bold," with a "remarkable memory" and the "wit to know how to apply it." Her judgment: "Roosevelt has charm; and the same is true of Huey Long."[66]

Huey spent time in the summer drafting his book, *My First Days in the White House,* probably getting the idea from Upton Sinclair, who wrote *I, Governor of California, and How I Ended Poverty: A True Story of the Future.*[67] As president, Huey appointed Governor Al Smith as Budget Director, Herbert Hoover as secretary of commerce, General Smedley Butler as secretary of war, and Franklin Roosevelt as secretary of the Navy. He thus declared a war against "partisanship, sectionalism and class prejudice." In this fantasy, Roosevelt said "What in the world do you mean by offering me a cabinet post, after all the things you have said about me as President?" with Huey replying, "I only offered you a position which I thought you were qualified to fill."[68] Outlined were plans for massive public works, criminal justice reform, and improvements in transportation and public health (under leadership of the Mayo brothers), all to be guided by experts. He even promised to depoliticize the post office!

Huey's book was whimsical, but its political purpose can be seen. H. G. Wells wrote a book based on his American visit, critical of the New Deal for lacking a coherent philosophy and of Huey for his backwardness.[69] Robert Brooks's *Deliver Us From Dictators!* said Roosevelt was already assuming dictatorial powers; Huey would do well, he thought, to read the Constitution's guaranty of a republican form of government.[70] John Franklin Carter's *American Messiahs* profiled many radicals, leading off with Huey, who was notable because he appealed to the southern sharecropper without use of racial prejudice.[71] Raymond Gram Swing thought Huey was a "plain dictator" and a forerunner of American fascism and published his book by that name, profiling Huey, Coughlin, Bilbo, Townsend, and Hearst. While none of them were fascists, they showed how fascism could arise. Roosevelt's NRA approached fascism, he said, and Roosevelt had failed to remedy the unequal distribution of economic power.[72] Deutsch's planned book, "Paradox in Pajamas," an incomplete draft of which is found in his papers, acknowledged Huey's schemes but portrayed his career as an amazing triumph in politics by a man of energy, genius, and spectacular benefits. The draft stops well before 1935.

*It Can't Happen Here* was Sinclair Lewis's take on Huey. Protagonist Berzelius "Buzz" Windrip's politics were more representative of Gene Talmadge, for Talmadge portrayed himself as a friend to farmers while rejecting most governmental programs that would help them. Huey was more colorful or, to Lewis, more dangerous, so he used disguised substitutes for Huey's potlikker and green pajamas episodes while portraying a leader who was a front for big business.[73]

Similarly, Benjamin Sokolsky, a socialist writer for the *Nation,* liked Huey and disliked Roosevelt, but worried that Huey would compromise with the big industrialists.[74] Leftist author Carleton Beals portrayed Huey's compromises as sellouts and his accomplishments as phony. His indiscriminate cynicism and his socialist views may have diminished Beals's credibility, but his exposure of Louisiana working conditions and racism were telling, and obscured Huey's advocacy of federal legislation to improve working conditions and reduce Black poverty. Nevertheless, Beals said Huey's patronage practices were necessary to dislodge the oligarchy, he excoriated Huey's Louisiana opponents, asserted that Roosevelt practiced dirty politics by relying on them in Louisiana and politicizing relief funds, and credited Huey with victory in his arguments with Johnson, Ickes, and Farley. "Unlike them, Huey presented a thoroughgoing diagnosis of our social ills."[75]

The fascism feared by Lewis, Sokolsky, and Beals is the fascism of big business. Unlike German and Italian fascists, Huey never advocated foreign conquests, and he criticized Hitler, Mussolini, and anti-Semitism, saying "there's never been a country that put its heel down on the Jews that ever lived afterward," and that anyone who let religious prejudice get mixed up with public policy was a "plain, goddamned fool."[76]

Beals nonetheless said Huey was a dictator, albeit with majority support. Beals failed to see that the concurrence of all three branches of Louisiana's government represented a consensus in support of Huey's program, a consensus that exceeded Huey's personal popularity; and that the necessity to *maintain* majority support *limited* Huey's ability to implement labor and racial reforms in Louisiana. A real dictatorship would have been required to impose them. Huey bargained with big businesses, epitomized by the compromise with Standard Oil. A good compromise keeps businesses incentivized while giving the people what they need. But leftists called Huey a dictator if he didn't compromise and a sellout when he did.

Author Forrest Davis concluded that Huey was a dictator, but he interviewed him at length, checked on his figures, questioned his associates and other leaders, and gave him his say. Huey induced no racial or religious hatred, was not hostile to civil liberties, and lacked any fascist dogma. He was an efficient administrator who ran a solvent state government despite the Depression and provided good roads, low utility costs, an affordable education, health care, and cheap gas prices (he compared the prices in other states) to the people. What was the problem?

Huey was a dictator, Davis thought, because he exerted himself over the Louisiana legislature as a matter of *will;* he vindicated "the right of a strong man to lead."[77] In other words, someone who believes in his proposals and convinces the legislature and the people to adopt them is a dictator. The difference between that and leadership is what? Had Huey been unable to convince the legislature of anything, he would have been a failure.

Huey's book did not consider such philosophical questions. He was kind, humorous, well-meaning, unthreatening, not dangerous, and certainly not a fascist. The book got favorable reviews after his death, and Deutsch says it would have been popular.[78] I speculate that it would have been edited more had he lived; some parts could have been excerpted and used against him in a presidential campaign.

These books would have made Huey a figure of compelling interest in 1936. And if he were of compelling interest, Huey would have had a chance to convince the people that Roosevelt was wrong, and he was right.

Included in Huey's book was a trial balloon for the plan to redistribute wealth. It began humorously. John D. Rockefeller gave his fortune away and agreed to chair the SOW committee. Huey had dinner with the industrialists, excluding the House of Morgan, including "old Andy Mellon," whose "fortune had become a tremendous bother and nuisance. . . . [H]e wanted above all to have the affection of the American people, which he believed he had lost." Huey named him "Vice-Chairman of the Committee, and his face lighted with real pleasure."

Rockefeller's committee proposed an SOW corporation to possess the wealth confiscated from the capital levy tax. Corporations affected would reorganize by issuing voting stock to remain in the hands of its current owners and nonvoting stock for the shares obtained by the tax. SOW stock would be distributed to the people who would share in dividends.[79] This kept the government from running the companies, retaining only the right to ask a court to intervene in the event of mismanagement, the same right shareholders had then and have today. Companies were not expropriated; rather their wealthy shareholders were taxed. Stock and asset collection meant that no one had to liquidate assets to pay the tax. Omitted was how to collect and hold real estate taxed under his plan, such as a $10 million farm. Real Estate Investment Trusts weren't invented until 1960.

Before seeing Huey's book, Forrest Davis asked how a homestead would be supplied to a city tenement dweller. Cooperatives then existed for the wealthy, Huey responded. There could be a group of homesteads within one building. Davis also wondered whether taxing the wealthy would lessen capital available to invest in new enterprises.[80] Brookings reported, however, that inequality might enhance capital formation but that consumption spending drove it, that capital was plentiful in 1935, and that commercial banks facilitated the flow of money for expanded production.[81] If money to invest had to be borrowed from banks, Davis thought this would result in dictatorship.[82] Huey supported an elected regional board to supervise banks and advocated easier credit.

Critics argued that America's wealth included highways, military equipment, museums, churches, and so forth and that the remainder had value only for the income that the wealth would produce,[83] so that a confiscatory tax of such wealth benefits no one. Wealth for highways or churches could not be taxed and redistributed, but to assert that only productive wealth was worth redistributing is false. If nonproducing wealth owned by individuals lacks "value," then they should not mind giving it up. If someone had a $5,000 painting, it produces nothing but could be traded for a house worth $5,000.

Some liberals advocating production for use stated that there was insufficient wealth for Huey to redistribute.[84] Under production for use, government boards of industry and labor would decide what goods to produce and their quantity. If workers were going to be paid to produce the necessary goods or if consumers were going to pay for those goods, where would the money come from? Insufficient wealth foils *either* SOW or production for use.

The insufficient-wealth argument also traps conservatives. If they believe that wealth was insufficient to feed and clothe everyone, and they must if they believe Huey's plan lacked the funds to work, they don't say what percentage

Table 2. The Number and Income of Families by Income Classes, 1929

| Income Class (In dollars) | Total in Each Class | | | | Cumulative Totals | | | |
|---|---|---|---|---|---|---|---|---|
| | Families* | | Income† | | Families | | Income | |
| | In Thousands | As Percentage of Total | In millions of dollars | As Percentage of Total | In Thousands | As Percentage of Total | In millions of dollars | As Percentage of Total |
| Under 0‡.... | 120 | 0.437 | -615 | -0.797 | 120 | 0.437 | -615 | -0.797 |
| 0 to 500‡.... | 1,982 | 7.214 | 596 | 0.773 | 2,102 | 7.651 | -19 | -0.024 |
| 500 to 1,000...... | 3,797 | 13.820 | 2,919 | 3.785 | 5,899 | 21.471 | 2,900 | 3.761 |
| 1,000 to 1,500...... | 5,754 | 20.943 | 7,197 | 9.333 | 11,653 | 42.414 | 10,097 | 13.094 |
| 1,500 to 2,000...... | 4,701 | 17.111 | 8,167 | 10.590 | 16,354 | 59.525 | 18,264 | 23.684 |
| 2,000 to 2,500...... | 3,204 | 11.626 | 7,153 | 9.276 | 19,558 | 71.187 | 25,417 | 32.960 |
| 2,500 to 3,000...... | 1,988 | 7.236 | 5,433 | 7.045 | 21,546 | 78.423 | 30,850 | 40.005 |
| 3,000 to 3,500...... | 1,447 | 5.267 | 4,678 | 6.066 | 22,993 | 83.690 | 35,528 | 46.071 |
| 3,500 to 4,000...... | 993 | 3.614 | 3,710 | 4.811 | 23,986 | 87.304 | 39,238 | 50.882 |
| 4,000 to 4,500...... | 718 | 2.613 | 3,041 | 3.943 | 24,704 | 89.917 | 42,279 | 54.285 |
| 4,500 to 5,000...... | 514 | 1.871 | 2,437 | 3.160 | 25,218 | 91.788 | 44,716 | 57.985 |
| 5,000 to 6,000...... | 666 | 2.424 | 3,632 | 4.710 | 25,884 | 94.212 | 48,348 | 62.695 |
| 6,000 to 7,000...... | 407 | 1.481 | 2,628 | 3.408 | 26,291 | 95.693 | 50,976 | 66.103 |
| 7,000 to 8,000...... | 252 | 0.917 | 1,883 | 2.442 | 26,543 | 96.610 | 52,859 | 68.545 |
| 8,000 to 9,000...... | 172 | 0.626 | 1,459 | 1.892 | 26,715 | 97.236 | 54,318 | 70.437 |
| 9,000 to 10,000...... | 128 | 0.466 | 1,218 | 1.579 | 26,843 | 97.702 | 55,536 | 72.016 |
| 10,000 to 15,000...... | 304 | 1.107 | 3,666 | 4.754 | 27,147 | 98.809 | 59,202 | 76.770 |
| 15,000 to 20,000...... | 108 | 0.393 | 1,856 | 2.407 | 27,255 | 99.202 | 61,058 | 79.177 |
| 20,000 to 25,000...... | 59 | 0.215 | 1,309 | 1.697 | 27,314 | 99.417 | 62,367 | 80.874 |
| 25,000 to 30,000...... | 35 | 0.127 | 965 | 1.251 | 27,349 | 99.544 | 63,332 | 82.125 |
| 30,000 to 40,000...... | 40 | 0.146 | 1,395 | 1.809 | 27,389 | 99.690 | 64,727 | 83.934 |
| 40,000 to 50,000...... | 22 | 0.080 | 984 | 1.276 | 27,411 | 99.770 | 65,711 | 85.210 |
| 50,000 to 75,000...... | 27 | 0.098 | 1,616 | 2.096 | 27,438 | 99.868 | 67,327 | 87.306 |
| 75,000 to 100,000...... | 12 | 0.044 | 1,036 | 1.343 | 27,450 | 99.912 | 68,363 | 88.649 |
| 100,000 to 250,000...... | 16 | 0.058 | 2,164 | 2.806 | 27,466 | 99.970 | 70,527 | 91.455 |
| 250,000 to 500,000...... | 4 | 0.015 | 1,500 | 1.945 | 27,470 | 99.985 | 72,027 | 93.400 |
| 500,000 and over...... | 4 | 0.015 | 5,089 | 6.600 | 27,474 | 100.000 | 77,116 | 100.000 |
| All classes.......... | 27,474 | 100.000 | 77,116 | 100.000 | 27,474 | 100.000 | 77,116 | 100.000 |

*Source:* From Leven, Moulton, and Warburton, *America's Capacity to Consume*, 54.

* All families of two or more persons.

† Includes income from occupation, investments, and from sale of property; also includes imputed income on owned homes, but does not include imputed income on durable consumption goods other than homes.

‡ The estimates for this class are highly tentative.

of the people were being, would be, or should be left to starve. During the prosperous "Roaring Twenties" (1929), $2,000 per year was deemed sufficient to supply *only basic necessities.* More startling: 60 percent of American families *fell below this standard.*[85] This might be why Huey never believed that his ideas depended on the Great Depression for their appeal.[86]

In 1929, 27.5 million families received $77 billion in income and 9 million unattached individuals received $15.8 billion. Twelve million families earned less than $1,500 (42 percent); 20 million families earned less than $2,500 (71 percent). Four thousand families (.015 percent of the total) earned more than $500,000.[87] See table 2.

Critic Beals said Huey's wealth taxes would only raise $50 billion, not the $165 billion Huey claimed. My own crude calculations reveal that the amount raised would be $15–19 billion at 1929 values.[88] And that assumes his tax proposals would not have been compromised. For these reasons, most historians dismiss Huey's plan as unrealistic or, worse, a lie.

Ironically, while the amounts Huey would *get* from his taxes on the rich were much less than he thought, the amounts Huey would *need* to provide his promised benefits were also much less than he thought. With $15 billion, Brookings said, 15 million families could be given $1,000 each in addition to the money they were already earning, $765 given to every family earning $2,500 or less, or $608 given to every family up to the $5,000 level.[89] Without saying how the $15 billion would be provided, Brookings calculated a sliding scale of increases to families—less generous than Huey's plan at the low levels and more generous at the higher levels—to show the effect on consumption per income group. In two tables (3 and 4 below), it showed that consumption in 1929 would have increased 25 percent.

Table 3. A Sliding-Scale Increase in Family Incomes

| Number of Families (in thousands) | Income in 1929 (in dollars) | Assumed Percentage Increase in Income | Average Income after Increase |
|---|---|---|---|
| 5,779 | 0 to 1,000 | 75 | $1,139 |
| 5,754 | 1,000 to 1,500 | 60 | 1,994 |
| 4,701 | 1,500 to 2,000 | 50 | 2,608 |
| 5,192 | 2,000 to 3,000 | 40 | 3,389 |
| 2,440 | 3,000 to 4,000 | 30 | 4,468 |
| 1,232 | 4,000 to 5,000 | 20 | 5,336 |
| 2,376 | Over 5,000 | 0 | — |

*Source:* Leven, Moulton, and Warburton, *America's Capacity to Consume,* 117.

*Note:* Families with losses more than current income in 1929, a large proportion of whom normally have incomes more than $5,000, were included in the first group.

Table 4. Effect of Increased Family Incomes upon Consumptive Expenditures

| Family Income in 1929 (in dollars) | Aggregate Consumptive Expenditures (In millions of dollars) | | | Percentage Increase in Consumptive Expenditures |
|---|---|---|---|---|
| | Actual, 1929 | With Increased Incomes* | Additional Expenditures | |
| 0 to 1,000 | 4,065 | 6,634 | 2,569 | 63 |
| 1,000 to 1,500 | 7,025 | 10,205 | 3,180 | 45 |
| 1,500 to 2,000 | 7,538 | 10,823 | 3,285 | 44 |
| 2,000 to 3,000 | 11,096 | 14,904 | 3,808 | 34 |
| 3,000 to 4,000 | 7,069 | 8,913 | 1,844 | 26 |
| 4,000 to 5,000 | 4,480 | 5,247 | 767 | 17 |
| Over 5,000 | 20,704 | 20,704 | — | — |
| All Classes | 61,977 | 77,430 | 15,453 | 25 |

*Source:* Leven, Moulton, and Warburton, *America's Capacity to Consume,* 118.

*Note:* Families with losses more than current income in 1929, a large proportion of whom normally have incomes more than $5,000, were included in the first group.

* At rate indicated in "A Sliding-Scale Increase in Family Incomes" table 2.

If all families' incomes were at least $2,500, a commensurate increase in consumption of $16 billion would occur. And Brookings noted that, until a family income of $3,000 was reached, families could not afford an adequate diet.[90]

Because Huey wanted to expand the money supply and was aware that the outstanding debt incurred by the government to pay for World War I had not hurt the economy, I believe he would have used deficit spending to the extent that his taxes failed to provide the revenues to pay for his promised benefits. Thus, Huey could have increased the money supply $20–30 billion or more to provide supplemental funds and public works to reach his family minimum earning levels. Perhaps he would have claimed that this money was borrowed from anticipated inheritance and capital tax collections.

One wonders whether it would have occurred to Huey to distribute the homes he promised by credit: 25 million $5,000 homes purchased with a 10 percent down payment would require only $12.5 billion (less the equity existing in some homes). If Huey had spent $20 billion to increase the money supply and $12.5 billion for down payments on homesteads, with or without money from high taxes on the wealthy, a permanent increase in incomes and wealth would have occurred.

Huey and his critics lacked the benefit of our experience in World War II, when the government increased both the supply of money and its spending to pay for the war. Inflating the supply of money and distributing it to, say, the bottom 80 percent of the people (directly, as with Huey's minimum-income plan or indirectly, as with employment on public works projects) redistributes wealth because the money of the wealthy is worth less and the people at the bottom now have more.

For purposes of production or consumption, there are adjustments in factory types or settings but not differences in effect between tanks or tractors, jeeps or cars, uniforms or clothes, boots or shoes, bomber planes or passenger planes, barracks or houses. The government deficit for 1935 was $2.8 billion. Because of World War II, the deficit of 1942 was $20.5 billion; of 1943 was $54.5 billion; of 1944 was $47.5 billion, of 1945 $47.5 billion.[91] Most of this deficit spending paid for tanks, jeeps, uniforms, boots, bombers, and barracks, much of which was destroyed. These amounts could have been distributed to the people to spend on tractors, cars, clothes, shoes, planes, and houses in the absence of a war. The free market would have allocated that money except for those billions paid to formerly idle or underemployed people to build dams, universities, hospitals, highways, and other public works. Once the money was distributed, whether to income and homestead recipients or to workers on public works projects, it would continue to circulate as the free market decided.

The World War II deficit spending jump-started the economy. The unemployment rate declined from 20 percent in 1938 to less than 2 percent in 1943. The economy performed well thereafter *without* significant deficit financing. To whatever extent Huey could have collected wealth and inheritance taxes, less debt would have been required than was incurred during World War II.

Income and wealth grew because of World War II spending. Inequality of wealth and income was lessened because the government war spending went to wages for people previously unemployed or underemployed. Between 1945 and the 1980s, no president significantly reduced taxes on the wealthy or repaid the deficit incurred during World War II. The ratios between rich and poor remained similar.

It is not that war is good for the economy, or that government spending is good for the economy. It depends on the circumstances. In the Great Depression, more government spending would have been good for the economy—and the war spending was good for the economy—because the economy was not working at capacity and because of the imbalance between the rich and everyone else.

Liberals and conservatives reached a truce over the issue of redistributive taxes after World War II, both focusing on productivity.[92] But a foundation for this consensus, perhaps unspoken or unrecognized, was that inequality was lessened by the war spending. When inequality was great and the economy depressed in the 1930s, Brookings noted: "The distribution of wealth and income in our modern society has become the central concern of those who would unleash our productive power and accelerate our economic progress."[93] Doane said the distribution of wealth strongly influences the distribution of income and its growth.[94]

Huey's plan would have established an economic ecosystem that eliminated outliers of rich and poor and provided children of poor parents the means to compete more effectively with the children of rich parents. The same principle forbids winners of a Monopoly game from carrying over their winnings to the next game, gives the worst football team the best draft pick and sets team salary caps, and causes companies to set a mandatory retirement age. Huey's system resembles a sports league insofar as the rules of the league are designed to enhance competition. Competition is enhanced if everyone has access to a similar education and at least the minimum amount of food, clothes, and shelter.

One wonders whether crop holidays would have eased the transition from the agricultural economy given that different jobs would be learned during the crop holiday years. Educational sabbaticals would facilitate the training necessary to move from obsolete jobs to modern ones. A shortened workweek would ensure full employment and allocate leisure time to all rather than just to the wealthy.

It is unfair to Huey's opponents to avoid criticism of his articulated plan by saying it would have been modified. Because so many details remained to be worked out, it might have failed. Acknowledging some likely and necessary modifications, however, does not impeach Huey's sincerity in presenting it. More astonishing is that he could have provided the benefits he promised had he been elected president.

Brinkley concludes that Huey failed to "confront the structure and process of economic consolidation" or to offer a "convincing picture of how the kind of society [he] envisioned could be achieved." His movement was a "timid" spasm in the "twilight" of a nostalgic populist struggle against the new economic order.[95] This is wrong. Huey stood up for those who were disadvantaged by economic consolidation, confronted the problem with a bold program of taxation and benefits to provide more equal opportunity, to improve competition, and to maintain capitalism, without a quixotic joust to restore the economy that had disappeared.

Hoover's laissez-faire approach was timid and unconvincing; Roosevelt's NRA was bold but wrong; production for use and socialism were bold but unconvincing. Huey's "picture" of a society that could be "achieved" was "convincing" to nine million people after a year and a half. He wasn't given the chance to convince more.

Many of Huey's fans had nostalgic notions, and Huey's rhetoric connected him to several populist and progressive traditions, but rhetoric in a social movement is *supposed* to bridge the past to the future.[96] Based on Huey's fans and rhetoric, Brinkley's critique is that Huey was old-fashioned, but this basis for criticism ignores Huey's actual proposals. The critical lens of old-fashioned, moreover, should focus on all leaders and their ideas in 1935: who was modern and who was nostalgic?

Conservative economists now assert that the money supply should have been expanded in the Great Depression. Huey, Wheeler, and Thomas were modern; Roosevelt and Morgenthau were not.

Modern economists believe that Roosevelt's public works spending was inadequate. Huey, LaFollette, Wagner, and others, not Roosevelt, advocated the modern theory of public works.

In 2017, *Utopia for Realists* by Rutger Bregman is considered brilliant and innovative because he advocates a shortened workweek. One chapter suggested a fifteen-hour workweek.[97] If the workweek could be shortened to fifteen hours, let the Lord be praised, Huey said in 1934.

The list of advocates of a universal basic family income—business titans, presidential cabinet members, economists—is lengthy and impressive.[98] Huey made this modern proposal in 1934.

Thomas Piketty created a stir in 2009 when he suggested that wealth inequality threatened democracy and proposed a capital levy tax, the tax Huey advocated in 1933.[99]

Bernie Sanders and Elizabeth Warren proposed to make college and vocational training affordable to everyone in 2016. Huey proposed this in 1934.

Social Security now more closely approximates Huey's vision in 1935, although the regressive tax remains.

Near the end of World War II, Congress implemented the G.I. Bill, which everyone approves of. The leading historian about veteran activism said this about it: "There would be one final but unspoken irony in [the 1944] GI Bill's provisions: the material benefits conferred by the GI Bill for farm and home ownership and education matched nearly exactly those found in Huey Long's Share Our Wealth program." After World War II, 5.6 million people used the educational and vocational benefits and another 2.2 million used the college benefits of the G.I. Bill,[100] a benefit that Huey advocated be given to everyone smart and energetic enough to do the work. How much of our economic success and social mobility in later decades resulted from that?

Concede for purposes of argument that Huey was intolerant or unbalanced, that he confused means and ends, that he was corrupted by power. Think, if you will, that Huey had, as Alex McManus wrote,[101] all the faults of a political fixer. Whatever his faults, nostalgia wasn't one of them. He was ahead of his time.

# *Thirty*

# ASSASSINATION

When Huey stopped drinking, he quit banquets, too, but the Senate official reporters invited him to speak at one in late August. He consented to attend "because they have gone through so much since" he arrived:

> I wish you might know how eloquent our Senate Official Reporters are. They are the ones who have made out of ordinary United States Senators more statesmen and more orators like Demosthenes than anyone else. Recently I read a speech I was supposed to have made in the Senate a while back, and the language was so perfect, and the words so "high-falutin" that I mailed it back to [my wife] in Louisiana and told her I wanted her to read it and see what an improvement I had made since I came to Washington to the Senate. The first thing she told me when she got to Washington afterwards was, "I want to meet those wonderfully educated reporters of the Senate who take those supposed quotations you are making from the Bible and fit them into your speeches exactly as they are in the Scripture.
>
> . . . If we want to quote from some ancient ruler who existed thousands of years ago, all we have to do is slip over it and say it a little faster so the newspapermen in the Gallery may not catch us in a mistake, if we make one. And then the Official Reporters go back and look up the ruler. They will find exactly what he said."

> To great audience laughter, Senator Long concluded, "or, [the Reporters] may find that there was never any such ruler, and they will 'dig up' a ruler to fit the speech."[1]

The reporters would shortly be drafted into action. The last bill up before the scheduled adjournment on August 26 was one for deficiency appropriations, to fund shortages because of programs omitted from the original budget.

Senator Byrnes added an amendment providing for government loans at 12 cents per bale of cotton, the price the industry had expected, but the bureaucrats in charge of the Agricultural Adjustment Administration had reduced to 9 cents. Roosevelt objected. Byrnes threatened a filibuster, and Cotton Ed Smith thundered that the whole southern economy depended on 12-cent cotton. Cotton state senators recruited senators from the wheat states to help them by tacking on an amendment for a minimum loan price for wheat. Over the weekend, Roosevelt brokered a compromise by which the bureaucrats agreed to guarantee ten-cent cotton loans; wheat was omitted. Byrnes was satisfied, but Senator Russell complained that it was "complete surrender."[2]

Robinson moved to strike the cotton and wheat amendments because there was no time to send an amended bill back to the House for a vote before the scheduled adjournment. In 1934, a similar problem with respect to the Frazier-Lemke bill was overcome by Huey's filibuster threat. Now, Huey claimed the floor and demanded that the House be allowed to vote on the amendments, or he would filibuster to defeat the bill. Extend the adjournment date one more day, he asked. Robinson refused.

The deficiency bill authorized funds to set up the new Social Security program and railroad pensions. No other senator was willing to defy Roosevelt or obstruct funds for these worthy purposes. Roosevelt, however, could allocate money from the relief bill for these purposes and had previously so stated.

Labor leaders in the galleries sent notes down asking him to stop. Huey said he was a friend of labor but would not help labor cut the throats of farmers any more than he would vote to let farmers cut the throats of labor. A quorum call was held to allow LaFollette and others to lobby Huey, but he refused their entreaties. Robinson taunted him: did he realize that he stood alone?

The Young Turks, Schwellenbach, most prominently, who had been quiet since Huey's June filibuster, now peppered Huey with loaded questions: did he intend to deny funds to crippled children; for railroad worker pensions; for Social Security for the aged? Smith, Russell, and George swallowed their principles in silence. Huey, the so-called dictator, prevented the Senate from voting to adjourn, but fought for the right of the House of Representatives to put the amendments to a vote. Roosevelt wouldn't let the House vote and dictated that the Senate adjourn.

A minute before adjournment, Schwellenbach got the last word, asking whether Huey's selfish desire for publicity defeated the hopes and desires of the people. Garner banged the gavel down so fast that Huey had no chance to respond.

Moley later wrote that Huey was like a wild boar being attacked by dogs in the Senate.[3] The *Congressional Record* reads that way, as if he were alone fighting numerous insults by the entire Senate, especially near the end. Huey's nemesis, Harold Ickes, was in the galleries, however, and had the opposite view: "I had never really seen [Huey] at his best, and he was at his best Saturday night. He waved his arms, he contorted, he swayed, and at all times he talked in a very loud voice. I must admit, however, that he was clever. Any Senator who ventured to cross swords with him was usually discomfited. He has a sharp, quick wit, even though he is a blatant and unconscionable demagogue."[4]

Some newspapers wrote the story from the point of view of the Young Turks: Huey had defeated a worthy appropriation for those in need. The *Times* noted that there was money for the other programs without the deficiency bill; the *Tribune* did not.[5] Drew Pearson wrote that Huey blundered because he was blinded by a pathological hatred for Roosevelt.[6] LaFollette's paper had a short story listing the programs that couldn't start for lack of money, and its columnist wrote that it was unclear whether the credit Huey would get from farmers would outweigh criticism from labor. Some agencies stated that they might have to delay benefits or deny them because of Huey's filibuster.[7] Robinson announced plans to change Senate rules to forbid filibusters. Huey responded that Robinson was on his way out.[8]

On August 28, Huey explained that there was no reason to adjourn the Senate without letting the House vote on the amendments and that there was sufficient money for all appropriations.[9] Friendly commentators explained that Huey strengthened his appeal to cotton and wheat farmers and could answer critics by pointing to the money available to fund Social Security, railroad pensions, and the other programs.[10] Huey was right as a matter of substance;[11] whether it was a political blunder was unclear.[12]

On August 30, Huey was serenaded "Happy Birthday" by Lila Lee, who was performing with Nick Lucas's ("Tiptoe Through the Tulips") band playing in the New Yorker Hotel. Huey; bodyguards Roden, Voitier, Landry; and Lila Lee tasted the birthday cake the hotel brought up, and Huey gave the rest of it to Lila Lee. That evening, he gave a radio speech sponsored by a labor union advocating higher wages for New Deal projects because the wages paid were less than what government statistics said was necessary to live. The mere announcement that Huey would speak caused the ubiquitous Hugh Johnson to announce a wage increase.[13]

That evening, theatrical agent Lou Irwin took Huey to dinner at an uptown location where he had booked a show. Passersby on the sidewalks shouted encouragement. At the show, radio star Phil Baker dropped by with his wife and his wife's niece. Huey danced with Mrs. Baker, who told him her niece was an artist. Huey asked the niece to sketch him on a napkin. They went to Baker's apartment to see her serious paintings. Huey hired her to illustrate *My First Days in the White House.*[14]

At three o'clock in the morning, Huey returned to his hotel. In the lobby was a publishing company agent referred by Earle Christenberry. They reached a tentative agreement at five o'clock in the morning to publish his book. Then Huey traveled by train to Harrisburg, Pennsylvania, to sign the contract, promising to cut 200 pages from the 340-page manuscript. Then he motored with Raymond Daniell of the *Times* to a Long family reunion in Long Grove, near Lebanon, Pennsylvania, where he claimed Pennsylvania Dutch ancestry to a crowd of two thousand; joked that a preacher forbear decided to leave Ohio when the congregation outlawed hard liquor during church hours; and said that half his family opposed slavery and the other half did not, but they all had to fight or get shot. There was loud cheering when Huey declared that he regretted attending the Chicago convention in 1932. The clan "took him to their hearts" and besieged him for autographs.[15] Huey then took a train to Oklahoma City to give a Labor Day speech arranged by a labor union. Accompanied by two stenographers and an editor, they worked through the night editing the book manuscript, finishing it as the train pulled into St. Louis the next morning. The station "was packed and jammed" by people who somehow learned that he would change trains there and "just wanted to catch one glimpse of the man while he was passing through."[16] The crowd almost made him miss his connection.

They reached Oklahoma City on September 1, 1935. Mayor Frank Martin greeted him, but Governor E. W. Marland boycotted his visit. The state labor commissioner labeled Huey a notorious scab who was out to destroy the only president who had tried to help labor.[17] Huey rode in the Labor Day parade in the morning and spoke to a crowd of six to ten thousand people in the afternoon. Deutsch and the local paper reported that he was applauded frequently and "even" his attacks on Roosevelt (he got laughs when he called him "Frankie") and Hoover were "cheered lustily." Either before or after the speech, Huey visited his old employer, K. W. Dawson, who had invited a big crowd to meet him.[18] A classmate from the University of Oklahoma, Charles Orr, joined him in his hotel room afterward as he was munching grapes and discussing a third-party challenge to defeat Roosevelt with local politicians and labor leaders. Huey asked Orr to draft a memorandum on the legal requirements to get an independent party on the ballot.[19]

Boarding a train to Dallas, a newspaper reported that he joked and teased crowd members, including the Black redcaps. In Dallas, he rented a car and drove to Shreveport. At the Washington Youree Hotel, he met political leaders that night and the next day. A state police car picked him up the morning of September 4 from Shreveport and drove him to Baton Rouge. "Tuesday far into the night, throughout Wednesday, and again Thursday until well past noon," Huey "labored with attorneys, officials, secretaries, and typists drafting and revising bills for the special session." On Thursday afternoon, he read Deutsch's article on his career in the *Saturday Evening Post* and then drove to New Orleans to make a three-hour radio speech, making it to the studio with only five minutes to spare. As he left, bystanders cheered and told him to "pour it on." On the radio, he announced a new program to increase enrollment at LSU: one thousand students with top credentials would attend LSU practically free.[20] "Every Man a King" was played at intervals, and he recited a chorus of "Sweetheart of LSU." He claimed that the state could not help New Orleans while Walmsley was mayor and answered questions submitted by listeners. Huey spent the night at home with his family.

Early the next day, he ate breakfast at the Roosevelt Hotel and talked with the stream of people there, and they followed him to his twelfth-floor suite. A call went out for a special session, and forty-two bills were introduced. Among them was one to gerrymander Judge Benjamin Pavy, an opponent, into a district where Huey's support was so strong that Pavy would lose. Another proposed to fine anyone spending money for political purposes in violation of the Tenth Amendment (reserving rights not given to the federal government to the states). George Wallace protested that it was unconstitutional. "I don't give a damn. . . . [D]raw it up anyway," Huey replied.[21]

The bills were introduced in Baton Rouge, but Huey remained for the day—Saturday, September 7—in New Orleans and played golf with Seymour

Weiss. Weiss worried about the lack of federal patronage and—one must believe—the pending tax indictments. Huey assured him that everything was in great shape. They had plenty of cash to campaign, affidavits of corruption to use against opponents, and the Tenth Amendment legislation, about which Weiss was dubious, would prevent or harass federal officials trying to campaign against them. Only the risk of a split in his faction of the party worried Huey.[22]

Associates urged him to stay in New Orleans, thinking he looked tired, and because of assassination rumors. Huey's wife asked him to stay home. Huey was tired and run down, fighting an attack of hay fever or a cold. Separately he told Chick Frampton and a bodyguard that, after the special session, he was going to take a long vacation, far away from politicians or newsmen, without even making any plans.[23]

Roosevelt was also tired. By the end of the congressional session, his eyes were ringed black, his hands shook as he lit cigarettes, and a visitor witnessed him telling his wife to shut up. In an undated remark, Tugwell said Huey had gotten on his nerves. Roosevelt's approval numbers had declined to 50 percent, high based on later standards, but the lowest point of his presidency. He had been depressed for weeks.[24]

Having passed the legislation of the second New Deal, Roosevelt should have felt on top of the world. There were two good indications to the contrary. First, he told Morgenthau that he wanted to reverse himself and pay the soldiers' bonus,[25] the one progressive bill that he hadn't backed after his May 14 meeting with progressives. Second, Roosevelt sent Frank Murphy as an emissary to Father Coughlin and then asked Joseph Kennedy to invite the priest to visit him in Hyde Park. Kennedy made the call and Coughlin accepted the invitation, scheduled for September 10.[26]

On Sunday morning, September 8, Huey kissed Rose goodbye, saying he might not come back but would die fighting,[27] and drove to Baton Rouge. Announcement of teacher discharges, including a school-principal relative of political opponent Pavy—and protests of the discharges—were in the news.[28] Additional security personnel were assigned to the capitol.[29] In Paraguay, Huey's picture, hung in a place of honor, fell off the wall and crashed to the floor.[30]

During the drive to Baton Rouge, they detoured to visit the construction site of the bridge over the Mississippi. "[Huey] left the car and walked as far as he could on the unfinished span."[31] Perhaps he was thinking of all that he had accomplished in Louisiana. Or maybe he was thinking of all those things he yet wanted to do.

Poor Earle Christenberry kept trying to corner Huey to fill out his tax returns for 1934, due September 15. A huge container of receipts was carried from Washington to New Orleans and then to Baton Rouge. After a couple of hours of review on Sunday, Huey waved off further effort with disgust. Christenberry should fill out the forms and he would sign them.[32] Christenberry went with Huey to the capitol cafeteria for lunch.[33] Huey was looking forward to the football season. The LSU band was going to play a new song that he had written with Castro Carazo, "Touchdown for LSU," for the first time during its first game in September. After lunch, Carazo and Huey worked on a new song. He told Carazo that he had found money to fund a new LSU school of music.[34]

Late in the afternoon he talked with politicians about the upcoming gubernatorial race because he had not decided on the candidate. Several of his allies wanted the nomination: Wade Martin of the Public Service Commission; House Leader Allen Ellender; Justice John Fournet; Governor Allen's former secretary, Richard Leche; and president of the Senate James Noe. Huey telephoned his printer in New Orleans and said he would later provide copy for a circular dealing with Judge Pavy.

At night, Huey snacked on cheese and crackers and fruit brought up from the cafeteria. With Jimmie O'Connor, another public service commissioner, Huey went down to the House of Representatives.[35] A new English professor at LSU, Robert Heilman, watched from the galleries:

> Huey appeared on the floor, and we saw him in operation—chatting with members at various desks, striding from spot to spot, gesturing, sitting on the speaker's dais, summoning and sending. It was my one experience of seeing a single political leader wholly in command—dispensing, almost magically it seemed, what T. Harry Williams has called "power in himself," exuding charisma; smiling, easy, almost urbane, yet falling a little short of it by a certain abruptness and thrust of nervous energy; tense, perhaps, but to the eye confident and even nonchalant; pressing, as we now know, ruthlessly toward political goals, and yet somehow managing to suggest a degree of aloof amusement at the show he was stage-managing.[36]

Huey spoke briefly to reporter Frampton. Frampton left for the governor's office to call his editor. Huey asked O'Connor to buy him some cigars. Surprised because Huey had quit smoking, O'Connor nevertheless departed. Allen Ellender was presiding at the speaker's dais. He and Huey were photographed talking. Huey asked Ellender to meet after the session in his apartment, probably about the governorship.[37]

Meanwhile Frampton's editor told him a hurricane had struck a CCC camp in Florida, marooning some of the men and drowning others, including veterans. Frampton called to a phone near the speaker's dais and asked Huey for a comment. Huey said that the deaths of the men lowered the number of votes that would be cast against Roosevelt and that he would request an investigation into whether criminal negligence caused the deaths.[38] Telling Frampton he would add to his statement, Huey strode out of the chamber. Bodyguard Coleman and Judge Fournet, just arrived from his home at Huey's request, saw Huey and Mason Spencer laugh.[39]

Exiting the chamber into the corridor leading to the governor's office, Huey asked Secretary A. P. White[40] the whereabouts of missing legislators. "Find them. If necessary, sober them up and have them at [the caucus the next morning]." Backing out into the corridor, he turned and announced to the group following him—including Fournet, Roden, and Coleman—that every representative should meet at the caucus tomorrow morning. It was 9:20 p.m.

The target of Huey's judicial gerrymandering bill, Judge Pavy, had a son-in-law named Dr. Carl Austin Weiss, an ear, nose, and throat specialist, married with a three-month-old son. He had studied medicine overseas in prestigious programs that guaranteed him a bright future. His family had a cabin outside of Baton Rouge on the Amite River. They spent the day there fishing and swimming. The family returned that evening. At 8:30 p.m., he called a colleague about a surgery scheduled for the next day. At 9:00 p.m., he told his wife that he was leaving to make sick calls. Instead, he drove to the capitol, about a stone's throw from his house. In the capitol he paced nervously and muttered, "It won't be long now."[41] Three teenagers seeking Huey's autograph saw him in the corridor.[42]

At 9:20 p.m., Weiss stepped from behind a pillar and toward Huey. A small gun in his right hand was at first concealed behind his hat. He aimed his gun at Huey's chest. Huey's eyes popped in terror. Fournet and Roden noticed the gun and struck Weiss's arm. Weiss's arm was deflected down, but he fired. Huey cried, "I'm shot!" and dashed toward the stairs leading to the street, holding his right side where he was hit. Roden wrestled Weiss, grabbing his gun hand, while Coleman tried to hit him. Weiss fired again, shooting off Roden's wristwatch. Then his gun jammed, perhaps because a mechanism was caught on Roden's hand. Either because Roden's leather soles slipped on the marble floor or because of a Fournet push on Weiss, Roden and Weiss fell, Weiss on top. Roden struggled to remove his own gun. Weiss got away and backed off, crouching. Both Roden and Coleman fired. Roden saw his shot enter Weiss's head. Coleman shot three or four times, seconds after Weiss's first shot. It is possible that one of Coleman's shots, rather than a Weiss second shot, hit Roden's wristwatch, and it is possible that Weiss only got off one shot before his gun jammed.

Weiss crumpled to the floor face down, head toward the wall and feet diagonally into the corridor. Bodyguards Messina and McQuiston fired maybe twenty-five rounds into Weiss, many as he lay inert on the floor, until he was shredded. Sixty-one (total of entry and exit) bullet holes were found in his body. When it was lifted, bullets dropped out and clanked on the marble floor. It was amazing that Roden wasn't hit himself when the other guards fired because of his proximity to Weiss. Roden's eyes were blinded by gun smoke. His skin had powder burns. His hand had a permanent scar. A week later a small piece of bullet casing was removed from his back.[43]

Huey made it down the inside capitol stairs, perhaps careening between the walls and the railing, finding O'Connor at the bottom of the stairs, where he had loitered with the cashier at the sundry shop. "What's the matter, Kingfish?" Spitting blood, Huey said "Jimmie, my boy, I've been shot." O'Connor flagged down Bill Fakier, a highway patrolman outside the building, and commanded him to drive them to the Our Lady of the Lake Catholic Hospital, adjacent to the capitol grounds. Along the way, Huey slumped into O'Connor and murmured: "I wonder why he shot me?" O'Connor got the Kingfish on a hospital cart and a nun met them. "Sister, how bad is it?" "Gunshot wounds are always serious," she said. "Pray for me, sister," Huey asked. "Pray with me," she said, and he did. Because Huey spit blood, O'Connor initially thought Huey was shot in the mouth. A hospital intern swabbed it and said it was only a small cut. O'Connor then assumed it resulted from Huey running into a wall or a railing as he stumbled down the stairs. Fournet said it was a fever blister.[44]

Frampton had heard the first shot as he opened the door from the governor's office to the hallway and saw Weiss and Roden wrestling. Bodyguard Jones, standing at the other end of the hallway, almost shot him by mistake. Frampton's editor was still waiting on the phone line. Frampton ran back and reported that Huey said he was shot and then ran out. Frampton ran all the way from the capitol to the hospital. Huey asked him the name of the assailant, but Frampton didn't know. A state policeman arrived a few minutes later and told Huey Weiss's name. "Weiss, Dr. Weiss," Huey said, "What did he want to shoot me for?" Later an attending doctor said Weiss was the son-in-law of Judge Pavy, but Huey said he didn't know him.[45]

Taken upstairs, Huey asked that his family, surgeons Russell Stone and Urban Maes in New Orleans, and Dr. Sanderson be called. A plane was chartered for Dr. Maes and his colleague, Dr. Rives. Colonel Roy, unable to reach anyone at the airport, drove out there, punched in a glass panel, and broke into the airport to turn on the lights. Drs. Maes and Rives decided to drive. Rose was called. With Russell driving, she and the children sped from New Orleans to Baton Rouge on the new Airline Highway. They broke down construction barriers to take a newly constructed spillway to shorten their trip. Seymour Weiss drove so fast from New Orleans that he blew out the engine in his new Cadillac. Politicians from the capitol rushed over after the shooting, and they crowded Huey's room.

Dr. Arthur Vidrine of Charity Hospital was in Baton Rouge for the legislative session. He arrived and took charge. Still conscious but nervous, Huey asked about his chances and said, "It doesn't matter how long it takes, as long as I recover." He instructed the coroner to conduct an inquest and his followers to issue no statements.

Huey's clothes were cut away. Dr. Vidrine found a bullet hole in Huey's right side underneath the rib cage below the nipple and a hole in his back where he thought the bullet exited. Refusing an anesthetic, Huey told Dr. Vidrine through gritted teeth to "go ahead and clean it."[46] Two other doctors, Cecil Lorio and William H. Cook, assisted Dr. Vidrine. Anesthesiologist Dr. Henry McKeown was called. He hated Huey and agreed to assist only if some other doctor watched his every move to vouch for him.

Dr. Lorio took Huey's pulse and blood pressure every fifteen minutes. Very matter-of-factly, Huey asked: "Am I going to die?" Caught off guard by the question and its tone, Lorio hesitated and then said he thought everything would work out in the end. His blood pressure kept decreasing, while his pulse quickened. "That's not good, is it?" Huey asked. "No, but it isn't too bad yet either," Dr. Lorio said. Huey asked, "It means there's an internal hemorrhage?" Dr. Lorio replied that it could mean just that he was in shock. Huey was in a cold sweat. Often, he asked for ice or water. Huey was given caffeine and sodium benzoate intravenously.

As Huey's pulse rate increased and his blood pressure dropped, Dr. Vidrine knew he would have to operate, but hoped to delay it until Drs. Maes and Stone arrived. Oddly, Huey was also aware of this relationship and knew it was necessary to operate.[47] Drs. Rives and Maes got into an automobile accident that caused at least a thirty-minute delay, and Dr. Stone was delayed, too. Dr. Vidrine should have cleared the room, but didn't, increasing the chance of infection, often lethal in those days without antibiotics. O'Connor thought the scene strange: Huey was possibly dying, and his hospital room was full of politicians.[48]

At 11:20 p.m., Huey's pulse was weak and faint although he still begged for ice. Dr. Vidrine learned that Drs. Maes and Rives had their accident. He told Huey he could operate. Huey said, "Come on, let's get operated upon." The operation began at 11:22 p.m.[49]

Dr. Vidrine opened the abdomen and found that the stomach, liver, and gall bladder were fine. The transverse colon (the bowel that crosses the abdomen before descending to carry waste to the rectum) had been nicked in two places. A hematoma the size of a silver dollar was found in the mesentery, the tissue connecting the small intestine with the posterior wall of the abdominal cavity. The medical records said there was a small perforation of the hepatic flexure, causing some soiling of the peritoneum. Blood and fecal matter were cleaned, and the colon was sutured. The operation was completed by 12:25 a.m. Bulletins were issued that Huey would probably recover.[50] Sympathetic messages poured in from Walmsley, Coughlin, Hugh Johnson, labor groups, SOW members, members of Roosevelt's administration, senators, and congressmen.

Drs. Maes and Rives arrived after 1:00 a.m., Dr. Stone shortly thereafter. Dr. Stone asked if Dr. Vidrine had seen the kidney. Dr. Vidrine said no, but he felt it. They got into an argument. Dr. Vidrine said, "well go on in and examine him yourself." Dr. Stone said: "Not I. This isn't my case, and this isn't my patient. Good night." He stalked out of the hospital. Drs. Maes and Rives asked if Dr. Vidrine had catheterized the kidney, but he hadn't. They did, and they found blood.

Bleeding from the renal duct had drained behind an abdominal wall and wasn't visible in the areas checked by Vidrine. Vidrine should have catheterized the kidney. If he had found blood in it, he could have tied off the kidney, killing the kidney but saving Huey. One doctor, however, believes that the bleeding hadn't occurred then, that a blood clot broke off, probably after one of the blood transfusions increased the blood pressure, causing the bleeding later, after the operation. Either way, Huey was bleeding internally and could not withstand another operation to tie off the kidney. One other doctor has written that sepsis, an infection, set in. Huey did run a fever, but if an infection existed, it was at the beginning stages.

By 6:00 a.m. Monday, September 9, the doctors estimated Huey's chances at 50/50, but Christenberry issued an optimistic assessment to the press.

For the rest of Monday, Huey grew weaker and unconscious, interrupted by moments of lucidity. Huey whispered to Fournet to be kind to Allen Ellender and Wade Martin because he was going to need them. He worried to Dr. Lorio about his plans to add a thousand students to LSU. At times he talked to his family, saying, "There's my sweetheart," when Rose arrived. He talked to politicians, his brothers, even Julius, his sisters, and, briefly, his father.[51] At 2:00 p.m., he awoke suddenly and asked Dr. Maes if he would be able to campaign in the upcoming elections. Dr. Maes said it was a little early to tell. Huey mentioned that his book would be a bestseller.[52] At intervals, he hallucinated:

> [T]he people out there, the poor people of America, a mass of faces, staring at him, needing him, wanting to give him power so that he could help them . . . the one-gallus farmers of the hill lands of the South . . . the white and black sharecroppers in the broad cotton fields . . . the gaunt and debt-ridden farmers of the Great Plains . . . the unemployed factory workers tramping the streets of the Northeast . . . the small businessmen all over the country pushed to the wall by big business . . . the pathetic elderly couples in countless towns and villages whose lifesavings had disappeared with the collapse of the banks . . . the fresh-faced boys and girls eager to gain an education . . . they looked at him and trusted him . . . and they would give him the power.[53]

Late Monday night, Dr. T. Jordan Kahle, an LSU urologist, arrived and thrust a needle under the retroperitoneal spaces surrounding the kidney and drew out a syringeful of blood. Only a miracle could save Huey now. He was put in an oxygen tent. It was removed because Huey thought photographers were taking his picture. Tuesday morning, early, Huey was back in an oxygen tent, barely breathing. His wife and children were brought in at 3:00 a.m. to say goodbye. He managed to weakly pat the hands of his wife and children in a "final, caressing gesture of farewell."[54] Russell said his mother looked like a little girl as she smiled and waved goodbye. Huey died at 4:06 a.m. on September 10, 1935. Hours earlier, he had spoken his last semiconscious words, either asking what the poor boys at LSU would do without him or "God, don't let me die. I have so much to do."[55]

# CONCLUSION

There is no one deader than a dead senator. So said Don Devol, Huey's assistant secretary.[1] The hospital cleared out fast and the infighting began. Seymour Weiss oversaw the funeral arrangements and let Gerald L. K. Smith deliver the eulogy. Between 100,000 and 200,000 people—Black and white—showed up for it or to pass by the open casket, the largest Louisiana funeral of all time.[2] Today Huey's statue is perched over his tomb, facing the state capitol. The Senate was represented at the service by Caraway, Overton, Schall, Thomas, and Wheeler.

John M. Parker, J. Y. Sanders Jr., former LSU Law School dean Robert Lee Tullis, District Attorney Fred Odom, and two thousand others attended Dr. Carl Austin Weiss's funeral, the largest funeral of all time for an assassin. Father Gassler presided.[3]

Robert Maestri and Seymour Weiss won the political infighting and nominated their candidates, Judge Richard Leche for governor, O. K. Allen for Huey's unexpired Senate term, Allen Ellender for the following full Senate term, and Earl Long for lieutenant governor. Noe and others were alienated.

In the fall of 1935, Cleveland Dear (for governor) and John Sandlin (for the Senate) opposed the Long slate.[4] Dear avoided criticism of Huey, promised old-age pensions, and charged that Win or Lose Corporation with Governor "Oily Oscar" Allen's help had bilked the state.[5] Leche reduced criticism of Roosevelt and promised cooperation with federal programs, defended lease

309 as aboveboard and the big fees as necessary to entice oilmen to lease state lands, and said pensions were a national issue and part of the SOW plan.

Dear and Sandlin were tagged with leading the "assassination" ticket. Dear counterattacked that a shot by one of Huey's bodyguards ricocheted into Huey. This theory has persisted. A videotaped conference about it was held as late as 2010.[6] Evidence cited included someone quoting a nurse who said that Huey pointed to his lip and said, "this is where he hit me"; the funeral director said a doctor removed large bullets (Weiss's gun was small caliber) from Huey's body while it was in the funeral home; Dr. Weiss's Sunday with his family and his call to set up a surgery the next morning seem to bely any premeditation; Weiss's car's glove compartment was rifled, so perhaps someone grabbed the gun and planted it. The head of the state police in the 1950s quoted bodyguard John DeArmond as saying the official version was wrong,[7] but DeArmond refused to confirm this under oath and didn't say this to Professor Williams.

Deutsch supported the official version, but books by Zinman, Reed, and Pavy opined that Dr. Weiss verbally confronted Huey—perhaps impulsively—and may have struck him, after which the bodyguards shot him, with a stray bullet hitting Huey. This requires believing the hearsay testimony of the nurse and disbelieving (1) eyewitnesses Roden, Coleman, and Fournet, who described what happened, and (2) O'Connor, Lorio, and Frampton, who said that Huey wondered why the man shot him. The medical records lacked any mention of other wounds or multiple bullets, so if more bullets were removed from Huey's body, the doctors—even the anesthesiologist who hated Huey—conspired in a cover-up. Even Huey's last words are disputed.[8]

Because of the Zinman and Reed books, the state police reopened the investigation into Huey's death in the 1990s. Pictures of Huey's clothes were found. They showed powder burns and a single bullet hole. A ricocheted bullet leaves no powder burns. Without additional holes in Huey's clothes, only one bullet must have hit him.

Weiss's gun, a unique Belgian pistol, was also recovered along with a gun clip and a previously fired bullet from the Guerre family. Ballistics tests concluded that the bullet was not fired from that gun. No care had been taken to safeguard the gun or bullets as evidence. Weiss's heirs won a court challenge against the Guerre family to recover the gun and then donated it *as the assassination weapon* to the Louisiana State Archives for a big tax deduction.

The issue of motive is still a puzzle. Some think that Weiss was told that Huey was going to smear a relative with being part Black, and that he killed

Huey to prevent this humiliation. Pavy's wife's father had a Black family on the side. Most people close to Huey never heard him say that he planned to so smear Pavy. It is at odds with his efforts to recruit Black voters in the North.[9] To speculate, maybe one or more of Huey's opponents or a traitor told this falsehood to Weiss, with the deadly consequences either unforeseen or intended.

Others think that, in Europe, Weiss observed Hitler, Dollfuss, and Mussolini and brooded that Huey, too, was a fascist. Witnesses say he cried or got angry whenever Huey was mentioned.[10]

The gerrymander of Weiss's father-in-law and the firing of a relative who was a school principal probably did not provide the motive. Pavy was considering retiring anyway. The family treated these matters lightly.

David Haas said that Weiss was a member of a group of five that plotted to kill Huey at the DeSoto conference. But Weiss was in Opelousas visiting with his wife's family on one day and in his office seeing patients the other day of the conference, which is when Haas said Weiss drew the deadly straw.[11]

Wallace, Ponder, and Roy quoted Weiss as saying that Huey must die and he might be the one to do it or that he was seen in the capitol the day before the assassination, casing the scene.[12] Weiss's mother reported that he left the home at 9:00 p.m., to go on a sick call. If that is what he said, it was likely a premeditated lie. He went straight to the capitol.

The idea that Weiss went to the capitol rather than to his stated appointment, decided to confront Huey, hit him, got killed, and then the guards identified him, located his car, searched it, stole his gun, which coincidentally was of the same size as the mortal weapon, and then fired it or just planted it near him, all without being seen by any anti-Long politician or spectator in the crowd that immediately assembled or even the next day, seems implausible. Preparation preceded the murder, but he made no plans for a getaway.[13] Jack McGuire's forthcoming book on the assassination is likely to be definitive.

Huey's political heirs won a smashing triumph, 362,502 votes to 176,150 in January 1936. All pro-Roosevelt, anti-Long congressmen were defeated. Allen died, however, and Noe, who succeeded briefly to the governorship, appointed Rose Long to Huey's unexpired Senate term, and Ellender took over when that term shortly ended. Martyrdom might explain the victory. But before the election Roosevelt thought Huey's machine would disintegrate, so he "reinvigorated" the tax prosecutions; expanded relief, CCC, and WPA programs; had work vouchers distributed by anti-Long candidates or their campaign managers; and had federal workers and relief recipients instructed to vote for Dear and Sandlin.[14]

Whereas Allen thought the results repudiated Roosevelt, Noe was a true SOW believer, and Smith wanted the national spotlight,[15] Weiss, Maestri, Ellender, Maloney, and Leche were practical. They coveted federal public works money and patronage, and Weiss feared criminal tax prosecutions.

In a cynical deal called the second Louisiana purchase, Roosevelt—concerned about the loss—dropped the remaining tax prosecutions (civil IRS cases collected additional tax payments from a variety of leaders) and Huey's heirs lined up behind Roosevelt. Through a series of machinations, Mayor Walmsley resigned, and Maestri became mayor of New Orleans.[16] Anti-Long politicians felt double-crossed by Roosevelt.[17]

Roosevelt even visited New Orleans in 1936. During the entire lunch with the president of the United States at Antoine's Restaurant, Maestri's only remark was, "How do you like them ersters?" When Roosevelt bloviated at length about their many great qualities, Maestri replied, "So you liked them, huh?" Neither man impressed the other.[18] Introduced as Huey's bodyguard, Landry met Roosevelt and got the coldest handshake of his life.[19] Perhaps because of Huey's absence, despite Roosevelt's 1936 electoral mandate, his reforms ended.

Leche quashed any effort to investigate Huey's death. A few of the power laws were repealed, but not most of them. Conservatives weren't for home rule so much as they were against Huey's rule. With Huey's death, the joy went out of politics, Leche said. In consolation, perhaps, or because the restraint of the IRS investigation was removed, Leche issued a contemptible quote: "When I took the oath of office, I didn't take any vows of poverty." The *American Progress,* owned by Leche, coerced advertising and subscriptions that made him rich. The superintendent of LSU Construction, George Caldwell, stole 2 percent of all contractual sums. Flaunting his wealth, he built a fancy house with gold fixtures.[20]

In the late 1930s, angry over the machine's betrayal of Huey's program and his exclusion from the ruling circle, and just as Roosevelt considered making Leche a federal judge, Noe collected hundreds of affidavits establishing theft of WPA money, materials, and labor and sent them to journalist Drew Pearson. Pearson's stories were sensational, the talk of the country.

Sixteen months after Huey's death, James Monroe Smith began grafting from LSU. Smith speculated on wheat futures with forged LSU bonds, betting that war in Europe would break out and the price of wheat would skyrocket.

When Neville Chamberlain appeased Hitler instead in 1939, announcing peace in our time, the price of wheat plummeted, and Smith lost the money.[21]

After ordering Smith arrested, Leche resigned the governorship, falsely claiming ill health. Grand juries defied machine prosecutors and judges to investigate corruption. Some of Huey's old leaders (such as Harvey Fields, as a U.S. attorney) helped ferret out the corruption,[22] but the most powerful ones were guilty: Leche, Weiss, and Shushan went to jail, although President Truman later pardoned Leche.[23]

The corruption centered on construction kickbacks and use of WPA money for private purposes, fees on the refinancing of bonds that provided no benefit to the government, and violations of production restrictions on oil. Fifty-nine indictments were filed against 149 individuals and forty-two companies and sought tax deficiencies of $6 million (the graft was multiples of this).[24] There were suicides. V. O. Key Jr. entitled his chapter on Louisiana "the seamy side of democracy."[25]

The number of Long leaders who stayed out of jail is not as impressive, but included Earle Christenberry, Don Devol, Allen Ellender (thoroughly investigated but spotless), John Fournet, Wade Martin, Harvey Fields, Paul Maloney, Bathtub Joe Fernandez, Alice Lee Grosjean Tharpe (fired by Leche), and Earl Long. Maestri's mayoral term started out good—with refinanced debt and economies—but investigation of his term as conservation commissioner and his business interests with Seymour Weiss resulted in prosecutions even though he was never convicted.[26]

Rumors persisted that Weiss got the deduct box money and laundered it through Ralph Hitz, who owned the New Yorker Hotel, or Hitz's lawyer, Max Stein, and used the funds to buy the Roosevelt Hotel or pay off its mortgage, held by his friend and Huey's enemy, Samuel Zemurray. When Williams asked Weiss about the deduct box, Weiss asked him to turn off the recorder until they decided what he would say. Weiss then told Williams (as he had previously told Deutsch) a fantastic tale that Huey had moved the deduct box and lost consciousness in the hospital without telling him where it was, murmuring "later, Seymour, later."[27] Unlike the Ark of the Covenant, it was not lost. The noncash items stored there, such as the original affidavits against Farley, have been acquired at private auctions.

The legacy of Weiss, Maestri, and Leche was depressing. There was no vision beyond plunder. Lieutenant Governor Earl Long served the rest of Leche's gubernatorial term. In 1940, reformer Sam Jones opposed Earl in the gubernatorial election, supported by Noe, Harvey Fields, and others enraged by the corruption. At one speech Earl said he hadn't always agreed with Huey. Someone in the crowd yelled, "We always did!"[28] Earl tried to deny knowledge of the graft, after which he was accused of being stupid for not seeing it, after which he said he could have gotten his but didn't, thereby inadvertently confessing that he knew what was going on and failed to stop it.[29] An FBI agent observing Earl Long in 1939 thought he was dumb, cocky without reason, and had opinions on subjects he knew nothing about.[30] Earl lost the race.

Earl ran for governor again in 1948 and this time defeated Sam Jones. While Earl was better than Huey at retail politics—one-on-one communications, aided by a great memory for names and faces—mostly Earl has been unfavorably compared to him. His derivative program included some solid accomplishments, however: old-age pensions, hot school lunches, and founding the University of New Orleans, among others. Once a group of politicians were extolling Huey and bemoaning his absence when Earl in a contemplative voice remarked, "Well, Huey ain't here, is he."[31]

Earl won the governorship again in 1956. While opposing virulent segregationists Leander Perez and Willie Rainach, he displayed the Long realism about the power of the federal government to compel civil rights: "Watcha gonna do now, Leander? The feds have got the atomic bomb." Later, during an infamous nervous breakdown in the legislature caused by a series of strokes, he spoke poetically: "After this [is] over, [Rainach will] probably go up there to Summerfield, get up on his front porch, take off his shoes, wash his feet, look at the moon and get close to God. And when you do, you got to recognize that n——s is human beings!"[32] He was led off the floor. Later he was photographed traveling with a bag over his head. Placed in a mental institution by his wife, he escaped, resumed the governorship, was seen with stripper Blaze Starr, and fired those who institutionalized him. A. J. Liebling of the *New Yorker* chronicled the drama sympathetically, and it was unconscionably fictionalized in the 1989 movie *Blaze*. Earl ran for Congress in 1960 against an incumbent to rehabilitate his standing. Jack McGuire's great book gives the best account of it.[33] Earl was determined to win the campaign or die trying. He did both.

With Earl's support in 1948, Huey's son Russell won a Senate seat, replacing John Overton, who had died. Russell's Senate career was the opposite of his father's. An insider as chairman of the powerful Finance Committee, his great memory made him the Kingfish of the intricacies of the tax code; he also fought to expand Social Security and enact Medicare. Ironically, he torpedoed the Nixon-Moynihan plan to provide a minimum income for families, a variant of Huey's idea, because he thought it would incentivize laziness, and advocated workfare instead of welfare. He kept an eye on the distribution of wealth statistics, however, which had improved after World War II government spending. Later, he helped pass employee stock-ownership legislation, quipping that his father wanted to make every man a king, but he wanted to make every man a capitalist. Russell defended the oil industry's tax breaks. Henry Wallace told him that a fascinating videotaped interview with his father predicted the future. They couldn't find it. Perhaps it is stored with the Ark of the Covenant.

Periodic public disagreements with his Uncle Earl were caused by Russell's alignment with aristocratic reformers in New Orleans that Earl disliked. In one of their spats, Earl said Russell was picked too green on the vine. Russell retorted that Earl was too ripe on the vine and should be picked at once.[34]

Some people die leaving tantalizing questions. How would Lincoln have handled Reconstruction? Would President Kennedy have ended the war in Vietnam? Would John Lennon have made music with Kurt Cobain?

Whether Huey could have become president in 1936 or 1940 is one of those questions. The soldiers' bonus bill was again passed and again vetoed by Roosevelt in January 1936, but this time without a speech and with a wink. Congress overrode the veto. The bonus checks were issued just in time for the 1936 elections. With $5 billion in relief money and $2 billion in the bonus, the economy had its best year under the New Deal and many thought that, with this money, Roosevelt was unbeatable. Huey had a great slogan as an antidote to politicized government expenditures: take the money and vote your conscience. In the New Mexico election of 1934,[35] the WPA workers had taken the WPA money and voted against Roosevelt's candidate. Agriculture Secretary Wallace was ordered to keep cotton prices at 12 cents a bale. One can imagine Huey in an improving economy attributing it to the soldiers' bonus, his fight for 12 cents cotton, and his support of other progressive legislation, and asking the voters to enact the rest of his plan, a classic case of incremental change giving way to radical change in a period of rising expectations. But the voters might have considered the improvements as evidence that the New Deal was working and that they should give it more time. Social scientists note that, when a pressure group succeeds, it might thereafter weaken now that its issue is removed from contention, or it might gain strength by claiming credit for the victory.[36]

It is easy to assume that Huey would have won reelection in Louisiana as his heirs did. He would have been helped by the success of the LSU football team—it won all its regular season games—and the completion of the spillway and the then-spectacular Mississippi River Bridge (now the Huey P. Long Bridge) in December and January 1936.

If Huey had won some presidential primaries,[37] Coughlin—who had flip-flopped *against* Roosevelt in August 1935[38]—and progressives such as Wheeler, LaFollette, Amlie, Maverick, Olson, and others might have been welcomed by Roosevelt to help him fight off Huey or might have thrown in with Huey once they thought he could win.

The experience of the Union Party that was formed by Coughlin, Smith, Townsend, and Representative William Lemke after Huey's death has no relevance to what would have happened had Huey lived. The party was formed at the last minute, on a whim of Coughlin. It failed to get on the ballot in Ohio, one of Coughlin's strongest states, or Louisiana. It lacked the SOW membership lists. (Christenberry gave them to Rose to keep them away from Smith.) It lacked money to campaign. Its presidential candidate, Lemke, was a poor speaker.

Reflecting conventional wisdom, Schlesinger wrote that Roosevelt would have been reelected if Huey had lived.[39] Conventional wisdom like this predicted Churchill's victory in the United Kingdom elections after his heroic leadership in World War II, Thomas Dewey's defeat of Truman in 1948, and Hillary Clinton's victory over Donald Trump in 2016.

Most contemporaries commenting on Huey's death acknowledged his intelligence and deplored both his assassination and his "dictatorship." Hugh Johnson and others respected his open advocacy. Some said he created the conditions that caused his own death. One congressman said Huey got what was coming to him.[40]

The demagogue charge has become a verdict, too. In 1916, Huey said any champion of the people would be called a demagogue, whereas defenders of the status quo would be christened as statesmen. There is truth in that, but many of those called demagogues have not been friends of the people.

"Demagogue" has been defined as one who appealed to the "rabble." Other definitions have emphasized evil traits of the leader. One academic paper listed these characteristics: simplicity; repetition; verbal perpetuation of problems; evasion of issues; invective; emotionalism; scapegoating; attacking a corporate enemy; appeals to religious, class, or race hatreds; exploitation of men and issues; common-man appeal, and anti-intellectualism.[41] This is too broad to be useful. Simplicity was one of Roosevelt's communication strengths. Repetition is required to break through the clutter of competing messages. The emotional identification with one's audience is useful.

Lies, irrelevancy, and destructiveness are hallmarks of demagoguery. Joseph McCarthy said he had in his hand a list of communists in the State Department, but he didn't. Chicago mayor William Hale Thompson said he would punch King George of England in the snout. It was a lie because he was not going to do it, and it was irrelevant because it wouldn't do anyone any good. James Vardaman, Thomas Heflin, and Theodore Bilbo played on demeaning stereotypes about Black people to incite hatred. The link from that to lynching can be drawn. Academics call it stochastic terrorism.

A leader denouncing racism might have moved public opinion one degree or more away from racism or toward tolerance, but Abraham Lincoln articulated a reason not to: "A universal feeling, whether well or ill-founded, cannot safely be disregarded."[42] A lawyer would call this a rule of necessity. During the 1932 Caraway campaign, Huey used the N-word and portrayed Black people as comical connivers in two anecdotes intended to be humorous. This wasn't constructive, but his anecdotes wouldn't have incited lynching.

A sense of humor can be irrelevant and conceal issue evasion, but when Huey said opponents of a new governor's mansion reminded him of the boardinghouse operator who told his boarders that his dirty towels were good enough for the prior boarders and therefore should be good enough for them, this humorous barb got right to the issue. While Hitler, Mussolini, and Joseph McCarthy, for example, sometimes displayed a sense of humor, more often their speeches were serious and fanatical. The clearest difference between Willie Stark of *All the King's Men* and Huey was that Willie didn't display much humor, joy, and enthusiasm. This shouldn't surprise. Willie was modeled after the bronze man of Greek mythology, Talos, an automaton who guarded the island of Crete and dispensed a remorseless justice, featured in book 5 of Spencer's *Faerie Queen*. Huey was no automaton; he had fun.

Divorced from the concepts of truth, relevancy, and destructiveness, scapegoating, invective, class-based appeals, and emotionalism are problematic indicators of demagoguery. If billionaires are paying no taxes, is it a demagogic appeal to argue that this is wrong? If England is occupying India, is it a demagogic appeal to say that India is for the Indians? Invective against injustice, oppression, crime, poverty, illiteracy, or colonialism ought to be applauded. Jesus could have approached the "moneychanger problem" in a "nuanced" way without calling them a den of robbers.

Beals said Huey was "called a demagogue too freely, or at least without proper examination of the word":

> Is the man who has the power to rouse the multitude necessarily a demagogue? Is the one who promises what he cannot fulfill more of a demagogue than the one who deceives the public without such promises? Certainly no President in the history of the Republic has so departed from his original campaign promises as has President Roosevelt. Is there any worse demagogue in America than Herbert Hoover with his inane platitudes about liberty. . . . Is not a demagogue a thousand times more desirable in public life than a gross machine politician like Mr. Farley?[43]

Ernest Bormann wrote an MA thesis about Huey's reply to Hugh Johnson—which included emotional, class-based appeals, invective, and simplifying analogies—and concluded that, while Huey was not a "good man" like Gandhi (who is?),[44] he used appropriate rhetorical techniques.[45]

Huey's program included relevant, realistic appeals for achievable goals, and then he delivered on his promises. Joseph McCarthy never delivered because he had nothing to deliver. Racist demagogues not only failed to deliver but led their followers down a path of inevitable defeat. The feds had the power, and Black people are human beings.

The relevance, specificity, and realism of Huey's program belies the demagogue label and frightens the ordinary politician. Most politicians follow the FDR model and straddle the issues. Huey's approach was to find some issue on which to confront his opponents, something on which they could not or would not retreat, and on which he believed that he could convince a majority of voters before the next election that he was right. Many historians believe that SOW was a lie, but it was closer to the truth than the economic orthodoxy of the time or other prescribed remedies such as the NRA. Huey offered his program two years before any presidential campaign, with plenty of time to debate it. Isn't that how democracy should work?

At every level of achievement, Huey fought on behalf of capitalist underdogs, challenged the biggest target, was attacked, capitalized on the attacks, won, overreached, was counterattacked, recovered, grew, gained new strength, and advanced to his next goal. At each stage, he used the tools of salesmen and lawyers, measured the circumstances, planned what to do, disregarded reprimands, refused to play it safe, and got things done.

It was a series of all-in gambles, akin to what Jim Collins in the business world calls the Big Hairy Audacious Goal (BHAG). Collins believes companies that make the jump from good companies to great companies have a BHAG, but he concedes that he hasn't measured the number of companies that had a BHAG and failed, when they might have survived as good companies.[46] Most politicians don't emulate Huey. The *Saturday Evening Post*'s article about Lost Leaders could be written today. It is safer to be mediocre or above average.

It is time to retire the historical caricature of Huey as a menace. It took Huey seventeen years to attain his preeminence in Louisiana (population 2.2 million), which is less significant than Mayor Daley's control over Chicago (in 1955 or so, population 3.5 million), and Huey endured an indictment, electoral defeats (1924 and January 1934), impeachment (1929), and legislative failure (1930). His opposition never bent, so, ultimately, he broke it. Huey could not have attained a similar preeminence over the Congress, representing forty-eight states.

Huey's humor, enthusiasm, optimism, perseverance, resilience, intelligence, energy, originality, and dedication to a worthy cause of helping 99 percent of the people are admirable. Huey proposed original but realistic ideas. Huey's realism included its cousin: cynicism. Ruthlessness was caused or necessitated in part by the unreasonable behavior of his opponents and in part was ingrained by heredity or environment. Huey had a temper and, for several years before 1934, a drinking problem. His concept of friendship approximated Cellini's extravagant description. Huey said he could handle his enemies; it was his friends who got him in trouble.[47] Huey had some strange ideas: that someone's deformities meant that the Lord had marked him[48] and that the state government and its agencies belonged to him. Faults shouldn't obscure Huey any more than describing Roosevelt's great qualities should blind us to his flaws.

Whether as caricature or not, Huey's memory has outlived most of his contemporaries: Ashurst, Barkley, Byrnes, Connally, Frazier, George, Harrison, Lewis, McKellar, Reynolds, Robinson, Tydings, Walsh, bit players all. Huey bent the national debate and forced Roosevelt to the best principles of the Banking Act and the second New Deal in ways that no one else did.

Tracing Huey's ideas from 1928 to 1935 (or from 1932 to 1935) shows a phenomenal analytical development. Huey's ideas wrapped around problems. They were big ideas. Many of them were obvious, or at least appear so now. For people unhappy with the Louisiana workers' compensation law, the obvious solution was to ask some expert what a better law would look like, draft a proposal, give it to a sympathetic representative, and ask others to support it. To promote LSU, Huey started with the obvious symbols: the band and the football team. In the Depression, too few had too much money and most of the people lacked it. The obvious solution was to tax the wealthy and provide everyone else with a minimum.

It is speculative to wonder whether Huey read the *Saturday Evening Post* story about Obvious Adams in April 1916. Obvious Adams was a fictional advertising executive who became successful because he developed big, obvious solutions. It became a small cult classic.[49] It required sustained, concentrated thought to produce big ideas. A big idea explodes in a listener or reader's consciousness. Whether Huey read that story or not, he had the capacity to think through a problem, and his proposals exploded into the public's consciousness. To a significant extent, he obtained power—rising from his inconsequential town and family—from his ideas.

Persistence and sincerity were other notable qualities. Huey advocated redistribution of wealth in 1918, 1919, and during the middle of the general prosperity during the Coolidge administration, long before the Depression. He outlawed mortgage deficiency judgments and restrictive employment covenants, which benefit the class of people Huey tried to help. He didn't have to pass these laws to portray himself as their champion.[50]

Huey was willing to face criticism, to be considered a nuisance, to fight for his ideas. There is something admirable about a man who would give a speech for hours and drop exhausted into his seat. There is something courageous about a man who would take on the entire U.S. Senate. There is something revolting about senators who agreed with him but stayed silent, leaving him to fight alone.

Resilience is easily stated as a trait. But to see someone engage in a sustained period of hard work to survive a bad time—even if self-inflicted—such as his post-impeachment work in 1929 and early 1930 and his exertions in 1934 after the disastrous events of 1933, is remarkable.

Huey's personal growth included ending his undisciplined life as a salesman to attend law school and curbing his overbearing conduct after his impeachment. When drinking got the best of him in 1933, he stopped. His relationship with his wife must have been strained between 1928 and 1933 but, if never normal, it improved in 1934 and 1935. Huey spent more time with his children than Williams relates, although not as much as they would have liked.[51]

Revolutions sometimes result in tyranny, and this was the charge leveled at Huey, despite the concession that he enjoyed majority support. The Jim Crow laws represented a majoritarian or legislative tyranny. The concentration camps set up by Roosevelt to imprison Japanese Americans during World War II were executive tyranny. The Supreme Court engaged in judicial tyranny by striking down all New Deal legislation and allowed the Jim Crow laws and concentration camps. While the three branches of government are designed to check and balance each other, if erroneous decisions are made by the president, Congress, or the Supreme Court, they can frustrate the legitimate decisions of the majority or permit the violation of individual rights.

In the aftermath of Roosevelt's politicization of relief funds and government officials, the Hatch Act was passed in 1939 to prohibit this. After Roosevelt left office, the Constitution was amended to restrict presidents to two terms. After Huey, some civil service and home rule protections were enacted, but nothing was done to improve the independence of the judiciary or tax assessors, and the state police force still exists. Criticism on these issues was overblown. The Supreme Court now believes that Jim Crow laws are unconstitutional. After Roosevelt, the government admitted that putting Japanese Americans in concentration camps was wrong. After Huey, LSU apologized for expelling students in the *Reveille* controversy.

Is Huey relevant now? A politician who today talked about a louse in Davy Crocket's eyebrow would be laughed off the stage and screen. Huey's style was a product of his times, as his *specific* plan resulted from the *general* ideas of William Jennings Bryan, Theodore Roosevelt, Woodrow Wilson, Henry Ford, John Truslow Adams, Felix Frankfurter, Rexford Guy Tugwell, Marriner Eccles, William Allen White, and many others. An article about Ford's ideas in *Collier's* in the early 1920s reads almost like Huey's SOW plan, although the author thought it would occur naturally and voluntarily.[52] Whether that idea is strong enough or prevalent enough today to support a political candidate or whether there is some other strong or prevalent idea that could support a political candidate now is well beyond the scope of this book.

Harry Truman in 1948 and Ronald Reagan in 1980 showed the power of advocating a program before an actual campaign, however, as Huey did.[53] Truman used Congress to dramatize his proposals to get elected. Reagan used his electoral mandate to get much of his program enacted by a Congress dominated by the opposing political party.

Former president Donald Trump has been compared to Huey. There are a few superficial similarities: domination of the media, a persuasive slogan, a warts-and-all-authenticity, demeaning nicknames for opponents, the violation of norms. But Trump's criticism of ethnic groups (Huey made ethnic groups feel appreciated),[54] incompetence in dealing with the COVID crisis, and solicitude for the wealthy distinguish him from Huey. Trump showed little growth or evidence of study. Without legal training, Trump failed to think like a lawyer when many of the issues he confronted were legal ones or had important legal components. People who worked closely with Huey never called him a moron, and opponents conceded Huey's legal skill, capacity for cold logic, and that he had a certain "genius" for governing. Huey's promised benefits were more specific than Trump's and were immediately achievable, and his legal skill, creativity, and energy in proposing and then implementing these solutions were evident.

Much like Trump, Huey capitalized on resentments held by farmers, laborers, and veterans, but he directed those resentments against the wealthy and powerful, and government bureaucrats. Huey wanted real jobs because, while relief was better than starvation, it often consisted of "sweeping leaves from one side of the street to the other." Huey had a way of blending resentments against big government with those against big business in ways that appeal to members of the left and the right.

Anti-Long senator Cecil Morgan and journalist Harnett Kane believed that Louisianans feared Huey because of his vindictiveness and his power over the courts, the banks, local government, the taxing authorities, and the police.[55] Facing Huey as inquisitor at the murder-plot hearings in February 1935, however, the anti-Longs displayed an insouciant, carefree insolence. The number of politicians who broke with Huey at various points, including in 1935, when he was at the height of his power, diminishes the accusation. Stories in 1935 described significant acceptance of Huey by the wealthy.

There was the fear that Huey could not be beaten. He was always one step ahead of his opponents, was resourceful and persistent, and would pay the price to win. Even after being appointed counsel for Standard Oil, Cecil Morgan "seethed" as he described Huey's cleverness.[56]

The various individuals and groups plotting to kill Huey or threatening to do so manifested fear and rage. Assassination plotter Dave Haas equated

Huey with the Kennedys. One is reminded of the newspaper ads accusing Kennedy of treason before his visit to Dallas in 1963.

Today, fear and rage—and an awful illogic—now infect *some* on *every* side of political issues. Discourse now often consists of shouting confirmatory facts that fit a predefined worldview and disregarding facts that don't. The left and the right often select ridiculous representatives of their opponent to mock, evading legitimate debate. Huey and the forces that made him helped usher in this distasteful aspect of modern politics. The lack of a sensible worldliness is now characteristic of American democracy. This could be a tragedy in the making, a tragedy *All the King's Men* reflected, a tragedy that Louisiana already experienced.

# Notes

## Abbreviations

| | |
|---|---|
| ACLU | American Civil Liberties Union |
| *ADN* | *Amarillo Daily News* |
| BCP | Bronson M. Cutting Papers |
| *BHMNP* | *News-Palladium* |
| *BMDH* | *Daily Herald* |
| *BMSH* | *Biloxi Sun Herald* |
| *BRA* | *Baton Rouge Morning Advocate* |
| *BRST* | *Baton Rouge State-Times* |
| *CDS* | *Corsicana Daily Sun* |
| CGP | Carter Glass Papers |
| CMP | Cecil Morgan Papers |
| Congress H.R. | Congress House of Representatives |
| CR | Congressional Record |
| *CT* | *Chicago Tribune* |
| CUOHC | Columbia University Oral History Collection |
| CUOHP | Columbia University Oral History Project |
| *DAL* | *Daily Argus Leader* |
| *DMR* | *Des Moines Register* |
| DNC | Democratic National Committee |
| *EDP* | *The Escanaba Daily Press* |
| *EMK* | *Every Man a King* |
| *EOA* | *Encyclopedia of Alabama* |
| *EONYS* | *The Encyclopedia of New York State* |
| FDR | Franklin D. Roosevelt |
| FDRL | Franklin D. Roosevelt Letters |
| FDROF | Franklin D. Roosevelt Official Files |
| FDROP | Franklin D. Roosevelt Official Papers |
| FDRPPF | Franklin D. Roosevelt, President's Personal File |
| GNP | George Norris Papers |
| HB | Harley Bozeman |
| HBDP | Hermann Bacher Deutsch Papers |

| | |
|---|---|
| HBP | Harry Byrd Papers |
| HJP | Hiram Johnson Papers |
| *HMHA* | *Hattiesburg American* |
| *HN* | *Hutchinson News* |
| HPL | Huey P. Long |
| HPLP | Huey P. Long Papers |
| HSTLOHIC | Harry S. Truman Library Oral History Interviews Collection |
| Int. | Interview |
| JAFP | James A. Farley Papers |
| JBAFP | James B. Aswell and Family Papers |
| JEUP | John Earle Uhler Papers |
| JMP | Jack McGuire Papers |
| *JNH* | *Joplin News Herald* |
| JR | Joseph Robinson |
| JTL | Julius T. Long |
| LBJ | Lyndon B. Johnson |
| *LDNL* | *Laurel Daily News Leader* |
| LFP | Lafollette Family Papers |
| LHA | Louisiana Historical Association |
| LHC | Louisiana Highway Commission |
| *LN* | *Lima News* |
| LOC | Library of Congress |
| LPSC | Louisiana Public Service Commission |
| LSBE | Louisiana State Board of Education |
| LSU | Louisiana State University |
| LTR | Letter |
| MBR | Mineral Board Report |
| MHM | Marvin H. McIntire |
| *MNS* | *Monroe News-Star* |
| NAACP | National Association for the Advancement of Colored People |
| *NOS* | *New Orleans States Magazine* |
| *NOTP* | *New Orleans Times-Picayune* |
| NRA | National Recovery Administration |
| NYBB | New York Ballantine Books |
| *NYT* | *New York Times* |
| OHI | Oral History Interviews |
| *PAN* | *Port Arthur News* |
| PSC | Public Service Commission |
| RBL | Russell B. Long |
| RBLP | Russell B. Long Papers |
| RORS | Records of Ross S. Sterling |
| Rpt. | Reprint |
| SC SOS | South Carolina Secretary of State |
| *SEP* | *Saturday Evening Post* |
| SHO | Senate Historical Office |
| SOHC | Southern Oral History Program Collection |
| THW | T. Harry Williams |
| THWC | T. Harry Williams Collection |

| | |
|---|---|
| THWCOH | T. Harry Williams Collection on Huey |
| THWP | T. Harry Williams Papers |
| TUDD | Tulane University Doctoral Dissertation |
| UPTW | United Press Transcontinental Wire |
| WBWC | William B. Wisdom Collection |
| *WDM* | *Winslow Daily Mail* |
| WEB | William E. Borah |
| WEBP | William E. Borah Papers |
| *WPE* | *Winn Parish Enterprise* |

## Introduction

1. Hair, *Realm,* 288.
2. Williams, *Huey Long,* 839–41; Haas int., THWP.
3. Spencer int., THWP.
4. Ortiz, *Beyond the Bonus March,* 199–201.
5. Heilman, *Southern Connection,* 61–62.

## 1. A Singularity

1. Gordon, *Rise and Fall,* 25–318. Chapter 7 is entitled "Nasty, Brutish, and Short: Illness and Early Death." McGerr, *Discontent,* 3–39.
2. Bogart and Thompson, *Readings,* 782.
3. Gordon, *Rise and Fall,* 57 (water), 94–128 (housing), 247–87 (working conditions). See Watts of Love (kerosene lamp danger).
4. Long, *EMK,* 2.
5. Gordon, *Rise and Fall,* 50–52, 62–85 (food), 65 (spending), 129–71 (transportation), 206–46 (health), 206–12 (life expectancy), 283 (contrasting rural and urban teenage life).
6. Chemerinsky, *Constitutional Law,* 13 (income tax), 255, 646 (minimum wages), 257–62 (antitrust law), 331 (child labor laws, struck down in 1918), 520–22, 638–39 (no right to practice trade or profession), 524–32 (Bill of Rights not applicable to states; First Amendment discussed at 525), 533–34 (law prohibiting race discrimination between private parties unconstitutional), 642 (maximum-hours law struck down for bakers but approved for coal miners and women), 732–34 (Jim Crow law passed in 1890, enforced in 1892, and approved in 1896); Hair, *Realm,* 1.
7. McGerr, *Discontent,* 4–5, 7.
8. Sindler, *Huey Long's Louisiana,* 1. For the following sketch of Louisiana's economic, social, and political characteristics, see Sindler, *Huey Long's Louisiana,* 1–5; Howard, *Political Tendencies,* 22, 104–210; Williams, *Huey Long,* 181–91; Hair, *Realm,* 1–23.
9. Istre, *Creoles,* 4, 1–42.
10. Ancelet, Edwards, and Pitre, *Cajun Country,* xiii–xxiv; 3–32.
11. Sindler, *Huey Long's Louisiana,* 45; Hair, *Realm,* 33; Gordon, *Rise and Fall,* 1–23, 172–205; Ancelet, Edwards, and Pitre, *Cajun Country,* 43–65.
12. Barry, *Rising Tide,* 218–19.
13. Hair, *Realm,* 9–10.
14. Chernow, *Grant,* 759–60 (Colfax massacre), 763, 790–95, 843 (atrocities: whipping, disemboweling, castration, torture, killing women and children), 847, 857.
15. Williams, *Huey Long,* 187; Barry, *Rising Tide,* 215–17.

16. Barnes, *Louisiana Populist Movement,* 128.

17. Howard, *Political Tendencies,* 176–78; Ancelet, Edwards, and Pitre, *Cajun Country,* 77–94.

18. See Barry, *Rising Tide,* 124–25, for an account of a Mississippi lynching.

19. Hair, *Realm,* 12–14.

20. Gordon, *Rise and Fall,* 241; Hyde, *Pistols and Politics,* 311–50.

21. "Manufacturing Interests of the United States," *St. Tammany Farmer,* June 14, 1902, 6.

22. Howard, *Political Tendencies,* 161–62, 165, 166; Hair, *Realm,* 1.

23. Margo, *Race and Schooling,* 6–32, tables 2.5 and 2.6, quote from 20.

24. Sindler, *Huey Long's Louisiana,* 2; Howard, *Political Tendencies,* 3–68; Williams, *Huey Long,* 12–14; Kane, *Hayride,* 37; Dew, "The Long-Lost Returns," 353.

25. Williams, *Huey Long,* 29–31; Jeansonne, *Messiah,* 6–7 (14 percent Black in 1893).

26. Howard, *Political Tendencies,* 153–87; Barnes, *Louisiana Populist Movement,* 142, 153, 167, 169, 175, 179, 182–83, 191, 206–9.

27. Barnes, *Louisiana Populist Movement,* 208–11.

28. Howard, *Political Tendencies,* 175–76, 202–4.

29. Sindler, *Huey Long's Louisiana,* 21.

30. Koenig, *Bryan,* passim; Kazin, *A Godly Hero,* 154 (insurance of bank deposits).

31. Berg, *Wilson,* 214.

32. Koenig, *Bryan,* 220–21, 231–32, 235, 243.

33. Herrick and Herrick, *Life of Bryan,* 29.

34. Friedman and Schwartz, *Monetary History,* 89–134 and note 52; Koenig, *Bryan,* 115–47, 178–208, 221–54.

35. For the history of the Long family and Winnfield, see Williams, *Huey Long,* 9–46; Hair, *Realm,* 24–38; Long, *EMK,* 1–7; and Eakin, *Little Hu.* Essential to these secondary accounts were Harley Bozeman's articles about Winn Parish and Huey published in *Winn Parish Enterprise;* most can be found in THWP, box 16: 22.

36. HB to RBL, March 10 and 29, 1957, RBLP, box 1: 21–22; Morgan, "Williams on Long," 676–82; Julius Long, *Real America,* September 1933, 30, 37.

37. Jeansonne, *Messiah,* 7.

38. Hair, *Realm,* 24, 40.

39. Long, *EMK,* 4–5; Field, "*Campaigns,*" 5–6.

40. Hunt int., THWP.

41. Hair, *Realm,* 29–30, 41.

42. Hair, *Realm,* 27–29.

43. Hess, "The Long, Long Trail."

44. Williams, *Huey Long,* 24.

45. Jeansonne, *Messiah,* 11.

46. *Huey Long, dir. Burns;* O. Stone to HPL, May 16, 2021, box 20: 33, HPLP.

47. Hair, *Realm,* 31.

48. Wallace int., THWP.

49. Long, *EMK,* 6.

50. Williams, *Huey Long,* 31–35.

51. Blackshear int., THWP.

52. HPL to Aline McConnell, September 13, 1921, box 1: 8, HPLP; box 1: 17, HPLP (Cellini excerpts, the Caesar advertisement, other poems, selections from *The Tempest,* and a short essay about the hardships of WWI soldiers).

53. Williams, *Huey Long,* 28–29; NOS, January 4, 1931, 1, clipping in box 20: 8, HBDP.

54. Hair, *Realm,* 34; Long, *EMK,* 6–7; F. Davis, *Huey Long,* 53.
55. HB, *WPE,* April 16, 2014, 3-A.
56. Eakin, *Little Hu,* 28.
57. Long, *EMK,* 3–5; F. Davis, *Huey Long,* 284; Field, "*Campaigns,*" 5.
58. Williams, *Huey Long,* 34.
59. Talbot int., THWP.
60. Long, *EMK,* 3–4, 6.
61. Hair, *Realm,* 28; Kane, *Hayride,* 39.
62. Long, *EMK,* 6.
63. Eakin, *Little Hu,* 43–44.
64. Williams, *Huey Long,* 30; HB, *WPE,* April 16, 2014, 3-A.
65. HPL to W. W. White, September 22, 1919, box 2: 17, 63, HPLP.
66. Hair, *Realm,* 35.
67. Peyton int., THWP.
68. Williams, *Huey Long,* 47.
69. Eakin, *Little Hu,* 12–18.
70. W. A. Friedman, *Birth,* 23–25, 36–38.
71. Hair, *Realm,* 42; HB, *WPE,* April 16, 2014, 3-A; Eakin, *Little Hu,* 87–89.
72. Williams, *Huey Long,* 37.
73. Hair, *Realm,* 36.
74. Kane, *Hayride,* 40.
75. Williams, *Huey Long,* 45–46.
76. Jeansonne, *Messiah,* 11–12.
77. Hanks (one of Huey's teachers) int., THWP; Deutsch, "*Paradox,*" 2. HB to Clara Knott (Huey's sister), November 1, 1965, box 8: 21–22, THWP. A fire destroyed grade transcripts.
78. Knott int., THWP.
79. Williams, *Huey Long,* 36.
80. J. L. Liggin to HB, March 5, 1958, box 8: 20–21, THWP.
81. Williams, *Huey Long,* 38–39; Hair, *Realm,* 38.
82. Deutsch, "Paradox," 3–4. While Huey later claimed to have started a secret society at school, Harley Bozeman didn't recall it. HB to T. Harry Williams, August 27, 1964, box 8: 20–21, TWHP.

## 2. Early Patterns

1. W. A. Friedman, *Birth,* 5, 7, 12–18, 23–32, 36–42, 51–65, 71–72, 80, 82–83, 86–87, 90, 150, 157–58, 180.
2. Kane, *Hayride,* 42; F. Davis, *Huey Long,* 56–57.
3. *Gideons International,* "About Us."
4. W. A. Friedman, *Birth,* 14.
5. Hiller, *Fifty-Two Sunday Dinners.*
6. Williams, *Huey Long,* 47–70; Hair, *Realm,* 39–54; Long, *EMK,* 8–14; Eakin, *Little Hu,* 91–131. Advertiser Claude Hopkins promoted Cotosuet—a competing product—by baking in each town the largest cake in the world (Hopkins, *My Life in Advertising,* 61–64).
7. *Kingsport Times,* September 12, 1935, 1.
8. Eakin, *Little Hu,* 93–94.
9. Williams, *Huey Long,* 51.
10. Hair, *Realm,* 43.

11. Jeansonne, *Messiah*, 15–16, 18.
12. Williams, *Huey Long*, 51–52, 65–67.
13. Williams, *Huey Long*, 53.
14. Hair, *Realm*, 39, 43 and note 13.
15. Jeansonne, *Messiah*, 15; Kane, *Hayride*, 42.
16. Williams, *Huey Long*, 54–55.
17. Long, *EMK*, 8.
18. Kane, *Hayride*, 43. Malone, *Hattie and Huey*, 28–29.
19. Long, *EMK*, 9.
20. Williams, *Huey Long*, 56.
21. Long, *EMK*, 9–10.
22. Long, *EMK*, 12.
23. Williams, *Huey Long*, 59.
24. Long, *EMK*, 13.
25. Housing Works Bookstore Cafe.
26. Williams, *Huey Long*, 61n1.
27. Deutsch, "Paradox," 15–16; Williams, *Huey Long*, 63.
28. Hair, *Realm*, 47–48.
29. Long, *EMK*, 14.
30. Williams, *Huey Long*, 63–65; Field, "*Campaigns*," 10.
31. Williams, *Huey Long*, 65.
32. Long, *EMK*, 14–15.
33. *Creston Advertiser*, January 26, 1928, 5.
34. Deutsch, "Paradox," 17; Harley Bozeman, "Huey Long as I Knew Him," part 3, *Winn Parish Enterprise*, June 18, 2014, 3-A; Hair, *Realm*, 49.
35. Williams, *Huey Long*, 66–67.
36. Hair, *Realm*, 50.
37. HPL to H. D. Chamberlain, December 29, 1917, box 2: 55, HPLP.
38. Hair, *Realm*, 51 and note 35; Field, "*Campaigns*," 11n13. Hadacol was a fraudulent medicine, too (Cruikshank and Schultz, *The Man Who Sold America*, 52–58, 95–99).
39. Long, *EMK*, 15; JTL to HPL, September 7, 1921, box 1: 8, HPLP.
40. Carazo int. (good dancer); Frampton int. (curing hangovers), THWP; Field, "*Campaigns*," 42–43 (bedbug poems).
41. Wheeler and Healy, *Yankee*, 411.
42. "Iowa a Cinch, Huey Believes," *DMR*, April 28, 1935.
43. Gamble int., THWP.
44. Roman and Maas, *How to Advertise*, 10.
45. Caples, *Tested Advertising Methods*, 141.
46. Hopkins, *My Life in Advertising*, 236–41, 254–58; Ogilvy, *Confessions*, 133–37.
47. Boswell, *Life of Samuel Johnson*, 1030–31: "'they consider it as a compliment to be talked to, as if they were wiser than they are.'"
48. HB to THW, April 8, 1966, box 8: 20–21, THWP.
49. Malone, *Hattie and Huey*, 28, 31–33. Arsenaul, "Davis, Jeff."
50. Street, "The Man Who Invented the Redneck"; Barry, *Rising Tide*, 117–31.
51. Holmes, "Vardaman, James Kimble."
52. Kirwan, *Revolt of the Rednecks*.
53. Boschert, "Williams, John Sharp"; Osborn, *John Sharp Williams*, 200.

### 3. Political Trends Huey Measured as He Came of Age

1. On Huey's law career, see Williams, *Huey Long,* 71–105; Hair, *Realm,* 52–54, 73–85, 99; Long, *EMK,* 15–36, 50–51.

2. Jeansonne, *Messiah,* 19.

3. Abstracts in box 1: 11 (Louisiana practice), 12 (federal practice), 13 (corporations), 14 (constitutional law), and 15 (succession), HPLP.

4. Jeansonne, *Messiah,* 12, 31, 60.

5. Williams, *Huey Long,* 74, 75; Debate cases, box 1: 16 has a typed debate speech, HPLP.

6. Long, *EMK,* 15.

7. HPL and C. D. Shaughnessy correspondence, box 2: 9, HPLP.

8. Williams, *Huey Long,* 77, 76; box 9: 27 (the document), WBWC; Woodrow Wilson also thought legal education should include literature courses (Berg, *Wilson,* 80).

9. Rivet int., THWP.

10. Williams, *Huey Long,* 79.

11. Williams, *Huey Long,* 106–7.

12. Roberts, *Churchill,* 32.

13. For the preceding and much of the following text, see Morris, *The Rise of Theodore Roosevelt* and *Theodore Rex;* Berg, *Wilson.*

14. Zoellick, *America in the World,* 112–33.

15. "Theodore Roosevelt—The Man with the Muck-rake."

16. Hofstadter, *American Political Tradition,* 232–35, 245.

17. Berg, *Wilson,* 175, 183, 214, 215.

18. Berg, *Wilson,* 223, 230–31.

19. Hofstadter, *American Political Tradition,* chap. 9 ("Theodore Roosevelt: The Conservative as Progressive"), 265–306, and chap. 10 ("Woodrow Wilson: The Conservative as Liberal"), 307–66.

20. Berg, *Wilson,* 78, 209, 240, 295; Hofstadter, *American Political Tradition,* 256–60.

21. Berg, *Wilson,* 297–301, 315–16, 399, 407.

22. Hofstadter, *American Political Tradition,* 258.

23. Scott, "Highway Building."

24. Berg, *Wilson,* 477–78; *NYT,* September 27, 1913; Long, *EMK,* 37–39 and note 10.

25. Howard, *Political Tendencies,* 188–89.

26. Schott, "Huey Long," 135, citing Dethloff, "The Longs," 401–12; Barry, *Rising Tide,* 123–25.

27. Woodward, *Origins,* 211.

28. Coverdale int., THWP.

29. Williams, *Huey Long,* 130.

30. Sindler, *Huey Long's Louisiana,* 16–25; Howard, *Political Tendencies,* 193–210.

31. Kane, *Hayride,* 30–35.

32. Marc Schneiberg and Sarah A. Soule, "Institutionalization as a Contested Multilevel Process," in *Social Movements and Organization Theory,* ed. Davis et al., 139; Dethloff, "The Longs, 401–12.

33. Hair, *Realm,* 12–14. Roosevelt "assembled a fairly small tableful of personal friends. Justice Holmes [of the U.S. Supreme Court], Elihu Root [secretary of state], General Leonard Wood [later army chief of staff] and John M. Parker. . . . Roosevelt fished the table like a fly fisherman, throwing to each guest. . . . [H]e asked Parker to tell the story of the

lynching of the Mafia in New Orleans, where the *good citizens* raided a jail, cleaned out and knifed a blackmailing secret society that had defied the courts, and Parker told a fine story" (W. A. White, *Autobiography*, 341 [emphasis added]).

34. Howard, *Political Tendencies*, 201–6; Morris, *Theodore Rex*, 47–48; Hair, *Realm*, 65–66, 75–78.

35. Berg, *Wilson*, 295–96. Laborde, *National Southerner*, 46–47.

36. Howard, *Political Tendencies*, 204, 207–10; Hair, *Realm*, 76–78, 93–94.

37. *State v. Smith*, 139 La. 442, 71 So. 734, 1916 La., LEXIS 1564 (Supreme Court of Louisiana, April 24, 1916).

38. Hair, *Realm*, 73; correspondence between Julius and Huey in box 1: 8, HPLP, discussed in chap. 4.

39. Long, *EMK*, 18; Williams, *Huey Long*, 80.

## 4. Rebukes, Ridicule, and Reprimands

1. HPL to R. O. Jackson, August 14, 1919, box 2: 20, HPLP.

2. HPL to J. A. Harps, October 31, 1915, box 2: 6–7, HPLP.

3. McConnell int., THWP; Williams, *Huey Long*, 81.

4. J. A. Harps to HPL, October 16, 1916; letters in box 2: 6–7, HPLP.

5. Boxes 9: 250; 22: 855, 861–63, HPLP.

6. Box 9: 252, 253, 254, 255, HPLP.

7. Long, *EMK*, 22–23.

8. Box 25: 1026, HPLP, has the trial transcript, from which quotations are taken, and the receipt for $25 of court costs; Long, *EMK*, 23–24; Williams, *Huey Long*, 85–87.

9. Long, *EMK*, 24–25.

10. Long, *EMK*, 25.

11. HPL to J. W. Payne, August 26, 1916, box 2: 9, HPLP.

12. Williams, *Huey Long*, 86–87.

13. Box 26: 1067, HPLP, for the illegal wage-deduction file.

14. Williams, *Huey Long*, 82, 87.

15. Long, *EMK*, 29.

16. Long, *EMK*, 29–31, 50–51.

17. See box 24: 957–58, HPLP, for the two cases.

18. Boxes 12: 386; 13: 412; 16: 615, HPLP.

19. Box 11: 353, HPLP.

20. Box 21: 833, HPLP.

21. Boxes 20: 785; 21: 835 (asked for $100 or the "amount you think I am entitled to"); 22: 868, 869; 10: 309, HPLP.

22. Box 11: 326 ("The court decided against you and we have to take our medicine"); box 12: 367 (defendant submitted a 77-page document on appeal; Huey submitted 12 pages), HPLP.

23. Box 10: 300, HPLP.

24. Box 14: 457, 458–59, 463–71; box 18: 663 (urging mother in 1917 to save the $131.25 she got for an award for the death of her son), HPLP.

25. Boxes 15: 563; 16: 577, HPLP.

26. Box 16: 589, 592; HPLP.

27. Box 11: 334, HPLP.

28. Box 12: 399–400, HPLP.

29. Box 13: 404–6, HPLP.

30. Hargrove int., THWP.

31. Hair, *Realm,* 99.

32. Long, *EMK,* 29.

33. Hair, *Realm,* 79; Landry int., THWP.

34. Williams, *Huey Long,* 105.

35. Russell Long int., THWP; *White v. Kavanaugh,* 140 La. 750 (1917); HPL to Judge Charles O'Niell, January 29, 1917, box 2: 55, HPLP.

36. Rivet int., THWP.

37. HPL to R. O. Jackson, August 14, 1919, box 2: 20, HPLP.

38. Box 1: 22 (in court eulogies about Huey as lawyer), HPLP.

39. Clifford, *Counsel to the President,* 35.

40. Fisher int., THWP.

41. *Creston Advertiser,* January 26, 1928, 5.

42. Box 2: 13, 17, 19, HPLP.

43. Box 9: 254, HPLP.

44. John Overton to HPL, August 14, 1915, box 2: 48b, HPLP.

45. HPL to Harry Gamble, January 14, 1916, box 2: 51, HPLP.

46. Box 3: 51, HPLP (letters of December 5 and 14, 1917).

47. Hair, *Realm,* 75.

48. Warren, *All The King's Men,* 180–81.

49. See Box 2: 51, HPLP.

50. HPL letters of March 2 and April 11, 1916, box 2: 52, HPLP. *Caldwell Watchman,* March 3, 1916, 1, listing Huey as "Leading Louisiana attorney"; *Winnfield Sentinel,* February 17, 1916, 1; "Huey P. Long Blames the Corporations," *Winnfield Sentinel,* March 30, 1916; *Labor Record,* March 10, 1916; *Dodson Times,* March 31, 1916; "Bienville Parish School Board," *Weekly Argus,* March 2, 1916, all in box 2: 54, HPLP.

51. Box 2: 51, 53, HPLP; HPL to Ruffin Pleasant, May 3, 1916, box 2: 53, HPLP.

52. HPL to J. W. Mansell, May 23, 1916, box 2: 51, HPLP.

53. Another legislator compared Huey to "a fly alighting on the hub of a wagon passing through a sand bed which said to itself: 'See what a dust I am raising!'" (Long, *EMK,* 27).

54. Long, *EMK,* 28.

55. Berg, *Wilson,* 216.

56. Williams, *Huey Long,* 109–12.

57. Copy in the author's possession; *Caldwell Watchman,* March 3, 1916, 1, listing Huey as "Leading Louisiana attorney."

58. Box 2: 50, HPLP.

59. Box 2: 48b, HPLP.

60. See HPL to R. O. Jackson, August 14, 1919, box 2: 20, HPLP, regarding Winnfield classmates; HPL to J. D. Pace, April 6, 1917, box 2: 56–57; HPL to Julius Long, January 10, 1919, box 1: 3; HPL to Charles Orr, March 13, 1919, box 2: 62, HPLP.

61. HPL to John D. Shireaf, March 17, 1933, RBLP, 3700, 2: 2

62. JTL to Senator Joseph E. Ransdell, April 14, 1917, box 2: 15, HPLP.

63. See box 2: 15, HPLP.

64. Ransdell to Mat Milam, April 2, 1917; Broussard to HPL, April 6, 1917, box 2: 15, HPLP.

65. Broussard to Sam A. Montgomery, April 13, 1917; Sam A. Montgomery to JTL, April 24, 1917, box 2: 15, HPLP.

66. JTL to J. Gunter, April 14, 1917; J. Gunter to JTL, April 13, 1917; Ransdell and Broussard to JTL April 13, 1917, box 2: 15, HPLP.

67. Long, *EMK,* 31.

68. JTL to Senator Joseph E. Ransdell, April 14, 1917, HPLP, box 2: 56–57.

69. JTL to J. Gunter, April 14, 1917, box 2: 15, HPLP; Hair, *Realm,* 80; Jeansonne, *Messiah,* 22; various letters, box 2: 13, 16, HPLP.

70. W. L. Stevens to HPL, February 19, 1917; HPL to W. L. Stevens, February 20, 1917; W. L. Stevens to HPL, February 21, 1917. Press release to the *NOTP,* December 4, 1917; Telegrams from the *New Orleans Item,* December 5, 1917. All in box 2: 16, HPLP.

71. McDaniel, "*Politics of Sedition,*" 51–67.

72. Deutsch, "*Paradox,*" 26.

73. Hair, *Realm,* 83.

74. Box 26: 1077, HPLP.

75. McDaniel, "*Politics of Sedition,*" 51–67.

76. Hair, *Realm,* 74; Huey P. Long, "Thinks Wealth Should Be More Evenly Distributed," *New Orleans Item,* March 1, 1918, box 2: 19, HPLP. In 1922, he wrote to Senator Albert J. Beveridge of Indiana about it (Williams, *Huey Long,* 116–17). A 1925 speech reiterated his view (box 1: 31, HPLP).

77. Long, *EMK,* 35; Harris, *Kingfish,* 19.

78. Long, *EMK,* 36; HPL to Duncan H. Chamberlain, March 21, 1918, box 2: 55, HPLP. HPL to R. O. Jackson, August 14, 1919, box 2: 20, HPLP.

79. Long, *EMK,* 34–35.

80. HPL to Biggest Little Store, March 22, 1918, box 2: 17, HPLP; see HPL to Hiram Johnson, April 6, 1918, box 2: 59, HPLP.

81. Hair, *Realm,* 83–85; HPL to R. O. Jackson, August 14, 1919, box 2: 62, HPLP. There are few papers pertaining to the Harper case in Huey's files. They might have been maintained by Julius. I have not located any repository of Julius's papers.

82. Louisiana Constitution of 1898, Art. 283, 284.

83. Long, *EMK,* 39.

84. Harris, *Kingfish,* 14. Charles Henderson served on the Alabama Public Service Commission from 1907 to 1915 and was elected governor in 1915 ("Charles Henderson, 1915–1919," *Alabama Governors*). Joe Brown was a member of the Georgia Public Service Commission from 1904 to 1907 and was elected governor in 1909 and 1912 ("Georgia: Gov. Joseph Mackey Brown," *National Governors Association*). J. J. McAlister was an Oklahoma public service commissioner from 1907 to 1910 and was then elected lieutenant governor in 1911.

85. HPL to C. A. McCoy, April 17, 1917, box 2: 57; HPL to the *Daily States,* January 21, 1918, and HPL to Burk Bridges, February 7, 1918, box 2: 58, HPLP.

86. Williams, *Huey Long,* 119–22; Field, "Campaigns," 18.

87. Smith, "Origins and Significance of Impeachment," 117.

88. Paul Y. Anderson, "Only Huey Could Be Sure of 100 Votes," *Milwaukee Journal,* November 12, 1935, 12.

89. Hair, *Realm,* 87.

90. Williams, *Huey Long,* 124–25.

91. HPL to R. O. Jackson, August 14, 1919, box 2: 62, HPLP. In Boston, opponents attacked James Michael Curley because he had been jailed for impersonating a friend to take

a civil service examination. His supporters replied that "'He did it for a friend,' and . . . the charge boomeranged" (Curley, *I'd Do It Again,* 68–70, 93–94, 119 [quote]).

92. Hair, *Realm,* 83; Draft Board Statement of October 15, 1923, box 3: 87, HPLP.

93. Box 2: 18, 19, 65, HPLP.

94. See chapter 6, *in this book.*

95. Perry, *Kingfish in Fiction,* 120–21, quoting MacLeish, *New Republic,* June 10, 1940, 789–90.

96. Williams, *Huey Long,* 115–16.

97. Rose named him Huey P. Long, III, while Huey was out campaigning, but he vetoed this, saying he had hated being called Little Huey all his life, and "if things go bad for me, he'll have his own name to make it on" (R. White, *Kingfish,* 38).

98. Field, "Campaigns," 19–21. Overton lost but ran well in the northern parishes (Sindler, *Huey Long's Louisiana,* 46n12).

99. Sindler, *Huey Long's Louisiana,* 47.

100. Jeansonne, *Messiah,* 26.

101. Sindler, *Huey Long's Louisiana,* 47. The old populist Hardy Brian wrote a letter endorsing Huey before the second primary (Bozeman to THW, June 29, 1965, box 8: 20–21, THWP).

102. Field, "Campaigns," 22–24.

## 5. Refusing to Play It Safe

1. Deutsch, "Paradox," 33, 34–41; Banta, "Regulation," chap. 3 and 107–14, 119; HPL to D.A. Hanrahan, February 25, 1920, box 2: 27, HPLP; Loos, *Oil on Stream!* 34–43, 82–86.

2. Williams, *Huey Long,* 117–19.

3. Banta, "Regulation," 116–20. The estimate is hard to verify.

4. Long, *EMK,* 42–43; Kane, *Hayride,* 49.

5. Loos, *Oil on Stream!* 52–59, 75–78 (ICC actions).

6. Banta, "Regulation," 107.

7. Loos, *Oil on Stream!* 82–85.

8. Loos, *Oil on Stream!* 86; Banta, "Regulation," 111–22.

9. J. Kendall, *History of New Orleans* 3: 942; Williams, *Huey Long,* 125–26.

10. Jeansonne, *Messiah,* 28; Kane, *Hayride,* 47. Michel and Taylor were hacks, but they had sense enough to reject Huey's early suggestion that they wear badges so that people would respect them.

11. Williams, *Huey Long,* 125–27; Banta, "Regulation," 121–23; Hair, *Realm,* 90.

12. Deutsch, "Paradox," 39.

13. Banta, "Regulation," 129.

14. Banta, "Regulation," 131; Deutsch, "*Paradox,*" 42–45; Williams, *Huey Long,* 127–28; Hair, *Realm,* 91–93.

15. Julius Long to HPL, July 17, 1919; HPL to Shan Long, July 30, 1919, box 1: 3, HPLP.

16. HPL to G. E. Long, September 19, 1919, box 2: 21; also boxes 1: 3; 2: 29 (HPL to B. Cuman, May 12, 2020), 3: 71 (letter of May 12, 2020), HPLP. Loos, *Oil on Stream!* 82–89 and note 13.

17. Deutsch, "Paradox," 121; Williams, *Huey Long,* 117–18.

18. HPL to S. Hendricks, October 4, 1920, box 2: 31, HPLP. August 6, 1919, HPL letters of August 6, 1919 (price was 75 cents/barrel; it was "difficult" to identify the cause for end-

ing the freeze-out, but "[p]olitically, I would get the credit"), and December 26, 1919 (price $1.25/barrel), box 27: 1090b, HPLP.

19. HPL to O. K. Allen, November 26, 2019, box 26: 1089b, HPLP.

20. "Economic See Saw Called Supply and Demand," box 28: 1139, booklet a "marvel," box 20: 1088b; regarding oil boom, boxes 26: 1090a and 28: 1119, HPLP.

21. Prospectus of Banks, March 26, 1918, and HPL to H. L. Mandevelle, April 2, 1919, box 26: 1087a, HPLP.

22. HPL to Mandevelle, July 2, 1919; Mandevelle to HPL, July 9, 1919, box 26: 1088a, HPLP (pipeline fight won but depressed at lack of sales by Mandeville; Mandeville promises big deal coming and small sales now).

23. Boxes 26–27: 1089b, 1090b, 1091–96, HPLP.

24. Box 27: 1093, HPLP (Mandeville sales decline; Homer well failed).

25. Article, May 21, 1920; H. L. Mandeville letter, May 13, 1920, box 27, HPLP.

26. HPL letter June 19, 1920, box 27: 1095a; HPL of September 16, 1920, box 27: 1096, HPLP.

27. Box 27: 1097–1103; 1104 (Huey's cross-examination of Payne), HPLP.

28. Kane, *Hayride*, 32–33.

29. Williams, *Huey Long*, 130–31.

30. Hair, *Realm*, 108–11; Howard, *Political Tendencies*, 211; Kane, *Hayride*, 32–33.

31. Deutsch, "*Paradox*," 50–61; Banta, "Regulation," 162–64.

32. Hair, *Realm*, 94–96; Williams, *Huey Long*, 132–34.

33. Julius Long to HPL, October 31, 1919, box 1: 3, HPLP (everyone there was for Stubbs); box 26: 1089b, HPLP.

34. Banta, "Regulation," 133–34.

35. Long, *EMK*, 47–48.

36. HPL to M. A. Kurz, November 28, 1919, box 26: 1090b, HPLP.

37. Kane, *Hayride*, 49; Long, *EMK*, 48.

38. Hair, *Realm*, 95–96; Williams, *Huey Long*, 134–35.

39. Calhoun, *Louisiana Almanac*, 454; Howard, *Political Tendencies*, 211–15.

40. HPL to John R. Hunter, January 26, 1920, box 2: 26; HPL to H. A. Avery, February 12, 1920, box 2: 27, HPLP.

41. Banta, "Regulation," 131–38 and note 72.

42. Long, *EMK*, 48–49.

43. Hair, *Realm*, 103; HPL to Leland Moss, November 11, 1920, box 3: 74, HPLP; HPL to Julius Long, January 24, 1920, box 1: 5, HPLP.

44. Williams, *Huey Long*, 138–40.

45. Loos, *Oil on Stream!* 87; Banta, "Regulation," 141.

46. Schott, "*John M. Parker*," 437n53.

47. Williams, *Huey Long*, 140–42 (quotations from Williams); Sindler, *Huey Long's Louisiana*, 42–43; Hair, *Realm*, 102; Banta, "Regulation," 148, 162–68.

48. HPL to C. Orr, November 24, 1920; Leland Moss to HPL, November 9, 1920; HPL to Leland Moss, November 11, 1920, box 2: 13, HPLP.

49. Long, *EMK*, 52–55.

50. Williams, *Huey Long*, 162–66; Hair, *Realm*, 118. See box 33: 1235a, HPLP, where Michel and Taylor noted that the "public and the press have been unsparing in denunciation of our action." There was an Anti-Increase Telephone Association that New Orleans's city attorney Kittridge and commissioner of utilities Paul Maloney spearheaded.

51. Williams, *Huey Long,* 164–66.
52. Box 3: 84, HPLP; Long, *EMK,* 55–56.
53. Williams, *Huey Long,* 142–44; Banta, "Regulation," 171–81.
54. Hair, *Realm,* 115.
55. Long, *EMK,* 57 and note 20.
56. Hair, *Realm,* 111; Williams, *Huey Long,* 133; Sindler, *Huey Long's Louisiana,* 41; Deutsch, "*Paradox,*" 52–61.
57. HPL to Arthur Long, August 29 and September 13, 1921; HPL to Aline McConnell, September 1, 1921; A. D. Long to HPL, September 7, 1921, box 1: 8, HPLP. L. Moss to HPL, September 7, 1921, box 20: 33, HPLP.
58. Long, *EMK,* 57; Williams, *Huey Long,* 145–46. Parker's letter to Huey of April 27, 1920, promised there would be "no lobby maintained at Baton Rouge."
59. HPL to Aline McConnell, October 25, 1921; A. D. Long to HPL, December 29, 1921, box 1: 8, HPLP.
60. Williams, *Huey Long,* 146–48 (quote at 148).
61. Undated statements regarding the hearing. Box 2: 40, HPLP.
62. Long, *EMK,* 56.
63. Williams, *Huey Long,* 147–48.
64. Long, *EMK,* 61–62 (emphasis in Huey's excerpt).
65. Williams, *Huey Long,* 149–50.
66. Field, "Campaigns," 29; see generally, box 3: 77–82, HPLP; Robert R. Reid to HPL, October 26, 1921; HPL to Robert R. Reid, October 28, 1921; John Overton to HPL, November 8, 1921, box 3: 77, HPLP; Sworn interrogatory statements of O. G. Thomas, Frank Looney, R. G. Pleasant, Ernest O'Bannon, Leland Moss, in box 3: 79, HPLP.
67. Williams, *Huey Long,* 151–52; Harris, *Kingfish,* 24–25; Banta, "Regulation," 176–88.
68. Long, *EMK,* 59–60; Banta, "Regulation," 189–92.

## 6. Getting Things Done

1. Hair, *Realm,* 113; Long, *EMK,* 66; Williams, *Huey Long,* 166–67; R. White, *Kingfish,* 24; Jeansonne, *Messiah,* 43.
2. HPL to Williams, July 31, 1922, box 33: 1231, HPLP.
3. Barry, *Rising Tide,* 344–45.
4. Williams, *Huey Long,* 168–71 (quotations); Long, *EMK,* 67–69. *Cumberland Tel. & Tel. Co. v. Louisiana P.S.C.,* 260 U.S. 212 (1922).
5. Long, *EMK,* 235, quoting *Vanity Fair* magazine.
6. Sindler, *Huey Long's Louisiana,* 47; Harris, *Kingfish,* 25–26; Williams, *Huey Long,* 170–73 (quotes); Long, *EMK,* 69.
7. HPL to Williams, January 23, 1923, box 33: 1232, HPLP. He wondered again whether he was wasting the best years of his life.
8. Williams, *Huey Long,* 174–75; Long, *EMK,* 70; Banta, "Regulation," 196–99.
9. Williams, *Huey Long,* 176–80.
10. Williams, *Huey Long,* 155–59.
11. Box 2: 67, HPLP.
12. Williams, *Huey Long,* 160–61.
13. Gleason and Todd, ints., THWP.
14. Williams, *Huey Long,* 161; Field, "*Campaigns,*" 30–31.

15. Rupert Peyton int., THWP.

16. Williams, *Huey Long,* 159.

17. Williams, *Huey Long,* 78–79 (Merrick), 173–80 (Standard Oil), 155–62 (smaller cases); Banta, "Regulation," 120–45; Long, *EMK,* 70, 79, 85–86. *Louisiana Public Service Commission v. Standard Oil Company of Louisiana,* 154 LA 557 (1923). The court held that the commission could find that pipelines were common carriers, subject to judicial review. No further case decided whether they were common carriers. But no freeze-out later took place.

18. Box 20: 23, HBDP.

19. Francis int., THWP.

20. HPL to Shan Long, August 19, 1919, box 1: 1, HPLP.

21. HPL to JTL, October 31, 1919, box 1: 1, HPLP.

22. HPL to Hotel Pennsylvania, May 17, 1920, box 2: 29, HPLP.

23. HPL to D. Hanrahan, February 24, 1920, box 2: 27, HPLP.

24. HPL to S. Hendricks, November 20, 1920, box 2: 32, HPLP.

25. HPL to C. Orr, November 24, 1920, box 2: 13; HPL to T. Burden, November 8, 1920, box 3: 74; HPL to S. Hendricks, October 31, November 8, November 9, and November 15, 1920, and S. Hendricks to HPL, October 27, November 10, November 13, and November 15, 1920, box 3: 74, HPLP.

26. HPL to JTL, January 10, 1919, box 1: 3, HPLP; HPL to JTL, January 24, 1920, box 1: 5, HPLP.

27. HPL to JTL, June 2, 1920, box 1: 6, HPLP.

28. HPL to JTL, January 24, 1920, box 1: 5, HPLP.

29. HPL to JTL, June 19, 1920, box 1: 6, HPLP.

30. HPL to C. Orr, November 24, 1920, box 2: 13, HPLP.

31. Box 1: 8, HPLP.

32. Hair, *Realm,* 107. HPL to A. D. Long, September 13, 1921, box 1: 8, HPLP.

33. JTL to HPL, September 7, 1921; HPL to JTL, September 8, 1921; HPL to JTL, November 12, 1921; HPL to JTL, October 2, 1922, box 1: 8–9, HPLP.

34. HPL to Aline McConnell, September 1, 1921, box 1: 8, HPLP.

35. Box 21: 822, box 22: 867, HPLP.

36. Box 13: 416, box 16: 573, HPLP.

37. Box 33: 1223, HPLP.

38. Box 1: 51, HBPLP (grossed $13,000 in 1921).

39. Williams, *Huey Long,* 96.

40. Williams, *Huey Long,* 88–90.

41. HPL to and from C. Orr, October 15, 1917; March 13 and April 5, 1919; November 24, 1920, box 2: 13, HPLP.

42. Gleason int., THWP.

43. Williams, *Huey Long,* 96.

44. Peyton int., THWP.

45. HPL to and from H. D. Chamberlain, box 2: 13, HPLP.

46. Box 1: 8, HPLP.

47. HPL to Aline McConnell, October 25, 1921; HPL to A. D. Long, October 25, 1921, box 1: 8, HPLP.

48. Williams, *Huey Long,* 96.

49. Boxes 7: 27–30 (Bankston), 8: 10–11 (Burrows), HPLP.

50. HPL to A. D. Long, May 23, 1921, box 1: 8, HPLP.

51. Hair, *Realm,* 106–7; HPL to Aline McConnell, October 25, 1921, box 1: 8, HPLP.

52. Box 2: 43 ("Moran matter"), HPLP. The imposter was John H. Morgan (Beals, *Story of Huey Long,* 37). "Moran" was one of the man's aliases.

53. HPL to Lottie Davis, March 18, 1920, box 1: 5, HPLP.

54. Hair, *Realm,* 103–6.

55. HPL to Shan Long, March 22, 1920, box 1: 5, HPLP.

56. HPL to Charles Orr, November 24, 1920, HPLP. box 2: 13, HPLP.

57. In September 1921, a New Orleans legislator said he had seen Huey in Baton Rouge "drunk and lit up like a Christmas tree. . . . If we make it any easier for him to get liquor, there will be no more living in this state" (Reed, *Requiem,* 99).

58. Box 2: 40, HPLP.

59. Hair, *Realm,* 144; Williams, *Huey Long,* 97.

60. HPL to Shan Long, August 19 and September 19, 1919; HPL to JTL, October 31, 1919, box 1: 1. Scott Hendricks to HPL, November 15, 1920, box 3: 74. HPL to Judge B. P. Mille, January 9, 1920, box 3: 75. All in HPLP.

61. Brothers int., THWP.

62. Box 31: 1194 (clippings of the stories), 1196 and 1198 (requests for briefs), 1201b (abstract of testimony),1205b (Treasury Department documents), 1208a (compromise of other lawsuit); box 32 (twenty folders of trial testimony), HPLP.

63. Peyton int., THWP; Hair, *Realm,* 144; Williams, *Huey Long,* 97.

64. HPL to Bernstein April 30, 1927, and Bernstein undated response. Huey had several cases for Bernstein. Bernstein paid Huey $4,000 in 1922, $4,700 in 1923, $4,500 in 1924, and $10,600 in 1925. Huey paid some of this money to his cocounsel, Robert L. Hunter, and advanced costs as well (box 31, HPLP).

65. Williams, *Huey Long,* 101, 105.

66. Long, *EMK,* 87; Williams and Price, "Huey P. Long Papers," 256–61.

67. Russell Long, "Why I Am for Earl Long," radio address, www.hueylong.com/legacy/russell-long-speech.php.

68. Hair, *Realm,* 144. Although Rose told Williams that Huey monogrammed the wrought iron railing over the front door with "CNB," and his notes include a drawing of it, the monogram is "HPL" (Williams, *Huey Long,* 105; Rose McConnell Long int., THWP; Peyton int., THWP).

69. Williams, *Huey Long,* 181.

70. Hair, *Realm,* 119; Harris, *Kingfish,* 25; box 2: 45 (August 5, 1923, statement), 50 (statement, n.d.), HPLP.

71. Hair, *Realm,* 128–30.

72. Schott, "*John M. Parker,*" 409–65, has an extensive discussion of Parker and the Klan, from which most of this account is taken.

73. HPL to Shan Long, December 22, 1921, box 1: 8, HPLP.

74. Field, "*Campaigns,*" 54–55. Parker appointed Samuel A. Leopold, a Jew, to replace the removed sheriff.

75. Hair, *Realm,* 130–34. Jeansonne's account differs on some details (*Messiah,* 32–33). Laborde differs on the sequence of events leading up to the request for federal intervention (*National Southerner,* 103–5). Schott's analysis seems more detailed and credible, but both analyses end up in the same place: Parker was denounced for seeking federal intervention.

76. Deutsch, "*Paradox,*" 65.

77. Williams, *Huey Long,* 191–96 (Parker integrity and impracticality at 195; roses/thorns quote at 193).

### 7. Election Day Rain

1. Deutsch, "Paradox," 67.

2. *Shreveport Times*, August 17, 1923, 1; *NOTP*, August 17, 1923, 1.

3. H. Ellis to HPL, November 3 and 5, 1923, box 2: 47, HPLP.

4. See Williams, *Huey Long*, 196–99; Deutsch, "Paradox," chap. 10; Field, "Campaigns," 36–43.

5. Long, *EMK*, 70–74 (reprinting the excerpts).

6. *NOTP*, August 31, 1923, 9.

7. Box 2: 49–50, HPLP; Jeansonne, *Messiah*, 66–67.

8. Long, *EMK*, 74–75.

9. Williams, *Huey Long*, 200–203; Field, "Campaigns," 39.

10. Jeansonne, *Messiah*, 45; H. Ellis to HPL, November 5, 1923, box 2: 47, HPLP.

11. Hair, *Realm*, 126; Williams, *Huey Long*, 254–55.

12. Peyton int., THWP.

13. Williams, *Huey Long*, 203–6; Field, "Campaigns," 36–39.

14. Racivitch int., THWP; Carriere int., THWP.

15. Williams, *Huey Long*, 205; Deutsch, "Paradox," chap. 8; Field, "Campaigns," 39; box 2: 49 (Pleasant rebuttal), HPLP.

16. Williams, *Huey Long*, 207–8.

17. *NOTP*, November 12, 1923, 1.

18. Williams, *Huey Long*, 206–8; Field, "Campaigns," 40–43.

19. Hair, *Realm*, 134–35.

20. Box 2: 48, HPLP.

21. Long, *EMK*, 77. Compare Boswell, *Life of Samuel Johnson*, 363: "There is no doubt, that if the poor should reason, 'we'll be poor no longer, we'll make the rich take their turn,' they could easily do it, were it not that they can't agree."

22. Hair, *Realm*, 136.

23. Field, "Campaigns," 44–49.

24. Williams, *Huey Long*, 210–11.

25. Long, *EMK*, 75–76.

26. *NOTP*, January 13, 1924, 1.

27. Williams, *Huey Long*, 211; H. Ellis to HPL, January 23, 1924, box 2: 47, and H. Jastrzemski to HPL, January 18, 1924, box 3: 1, HPLP.

28. Kim Voss, "Collapse of a Social Movement," in *Comparative Perspectives*, ed. McAdam, McCarthy, and Zald, 253–56.

29. Field, "Campaigns," 51; *NOTP*, January 16, 1924, 1.

30. Sindler, *Huey Long's Louisiana*, 49–50.

31. Thompson int., THWP; Williams, *Huey Long*, 213.

32. Deutsch, "Paradox," 75.

33. Williams, *Huey Long*, 211–15 (quote at 213); Hair, *Realm*, 136–38; Howard, *Political Tendencies*, 217, 227–29.

34. Lawson, *Anatomies of Revolution*, 64.

35. Barnes, *Louisiana Populist Movement*.

36. McAdam, McCarthy, and Zald, "Introduction," in *Comparative Perspectives*, 1–22; Barnes, *Louisiana Populist Movement*, 4.

37. Gordon, *Rise and Fall*, 113.

38. Williams, *Huey Long*, 186.

39. Jeansonne, *Messiah*, 68; see chapter 3.

40. Workers of the Writers' Program of the WPA, *Louisiana: A Guide to the State*, 84, said there were 51 miles of hard-surfaced roads constructed between 1922 and 1928; Scott, "Highway Building," 5–38.

41. Hair, *Realm*, 162.

42. Sindler, *Huey Long's Louisiana*, 5.

43. See Timothy J. Vogus and Gerald F. Davis, "Elite Mobilizations for Antitakeover Legislation, 1982–1990," in *Social Movements and Organization Theory*, ed. Davis et al., 104, 119.

44. Geddes, Wright, and Frantz, *How Dictatorships Work*, 35.

45. William A. Gamson and David S. Meyer, "Framing Political Opportunity," in *Comparative Perspectives*, ed. McAdam, McCarthy, and Zald, 278, 283; Lawson, *Anatomies of Revolution*, 67 ("inert backdrop").

46. Lawson, *Anatomies of Revolution*, 40–47, 52–61, 74–93, 100–124 (changing economy, population growth, urbanization, malfeasance, and systemic crises can cause a revolutionary situation); Harry Eckstein, "On the Etiology of Internal Wars," in *Revolution*, ed. Mazlish, Kaledin, and Ralston, 18; DeFronzo, *Revolutions*, chaps. 1, 10, and 12 (growth of mass frustration [disequilibrium or grievances], elite dissidence [examination of their leadership], unifying motivations [depends on issue framing], a crisis, and a permissive environment [whether structural political processes permit change]); Goldstone, *Revolutions*, introduction, chaps. 1–3, 5. Compare McAdam, McCarthy, and Zald, "Introduction," in *Comparative Perspectives*, 7 (material and ideological inconsistencies; social changes); McAdam, "Conceptual Origins," in *Comparative Perspectives*, ed. McAdam, McCarthy, and Zald, 24–25 (contradiction between cultural values and social practices, suddenly imposed grievances, dramatization of system vulnerability or illegitimacy).

47. Mayer N. Zald, "Culture, Ideology, and Strategic Framing," in *Comparative Perspectives*, ed. McAdam, McCarthy, and Zald, 261–74; William A. Gamson and David S. Meyer, "Framing Political Opportunity," in *Comparative Perspectives*, ed. McAdam, McCarthy, and Zald, 275–90; Barnes, *Louisiana Populist Movement*, 5–7, 24–30.

48. Doug McAdam and W. Richard Scott, "Organizations and Movements," in *Social Movements and Organization Theory*, ed. Davis et al., 4–40; Hoffer, *The True Believer* (reform movement followers were often fanatics); Barnes, *Louisiana Populist Movement*, 6–7 (movement followers made rational cost-benefit analyses before deciding whether to join a movement); Lawson, *Anatomies of Revolution*, 84–85; Donatella Della Porta, "Opportunities and Framing in the Eastern European Revolts of 1989," in *Comparative Perspectives*, ed. McAdam, McCarthy, and Zald, 97; Elena Zdravomyslova, "Opportunities and Framing in the Transition to Democracy: The Case of Russia," in *Comparative Perspectives, ed.* McAdam, McCarthy, and Zald, 125, 134; Elisabeth S. Clemens, "Organizational Form as Frame: Collective Identity and Political Strategy in the American Labor Movement, 1880–1920," in *Comparative Perspectives*, ed. McAdam, McCarthy, and Zald, 210–11; John D. McCarthy, Jackie Smith, and Mayer N. Zald, "Accessing Public, Media, Electoral, and Governmental Agendas," in *Comparative Perspectives*, ed. McAdam, McCarthy, and Zald, 309–11; Bert Klandermans and Sjoerd Goslinga, "Media Discourse, Movement Publicity, and the Generation of Collective Action Frames," in *Comparative Perspectives*, ed. McAdam, McCarthy, and Zald, 319.

49. John D. McCarthy, "Constraints and Opportunities in Adopting, Adapting, and Inventing," in *Comparative Perspectives*, ed. McAdam, McCarthy, and Zald, 141–51; Dieter Rucht, "The Impact of National Contexts on Social Movement Structures," in *Comparative*

*Perspectives,* ed. McAdam, McCarthy, and Zald, 185–204; Kim Voss, "Collapse of a Social Movement," in *Comparative Perspectives,* ed. McAdam, McCarthy, and Zald, 227–58; Timothy J. Vogus and Gerald F. Davis, "Elite Mobilizations for Antitakeover Legislation," in *Social Movements and Organization Theory, ed. Davis et al.,* 96–121; Marc Schneiberg and Sarah A. Soule, "Institutionalization as a Contested, Multilevel Process: The Case of Rate Regulation in American Fire Insurance," in *Social Movements and Organization Theory, ed. Davis et al.,* 122–160; Barnes, *Louisiana Populist Movement,* 8–17.

50. See Doug McAdam, "Conceptual Origins, Current Problems, Future Directions," in *Comparative Perspectives,* ed. McAdam, McCarthy, and Zald, 23–40; John L. Campbell, "Where Do We Stand," in *Social Movements and Organization Theory,* ed. Davis et al., 41–68.

51. William A. Gamson and David S. Meyer, "Framing Political Opportunity," in *Comparative Perspectives,* ed. McAdam, McCarthy, and Zald, 285. Barnes details the counterarguments made to the framing of the populists in Louisiana in detail over time (*Louisiana Populist Movement*).

52. Scott, "Highway Building," 9–10. Parker opposed bond financing (Schott, "John M. Parker," 376–78).

53. Sindler, *Huey Long's Louisiana,* 43–44; Field, "Campaigns," 32 (Parker's administration fell "far short of [his] lofty platform" and "left much unfinished business.").

54. Scott, "Highway Building," 8–9.

55. Kidd, "Louisiana Highways," 7.

56. Scott, "Highway Building," 6.

57. McKinney, "Getting Out of the Mud," 289–332.

58. McKinney, "Getting Out of the Mud," 321.

59. Lawson, *Anatomies of Revolution,* 4.

60. Goldstone, *Revolutions,* 5 (incumbent attempts at reform may be resisted by part of the elite, weakening the governing class, and presenting revolutionary forces with a divided, conflict-ridden, and consequently vulnerable leadership), 19 ("Chinese rulers who attempted to modernize their country in the late 19th Century were frustrated by wealthy landowners and other conservatives" who prevented sufficient reforms, fostering a revolution).

## 8. Winning the Governorship in 1928

1. Williams, *Huey Long,* 215–20.

2. LaBorde, *National Southerner,* 1–4, 8–10, 31–32, 48–49, 56–57, 113, 121; Field, "Campaigns," 59–60.

3. Field, "Campaigns," 56–57; Hair, *Realm,* 140–41; Jeansonne, *Messiah,* 40–41.

4. Williams, *Huey Long,* 219–22; Jeansonne, *Messiah,* 37; Long, *EMK,* 80–81.

5. Field, "Campaigns," 62–63.

6. Williams, *Huey Long,* 222.

7. The Ring turned out 33,000 votes for Fuqua in the 1924 gubernatorial election (Sindler, *Huey Long's Louisiana,* 49).

8. Field, "Campaigns," 63.

9. Hair, *Realm,* 141.

10. HPL to Williams, December 15, 1924, with copies to Ewing, box 3: 95, HPLP.

11. Williams, *Huey Long,* 223–24; Boulard, *Huey Long Invades,* 40.

12. Deutsch, "Paradox," 77–78.

13. Williams, *Huey Long,* 225–26.

14. Long, *EMK,* 88–89; Williams, *Huey Long,* 227–29.
15. Field, "Campaigns," 67–68; Long, *EMK,* 88–92.
16. Williams, *Huey Long,* 227–30.
17. Deutsch, "Paradox," 89.
18. Williams, *Huey Long,* 231. Watson-Williams would have a monopoly for twenty years; the tolls depended on the amount of traffic; and the state could buy the bridge after twenty years by paying $5.5 million.
19. Williams, *Huey Long,* 231–33; Long, *EMK,* 88–93.
20. Long, *EMK,* 88–93 (quote at 92).
21. Long, *EMK,* 225–27; Deutsch, "Paradox," 78–79.
22. Williams, *Huey Long,* 233–35.
23. Williams, *Huey Long,* 145.
24. Laborde, *National Southerner,* 43.
25. Williams, *Huey Long,* 235; Banta, "Regulation," 273–74.
26. Hair, *Realm,* 142.
27. Deutsch, "Paradox," 82.
28. Long, *EMK,* 83.
29. Deutsch, "Paradox," 81–82.
30. John St. Paul int., THWP.
31. Hair, *Realm,* 143 (sapsucker); Williams, *Huey Long,* 237–38; Banta, "Regulation," 275–84, 299–305, 316; Deutsch, "Paradox," 83 (possum watchers).
32. Carbon black was produced by burning natural gas under channel bars. The carbon on the bars was scraped off and used in printing ink and automobile tires to give the rubber more resilience, traction, and heat tolerance (Banta, "Regulation," 203–4, 207–50, 325–40; *NYT,* July 29, 1928, 36). By 1924, Louisiana had thirty-five plants producing over 144 million pounds of carbon black, 77 percent of the national total.
33. Banta, "Regulation," 273–74, 316.
34. Field, "Campaigns," 71–72.
35. Williams, *Huey Long,* 239–40; Hair, *Realm,* 145 and note 21. Huey's friends signed a statement that Prophit assaulted Huey from behind, and that Huey told them to go easy on Prophit.
36. Williams, *Huey Long,* 240 and note 2; Deutsch, "Paradox," 85–86.
37. Long, *EMK,* 84; Field, "Campaigns," 74.
38. HPL to Jastrzemski, December 16, 1926; January 13, 1927, box 33: 1225, HPLP. Williams, *Huey Long,* 242–43.
39. Field, "Campaigns," 76–78.
40. Long, *EMK,* 93.
41. Hair, *Realm,* 150; Williams, *Huey Long,* 245–46.
42. Jeansonne, *Messiah,* 41; R. White, *Kingfish,* 21–22.
43. Williams, *Huey Long,* 246 (Hardtner as a potential candidate); Hair, *Realm,* 149–50; Jeansonne, *Messiah,* 41; Field, "Campaigns," 79.
44. JBAFP, Range U: 172, box 1: 6–9.
45. Hair, *Realm,* 148.
46. Barry, *Rising Tide,* 213–38, 344–53; Hair, *Realm,* 146–49; Williams, *Huey Long,* 247–50.
47. Hair, *Realm,* 150; Howell int., THWP.
48. *Town Talk* (Alexandria), July 9, 1927, 1; *Shreveport Times,* July 9, 1927, 1.
49. Williams, *Huey Long,* 249.

50. Williams, *Huey Long*, 244–79; R. White, *Kingfish*, 26–35; Hair, *Realm*, 149–60; Long, *EMK*, 97–98; and Field, "Campaigns," 79–95, all cover the campaign. *Town Talk* (Alexandria), August 4, 1927, 1.

51. Long, *EMK*, 98.

52. Williams, *Huey Long*, 263–64.

53. Wilson placed more newspaper advertisements (Hair, *Realm*, 154).

54. Williams, *Huey Long*, 252–53; Schott, "John M. Parker," 444, 454; Habans int., THWP (Moss).

55. Hair, *Realm*, 155.

56. Williams, *Huey Long*, 255.

57. Williams, *Huey Long*, 255 (campaign cash), 264 (circular paper), 454 (six-year-old); Hair, *Realm*, 153; Field, "Campaigns," 84.

58. Remas, "Once Proud Princes," 192–98.

59. Williams, *Huey Long*, 257–59, 261 (quotations); Long, *EMK*, 96.

60. Hair, *Realm*, 157.

61. Kane, *Hayride*, 56; Jeansonne, *Messiah*, 44.

62. Williams, *Huey Long*, 251.

63. Deutsch, "Paradox," 95.

64. Long, *EMK*, 100–101.

65. Williams, *Huey Long*, 417.

66. Kane, *Hayride*, 55.

67. Hair, *Realm*, 156.

68. Williams, *Huey Long*, 250; Deutsch, "Paradox," 92–93.

69. Field, "Campaigns," 86–95.

70. R. White, *Kingfish*, 30; *Shreveport Times*, November 12, 1927, 1–2.

71. Hair, *Realm*, 152.

72. Newspaper clipping on speeches in Crowley, LA, box 3, JMP.

73. Williams, *Huey Long*, 270–71.

74. Hair, *Realm*, 157. *NOTP*, November 16, 1927, 1–2. The *Daily Caucasian*, November 16, 1927, had a satirical rendition of Huey's account of the fight.

75. Hair, *Realm*, 158.

76. Williams, *Huey Long*, 272.

77. Field, "Campaigns," 87 (forty-two states had free-schoolbooks laws); Timothy J. Vogus and Gerald F. Davis, "Elite Mobilizations for Antitakeover Legislation, 1982–1990," in *Social Movements and Organization Theory*, ed. Davis et al., 105–7, 110–11, 115–21.

78. Clipping, *Q'Fort Times*, October 3, 1927, reporting on an October 2 speech in Lafayette, in possession of the author.

79. *NOTP*, August 4, 1927, 3–4, 19, 29.

80. Brooks int.; Bauer int., THWP. Both individuals *opposed* Huey.

81. Good Roads Association, Bulletin 1, box 3: circulars, CMP.

82. Williams, *Huey Long*, 272–75; Long, *EMK*, 99.

83. Long, *EMK*, 101–2.

84. Hair, *Realm*, 158.

85. Williams, *Huey Long*, 265; Kane, *Hayride*, 55; R. White, *Kingfish*, 33.

86. *MNS*, January 3, 1928, 2, 7; January 4, 1928, 2. *NOTP*, January 5, 1928, 3.

87. *MNS*, January 10, 1928, 6; January 12, 1928, 12.

88. *NYT*, January 18, 1928, 3.

89. Williams, *Huey Long*, 275–76. *NYT*, January 19, 1928, 2.

90. *Biloxi Daily Herald,* January 28, 1928, 4 (a man who can poll a plurality of 40,000 in the first primary "must be a power among the people"); *NYT,* January 23, 1928, 2.

91. *MNS,* January 21, 1928, 1.

92. *NOTP,* January 20, 1928, 1.

93. Williams, *Huey Long,* 277–78.

94. Hair, *Realm,* 160; Basso, "Huey Long and His Background"; Perry, *Kingfish in Fiction,* 82–83.

95. Deutsch, "Paradox," 97; Jeansonne, *Messiah,* 57.

96. For example, *Altoona Mirror,* March 22, 1928, 20; *Frederick Daily News,* March 21, 1928, 7.

97. Hunt int., THWP.

98. *NYT,* January 29, 1928, 52; Hair, *Realm,* 161.

99. Winter, "Governor Mike Conner and the Sales Tax."

100. Hair, *Realm,* 161; Long, *EMK,* 107; Harris, *Kingfish,* 33.

## 9. Early Legislative Success

1. Williams, *Huey Long,* 278–79.

2. R. White, *Kingfish,* 43.

3. *MNS,* February 15, 1928, 7; R. White, *Kingfish,* 43–44; Williams, *Huey Long,* 280–81.

4. The week of revelry, drinking and parades began with a great parade of King Momus, the "God of Mirth and Dispeller of Doom." Exclusive balls featured grand orchestras, ornate costumes, and the best cuisine, hosted by private, invitation-only Krewes (R. White, *Kingfish,* 42). Barry, *Rising Tide,* 215–21, traces the interrelationships between the exclusive clubs, Mardi Gras, and the ruling powers in New Orleans. Rex is the King of Carnival, with the motto: "For the good of the public." In an elaborate ceremony, Rex pays homage to Comus, whose motto is "As I wish, thus I command." Sometime before 1920, Rex snubbed the Jewish club during the parade, and thereafter the clubs excluded Jews. J. Blanc Monroe's law partner was Jewish, so he and other prominent Jews always took vacations during Mardi Gras.

5. Harris, *Kingfish,* 34–35.

6. Williams, *Huey Long,* 281.

7. Kane, *Hayride,* 62–63.

8. Williams, *Huey Long,* 282–83; R. White, *Kingfish,* 39; Harris, *Kingfish,* 35–36.

9. *MNS,* April 4, 1928, 11.

10. *MNS,* April 6, 1928, 3 and 22.

11. *MNS,* April 16, 1928, 2; May 4, 1928, 1; and May 21, 1928, 7.

12. *MNS,* April 19, 1928, 1

13. *MNS,* May 8, 1928, 1, and May 18, 1928, 1.

14. *MNS,* May 10, 1928, 2.

15. *MNS,* April 21, 1928, 3, and May 11, 1928, 14.

16. *MNS,* February 2, 1928, 1, 10; February 3, 1928, 6.

17. *BHMNP,* February 3, 1928, 13; *BMDH,* February 3, 1928, 1; Bukowski, *Big Bill Thompson,* 195–96.

18. Williams, *Huey Long,* 288.

19. Williams, *Huey Long,* 287–88.

20. *MNS,* May 8, 1928, 2.

21. *MNS,* May 11, 1928, 20.

22. Williams, *Huey Long,* 288–89; Deutsch, "Paradox," 102–3; Fournet letter, March 26, 1928, box 1: 3, CMP.

23. Long, *EMK,* 106–7.

24. Harris, *Kingfish,* 36–37.

25. Norman Bauer didn't support Huey, but he voted for Fournet because they were LSU classmates. Bauer int., THWP.

26. *MNS,* May 19, 1928, 3.

27. *MNS,* May 19, 1928, 1.

28. Williams, *Huey Long,* 289–90; Hair, *Realm,* 162; R. White, *Kingfish,* 41.

29. R. White, *Kingfish,* 36–38. See also, *MNS,* May 19, 1928, 1 (explaining the plans); *HMHA,* May 21, 1928, 1.

30. *BMDH,* May 21, 1928, 1; *MNS,* May 21, 1928, 1.

31. *MNS,* May 21, 1928, 1, 7.

32. R. White, *Kingfish,* 44.

33. Deutsch, "Paradox," 99.

34. Williams, *Huey Long,* 307; R. White, *Kingfish,* 44, 51.

35. Williams, *Huey Long,* 455.

36. Williams, *Huey Long,* 287.

37. Williams, *Huey Long,* 297, 522 (malt syrups tax); Hair, *Realm,* 162.

38. Rorty, "Callie Long's Boy Huey."

39. Williams, *Huey Long,* 298–99.

40. McManus, "Sharing the Hate," 32–34, 51, 78, 83, 130, 134; Hair, *Realm,* 164.

41. *NYT,* July 29, 1928, 36.

42. Williams, *Huey Long,* 307–8; R. White, *Kingfish,* 51.

43. Sindler, *Huey Long's Louisiana,* 59.

44. *MNS,* June 19, 1928, 4 (editorial).

45. *MNS,* June 6, 1928, 1; June 11, 1928, 1. *NYT,* July 29, 1928, 36. Banta, "Regulation," 338.

46. Julius charged that Huey had insulted their mother by lying about their lack of shoes.

47. *MNS,* June 20, 1928, 1.

48. Williams, *Huey Long,* 309; R. White, *Kingfish,* 52.

49. Banta, "Regulation," 337.

50. *MNS,* June 10, 1928, 1, 8; June 16, 1928, 10; *NOTP,* July 1, 1928, 1.

51. *MNS,* February 21, 1928, 1–2, and May 23, 1928, 1, 6.

52. Williams, *Huey Long,* 285.

53. Williams, *Huey Long,* 300–303; Sindler, *Huey Long's Louisiana,* 58 ("Huey both had fulfilled his campaign pledge and had beaten the Ring"); Kane, *Hayride,* 65 (rate was too high); Jeansonne, *Messiah,* 66–67 (same); *NYT,* July 29, 1928, 36 ("The Governor made this demand at a time when there was reason to believe a much lower rate could be obtained," but also noting the company's demand for a higher price, its "large lobby," and that Huey's intervention speeded the negotiations). Harris quotes a paragraph of the "deck of cards" speech, viewing it as dictatorial (*Kingfish,* 42–43).

54. Long, *EMK,* 112.

55. *NYT,* July 29, 1928, 36. *MNS,* June 19, 1928, 1, 6; June 21, 1928, 1, 8.

56. *MNS,* June 7, 1928, 1, 11; June 19, 1928, 1, 6; June 22, 1928, 1, 6.

57. Vandervoort, *NOTP,* June 8, 1929, 1, 13.

58. Long, *EMK,* 113–14 ; *MNS,* June 21, 1928, 1, 8.

59. Williams, *Huey Long,* 303–6.

60. Long, *EMK,* 108, 110.

61. Long, *EMK,* 109; R. White, *Kingfish,* 45–46, 49; *NYT,* July 29, 1928, 36. *BMDH,* July 14, 1928, 1.

62. *MNS,* June 1, 1928, 7.

63. MNS, May 28, 1928, 1, May 29, 1928, 1, June 16, 1928, 2.

64. *BMDH,* August 16, 1928, 1.

65. Williams, *Huey Long,* 291–92.

66. Peterman and Hughes, ints., THWP.

67. Banta, "Regulation," 316.

68. Williams, *Huey Long,* 292–93.

69. Kane, *Hayride,* 62.

70. R. White, *Kingfish,* 46; Hair, *Realm,* 165. Act No. 99 of 1928.

71. Schlesinger, *Age of Jackson,* 25–26; James, *Life of Andrew Jackson,* 520–23.

72. Morris, *Rise of Theodore Roosevelt,* 398–99.

73. Sindler, *Huey Long's Louisiana,* 41, 61; Howard, *Political Tendencies,* 212.

74. Beals, *Story of Huey Long,* 92, 122.

75. R. White, *Kingfish,* 50.

76. Williams, *Huey Long,* 293–95.

77. Fisher int., THWP. Beals, *Story of Huey Long,* 188.

78. Rivet int., THWP.

79. Williams, *Huey Long,* 296 and note 7.

80. Hair, *Realm,* 163.

81. Compare Harris, *Kingfish,* 42 (control "somewhat spotted"); *NYT,* June 10, 1928, 130; June 24, 1928, 50 (lacked majority for all matters); July 29, 1928, 50 (same and listing compromises).

82. R. White, *Kingfish,* 49. Huey's bill would have allowed him to appoint a lot of judges (box 1: 10, CMP).

83. Alford int., THWP.

84. Cooper int., THWP.

85. Weiss int., THWP.

86. *MNS,* June 22, 1928, 1; June 23, 1928, 8; June 27, 1928, 7. *PAN,* June 27, 1928, 2. *LN,* June 27, 1928, 1.

87. Williams, *Huey Long,* 283. Earlier in February, Colonel Ewing had publicly expressed his support for Smith (*NYT,* February 20, 1928, 3; Deutsch, "Paradox," 100–102).

88. R. White, *Kingfish,* 45.

89. *NYT,* January 29, 1933, 85.

90. Long, *EMK,* 155.

91. R. White, *Kingfish,* 45.

92. Berg, *Wilson,* 210–11, 292–301 (lobbying as president).

93. Williams, *Huey Long,* 298.

## 10. Overcoming an Intransigent Opposition

1. *ADN,* July 12, 1928, 1. *BMDH,* July 12, 1928, 10; July 26, 1928, 1. *NYT,* July 15, 1928, 30. Appel, "Free State of New Orleans."

2. *PAN,* August 1, 1928, 1; *CDS,* August 1, 1928, 1; *HMHA,* August 1, 1928, 1; *BMDH,* August 2, 1928, 1; *EDP,* August 2, 1928, 2; UPTW, *WDM,* August 4, 1928, 4.

3. UPTW, *WDM,* August 4, 1928, 4.

4. R. White, *Kingfish,* 52.

5. Williams, *Huey Long*, 342. R. White, *Kingfish*, 53. Appel says $6,000 was taken from the two clubs ("Free State of New Orleans," 19).

6. *NYT*, August 13, 1928, 1.

7. *Bradford Era*, August 13, 1928, 1; *Danville Bee*, August 13, 1928, 1; *Morning Herald*, August 17, 1928, 10.

8. Deutsch, "Paradox," 132; Appel, "Free State of New Orleans," 20.

9. *MNS*, September 17, 1928, 7, September 27, 1928, 1. Deutsch, "Paradox," 130.

10. Long, *EMK*, 113–114.

11. R. White, *Kingfish*, 56.

12. R. White, *Kingfish*, 55–56; Hair, *Realm*, 171–72.

13. Williams, *Huey Long*, 325–26.

14. *BMDH*, September 12, 1928, 1; *Joplin Globe*, September 13, 1928, 7; *MNS*, September 12, 1928, 1.

15. *Bossier Parish School Board v. LSBE*, 168 La. 1033, 123 So. 665 (1929); *Borden v. LSBE*, 168 La. 1005 (1928); Finkelman, ed., *Religion and American Law.*

16. Banta, "Regulation," 341–44; *Ohio Oil Co. v. Conway*, 34 F.2d 47 (1928); *Cochran v. LSBE*, 168 La. 1030 (1928); *Cochran v. LSBE*, 281 U.S. 370, 50 S. Ct. 335 (1930).

17. Long, *EMK*, 117–18.

18. *MNS*, October 11, 1928, 2.

19. *MNS*, October 17, 1928, 3; *LDNL*, November 9, 1928, 9; *HMHA*, November 12, 1928, 4.

20. *HMHA*, September 25, 1928, 1; *MNS*, October 2, 1928, 9.

21. Wingo, "1928 Presidential Election in Louisiana," 405–35; Purdy, "Presidential Race of 1928."

22. Slayton and Eisenstadt, eds., *EONYS*, 1424–25.

23. Williams, *Huey Long*, 327.

24. *MNS*, October 8, 1928, 1.

25. Williams, *Huey Long*, 328.

26. Hair, *Realm*, 164–65; Wingo, "1928 Presidential Election in Louisiana." *Plessy v. Ferguson*, 163 U. S 537 (1896).

27. Smith lost Texas, Oklahoma, Tennessee, Virginia, North Carolina, and Florida, each of which John Davis, the lackluster Democratic candidate in 1924, had won.

28. Sindler, *Huey Long's Louisiana*, 60; Williams, *Huey Long*, 328.

29. *JNH*, November 12, 1928, 2; *Kingsport Times*, November 12, 1928, 1.

30. *Sheboygan Press*, November 17, 1928, 2; *PAN*, November 17, 1928, 1; Deutsch, "Paradox," 131.

31. *NYT*, November 21, 1928, 3; *BMSH*, November 20, 1928, 1; UPTW, *WDM*, November 23, 1928, 6.

32. Long, *EMK*, 114–15.

33. Hair, *Realm*, 172.

34. Williams, *Huey Long*, 329–32; Deutsch quotes a later speech by Huey: "They say, friends, I coerced (stiltedly pronounced coe-urst) 'em into doing it, and I'd do it again, any time the oil trust tried to keep me from giving free schoolbooks to your children" ("Paradox," 184).

35. Deutsch, "Paradox," 142.

36. Turner, *Paving Tobacco Road.*

37. Long, *EMK*, 201.

38. LHC, 5th Biennial Report, 1930, 11–13.

39. Lant int., THWP; Williams, *Huey Long*, 333.

40. *NYT,* July 7, 1991, 176: "Unlike most blackface characters, those in 'Amos 'n' Andy' reflected many values common to lower middle-class Americans. White audiences could empathize with the universal aspects of the experiences of the black people depicted on the program—financial problems, personal relationships, even reactions to contemporary events—while laughing at their supposed ethnic traits. As Mr. Ely points out, Gosden and Correll walked a tightrope, plying white audiences with traditional racial stereotypes but cleverly muting their harsher overtones. As the show evolved . . . its central comic characters became George Stevens, the Kingfish of the Mystic Knights of the Sea lodge; Lightnin', the shiftless handyman; Algonquin J. Calhoun, a bogus lawyer, and Sapphire, Kingfish's wife." See also Peters, *Five Days in Philadelphia,* 7–8.

41. Long, *EMK,* 277–78; Williams, *Huey Long,* 312–13.

42. Hair, *Realm,* 168–69; Williams, *Huey Long,* 374–75.

43. Hair, *Realm,* 165–66; Williams, *Huey Long,* 321–23. Brocato had brief careers as a barber and prizefighter before turning to gambling and bootlegging. In 1930, he was sentenced to a year in prison for a second violation of Prohibition laws. Brocato was thereafter welcomed back into Huey's retinue. His son continued Brocato's La Louisiane Restaurant and added Moran's Riverside Restaurant and Acme Oyster House (*NOTP,* January 20, 1995).

44. Williams, *Huey Long,* 323.

45. H. L. Bozeman to RBL, February 12 and 18, 1957, box 1: 21–22, RBLP.

46. Williams, *Huey Long,* 316–18; Spencer int., THWP; Fournet int., THWP; Fisher int., THWP; Leche int., THWP.

47. Four witnesses related a train trip in which Huey met someone and then attacked the man's daughter (Williams, *Huey Long,* 318 and note 4). Williams thought Huey's energy gave rise to periodic sexual impulses. Richard Leche said Seymour Weiss had to pay off a woman in New York after an affair, but Williams did not ask Weiss about it. Williams did not interview Alice Lee Grosjean or ask Rose Long about infidelity. A female journalist said Huey was not interested in affairs, but this was in 1935 (St. Johns, *The Honeycomb,* 389).

48. Old Hu had remarried and was living in Dry Prong. His new wife eventually sued him for divorce on grounds of desertion (Williams, *Huey Long,* 312 and note 3).

49. Huey had suggested that a new tuberculosis hospital could be built with the money saved. One newspaper ran a picture of Earl with the caption "new TB hospital" (Long, *EMK,* 259–60; Hair, *Realm,* 220).

50. Williams, *Huey Long,* 314–16; Long, *EMK,* 259. The governorship paid a salary of $7,500; Earl's job paid twice that much.

51. Jeansonne, *Messiah,* 52–53.

52. *Advocate,* May 21, 1928.

53. Rose McConnell Long int., THWP.

54. Deutsch, "Paradox," 14.

55. Williams, *Huey Long,* 319–20; Broussard int., THWP.

56. Hallack int., THWP; Gary int., THWP.

57. Williams, *Huey Long,* 268, 436.

58. *NYT,* February 27, 1994, 21 (Mutual deposited its files in Tulane University).

59. Hair, *Realm,* 175–76, 213.

60. Wimberly int., THWP; Bauer int., THWP.

61. Hair, *Realm,* 168.

62. Williams, *Huey Long,* 334.

63. Long, *EMK,* 224–25; Williams, *Huey Long,* 333–35.

64. Bourg int., THWP. Hair says Joe Messina supervised its destruction (*Realm,* 169).

65. *MNS,* October 6, 1928, 1.

66. Hargroder, *Ada and the Doc.*

67. Even a song was written about it, "Don't you angle iron me." Long, *EMK,* 126–31; Williams, *Huey Long,* 336–40; *Brownwood Bulletin,* July 2, 1928, 1.

68. Williams, *Huey Long,* 340; Long, *EMK,* 129–30; *Waterloo Evening Courier,* January 3, 1929, 1. Rose McConnell Long int., THWP.

69. R. White, *Kingfish,* 59. Justice Charles O'Niell of the Louisiana Supreme Court resided in the parish where the crime occurred, knew the Dreher family, and attended the trial.

70. Long, *EMK,* 131–32; Beals, *Story of Huey Long,* 108–9; *MNS,* January 4, 1929, 1; January 5, 1929, 1. Huey's opponents Cyr and Saint approved this pardon.

71. *MNS,* January 8, 1929, 1; January 12, 1929, 1. *Joplin Globe,* January 11, 1929, 2.

72. Long, *EMK,* 130 and note 49, quoting a January 11, 1929, newspaper.

73. Williams, *Huey Long,* 340 and note 4, citing John Nuckolls.

74. *MNS,* January 28, 1929, 1.

75. Huey claimed that the younger Ewing got arrested because of his drinking, that he prevented Ewing's incarceration, never got a thank-you, and faced Ewing's hostility because he told his father (Long, *EMK,* 94–96).

76. Williams, *Huey Long,* 340–41; Hair, *Realm,* 175.

77. Williams, *Huey Long,* 344–45; *MNS,* February 9, 1929, 1; *Daily Herald* (Biloxi), February 14, 1929, 1.

78. R. White, *Kingfish,* 53–54.

79. Williams, *Huey Long,* 344–45. *MNS,* February 18, 1929, 1; February 19, 1929, 1; February 21, 1929, 10; February 22, 1929, 1. *NYT,* March 3, 1929, 53. Appel, "Free State of New Orleans," 24.

80. *MNS,* January 28, 1929, 1; February 4, 1929, 1; February 6, 1929, 1; February 7, 1929, 1; February 13, 1929, 1.

81. Williams, *Huey Long,* 345; Hair, *Realm,* 176–77.

82. Williams, *Huey Long,* 331–32, 335–36.

83. P. Kendall, *Louis XI,* 313–14.

84. *MNS,* February 26, 1929, 1.

85. Banta, "Regulation," 343–44; *Ohio Oil Co. v. McFarland,* 28 F.2d 441 (1928); *Cochran v. LSBE,* 168 La. 1030 (1928); *Cochran v. LSBE,* 281 U.S. 370, 50 S. Ct. 335 (1930).

86. Long, *EMK,* 122–23.

87. Williams, *Huey Long,* 348; R. White, *Kingfish,* 63; McManus, "Sharing the Hate," 63.

88. Williams, *Huey Long,* 346.

## 11. The Opposition Strikes Back

1. *MNS,* March 16, 1929, 1.

2. Williams, *Huey Long,* 347–48, 354, 370.

3. Long, *EMK,* 123.

4. *MNS,* March 19, 1929, 1, 9.

5. Williams's account was based on the recollections of three men on the scene. "Other surviving legislators who were asked about the incident," Williams wrote, "smiled knowingly but refused to say anything" (*Huey Long,* 354n1). Fred Blanche voted to impeach Huey but provided information on Snyder and the money spent. One legislator, Huey wrote, re-

fused to expose a bribery offer because the man who made the offer was closer to him than Huey ever was or would be (*EMK*, 165–67).

6. *MNS*, March 19, 1929, 1, 9.

7. *NYT*, March 22, 1929, 9. Compare Huey's forty votes here with seventy-two for Fournet and sixty-seven for the road bond bill in 1928.

8. Long, *EMK*, 123.

9. Long, *EMK*, 146. Beals said the legislature censured Harris for politicizing the school system (*Story of Huey Long*, 111).

10. *MNS*, March 19, 1929, 1, 9.

11. *MNS*, March 21, 1929, 1 (losing support of T. T. Webb, for example); March 23, 1929, 1. R. White, *Kingfish*, 62.

12. *MNS*, March 21, 1929, 1, 6; R. White, *Kingfish*, 64–65. Williams wrongly suggests that Cyr's charges were illogical (*Huey Long*, 350–51 and note 6). Huey opposed Standard Oil by championing independent oil drillers, also oilmen, in whose companies Huey owned stock. Favoring a Texas company that wasn't fighting him in state politics would not be inconsistent or illogical to his fight against Standard Oil. In his autobiography, Huey said the oil lands had been leased by Governor Parker and all he did was permit the leaseholder to drill (*EMK*, 146). This is not right either. The lease was transferred from someone who could not or would not drill and wanted to assign it to someone who could, reaping a profit on the assignment. At the time, Huey said the state's word was at stake; it had leased the land and should keep the terms it agreed to, whether with the original leaseholder or assignee. In Huey's papers, there is a suggestion that, as a condition of the assignment, he required drilling of wells, absent from the original lease. This would aid the state's severance tax revenues (box 37: 1349, HPLP). Enemies of Huey heard rumors that Huey received a payoff for permitting the assignment. W. D. Robinson (Huey's old press agent and now enemy) searched for such evidence, finding nothing. Cyr's speech led to no action either by those law enforcement authorities who opposed Huey or by the impeachers.

13. *MNS*, March 21, 1929, 1.

14. *Hattiesburg American*, March 22, 1929, 1; *PAN*, March 23, 1929, 1; *NYT*, March 23, 1929, 16.

15. Deutsch, "Paradox,"108.

16. *MNS*, March 23, 1929, 1; R. White, *Kingfish*, 66–67.

17. Hair, *Realm*, 178–79; R. White, *Kingfish*, 66–67.

18. Williams, *Huey Long*, 352–55; *MNS*, March 25, 1929, 1.

19. Williams, *Huey Long*, 356–58; *MNS*, March 26, 1929, 1, 6; R. White, *Kingfish*, 68–69; Deutsch, "Paradox," 163–64; *NYT*, March 26, 1929, 1.

20. Hair, *Realm*, 180.

21. *MNS*, March 27, 1929, 1.

22. R. White, *Kingfish*, 70.

23. *NYT*, March 27, 1929, 1 (charges), 21 (very good show).

24. Long, *EMK*, 139–42. Williams, *Huey Long*, 360–63. *MNS*, March 27, 1929, 1; March 28, 1929, 1. R. White, *Kingfish*, 72.

25. Williams, *Huey Long*, 365. *MNS*, March 28, 1929, 1. *NYT*, March 28, 1929, 5; March 30, 1929, 10. Fruge int., THWP.

26. R. White, *Kingfish*, 69; Harris, *Kingfish*, 62.

27. Larcade int., THWP.

28. Harris, *Kingfish*, 62.

29. Rose McConnell Long int., THWP.

30. Long, *EMK,* 152–53.

31. *PAN,* March 31, 1929, 1, 2; *NYT,* March 29, 1929, 17.

32. Beals, *Story of Huey Long,* 121.

33. *NYT,* March 31, 1929, 47.

34. Williams, *Huey Long,* 367–68; *MNS,* March 28, 1929, 1, 11; *PAN,* April 2, 1929, 1; *NYT,* April 2, 1929, 14.

35. *NYT,* April 3, 1929, 11; *MNS,* April 2, 1929, 1, 8; Williams, *Huey Long,* 364–65, 370.

36. *Daily Herald,* April 2, 1929, 1 (remarks of Leon Law).

37. *NYT,* March 29, 1929, 17; March 30, 1929, 9; March 31, 1929, 19. *Daily Herald,* April 4, 1929, 1.

38. R. White, *Kingfish,* 75.

39. Long, *EMK,* 149; R. White, *Kingfish,* 75; Williams, *Huey Long,* 367.

40. Kane, *Hayride,* 75.

41. R. White, *Kingfish,* 76; Long, *EMK,* 150; *Kingsport Times,* April 5, 1929, 1.

42. Williams, *Huey Long,* 370.

43. R. White, *Kingfish,* 78.

44. McManus, "Sharing the Hate," 72.

45. Long, *EMK,* 145.

46. Williams, *Huey Long,* 370 and note 4.

47. Williams, *Huey Long,* 371.

48. Hair, *Realm,* 178.

49. R. White, *Kingfish,* 66. Box 37: 1349, HPLP.

50. Deutsch, "Paradox," 168–69.

51. Jeansonne, *Messiah,* 77; *PAN,* April 3, 1929, 1 (bribery); *Daily Herald,* April 3, 1929, 1 (Bennett); *NYT,* April 4, 1929, 5.

52. Williams, *Huey Long,* 380.

53. Deutsch doubted that more than $500 could have been spent on liquor ("Paradox," 186). The governors who attended the conference denied that there was a party (Jeansonne, *Messiah,* 78). But they couldn't be expected to admit that they were on a big drunken spree. Weiss int., THWP.

54. Hair, *Realm,* 182; R. White, *Kingfish,* 78–79.

55. Long, *EMK,* 143.

56. *Daily Herald,* April 24, 1929, 1.

57. R. White, *Kingfish,* 47; Deutsch, "Paradox," 183–88.

58. *NYT,* April 5, 1929, 30.

59. Williams, *Huey Long,* 375–77 and note 5. West Publishing Company supported Huey's defense, writing that it separated his private law books paid for individually from his public law books paid for by the state (box 37: 1349, HPLP).

60. Long, *EMK,* 144–45.

61. Williams, *Huey Long,* 378. *Kingsport Times,* April 9, 1929, 1.

62. Hair, *Realm,* 182; *NYT,* April 25, 1929, 24.

63. Williams, *Huey Long,* 379; McManus, "Sharing the Hate," 122; Thomas W. Robertson letter of April 14, 1929, box 1: 16, CMP.

64. R. White, *Kingfish,* 50; *Kingsport Times,* April 12, 1929, 3; Porterie int., THWP.

65. Hair, *Realm,* 181.

66. Long, *EMK,* 143.

67. See Baker, "Some Legal Aspects of Impeachment in Louisiana," 359–87.

68. Louisiana Constitution of 1921, Article V, Section 14 ("It shall become [the Governor's] duty to convene the Legislature in extraordinary session whenever petitioned to do so by two-thirds of the members elected to each house. . . . If the Governor should fail to . . . [convene the legislature, then the Lieutenant Governor or Speaker of the House shall do so]).

69. Williams, *Huey Long*, 381.

70. Williams, *Huey Long*, 381–82.

71. Williams, *Huey Long*, 383.

72. Williams, *Huey Long*, 380. R. White, *Kingfish*, 84. *Daily Herald*, April 11, 1929, 3; April 12, 1929, 1. *NYT*, April 11, 1929, 25; April 12, 1929, 11; April 25, 1929, 24.

73. R. White, *Kingfish*, 84.

74. Williams, *Huey Long*, 384–85 and note 2.

75. Gottlieb int., THWP.

76. Fisher int., THWP.

77. Boone int., THWP.

78. Long, *EMK*, 168–69.

79. Bahan int., THWP.

80. Williams, *Huey Long*, 390.

81. Harris, *Kingfish*, 74–76.

82. Williams, *Huey Long*, 391–93.

83. Deutsch says an investigation cleared Cutrer ("Paradox," 186–87), but Huey remained convinced that he had sold him out.

84. *NYT*, May 10, 1929, 20; Williams, *Huey Long*, 395–96; Deutsch, "Paradox," 180.

85. Long, *EMK*, 156.

86. Deutsch, "Paradox," 191–97.

87. Williams, *Huey Long*, 398.

88. *Daily Herald*, May 13, 1929, 1; May 14, 1929, 1. *NYT*, May 16, 1929, 14.

89. Williams, *Huey Long*, 400–405.

90. *NYT*, May 26, 1929, 47.

91. *Daily Herald*, May 9, 1929, 1; May 17, 1929, 1. Beckcom and Gleason ints., THWP.

## 12. Stalemate

1. Williams, *Huey Long*, 409–10; McManus, "Sharing the Hate," 76.

2. Long, *EMK*, 79.

3. Excerpt from the "Barbecue Speech," delivered December 1934 or spring 1935, probably to members of the press in Washington, DC. This excerpt was shown in the Ken Burns film.

4. Williams, *Huey Long*, 406. *Daily Herald*, May 22, 1929, 1. *PAN*, May 27, 1929, 1. *Daily Herald*, June 6, 1929, 10; July 19, 1930, 1.

5. Bahan int., THWP. Slade was a drugstore clerk who treated Willie Stark kindly when he was a nobody and thereafter obtained lucrative state business.

6. Long, *EMK*, 172.

7. Williams, *Huey Long*, 422.

8. Long, *EMK*, 182, 186.

9. Compare Williams, *Huey Long*, 420, with *Daily Herald*, October 23, 1929, 1.

10. Williams, *Huey Long*, 421.

11. *Daily Herald*, October 23, 1929, 5; October 25, 1929, 7.

12. *PAN*, September 17, 1929, 1.

13. *Daily Herald,* October 23, 1929, 1.

14. Gleason int., THWP; Williams, *Huey Long,* 407–8.

15. *PAN,* July 10, 1929, 6; *Daily Herald,* July 9, 1929, 7; Deutsch, "Paradox," 242.

16. Ginsberg int., THWP; Thomas int., THWP.

17. Long, *EMK,* 180, 183–84; *NYT,* May 26, 1929, 51–52; founding document, July 1, 1929, box 1: 76, CMP.

18. McManus, "Sharing the Hate," 80.

19. Long, *EMK,* cartoons at 185, 189.

20. Long, *EMK,* 189–90.

21. *PAN,* July 20, 1929, 2; July 26, 1929, 5. *Kingsport Times,* July 21, 1929, 1. *Daily Herald,* July 24, 1929, 1; July 31, 1929, 1. Williams, *Huey Long,* 423–24. *NYT,* July 22, 1929, 18; July 28, 1929, 49.

22. Banta, "Regulation," 324.

23. *Kingsport Times,* December 3, 1929, 1; *Daily Herald,* December 3, 1929, 1.

24. *Daily Herald,* September 30, 1929, 1.

25. Long, *EMK,* 187.

26. *NYT,* November 13, 1929, 30.

27. *PAN,* August 6, 1929, 12; *Daily Herald,* August 7, 1929, 1; *NYT,* August 8, 1929, 5.

28. *Daily Herald,* September 28, 1929, 2.

29. *Daily Herald,* September 12, 1929, 1 (New Orleans's inadequate drainage system).

30. *Daily Herald,* November 23, 1929, 1; December 10, 1929, 1; December 17, 1929, 12.

31. *Daily Herald,* November 26, 1929, 1.

32. *Daily Herald,* December 18, 1929, 7.

33. *Kingsport Times,* December 27, 1929, 2.

34. *Daily Herald,* September 18, 1929, 9 (Chef Menteur Bridge); September 13, 1929 (Huey urged paving near the bridge welcomed by travelers).

35. *PAN,* October 26, 1929, 5 ($5,000,000 more in bonds authorized); October 25, 1929, 11. *Daily Herald,* November 28, 1929, 1.

36. *Daily Herald,* October 28, 1929, 5.

37. *Daily Herald,* November 27, 1929, 3.

38. *Daily Herald,* September 28, 1929, 6.

39. *PAN,* September 26, 1929, 1; *Daily Herald,* September 28, 1929, 1.

40. *Daily Herald,* September 4, 1929, 1.

41. *Daily Herald,* October 1, 1929, 7.

42. Long, *EMK,* 325, reprinting November 15, 1929, article of the *Baton Rouge State Times.*

43. Long, *EMK,* 179–80; Banta, "Regulation," 47–50.

44. *Daily Herald,* June 26, 1929, 7; Banta, "Regulation," 47–50.

45. *Daily Herald,* November 28, 1929, 6.

46. *Daily Herald,* January 31, 1930, 5.

47. Gamble int., THWP; Williams, *Huey Long,* 426; *Daily Herald,* January 31, 1930, 5.

48. *Daily Herald,* January 6, 1930, 3 (contracts for 1,300 more miles planned; goal of 3,000 miles); *Daily Herald,* March 19, 1930, 5 ($2 million in contracts).

49. *Daily Herald,* January 15, 1930, 2; January 29, 1930, 1 (intracoastal canal); February 17, 1930, 1 (Rigolets bridge); March 14, 1930, 3; April 18, 1, April 26, 1930, 1; March 24, 1930, 7. *PAN,* March 5, 1930, 16; April 5, 1930, 1.

50. *Daily Herald,* April 8, 1930, 10.

51. *PAN,* April 25, 1930, 14.

52. *Daily Herald,* February 3, 1930, 5.

53. *Daily Herald,* January 22, 1930, 3. He also told the man that he hoped to remain his friend.

54. *Daily Herald,* March 29, 1930, 12.

55. Williams, *Huey Long,* 439–40; *Daily Herald,* March 11, 1930, 1.

56. Williams, *Huey Long,* 440–44; Deutsch, "Paradox," 214–19.

57. Hughes int., THWP.

58. Williams, *Huey Long,* 428, 433; Deutsch, "Paradox," 237–38.

59. Deutsch, "Paradox," 219–20.

60. Williams, *Huey Long,* 424–25; *NYT,* February 23, 1930, 146.

61. Williams, *Huey Long,* 428 and note 2, citing *BRST,* February 27, 1930.

62. Sheire, "Louisiana State Capitol." The old capitol is now a museum.

63. *Daily Herald,* February 4, 1930, 7.

64. Williams, *Huey Long,* 429–32.

65. Long, *EMK,* 194–99; Deutsch, "Paradox," 234; *NYT,* March 4, 1930, 2.

66. *Daily Herald,* March 4, 1930, 1; R. White, *Kingfish,* 92–93.

67. *Daily Herald,* March 11, 1930, 5; *NYT,* March 11, 1930, 8.

68. Liebling, *Earl of Louisiana,* 7–8; Williams, *Huey Long,* 432–33.

69. Hair, *Realm,* 192–93.

70. Williams, *Huey Long,* 441–44; R. White, *Kingfish,* 97; *Daily Herald,* March 26, 1930, 1.

71. Williams, *Huey Long,* 455–60; R. White, *Kingfish,* 97–99.

72. *PAN,* April 14, 1930, 1.

73. *NYT,* May 4, 1930, 58.

74. *NYT,* May 25, 1930, 172.

75. Sindler, *Huey Long's Louisiana,* 69.

76. R. White, *Kingfish,* 100–101.

77. Sindler, *Huey Long's Louisiana,* 69; Cowan and McGuire, *Louisiana Governors,* chapter on Alvin O. King.

78. *NYT,* July 13, 1930, 120.

79. Williams, *Huey Long,* 445–47.

80. Long, *EMK,* 205. Williams, *Huey Long,* 447–48. *Daily Herald,* May 17, 1930, 11. *PAN,* May 21, 1930, 13. Clipping, Associated Press wire story, May 31, 1930. *Daily Herald,* June 9, 1930, 1. *NYT,* June 1, 1930, 28; June 15, 1930, 50.

81. R. White, *Kingfish,* 97–99.

82. Deutsch, "Paradox," 243, 245–46.

83. Long, *EMK,* 204.

84. Williams, *Huey Long,* 448–50; *Daily Herald,* June 19, 1930, 1; R. White, *Kingfish,* 96–97; Hair, *Realm,* 194–95.

85. Deutsch, "Paradox," 250.

86. Williams, *Huey Long,* 452. Harris, *Kingfish,* 81–85. *NYT,* June 23, 1930, 2; July 6, 1930, 44.

87. *Daily Herald,* June 10, 1930, 1.

88. Larcade int., THWP.

89. R. White, *Kingfish,* 100.

90. *Daily Herald,* January 2, 1930, 1; January 3, 1930, 1. R. White, *Kingfish,* 91. Pleasant, "Ruffin G. Pleasant and Huey P. Long," 357–66.

91. *Daily Herald,* February 7, 1930, 1; Williams, *Huey Long,* 406, 548. *Kingsport Times,* August 31, 1930, 1.

92. Williams, *Huey Long,* 452; *NYT,* July 20, 1930, 46.

93. Long, *EMK,* 207–9.

94. Williams, *Huey Long,* 452–53.

95. R. White, *Kingfish,* 101.

96. Long, *EMK,* 210. Beals said Huey later secretly repaid the banks from the general fund (*Story of Huey Long,* 183).

### 13. There Was No Middle Ground

1. Ransdell was elected senator in 1912 and had served in the House of Representatives before that from 1899 to 1913 (Laborde, *National Southerner,* 10–18, 43–44).

2. Long, *EMK,* 211; Williams, *Huey Long,* 453; *Daily Herald,* July 16, 1930, 1; *NYT,* July 17, 1930, 2.

3. Hair, *Realm,* 196.

4. Laborde, *National Southerner,* 43–53, 167–74 (tariff, divorce); 53–61 (League of Nations); 61–70, 122–33, 154–67, 174–85 (public health projects); 131–53 (flood control).

5. Williams, *Huey Long,* 462; Laborde, *National Southerner,* 174–85.

6. Galbraith, *Great Crash,* 95–141; Brooks, *Once in Golconda,* 109–10; Schlesinger, *Age of Roosevelt: The Crisis,* 159–67; Chandler, *America's Greatest Depression,* 1.

7. Aaron and Bendiner, *Strenuous Decade,* 38–39.

8. Leuchtenburg, *Franklin D. Roosevelt,* 3, 21.

9. Hair, *Realm,* 191–92.

10. Laborde, *National Southerner,* 187–88.

11. Williams, *Huey Long,* 465.

12. Hair, *Realm,* 199.

13. Williams, *Huey Long,* 465–67; Caro, *Years of Lyndon Johnson: Means,* 211–23, 232–34.

14. Hair, *Realm,* 200; Harris, *Kingfish,* 85–87.

15. Laborde, *National Southerner,* 185–92; *PAN,* August 22, 1930, 17.

16. Williams, *Huey Long,* 466.

17. Williams, *Huey Long,* 466. Long, *EMK,* 213–19. *Daily Herald,* August 20, 1930, 1; August 23, 1930, 1.

18. R. White, *Kingfish,* 110.

19. Hair, *Realm,* 200–201; Williams, *Huey Long,* 468.

20. *Kingsport Times,* September 7, 1930, 5; R. White, *Kingfish,* 109.

21. *Daily Herald,* August 23, 1930, 5.

22. Williams, *Huey Long,* 470–501; Hair, *Realm,* 197–98; *Daily Herald,* August 26, 1930, 1. The *Times* said the epithets against Huey could not be printed (August 31, 1930, 37).

23. Williams, *Huey Long,* 468–69.

24. Williams, *Huey Long,* 471–74 (quotes from 473, 474); Hair, *Realm,* 203–5.

25. Jeansonne, *Messiah,* 89; Fisher int., THWP.

26. Williams, *Huey Long,* 474; Hair, *Realm,* 204; *Daily Herald,* September 8, 1930, 1; *NYT,* September 7, 1930, 15.

27. Williams, *Huey Long,* 476.

28. *Daily Herald,* September 6, 1930, 1; September 8, 1930, 1, 8. *NYT,* September 8, 1930, 3; September 9, 1930, 29. Deutsch, "Paradox," 260–64.

29. *NYT,* September 14, 1930, 57.

30. *NYT,* September 11, 1930, 21.

31. Fisher int, McConnell int., THWP.

32. Hair, *Realm,* 205 and note 53. Williams, *Huey Long,* 477–79. *CT,* September 10, 1932, 2; September 23, 1932, 13. Deutsch, "Paradox," 264.

33. Hair, *Realm,* 203.

34. Williams, *Huey Long,* 479–80; R. White, *Kingfish,* 110; Reyer int., THWP.

35. Hair, *Realm,* 205.

36. Deutsch, "Paradox," 265; Landry int., THWP.

37. R. White, *Kingfish,* 113–14.

38. Williams, *Huey Long,* 481–82; Hair, *Realm,* 206; Long, *EMK,* 230; *NYT,* October 5, 1930, 53.

39. Hair, *Realm,* 206–7; Williams, *Huey Long,* 482.

40. R. White, *Kingfish,* 119.

41. R. White, *Kingfish,* 120.

42. Williams, *Huey Long,* 484–85; Long, *EMK,* 239. Williams omits Huey's remark that Dupre was amused, and Huey omits that he drilled the hole in the roof. Because Dupre was allied with Huey when Huey wrote his autobiography, he may have said Dupre was amused when he wasn't. In 1931, Dupre lost his legislative seat because the Pavys supported a family member for the position. Huey had promised a road in their district and to support the family member against Dupre. Recognizing inevitable defeat, Dupre withdrew and, without his legislative salary, lacked an income (Williams, *Huey Long,* 535). Huey then gave Dupre a job on the *Louisiana Progress.* On Thanksgiving Day, 1931, after he began his new job as a pro-Long columnist, an acquaintance stopped him on the street and wrote on his pad, "you thought [Huey's ally and later governor] Allen was a crook three months ago. What do you think of him now?" The suggestion of hypocrisy enraged Dupre, who walked home and retrieved his .38 revolver and returned to town. Running into the same man again, Dupre pulled his gun and shot him dead. Huey engaged a criminal defense attorney for him, and he was acquitted on a self-defense plea (R. White, *Kingfish,* 140; Hair, *Realm,* 208). Williams omits the shooting, and Hair and White implicitly suggest improper resolution of the case. Contemporary newspaper accounts report that, when Dupre went back to town, he was threatened by the man, backed up against a wall, but warned him that if he continued to advance, he would be shot. Dupre was small and said, "I couldn't physically fight a man of that size" (*NYT,* November 27, 1931, 18; November 28, 1931, 20). If that is true, the shooting was self-defense.

43. Williams, *Huey Long,* 485. Later, Earl said he was worried about kickbacks during construction or the capitol's design.

44. Hughes int., THWP.

45. *NYT,* November 9, 1930, 55.

46. Deutsch, "Paradox," 274–75.

47. Long, *EMK,* 239–40; Williams, *Huey Long,* 486–88; Bozeman int., THWP.

48. F. Davis, *Huey Long,* 26–27; "Virginia's Road Problem," speech of January 6, 1923, box 397, HBP.

49. Deutsch, "Paradox," 270; Gamble int., THWP.

50. Anders int., THWP.

51. R. White, *Kingfish,* 129.

52. *NYT,* March 20, 1932, 54.

53. Long, *EMK,* 240–41.

54. Williams, *Huey Long,* 546.

55. Sharp, "Study of the Counter-Cyclical Aspects of Total Government Fiscal Policy, 1929–1940," 203–10.

56. Hair, *Realm,* 210.

57. F. Davis, *Huey Long,* 11–12.

58. *NYT,* December 27, 1930, 22.

59. R. White, *Kingfish,* 117; Williams, *Huey Long,* 488–89.

60. Hair, *Realm,* 208–9; *Chicago Tribune,* April 23, 1932, 16; *NYT,* April 24, 1932, 26. The secretary of State was a member of a disbursing board for the PSC. She promptly voted to prevent it from operating (Deutsch, "Paradox," 269).

61. R. White, *Kingfish,* 121.

62. Williams, *Huey Long,* 483; Long, *EMK,* 227–34, reprinting *New Orleans Item* article of September 18, 1930.

63. Williams, *Huey Long,* 523; Long, *EMK,* 232.

64. Long, *EMK,* 235; R. White, *Kingfish,* 121.

65. Williams, *Huey Long,* 522. Harris wanted the whole cent from the tax, but Huey said, "If I did, you'd want two cents. When you can get a bushel, you want a barrel. No. Half a cent is all I can do right now."

## 14. LSU

1. Long, *EMK,* 184–86, 246–47.

2. Williams, *Huey Long,* 493.

3. Mann, *Kingfish U,* 28–29, 49–54.

4. Box 14: 457–59, HPLP.

5. Mann, *Kingfish U,* 55–56.

6. R. White, *Kingfish,* 147–48; Mann, *Kingfish U,* 58–59.

7. Williams, *Huey Long,* 497–98.

8. Frey and Middleton ints., THWP.

9. Long, *EMK,* 247.

10. Mann, *Kingfish U,* 64, 70–71. Everett led the tick eradication drive that passed the bill Huey vetoed in 1928 (box 1: 5, 13, CMP).

11. Williams, *Huey Long,* 500–502 (quote at 502); R. White, *Kingfish,* 270–71; Heilman, *Southern Connection,* 12.

12. Frey int., THWP.

13. Warren, "*All the King's Men:* The Matrix of Experience," 163.

14. Williams, *Huey Long,* 503.

15. Williams, *Huey Long,* 504–5.

16. Williams, *Huey Long,* 506–8.

17. Long, *EMK,* 247–48.

18. Bauer int., THWP.

19. Deutsch, "Paradox," 271–72.

20. *NYT,* February 3, 1931, 20.

21. Long, *EMK,* 271–72.

22. Williams, *Huey Long,* 489–91.

23. Williams, *Huey Long,* 514, 517–18.

24. Mann, *Kingfish U,* 230.

25. Jeansonne, *Messiah,* 95.

26. Williams, *Huey Long,* 518–20. F. Davis, *Huey Long,* 38–40. *NYT,* September 29, 1935, 162. Mann states that 6,065 students were enrolled for the 1935–36 school year (*Kingfish U,* 226).

27. R. White, *Kingfish,* 124–26.

28. "Death Valley Dorms," *Daily Reveille,* April 27, 2005; Mann, *Kingfish U,* 129.

29. R. White, *Kingfish,* 125.

30. Mann, *Kingfish U,* 168.

31. Heilman, *Southern Connection,* 11.

32. Heilman, *Southern Connection,* 24.

33. McSween, "Huey Long At His Centenary."

34. Heilman, *Southern Connection,* 35–36. Cutrer, *Parnassus,* 176, 180, 204–12.

35. R. White, *Kingfish,* 124; McSween, "Huey Long At His Centenary."

36. Warren, "*All the King's Men:* The Matrix of Experience."

37. Heilman, *Southern Connection,* 24.

38. Cutrer, *Parnassus,* 70, 78, 87, 110.

39. Long, *EMK,* 266–70, reprinting excerpts from several newspapers.

40. R. White, *Kingfish,* 129.

41. Williams, *Huey Long,* 437–39. Hair, *Realm,* 211–12. Jeansonne, *Messiah,* 100–101. *NYT,* February 17, 1931, 52; February 18, 1931, 6; February 19, 1931, 17; February 20, 1931 3; February 23, 1931, 3; February 26, 1931, 19; March 1, 1931, 57; March 5, 1931, 2. *Chicago Tribune,* March 3, 1931, 3 (including picture of Huey in a kitchen with various chefs); May 6, 1932, 20 (Chef Pierre Berard says potlikker is "atrocious" and he would like a "good hot argument" with Huey).

42. Weinzweig, "Potlikker."

43. R. White, *Kingfish,* 130.

44. *NYT,* March 26, 1931, 39; May 19, 1932, 28.

45. *NYT,* May 25, 1931, 2.

46. Williams, *Huey Long,* 514–15, 500.

47. R. White, *Kingfish,* 123–24, 126.

48. Williams, *Huey Long,* 515–16, 517.

49. Mann, *Kingfish U,* 39, 42, 97, 133, 165, 223, 231, 244.

50. Williams, *Huey Long,* 492.

51. Frey int., THWP; Cutrer, *Parnassus,* 23–24.

52. Sindler, *Huey Long's Louisiana,* 104n23, quoting a non-Longite observer; Carter, *American Messiahs,* 15–16; Williams, *Huey Long,* 781.

53. Mann, *Kingfish U,* 167, 202–3.

54. Heilman, *Southern Connection,* 13, 21.

55. R. White, *Kingfish,* 126.

56. Warren, "*All the King's Men:* The Matrix of Experience," 161; Warren, "In the Time of 'All the King's Men,'" *NYT,* May 31, 1981, section 7, 9.

57. The publicity helped sell fifty thousand copies (R. White, *Kingfish,* 147–48).

58. *NOTP,* November 24, 1962, box 1: 33, RBLP.

59. Cutrer, *Parnassus,* 19. John Uhler to Baldwin (his attorney), November 5, 1931; John Uhler to Baldwin, November 6, 1931; draft ACLU news release, November 15, 1931; H. W. Tyler to John Uhler, November 30, 1931; John Uhler to A. Young, December 15, 1931; John Uhler to Arthur Sheldon, March 1, 1932, box 1: 1, JEUP.

60. R. White, *Kingfish,* 125; Jeansonne, *Messiah,* 95–96.

61. Tamny, "Extolling Jim Harbaugh's Virtues."

62. R. White, *Kingfish*, 126; Jeansonne, *Messiah*, 94.
63. R. White, *Kingfish*, 125.
64. L. Williams and Broussard ints., THWP.
65. Williams, *Huey Long*, 504; Hood int., THWP.
66. Bowman int., THWP.
67. R. White, *Kingfish*, 130–31.
68. Gottlieb int., THWP.
69. Cawthorn int., THWP; R. White, *Kingfish*, 126.
70. Heilman, *Southern Connection*, 12, 44.
71. McSween, "Huey Long At His Centenary."
72. Cutrer, *Parnassus*, 248–55.
73. Heilman, "Cutrer on the *Southern Review*," 40, 41–44.
74. Heilman, *Southern Connection*, 85–86; Cutrer, *Parnassus*, 234–55.

## 15. The Vision Thing

1. R. White, *Kingfish*, 129–30.
2. *NYT*, March 15, 1931, 53.
3. Williams, *Huey Long*, 526.
4. Gottlieb int., THWP.
5. Weiss int., THWP.
6. *MNS*, April 18, 1931, 1.
7. Williams, *Huey Long*, 548–49; Carleton, *Politics and Punishment*, 111–12.
8. Long, *EMK*, 270; *NYT*, June 5, 1931, 7.
9. Deutsch, "Paradox," 288.
10. Williams, *Huey Long*, 527.
11. *NYT*, August 16, 1931, 50; Deutsch, "Paradox," 291–92, 294.
12. *NYT*, July 12, 1931, 45; August 2, 1931, 48.
13. Long, *EMK*, 275–76.
14. Snyder, *Cotton Crisis*, xiii, xv–xvi; Snyder, "Huey Long and the Cotton-Holiday Plan," 133–60.
15. R. White, *Kingfish*, 126–27; Hair, *Realm*, 213–14.
16. Snyder, *Cotton Crisis*, 3–16.
17. Snyder, *Cotton Crisis*, 17–32.
18. *CT*, August 14, 1931, 8; August 28, 1931, 3.
19. Williams, *Huey Long*, 531 (seven cotton growing states); R. White, *Kingfish*, 127 (twelve). *CT*, August 14, 1931, 8 (fourteen states: Texas, Georgia, Arkansas, Mississippi, North Carolina, Tennessee, Arizona, Missouri, Alabama, California, South Carolina, Florida, Oklahoma, and Louisiana).
20. HPL to Ross S. Sterling, August 16, 1931, RRSS; *NYT*, August 17, 1931, 34.
21. Snyder, *Cotton Crisis*, 37–38; Hair, *Realm*, 239; Williams, *Huey Long*, 535.
22. Malone, *Hattie and Huey*, 1. *NYT*, August 18, 1931, 6; August 23, 1931, 37. Snyder, *Cotton Crisis*, 39–40.
23. Malone, *Hattie and Huey*, 1–2 and note 5; Snyder, *Cotton Crisis*, 40–43.
24. Ross S. Sterling to HPL, August 21, 1931, RORS.
25. HPL to Ross S. Sterling, August 24, 1931, RORS; Snyder, *Cotton Crisis*, 43–45.
26. Judge Dupre said it was unconstitutional, but then abstained when the vote was taken (R. White, *Kingfish*, 128). Another legislator spoke against it but changed his vote to

present a united front (*CT,* August 27, 1931, 9, August 28, 1931, 3; *NYT,* August 28, 1931, 12, August 30, 1931, 2).

27. Snyder, *Cotton Crisis,* 45–53, 92; Williams, *Huey Long,* 532–33.

28. *CT,* September 5, 1931, 4.

29. Snyder, *Cotton Crisis,* 93–98.

30. Hair, *Realm,* 215–16.

31. Snyder, *Cotton Crisis,* 101.

32. Sterling, *Ross Sterling, Texan,* 168. *CT,* September 9, 1931, 13; September 12, 1931, 16. *NYT,* September 5, 1931, 23.

33. Snyder, *Cotton Crisis,* 99–102.

34. *NYT,* September 6, 1931, 39.

35. *CT,* August 26, 1931, 18; August 29, 1931, 16; August 30, 1931, 19.

36. *NYT,* September 13, 1931, 57.

37. Brinkley, *Voices of Protest,* 39.

38. *NYT,* September 8, 1931, 44.

39. *CT,* October 4, 1931, 14.

40. Snyder, "Huey Long and the Cotton-Holiday Plan," 156.

41. Jeansonne, *Messiah,* 102. *CT,* September 15, 1931, 14. *NYT,* September 11, 1931, 7; September 12, 1931, 2; September 13, 1931, 57; September 15, 1931, 4; September 17, 1931, 1. Snyder, *Cotton Crisis,* 102–7, 111–12.

42. Jeansonne, *Messiah,* 102; *CT,* August 31, 1931, 7; Snyder, *Cotton Crisis,* 63–72, 103; 78 CR 3972 (Byrd).

43. Snyder, "Huey Long and the Cotton-Holiday Plan," 147.

44. Schlesinger, *Age of Roosevelt: The Coming of the New Deal,* 71–83. Commenting on criticism that Huey "never once confronted the really significant problems" of tenancy and sharecropping, Alex McManus asked, "Who did?" ("Sharing the Hate," 17).

45. Jeansonne, *Messiah,* 102; *CT,* August 28, 1931, 12.

46. Louisiana Constitution, Art. 6, Sec. 14, allowed prohibiting the cultivation of crops (Snyder, *Cotton Crisis,* 57–59).

47. *Horne v. United States Dept. of Agriculture,* 576 U.S. 351 (2015).

48. Snyder, "Huey Long and the Cotton-Holiday Plan," 149–50.

49. Brinkley, *Voices of Protest,* 39; *NYT,* September 27, 1931, 78.

50. *CT,* September 18, 1931, 15.

51. Daniel, review of *Cotton Crisis,* by Snyder, 441–43.

52. Snyder, "Huey Long and the Cotton-Holiday Plan," 158–59.

53. "No More Cotton?" *Time,* August 31, 1931.

54. Snyder, "Huey Long and the Cotton-Holiday Plan," 160.

55. R. White, *Kingfish,* 138. Hair, *Realm,* 216–17, 239. Williams, *Huey Long,* 533–35. *NYT,* September 18, 1931, 25; October 11, 1931, 31.

56. *CT,* January 13, 1931, 10.

57. Williams, *Huey Long,* 488; *Newton Record,* May 22, 1930, 1.

58. *NYT,* August 16, 1931, 31;Williams, *Huey Long,* 510–11; *CT,* August 23, 1931, 6. Huey phoned frequently to check on their reception during the trip (Hood int., THWP).

59. Williams, *Huey Long,* 511–12.

60. *NYT,* January 5, 1932, 22.

61. *NYT,* July 27, 1931, 19 (Broussard).

62. Williams, *Huey Long,* 540–43.

63. Hair, *Realm,* 222.

64. Harris, *Kingfish,* 102. *CT,* October 16, 1931, 16. *NYT,* October 14, 1931, 1 ("opera bouffe"); October 15, 1931, 1–2.

65. *NYT,* October 16, 1931, 7; October 17, 1931, 13.

66. *NYT,* October 25, 1931, 59; October 30, 1931, 36.

67. *CT,* October 16, 1931, 16.

68. R. White, *Kingfish,* 134. *NYT,* October 15, 1931, 1–2; October 20, 1931, 26.

69. *NYT,* November 4, 1931, 12; November 19, 1931, 13.

70. Williams, *Huey Long,* 528.

71. Hair, *Realm,* 219; Williams, *Huey Long,* 566; Deutsch, "Paradox," 330.

72. Deutsch, "Paradox," 288.

73. Long, *EMK,* 261–62.

74. Knott int., THWP.

75. Larcade int., THWP.

76. Leche int., THWP. In *Dubuisson v. Long,* 143 So. 494 (La 1932), it was alleged that Huey dictated the transfer of a failing bank's assets to a new bank, but the lawsuit was not pursued.

77. Long, *EMK,* 242–45; Williams, *Huey Long,* 543–45; 77 CR 5269–70.

78. Hair, *Realm,* 223.

79. R. White, *Kingfish,* 137–38; Williams, *Huey Long,* 536–38.

80. Williams, *Huey Long,* 539–40.

81. Sindler, *Huey Long's Louisiana,* 77–80.

82. Hair, *Realm,* 225–26. *NYT,* January 10, 1932, 35; January 20, 1932, 3. R. White, *Kingfish,* 138–39.

83. *NYT,* January 23, 1932, 8.

84. *CT,* January 21, 1932, 9.

85. Long, *EMK,* 280, 284, 287–88.

86. *CT,* January 27, 1932, 5. *NYT,* January 26, 1932, 5; January 27, 1932, 3; January 31, 1932, 3; February 2, 1932, 3.

87. *NYT,* January 30, 1932, 6.

88. *CT,* January 30, 1932, 11; *NOTP,* February 1, 1932, 1; Long, *EMK,* 288.

89. *BRA,* February 2, 1932, 2; February 3, 1932, 1; February 5, 1932, 1; February 6, 1932, 1; March 15, 1932, 1; April 6, 1932, 1.

90. *NYT,* January 31, 1932, 8.

91. *NOTP,* February 7, 1932, 7; Williams, *Huey Long,* 555.

92. Williams, *Huey Long,* 489.

93. Jeansonne, *Messiah,* 105.

94. Patterson, "Mastering the Senate Maze."

95. *BRA,* February 10, 1932, 2.

96. *CT,* February 12, 1932, 27. *NYT,* February 12, 1932, 30. Long shot a duffer's 128 (*BRA,* February 12, 1932, 1; *NOTP,* February 12, 1932, 11, 12).

97. *NOTP,* February 7, 1932, 4.

98. *BRA,* February 17, 1932, 19; February 24, 1932, 11.

99. *NOTP,* February 12, 1932, 3.

100. *BRA,* February 14, 1932, 1; *NOTP,* February 14, 1932, 1.

101. *NOTP,* February 27, 1932, 11.

102. F. Davis, *Huey Long,* 10.

103. Sindler, *Huey Long's Louisiana,* 41–44.

104. P. Kendall, *Louis XI,* 296.

105. Sindler, *Huey Long's Louisiana*, 40–45; Schott, "Huey Long," 141–45; Howard, *Political Tendencies*, 217–27.

106. Schott, "Huey Long," 141; Barry, *Rising Tide*, 111–13, 218–19.

107. Harris, *Kingfish*, 112–13.

108. Sindler, *Huey Long's Louisiana*, 44–45.

109. 75 CR 1185–87; 75 CR 3660–70.

110. 75 CR 12,521.

111. F. Davis, *Huey Long*, 240–42.

112. Jeansonne, *Messiah*, 4.

113. Mayer, *Political Career of Floyd B. Olson*, 242–44, 259; Key, *Southern Politics*, 27n8 (pay-as-you-go road construction postponed Virginia's rural development for twenty years).

114. Sansing, "Paul B. Johnson Sr."

115. Sindler, *Huey Long's Louisiana*, 40–45 (quote at 45); Howard, *Political Tendencies*, 217–27.

116. Williams, "Politics of the Longs," 28.

117. Long, *EMK*, 280–84.

118. Jennings, "Some Policy Consequences of the Long Revolution," 225–46.

## 16. Magnificent Defiance

1. Much of this chapter and a portion of the following one are based on my article "Mastering the Senate Maze," 321–72. *CT*, January 22, 1932, 12. *NYT*, January 24, 1932, 36. Senator Carter Glass was also on alert—for another "demagogue" (letters between Charles T. Wortham and Glass, May 14, 1931; May 18, 1931, box 47: 19, CGP).

2. R. White, *Kingfish*, 140–41; *NYT*, January 25, 1932, 3.

3. Hamblin, "Mapped History of Taking a Train Across the United States."

4. *CT*, January 26, 1932, 3. *NYT*, January 26, 1932, 5. Huey's views on FDR probably reflected those of Harvey Couch (Burton K. Wheeler to Louis Howe, February 2, 1932, PPF 2337, FDRL).

5. *NYT*, January 26, 1932, 5, 22; January 31, 1932, 137. Watson, *As I Knew Them*, 304.

6. Historycomestolife, "Huey Long (1893–1935)."

7. Reconstruction Finance Corporation Act, 72nd Congress, H.R. 7360, 4.

8. 75 CR 2632–41, 2645.

9. 75 CR 2642.

10. *CT*, January 28, 1932, 4; *NYT*, January 28, 1932, 2, 20.

11. 75 CR 2790–92 (1932).

12. 75 CR 3313–23 (1932).

13. 75 CR 3939, 4008 (1932).

14. *NYT*, February 10, 1932, 22.

15. *CT*, February 7, 1932, 19; *NYT*, February 5, 1932, 5; *NOTP*, February 7, 1932, 4; *BRA*, February 6, 1932, 1.

16. Adams, *Epic of America*, 404: the American Dream is "that dream of a land in which life should be better and richer and fuller for every man [later editions changed this to everyone], with opportunity for each according to ability or achievement."

17. Cullen, *The American Dream*, 7; "What the Man Behind the 'American Dream' Really Meant."

18. Adams, *Epic of America*, 344, 410–14.

19. *BRA*, March 4, 1932, 1.

20. Box 2: 37 and 39, HPLP.

21. 75 CR 4682 (excellent question of Senator Herbert but Senator Norris followed up); 4769 (question to Wheeler); 4773 (Senator George denied need for Huey's amendment); 4775 (question of Norris, answered); 4776–77 (describing potential injunction against restaurant sympathetic to strikers, but no response from senators); 4778 (question of King; answer by Wagner), 4778–80 (Connally supported making "threats" actionable in injunction actions; Huey thought this was covered by other criminal laws); 4917–18 (inconsequential question of Wagner).

22. 75 CR 4985 (present at start of day), 4996 (start of debate); absent from later roll calls.

23. *BRA*, March 15, 1932, 1.

24. *NOTP*, February 1, 1932, 1.

25. *BRA*, February 6, 1932, 1.

26. Huey supposedly disgusted Smith because of his racial attitudes (Finan, *Alfred E. Smith*, 297–98), hard to credit given Smith's friendship with racist Democratic southern politicians. Smith supported a national sales tax that Huey opposed.

27. *NYT*, March 4, 1932, 21; *CT*, March 12, 1932, 12, reprinting editorial of *New York Herald Tribune*.

28. *NOTP*, March 11, 1932, 6.

29. *BRA*, March 15, 1932, 1.

30. *NYT*, March 16, 1932, 32; March 20, 1932, 54. *NOTP*, March 16, 1932, 1.

31. *NOTP*, March 23, 1932, 1.

32. *NOTP*, March 24, 1932, 1; *BRA*, March 24, 1932, 1.

33. *BRA*, March 25, 1932, 1; *NOTP*, March 25, 1932, 1.

34. *NOTP*, March 26, 1932, 1, 7 (letter to creditors).

35. *BRA*, March 29, 1932, 2.

36. 75 CR 5987–89, 5991–92.

37. *CT*, March 22, 1932, 2; 75 CR 6538–45.

38. 75 CR 6628–29.

39. 75 CR 6648; *CT*, March 23, 1932, 5.

40. 75 CR 7192 (oil wells), 7193 (interruption of Thomas), 7196 (further interruption, better received), 7196 (interruption ignored).

41. 75 CR. 6636–37; *NYT*, March 23, 1932, 1, 16.

42. 75 CR 7372–77.

43. *Baltimore Sun*, April 5, 1932, clipping in box 2: 6, Devol Collection on Huey P. Long.

44. *NYT*, April 5, 1932, 1, 18. *CT*, April 5, 1932. Harrison conceded that he might change his views after committee study (75 CR 7378–81).

45. 75 CR 7535–37, 7574–75.

46. *CT*, April 8, 1932, 25 (with picture); April 9, 1932, 1. *NYT*, April 8, 1932, 6. *BRA*, April 9, 1932, 2.

47. 75 CR 7660, 7665.

48. 75 CR 7746.

49. 75 CR 7879.

50. 75 CR 8556; *NYT*, April 22, 1932, 2.

51. 75 CR 8124–25.

52. *NYT*, April 17, 1932, 32.

53. 75 CR 8671–73.

54. Lafferty to HPL, April 28, 1932; *Cleveland Plain Dealer*, April 24, 1932, 4, box 1: 2, RBLP. Potlikker was served at lunch.

55. 75 CR 8687–88, 9110.
56. 75 CR 9212–20 (entire debate).
57. Darrell St. Claire, OHI, SHO.
58. R. White, *Kingfish,* 144; Weller, *Joe T. Robinson,* 121, 131, 132–37, 166.
59. 75 CR, 9217.
60. 75 CR, 9220.
61. *NYT,* April 30, 1932, 1; *CT,* April 30, 1932, 1.
62. R. White, *Kingfish,* 145.
63. *NYT,* May 1, 1932, 51; May 22, 1932, 123.
64. Maloney int., THWP; Christenberry int., THWP.
65. 75 CR 4907–12 (Connally), 5076 (Barkley), 5228 (Harrison), 5383 (McKellar advocating economy), 4383 (Robinson on economy bill).
66. 75 CR 10394.
67. 75 CR 10549–54.
68. *Reading Eagle,* May 1, 1932, 3; *NYT,* May 1, 1932, 26.
69. 75 CR 9453. *NYT,* May 4, 1932, 2. The subheading: "He Returns to Attack" (with list of Robinson's corporate clients).
70. *CT,* May 4, 1932, 8.
71. K. Davis, *FDR,* 390, 394.
72. Neal, *Happy Days,* 26–36, 115–18.
73. Neal, *Happy Days,* 81–95. While conservative on race relations, Garner had denounced the Klan in 1922.
74. Neal, *Happy Days,* 65–79; 75 CR 1562–63 (article).
75. Neal, *Happy Days,* 96–107.
76. Neal, *Happy Days,* 133–39.
77. Neal, *Happy Days,* 38–40.
78. *BRA,* February 6, 1932, 1.
79. Schlesinger, *Age of Roosevelt: The Crisis,* 289.
80. Long, *EMK,* 301–3. Wheeler and Healy, *Yankee,* 284–85. Burton K. Wheeler, CUOHP, int. 1, March 18, 1968, by Paul Hopper, 15–16.
81. *CT,* May 6, 1932, 5. *NYT,* May 7, 1932, 3. Norris agreed with Huey that concentration of wealth diminished mass purchasing power (75 CR 9616).
82. Long, *EMK,* 298; 75 CR 10,872 (article of *New York Herald Tribune).*
83. Compare 75 CR 8282–84 with 75 CR 9969–70. Wagner later justified Robinson's new bills because conditions had worsened since February and the legislation had been improved (75 CR 12513–16).
84. *CT,* May 11, 1932, 15.
85. *NYT,* May 22, 1932, 51.
86. 75 CR 10062–68.
87. *CT,* May 13, 1932, 6.
88. *NYT,* May 13, 1932, 13. Huey might have gotten more press, but Charles Lindbergh's kidnapped baby was found dead that day, which dominated the news.
89. Williams, *Huey Long,* 563.
90. *NYT,* May 8, 1932, 52.
91. Brinkley, *Voices of Protest,* 43; Jeansonne, *Messiah,* 106.
92. Weller, *Joe T. Robinson,* 106–8. Weller was unable to determine why Robinson left his prior firm.
93. *CT,* May 14, 1932, 6; May 15, 1932, 8. *NYT,* May 15, 1932, 39.

94. 75 CR 10281–10304 (1932) (poem at 10301–10302).

95. *Santa Fe New Mexican,* May 21, 1932, 4.

96. *NYT,* May 17, 1932; *CT,* May 17, 1932, 1.

97. Huey favored an amendment, appealing to Norris that it would smoke out the opponents. Huey thought too fast; Norris voted against it. The next day, Huey offered an amendment for the same purpose. This time, Norris spoke and voted for it (75 CR 10272–75, 10295–96, and 10390–99, 10420–21).

98. Patterson, "Mastering the Senate Maze," 368.

99. *NYT,* April 8, 1932, 20. Beals, *Story of Huey Long,* 232.

100. *NYT,* May 17, 1932, 8.

101. *NYT,* May 18, 1932, 1, 10. 75 CR 10399, 10421, 11588 (Huey voted yes by telegram).

102. M. Friedman, *Capitalism and Freedom,* 56–74, 128–30.

103. 75 CR 10526–57 (first day), 10617–77 (second day, beginning with Tydings), 10748–82 (third day and vote).

104. 75 CR 10626.

105. 75 CR 10685.

106. M. Friedman, *Capitalism and Freedom,* 129 (he "takes the individual, not the nation or citizen of a particular nation, as his unit.").

107. Neal, *Happy Days,* 181.

108. 75 CR 10668–69, 10676–77.

109. 75 CR 10750–52. Foreign oil production cost $1.03 less per barrel than domestic production. The tax was $0.42 per barrel.

110. 75 CR 10756–61.

111. 75 CR 10662–63, 10808–11 (1932).

112. *CT,* May 29, 1932, E3.

113. Williams, *Huey Long,* 565; 75 CR 13471–83, 13485–87 (1932).

## 17. Nominating a President

1. Harris, *Kingfish,* 247–48.

2. *NYT,* May 15, 1932, 54. *BRA,* May 16, 1932.

3. *NOTP,* April 23, 1932, 1.

4. Talbot int., THWP.

5. *BRA,* May 28, 1932, 1; May 31, 1932, 1. *NOTP,* May 22, 1932, 1, 12 (nine revenue bills); May 30, 1932, 1 (tax program goal to raise $4 million).

6. *NOTP,* June 7, 1932, 7.

7. *CT,* June 1, 1932, 18. *NYT,* July 3, 1932, 49. *BRA,* June 2, 1932, 1.

8. *NYT,* June 3, 1932, 1. *CT,* June 3, 1932, 9. *NOTP,* June 3, 1932, 2; June 4, 1932, 3.

9. *CT,* June 4, 1932, 11.

10. *NOTP,* June 8, 1932, 1.

11. Long, *EMK,* 299.

12. *BRA,* June 18, 1932, 1, 6. *NOTP,* June 23, 1932, 1; July 14, 1932, 4.

13. *CT,* June 8, 1932, 13. *NYT,* June 15, 1932, 21. *BRA,* June 7, 1932, 1; June 9, 1932, 1; June 10, 1932, 1; June 15, 1932, 1; June 16, 1932, 2; June 17, 1932, 1, 12. *NOTP,* June 3, 1932, 2; June 10, 1932, 1; June 11, 1932, 1; June 14, 1932, 1; June 15, 1932, 1.

14. *CT,* June 14, 1932, 16.

15. *BRA,* June 9, 1932, 1; June 11, 1932, 1. *NOTP,* June 8, 1932, 1. Williams, *Huey Long,* 570–71.

16. *NOTP,* June 19, 1932, 1; June 22, 1932, 2.

17. *NYT,* July 3, 1932, 49.

18. 75 CR 13443–46. 79 CR 150–59.

19. *BRA,* June 12, 1932, 1; *NOTP,* June 11, 1932, 1.

20. Williams, *Huey Long,* 574–76. *BRA,* June 16, 1932, 1; June 17, 1932, 6.

21. *CT,* June 23, 1932, 5; June 24, 1932, 5; June 25, 1932, 2.

22. *NOTP,* June 20, 1932, 1; June 21, 1932, 11.

23. *NOTP,* May 3, 1932, 1; June 14, 1932.

24. 75 CR 13010–11, 13443–46, 13485–87.

25. *NYT,* June 21, 1932, 45; *BRA,* June 21, 1932, 1; *NOTP,* June 21, 1932, 1.

26. 75 CR 13471–83, 13485–87.

27. *CT,* June 22, 1932, 6. *NYT,* June 22, 1932, 8; June 23, 1932, 11 (picture). *Kingsport Times,* September 12, 1935, 1 (Thorssen). Williams, *Huey Long,* 576.

28. Farley, *Behind the Ballots,* 114.

29. Farley, *Behind the Ballots,* 112. *NOTP,* June 28, 1932, 1; June 30, 1932, 1.

30. Farley, *Behind the Ballots,* 116–18.

31. *NYT,* June 23, 1932, 1; June 24, 1932, 1 (nine prominent leaders spoke against the rule); June 28, 1932, 1, 12 (Roosevelt favored rule change in several statements after Huey's action; Wheeler and Dill along with Huey swept the conferees off their feet); June 27, 1932, 11; June 29, 1932, 1 (Huey and Dill prompted abolition movement without consulting Roosevelt).

32. Neal, *Happy Days,* 228–29; Oulahan, *The Man Who . . . ,* 86.

33. Long, *EMK,* 306–11; *NYT,* June 27, 1932, 11; *BRA,* June 23, 1932, 1; Neal, *Happy Days,* 228–29.

34. Wheeler and Healy, *Yankee,* 286. Neal, *Happy Days,* 229–31. Farley, *Behind the Ballots,* 124–25. *NYT,* June 25, 1932, 7; June 28, 1932, 12. *BRA,* June 26, 1932, 1; June 28, 1933, 1. *NOTP,* June 25, 1932, 2; June 28, 1932, 1.

35. *CT,* June 28, 1932, 3.

36. Neal, *Happy Days,* 231–33; Oulahan, *The Man Who . . . ,* 83.

37. Hair, *Realm,* 244. *NYT,* June 26, 1932, 24; June 27, 1932, 11.

38. Oulahan, *The Man Who . . . ,* 82; *NYT,* June 25, 1932, 5.

39. Neal, *Happy Days,* 228.

40. *CT,* June 30, 1932, 6.

41. *CT,* June 26, 1932, 5; *NYT,* June 26, 1932, 24.

42. *NYT,* June 26, 1932, 22.

43. Long, *EMK,* 304–5; Neal, *Happy Days,* 226; Farley, *Behind the Ballots,* 125; *NYT,* June 26, 1932, 23.

44. *NYT,* June 30, 1932, 16.

45. Austin int., THWP.

46. *CT,* June 26, 1932, 5; June 27, 1932, 3; June 28, 1932, 5; June 29, 1932, 3.

47. *NYT,* June 25, 1932, 6; June 26, 1932, 24.

48. Hair, *Realm,* 244–45; *NYT,* June 29, 1932, 15.

49. Williams, *Huey Long,* 578.

50. Neal, *Happy Days,* 225.

51. Wheeler and Healy, *Yankee,* 285–86; *NOTP,* June 29, 1932, 1, 2.

52. Williams, *Huey Long,* 579–81; Neal, *Happy Days,* 233; *NYT,* June 29, 1932, 1, 14, 16.

53. *NOTP,* June 29, 1932, 1, 2. *CT,* June 29, 1932, 5, 8, 12; July 8, 1932, 6.

54. Neal, *Happy Days,* 235.

55. Neal, *Happy Days,* 177–81.

56. Mike Conner supported Newton Baker (Farley, *Behind the Ballots,* 118, 143–45, 152; Stokes, *Chip Off My Shoulder,* 321).

57. Neal, *Happy Days,* 269–70. Joe Robinson didn't attend the convention (75 CR 13601).

58. Neal, *Happy Days,* 273–94, 302; Farley, *Behind the Ballots,* 131–36, 144–51.

59. Ortiz, *Beyond the Bonus March,* 21–65. 75 CR 1159, 2233–37, 6564, 7193–96, 9617–18, 12958–84, 13140–46, 13224–74.

60. Neal, *Happy Days,* 259–62; Oulahan, *The Man Who . . . ,* 98, 107; *NYT,* July 1, 1932, 1, 15.

61. Neal, *Happy Days,* 305; Oulahan, *The Man Who . . . ,* 134; *NYT,* July 3, 1932, 8.

62. *NYT,* June 30, 1932, 16.

63. Neal, *Happy Days,* 310; 75 CR 14637–38 (acceptance speech).

64. *NYT,* July 5, 1932, 4.

65. Austin int., THWP.

66. *BRA,* June 24, 1932, 1; June 25, 1932, 1. *NOTP,* June 24, 1932, 1; June 26, 1932, 1.

67. Williams, *Huey Long,* 569–71; R. White, *Kingfish,* 154–55; Hair, *Realm,* 238. Talbot int., THWP. LeBlanc biographies don't mention a fire.

68. *NOTP,* July 2, 1932, 2.

69. *NOTP,* June 30, 1932, 1.

70. *NOTP,* June 17, 1932, 1, 9.

71. *NOTP,* May 24, 1932, 3.

72. *NOTP,* July 10, 1932, 1; July 13, 1932, 1.

73. 75 CR 14647–51; *NOTP,* July 7, 1932, 6.

74. 75 CR 14736–68, 14959; *NOTP,* July 13, 1932, 1.

75. 75 CR 15007; *NYT,* June 21, 1932, 45.

76. 75 CR 15080.

77. *NYT,* November 23, 1932, 12. *NOTP,* July 12, 1932, 3; July 14, 1932, 4; July 15, 1932, 6.

78. 75 CR 15341.

79. 75 CR 15437–38.

80. Williams, *Huey Long,* 555–56, 560; Hair, *Realm,* 234–37; Jeansonne, *Messiah,* 104–6; White, *Kingfish,* 142–44; Brinkley, *Voices of Protest,* 42–45; Cushman, "Huey Long's First Session," 131. See, generally, Patterson, "Mastering the Senate Maze," 321–72.

81. 75 CR 10549–57 (At 10555, getting a laugh at Huey's expense by playing on the word "gas").

82. 75 CR 10801 (Senator Jones appreciating Huey's supportive interruption).

83. 75 CR 10912–16.

84. Leche int., THWP.

85. 75 CR 10928.

## 18. An Over-the-Border Raid

1. *NYT,* June 19, 1932, 83.

2. Malone, *Hattie and Huey,* 3.

3. Wheeler and Healy, *Yankee,* 280–81; Deutsch, "Hattie and Huey," 7, 88.

4. Williams, *Huey Long,* 586; Malone, *Hattie and Huey,* 6–7.

5. Malone, *Hattie and Huey,* 17.

6. 75 CR 15192–93.

7. Malone, *Hattie and Huey*, 18.
8. R. White, *Kingfish*, 156.
9. Weiss int., THWP.
10. Malone, *Hattie and Huey*, 40.
11. Malone, *Hattie and Huey*, 19–22. Other progressives believed this. See 75 CR 1472–94 (remarks of Blaine, Brookhart, and Wheeler).
12. Weiss and Peltier ints., THWP.
13. Malone, *Hattie and Huey*, 23–24, 40–41.
14. Malone, *Hattie and Huey*, 24–25. One of these circulars was framed and hung in President Clinton's office.
15. Williams, *Huey Long*, 583.
16. Brinkley, *Voices of Protest*, 49; Williams, *Huey Long*, 588.
17. Malone, *Hattie and Huey*, 26.
18. Malone, *Hattie and Huey*, 42, picture after page 112.
19. Malone, *Hattie and Huey*, 25–26.
20. Ortiz, *Beyond the Bonus March*, 56.
21. MacArthur, *Reminiscences*, 96–97; Lynd and Lynd, *Middletown in Transition*, 110, 117.
22. Malone, *Hattie and Huey*, 27–28.
23. Brinkley, *Voices of Protest*, 49; *NYT*, July 31, 1932, 32.
24. Malone, *Hattie and Huey*, 44.
25. Malone, *Hattie and Huey*, 67–68; Williams, *Huey Long*, 587–88.
26. Malone, *Hattie and Huey*, 57–58 (quoting Deutsch in a 1952 interview), 81.
27. Deutsch, "Hattie and Huey," 90.
28. Deutsch's stenographic report, box 20: 3, HBDP. Unless otherwise noted, this is the source for the report of Huey's speech.
29. See Deutsch, "Hattie and Huey," 90.
30. Malone, *Hattie and Huey*, 83. The stenographic report rendered the same idea a little differently.
31. Lincoln had used this illustration (*Lincoln Evening Journal*, March 8, 1935, 8).
32. Malone, *Hattie and Huey*, 76–78 and note 11.
33. Malone, *Hattie and Huey*, 54. The rest of the quoted remarks in this chapter are not from the stenographic report.
34. Malone, *Hattie and Huey*, 55. Compare Donald Trump's expulsion of a baby from one of his rallies in August 2016.
35. Malone, *Hattie and Huey*, 86.
36. Roden int., THWP.
37. Malone, *Hattie and Huey*, 66; Deutsch, "Paradox," 14–15, 35–36, 38, 40.
38. Malone, *Hattie and Huey*, 68–69.
39. Malone, *Hattie and Huey*, 56.
40. Malone, *Hattie and Huey*, 48. "After the broadcast, Mayor McLaughlin was deluged with letters announcing reception of the broadcast. . . . A card received from . . . Iowa, was typical. . . . It said, 'We got quite a kick when Senator Long said you used up about $20 worth of his time advertising Hot Springs.'"
41. Malone, *Hattie and Huey*, 57.
42. Malone, *Hattie and Huey*, 75–76.
43. Malone, *Hattie and Huey*, 93.
44. Malone, *Hattie and Huey*, 65, 67–68.
45. Malone, *Hattie and Huey*, 60–61.

46. Williams, *Huey Long,* 590–91; Malone, *Hattie and Huey,* 95.
47. Malone, *Hattie and Huey,* 33, 89–91.
48. Malone, *Hattie and Huey,* 86.
49. Brinkley, *Voices of Protest,* 51.
50. Malone, *Hattie and Huey,* 52.
51. Malone, *Hattie and Huey,* 73; Williams, *Huey Long,* 590.
52. Malone, *Hattie and Huey,* 49.
53. Malone, *Hattie and Huey,* 56–60.
54. Brinkley, *Voices of Protest,* 49; Roden int., THWP.
55. Malone, *Hattie and Huey,* 60.
56. Malone, *Hattie and Huey,* 86–87.
57. Williams, *Huey Long,* 591–92; Hair, *Realm,* 248 and note 43.
58. Williams, *Huey Long,* 593.
59. Hattie lost three counties where Huey spoke: one was a machine-dominated county, one was where they hastily added a speech and lacked the time to draw a crowd, and the other was the hometown of an opponent (Malone, *Hattie and Huey,* 98).
60. Brinkley, *Voices of Protest,* 53.
61. *NYT,* July 31, 1932, 54; August 2, 1932, 6; August 9, 1932, 2; August 10, 1932, 5; August 11, 1932, 4; August 13, 1932, 3; August 15, 1932, 2.
62. *NYT,* August 14, 1932, 101.
63. Deutsch, *Hattie and Huey,* 7.
64. T. White, *Making of the President, 1960,* 164.
65. Williams, *Huey Long,* 597.
66. Williams, *Huey Long,* 594–98.
67. *NYT,* September 11, 1932, 38; September 25, 1932, 47.
68. Williams, *Huey Long,* 598–600.
69. Williams, *Huey Long,* 763–66.
70. Williams, *Huey Long,* 765–66.
71. *NYT,* October 6, 1932, 17.
72. Roosevelt's other dangerous man was General Douglas MacArthur (Tugwell, *Democratic Roosevelt,* 349).
73. Farley, *Behind the Ballots,* 170–71.
74. *NYT,* October 11, 1932, 10.
75. *NYT,* November 1, 1932, 12; November 3, 1932, 14; November 5, 1932, 1; November 6, 1932, 13.
76. Rose McConnell Long int., THWP. She was not asked why she declined.
77. *NYT,* October 10, 1932, 1; Williams, *Huey Long,* 601; McSween, "T. Harry Williams."
78. Williams, *Huey Long,* 602 and note 2.
79. Mann, *Kingfish U,* 139.
80. *NYT,* October 16, 1932, 30.
81. Williams, *Huey Long,* 603; *DAL,* October 22, 1932, 2.
82. *Bismarck Tribune,* October 24, 1932, 4.
83. *DAL,* October 24, 1932, 8; *NYT,* October 25, 1932, 11; "Hubert Humphrey's Year in Baton Rouge."
84. *Lincoln Star,* October 21, 1932, 1; Weiss int., THWP.
85. *HN,* October 26, 1932, 1.
86. *CT,* October 28, 1932.
87. *HN,* October 27, 1932, 10.

88. *HN*, October 26, 1932, 1.
89. *NYT*, October 25, 1932, 11.
90. *DAL*, October 24, 1932, 8.
91. *SEP*, October 12, 1935.
92. *DAL*, October 25, 1932, 6.
93. Brinkley, *Voices of Protest*, 46.
94. *CT*, October 21, 1932, 3. In a separate story on the same page, Republican leaders said Nebraska and Iowa were safe for Hoover.
95. Williams, *Huey Long*, 602–3; Farley, *Behind the Ballots*, 170–71.

## 19. The Senate Strikes Back

1. Chandler, *America's Greatest Depression*, 25, 36. (The exact figures in millions: $87,814, $40,130, $50,423, and $28,993.)
2. Chandler, *America's Greatest Depression*, 36–45.
3. Chancler, *America's Greatest Depression*, 57. (Figures in millions: $13,985, $7,081. For net income: $7,024 to $3,012.)
4. Hofstadter, *American Political Tradition*, chap. 11 ("Herbert Hoover and the Crisis of American Individualism").
5. 75 CR 10919–20, 11537–38.
6. Letter, May 31, 1932, probably to N. D. Mackenzie, box 1C10: Mackenzie, N. D., LFP.
7. Leuchtenburg, *Franklin D. Roosevelt*, 10–11; Hofstadter, *American Political Tradition*, 329.
8. Schlesinger, *Age of Roosevelt: The Crisis*, 420, 427–28.
9. *Lewiston Daily Sun*, October 31, 1932, 4.
10. *NYT*, November 9, 1932, 1, 6.
11. *CT*, December 1, 1932, 3. Connally met with Roosevelt and was appalled that he was discussing economy in government (Schlesinger, *Age of Roosevelt: The Crisis*, 452). Along with other southern leaders, Huey proposed James Thomson, publisher of the *New Orleans Item*, as secretary of war (*NYT*, December 1, 1932, 1–2).
12. 76 CR 54–59.
13. *CT*, December 7, 1932, 9; *NYT*, December 7, 1933, 14; Williams, *Huey Long*, 620; Brinkley, *Voices of Protest*, 54.
14. 76 CR 156.
15. *NYT*, December 9, 1933, 3.
16. 76 CR 176–96, 254–72, 308–34, 372–93, 424–28, 483–89, 538–65, 612–31.
17. 76 CR 876–85.
18. *CT*, December 17, 1932, 4; *NYT*, December 17, 1932, 10.
19. 76 CR 1156–69.
20. 76 CR 1279–83.
21. 76 CR 1284–94.
22. *CT*, January 6, 1933, 6; *NYT*, January 6, 1933, 27.
23. Schlesinger, *Age of Roosevelt: The Politics of Upheaval*, 296.
24. Berg, *Wilson*, 300, 315–16. 76 CR 1938–39.
25. Chandler, *America's Greatest Depression*, tables 5–6, 83–84.
26. Williams, *Huey Long*, 620–21; Brinkley, *Voices of Protest*, 55–56.
27. Deutsch, "Paradox," 326.
28. Williams, *Huey Long*, 621; *CT*, January 6, 1933, 6; 76 CR 1330–36.

29. 76 CR 1404–21, 1449–64, 1555–81 (comments on protecting bank depositors at 1575), 1623–49; Williams, *Huey Long*, 624, 626.

30. *NYT*, January 13, 1933, 1. Huey prepared a redline of the old law with the new, a useful reference to senators (76 CR 1646; denial of a recess is at 1649; 76 CR 1724–56).

31. *CT*, January 14, 1933, 7 (Thomas holding the floor).

32. *NYT*, January 14, 1933, 15.

33. *NYT*, January 15, 1933, 112 (editorial); January 17, 1933, 18 (editorial). *CT*, January 14, 1933, 8; January 15, 1933, 2. 76 CR 1782–1802.

34. *NYT*, January 17, 1933, 12 (story); January 17, 1933, 18 (editorial).

35. *CT*, January 17, 1933, 6; January 20, 1933, 2. 76 CR 1835–67.

36. *CT*, January 29, 1933, 9. The Illinois Bankers Association said 90 percent of Illinois Banks opposed branch banking (statement of December 31, 1932, WEBP, LOC, box 788: Branch Banking).

37. *CT*, January 18, 1933, 6. Glass had received an anonymous letter that made this charge (box 159: 25, CGP).

38. 76 CR 1797 (Huey's resolution); 76 CR 1937.

39. 76 CR 1993–2003, 2074–96.

40. 76 CR 1933–35.

41. *NYT*, January 19, 1933, 1. Robinson responded, to no applause, that the election returns had removed the Republican leaders who were now cooperating with the filibuster (76 CR 1987–2027).

42. 76 CR 2140–45, 2158, 2205–8, 2263–94, 2349–2407.

43. Williams, *Huey Long*, 625; *NYT*, January 20, 1933, 1.

44. Williams, *Huey Long*, 619; Schlesinger, *Age of Roosevelt: The Crisis*, 452; *NYT*, January 22, 1933, 56. Other progressives were unsure of Roosevelt, too (box IA43: Phil '33 (various letters), LFP. But Roosevelt told LaFollette that he viewed Democratic Senate leaders as out of harmony with his party's policies (Bob to Phil, January 24, 1933, box IA43: Phil '33, LFP).

45. *CT*, February 2, 1933, 7; box 119: 7 (newspaper clipping), CGP. Glass refused the Treasury job, telling Roosevelt that it was on the advice of his doctor, but telling the public that he would be of more use to Roosevelt in the Senate (box 119: 51, CGP).

46. 76 CR 2263–66, 2275–83.

47. *NYT*, January 22, 1933, 113.

48. Scroop, "Anti-Chain Store Movement," 925–49.

49. 76 CR 1333–34.

50. 76 CR 1575, 2289–92.

51. 76 CR 1845–49. *NYT*, January 24, 1933, 5; January 25, 1933, 1.

52. *CT*, January 15, 1933, 3; January 17, 1933, 6 (refusing to say what he wanted with respect to farm aid). *NYT*, January 16, 1933, 2.

53. Johnson to Archibald, January 21, 1933, Diary Letters, HJP. I suspect that Roosevelt also denounced Huey to LaFollette (Robert LaFollette to Phil LaFollette, January 20, 1933, IA43: Phil 33, LFP).

54. Hofstadter, *American Political Tradition*, 326–27. Friedman and Schwartz, *Monetary History*, 309–11 and note 9, remark that a merger plan might have saved the Bank of the United States. Whether Roosevelt failed to intervene to save it or failed to prevent abuses before they occurred, it is safe to infer that banking was not his strong suit.

55. *NYT*, January 27, 1933, 5.

56. *NYT*, January 29, 1933, 85.

57. *CT*, January 22, 1933, 5.
58. Williams, *Huey Long*, 624.
59. *NYT*, January 22, 1933, 56.
60. *CT*, March 3, 1933, 15; March 7, 1933, 8.
61. *CT*, January 29, 1933, G1.
62. Williams, *Huey Long*, 559.
63. Williams, *Huey Long*, 604–18, describes the Overton investigation.
64. Williams, *Huey Long*, 607. *CT*, October 7, 1932, 20.
65. *NYT*, January 28, 1933, 3; January 31, 1933, 9. 76 CR 2809–19.
66. *NYT*, February 8, 1933, 2; February 10, 1933, 2.
67. Williams, *Huey Long*, 616; R. White, *Kingfish*, 212.
68. Deutsch, "Paradox," 40. *NYT*, February 6, 1933, 10; February 7, 1933, 27.
69. *NYT*, February 12, 1933, 61.
70. *NYT*, February 7, 1933, 8.
71. Williams, *Huey Long*, 613; *NYT*, February 9, 1933, 23 (5 percent of salaries collected).
72. Williams, *Huey Long*, 610.
73. See Chemerinsky, *Constitutional Law*, sec. 3.9, 324–26.
74. *CT*, February 15, 1933, 11. *NYT*, February 15, 1933, 3; February 17, 1933, 6.
75. *CT*, February 16, 1933, 9.
76. Williams, *Huey Long*, 610–11.
77. *CT*, February 18, 1933, 11; February 20, 1933, 5
78. *NYT*, February 7, 1933, 8; February 9, 1933, 23; February 11, 1933, 6; February 12, 1933, 25; February 14, 1933, 2; February 15, 1933, 3; February 16, 1933, 42.
79. *CT*, February 25, 1933, 10.
80. Harris, *Kingfish*, 121, reprinting the circular after 184.
81. Rose McConnell Long int., THWP.
82. Williams, *Huey Long*, 655–58.
83. Wheeler and Healy, *Yankee*, 289–91.
84. Long, *EMK*, 318–19, reprinting the article.
85. *CT*, February 22, 1933, 9; 76 CR 4993–5002.
86. 76 CR 4657–90.
87. *CT*, March 2, 1933, 2. *NYT*, March 2, 1933, 2; May 10, 1933, 7.
88. *CT*, March 26, 1933, 4; March 28, 1933, 2; April 2, 1933, 6.
89. *CT*, March 5, 1933, 5.
90. Williams, *Huey Long*, 796; Wheeler and Healy, *Yankee*, 289–91; Talbot int., THWP.
91. *CT*, March 22, 1933, 13; June 10, 1933, 2.
92. Moley, *27 Masters of Politics*, 227–28.
93. *NYT*, February 19, 1933, 35.

## 20. A Right to Complain

1. K. Davis, *FDR*, 26; *NYT*, March 8, 1933, 2. Chandler, *America's Greatest Depression*, 83.
2. "Franklin Delano Roosevelt—First Inaugural Address."
3. K. Davis, *FDR*, 28.
4. *NYT*, February 23, 1933, 9 (Frankfurter); Schlesinger, *Age of Roosevelt: The Crisis*, 451 (Tugwell).
5. K Davis, *FDR*, 30, 32, 36–37, 65–67; Schlesinger, *Age of Roosevelt: The Coming of the New Deal*, 1–3.

6. 77 CR 6–7 (1933). Leuchtenburg, *Franklin D. Roosevelt,* 44 and note 7. Schlesinger, *Age of Roosevelt: The Coming of the New Deal,* 5.

7. Friedman and Schwartz, *Monetary History,* 420–34; Chandler, *America's Greatest Depression,* 145–60; K. Davis, *FDR,* 42–56, 60–62; Schlesinger, *Age of Roosevelt: The Coming of the New Deal,* 4–8, 426; Leuchtenburg, *Franklin D. Roosevelt,* 42–48.

8. Friedman and Schwartz, *Monetary History,* 421–22; K. Davis, *FDR,* 26, 42–49, 52–53; Smith, *FDR,* 306.

9. *NYT,* March 10, 1933, 10.

10. 77 CR 46–48, 50–52 (1933).

11. Schlesinger, *Age of Roosevelt: The Coming of the New Deal,* 5–8; LaFollette/Costigan to FDR, March 9, 1933, box 1 C 11: 1933 FDR, LFP.

12. There were 6,080 national and 824 state banks in the Federal Reserve System and 11,890 state banks outside of the system (*NYT,* March 12, 1933, 1, 7; *CT,* March 12, 1933, 7; 77 CR 45–67).

13. 77 CR 54–59.

14. *NYT,* March 11, 1933, 1.

15. 77 CR 128; *CT,* March 10, 1933, 1.

16. 77 CR 178–93; *NYT* clipping of March 13, 1933, box 47: 9, CGP.

17. 77 CR 178–79.

18. *CT,* March 12, 1933, 7; *NYT,* March 12, 1933, 1, 7; 77 CR 174–92.

19. Franklin D. Roosevelt Day By Day, March 11, 1933; Williams, *Huey Long,* 628 and note 9, citing *NOTP,* March 12, 1933.

20. "Franklin Delano Roosevelt—First Fireside Chat."

21. 77 CR 249.

22. 77 CR 422.

23. 77 CR 331–32.

24. Smith, *FDR,* 316.

25. Leuchtenburg, *Franklin D. Roosevelt,* 44n6, 47–48.

26. 77 CR 422–23, 426–33, 540–41.

27. 77 CR 789–814 (1933).

28. For example, Smith, *FDR,* 311.

29. Moley, *After Seven Years,* 133.

30. K. Davis, *FDR,* 57–59, 63–64; Schlesinger, *Age of Roosevelt: The Coming of the New Deal,* 10–11; Leuchtenburg, *Franklin D. Roosevelt,* 45; Ortiz, *Beyond the Bonus March,* chap. 3.

31. Box 426: letters of February 2, 6, and 27, 1933, HBP; K. Davis, *FDR,* 58–59, 63–64; *NYT,* March 17, 1933, 19.

32. 77 CR 274–76.

33. 77 CR 310–70.

34. Christenberry int., THWP.

35. *NOTP,* March 14, 1933, 1; 77 CR 442–71.

36. 77 CR 539, 625.

37. 77 CR 438–39 (Huey suggested that Insull, a fugitive in Greece, be appointed ambassador to Greece).

38. *NYT,* March 26, 1933, 7.

39. *NYT,* April 1, 1933, 13; April 16, 1933, 64.

40. 77 CR 786–89.

41. Form letter, File 2–2, Part A. Correspondence, 1923–85, RBLP.

42. 77 CR 2211–12 (speech of April 21, 1933). The April 4, 1933, speech was not transcribed, but a recording of it is in the LOC, 200–2491.

43. K. Davis, *FDR*, 68; 77 CR 861–62.

44. K. Davis, *FDR*, 77–79; Schlesinger, *Age of Roosevelt: The Coming of the New Deal*, 336–41; Smith, *FDR*, 319–22; 77 CR. 860–62, 936.

45. LFP, box IC10: Thomas A. Duncan, letter of March 17, 1933.

46. K. Davis, *FDR*, 79–80; 77 CR 1020–42; *CT*, March 31, 1933, 2; *NYT*, March 31, 1933, 4.

47. On the farm bill, see Schlesinger, *Age of Roosevelt: The Coming of the New Deal*, 27–84; K. Davis, *FDR*, 69–76; Chandler, *America's Greatest Depression*, 209–21. The processing tax was ruled unconstitutional. *United States v. Butler*, 297 U.S. 1 (1936).

48. Chandler, *America's Greatest Depression*, 219.

49. 77 CR 1380–93.

50. 77 CR 1441–47. *CT*, April 11, 1933, 2; April 15, 1933, 8. *NYT*, April 12, 1933, 1–2.

51. 77 CR 1474–79; *CT*, April 12, 1933, 4; 77 CR 1949.

52. K. Davis, *FDR*, 77–79; Schlesinger, *Age of Roosevelt: The Coming of the New Deal*, 340–41; Smith, *FDR*, 322.

53. 77 CR 1481–90.

54. Letter to Fola, April 3, 1933, box IA43: Phil '33, LFP.

55. Schlesinger, *Age of Roosevelt: The Coming of the New Deal*, 42, 64–67; K. Davis, *FDR*, 69–76.

56. 77 CR 1548–70; 1618–49.

57. 77 CR 1741–42; 1817–20; Schlesinger, *Age of Roosevelt: The Coming of the New Deal*, 42.

58. *CT*, April 12, 1933, 4; April 16, 1933, 5; April 17, 1933, 1. 77 CR 1817–44, 1864.

59. *NYT*, April 17, 1933, 1; April 29, 1933, 1, 4. 77 CR 1820–26.

60. K. Davis, *FDR*, 104–7; Schlesinger, *Age of Roosevelt: The Coming of the New Deal*, 41–42.

61. 77 CR 2073–82.

62. 77 CR 1978, 2164–66.

63. 77 CR. 2457–60 (*Washington Post* editorial advocating inflation), 2569–70 (*Philadelphia Record* article of April 13, 1933, supporting Huey); *CT*, April 21, 1933, 14 (editorial).

64. 77 CR 2522–31(Robinson's remark at 2523).

65. K. Davis, *FDR*, 110; Schlesinger, *Age of Roosevelt: The Coming of the New Deal*, 41–44, 249; 77 CR 2401–9, 2522–62.

66. 77 CR 3114–24; Leuchtenburg, *Franklin D. Roosevelt*, 51.

67. 77 CR 2460–67; Schlesinger, *Age of Roosevelt: The Coming of the New Deal*, 44.

68. K. Davis, *FDR*, 108; Schlesinger, *Age of Roosevelt: The Coming of the New Deal*, 233–52.

69. Ivy Lee Papers, box 29: 17, int. FDR, December 1933.

70. 77 CR 1113–28.

71. 77 CR 1172–98 (canning industry exempted despite Huey's opposition); 77 CR 1244–48, 1282–94, 1333–48 (1933).

72. 77 CR 1249, 1348; K. Davis, *FDR*, 95–103, 115–22, 132–45; Smith, *FDR*, 330–31; Leuchtenburg, *Franklin D. Roosevelt*, 55–58. Roosevelt's secretary of labor, Frances Perkins, testified for Black's bill, advocating some flexibility in its application (K. Davis, *FDR*, 100–103).

73. K. Davis, *FDR*, 95–99; Schlesinger, *Age of Roosevelt: The Coming of the New Deal*, 90–92, 95; *NYT*, April 16, 1933, 1; *CT*, April 16, 1933, 5.

74. 77 CR 1460–61,1538, 1546, 1779, 1806–8, 2845, 3210 (article by Frank Kent in the *Baltimore Sun*).

75. *CT*, May 12, 1933, 4. *NYT*, May 12, 1933, 25; May 15, 1933, 2. 77 CR 3318–24, 3329. Those favoring Huey's resolution aside from Overton and Huey included Senators Bone and Dill (Washington), Caraway (Arkansas), Cutting (New Mexico), Frazier and Nye (North Dakota), McGill (Kansas), Neely (West Virginia), Norris (Nebraska), LaFollette (Wisconsin), Pope (Idaho), Reynolds (North Carolina), A. Robinson (Indiana), Shipstead (Minnesota), Trammel (Florida), Wheeler (Montana). Significant nonvoters included Borah (Idaho), Clark (Missouri), McAdoo (California), Russell (Georgia), and Thomas (Oklahoma). Significant no votes included Connally, Couzens, and Johnson, who had voted for the Couzens amendment for higher taxes on the rich in May 1932, and Senator Black, who said that labor was paid too little and capital too much (77 CR 10275).

76. Schlesinger, *Age of Roosevelt: The Coming of the New Deal*, chaps. 6–7.

77. 77 CR 3800 (*New Orleans Item* editorial for $6 billion in public works and higher taxes for the rich).

78. 77 CR 5174–85. Continuing: "Every crime of monarchy is in there, without one of the things that would give it credit. It is a combination of everything that is impracticable and impossible under the socialist system, and everything that has robbed us in disasters under the monarchial system."

79. 77 CR 5152–67 (initial explanation); 5229–49 (planning remark at 5245).

80. 77 CR 5247–48.

81. 77 CR 5249–50.

82. 77 CR 5152–86, 5251–53.

83. *NYT*, August 16, 1933, 15.

84. 77 CR 5278–5307, 5383–89.

85. 77 CR 5308.

86. 77 CR 5420–25.

87. 77 CR 5764.

88. K. Davis, *FDR*, 132–45; Schlesinger, *Age of Roosevelt: The Coming of the New Deal*, 96–102; Williams, *Huey Long*, 634–36; 77 CR 5764–68, 5834–61.

89. 77 CR 3725.

90. 77 CR 4148–52, 4159, 4166–82.

91. 77 CR 4260–66, 4583–90.

92. *CT*, May 31, 1933, 2; *NYT*, May 28, 1933, 1.

93. 77 CR 1020, 1028–30, 1038, 1160 (American Bankers Association criticizing Wall Street oligarchy), 1821 (Wheeler: thousands of banks still closed and billions still frozen), 2079 (Connally: inflating by $6 billion just regains ground lost because $6 billion is frozen in closed banks), 2084–85 (Vandenberg: 250 Michigan banks still closed; Huey said we need a more liberal administration by the Federal Reserve Board), 2434–35 (Capper: resolutions of fourteen midwestern states complaining about closed banks, concentration of wealth, and Wall Street control destroying state banks), 4260–65 (Huey's speech "Our Constant Rulers").

94. Friedman and Schwartz, *Monetary History*, 420–34, 432 (money supply of 1933), 302 (1929 money supply); Chandler, *America's Greatest Depression*, 145–56.

95. 77 CR 4839–43.

96. 77 CR 4995.

97. 77 CR. 5082–85. Huey cited the *Philadelphia Record* dated June 6, 1933. *NYT*, June 7, 1933, 4.

98. NYT, June 10, 1933, 1, 7 (contains questions and answers). Hostile critic T. O. Harris thought Huey got the best of *Colliers* (*Kingfish*, 280–81).

99. *NYT*, June 7, 1933, 4; June 14, 1933, 1. *CT*, June 14, 1933, 5 (objections of Huey and Vandenberg solved).

100. K. Davis, *FDR*, 150; Friedman and Schwartz, *Monetary History*, 434–40. Hofstadter, *American Political Tradition*, 327. Schlesinger, *Age of Roosevelt: The Coming of the New Deal*, 443. Leuchtenburg, *Franklin D. Roosevelt*, 60 (deposit insurance a New Deal "stepchild").

101. K. Davis, *FDR*, 113–14; 77 CR 4406–19, 4429–41.

102. K. Davis, *FDR*, 82–90; Schlesinger, *Age of Roosevelt: The Coming of the New Deal*, 440–42; 77 CR 2978, 2996–3000 (text).

103. K. Davis, *FDR*, 90–93; 77 CR 2777, 2808.

104. *CT*, June 12, 1933, 3; Ortiz, *Beyond the Bonus March*, chap. 3.

105. Schlesinger, *Age of Roosevelt: The Coming of the New Deal*, 14–15.

106. 77 CR 1705–6 (complaints of Illinois Governor Horner), 2311–16 (Wheeler complaints), 2457–58 (*Washington Post* editorial: Economy Bill was mistake), 2672–75 (articles relating suicides; Douglas letter when he was running for office opposing veteran benefit cuts), 3106 (North Carolina resolution protesting closure of veterans facility), 3210–11 (1933) (*Dayton Jour*nal article: veteran gave up his government-issued clothes and left the office in his underwear, 3393, 3388–90 (letters revealing hardships and distress), 3474 (California petition for veterans benefits), 4237–91 (George, Huey, Reed, and Clark criticizing the economy bill), 4406 (article on suicides), 4457 (Johnson petitions to restore benefits), 4599–4620 (several said that when passed it was promised that the Economy Bill would be administered liberally); 77 CR 4658–68.

107. 77 CR 5378–79.

108. 77 CR 4811.

109. 77 CR 4662.

110. 77 CR 4667.

111. K. Davis, *FDR*, 147–48.

112. 77 CR 5731–62.

113. 77 CR 6014–15.

114. K. Davis, *FDR*, 146–48; 77 CR 6130.

115. 77 CR 6108–10.

## 21. Inevitable Conflict

1. R. White, *Kingfish*, 181–82.

2. Schlesinger, *Age of Roosevelt: The Crisis*, 457–58.

3. Friedman and Schwartz, *Monetary History*, 408, 410.

4. Galbraith, *Great Crash*, 182–86.

5. Galbraith, *Great Crash*, 78, 186–88. Stock market losers were a small percentage of the population but had provided most of the money that fueled investment and consumption.

6. Romer and Romer, "The Missing Transmission Mechanism," 66–72.

7. Chandler, *America's Greatest Depression*, 105–6; McElvaine, *The Great Depression*, 34–37, 83–84.

8. Telser, "The Reconstruction Finance Corporation and the Great Depression," 1–2; Telser, "Lessons from the United States Great Depression," 5. Telser says bank failures caused the Depression and the decline in the money supply was only a symptom of distress.

9. Leven, Moulton, and Warburton, *America's Capacity to Consume*, 54.

10. McElvaine, *The Great Depression*, 38–50 (maldistribution of wealth was the "taproot" of the Depression); Galbraith, *Great Crash*, chap. 9 (first probable cause).

11. Chandler, *America's Greatest Depression*, 15–29.

12. Smiley, "Some Austrian Perspectives," 162–63.

13. "Minsky's Moment."

14. Posner, *Crisis of Capitalist Democracy*, 115–16.

15. Smiley, "Some Austrian Perspectives," 145–55, and appendix, 167–69.

16. Posner, *Crisis of Capitalist Democracy*, 353–60; Geithner, *Stress Test*, 390–91, 413–15.

17. C. Romer, "What Ended the Great Depression?" 757–784.

18. Telser, "The Reconstruction Finance Corporation and the Great Depression," 1.

19. Chandler, *America's Greatest Depression*, 141, quoting Brown, "Fiscal Policy in the 'Thirties," 857–79.

20. K. Davis, *FDR*, 260.

21. Brinkley, *Voices of Protest*, 60.

22. Black, "Truth About FDR"; Black, "FDR's Triumph."

23. Schlesinger, *Age of Roosevelt: The Coming of the New Deal*, 112–16, 120–35, 152–76, quotes at 172 and 174; K. Davis, *FDR*, 250. Schlesinger, *Age of Roosevelt: The Politics of Upheaval*, 212–19.

24. Schlesinger, *Age of Roosevelt: The Coming of the New Deal*, 73.

25. K. Davis, *FDR*, 269.

26. Schlesinger, *Age of Roosevelt: The Coming of the New Deal*, 63–66, 71, 82–83.

27. K. Davis, *FDR*, 471–86, 490.

28. Schlesinger, *Age of Roosevelt: The Coming of the New Deal*, 11 (one paragraph on the Economy Act), 15 (one paragraph on the Economy Act).

29. Ortiz, *Beyond the Bonus March*, 75, 83.

30. *NYT*, June 10, 1933, 12 (editorial).

31. Farley has the meeting date wrong (*Behind the Ballots*, 238–49).

32. *NYT*, July 26, 1933, 5. Before their showdown, *Barron's* quoted Huey as saying Roosevelt "is a real salesman. Every time I go there he sells me a bill of goods. I don't like to go" (June 19, 1933). Forrest Davis said Huey looked "dazed" when he left the Roosevelt conference (*Huey Long*, 193).

33. Byrnes didn't mention Huey by name (James F. Byrnes to FDR, July 24, 1933, PPF 2786–2818, FDRPPF).

34. Williams, *Huey Long*, 636–37, 640.

35. Williams, *Huey Long*, 637, citing *NOTP*, August 23, 1933.

36. 77 CR 5599–5605.

37. *NYT*, April 23, 1933, 1, 7.

38. Roosevelt said that, if you eat with Huey, it had better be with a long spoon (R. White, *Kingfish*, 179). *CT*, April 15, 1933, 15; April 16, 1933, 8. *NYT*, April 14, 1933, 1. W. D. Robinson to FDR, April 12 and 13, 1933; letter from Oscar R. Whilden, April 15, 1933; letter from John M. Parker, April 21, 1933, in PPF 2337, FDRPPF.

39. *NYT*, April 18, 1933, 2.

40. *NYT*, May 31, 1933, 11. She died before the case concluded.

41. *NYT*, June 11, 1933, 6.

42. The 1940 Republican presidential nominee Wendell Willkie's hard drinking was seen as a sign of masculinity (Peters, *Five Days in Philadelphia*, 65).

43. Wheeler and Healy, *Yankee,* 283.
44. Malone, *Hattie and Huey,* 100.
45. Colman, *Mrs. Wheeler Goes to Washington,* 144–45.
46. Boulard, *Huey Long Invades,* 131.
47. Edmund Talbot int., THWP; Don Devol int., OHI, LSU.
48. *NYT,* June 4, 1933, 28; June 11, 1933, 33. Brinkley, *Voices of Protest,* 63–64.
49. *NYT,* April 15, 1933, 1–2.
50. Brinkley, *Voices of Protest,* 60; *CT,* April 12, 1933, 4.
51. *NYT,* October 8, 1933, 69.
52. *Time* magazine wrote: "To the Chicago convention which had just nominated him for President in 1932, Franklin D. Roosevelt made a speech of acceptance in which the following passage fairly raised the roof with applause: 'Throughout the nation men and women . . . look to us here for guidance and a more equitable opportunity to share in the distribution of national wealth.' *To most Chicago delegates those words were just mouth filling rhetoric, a noble sentiment to be approved but not literally practiced*" (April 1, 1935, 17–23 [emphasis added]).
53. Schlesinger, *Age of Roosevelt: The Coming of the New Deal,* 14; Smith, *FDR,* 311; Dallek, *Franklin D. Roosevelt,* 15. Wheeler and Healy, *Yankee,* 425; Neal, *Happy Days,* 68; Hofstadter, *American Political Tradition,* 327–28; Moley, *27 Masters of Politics,* 31–33.
54. FDR to Ray Stannard Baker, March 20, 1935, PPF 2337, FDRPPF.
55. Schlesinger, *Age of Roosevelt: The Coming of the New Deal,* 511–88.
56. R. White, *Kingfish,* 183.
57. Brinkley, *Voices of Protest,* 64.
58. Moley, *After Seven Years,* 395–96; Moley, *27 Masters of Politics,* 221.
59. Neal, *Happy Days,* 222, quoting Childs, *I Write from Washington,* 16–17.
60. *Daily Reporter,* September 10, 1935, 2. Vandenberg would raptly listen to Huey's speeches (Darrell St. Claire, OHI, SHO). Jeansonne, *Messiah,* 60.
61. Huey impressed Montana visitors to Wheeler's Senate office by comparing Senator Walsh to a guinea hen, a "very peculiar bird." Walsh dropped ideas as the guinea hen dropped eggs and Joe Robinson used a long-handled rake to collect them (Wheeler and Healy, *Yankee,* 283).
62. Congressman John J. O'Connor to THW, October 18, 1956, box 3: 21, RBLP (describing bull sessions in the hotel where Huey and other congressmen stayed).
63. Wheeler and Healy, *Yankee,* 282.
64. Smith, *FDR,* 71, 78.
65. Don Devol, int., OHI, LSU; George Maines to his mother, June 21, 1935 (buying some good books for Huey to read), RBLP, 1–30; Leche int., THWP.
66. Sokolsky, "Dr. Huey and Mr. Long." Huey was reading about the likely European War in September 1935. Cawthorn int., THWP.
67. R. White, *Kingfish,* 183; Anders int., THWP.
68. Krock, *Memoirs,* 167. This was a show Huey put on. He tried it on Leche, but Leche figured it out. While being dressed down over the phone, Leche said, "you have an audience?" Huey said yes and then goodbye (Leche int., THWP).
69. Hair, *Realm,* 240–41.
70. Wheeler and Healy, *Yankee,* 285. Louie Jones int., THWP.
71. Gottlieb int., THWP.
72. Don Devol, int OHI, LSU.

73. *NYT,* September 11, 1935, 17.

74. Fisher int., THWP.

75. Deutsch, "Paradox," 32; Peyton int., THWP.

76. Huey told Leche he berated one man to make sure he remained a good man (Leche int., THWP; Blanche int., THWP).

77. Sutton, *The No Asshole Rule,* chap. 6, "The Virtues of Assholes"; Caro, *Years of Lyndon Johnson: Means,* 239–40.

78. *CT,* February 10, 1935, 21; *Wisconsin State Journal,* September 15, 1935, 13.

79. Diaries of Henry Morgenthau Jr., January 1, 14, and 22, 1935, Ickes, *Secret Diary,* 606.

80. K. Davis, *FDR,* 210; Schlesinger, *Age of Roosevelt: The Coming of the New Deal,* 537.

81. Jeansonne, *Messiah,* 148.

82. Smith, *FDR,* 181.

83. Peterman int., THWP; Bauer int., THWP.

84. Burns, *Roosevelt,* 486–87 and note 19.

85. Williams, *Huey Long,* 759, quoting reporter Paul Y. Anderson in the *St. Louis Post Dispatch* of February 10, 1935.

86. Smith, *FDR,* 230–33; Dallek, *Franklin D. Roosevelt,* 101–3.

87. Roosevelt approved a Moley draft article relating to the London Conference without noticing it was inconsistent with Hull's position. While Moley says this evidenced Roosevelt's mediocre intellect, this should condemn Moley, who never pointed this out to Roosevelt (Moley, *After Seven Years,* 224–38 [conference], 270–77 [resignation], 280 [*Newsweek*]). Schlesinger, *Age of Roosevelt: The Coming of the New Deal,* 181–82, 207–8, 213–32. Dallek, *Franklin D. Roosevelt,* 161–65.

88. Lowitt, *Bronson M. Cutting,* 293–306; box 11: "Dear Partner" letter of February 7, 1935, February 1935, BCP.

89. Schlesinger, *Age of Roosevelt: The Politics of Upheaval,* 140–41; Ickes, *Secret Diary,* 217, 358–59; Lowitt, *Bronson M. Cutting,* 307–16.

## 22. The Kingfish Gets a Black Eye

1. *Collier's,* May 27, 1933, 20.

2. *NYT,* August 16, 1933, 15.

3. Williams, *Huey Long,* 640–41, and note 5, citing Lonergan, *Labor,* and Bealle, "Kingfishophobia." The papers of Ivy Lee—the publicist—at Princeton contain nothing about this. Huey believed Ivy Lee was an opponent, however, and investigated his ties to Hitler (Christenberry to G. Maines, October 8, 1934, RBLP, 3700, 1–30).

4. *CT,* June 25, 1933, 11. Williams, *Huey Long,* 654–60.

5. Long, *EMK,* 322. Eleven jurors tried to cite one juror and the newspaper for contempt for disclosing the workings of the grand jury, which are supposed to be secret (*CT,* August 2, 1933, 19; August 3, 1933, 16). *NYT,* August 3, 1933, 20.

6. Long, *EMK,* 329–30.

7. *NYT,* August 6, 1933, 50. The discrepancy was 18,000 votes. In Mayor Walmsley's precinct, the vote count changed from 177–68 to 59–154 (Williams, *Huey Long,* 658).

8. *CT,* December 20, 1933, 15.

9. *NYT,* August 23, 1933, 19.

10. Williams, *Huey Long,* 640–47; Hair, *Realm,* 259–60; R. White, *Kingfish,* 213; Brinkley, *Voices of Protest,* 70–71.

11. Williams, *Huey Long*, 641–42; Maines to Marvin MacIntyre, May 22, 1934, PFF 2337, FDRPPF; Maines to RBL, September 12, 1963, box 1: 33, RBLP.

12. A manuscript draft is in box 1: 24, HPLP.

13. Williams, *Huey Long*, 645.

14. *CT*, October 19, 1933, 10.

15. Williams, *Huey Long*, 644–47. *NYT*, October 19, 1933, 21; October 24, 1933, 1; December 17, 1933, 83.

16. Darrell St. Claire, OHI, SHO, 21, 24. Lyndon Johnson read it and told his friends that Huey was too radical (Caro, *Years of Lyndon Johnson: The Path*, 272).

17. Charles McCain, post of October 15, 2015.

18. Steel, *Walter Lippmann*, 314.

19. Liebling, *Earl of Louisiana*, 7–8.

20. Krock, *Memoirs*, 167.

21. Hair, *Realm*, 257–58.

22. *NYT*, August 23, 1933, 19.

23. Thurber, "Rough on Rats."

24. *NYT*, August 29, 1933, 1. Williams, *Huey Long*, 648–54. Hair, *Realm*, 258 (citing the *New York Herald Tribune*, August 30, 1933, and *Time* magazine, September 11, 1933, 16–17; one witness said, "Senator Long is just a pig!"). *CT*, September 1, 1933, 7; September 2, 1933, 1, 3. Reporter Adela Rogers St. John said later: "I liked [Huey] the night I met him at the Sands Point Club. He wasn't all that drunk, you know. I danced with him, and even sober men have difficulty dancing with me. He didn't" (St. Johns, *The Honeycomb*, 370). A Black newspaper, *the Chicago Defender*, reported the rumor that a Black musician had socked Huey for using racial slurs.

25. Butler, *War Is a Racket*.

26. Ortiz, *Beyond the Bonus March*, 87.

27. Ortiz, *Beyond the Bonus March*, 75–84 (radicalization), 88–89 and note 47 (convention speech), 90–93 (fury at Roosevelt's remark); *NYT*, August 30, 1933, 21; *CT*, August 30, 1933, 3.

28. *NYT*, August 30, 1933, 21; August 31, 1933, 16 (editorial), 18, 20; September 1, 1933, 3. *CT*, August 31, 1933, 5.

29. *CT*, September 1, 1933, 7. *NYT*, September 1, 1933, 3; September 21, 1933, 21.

30. Williams, *Huey Long*, 653 and note 9.

31. *Miami News*, August 29, 1934, 11.

32. Lynd and Lynd, *Middletown in Transition*, 497 and note 5.

33. *NYT*, September 10, 1933, 132.

34. *NYT*, September 14, 1933, 4. Williams, *Huey Long*, 670 and note 3. Paul Wooten letter of September 14, 1933 (claiming the circular was a ruse), OF 1403, container 1, FDROP.

35. *NYT*, October 1, 1933, 74.

36. *NYT*, October 4, 1933, 26.

37. Williams, *Huey Long*, 661–65; Hair, *Realm*, 261–63; R. White, *Kingfish*, 186–87; Brinkley, *Voices of Protest*, 67; *NYT*, November 5, 1933, 135 (summarizing several speeches and the crowd's reaction).

38. *NYT*, October 17, 1933, 9; October 19, 1933, 21.

39. *NYT*, October 22, 1933, 3.

40. Williams, *Huey Long*, 663 and note 9.

41. Hair, *Realm*, 262; Roden int., THWP.

42. *NYT,* November 3, 1933, 16.

43. *NYT,* November 10, 1933, 4.

44. *NYT,* November 11, 1933, 2; *CT,* November 11, 1933, 2.

45. *CT,* September 12, 1933, 16.

46. *CT,* September 28, 1933, 8.

47. *NYT,* November 19, 1933, 71.

48. *NYT,* November 15, 1933, 22.

49. *CT,* November 19, 1933, 9, 19 (picture of Connally climbing the fire escape to get in); November 26, 1933, 12; November 28, 1933, 14; November 29, 1933, 7.

50. *NYT,* November 16, 1933, 18; November 17, 1933, 3. *CT,* November 16, 1933, 3.

51. *NYT,* November 18, 1933, 18; November 19, 1933, 23. *CT,* November 21, 1933, 13.

52. *NYT,* November 22, 1933, 22; *CT,* November 21, 1933, 13. The seventy-five men weren't needed and were paid and sent home.

53. *NYT,* November 23, 1933, 3; November 26, 1933, 24; November 29, 1933, 13.

54. *NYT,* November 30, 1933, 38; *CT,* November 30, 1933, 24.

55. *NYT,* December 10, 1933, 81.

56. *CT,* November 21, 1933, 14.

57. *NYT,* November 23, 1933, 20.

58. Williams, *Huey Long,* 665–69.

59. *NYT,* November 29, 1933, 13; *CT,* December 4, 1933, 8.

60. *NYT,* December 1, 1933, 6.

61. *NYT,* December 4, 1933, 7.

62. *NYT,* December 5, 1933, 9; *CT,* December 4, 1933, 8.

63. *NYT,* December 6, 1933, 48; *CT,* December 6, 1933, 6.

64. *NYT,* December 7, 1933, 24.

65. *NYT,* December 17, 1933, 32.

66. *CT,* December 8, 1933, 19; December 9, 1933, 9. Williams, *Huey Long,* 668–69.

67. *NYT,* December 15, 1933, 23; *CT,* December 15, 1933, 30.

68. *NYT,* December 21, 1933, 2; *CT,* December 21, 1933, 12.

69. *NYT,* December 22, 1933, 7; *CT,* December 23, 1933, 8 (editorial: it wanted Huey removed, but worried that the IRS investigation was political).

70. Williams, *Huey Long,* 661–65; Hair, *Realm,* 260–63; R. White, *Kingfish,* 186–88.

71. Sharp, "Study of the Counter-Cyclical Aspects of Total Government Fiscal Policy," 181, 211–12.

72. *NYT,* December 16, 1933, 1.

73. *NYT,* December 25, 1933, 22.

74. *NYT,* December 8, 1933, 1; December 9, 1933, 34. *CT,* December 6, 1933, 31.

75. 78 CR 58 (antitrust), 60 (tax) (1934).

76. *NYT,* January 4, 1934, 3.

77. 78 CR 72–73 (1934); *CT,* January 5, 1934, 4.

78. Franklin D. Roosevelt Day By Day, January 8, 1934.

79. F. Davis, *Huey Long,* 206–7; 78 CR 3693–96.

80. Williams, *Huey Long,* 7, 639.

81. 78 CR 216–19.

82. 78 CR 194–96, 216–19.

83. *NYT,* January 9, 1934, 23; January 12, 1934, 34; January 17, 1934, 2, 26. *CT,* January 9, 1934, 1.

84. Williams, *Huey Long*, 669–75; Boulard, *Huey Long Invades*, 79–93; Hair, *Realm*, 264–65; R. White, *Kingfish*, 193–95.

85. R. White, *Kingfish*, 193; Boulard, *Huey Long Invades*, 82.

86. Williams, *Huey Long*, 673.

87. Boulard, *Huey Long Invades*, 85–87; Leche int., THWP.

88. *NYT*, January 23, 1934, 21.

89. Boulard, *Huey Long Invades*, 83–84.

90. 78 CR 3189 (1934); Field, "Politics," 72–73.

91. *CT*, January 17, 1934, 3; Boulard, *Huey Long Invades*, 88–89.

92. Boulard, *Huey Long Invades*, 91–92.

93. *CT*, January 24, 1934, 3; January 25, 1934, 9.

94. *NYT*, January 24, 1934, 1; February 3, 1934, 30. *CT*, January 28, 1934, 11.

95. Boulard, *Huey Long Invades*, 92.

96. Boulard, *Huey Long Invades*, 112.

97. *NYT*, January 26, 1934, 16; January 27, 1934, 30. *CT*, January 27, 1934, 11.

98. Burke showed up at his suite. Huey apologized: Burke was not as bad as the other Old Regulars. Burke handed him a bullet, his calling card. When asked, Burke said he had a gun in each pocket and would have shot Huey if he did not get the apology (Jack McGuire, letter to author, September 26, 2019).

99. 78 CR 699–714 (1934). *CT*, January 17, 1934, 3; January 18, 1934, 10 (editorial critical of the Connally report).

100. When Huey proposed a law to equalize election commissioners, the *Times-Picayune* opposed it (Leche int., THWP).

101. 78 CR 1552–67 (1934); Williams, *Huey Long*, 687.

102. Boulard, *Huey Long Invades*, 95–97; *CT*, February 2, 1934, 8.

103. Williams, *Huey Long*, 678–79.

104. Adams, *Select Correspondence*, 255–56.

105. Moley, *After Seven Years*, 308.

106. Telser, "The Veterans' Bonus of 1936," cited in Posner, *Crisis of Capitalist Democracy*, 114 and note 4.

## 23. The Command of the Lord

1. Williams, *Huey Long*, 686, 692–93. Huey incorporated Share-Our-Wealth and copyrighted "Every Man a King" (R. White, *Kingfish*, 197).

2. *NYT*, February 4, 1934, 123; *CT*, January 14, 1934, 88–89.

3. 78 CR 1920–21, 2088 (1934).

4. *NYT*, February 11, 1934, 37; March 2, 1934, 3.

5. *NYT*, March 3, 1934, 7.

6. Williams, *Huey Long*, 694, citing the *New York Sun*, *New York Herald-Tribune*, and the *Washington Post*, all March 3, 1934.

7. Schlesinger, *Age of Roosevelt: The Politics of Upheaval*, 230–33.

8. Coyle, "Recovery and Finance"; Coyle, "Decentralize Industry."

9. Long, "Share Our Wealth" pamphlet. The earliest version is contained in box 13: 18 of WBWC.

10. 78 CR 1920–21.

11. "Huey Pierce Long—Every Man a King," *American Rhetoric;* Safire, *Lend Me Your*

*Ears*, 696. The LOC has a recording of the speech. Huey used the word "Dago" (sympathetically); it provoked protests, and "Italian" was substituted in the reports (*Afro American*, March 16, 1935, 1, 2).

12. Frank Russell to Steve Early, February 13, 1934, PPF 2337, FDRPPF.

13. Reminiscences of Arthur Krock, CUOHC; notes contained in THWC, LSU.

14. Sindler, *Huey Long's Louisiana*, 84.

15. Ogilvy, *Confessions*, 121, quoting Samuel Johnson.

16. Brinkley, *Voices of Protest*, 74, 168; Schlesinger, *Age of Roosevelt: The Politics of Upheaval*, 11.

17. R. White, *Kingfish*, 198.

18. 78 CR 6187–93.

19. Box 2: 40, FBI Files on Huey Long.

20. R. White, *Kingfish*, 197 (twenty-five secretaries); Wall int., THWP (thirty secretaries).

21. Williams, *Huey Long*, 698. Examples in HPLP Series, 1912–93, undated, Part A. Correspondence, 1923–85, RBLP.

22. Jeansonne, *Minister*, 11–32.

23. The "most reasonable conclusion is that Smith flirted briefly with Pelley after resigning the pulpit [in Shreveport], developed grandiose plans, grew disillusioned quickly, and then denied any alliance" (Jeansonne, *Minister*, 28). Intriguingly, Don Devol's papers include a memorandum that says Smith was affiliated with Pelley (Devol Collection on Huey P. Long, box 2: 6); Brinkley, *Voices of Protest*, 171–72; Hair, *Realm*, 273–74.

24. G. Smith, "Or Superman?" 14–15.

25. Williams, *Huey Long*, 700; Brinkley, *Voices of Protest*, 172. R. White, *Kingfish*, 199.

26. Ainsworth, "Gerald L. K. Smith," YouTube.

27. Williams, *Huey Long*, 700.

28. Brinkley, *Voices of Protest*, 173.

29. R. White, *Kingfish*, 198–99.

30. Hair, *Realm*, 273.

31. Leche int., THWP.

32. Jeansonne, *Minister*, 33–45. Circulars advertising Smith's speeches make different claims about his crowds (April 29th says 125,000 people, May 5th says 200,000 people, June 5th says over a million). The towns he spoke in were too small to aggregate an audience of one million (Tim Landry, email to author, June 26, 2018).

33. Williams, *Huey Long*, 697.

34. Jeansonne, *Minister*, 37–40.

35. *NYT*, February 21, 1934, 6; 78 CR 2831–41, 2845.

36. 78 CR 2104; 78 CR 2195, 2197, 2198; 78 CR 2414.

37. 78 CR 2445–52; 78 CR 2492.

38. 78 CR 2489–90.

39. *NYT*, February 28, 1934, 1 (long story with roll call votes).

40. 78 CR 5572–73.

41. 78 CR 5573–5606; *CT*, April 1, 1934, 8.

42. 78 CR 672; 78 CR 3439. *CT*, January 11, 1934, 5; January 30, 1934, 3; January 26, 1934, 6; February 6, 1934, 15; February 10, 1934, 12; March 7, 1934, 23; March 8, 1934, 14; March 21, 1934, 16. *NYT*, February 6, 1934, 13; February 15, 1934, 18.

43. Williams, *Huey Long*, 687. *CT*, March 20, 1934, 6; March 21, 1934, 16 (editorial).

44. 78 CR 4231–35 (Norris); 78 CR 3978–94 (1934) (Wheeler).

45. *CT*, March 9, 1934, 12. 78 CR 4106–10, 4373–75 (Overton), 4379–87; 4399–4400.

46. 78 CR 603 and following; 78 CR 714; 78 CR 789 and many following days.
47. 78 CR 4253–57.
48. 78 CR 4260.
49. 78 CR 4475. The vote was forty-six to forty-two in favor, short of the two-thirds required.
50. *NOTP*, February 15, 1934, 9; H. Cummings to FDR, November 16, 1933; May 8, 1934, OF 300, DNC Box 46: 3, FDROF.
51. Confirmation of Daniel D. Moore to Be Collector of Internal Revenue, Hearing before a Subcommittee of the Committee on Finance, 73rd Congress, February 19, 1934.
52. *CT*, March 24, 1934, 15; 78 CR 5233–52.
53. *NYT*, March 31, 1934, 7; *CT*, March 31, 1934, 19.
54. 78 CR 5882–93.
55. *CT*, April 5, 1934, 2; *NYT*, April 5, 1934, 3.
56. *NYT*, April 6, 1934, 1.
57. 78 CR 5972–73 (LaFollette), 5977–84 (Bone), 5984–85 (Borah), 5985–96 (Huey).
58. 78 CR 6081–83.
59. 78 CR 6092–99.
60. 78 CR 6104–8.
61. *NYT*, April 6, 1934, 22; *CT*, April 6, 1934, 23.
62. Darrell St. Claire, OHI, 50–51, said he might have the original record in his basement, but the interviewer did not ask him for it.
63. *NYT*, April 7, 1934, 4; *CT*, April 7, 1934, 6.
64. R. White, *Kingfish*, 196.
65. Hair, *Realm*, 268 and note 46.
66. *NYT*, April 6, 1934, 22.
67. *NYT*, April 7, 1934, 14 (editorial).
68. 78 CR 6091.
69. 78 CR 6198–99, 6300, 6400–6402.
70. 78 CR 6232–38, 6479–82; *CT*, April 10, 1934, 6 (brief mention only).
71. 78 CR 6536–39, 8714, 10185–10886. Huey telegrammed Roosevelt that he was "ringing right" on this legislation and should not "give an inch" (HPL to FDR, May 16, 1934, PPF 2337, FDRPPF).
72. *NYT*, May 31, 1934, 16; 78 CR 9942–45.
73. *NYT*, June 3, 1934, 28; *CT*, June 3, 1934, 7.
74. Gillette, "Huey Long and the Chaco War," 293–311; *NYT*, August 19, 1934, 9; *CT*, August 19, 1934, 1. The fort was later recaptured by Bolivia, then recovered by Paraguay, and finally abandoned after the war. A city street in Asuncion is named after Huey, and a plaque commemorates his defense of Paraguay.
75. Williams, *Huey Long*, 713; R. White, *Kingfish*, 190; *NYT*, April 18, 1934, 16; *CT*, April 24, 1934, 17.
76. *NYT*, May 14, 1934, 2.
77. *NYT*, dispatch of May 10, 1934, published May 13, 1934, 73.
78. On the reconciliation with Earl, see Williams, *Huey Long*, 689–91.
79. Harris, *Kingfish*, 160–65; Boulard, *Huey Long Invades*, 100–102; Williams, *Huey Long*, 713–15; *CT*, May 14, 1934, 8; *NYT*, May 15, 1934, 13.
80. *CT*, May 4, 1934, 3.
81. *CT*, May 30, 1934, 7.
82. Williams, *Huey Long*, 688–89.
83. *NYT*, June 4, 1934, 1; June 14, 1934, 25 ("heirlooms include oriental rugs . . . a spun

gold card case, an inlaid tortoise shell patch box and a hair bracelet mounted in gold and with a pendant gold heart, symbol of a long-forgotten romance"). *CT,* June 14, 1934, 16 (editorial: "Delicate mahogany escritoires, inlaid with mother-of-pearl, silently told the story of many a love letter written on them by daughters of Dixie in crinolines"; the sale should "touch the heart and conscience of every American" because they were fighting a "desperate battle against corruption and misgovernment"), 17.

84. 78 CR 7804, 8205.

85. *CT,* May 24, 1934, 7.

86. *NYT,* May 2, 1934, 6; May 26, 1934, 5; June 5, 1934, 1.

87. *NYT,* May 4, 1934, 2; May 25, 1934, 8; June 10, 1934, 6. *CT,* June 10, 1934, 13.

88. 78 CR 5848.

89. 78 CR 10816–37.

90. 78 CR 10927–28.

91. *CT,* June 15, 1934, 3; 78 CR 11451–52.

92. 78 CR 7900–7907.

93. 78 CR 7992–8005, 8056–78, 8151 (motion to reconsider); *CT,* May 3, 1934, 8.

94. WEB to R. N. Reed, April 23, 1934 (FDR unalterably opposes); May 23, 1934 (leadership opposes), "Currency Question," April–May 1934, WEBP.

95. 78 CR 10184–85, 12063.

96. 78 CR 12062–72.

97. 78 CR 12055–60.

98. 78 CR 12074–77 (1934).

99. 78 CR 12083–12105 (1934).

100. Williams, *Huey Long,* 709–11.

101. 78 CR 12361. Nevertheless, some reported that Huey had coerced Robinson to back down (*Fairfield Daily Ledger,* June 19, 1934, 1).

102. 78 CR 12356–62, 12376.

103. *NYT,* June 20, 1934, 20.

104. 78 CR 12596.

105. 79 CR 9125.

106. 78 CR 6097.

107. Heilman, *Southern Connection,* 58–59.

## 24. No Quarter for the French Quarter

1. Boulard, *Huey Long Invades,* 103–5; Williams, *Huey Long,* 716; *NYT,* July 4, 1934, 10. Joe Fisher proposed a state-run lottery to raise $50 million annually (*CT,* June 21, 1934, 7).

2. Boulard, *Huey Long Invades,* 110.

3. *CT,* June 14, 1934, 17. Boulard, *Huey Long Invades,* 107–8.

4. *CT,* June 22, 1934, 3.

5. *CT,* June 27, 1934, 11.

6. Williams, *Huey Long,* 717–18, 721 (replacement of leaders).

7. Boulard, *Huey Long Invades,* 110–11.

8. R. White, *Kingfish,* 203–4; Williams, *Huey Long,* 721.

9. *NYT,* July 22, 1934, 56.

10. *NYT,* August 2, 1934, 1, 14.

11. *NYT,* July 4, 1934, 10; *CT,* July 4, 1934, 7. Alice Lee Grosjean's office was put in charge of the licenses (F. Davis, *Huey Long,* 213).

12. Williams, *Huey Long*, 720.

13. R. White, *Kingfish*, 202.

14. *NYT*, July 8, 1934, 2.

15. *NYT*, August 14, 1934, 4. The BCI legislation was referred to as the "Cossack bill."

16. *NYT*, August 12, 1934, 5. *CT*, August 12, 1934, 6; July 10, 1934, 18.

17. *NYT*, July 22, 1934, 56. The *Times* said people wrote about guns and rope, but no one appeared to be "really fighting mad."

18. Field, "Politics," 74–87.

19. *NYT*, July 12, 1934, 2.

20. *NYT*, July 5, 1934, 8; *CT*, July 5, 1934, 7.

21. R. White, *Kingfish*, 205–6.

22. *NYT*, July 21, 1934, 3; *CT*, July 18, 1934, 10.

23. *NYT*, August 6, 1934, 2; August 11, 1934, 2; November 18, 1934, 139.

24. Williams, *Huey Long*, 726; R. White, *Kingfish*, 208.

25. *NYT*, August 6, 1934, 2; September 15, 1934, 32.

26. Boulard, *Huey Long Invades*, 156.

27. *NYT*, August 10, 1934, 14. It is difficult to reconcile the different accounts of the likelihood of violence. See note 17, above.

28. *NYT*, August 1, 1934, 16 (editorial); August 2, 1934, 1, 14. *CT*, July 31, 1934, 6; August 1, 1934, 7.

29. Williams, *Huey Long*, 724.

30. *NYT*, August 3, 1934, 1; *CT*, August 5, 1934, 4.

31. *NYT*, August 6, 1934, 2.

32. *NYT*, August 5, 1934, 1.

33. *NYT*, August 11, 1934, 2.

34. *NYT*, August 12, 1934; August 13, 1934, 11; August 14, 1934, 4.

35. *NYT*, August 7, 1934, 13; August 12, 1934, 5.

36. *NYT*, August 13, 1934, 11.

37. *NYT*, August 20, 1934, 1–2.

38. Williams, *Huey Long*, 726.

39. Williams, *Huey Long*, 726; *NYT*, August 16, 1934, 1; *CT*, August 15, 1934, 3; Sindler, *Huey Long's Louisiana*, 88–91.

40. Williams, *Huey Long*, 737.

41. *NYT*, August 18, 1934, 5.

42. *NYT*, August 17, 1934, 1.

43. *NYT*, August 18, 1934, 5.

44. *NYT*, August 18, 1934, 5; *CT*, August 18, 1934, 1–2.

45. *NYT*, August 16, 1934, 1.

46. *NYT*, August 1, 1934, 9; August 2, 1934, 1, 14; August 3, 1934, 1; August 5, 1934, 1; August 6, 1934, 2; August 26, 1934, 4.

47. *NYT*, August 8, 1934, 12.

48. *NYT*, August 10, 1934, 14; August 13, 1934, 11; August 16, 1934, 1; August 18, 1934, 5; August 19, 1934, 17; August 20, 1934, 1; September 2, 1934, 98 (lengthy, harsh article).

49. *NYT*, August 16, 1934, 1; August 21, 1934, 2; August 29, 1934, 19; September 1, 1934, 1 (three reporters had been beaten by Long partisans since August 1). *CT*, September 1, 1934, 1. Walmsley threatened to pass a city ordinance that would forbid armed bodyguards.

50. *NYT*, August 9, 1934, 10; *CT*, August 9, 1934, 5.

51. *NYT*, August 10, 1934, 14.

52. *NYT,* August 14, 1934, 4; *CT,* August 14, 1934, 11.

53. Boulard, *Huey Long Invades,* 153–54.

54. *NYT,* August 6, 1934, 2.

55. *NYT,* August 31, 1934, 3; *CT,* August 30, 1934, 6.

56. *NYT,* September 2, 1934, 1; *CT,* September 3, 1934, 3.

57. *NYT,* September 6, 1934, 7; *CT,* September 6, 1934, 3.

58. *NYT,* September 4, 1934, 11.

59. *NYT,* September 5, 1934, 1; *CT,* September 5, 1934, 1.

60. Reyer int., THWP.

61. Williams, *Huey Long,* 728, 730.

62. *NYT,* September 3, 1934, 20; September 5, 1934, 1; September 6, 1934, 7; September 7, 1934, 16.

63. Boulard, *Huey Long Invades,* 157–61; *NYT,* September 8, 1934, 1, 7.

64. Boulard, *Huey Long Invades,* 163–65.

65. *NYT,* September 7, 1934, 16; *CT,* September 7, 1934, 1, 6; Boulard, *Huey Long Invades,* 165–67.

66. *NYT,* September 8, 1934, 1, 7; *CT,* September 8, 1934, 1, 8.

67. Boulard, *Huey Long Invades,* 149.

68. "Huey Long Collection—Hostility with T. Semmes Walmsley—1930–1935," YouTube video.

69. Boulard, *Huey Long Invades,* 161–62; Williams, *Huey Long,* 732–33.

70. *NYT,* September 9, 1934, 33; *CT,* September 9, 1934, 10.

71. Boulard, *Huey Long Invades,* 161; Williams, *Huey Long,* 730.

72. *NYT,* September 12, 1934, 5.

73. LBJ to "Lady Bird" Johnson, September 11, 1934.

74. Williams, *Huey Long,* 733.

75. *NYT,* September 12, 1934, 1; *CT,* September 12, 1934, 4.

76. *NYT,* September 30, 1934, 30; *CT,* September 30, 1934,14; *NYT,* November 10, 1934, 2.

77. *NYT,* September 13, 1934, 19; September 19, 1934, 2; September 20, 1934, 4. *CT,* September 13, 1934, 4; September 19, 1934, 9.

78. *NYT,* September 15, 1934, 32.

79. Williams, *Huey Long,* 736.

80. Huey said the statute was silent on what to do (*NYT,* September 10, 1934, 6; *CT,* September 10, 1934, 5).

81. Circular, box 2: 88, WBWC.

82. Williams, *Huey Long,* 734–36.

83. R. White, *Kingfish,* 211.

84. *NYT,* October 8, 1934, 35; *CT,* October 7, 1934, 4.

85. *NYT,* October 10, 1934, 4.

86. Fruge int., THWP.

87. *NYT,* September 16, 1934, 3.

88. Mann, *Kingfish U,* 155, says the story is apocryphal, based on newspaper advertisements two weeks ahead of the game that show it was not scheduled on any game day, but it is possible that the call took place ahead of the newspaper ads. In addition to interviews, Williams cited "Trost," *Brooklyn Eagle,* November 13, 1934, a contemporaneous account though not from Louisiana (*Huey Long,* 767–68 and note 7). "Trost" said Huey convinced the circus to play in New Orleans instead on the day of the game. The ads cited by Mann show the circus played in New Orleans on the day of the Southern Methodist game and

went to Baton Rouge two days after the game on October 8. "Trost" also related the Vanderbilt train journey discussed *below* and said these two events proved that Huey would either become President or get "punctured by bullets."

89. *NYT*, October 16, 1934, 8.

90. *NYT*, October 24, 1934, 23; November 6, 1934, 3. *CT*, October 24, 1934, 19; November 6, 1934, 19.

91. *NYT*, October 25, 1934, 25; *CT*, October 25, 1934, 21, *NYT*, October 26, 1934, 1; *CT*, October 26, 1934, 1.

92. *CT*, October 27, 1934, 19.

93. *Nashville Tennessean*, October 23, 1934, 10; October 24, 1934, 10; October 25, 1934, 1, 11; October 26, 1934, 15, 16; October 27, 1934, 1.

94. "Huey Long Collection—Huey and LSU," YouTube video. Williams, *Huey Long*, 768–70. Traughber, "LSU parades into Nashville." Rabalais, "The Kingfish, Biff & the Golden Thirties."

95. *CT*, October 28, 1934, 3.

96. *Nashville Tennessean*, October 28, 1934, 1.

97. *NYT*, October 28, 1934, 59; October 29, 1934, 19. *CT*, October 28, 1934, A2.

98. *NYT*, October 29, 1934, 11.

99. *NYT*, November 14, 1934, 5; *CT*, November 14, 1934, 23.

100. *NYT*, November 18, 1934, 30. *CT*, November 18, 1934, 23.

101. *NYT*, November 18, 1934, 65; *CT*, November 18, 1934, 23.

102. *NYT*, November 7, 1934, 18; *CT*, November 7, 1934, 12.

103. *NYT*, November 7, 1934, 23.

## 25. Strange, Ruthless, and Cynical Things

1. Williams, *Huey Long*, 797–98, 820; Christenberry int., THWP; Maines int., THWP.

2. Field, "Politics," 172–77, 182; R. White, *Kingfish*, 223; Irey and Slocum, *Tax Dodgers*, 94–97.

3. Examination (1934), box 1: 23, 24–25, 54, HPLP.

4. Irey and Slocum, *Tax Dodgers*, 99–100; Field, "Politics," 171.

5. Deutsch, *Huey Long Murder Case*, 57.

6. Field, "Politics," 187–88.

7. Field, "Politics," 382.

8. Talbot int., THWP.

9. Boulard, *Huey Long Invades*, 167; R. White, *Kingfish*, 217; box 1: 16–18, FBI Files on Huey Long.

10. Williams, *Huey Long*, 689–90, 708.

11. Associated Press News, October 14, 1985; "Long, Huey," unsigned, undated memo, JAFP, box 51.

12. *Town Talk*, September 18, 1934, 1; Field, "Politics," 11.

13. *CT*, December 25, 1933, 30.

14. J. Tom Daniel, May 22, 1935, box IC12: "1935 D–H," LFP.

15. 78 CR 3189.

16. Sindler collapses the time frame from 1930 to 1935; Boulard says the descent into dictatorship began in September 1934.

17. Williams, *Huey Long*, 748–52, 858.

18. Field, "Politics," 69–70.

19. Reyer and Labbe ints., THWP.

20. Provost int., THWP.

21. Williams, *Huey Long,* 751 (list of one hundred men), 752 (controlling votes), 752–53 (deducts and organization), 754–55 (control over local leaders).

22. Fournet int., THWP; Roy int., THWP.

23. Jeansonne, *Leander Perez.*

24. Williams, *Huey Long,* 755–56.

25. Amendments to tax laws passed during the special session: No. 5: Levying/collection of taxes on automobiles; No. 7: Amending income tax law of 1934; No. 11: Amending liquor tax law; No. 20: LPSC could collect "fees"; No. 33: Tobacco tax amended (*NOTP,* November 13, 1933,1, 6).

26. *NYT,* November 11, 1934, 1; November 14, 1934, 5; November 15, 1934, 16. There were, nevertheless, disagreements among his supporters (*NYT,* November 16, 1934, 6, 25; November 17, 1934, 30; November 18, 1934, 30, 49 [debt moratorium law disquieted investors], and 139; *CT,* November 17, 1934, 8).

27. *CT,* November 17, 1934, 8; November 15, 1934, 13. Boulard says there were forty-five bills (*Huey Long Invades,* 175–77); Williams, *Huey Long,* 738–41.

28. *CT,* November 13, 1934, 4; November 15, 1934, 7; November 18, 1934, 5; November 20, 1934, 10. *NYT,* November 15, 1934, 16; November 17, 1934, 30; November 18, 1934, 2.

29. *NYT,* November 11, 1934, 1; November 12, 1934, 7. *CT,* November 13, 1934, 1. *NOTP,* November 13, 1934, 1; November 20, 1934 ("The . . . young college man is more representative of Louisiana than are Huey Long and his contemptibles"). Williams, *Huey Long,* 773–74.

30. *NYT,* November 14, 1934, 21.

31. Mann, *Kingfish U,* 188–89.

32. Another version: "If that little ——— prints that, we gonna have a new editor. And as for the little ——— who wrote this, why he's not gonna be in school. That's my university and I'll fire any student that dares to say a word against Huey Long. I'll fire a thousand, we've got 10,000 to take their place" (Cutrer, *Parnassus on the Mississippi,* 21; Williams, *Huey Long,* 774–75).

33. Williams, *Huey Long,* 776; R. White, *Kingfish,* 216.

34. R. White, *Kingfish,* 216; Cutrer, *Parnassus on the Mississippi,* 21; Mann, *Kingfish U,* 199.

35. Cutrer, *Parnassus on the Mississippi,* 21–22 (five students dismissed). *NOTP,* December 6, 1934, 1 (seven students dismissed); Williams, *Huey Long,* 778–79 (seven dismissed).

36. Troy Middleton int., THWP; Price, *Troy H. Middleton,* 114–16.

37. Cutrer, *Parnassus on the Mississippi,* 22, 219–20.

38. *NYT,* November 18, 1934, 30; November 27, 1934, 6 (resignations and sign on print shop door: "killed by suppression."); November 28, 1934, 2 (demand for reinstatement); November 28, 1934, 2 (suspension); November 29, 1934, 27 (journalism students strike; classes deserted). *CT,* November 22, 1934, 4; November 28, 1934, 1.

39. *NYT,* July 4, 1934, 10.

40. Hair, *Realm,* 279. *NOTP,* July 6, 1934, 1, 9. *Shreveport Times,* July 6, 1934, 1, 16. *Town Talk,* July 7, 1934, 1, 6. *Daily Signal,* July 7, 1934, 1, 3. *MNS,* July 8, 1934, 1, 6; July 10, 1934, 1. *Shreveport Times,* July 10, 1934, 5.

41. *Grosjean v. American Press Co.,* 297 U.S. 233 (1936).

42. *New York Times Co. v. Sullivan*, 376 U.S. 254 (1964).

43. *NYT*, April 26, 1935, 7; May 6, 1935, 17 (review of *Handout*, a book by two correspondents charging that Roosevelt manipulated the media, saying the book was too "overheated" but "just plausible enough . . . to make me uncomfortable"). *CT*, May 9, 1935, 14.

44. *CT*, March 29, 1935, 14.

45. Cutrer, *Parnassus on the Mississippi*, 24.

46. Swing, *Forerunners of American Fascism*, 104.

47. F. Davis, *Huey Long*, 287; but see H. Carter, *Huey Long: American Dictator*, who wrote—without quantification—that Huey took over local control of printing legal notices, which gave him the means to hurt small papers.

48. *NYT*, July 16, 1935, 22. The board was to get better movies and the return of vaudeville to New Orleans.

49. *NYT*, August 6, 1935, 15.

50. Middleton int., THWP.

51. F. Davis, *Huey Long*, 227.

52. Mann, *Kingfish U*, 199–201; Williams, *Huey Long*, 775–80.

53. *NYT*, November 23, 1934, 2; November 24, 1934, 5. *CT*, November 23, 1934, 5.

54. *NYT*, November 26, 1934, 2; November 28, 1934, 2. *NOTP*, November 29, 1934, 12.

55. Maines int., THWP; F. Davis, *Huey Long*, 225; *Shreveport Times*, August 21, 1934, 1–2.

56. Cutrer, *Parnassus on the Mississippi*, 15–16, 23.

57. Mann, *Kingfish U*, 208.

58. *Shreveport Times*, December 2, 1934, 21. Huey lost a bet with the young son of a supporter; he sent the boy his tie in payment (Fruge int., THWP; Knott [Huey's sister] int., THWP).

59. *Monroe Morning World*, December 9, 1934, 14–15.

60. "Sugar Bowl," Wikipedia.

61. *Shreveport Times*, December 18, 1934,14. *NYT*, December 18, 1934, 29; December 19, 1934, 30. *NOTP*, December 18, 1934, 2. *CT*, December 19, 1934, 21; December 21, 1934, 34; December 22, 1934, 17. Williams, *Huey Long*, 771–72.

62. Mann, *Kingfish U*, 215.

63. *NYT*, December 20, 1934, 32; *CT*, January 4, 1935, 23.

64. *MNS*, December 24, 1934, 1; *CT*, December 25, 1934, 33; *Shreveport Times*, December 28, 1934, 13.

65. Warren, "*All the King's Men*: The Matrix of Experience," 161–67; Payne, "Willie Stark and Huey Long," 580–95; 75th anniversary of LSU, box 7, CMP; Beals, *Story of Huey Long*, 379–80.

66. He had proposed thirty-five bills, but two (which dealt with firefighters' pensions) were withdrawn (*NOTP*, December 19, 1934, 1, 14–15).

67. *NOTP*, December 20, 1934, 1; *CT*, December 20, 1934, 18; R. White, *Kingfish*, 219–20. In a thinly reasoned decision, Judge Borah held the pro rata pension law unconstitutional, emphasizing that Standard Oil would have to contribute more than $1 million to fund the pro rata pensions. One wonders whether Standard Oil's policy was to discharge employees before their pensions vested to save this $1 million. *Standard Oil v. Porterie*, 12 F. Supp. 100 (August 30, 1935).

68. *Clinton v. Cedar Rapids and the Missouri River Railroad*, 24 Iowa 455 (1868).

69. FDR was aware of this principle and said there was nothing he could do about these laws (Boulard, *Huey Long Invades*, 146 and notes 20, 21).

70. Key, *Southern Politics*, 20–23.

71. Williams, *Huey Long*, 719; *NYT*, August 6, 1934, 2. Police Chief Reyer said this law was like that of other states (int., THWP).

72. *Weekly Town Talk*, December 22, 1934, 1; Williams, *Huey Long*, 746.

73. *CT*, January 4, 1935, 16.

74. Sehrt int., THWP.

75. *NYT*, January 4, 1935, 8; January 5, 1935, 13.

76. *Shreveport Times*, January 6, 1935, 1, 10; *NYT*, January 7, 1935, 1. Williams, *Huey Long*, 783–85.

77. Beals, *Story of Huey Long*, 334–35; Williams, *Huey Long*, 741.

78. Slaughter, *Income Received in the Various States*, 22, chart 6.

79. Hamlin and Wimberly ints., THWP.

80. Williams, *Huey Long*, 854; Racivitch int., THWP..

81. F. Davis, *Huey Long*, 245.

82. *NYT*, January 4, 1935, 16.

83. *CT*, January 2, 1935, 9. *NYT*, January 2, 1935, 1, 8; January 5, 1935, 13.

## 26. The Pied Piper

1. *NYT*, January 8, 1935, 1; *CT*, January 8, 1935, 7; 79 CR 150–59; F. Davis, *Huey Long*, 245; 79 CR 965.

2. *NYT*, January 10, 1935, 1, 6. Stenographic record, "Redistribution of Wealth," box 1: 26, HPLP.

3. *NYT*, January 10, 1935, 18.

4. *NYT*, January 11, 1935, 25.

5. *NYT*, January 12, 1935, 3.

6. *NYT*, January 17, 1935, 2.

7. *NYT*, January 20, 1935, 26.

8. *NYT*, January 18, 1935, 22; January 20, 1935, 65; January 30, 1935, 5.

9. *NYT*, February 10, 1935 (Sunday), 99.

10. *CT*, January 16, 1935, 10. Huey also denounced the munitions manufacturers (*NYT*, January 16, 1935, 4).

11. *CT*, January 18, 1935, 1, 10; *NYT*, January 18, 1935, 5.

12. Gillette, "Huey Long and the Chaco War," 293–311, 310–11. Gillette doesn't think Standard Oil motivated the war. Huey had "a remarkable faculty for giving pertinence to the irrelevant, for emphasizing the few facts he did have, and for stretching his contentions to bridge the inherent gaps . . . a talent characteristic of Long's unique brilliance." See, however, DeFronzo, *Revolutions*, 398 ("A conservative Bolivian government, seeking a river route to the Atlantic Ocean and a new source of oil, provoked the Chaco War (1932–1935) with Paraguay, fought it incompetently, was defeated, and lost more territory").

13. 79 CR 432–37 (Robinson); 479–90 (Johnson); 563–79; 636–48 (Vandenberg, Logan and Huey, Huey's resolution); 695–703 (Borah); 704–5 (Robinson); 771–77 (Reynolds); 964–66 (Norris); 966–72 (Robinson); 1114–48. *NYT*, January 18, 1935, 5; January 29, 1935, 1. *CT*, January 29, 1935, 1–2. A book written by the Paraguayan consul about the conflict, with a foreword by Smedley D. Butler, featured the default of $60 million in Bolivian bonds on Wall Street that induced some to favor Bolivia. Huey had mentioned this but not prominently (De Ronde, *Paraguay*). *NYT*, January 6, 1935, 80 (book review).

14. Ickes, *Secret Diary*, 284–85; K. Davis, *FDR*, 493–96; *CT*, January 30, 1935, 1; *NYT*,

February 3, 1935, 59. Compare FDR to JR, January 30, 1935, FDR, PPR 473, with Johnson's letters to his son dated January 13, 26, and 31, 1935, HJP.

15. *NYT,* January 9, 1935, 7 (Square Dealers, the "blue shirts"); January 16, 1935, 14; January 19, 1935, 3; January 20, 1935, 1, 26. *CT,* January 19, 1935, 11; January 20, 1935, 14.

16. *NYT,* January 23, 1935, 7.

17. Williams, *Huey Long,* 785–86; *NYT,* January 24, 1935, 14; *CT,* January 25, 1935, 7.

18. R. White, *Kingfish,* 226–27.

19. *NYT,* February 1, 1935, 3. *CT,* February 1, 1935,11; February 2, 1935, 14 (letter to the editor). Another letter was critical: Louisiana "will now deserve the name Huesiana."

20. Reed, *Requiem,* 115–16; *CT,* January 26, 1935, 1; *NYT,* January 27, 1935, 55.

21. *CT,* February 2, 1935, 1.

22. *NYT,* January 27, 1935, 1, 2, 55; January 27, 1935, 61. *CT,* January 27, 1935, 1–2.

23. Williams, *Huey Long,* 791.

24. Reed, *Requiem,* 115–17. *CT,* January 29, 1935, 2; January 30, 1935, 2.

25. *NYT,* January 28, 1935, 1, 16; February 1, 1935, 3. *CT,* January 27, 1935, 1–2.

26. *NYT,* January 30, 1935, 4; January 31, 1935, 2 (asking for congressional investigation).

27. *NYT,* January 31, 1935, 2.

28. Ernest Bourgeois to J. Edgar Hoover, March 8, 1935, box 1: 2, FBI Files on Huey Long. *NYT,* March 11, 1935, 3.

29. *CT,* January 28, 1935, 1. As Jack McGuire points out, this is a great story, but she would have needed a ladder to touch Huey's bronze plaque above the elevators.

30. *NYT,* February 1, 1935, 3; February 2, 1935, 5. *CT,* January 28, 1935, 2 (picture).

31. *NYT,* February 2, 1935, 1, 5; February 3, 1935, 1, 24. *CT,* February 2, 1935, 1.

32. Proceedings, box 1: 22, HPLP.

33. Landry int., THWP.

34. *NYT,* February 4, 1935, 3; February 5, 1935, 3. *CT,* February 3, 1935, 1; February 4, 1935, 3 (neighboring parishes defied the threat to send in troops).

35. *NYT,* February 6, 1935, 3. *CT,* February 6, 1935, 7. Williams, *Huey Long,* 814. Anderson, *Wild Man from Sugar Creek,* 92, 117–19. Huey also asked someone if he had heard the story of the fisherman who ate his bait; Talmadge was Huey's "bait." *NYT,* February 7, 1935, 5 (Alabama representative proposed inviting Huey "as a substitute for a circus"); February 10, 1935, 29 (Arkansas); February 12, 1935, 19 (Kansas); February 15, 1935, 2 (Tennessee); April 16, 1935, 12 (Florida). Talmadge's son disagreed with biographer Anderson's judgment that Huey held a harsh opinion of his father, Herman Talmadge (int. A-0331-1, SOHC [#4007]).

36. Schlesinger, *Age of Roosevelt: The Politics of Upheaval,* 243–44; K. Davis, *FDR,* 494.

37. OF 1403, FDROF.

38. *CT,* February 7, 1935, 10.

39. *NYT,* February 10, 1935, 63, 68 (editorial), 99 (Owen).

40. *NYT,* February 19, 1935, 2; *CT,* February 19, 1935, 14.

41. See, for example, *Mobile Post,* February 8, 1935, rpt. in 79 CR 1820.

42. Talbot int., THWP.

43. Brothers int., THWP; Jones, "*Administration Under Fire,*" 5–17; Schlesinger, *Age of Roosevelt: The Politics of Upheaval,* 242–43; *CT,* February 12, 1935, 3.

44. *CT,* February 13, 1935, 4.

45. *CT,* February 15, 1935, 17; February 16, 1935, 7; February 18, 1935, 10 (editorial recommended investigation). Republicans laughed; Democrats were "disgusted" (*NYT,* February 15, 1935, 2; February 16, 1935, 1; Landry and Christenberry ints., THWP). Roosevelt's

papers reflect concerns about leaks to Huey. See, for example, letter, April 30, 1935, box 1: April 1935, FDROP, 1403.

46. Williams, *Huey Long,* 804–5.

47. Ickes, *Secret Diary,* 294–97, 302; Watkins, *Righteous Pilgrim,* 434 (Roberts said Farley knew nothing about the destruction of the letter).

48. *NYT,* February 16, 1935, 1, 2; February 17, 1935, 19; February 18, 1935, 8; February 20, 1935, 3; February 21, 1935, 15; March 3, 1935, 2. *CT,* February 18, 1935, 10; March 5, 1935, 1, 6.

49. Ickes, *Secret Diary,* 302; Schlesinger, *Age of Roosevelt: The Politics of Upheaval,* 269. Roosevelt said it would cost $1 billion more and this would threaten the credit of the United States. Huey said this was ridiculous: was the United States only a billion dollars away from insolvency?

50. *NYT,* February 22, 1935, 1, 15; *CT,* February 22, 1935, 1, 8.

51. *NYT,* February 23, 1935, 1, 6.

52. *NYT,* February 24, 1935, 2. Huey said state highway agencies were already set up with plans; spending therefore could take place now and would spur the "purchase of gasoline and cotton fiber tires and steel mills to sending tin to factories for building automobiles," as opposed to current spending that was wasted and bred a spirit of idleness (*CT,* February 24, 1935, 3). Government spending in a Depression should be quick (Posner, *Crisis of Capitalist Democracy,* 115–16).

53. *Circleville Herald,* February 27, 1935, 1, 6 (Drew Pearson).

54. *NYT,* March 3, 1935, 63; *CT,* March 1, 1935, 8.

55. *NYT,* February 22, 1935, 1, 17; *CT,* February 23, 1935, 6; 79 CR 2396–2401 (1935).

56. *NYT,* February 24, 1935, 6; Field, "*Politics,*" 187–88.

57. *NYT,* February 26, 1935, 12.

58. 79 CR 2838–49; *CT,* March 5, 1935, 1, 6.

59. K. Davis, *FDR,* 412–14, 497.

60. Schlesinger, *Age of Roosevelt: The Politics of Upheaval,* 244.

61. *CT,* March 5, 1935, 3.

62. F. Davis, *Huey Long,* 249–50.

63. NYT, March 5, 1935, 10 (speech).

64. *NYT,* March 6, 1935, 18 (Krock).

65. Williams, *Huey Long,* 808–9. *NYT,* March 5, 1935, 10.

66. *DMR,* March 6, 1935, 1, 16.

67. *NYT,* March 6, 1935, 1, 6, 7; *CT,* March 6, 1935, 1; F. Davis, *Huey Long,* 262; Landry int., THWP.

68. 79 CR 2953–55.

69. Sen. Johnson letter to Jack, March 17, 1935, HJP, Diary Letters; Beals, *Story of Huey Long,* 304–7.

70. *NYT,* March 7, 1935, 1, 4 (two stories); *CT,* March 7, 1935, 2, 12. Caro, *Power Broker,* 287–93, 426, 437; K. Davis, *FDR,* 497–501.

71. The speech in the *Congressional Record* and on the American Rhetoric website is not quite the version delivered. The *Times* printed it verbatim on March 8, 1935, 16, and recordings of it are available at the Museum of Broadcasting and the Library of Congress.

72. Rhetoricians noted Huey's appropriation of the war metaphor at the beginning of his speech and these messianic overtones and light-dark imagery (Ryan, ed., *Oratorical Encounters,* 42–43).

73. Ryan, ed., *Oratorical Encounters,* 38. *NYT,* March 8, 1935, 1, 17; March 8, 1935, 16;

March 8, 1935, 20; March 10, 1935, 67 (he "has a certain genius for government."), 72 (reprinting *San Francisco Chronicle,* 74); March 11, 1935, 13. *CT,* March 8, 1935, 1. Schlesinger, *Age of Roosevelt: The Politics of Upheaval,* 247.

74. K. Davis, *FDR,* 501. *NYT,* March 11, 1935, 14; March 12, 1935, 20; March 16, 1935, 19.

75. Walter Lippmann, *New York Herald-Tribune,* March 14, 1935.

76. A few weeks later, Huey cited General Motors as an example of stock ownership being divorced from management (F. Davis, *Huey Long,* 282). In 1932, Adolf Berle and Gardiner Means noted that stock ownership was divorced from management (*Modern Corporation).*

77. Senator Norris advanced a similar idea while advocating high inheritance taxes (*NYT,* February 24, 1935, 66; 79 CR 2180–83 [1935]).

78. *NYT,* March 9, 1935, 9.

79. Landry int., THWP. *NYT,* March 15, 1935, 4; March 27, 1935, 20 (Krock). Anonymous, March 15, 1935 (flop); Sgt. M. F. Doyle to James Farley, March 15, 1935 (something must be done); OF 1403: 2, FDROF.

80. *NYT,* March 9, 1935, 1; March 10, 1935, 33, 67; April 7, 1935, 1, 18; April 8, 1935, 18. *CT,* March 10, 1935, 3.

81. *NYT,* March 9, 1935, 9; *CT,* March 9, 1935, 1, 6.

82. *CT,* March 12, 1935, 8; March 14, 1935, 4; March 15, 1935, 1.

83. *NYT,* March 15, 1935, 1; March 16, 1935, 2. 79 CR 3447–49, 3452; 3592–95.

84. *CT,* March 16, 1935, 1.

85. *NYT,* March 24, 1935, 32.

86. Beals, *Story of Huey Long,* 318–19.

87. Cawthorn int., THWP.

88. *NYT,* March 24, 1935, 2. *CT,* March 17, 1935, 5; March 18, 1935, 6; March 24, 1935, 1, 6; March 25, 1935, 5; March 27, 1935, 4. Expansion of the money supply was popular with progressives of every region (*NYT,* March 26, 1935, 1, 12).

89. "Statement . . . of Votes Cast for Presidential and Vice-Presidential Electors . . . on November 8th, 1932," SC SOS. Williams, *Huey Long,* 816 (60,000 Carolinians joined SOW).

90. *NYT,* April 1, 1935, 13; *DMR,* April 7, 1935, 1; box 1: 26, HPLP (excerpts of speech).

## 27. FDR Drifts on the *Nourmahal*

1. *NYT,* March 14, 1935, 31; March 15, 1935, 20 (Krock). *CT,* March 14, 1935, 4.

2. *NYT,* April 21, 1935, 53 (Krock); *DMR,* April 28, 1935, 10 (Mark Sullivan).

3. *NYT,* March 22, 1935, 5; *CT,* March 22, 1935, 14.

4. 79 CR 5727–30.

5. *NYT,* April 23, 1935, 1.

6. *NYT,* April 28, 1935, 1, 31.

7. *NYT,* March 15, 1935, 22.

8. *NYT,* April 2, 1935, 16.

9. "Huey a Film Censor Now? Kidding Subject Deleted From 'Time' in N.O." *Variety,* April 24, 1935, 1, 58. Fielding, *March of Time,* 46–53.

10. *Huey Long,* dir. Burns; "Huey Long Seen as Threat to FDR in 1930s," YouTube video.

11. *DMR,* April 13, 1935, 1.

12. *NYT,* May 6, 1935, 17.

13. *NYT,* May 8, 1935, 1; *CT,* May 6, 1935, 4.

14. *NYT,* May 16, 1935, 25, May 17, 1935, 20.

15. *NYT*, April 6, 1935, 23; *CT*, April 6, 1935, 1–2, 10.
16. 79 CR 5727–30.
17. Leighninger, *Building Louisiana*, 33; Field, "Politics," 95, 107n11.
18. Field, "Politics," 93–94.
19. *CT*, January 9, 1935, 11. *NYT*, January 9, 1935, 7 (federal judge enjoins Huey's takeover of New Orleans sewer and water district because federal law preempted it); January 15, 1935, 3 (Walmsley gets federal financing to evade Huey's laws); January 15, 1935, 3 (court nullifies Huey's takeover of Baton Rouge); April 14, 1935, 99.
20. *NYT*, May 5, 1935, 61.
21. *NYT*, April 15, 1935, 7; *CT*, April 16, 1935, 7.
22. *CT*, April 11, 1935, 15.
23. *NYT*, April 21, 1935, 22; *CT*, April 18, 1935, 1.
24. Williams, *Huey Long*, 850.
25. *CT*, April 19, 1935, 8. *DMR*, April 17, 1935, 1; April 18, 1935, 15; April 19, 1935, 1.
26. *CT*, April 17, 1935, 9.
27. *NYT*, April 21, 1935, 51; *DMR*, April 21, 1935, 5.
28. Ickes, *Secret Diary*, 345–46. Congressman Maury Maverick of Texas remarked that Ickes's retort was unnecessary and counterproductive (*DMR*, April 20, 1935, 2).
29. *NYT*, April 19, 1935, 1.
30. *NYT*, April 20, 1935, 1. *CT*, April 20, 1935, 4; April 21, 1935, 14. *NYT*, April 20, 1935, 12; April 21, 1935, 56.
31. Ickes, *Secret Diary*, 352–53; Schlesinger, *Age of Roosevelt: The Politics of Upheaval*, 249–51; *NYT*, April 23, 1935, 1, 11. Huey told Drew Pearson that Ickes only acted against him because Roosevelt told him to (*DMR*, May 1, 1935, 6). Huey also liked Cordell Hull, so sincere that he was not heeded.
32. *NYT*, April 2, 1935, 8; April 3, 1935, 4; April 4, 1935, 11. *CT*, April 27, 1935, 2. *Shreveport Times*, April 27, 1935, 1 (Fisher was "swarthy little Jefferson Parish leader" who showed no emotion). Kane, *Hayride*, 166–67, 174–76.
33. Williams, *Huey Long*, 819.
34. Talbot int., THWP.
35. Box 1, anonymous to John Rogge, August 1, 1939, FBI Files on Huey Long.
36. Field, "Politics," 186–99, 215–21.
37. Field, "Politics," 182–85, 221–24.
38. *NYT*, March 13, 1935, 11.
39. *NYT*, March 17, 1935, 35.
40. *DMR*, April 21, 1935, 10.
41. *NYT*, April 25, 1935, 2; *CT*, April 25, 1935, 3; *DMR*, April 25, 1935, 9.
42. *NYT*, April 23, 1935, 8.
43. *DMR*, April 21, 1935, 13; April 26, 1935, 12, 14; April 28, 1935, 6.
44. *DMR*, April 28, 1935, 3 (California); May 4, 1935, 2.
45. *DMR*, April 22, 1935, 11.
46. *CT*, April 27, 1935, 2.
47. *CT*, April 28, 1935, 4.
48. "Huey Long and Father Charles Coughlin Speak 1935," YouTube video.
49. "Huey P Long on the difference between Democrats and Republicans," YouTube video.
50. *CT*, April 28, 1935, 4; Williams, *Huey Long*, 817.
51. *DMR*, April 28, 1935, 1, 9. Compare with *NYT*, April 28, 1935, 1, 24 ("hearty booing").

52. *CT,* April 28, 1935, 4.
53. *DMR,* April 28, 1935, 1, 8, 9.
54. *DMR,* April 29, 1935, 4.
55. *DMR,* April 29, 1935, 1, 12.
56. Rpt. in *DMR,* May 5, 1935, 10.
57. "Huey Long Speech 1935," YouTube video. "Huey Pierce Long—Radio Address: St. Vitus Dance Government."
58. The personal reference to Rockefeller was omitted from the printed copy of his speech, but the quote is taken from the recording.
59. F. Davis, *Huey Long,* 299–307.
60. Ogilvy, *Unpublished David Ogilvy,* 3.
61. Bible verses cited: Acts 4:32–36; Micah 4:3–4; Proverbs 20:8–9; Nehemiah 5; Leviticus 26; Deuteronomy 15:1–2.
62. William More, April 1935, OF 1403, FDROF; OF 300, box 36, MHM to S Early, March 26, 1935, FDROF.
63. *NYT,* May 12, 1935, 10; *Town Talk,* May 11, 1935, 1.
64. *NYT,* May 15, 1935, 1; *CT,* May 16, 1935, 4.
65. *NYT,* May 5, 1935, 33; *CT,* May 5, 1935, 4.
66. Swing, "Build-up of Long and Caughlin," 325–26; Brinkley, *Voices of Protest,* 211. Farley analyzed Coughlin's mail receipts in March 1935 to gauge his impact. The *National Whirligig* said on March 16, 1935, that Coughlin had four million members, that he was not close to Huey, but that they shared information (box 2: January–May 1935, FDR OF 306).
67. Box 1: Charles E. Coughlin, folders February 1933–May 1935, FDROF 306; box 1, Morganthau correspondence, Coughlin, July 6, 1934, July 9, 1934, FDROF 603.
68. *NYT,* March 12, 1935, 1; March 13, 1935, 11; March 19, 1935, 11; March 29, 1935, 18; March 31, 1935, 16. *CT,* March 12, 1935, 2; March 31, 1935, 5.
69. O'Connor and Christenberry ints., THWP.
70. *DMR,* April 22, 1935, 2; April 25, 1935, 1, 9. *NYT,* April 27, 1935, 9.
71. *DMR,* April 27, 1935, 1; April 27, 1935, 5 (two stories); *NYT,* April 28, 1935, 24, 66; *CT,* April 27, 1935, 2.
72. 79 CR 1542.
73. *DMR,* May 22, 1935, 2.
74. Brinkley, *Voices of Protest,* 194–241.
75. Ortiz, *Beyond the Bonus March,* 118–19.
76. *NYT,* May 3, 1935, 1; *CT,* May 3, 1935, 9.
77. Williams, *Huey Long,* 829; *NYT,* May 5, 1935, 61.
78. *CT,* May 4, 1935, 1.
79. *NYT,* May 11, 1935, 1, 2. *CT,* May 11, 1935, 2; May 12, 1935, 1.
80. Ortiz, *Beyond the Bonus March,* 109–27.
81. *NYT,* May 12, 1935, 2; 79 CR 7301–14.
82. Huey made this argument in the Senate, and "administration defenders could not answer him" (*CT,* May 11, 1935, 2).
83. "[HPL] A Fair Deal for the Veterans," *American Rhetoric*; copies also available at the Museum of Broadcasting and the Library of Congress.
84. *DMR,* May 9, 1935, 2; *NYT,* May 9, 1935, 7.
85. Ickes, *Secret Diary,* 356.

86. Christenberry int., THWP.

87. *NYT,* May 13, 1935, 2; May 14, 1935, 8; May 15, 1935, 1, 10. *CT,* May 14, 1935, 1 (summarizing charges); May 15, 1935, 2.

88. Hair, *Realm,* 289; Jones, "Administration Under Fire," 5–17 (serious questions never explained); Christenberry int., THWP.

89. Schlesinger, *Age of Roosevelt: The Politics of Upheaval,* 11, 211–14.

90. Ickes, *Secret Diary,* 316.

91. *NYT,* September 22, 1935, 69, 73; September 23, 1935, 11; September 24, 1935, 8. Cawthorn int., THWP.

92. Don Devol int., OHI, LSU.

93. Amenta, Dunleavy, and Bernstein, *"Stolen Thunder?"* 687; Brinkley, *Voices of Protest,* 173, 203.

94. Ickes, *Secret Diary,* 462; Brinkley, *Voices of Protest,* 207–8; Hair, *Realm,* 307; Schlesinger, *Age of Roosevelt: The Politics of Upheaval,* 251.

95. *DMR,* April 27, 1935, 6.

96. "Statement . . . of Votes Cast for Presidential and Vice-Presidential Electors . . . on November 8th, 1932," SC SOS.

97. Brinkley, *Voices of Protest,* 243.

98. Ickes, *Secret Diary,* 360, 363, 462; Schlesinger, *Age of Roosevelt: The Politics of Upheaval,* 243, 271–74.

99. Schlesinger, *Age of Roosevelt: The Politics of Upheaval,* 219–25; 233–35.

100. Ickes, *Secret Diary,* 363–64.

101. Ortiz, *Beyond the Bonus March,* 130–32, 138–42; Schlesinger, *Age of Roosevelt: The Politics of Upheaval,* 11.

102. *NYT,* May 18, 1935, 1; *CT,* May 18, 1935, 1.

103. 79 CR 7919–24.

104. *NYT,* May 22, 1935, 1, 2; *CT,* May 22, 1935, 1.

105. Ortiz, *Beyond the Bonus March,* 144–45; *NYT,* May 23, 1935, 1; *CT,* May 23, 1935, 1.

106. *NYT,* May 27, 1935, 20. "President Roosevelt Reads Bonus Veto to Joint Congress," YouTube video of silent film footage.

107. *NYT,* May 23, 1935, 1.

108. Ortiz, *Beyond the Bonus March,* 151.

109. *NYT,* May 26, 1935, 10; *CT,* May 27, 1935, 34 (picture).

110. *A.L.A. Schechter Poultry Corp. v. United States,* 295 U.S. 495 (1935); *Louisville Joint Stock Land Bank v. Radford,* 295 U.S. 555 (1935); *CT,* May 28, 1935, 2.

111. K. Davis, *FDR,* 516. *CT,* May 11, 1935, 2; May 15, 1935, 1. *NYT,* May 16, 1935, 22 (editorial).

112. Schlesinger, *Age of Roosevelt: The Politics of Upheaval,* 283; K. Davis, *FDR,* 517–21; *NYT,* May 28, 1935, 24.

## 28. Stealing Huey's Thunder

1. Schlesinger, *Age of Roosevelt: The Politics of Upheaval,* 326; Moley, *After Seven Years,* 305.

2. Krock, *Memoirs,* 163–64.

3. Dallek, *Franklin D. Roosevelt,* 221.

4. Schlesinger, *Age of Roosevelt: The Politics of Upheaval,* 6–8.

5. 79 CR 8933–36, 8942–43.

6. 79 CR 9040–51, 9053, 9062–63.

7. 79 CR 8933–50, 9037–65. *NYT,* June 12, 1935, 1. *CT,* June 12, 1935, 1, 6. Schlesinger, *Age of Roosevelt: The Politics of Upheaval,* 302–24. The bill was eviscerated in the House and then a compromise passed late in the session.

8. *CT,* June 12, 1935, 7.

9. *NYT,* June 12, 1935, 1, 2; 79 CR 9066–68.

10. G. Maines to his mother, June 21, 1935, box 1: 30, RBLP; Mann, *Legacy to Power,* 39.

11. 79 CR 9089–9179.

12. *CT,* June 13, 1935, 1, 6; June 14, 1935, 10.

13. *CT,* June 13, 1935, 6; *St. Louis Post-Dispatch,* June 13, 1935, 7C; *Miami News,* June 13, 1935, 1.

14. *NYT,* June 13, 1935, 2.

15. *NYT,* June 14, 1935, 2.

16. Will Rogers, "Daily Telegram #2763: Mr. Rogers Must Admit That a 'Hero' Is Slipping."

17. *NYT,* June 14, 1935, 2, 22; June 16, 1935, 49, 51. *Barron's* said Senator Black was the hero of Congress's craziest week (vol. 15, no. 24 [June 17, 1935]: 4). Senator Hiram Johnson thought the filibuster pointless (R. White, *Kingfish,* 255).

18. Schlesinger, *Age of Roosevelt: The Politics of Upheaval,* 291.

19. Tugwell, *Democratic Roosevelt,* 348.

20. 79 CR 9510–38, 9625–34, 9648–50.

21. *NYT,* June 15, 1935, 2; *CT,* June 15, 1935, 9; 79 CR 9291–97.

22. Darrell St. Claire, OHI.

23. *NYT,* June 16, 1935, 1, 24. *CT,* June 16, 1935, 1, 8. The record shows neither man getting laughs or applause (79 CR 9363–66).

24. Johnson, "Strategy of the Extremists," 36, 112.

25. Schlesinger, *Age of Roosevelt: The Politics of Upheaval,* 325.

26. *CT,* June 20, 1935, 2.

27. Williams, *Huey Long,* 836.

28. 79 CR 9365–66.

29. *NYT,* June 23, 1935, 1, 24 (Huey's letter sarcastic between the lines). *CT,* June 23, 1935, 1. 79 CR 9905–9914 (letter to Roosevelt at 9906–7). Harry Hopkins advised Roosevelt not to respond (Harry Hopkins to FDR, June 28, 1935, PPF 200, container 22, FDRPPF).

30. *CT,* June 27, 1935, 2.

31. Schlesinger, *Age of Roosevelt: The Politics of Upheaval,* 325–33. Williams, *Huey Long,* 836–37. *NYT,* June 23, 1935, 51; June 25, 1935, 18; July 28, 1935, 47.

32. *NYT,* June 26, 1935, 1, 2.

33. *NYT,* July 9, 1935, 2; *CT,* July 9, 1935, 1; *NOTP,* July 9, 1935, 1, 3.

34. "Washington: Both Sides of the Curtain," *Barron's* 15, no. 28 (July 15, 1935): 4.

35. *NYT,* June 23, 1935, 60; *CT,* June 21, 1935, 9.

36. *NYT,* July 4, 1935, 1. A bodyguard held Ansell—courteously—until Huey disappeared and Ansell "dismissed the incident without further thought." Huey was a regular on this terrace all summer without incident (*CT,* July 4, 1935, 4).

37. *NYT,* July 2, 1935, 13; July 3, 1935, 6. 79 CR 10595–10619; 10690–92.

38. Schlesinger, *Age of Roosevelt: The Politics of Upheaval,* 290; Hofstadter, *American Political Tradition,* 338.

39. *CT,* July 25, 1935, 21; July 26, 1935, 25. Chandler, *America's Greatest Depression,* 176. Schlesinger, *Age of Roosevelt: The Politics of Upheaval,* 291–301. *NYT,* March 7, 1935, 1, 15.

40. *NYT,* August 23, 1935, 8; *CT,* August 23, 1935, 7.

41. Amenta, Dunleavy, and Bernstein, "*Stolen Thunder?*" 678–702; Burns, *Roosevelt,* 210–15, 220–26.

42. Schlesinger, *Age of Roosevelt: The Politics of Upheaval,* 387–98.

43. Brinkley, *End of Reform,* 34–39 (recapping NRA theories), 39–47 (discussing continued NRA-type approaches after 1936), 89 (same), 127 (new agency accused of resurrecting the NRA).

44. FDR to Ray Stannard Baker, March 20, 1935, PPF 2337, FDRPPF.

45. Horan, *Desperate Years,* 178.

46. "Huey Long (1893–1935)," YouTube video.

47. Roden int., THWP.

48. Boulard, *Huey Long Invades,* 180–82.

49. *NYT,* July 4, 1935, 2; July 5, 1935, 14; July 6, 1935, 2; July 7, 1935, 3 ("lying crook"); July 8, 1935, 5; July 10, 1935, 5. *CT,* July 6, 1935, 6.

50. *NYT,* July 21, 1935, 91, 98; *NOTP,* July 7, 1935, 1, 12.

51. Boulard, *Huey Long Invades,* 182–88. Williams, *Huey Long,* 852–54. *NYT,* July 13, 1935, 3; July 14, 1935, 23; July 17, 1935, 14; July 19, 1935, 6; July 21, 1935, 3; July 21, 1935, 58; July 30, 1935, 14. *CT,* July 11, 1935, 23; July 12, 1935, 5; July 13, 1935, 4; July 14, 1935, 15; July 16, 1935, 9; July 21, 1935, 2. *NOTP,* July 13, 1935, 1, 3 (Old Regular pledge).

52. *NYT,* July 25, 1935, 20; *NOTP,* July 25, 1935, 1, 3.

53. *CT,* July 20, 1935, 4.

54. 79 CR 11517–19 (radio speech); 11523–24, and 11556–57 (tariffs).

55. 79 CR 11618 (speech), 11658 (vote).

56. *NYT,* July 26, 1935, 5; *NOTP,* July 26, 1935, 1–2.

57. *NYT,* July 25, 1935, 20; July 26, 1935, 5. *CT,* July 27, 1935, 5 (Julius humorlessly denying that their grandfather introduced the Ramos gin fizz to New Orleans). "Huey Long Collection—Making a Gin Fizz," YouTube video. "Huey Long Collection—Drinking and Talking," YouTube video.

58. *NYT,* August 6, 1935, 2.

59. *NYT,* August 14, 1935, 13; *CT,* August 15, 1935, 3.

60. *NYT,* August 16, 1935, 36; *CT,* August 16, 1935, 6.

61. *NYT,* August 18, 1935, 56.

62. *NYT,* August 21, 1935, 13.

63. *CT,* August 21, 1935, 1; August 24, 1935, 1.

64. Williams, *Huey Long,* 839–41; Haas int., THWP.

65. Field, "Politics," 200–202, 228–70.

66. Schlesinger, *Age of Roosevelt: The Politics of Upheaval,* 250.

67. *NYT,* August 28, 1935, 1. *CT,* August 28, 1935, 7; August 29, 1935, 8.

68. Williams, *Huey Long,* 751.

69. HPL circular, "Take the Money—Vote As You Please," April 1935, OF 1403, box 2: April 1935, FDROF.

70. Cohen and Taylor, *American Pharaoh,* 158–60.

71. Royko, *Boss,* 78.

72. *CT,* June 23, 1935, 77; *NYT,* May 26, 1935, 54.

73. Williams, *Huey Long,* 822–24.

74. *NYT,* May 31, 1935, 30; June 2, 1935, 54.

75. *NOTP,* June 4, 1935, 1.

76. A Kennedy biographer disagrees (Nasaw, *Patriarch*, 80).

77. *NYT*, July 5, 1935, 15; *NOTP*, June 5, 1935, 9.

78. *NOTP*, May 9, 1940, 1, 13–14; DeStefano, *Top Hoodlum*, 112.

79. Reed, *Requiem*, 110.

80. RBL to THW, RBLP; Fisher int., THWP; L. Jones int., THWP; Williams, *Huey Long*, 824–25.

81. See DeStefano, *Top Hoodlum*, 107–15; M. Kurtz, "Longism and Organized Crime," in *Huey at 100*, ed. Jeansonne, 111–26, for a variety of theories about Huey and Costello. With respect to Huey, these authors are loose on dates and depend on Mafia sources that are difficult to credit. The evidence against Maestri and Earl Long is stronger.

82. Congressman John J. O'Connor to T. Harry Williams, October 18, 1956, box 3: 21, RBLP.

83. *NOTP*, July 18, 1935, 1; July 19, 1935, 3.

84. *NOTP*, August 19, 1935; August 23, 1935; August 29, 1935, 1 (reporter called manufacturer in Chicago who said that two hundred machines were sent to New Orleans, and he hoped to sell more).

85. *NOTP*, September 5, 1935, 1; September 7, 1935, 8.

86. Guerre int., THWP.

87. *NOTP*, September 6, 1935, 1, 11.

88. Reed, *Requiem*, 105–11.

89. Seidemann, et al., "Analysis of the Legality and Viability of Mineral Leases Granted to W. T. Burton and James A. Noe During the Years 1934–1936" (MBR). Appendix 9 contained trial transcripts from a related tax prosecution of Noe, and I relied on those transcripts. See also Banta, "Regulation," 490–93; *Roussel v. Noe* 42,338, James A. Noe, Memorandum in Support of Joint Motion for Summary Judgment, in possession of the author; RBL to THW, September 15, 1966, in response to THW to RBL, March 28, 1966, box 2: 1, RBLP; *Shreveport Times*, October 15, 1939, 1, 20; Seidemann, "Did the State Win or Lose," 196–225.

90. MBR, appendix 14.

91. Dodd, *Peapatch Politics*, 97–98.

92. MBR, 19, 37n175.

93. Royko, *Boss*, 51–52.

94. See, for example, *Vendo v. Stoner*, 58 Ill. 2d 289, 321 N.E. 2d 1 (1974); *Plaquemines Parish Commission Council v. Delta Development Co.*, 502 So.2d 1034 (La 1987). A few more than thirty wells were drilled, but not enough to change the point.

95. RBL to THW, September 15, 1966, THWP, range 34: 17–69; also box 2: 1, RBLP.

96. Sacket to Viosca, July 20, 1939, box 2, FBI Files on Huey Long.

97. Barbecue speech, portions of which were shown in the Ken Burns documentary. A video of most of the speech used to be available on the Louisiana Secretary of State's website. At the beginning of the speech, Huey said he had refused fees to speak in Cleveland and New York.

98. Leche (crooked judge no credit), White (hated petty grafters), Weiss, Gleason, and Fleming (indifference to money), Smith (could earn money if defeated) ints., THWP.

99. Christenberry, Lorio, Ellender, and Fields ints., THWP.

100. RBL to THW, September 15, 1966, THWP, range 34: 17–69; also box 2: 1, RBLP.

101. LaFollette, *Adventure in Politics*, 223–24.

102. Warren, *All the King's Men*, 548, 606.

103. Bethge, *Dietrich Bonhoeffer,* 830, 845–46, 868–70, 927–30.

104. Sehrt and Landry ints., THWP.

## 29. Conceiving Huey's First Days in the White House

1. Williams, *Huey Long,* 843–45.

2. *NYT,* August 14, 1935, 13; August 16, 1935, 36; August 18, 1935, 56. *CT,* August 15, 1935, 3; August 16, 1935, 6.

3. Sindler, *Huey Long's Louisiana,* 86 and note 31.

4. Christenberry int., THWP.

5. Brinkley, *Voices of Protest,* 197–98; Snyder, "Huey Long and the Presidential Election of 1936," 122; OF 1403, box 2: February 1935, FDROF; PPF 200, FDRPPF; Fruge int., THWP; Gamble int., THWP; RBL, 3700, 1: 24, 34, 37.

6. Letter of March 22, 1935, OF 1403, box 2: March 16–31, FDROF.

7. *American Progress,* May 1935, box 51: "Long, Huey," JAFP.

8. Deutsch, *Huey Long Murder Case,* 177 (sound trucks); Williams, *Huey Long,* 844 (plane); Sehrt int., THWP.

9. Brothers int., THWP.

10. Maines int., THWP; Brothers int., THWP; Hunt int., THWP.

11. Hughes int., THWP.

12. L. Jones int., THWP; Noe int., THWP.

13. Jeansonne, *Minister,* 41.

14. Marshburn to RBL, April 1, 1954, RBL 3700, 52: 53.

15. *Phoenix Nest,* October 17, 1964, 6, 8, in Part F. Clippings, 1923–93, RBLP.

16. Box 2: 50, FBI Files on Huey Long.

17. OF 1403, box 2: March 16–31, 1935, FDROF. LFP, LOC, box I C 12, folder "1935 Ev-jue," letter from John A. Busch.

18. Letter from Mayor, June 27, 1935, PPF 2337, FDRPPF. Roosevelt thanked him.

19. *CT,* July 2, 1935, 9.

20. HPL to Klorer August 16, 1935, box 7: 225, HPLP.

21. *NYT,* August 8, 1935; August 9, 1935, 5; August 11, 1935, 32; August 26, 1935, 10; August 27, 1935, 14. *NOTP,* August 21, 1935.

22. *NYT,* August 11, 1935, 54; Marvin McIntyre to James Farley, May 25, 1935, OF 300, box 46: 2, FDROF.

23. DNC Files on Kentucky, 1933–45, OF 300, box 18: 4, FDROF.

24. Brinkley, *Voices of Protest,* chap. 8.

25. *Progressive,* August 3, 1935.

26. *DMR,* May 4, 1935, 2; *NYT,* April 14, 1935, 66.

27. See LFP, box OV 14, LOC, for the *Progressive.*

28. *Progressive,* February 23, 1935.

29. *Progressive,* March 16, 1935.

30. *Progressive,* May 4, 1935. Johnson to Jack, April 28, 1935, Diary letters, HJP.

31. *Progressive,* May 25, 1935; November 2, 1935.

32. Box 37: "Third Party 1926–1930," letter March 4, 1925; box 38: "Progressive Conference 1931," letter December 7, 1931; and box 29: "6F-8," letter of March 14, 1936, GNP.

33. Compare the *Progressive* of July 13, 1935, with Robert LaFollette to Phil LaFollette, July 23, 1935, ser. A, box 44, LFP. Cutting to Borah, November 16, 1934 (letter is misfiled), box 11: General Correspondence Folder, Nov 1935, BCP.

34. Postcard from M & M Hicks, January 9, 1935, OF 1403, box 2: January 1935, FDROF. Seymour Weiss Papers, box 1: 9 (three-state convocation planned).

35. *Big Spring Daily Herald*, March 26, 1936, 6 (Drew Pearson).

36. F. Davis, *Huey Long*, 239–41, 287.

37. NAACP files, box F-4, November–December 1934, LOC, Walter White to Roy Wilkins, December 11, 1934.

38. *Afro American*, March 16, 1935, 1, 2; *Hope Star*, January 14, 1935, 1.

39. Walter L. Lowe, "Huey Long and the 'N——s,'" *Chicago Defender*, March 23, 1935, 12. The columnist analogized the situation to a story: a customer finished a restaurant meal and asked for the head waiter but used the slur instead of "waiter." The Black waiter ignored him until the man said he wanted to give a large, $50 tip. The waiter went right over to collect.

40. Cohen and Taylor, *American Pharaoh*, 94.

41. Christenberry to Mary and Mildred Hicks, April 30, 1934, and their response dated May 4, 1934, copies in author's possession, courtesy of E. Kathleen Shoemaker, Robert W. Woodruff Library, Emory University.

42. Gaines, *Autobiography of Miss Jane Pittman.* Black Panther Party co-founder Huey P. Newton was named after Huey.

43. *Chicago Defender*, November 17, 1934, 3.

44. NAACP files, G-82, LOC: New Orleans, August–December 1932.

45. *Bunkie Record, box* 1: PPF-200-tax message, FDRPPF 1403.

46. Deutsch, *Huey Long Murder Case*, 165–67.

47. Devol int., OHI, LSU.

48. Lant int., THWP.

49. Porterie int., THWP.

50. McGuire Papers at Tulane, box 231, April 1, 1937; Landry int., THWP.

51. *New Castle News*, April 26,1935, 9.

52. Maines int., THWP. G. Maines to RBL, February 28, 1953; September 12, 1963, RBLP 3700, boxes 1: 33, 2: 1.

53. St. Johns, *The Honeycomb*, 367–70, 387–92, 397–99. She got Huey to meet her by writing a story about him that was violently good and bad. He showed her articles in which he had added criticisms of himself to ensure they got published. She resisted his political entreaties, recognized his talents, was convinced of his sincerity, but thought his program was crude and his methods dangerous. A lot of what she says about Huey is incredible (for example, Huey named his assassin months before his death).

54. *NYT*, March 9, 1935, 17; March 13, 1935, 11. *CT*, March 9, 1935, 8.

55. Boulard, *Huey Long Invades*, 114; *New York Sun*, February 22, 1935 ("Gertrude Stein for Huey Long"); Rebecca West, *NYT*, May 12, 1935, 103, 117; West to Arthur Schlesinger Jr., January 20, 1959, in *Selected Letters of Rebecca West;* Rollyson, *Rebecca West*, 3, 27.

56. Bellow, *Ravelstein*, 1–2.

57. Kauffman, "The Populist Patriotism of Gore Vidal."

58. Lamster, *Man in the Glass House*, 131–45.

59. Bergman, ed., *Iowa History Reader*, 340; Barlow int., THWP.

60. G. Maines letter, "Tuesday," in RBL 3700, 1–30. Huey also had a fine reception in New York, he said.

61. F. Davis, *Huey Long*, 278.

62. Truman, *Memoirs* 1: 145–46.

63. Faris int., HSTLOHIC, 34–36.

64. Lowitt, *George W. Norris,* 136n29 (Huey voted more right than Norris and it took Huey to put the fear of God into the "lousy" Southern Democrats).

65. "The Huey Long Boy," May 11, 1935.

66. Alice Roosevelt Longworth, *Women's Wear Daily,* October 1935, clipping in box 273: 31, CGP; Plummer, n.d., in RBL 3700, 52–53. Equally surprising was that Senator Tydings held twenty dollars for an unknown bet between Huey and Norris (Lowitt, *George W. Norris,* 136n29). Huey's unpopularity in the Senate has been overstated.

67. K. Davis, *FDR,* 403–4, 409, 423–28.

68. Long, *My First Days in the White House,* 6–9, 18.

69. *NYT,* June 19, 1935, 17 (review).

70. *NYT,* June 16, 1935, 79 (summary); March 19, 1935, 19 (review); June 23, 1935, 71, 82.

71. *NYT,* June 5, 1935, 17 (review).

72. Swing, *Forerunners of American Fascism,* 13–33, 62–107. *NYT,* April 30, 1935, 15 (review); May 19, 1935, 83.

73. Perry, *Kingfish in Fiction,* 54–55.

74. Sokolsky, "Dr. Huey and Mr. Long," October 1935.

75. Beals, *Story of Huey Long,* 25–26, 297, 300–301, 304, 314 (quote), 317–18, 328–30, 398–99, 410.

76. Williams, *Huey Long,* 761.

77. F. Davis, *Huey Long,* 286–87.

78. *NYT,* September 11, 1935, 15; Deutsch, *Huey Long Murder Case,* 141.

79. Long, *My First Days in the White House,* chap. 5.

80. F. Davis, *Huey Long,* 280–82.

81. Moulton, *Income and Economic Progress,* 40–45; Moulton, *Formation of Capital,* 157–60; Moulton, *Recovery Problem,* 535–37.

82. F. Davis, *Huey Long,* 282.

83. Moulton, *Income and Economic Progress,* 75–77 (churches, museums, and so forth: $22.6 billion; naval vessels: $1.5 billion; highways, and so forth: $2.5 billion, plus gold in the treasury and other items not valued).

84. Zinn, *New Deal Thought,* essay 58. See also Brinkley, *Voices of Protest,* 73 and note 42; Beals, *Story of Huey Long,* 311–13.

85. Leven, Moulton, and Warburton, *America's Capacity to Consume,* 50–58.

86. Kane, *Hayride,* 125.

87. Leven, Moulton, and Warburton, *America's Capacity to Consume,* 54.

88. Doane, *Measurement of American Wealth,* 15–16, 32–33, 199; Moulton, *Income and Economic Progress,* 72–73. Using the 80/20 rule and the Brookings table for 1929, 20 percent of the 4,000 families in the top .015 percent of the income earners is 800, and 80 percent of their combined income of $5.089 billion is $4.071 billion, with an average per such family of $5,088,750, meaning that each would surrender about $4,000,000 of annual income, for a total (800 x $4,000,000) of $3.2 billion obtained from Huey's proposed income tax. At a capitalization rate of 4, about $12 billion would be obtained from a wealth tax. If the capitalization rate were 5, or if there were significant non-income-producing wealth obtained, the amount collected could be $16 billion or more. The ratio between the top .015 percent and the next .015 percent is not quite 80/20, but is 77/23, close.

89. Leven, Moulton, and Warburton, *America's Capacity to Consume,* 117–18; Nourse, *America's Capacity to Produce,* 117–32.

90. Leven, Moulton, and Warburton, *America's Capacity to Consume,* 119–24.

91. Federal Reserve Bank of St. Louis, "Federal Surplus or Deficit."

92. Galbraith, *Affluent Society,* 72–83.
93. Moulton, *Income and Economic Progress,* 12.
94. Doane, *Measurement of American Wealth,* 36.
95. Brinkley, *Voices of Protest,* 143–68, 262.
96. Kim Voss, *"Collapse of a Social Movement," in Comparative Perspectives,* ed. McAdam, McCarthy, and Zald, 234; Campbell, "*Where Do We Stand*," in *Social Movements and Organization Theory,* ed. Davis, McAdam, Scott, and Zald, 49.
97. Bregman, *Utopia,* 25–50.
98. "List of advocates of universal basic income," Wikipedia.
99. Piketty, *Capital,* 515–539.
100. Ortiz, *Beyond the Bonus March,* 199–201.
101. McManus, "*Sharing the Hate,*" 57.

## 30. Assassination

1. "Huey Long Praises the Official Reporters of Debates," SHO.
2. *CT,* August 25, 1935, 1, 4; August 27, 1935, 1. *NYT,* August 27, 1935, 1, 9.
3. Moley, *27 Masters of Politics,* 228.
4. Ickes, *Secret Diary,* 423.
5. *NYT,* August 27, 1935, 1; September 1, 1935, 39. *CT,* September 1, 1935, 11.
6. *Joplin Globe,* September 8, 1935, 19.
7. Lafollette's *Progressive,* September 7, 1935 (Albert Beveridge Jr. column: it angered labor but appealed to farmers); August 31, 1935 (listing programs and appropriations nullified until 1936). *NOTP,* August 29, 1935 (Roosevelt blaming filibuster). *CT,* August 28, 1935, 6.
8. *CT,* August 29, 1935, 1, 8; *NYT,* August 29, 1935, 1, 10.
9. *NYT,* August 28, 1935, 1, 10; August 30, 1935, 2.
10. Sokolsky, "Dr. Huey and Mr. Long"; Beals, *Story of Huey Long,* 401.
11. *NYT,* September 10, 1935, 1, 3.
12. LaFollette asked the editor of his newspaper not to reprint an editorial criticizing Huey but approved a factual story to let the readers draw their own conclusions. Box 1 C 12: "1935 Evjue, WT—August," August 19 to LaFollette and August 29 to Evjue, LFP. Evjue mentioned two letters from labor leaders predicting "disastrous consequences" from Huey's filibuster.
13. *CT,* August 31, 1935, 3; Hair, *Realm,* 314.
14. For this account of Huey's activities, see Deutsch, *Huey Long Murder Case,* 46–57; Williams, *Huey Long,* 846–47, 859–63; Landry int., THWP; Roden int., THWP.
15. *NYT,* September 1, 1935, 5.
16. Deutsch, *Huey Long Murder Case,* 49–51.
17. *CT,* August 25, 1935, 7; *NYT,* September 3, 1935, 19.
18. Deutsch, *Huey Long Murder Case,* 49–51; *Daily Oklahoman,* September 3, 1935, 1, 4.
19. Orr to THW, undated letter fragment from THWP, in author's possession. Orr estimated the crowd at ten to twelve thousand.
20. Deutsch, *Huey Long Murder Case,* 54–57.
21. R. White, *Kingfish,* 260–62; Hair, *Realm,* 316–17.
22. Deutsch, *Huey Long Murder Case,* 59–64 (quoting conversation with Weiss).
23. Frampton int., THWP; Landry int., THWP.
24. Steel, *Walter Lippman,* 316–17. K. Davis, *FDR,* 543–79. Tugwell, *Democratic Roosevelt,* 350–51. Dallek, *Franklin D. Roosevelt,* 232–33.

25. Diaries of Henry Morgenthau Jr., September 6, 1935. Morganthau talked him out of it for the moment, but the bonus was passed over Roosevelt's winking veto in January 1936.

26. Beschloss, *Kennedy and Roosevelt,* 118–20.

27. Reed, *Requiem,* 203.

28. *NOTP,* August 23, 1935, 3.

29. Fournet int., THWP.

30. *South Haven Daily Tribune,* November 24, 1936, 1.

31. Reed, *Requiem,* 203.

32. Deutsch, *Huey Long Murder Case,* 72–73.

33. Fred Frey said the cafeteria was empty and the bodyguards were tense. Christenberry said people stopped by to chat the whole time (Frey int., THWP; Christenberry int., THWP).

34. Deutsch, *Huey Long Murder Case,* 59–64; *NYT,* September 8, 1935, 1, 23.

35. Williams, *Huey Long,* 863.

36. Heilman, *Southern Connection,* 5–6.

37. Williams, *Huey Long,* 863.

38. Frampton int., THWP.

39. Coleman int., THWP; Fournet int., THWP.

40. Leche had resigned as Allen's secretary to become a judge and was replaced by White (Leche int., THWP).

41. *NYT,* September 10, 1935, 1, 2. Williams, *Huey Long,* 863–66. See also *NYT,* September 11, 1935, 15; September 13, 1935, 18; September 14, 1935, 20.

42. Reed, *Requiem,* 201.

43. Roden int., THWP.

44. O'Connor int., THWP; Deutsch, *Huey Long Murder Case,* 99, 131, 146; Zinman, *The Day Huey Long Was Shot,* 203–4 and note 4.

45. Frampton int., THWP.

46. *NYT,* September 9, 1935, 1, 3.

47. Lorio int., THWP.

48. O'Connor int., THWP.

49. *NYT,* September 10, 1935, 3; September 11, 1935, 1, 17.

50. Reed, *Requiem,* 218–26; Williams, *Huey Long,* 873–74; Trotter, *Huey P. Long's Last Operation.*

51. *NYT,* September 11, 1935, 15.

52. *NYT,* September 10, 1935, 1, 2.

53. Williams, *Huey Long,* 875–76; *NYT,* September 10, 1935, 1, 2.

54. Deutsch, *Huey Long Murder Case,* 124–26.

55. *NYT,* September 11, 1935, 15; Fournet int., THWP.

## Conclusion

1. Devol int., OHI, LSU.

2. "Huey Long Collection—Eulogy—1935," YouTube video.

3. Hair, *Realm,* 324.

4. The campaign is covered by Kane, *Hayride,* 147–62; Field, *"Politics,"* 196–281.

5. *BRA,* November 28, 1935, 1, 5.

6. Deutsch, *Huey Long Murder Case.* Zinman, *The Day Huey Long Was Shot.* Reed,

*Requiem*. Pavy, *Accident and Deception*. "The Death of Huey Long," C-SPAN video. King, "A Fresh Look at the Shooting of Huey P. Long," website. Ed Reed's researcher, Ernie Gremillion, kindly met with me and shared his file, but he disagrees with my conclusions.

7. Grevemberg and Angers, *My Wars*, 119–26. I am grateful to W. Thomas Angers for sending this book to me.

8. Compare Christenberry int., THWP, with Christenberry, statement on Huey P. Long's death, Devol Collection on Huey P. Long, box 1: 4. Hair and Jeansonne imply that Huey lacked any last words—an impossibility. But Huey's last words could not have been uttered as he died or for hours before then. O'Connor said that he never spoke after the operation, but Frampton and the newspapers said he had some lucid intervals. Fournet quoted him as I did in chapter 30, above. See also *NYT*, September 10, 1935, 1; September 11, 1935, 15; September 13, 1935, 18; September 14, 1935, 20.

9. Guillory int., THWP; Deutsch, *Huey Long Murder Case*, 159, 167–69.

10. Lorio int., THWP.

11. Haas int., THWP. Reed found other witnesses who said they plotted the assassination at the DeSoto conference without being recorded but did not identify Weiss as one of the plotters (*Requiem*, 29, 119, 122, 208–9). Haas told Norman Bauer that he was going to kill Huey (Bauer int., THWP).

12. Wallace, Ponder, and Roy ints., THWP.

13. He might have thought he could surrender and be acquitted by a Baton Rouge jury (Kavanaugh int., THWP).

14. Field, "*Politics*," 276–78, 316–22; Spinks int., THWP.

15. Kane, *Hayride*, 255; Field, "*Politics*," 282.

16. Boulard, *Huey Long Invades*, 202–4.

17. Ginsberg int., THWP.

18. Kane, *Hayride*, 251.

19. Landry int., THWP.

20. Kane, *Hayride*, 194, 198–99 (power laws), 199–207 (Leche and *American Progress*), 230–32, 271, 281, 286, 355, 383 (corruption).

21. Kane, *Hayride*, 275–83.

22. Kane, *Hayride*, 256–78.

23. McGuire, *Win the Race*, 99–102.

24. Field, "Politics," 400; Kane, *Hayride*, 335–55.

25. Key, *Southern Politics*.

26. Kane, *Hayride*, 241–46, 317–34.

27. See box 1: 7, FBI Files on Huey Long. Rose Long sent agents looking for it all over the country, unsuccessfully (Rivet int., THWP). The Roosevelt Hotel today will show visitors where the deduct box was held, but in Weiss's tale, Huey had the deduct box with him in Washington at the Riggs National Bank. If this were true, then Huey would not have told Noe on September 6, 1935, to give the Win or Lose cash to Weiss. Perhaps there were two deduct boxes, one at the Roosevelt to collect the deducts, and another in Washington, DC, to be tapped when funds were needed or to accept contributions made there.

28. Kane, *Hayride*, 430.

29. Kane, *Hayride*, 289–316, 427–55.

30. Earl K. Long, 1939–1940, box 1: 8, FBI Files on Huey Long.

31. Deutsch, *Huey Long Murder Case*, 174.

32. Liebling, *Earl of Louisiana*, 29. Jack McGuire quotes him differently: "After this is

all over, you can go home with your mind at peace, put your feet up on the rail, look at the moon, and talk to your God. And when you do, you'll know that n——s are human too! There's no longer any slavery!" (McGuire, *Win the Race,* 41, 61).

33. McGuire, *Win the Race.*

34. Mann, *Legacy to Power,* 135–36 (fighting with Earl), 299–302 (opposition to Nixon-Moynihan plan), 323–24 (employee stock ownership), 413–14 (Win or Lose); Martin, *Russell Long,* 182–87, 192–96 (employee stock ownership plans).

35. LTR J. Tom Daniel, May 22, 1935, LFP, box C-12: 1935, D-H.

36. Amenta, Dunleavy, and Bernstein, "*Stolen Thunder?*" 684–91.

37. *NYT,* April 9, 1935, 11 (discussing expected primary challenges); *DMR,* April 9, 1935, 6 (Drew Pearson).

38. Compare *CT,* August 14, 1935, 1 (Coughlin would not support a third party), with *CT,* August 31, 1935, 7 (Coughlin would support opposing presidential candidate). Leuchtenburg, "FDR and The Kingfish"; Ortiz, *Beyond the Bonus March,* 83.

39. Schlesinger, *Age of Roosevelt: The Politics of Upheaval,* 341–42.

40. *NYT,* September 20, 1935, 4.

41. Ash, "*Contemporary Examination of Demagogic Techniques,*" 37–38, 65–66.

42. Lincoln, qtd. in Woodward, *The Strange Career of Jim Crow,* 21.

43. Beals, *Story of Huey Long,* 410.

44. Bormann, "Analysis of the March 7, 1935, Radio Address of Senator Huey P. Long," 41–43, 225.

45. Bormann, "Analysis of the March 7, 1935, Radio Address," chap. 6.

46. Collins, *From Good to Great,* 197–204.

47. R. Long and Larcade ints., THWP.

48. Racivitch and Gardiner ints., THWP.

49. Updegraff, *Obvious Adams;* Ogilvy, *Ogilvy on Advertising,* 218.

50. In one special session, Huey saw an opponent's bill to cap consumer interest rates, hastily read it, and just as quickly had it passed.

51. Landry, Pierson, Talbot, Roden, Fisher ints., THWP.

52. Filene, "Shall We Fordize America?" 5, 29.

53. Ross, *The Loneliest Campaign.*

54. Reggie int., THWP.

55. Kane, *Hayride,* 128–31; Morgan, "Williams on Long," 676–82.

56. Boulard, *Huey Long Invades,* 103.

# Bibliography


## Archives and Private Collections

**Columbia University Oral History Collection, Part 1, New York City.**

Will W. Alexander.

**Columbia University Oral History Project, Int. 1, March 18, 1968 by Paul Hopper.**

Burton K. Wheeler.

**Franklin D. Roosevelt Presidential Library, Hyde Park, NY.**

Diaries of Henry Morgenthau Jr., April 27, 1933–July 27, 1945, ser. 1, vol. 3.
Franklin D. Roosevelt Papers.

**Library of Congress.**

William E. Borah Papers.
Bronson Cutting Papers.
James A. Farley Papers.
LaFollette Family Papers.
NAACP Files.
George Norris Papers.

**LSU Libraries, Baton Rouge.**

Special Collections Hill Memorial Library.
James B. Aswell & Family Papers.
H. Donald Devol Collection on Huey P. Long, MS 3653.
Huey P. Long Papers, MS 2005.
Russell B. Long Papers, MS 3700.
John Earle Uhler Papers 1921–60, MS 1902.
Seymour Weiss Papers.

U.S. Department of Justice.
Federal Bureau of Investigation Files on Huey P. Long, 1932–69.
T. Harry Williams Center for Oral History, MS 4700.0009.
T. Harry Williams Papers, MSS 2489, 2510.

**Lyndon B. Johnson Presidential Library, Austin, TX.**

Personal Papers of Lyndon B. and Lady Bird Johnson.

**Princeton University.**

Ivy Lee Papers.

**Tulane University, New Orleans.**

Louisiana Research Collection.
LA Research Collection.
Cecil Morgan Papers.
LaRC/Manuscripts Collection 282.
William B. Wisdom Collection on Huey P. Long, 1924–75.
Special Collections Howard-Tilton Memorial Library.
Hermann Bacher Deutsch Papers, 1827–1970.
Jack McGuire Papers.

**University of California at Berkeley.**

Papers of Hiram Johnson, Diary Letters.

**University of California at Los Angeles.**

Film Library.

**University of Virginia, Charlottesville.**

Harry Byrd Papers.
Carter Glass Papers.

## Government Documents

**Louisiana.**

Louisiana Department of Justice, Office of the Attorney General.
Louisiana Highway Commission.
Biennial Report 1922–24.
2nd Biennial Report.
3rd Biennial Report 1924–26.
4th Biennial Report 1926–28.
5th Biennial Report 1930.
Louisiana State Mineral and Energy Board.
Ryan M. Seidemann et al., "An Analysis of the Legality and Viability of

Mineral Leases Granted to W. T. Burton and James A. Noe During the Years 1934–1936."

**Mississippi.**

Mississippi Biennial Report: 1923, 1925, 1927, and 1929.

**North Carolina.**

North Carolina Biennial Report: 1922, 1924, and 1926.

**South Carolina.**

Report of the Secretary of State to the General Assembly of South Carolina Election, November 8, 1932 (Columbia, 1933).

**Virginia.**

Virginia 1921–22, 15th and 16th Annual Reports.
Virginia 1923–24, 17th and 18th Annual Reports.
Virginia 1925–28, 19th and 20th Annual Reports.

**Washington, DC.**

Congressional Record
U.S. Department of Labor, Bureau of Labor Statistics.
*History of Wages in the United States from Colonial Times to 1928*, by Estelle May Stewart and Jesse Chester Bowe (Washington DC: Government Printing Office, 1934).
U.S. Senate Historical Office.
Oral History Interviews, December 1976 to April 1978.

## Louisiana Newspapers

*Advocate* (Baton Rouge) (1928).
*Baton Rouge Advocate* (1932).
*Baton Rouge State Times* (1929).
*Caldwell Watchman* (Columbia) (1916).
*Daily Reveille* (Baton Rouge) (2005).
*Daily Signal* (Crowley) (1934).
*Dodson Times* (1916).
*Monroe Morning World* (1934).
*Monroe News-Star* (1928–34).
*Morning Advocate* (Baton Rouge) (1935).
*New Orleans Item* (1917–33).
*New Orleans States.*
New Orleans *Times-Picayune* (1917–62).
*Shreveport Journal* (1926).
*Shreveport News American* (1919).
Shreveport *Times* (1923–39).
*St. Tammany Farmer* (Covington) (1902).
*Town Talk* (Alexandria) (1927–35).
*Weekly Argus* (Arcadia) (1916).
*Weekly Town Talk* (Alexandria) (1934).
*Winn Parish Enterprise* (Winnfield) (2014).
*Winnfield News-American* (1946).
*Winnfield Sentinel* (1916).

## Other Newspapers

*Afro American* (Baltimore) (1935).
*Altoona Mirror* (PA) (1928).
*Amarillo Daily News* (TX) (1928).
*Baltimore Sun* (1932–1934).
*Barron's* (New York) (1933–35).
*Battle Creek Enquirer* (MI) (1935).
*Big Spring Daily Herald* (TX) (1936).
Biloxi *Daily Herald* (MS) (1928–36).
*Bismarck Tribune* (ND) (1932).
*Boston Globe* (2015).
*Bradford Era* (PA) (1928).
*Brownwood Bulletin* (TX) (1928).
*Burlington Hawk-Eye* (IA) (1928).
*Capital Times* (Madison, WI) (1928).
*Chicago Defender* (1930–35).
*Chicago Tribune* (1931–35).
*Circleville Herald* (OH) (1935).
*Cleveland Plain Dealer* (1932).
*Corsicana Daily Sun* (TX) (1928).
*Creston Advertiser* (IA) (1928).
*Cumberland Evening Times* (MD) (1928).
*Daily Ardmoreite* (Ardmore, OK) (1928).
*Daily Argus Leader* (Sioux Falls, SD) (1932).
*Daily Caucasian* (Clinton, NC) (1927).
*Daily Gazette* (Gastonia, NC) (1928).
*Daily Oklahoman* (Oklahoma City) (1935–36).
*Daily Reporter* (Greenfield, IN) (1935).
*Danville Bee* (VA) (1928).
*Des Moines Register* (IA) (1935).
*Des Moines Tribune* (IA) (1935).
*Detroit Free Press* (1934).
*Emporia Daily Gazette* (KS) (1928).
*Escanaba Daily Press* (MI) (1928).
*Fairfield Daily Ledger* (IA) (1934).
*Frederick Daily News* (MD) (1928).
*Galveston Daily News* (TX) (1928).
*Hattiesburg American* (MS) (1928–29).
*Herald Tribune* (New York) (1932–34).
*Hope Star* (AR) (1935).
*Hutchinson News* (KS) (1932).
*Joplin Globe* (MO) (1928–35).
*Joplin News Herald* (MO) (1928).
*Kingsport Times* (TN) (1928–35).
*Labor Record* (Joliet, IL) (1916).
*Lafollette's Progressive* (1935) (collection in Library of Congress).
*Laurel Daily News Leader* (MS) (1928).
*Lewiston Daily Sun* (ME) (1932).
*Lima News* (OH) (1928).
*Lincoln Evening Journal* (NE) (1935).
*Lincoln Star* (NE) (1932).
*Manitowoc Herald News* (WI) (1928).
*Mason City Globe-Gazette* (IA) (1934).
*Miami News* (1935).
*Milwaukee Journal* (1935).
*Mobile Post* (AL) (1935).
*Morning Herald* (Hagerstown, MD) (1928).
*Nashville Tennessean* (1934).
*New Castle News* (PA) (1928).
*New Republic* (New York) (1935–40).
*New York Herald Tribune* (1932–35).
*New York Sun* (1934–35).
*New York Times* (1913–2017).
*New Yorker* (1933–35).
*News-Palladium* (Benton Harbor, MI) (1928).
*Newton Record* (MS) (1930).
*Olean Times*, (NY) (1928).
*Philadelphia Record* (1933–34).
*Phoenix Nest* (AZ) (1964).
*Port Arthur News* (TX) (1928–30).
*The Progressive* (Madison, WI) (1935).
*Qu'Appelle Fort Times*, (Melville, Saskatchewan) (1927).
*Reading Eagle* (PA) (1932).
*San Antonio Express* (TX) (1928).
*San Francisco Chronicle* (1935).

*Santa Fe New Mexican* (1932).
*Saturday Evening Post* (Indianapolis) (1932–35).
*Semi-Weekly Spokesman Review* (Spokane, WA) (1936).
*Sheboygan Press* (WI) (1928).
*South Haven Daily Tribune* (MI) (1936).
*St. Louis Post-Dispatch* (1934–35).
*Stevens Point Daily Journal* (WI) (1928).
*The Times* (Lake County, IN) (1928).
*Variety* (New York) (1935).
*Washington C.H. Herald* (Washington Court House, OH) (1928).
*Washington Post* (1932–34).
*Waterloo Evening Courier* (IA) (1929).
*Winslow Daily Mail* (AZ) (1928).
*Wisconsin State Journal* (Madison) (1935).

## Articles and Periodicals

"About Us." *Saturday Evening Post.* www.saturdayeveningpost.com/about.
Amenta, Edwin, Kathleen Dunleavy, and Mary Bernstein. "Stolen Thunder? Huey Long's 'Share our Wealth,' Political Mediation, and the Second New Deal."
*American Rhetoric.* "Franklin Delano Roosevelt: First Fireside Chat." www.americanrhetoric.com/speeches/fdrfirstfiresidechat.html. Baker, Newman F. "Some Legal Aspects of Impeachment in Louisiana." *Southwestern Political and Social Science Quarterly* 10, no. 4 (1930): 359–87.
Baker, Newman F. "Some Legal Aspects of Impeachment in Louisiana." *Southwestern Political and Social Science Quarterly* 10, no. 4 (1930): 359–87.
Banta, Brady Michael. "The Pine Island Situation: Petroleum, Politics and Research Opportunities in Southern History." *Journal of Southern History* 52 (November 1986): 589–610.
Basso, Hamilton. "Huey Long and His Background." *Harpers Monthly,* May 1935.
Bealle, Morris A. "Kingfishophobia." *Plain Talk* 10 (January 1934): 6–7, 46–47.
Brown, E. Cary. "Fiscal Policy in the 'Thirties: A Reappraisal." *American Economic Review* 46, no. 5 (December 1956): 857–79. www.jstor.org.ezproxy.depaul.edu/stable/1811908.
Coyle, David Cushman. "Decentralize Industry." *Virginia Quarterly Review* 11, no. 4 (Summer 1935): 321–38.
Cushman, M. S. "Huey Long's First Session in the United States Senate." *Proceedings of the West Virginia Academy of Science* 11 (1937): 123.
Daniel, Peter. Review of *Cotton Crisis* by Robert E. Synder. *Georgia Historical Quarterly* 68, no. 3 (Fall 1984): 441–43.
Dethloff, Henry C. "The Longs: Revolution or Populist Retrenchment?" *Louisiana History* 19 (1978): 401–12.
Deutsch, Hermann B. "Hattie and Huey." *Saturday Evening Post,* October 15, 1932, 6–7, 88–90, 92.
———. "Huey Long—The Last Phase." *Saturday Evening Post,* October 12, 1935.
———. "Paradox in Pajamas." *Saturday Evening Post,* October 5, 1935, 40.

Dew, "The Long-Lost Returns: The Candidates and Their Totals in Louisiana's Secession Election," *Louisiana Historical Journal* 10, no. 4 (1969): 353.

Filene, Edward A. "Shall We Fordize America?" *Collier's,* December 29, 1923, 5, 29.

"Franklin Delano Roosevelt—First Fireside Chat." *American Rhetoric.* www.americanrhetoric.com/speeches/fdrfirstfiresidechat.html (last updated February 26, 2017).

"Franklin Delano Roosevelt—First Inaugural Address." *American Rhetoric.* www.americanrhetoric.com/speeches/fdrfirstinaugural.html (last updated February 25, 2017).

Gilbert, Clinton. "Long Chances." *Collier's,* May 27, 1933: 20.

Gillette, Michael L. "Huey Long and the Chaco War." *Louisiana History* 11, no. 4 (Autumn 1970): 293–311.

Haas, Edward F. "Huey Long and Historical Speculation." *History Teacher* (1994): 125–31.

———. "Huey Long and the Communists." *Louisiana History* (1991): 29–46.

———. "Huey Long and the Dictators." *Louisiana History* (2006): 133–51.

Hess, Stephen. "The Long, Long Trail." *American Heritage,* August 1966.

"The Huey Long Boy." *New Yorker,* May 11, 1935.

"Huey Pierce Long—Every Man a King." *American Rhetoric.* www.americanrhetoric.com/speeches/hueyplongking.html (last updated February 26, 2017).

"Huey Pierce Long—Radio Address: St. Vitus Dance Government." *American Rhetoric.* americanrhetoric.com/speeches/hueyplongstvitusdancegovernment.html (last updated August 4, 2018).

Huey Pierce Long—"A Fair Deal for the Veterans," *American Rhetoric.* www.americanrhetoric.com/speeches/hueyplongafairdealforveterans.htm

Jennings, Edward T. "Some Policy Consequences of the Long Revolution and Bifactional Rivalry in Louisiana." *American Journal of Political Science* 21, no. 2 (May 1977): 225–46.

Johnson, Hugh. "Strategy of the Extremists." *American Magazine,* May 1935, 36, 112.

Jones, Terry L. "An Administration Under Fire: The Long-Farley Affair of 1935." *Louisiana History* 28 (1987): 5–17.

Leuchtenburg, William E. "FDR and The Kingfish." *American Heritage,* October 1985.

Long, Julius. "What I Know About My Brother." *Real America,* September 1933, 30.

McDaniel, Tammie A. "The Politics of Sedition: The Trial of Winnfield's Senator S. J. Harper." *Louisiana History* 53 (2012): 51–67.

McKinney, Karen J. S. "Getting Out of the Mud: Louisiana and Good Roads before 1928." *Louisiana History* 60, no. 3 (2019): 289–332.

McSween, Harold B. "T. Harry Williams: A Remembrance." *Virginia Quarterly Review* 76, no. 4 (Autumn 2000).

Morgan, Cecil. "Williams on Long: Review of Huey Long by T. Harry Williams." *Tulane Law Review* 45 (1971): 676–82.
Patterson, Thomas E. "Mastering the Senate Maze: Mr. Long Goes to Washington." *Louisiana History* 63, no. 3 (2022): 321–72.
Payne, Ladell. "Willie Stark and Huey Long: Atmosphere, Myth or Suggestion?" *American Quarterly* 20 (1968): 580–95.
Pleasant, John R., Jr. "Ruffin G. Pleasant and Huey P. Long on the Prisoner-Stripe Controversy." *Louisiana History* 15, no. 4 (1974): 357–66.
"Political Notes: In a Washroom." *Time*, September 11, 1933.
Rogers, Will. "Daily Telegram #2763: Mr. Rogers Must Admit That a 'Hero' Is Slipping." June 13, 1935. archive.org/details/willrogersdailyt0002roge.
Romer, Christina. "The Great Crash and the Onset of the Great Depression." *Quarterly Journal of Economics* 105 (1990): 597–624.
———. "The Nation in Depression." *Journal of Economic Perspectives* 7 (1993): 19–39.
———. "What Ended the Great Depression?" *Journal of Economic History* 52, no. 4 (1992): 757–84.
———, and David Romer. "The Missing Transmission Mechanism in the Monetary Explanation of the Great Depression." *American Economic Review* 103, no. 3 (May 2013): 66–72.
Rorty, James. "Callie Long's Boy Huey." *Forum*, August 1935.
Sansing, David G. "Martin Sennet (Mike) Conner: Forty-fourth Governor of Mississippi, 1932–1936." *Mississippi History Now*, January 2004.
———. "Paul B. Johnson Sr.: Forty-sixth Governor of Mississippi: 1940–1943." *Mississippi History Now*, January 2004.
Sanson, Jerry P. "What He Did and What He Promised to Do: Huey Long and the Horizons of Louisiana Politics." *Louisiana History* (2006): 261–76.
Schott, Matthew J. "Huey Long: Progressive Backlash?" *Louisiana History* 27 (1986): 133–45.
Scott, John W. "Highway Building in Louisiana before Huey Long: An Overdue Re-Appraisal." *Louisiana History* 44, no. 1 (2003): 5–33.
Scroop, Daniel. "The Anti–Chain Store Movement and the Politics of Consumption." *American Quarterly* 60, no. 4 (2008): 925–49. www.jstor.org/stable/40068556.
Seidemann, Ryan M. "Did the State Win or Lose in Its Mineral Dealings with Huey Long, Oscar Allen, James Noe, and the Win or Lose Oil Co.?" *Louisiana History* 59 (2018): 196–225.
"Share-the-Wealth Wave." *Time Magazine*, April 1, 1935, 17–23.
Smiley, Gene. "Some Austrian Perspectives on Keynesian Fiscal Policy and the Recovery in the Thirties." *Review of Austrian Economics* 1 (1987): 145–79.
Smith, Gerald L. K. "Or Superman?" *New Republic* 82 (February 13, 1935): 14–15.
Snyder, Robert E. "Huey Long and the Cotton-Holiday Plan of 1931." *Louisiana History* 18, no. 2 (Spring 1977): 133–60.

——. "Huey Long and the Presidential Election of 1936." *Louisiana History* 16, no. 2 (Spring 1975): 117–43.

Sokolsky, George E. "Dr. Huey and Mr. Long," *The Nation* 141 (September 18, 1935).

Strom, Claire. "Editorials and Explosions: Insights into Grassroots Opposition to Tick Eradication in Georgia, 1915–1920." *Georgia Historical Quarterly* (2004): 210.

Swing, Raymond Gram, "The Build-up of Long and Caughlin." *The Nation,* March 20, 1935, 325–26.

Tamny, John. "Extolling Jim Harbaugh's Virtues, Colin Cowherd Explains Basic Economics." *Forbes,* December 21, 2014. www.forbes.com/sites/johntamny/2014/12/21/extolling-jim-harbaughs-virtues-colin-cowherd-explains-basic-economics/#4fc7ce715167 (accessed July 11, 2018).

Telser, Lester G. "The Veterans' Bonus of 1936." *Journal of Post Keynesian Economics* 26 (2003).

"Theodore Roosevelt—The Man with the Muck-rake." *American Rhetoric.* www.americanrhetoric.com/speeches/teddyrooseveltmuckrake.htm (last updated September 29, 2018).

Thurber, James. "Rough on Rats." *The New Yorker,* September 2, 1933.

Warren, Robert Penn. "All the King's Men: The Matrix of Experience." *Yale Review* 53 (1963): 161–67.

——. "In the Time of 'All the King's Men,'" *NYT,* May 31, 1981, section 7, 9.

Weinzweig, Ari. "Potlikker: From Slave Plantations to Today." *The Atlantic,* April 16, 2009.

Williams, T. Harry. "The Politics of the Longs." *Georgia Review* 15, no. 1 (Spring 1961): 28.

——, and John Milton Price. "The Huey P. Long Papers at Louisiana State University." *Journal of Southern History* 36 (1970): 256–61.

Wingo, Barbara C. "The 1928 Presidential Election in Louisiana." *Louisiana History* 18, no. 4 (Autumn 1977): 405–35.

Winter, William A. "Governor Mike Conner and the Sales Tax, 1932." *Journal of Mississippi History* 41 (August 1979): 213–30.

## Transcripts of Interviews

Devol, Don. THWCOH, MS 4700.0009.

Faris, Edgar C., Jr. Int. HSTLOHIC, 34–36. www.trumanlibrary.gov/library/oral-histories/faris.

St. Clair, Darryl, OHI, SHO.

Talmadge, Herman. Int. by Jack Nelson, July 15 and 24, 1975. Interview A-0331-1, Southern Oral History Program Collection (#4007), Wilson Library, University of North Carolina at Chapel Hill.

Wheeler, Burton K. Int. 1, March 18, 1968, by Paul Hopper, CUOHP.

### Interviews by T. Harry Williams

*(T. Harry Williams Papers, box 19, Louisiana and Lower Mississippi Valley Collections, LSU Libraries)*


Alford, W. C. (April 1, 1960).
Anders, D. J. (January 19, 1960).
Austin, Gene (November 14, 1958).
Bahan, L. P. (December 15, 1956).
Barlow, Lester.
Bauer, Norman (May 4, 1962).
Beckcom, George (August 7, 1957).
Blackshear, David (June 27, 1957).
Blanche, Fred (May 19, 1961).
Boone, William C. (June 3, 1960).
Bourg, E. J. (July 16, 1963).
Bowman, Sidney (February 20, 1961).
Bozeman, Harley (January 7, 1959; February 9, 1961).
Brooks, Overton (April 16, 1960).
Brothers, Robert (July 19, 1958).
Broussard, Alton E. (May 4, 1960)
Broussard, J. C. (October 3, 1960).
Carazo, Castro (March 26, 1961).
Carriere, Oliver P. (May 29, 1961).
Carson, W. P.
Cawthorn, Joe (May 5, 1960).
Christenberry, Earle (July 11, 1957).
Cleveland, William.
Cole, Clegg.
Coleman, Elliott (January 2, 1960).
Comiskey, James.
Cooper, W. A. (July 16, 1963).
Copeland. R. S.
Corbin, Carl.
Coverdale, Milton.
Craddock, Perry.
Dalferes, A. Wilmot.
David, Joseph.
Davis, Harry.
Davidson, Charles.
Davis, Mr. R. W. (Lottie) (April 11, 1960).
DeArmond, John.
Delatte, Norbert.
Dent, Fred.
Deutsch, Hermann B.
Digby, Fred.
Dillon, William.
Dodd, William J.
Doles, John J.
Doucet, D. J.
Dugas, Bobby.
Dugas, Patrick (March 23, 1960).
Dugas, Waldo.
Dunbar, Charles E.
Ellender, Allen J.
Favrot, St. Clair.
Fields, Harvey G. (January 9, 1960).
Fisher, Joe (July 10, 1957).
Fleming, Raymond H.
Fournet, John (July 4, 1957).
Frampton, Charles "Chick" (June 24, 1957).
Francis, Fred (April 21, 1960).
Frazar, L. (October 22, 1958).
Frey, Fred (February 2, 1957).
Fruge, J. Cleveland (April 1, 1960).
Gamble, Harry (July 12, 1957).
Gardiner, Lessley P. (June 10, 1953).
Gary, Leon (December 10, 1960).
Gilbert, Harry (January 19, 1960).
Ginsberg, George (October 13, 1959).
Gleason, Ira (December 26, 1956).
Gottlieb, Lewis (July 23, 1963).
Guidry, Oscar (March 29, 1960).
Guerre, Louis F.
Guillory, Isom (March 28, 1960).
Haas, David (April 10, 1963).
Habans, Paul (Moss) (October 24, 1960).
Haggerty, Edward A., Sr. (July 16, 1957).
Hallack, W. M. (March 16, 1964).
Hamlin, Judge Walter (July 2, 1957).

Hanks, Mrs. Ruby (February 10, 1961).
Hargrove, F. Leonard (March 15, 1960).
Hood, Judge John T. (April 3, 1961).
Howell, Roland B. (May 22, 1965).
Hughes, H. Lester (March 18, 1960).
Hunt, Lucille Long (April 11, 1960).
Hunter, Robert A. (March 14, 1960).
Hutcheson, J. L. (April 12, 1960).
James, Trent (October 14, 1959).
Jones, Lawrence M. (December 28, 1961).
Jones, Louie A. (March 2, 1962).
Jones, Robert D. (December 19, 1960).
Jones, Sam H. (April 3, 1961).
Jordan, Harrison (October 26, 1959).
Kahn, Marion (March 4, 1966).
Kavanaugh, M. J. (April 12, 1960).
Kidd, Shelby (October 27, 1959).
Kilpatrick, A. K. (January 8, 1960).
Knott, Clara (April 18, 1960).
Labbe, Donald (May 4, 1960).
Landry, Theophile (July 10, 1957).
Lant, Norman (March 25, 1966).
Larcade, Henry (July 29, 1958).
Lautenshlaeger, Lester (July 9, 1957).
Lawrence, Rolo C. (October 14, 1959).
Leche, Richard (June 30, 1957; January 30 and April 4, 1960).
Long, Otho (February 10, 1961).
Long, Russell (November 26, 1956).
Long Hunt, Lucille (April 11, 1960).
Lorio, Dr. Cecil L. (April 19, 1965).
Maines, George (November 14, 1958).
Maloney, Paul (June 26, 1957).
Manetta, Manuel (July 1958).
McConnell, David (March 14, 1960).
McConnell Long, Rose (March 17, 1960).
Middleton, Troy (September 28, 1961).
Noe, James (December 31, 1956).
O'Connor, James (June 28, 1957).
Peltier, Harvey A.
Peterman, Frank (October 13, 1959).
Peyton, Rupert (January 28, 1958).
Picciola, Marc (August 23, 1961).
Pierson, Mrs. Clarence (October 13, 1959).
Planche, Maurice (June 1, 1960).
Polmer, Irvin F. (November 20, 1960).
Ponder, Amos Lee (July 14, 1958).
Porterie, Mrs. Gaston (October 13, 1959).
Prophit, Robert L. (January 7, 1959).
Provost, C. Arthur (May 6, 1960).
Quaw, Gene (June 27, 1961).
Rabby, Carlos (October 28, 1959).
Rabenhorst, Henry (July 3, 1963).
Racivitch, Herve (May 29, 1961).
Rappelet, A. O. (March 5, 1963).
Rathbone, M. J. (February 11, 1966).
Reggie, Edmund T. (May 6, 1960).
Reyer, George (July 15, 1957).
Rivet, Charles J. (June 27, 1959).
Roberts, Jesse (February 10, 1961).
Robertson, Edward S. (February 10, 1965).
Roden, Murphy (September 25, 1961).
Roy, E. P. (March 20, 1961).
Roy, J. Maxine (May 5, 1960).
Sanders, J. Y., Jr. (November 6, 1959).
Sehrt, Clem (1957).
Sevier, Andrew (June 21, 1960).
Sevier, H. C. (January 9, 1960).
Sheffield, Frank (May 10, 1961).
Sheffield, Ollie (May 10, 1961).
Slack, J. Stewart (May 18, 1963).
Smith, Charles L. (February 10, 1961).
Spencer, Mason (January 20, 1960).
Spinks, Leonard (May 18, 1960).
St. Paul, John (July 20, 1958).
Stagg, George (March 28, 1960).
Stanley, Eugene (July 16, 1957).
Stich, Frank J. (July 17, 1957).
Talbot, Edmund (May 18, 1960).

Talbot, Eva (June 26, 1957).
Talbot, W. Harry (June 26, 1957).
Taylor, Robert (May 10, 1960).
Terzia, Mrs. Theo (January 18, 1960).
Thomas, Orlean (October 13, 1959).
Thompson, O. B. (February 11, 1961).
Todd, Will Harvey (January 8, 1960).
Truman, Harry S. (November 24, 1959).
Wall, Miss Mary (February 20, 1961).
Wallace, A. M. (July 21, 1959).
Wallace, George M. (December 3, 1956).
Watts, Kenneth (February 10, 1961).
Weiss, Seymour (July 3, 1957).
White, A. P. (June 13, 1960).
Whitley, Rupert S. (March 15, 1960).
Wiegand, William.
Williams, E. H. (March 17, 1960).
Williams, Llewelyn B.
Williams, Louis (May 4, 1960).
Wimberly, Shirley G. (July 9, 1957).
Wingrave, John J. (July 30, 1957).
Whittington, V. V. (January 25 and March 16, 1960).
Womack, Mrs. Frank (March 23, 1960).

## Dissertations and Unpublished Manuscripts

Appel, Edward James, Jr. "The Free State of New Orleans: Local Law Enforcement and Illegal Gambling in the 1920s." MA thesis, University of New Orleans, 2010.
Ash, Morgan. "A Contemporary Examination of Demagogic Techniques: Selected Speeches From the 2008 Presidential Campaign." MA thesis, University of Houston, 2010.
Banta, Brady. "The Regulation and Conservation of Petroleum Resources in Louisiana, 1901–1940 (Volumes I and II)." PhD diss., LSU, 1981.
Bormann, Ernest Gorden. "An Analysis of the March 7, 1935 Radio Address of Senator Huey P. Long." MA thesis, State University of Iowa, 1951.
Deutsch, Hermann B. "Paradox in Pajamas." Unpublished manuscript. HBDP, Tulane University.
Field, Betty Marie. "The Campaigns of Huey Long, 1918–1928." MA thesis, Tulane University, 1969.
———. "The Politics of the New Deal in Louisiana, 1933–1939." PhD diss., Tulane University, 1973.
Gordon, Michael Lawrence. "The Development of Louisiana's Public Mental Institutions, 1735–1940." PhD diss., LSU 1974.
Jefferson E. Kidd. "Louisiana Highways—Their History, Construction and Maintenance." BS thesis, Georgia School of Technology, 1924. smartech.gatech.edu.
McManus, Alex J. "Sharing the Hate: The Louisiana Establishment and Huey Long." PhD diss., Tulane University, 2016.
Remas, James Matthew. "Once Proud Princes: Planters and Plantation Culture in Louisiana's Northeast Delta, from the First World War through the Great Depression." PhD diss., LSU, 2006.
Schott, Matthew J. "John M. Parker of Louisiana and the Varieties of American Progressivism." PhD diss., Vanderbilt University 1969.

Sharp, Ansel Miree. "A Study of the Counter-Cyclical Aspects of Total Government Fiscal Policy, 1929–1940." PhD diss., LSU, 1956.

Smith, Diane. "The Origins and Significance of Impeachment in the Career of Governor Huey P Long." PhD diss., Brunel University, London, 2019.

## Books

Aaron, Daniel, and Robert Bendiner. *The Strenuous Decade: A Social and Intellectual Record of the Nineteen-Thirties.* New York: Anchor Books, 1970.

Adams, James Truslow. *The Epic of America.* Boston: Little, Brown & Co., 1932.

——. *Select Correspondence.* Ed. Allan Nevins. New York: Routledge, 2017.

Ancelet, Barry Jean, Jay D. Edwards, and Glen Pitre. *Cajun Country.* Jackson: University Press of Mississippi, 1991.

Anderson, William. *The Wild Man from Sugar Creek: The Political Career of Eugene Talmadge.* Baton Rouge: LSU Press, 1975.

Barnes, Donna A. *The Louisiana Populist Movement, 1881–1900.* Baton Rouge: LSU Press, 2011.

Barry, John M. *Rising Tide: The Great Mississippi Flood of 1927 and How It Changed America.* New York: Simon & Schuster, 1997.

Beals, Carleton. *The Story of Huey Long.* Westport, CT: Greenwood Press, 1935.

Bellow, Saul. *Ravelstein.* New York: Viking, 2000.

Berg, A. Scott. *Wilson.* New York: Berkley, 2014.

Bergman, Marvin, ed. *Iowa History Reader.* Iowa City: University of Iowa Press, 1996.

Berle, Adolf A., Jr., and Gardiner C. Means. *The Modern Corporation and Private Property.* New Brunswick, NJ: Transaction, 1932.

Beschloss, Michael. *Kennedy and Roosevelt: The Uneasy Alliance.* Open Road Media, 1980.

Bethge, Eberhard. *Dietrich Bonhoeffer: A Biography.* Minneapolis: Fortress Press, 2000.

Bogart, Ernest Ludlow, and Charles Manford Thompson. *Readings in the Economic History of the United States.* New York: Longmans, Green and Co., 1917.

Boswell, James. *The Life of Samuel Johnson.* Ed. Bennett A. Cerf and Donald S. Klopfer. New York: Modern Library, 1931.

Boulard, Garry. *Huey Long Invades New Orleans: The Siege of a City 1934–1936.* Gretna, LA: Pelican Publishing, 1998.

Bregman, Rutger. *Utopia for Realists: And How We Can Get There.* New York: Back Bay Books, 2017.

Brinkley, Alan. *The End of Reform: New Deal Liberalism in Recession and War.* New York: Vintage Books, 1996.

——. *Voices of Protest: Huey Long, Father Coughlin and the Great Depression.* New York: Alfred C. Knopf, 1982.

Brooks, John. *Once in Golconda: A True Drama of Wall Street, 1920–1938.* New York: Harper & Row, 1969.

Bukowski, Douglas. *Big Bill Thompson, Chicago, and the Politics of Image.* Champaign: University of Illinois Press, 1997.

Burns, James MacGregor. *Roosevelt: The Lion and the Fox.* New York: Harcourt, Brace & Co., 1956.

Butler, Smedley. *War Is a Racket.* New York: Round Table Press, 1935.

Caldwell, Erskine. *Deep South, Memory and Observation.* Athens: University of Georgia Press, 1995.

Calhoun, Milburn. *Louisiana Almanac, 2002–2003.* Gretna, LA: Pelican Publishing Co., 2002.

Caples, John. *Tested Advertising Methods.* Upper Saddle River, NJ: Prentice Hall, 1998.

Carleton, Mark. *Politics and Punishment: The History of the Louisiana State Penal System.* Baton Rouge: LSU Press, 1984.

Caro, Robert. *The Power Broker: Robert Moses and the Fall of New York.* New York: Alfred A. Knopf, 1974.

———. *The Years of Lyndon Johnson: Means of Ascent.* New York: Vintage Books, 1990.

———. *The Years of Lyndon Johnson: The Path to Power.* New York: Alfred A. Knopf, 1982.

Carter, Hodding. *Huey Long: American Dictator*, in *The Aspirin Age, 1919–1941.* Simon & Schuster, 1949.

Carter, John. *American Messiahs.* New York: Schuster & Schuster, 1935.

Chandler, Lester. *America's Greatest Depression, 1929–1941.* New York: Harper and Row, 1970.

Chemerinsky, Erwin. *Constitutional Law: Principles and Policies.* New York: Wolters Kluwer, 2015.

Chernow, R. *Grant.* New York: Penguin Press, 2017.

Childs, Marquis William. *I Write from Washington.* New York: Harper & Row, 1942.

Clay, Floyd Martin. *Coozan Dudley LeBlanc: From Huey Long to Hadacol.* Pelican Publishing Co, Inc. 1982.

Clifford, Clark, with Richard Holbrooke. *Counsel to the President: A Memoir.* New York: Doubleday, 1991.

Cohen, Adam, and Elizabeth Taylor. *American Pharoah: Mayor Richard J. Daley, His Battle for Chicago and the Nation.* New York: Back Bay Books, 2001.

Collins, Jim. *From Good to Great.* New York: Harper Business, 2001.

Cortner, Richard C. *The Kingfish and the Constitution: Huey Long, The First Amendment, and the Emergence of Modern Press Freedom in America.* Greenwood Press, 1996.

Cowan, Walter Greaves, and Jack B. McGuire. *Louisiana Governors: Rulers, Rascals and Reformers.* Jackson: University Press of Mississippi, 2008.

Cruikshank, Jeffrey, and Arthur Schultz. *The Man Who Sold America: The Amazing (but True!) Story of Albert D. Lasker and the Creation of the Advertising Century.* Cambridge, MA: Harvard Business Review Press, 2010.

Cullen, Jim. *The American Dream: A Short History of an Idea That Changed a Nation.* Oxford, UK: Oxford University Press, 2004.

Curley, James Michael. *I'd Do It Again: A Record of All My Uproarious Years.* Englewood Cliffs, NJ: Prentice-Hall, Inc. 1957.

Cutrer, Thomas W. *Parnassus on the Mississippi: The Southern Review and the Baton Rouge Community, 1935–1942.* Baton Rouge: LSU Press, 1984.

Dallek, Robert. *Franklin D. Roosevelt: A Political Life.* New York: Viking, 2017.

———. *An Unfinished Life: John F. Kennedy, 1917–1963.* Boston: Little, Brown and Co., 2003.

Davis, Forrest. *Huey Long: A Candid Biography.* Rpt. New York: Dodge Publishing Co., 1935.

Davis, Gerald F., Doug McAdam, Richard W. Scott, and Mayer N. Zald, eds. *Social Movements and Organization Theory.* Cambridge, UK: Cambridge University Press, 2005.

Davis, Kenneth S. *FDR: The New Deal Years: 1933–1937.* New York: Random House, 1986.

DeFronzo, James. *Revolutions and Revolutionary Movements.* Boulder, CO: Westview Press, 2015.

De Ronde, Philip. *Paraguay: A Gallant Little Nation.* New York: G. P. Putnam's Sons, 1935.

DeStefano, Anthony M. *Top Hoodlum: Frank Costello, Prime Minister of the Mafia.* New York: Kensington Publishing Corp., 2018.

Deutsch, Hermann B. *The Huey Long Murder Case.* Lafayette: University of Louisiana Press, 1993.

Doane, Robert R. *The Measurement of American Wealth: A Study of the Total Wealth, Income, Expenditures, Profits, Losses, Debts and Savings of American Producers, Consumers and Institutions, from 1860 to 1933.* New York: Harper & Brothers, 1933.

Dodd, William J. *Peapatch Politics: The Earl Long Era in Louisiana Politics.* Baton Rouge: Claitor's Publishing, 1991.

Dumas, Alexandre. *The Count of Monte Cristo.* 1844. London: Penguin Books, 2003.

Eakin, Sue L. *Little Hu: The Little Boy Who Planned to Be Governor of Louisiana.* Winnfield, LA: Louisiana Political Museum, 1995.

Farley, James A. *Behind the Ballots: The Personal History of a Politician.* New York: Harcourt, Brace and Co., 1938.

Fielding, Raymond. *The March of Time, 1935–1951.* New York: Oxford University Press, 1978.

Fields, Thomas T. J. *I Called Him Grandad: The Lost Political Papers of Harvey G. Fields.* Xdetris Corp., 2009.

Finan, Christopher M. *Alfred E. Smith: The Happy Warrior.* New York: Hill and Wang, 2002.

Finkelman, Paul, ed. *Religion and American Law: An Encyclopedia.* New York: Routledge, 2000.

Flynn. *You're The Boss.* New York: Viking Press, 1947.

Friedman, Milton. *Capitalism and Freedom.* Chicago: University of Chicago Press, 1962.

——, and Anna Jacobson Schwartz. *A Monetary History of the United States, 1867*–1960. Princeton, NJ: Princeton University Press, 1971.

Friedman, W. A. *Birth of a Salesman.* Cambridge, MA: Harvard University Press, 2005.

Gaines, Ernest J. *The Autobiography of Miss Jane Pittman.* New York: Bantam, 1972.

Galbraith, John Kenneth. *The Affluent Society.* Boston: Houghton Mifflin, 1958.

——. *The Great Crash, 1929.* New York: Mariner Books, 2009.

Geddes, Barbara, Joseph Wright, and Erica Frantz. *How Dictatorships Work.* Cambridge, UK: Cambridge University Press, 2018.

Geithner, Timothy F. *Stress Test.* New York: Crown Publishing, 2014.

Goldstone, Jack A. *Revolutions: Theoretical, Comparative and Historical Studies.* Belmont, CA: Thomson Wadsworth, 2003.

Gordon, Robert. *The Rise and Fall of American Growth: The U.S. Standard of Living Since the Civil War.* Princeton, NJ: Princeton University Press, 2016.

Grevemberg, Col. Francis C., and W. Thomas Angers. *My Wars: Nazis, Mobsters, Gambling and Corruption.* Lafayette: Beau Bayou Publishing Co., 2004.

Hair, William Ivy. *The Kingfish and His Realm: The Life and Times of Huey P. Long.* Baton Rouge: LSU Press, 1991.

Hargroder, Charles M. *Ada and the Doc: An Account of the Ada LeBoeuf–Thomas Dreher Murder Case.* Lafayette: University of Louisiana Press, 2000.

Harris, Thomas, O. *The Kingfish: Huey P. Long, Dictator.* Gretna, LA: Pelican, 2001.

Heilman, Robert Bechtold. *The Southern Connection: Essays.* Baton Rouge: LSU Press, 1991.

Herrick, Genevieve Forbes, and John Origen Herrick. *The Life of William Jennings Bryan.* Chicago: Grover C. Buxton, 1925.

Hiller, Elizabeth O. *Fifty-Two Sunday Dinners: A Book of Recipes.* Chicago: N. K. Fairbank Co., 1913.

Hoffer, Eric. *The True Believer: Thoughts on the Nature of Mass Movements.* New York: Harper & Brothers, 1951.

Hofstadter, Richard. *The American Political Tradition: And the Men Who Made It.* New York: Vintage Books, 1948.

——. *Anti-Intellectualism in American Life.* New York: Vintage Books, 1966.

Hopkins, Claude. *My Life in Advertising and Scientific Advertising.* Lincolnwood, IL.: NTC Business Books, 1998.

Horan, James D. *The Desperate Years: A Pictorial History of the Thirties.* New York: Bonanza Books, 1962.

Howard, Perry H. *Political Tendencies in Louisiana.* Baton Rouge: LSU Press, 1971.

Hyde, Samuel C., Jr. *Pistols and Politics: Feuds, Factions, and the Struggle for Order in Louisiana's Florida Parishes, 1810–1935.* Baton Rouge: LSU Press, 2018.

Ickes, Harold L. *The Secret Diary of Harold L. Ickes: The First Thousand Days, 1933–1936.* New York: Simon and Schuster, 1953.

Irey, Elmer L., and William J. Slocum. *The Tax Dodgers: The Inside Story of the T-Men's War with America's Political and Underworld Hoodlums.* New York: Greenberg, 1948.

Istre, Elista. *Creoles of South Louisiana: Three Generations Strong.* Lafayette: University of Louisiana Press, 2018.

James, Marquis. *The Life of Andrew Jackson.* Indianapolis: Bobbs-Merrill Co., 1938.

Jeansonne, Glen. *Leander Perez: Boss of the Delta.* Jackson: University Press of Mississippi, 2006.

———. *The Messiah of the Masses: Huey P. Long and the Great Depression.* New York: HarperCollins, 1993.

———. *Minister of Hate.* Baton Rouge: LSU Press, 1997.

———, ed. *Huey at 100: Centennial Essays on Huey P. Long.* Ruston, LA: McGinty Publications, 1995.

Kane, Harnett. *Louisiana Hayride: The American Rehearsal for Dictatorship, 1928–1940.* Gretna, LA: Pelican, 1986.

Kazin, Michael. *A Godly Hero: The Life of William Jennings Bryan.* New York: Anchor Books, 2007.

Kendall, John Smith. *History of New Orleans.* Vol. 3. Chicago: Lewis Publishing Co., 1922.

Kendall, Paul Murray. *Louis XI: The Universal Spider.* New York: W. W. Norton & Co, 1971.

Key, V. O., Jr. *Southern Politics in State and Nation.* New York: Alfred A. Knopf, 1949.

Koenig, Louis W. *Bryan: A Political Biography of William Jennings Bryan.* New York: Putnam, 1971.

Krock, Arthur. *Memoirs: Sixty Years on the Firing Line.* New York: Popular Library, 1968.

Laborde, Adras. *A National Southerner: Ransdell of Louisiana.* New York: Benziger, 1951.

LaFollette, Philip. *Adventure in Politics.* New York: Holt, Rinehart and Winston, 1970.

Lamster, Mark. *The Man in the Glass House: Philip Johnson, Architect of the Modern Century.* New York: Little Brown, 2018.

Lawson, George. *Anatomies of Revolution*. Cambridge, UK: Cambridge University Press, 2019.

Leighninger, Robert, Jr. *Building Louisiana: The Legacy of the Public Works Administration*. Jackson: University Press of Mississippi, 2007.

Leuchtenburg, William E. *Franklin D. Roosevelt and the New Deal: 1932–1940*. New York: Harper & Row, 1963.

Leven, Maurice, Harold G. Moulton, and Clark Warburton. *America's Capacity to Consume*. Washington, DC: Brookings Institution, 1934.

Liebling, A. J. *The Earl of Louisiana*. Baton Rouge: LSU Press, 1978.

Long, Huey P. *Every Man a King*. New Orleans: National Book Co., 1933.

———. *My First Days in the White House*. New York: Da Capo Press, 1972.

Loos, John L. *Oil On Stream! A History of Interstate Oil Pipe Line Company, 1909–1959*. Baton Rouge: LSU Press, 1959.

Lowitt, Richard. *Bronson M. Cutting, Progressive Politician*. Albuquerque: University of New Mexico Press, 1992.

———. *George W. Norris: The Triumph of a Progressive, 1933–1944*. Champaign: University of Illinois Press, 1978.

Luthin, Reinhard H. *American Demagogues: Twentieth Century*. Boston: Boston Press 1954.

Lynd, Robert S., and Helen Merrell Lynd. *Middletown in Transition: A Study in Cultural Conflicts*. New York: Harcourt Brace, 1937.

MacArthur, Douglas. *Reminiscences*. Annapolis, MD: Bluejacket Books, 1964.

Malone, David. *Hattie and Huey: An Arkansas Tour*. Fayetteville: University of Arkansas Press, 1989.

Mann, Robert. *Kingfish U: Huey Long and LSU*. Baton Rouge: LSU Press, 2023.

———. *Legacy to Power: Senator Russell Long of Louisiana*. New York: Paragon House, 1992.

Margo, R. A. *Race and Schooling in the South, 1880–1950: An Economic History*. Chicago: University of Chicago Press, 1990.

Martin, Michael S. *Russell Long: A Life in Politics*. Jackson: University Press of Mississippi, 2014.

Mayer, George H. *The Political Career of Floyd B. Olson*. Minneapolis: University of Minnesota Press, 1951.

Mazlish, Bruce, Arthur D. Kaledin, and David B. Ralston. *Revolution: A Reader*. New York: Macmillan Co., 1971.

McAdam, Doug, John D. McCarthy, and Mayer N. Zald. *Comparative Perspectives on Social Movements: Political Opportunities, Mobilizing Structures, and Cultural Framings*. Cambridge, UK: Cambridge University Press, 1996.

McElvaine, Robert S. *The Great Depression: America, 1929–1941*. New York: Times Books, 1993.

McGerr, Michael. *A Fierce Discontent: The Rise and Fall of the Progressive Movement in America, 1870–1920*. Oxford, UK: Oxford University Press, 2003.

McGuire, Jack. *Win the Race or Die Trying: Uncle Earl's Last Hurrah:* Jackson: University of Mississippi Press, 2016.

Moley, Raymond. *After Seven Years.* New York: Harper & Brothers, 1939.

———. *27 Masters of Politics, in a Personal Perspective.* New York: Funk & Wagnalls Co., 1949.

Morris, Edmund. *The Rise of Theodore Roosevelt.* New York: Ballantine Books, 1980.

———. *Theodore Rex.* New York: Modern Library, 2002.

Moulton, Harold G. *The Formation of Capital.* Washington DC: Brookings Institution Press, 1935.

———. *Income and Economic Progress.* Washington, DC: Brookings Institution, 1935.

———. *The Recovery Problem in the United States.* Washington, DC: Brookings Institution, 1936.

Nasaw, David. *The Patriarch: The Remarkable Life and Turbulent Times of Joseph P. Kennedy.* New York: Penguin Press, 2012.

Neal, Steve. *Happy Days Are Here Again: The 1932 Democratic Convention, the Emergence of FDR—and How America Was Changed Forever.* New York: HarperCollins, 2004.

Nourse, Edwin G. *America's Capacity to Produce.* Washington, DC: Brookings Institution, 1934.

Ogilvy, David. *Confessions of an Advertising Man.* London: Southbank Publishing, 2004.

———. *Ogilvy on Advertising.* New York: Vintage Books, 1985.

———. *The Unpublished David Ogilvy.* Crown Publishers, Inc., 1986.

Ortiz, Stephen R. *Beyond the Bonus March and GI Bill: How Veteran Politics Shaped the New Deal Era.* New York: NYU Press, 2009.

Osborn, George C. *John Sharp Williams: Planter-Statesman of the Deep South.* Baton Rouge: LSU Press, 1943.

Oulahan, Richard. *The Man Who . . . : The Story of the 1932 Democratic National Convention.* New York: Dial Press, 1971.

Pavy, Donald A. *Accident and Deception: The Huey Long Shooting.* New Iberia, LA: Cajun Publishing, 1999.

Perry, Keith. *The Kingfish in Fiction: Huey P. Long and the Modern American Novel.* Baton Rouge: LSU Press, 2004.

Peters, Charles. *Five Days in Philadelphia: The Amazing "We Want Willkie!" Convention of 1940 and How It Freed FDR to Save the Western World.* New York: Public Affairs, 2005.

Piketty, Thomas. *Capital in the Twenty-First Century.* Cambridge, MA: Harvard University Press, 2014.

Posner, Richard A. *The Crisis of Capitalist Democracy.* Cambridge, MA: Harvard University Press, 2010.

Price, Frank James. *Troy H. Middleton: A Biography.* Baton Rouge: LSU Press, 1974.

Reed, Ed. *Requiem for a Kingfish.* Baton Rouge: Award Publications, 1986.
Roberts, Andrew. *Churchill: Walking with Destiny.* New York: Viking, 2018.
Rollyson, Carl. *Rebecca West and the God That Failed: Essays.* Bloomington, IN: Universe, 2005.
Roman, Kenneth, and Jane Maas. *How to Advertise.* New York: St. Martin's Griffin, 1997.
Ross, Irwin. *The Loneliest Campaign: The Truman Victory of 1948.* Westport, CT: Greenwood Press, 1977.
Royko, Mike. *Boss: Richard J. Daley of Chicago.* New York: E. P. Dutton & Co., 1977.
Ryan, Halford Ross. *Oratorical Encounters: Selected Studies and Sources of Twentieth-Century Political Accusations and Apologies.* Westford, CT: Greenwood Press, 1988.
Safire, William. *Lend Me Your Ears: Great Speeches in History.* New York: W. W. Norton & Co., 2004.
Salmond, John. *A Southern Rebel: The Life and Times of Aubrey Willis Williams, 1860–1965.* University of North Carolina Press, 1983.
Schlesinger, Arthur M., Jr. *The Age of Jackson.* New York: Mentor Books, 1949.
———. *The Age of Roosevelt: The Coming of the New Deal.* Boston: Houghton Mifflin, 1959.
———. *The Age of Roosevelt: The Crisis of the Old Order, 1919–1933.* Boston: Houghton Mifflin, 1957.
———. *The Age of Roosevelt: The Politics of Upheaval.* Boston: Houghton Mifflin, 1960.
Schweiger, Beth Barton. *Religion in the American South: Protestants and Others in History and Culture.* Chapel Hill: University of North Carolina Press, 2004.
Sindler, Allan P. *Huey Long's Louisiana: State Politics, 1920–1952.* Baltimore: Johns Hopkins University Press, 1956.
Slaughter, John A. *Income Received in the Various States 1929–1935.* New York National Industrial Conference Board, Inc., 1937.
Slayton, Robert A., and Peter Eisenstadt. *The Encyclopedia of New York State.* Syracuse: Syracuse Press, 2005.
Smith, Jean Edward, *FDR.* New York: Random House, 2008.
Snyder, Robert E. *Cotton Crisis.* Chapel Hill: University of North Carolina Press, 1984.
Spain, Rufus B. *At Ease in Zion: A Social History of Southern Baptists, 1865–1900.* Nashville: Vanderbilt University Press, 1967.
Spears, T. B. *100 Years on the Road.* New Haven, CT: Yale University Press, 1995.
Steel, Ronald. *Walter Lippmann and the American Century.* New Brunswick, NJ: Transaction Publishers, 2008.
Sterling, Ross. *Ross Sterling, Texan.* Austin: University of Texas Press, 2007.
St. Johns, Adela Rogers. *The Honeycomb.* Garden City, NY: Doubleday & Co., 1969.

Stokes, Thomas L. *Chip Off My Shoulder.* Princeton, NJ: Princeton University Press, 1940.

Sutton, Robert I. *The No Asshole Rule: Building a Civilized Workplace and Surviving One That Isn't.* New York: Business Plus, 2007.

Swain, Martha H. *Pat Harrison: The New Deal Years.* Jackson: Mississippi University Press, 1978.

Swing, Raymond Gram. *Forerunners of American Fascism.* New York: Julian Messner, 1935.

Truman, Harry S. *Memoirs by Harry S. Truman: Year of Decisions, Vol. 1.* New York: Doubleday, 1955.

Tugwell, Rexford G. *The Democratic Roosevelt.* New York: Doubleday & Co. 1957.

Turner, Walter R. *Paving Tobacco Road: A Century of Progress by the North Carolina Department of Transportation.* Raleigh: North Carolina Office of Archives and History, 2003.

Tyler, Pamela. *Silk Stockings and Ballot Boxes: Women in Politics, 1920–1963.* Athens: University of Georgia Press, 1996.

Updegraff, Richard. *Obvious Adams.* Louisville, KY: Updegraff Press, 1916.

Walkiewicz, E. P., and Hugh Witemeyer. *Ezra Pound and Senator Bronson Cutting: A Political Correspondence, 1930–1935.* Albuquerque: University of New Mexico Press 1995.

Warren, Robert Penn. *All The King's Men.* Restored edition. 1946. New York: Harcourt, Inc., 2001.

Watkins, T. H. *Righteous Pilgrim: The Life and Times of Harold Ickes, 1874–1952.* New York: Henry Holt & Co. 1990.

Watson, James E. *As I Knew Them: Memoirs of James E. Watson.* Indianapolis: Bobbs Merrill Co., 1936.

Weller, Cecil Edward, Jr. *Joe T. Robinson: Always A Loyal Democrat.* Fayetteville: University of Arkansas Press, 1998.

West, Rebecca. *Selected Letters of Rebecca West.* New Haven, CT: Yale University Press, 2000.

Wheeler, Burton K., and Paul F. Healy. *Yankee from the West: The Candid, Turbulent Life Story of the Yankee-born U.S. Senator from Montana.* London: Octagon Press, 1977.

Wheeler Colman, Elizabeth. *Mrs. Wheeler Goes to Washington.* Helena, MT: Falcon Press Publishing Co., 1989.

White, Richard D., Jr. *Kingfish: The Reign of Huey P. Long.* New York: Random House, 2006.

White, Theodore. *The Making of the President, 1960.* New York: Signet, 1961.

White, William Allen. *The Autobiography of William Allen White.* New York: Macmillan Co., 1946.

Williams, T. Harry. *Huey Long.* New York: Alfred A. Knopf, 1969.

———. *Romance and Realism in Southern Politics.* Athens: University of Georgia Press, 1961.

Wilson, Charles Reagan. *Baptized in Blood: The Religion of the Lost Cause, 1865–1920*. Athens: University of Georgia Press, 2009.
Woodward, C. Vann. *Origins of the New South: 1877–1913*. Baton Rouge: LSU Press, 1951.
———. *The Strange Career of Jim Crow*. Oxford, UK: Oxford University Press, 1974.
Workers of the Writers' Program of the Works Progress Administration in the State of Louisiana. *Louisiana: A Guide to the State*. New York: Hastings House, 1941.
Zinman, David. *The Day Huey Long Was Shot*. Lafayette: University of Louisiana Press, 1993.
Zinn, Howard. *New Deal Thought*. Indianapolis: Hackett Publishing Co., 2003.
Zoellick, Robert B. *America in the World: A History of U.S. Diplomacy and Foreign Policy*. New York: Hachette Book Group, 2020.

## Internet and Other Media Sources

Ainsworth, Laura. "Gerald L. K. Smith." May 23, 2017. www.youtube.com/watch?v=aE3pFq4VeDA.
*American Presidency Project*. "1932 Presidential Election." www.presidency.ucsb.edu/showelection.php?year=1932 (accessed July 12, 2018).
Arsenaul. "Davis, Jeff." *American National Biography Online*. www.anb.org/articles/06/06-00139.html.
Black, Conrad. "FDR's Triumph." *National Review*, March 26, 2009. www.nationalreview.com/2009/03/fdrs-triumph-conrad-black/ (accessed July 20, 2016).
———. "Truth About FDR." *National Review*, March 18, 2009. www.nationalreview.com/2009/03/truth-about-fdr-conrad-black/.
Boschert, Thomas N. "Williams, John Sharp." *American National Biography Online*. www.anb.org/articles/06/06-00716.html.
"Charles Henderson, 1915–1919." *Alabama Governors*. legacy.archives.alabama.gov/govs_list/g_hender.html.
Coyle, David Cushman. "Recovery and Finance." *VQR Online*, Autumn 1934. www.vqronline.org/essay/recovery-and-finance.
"The Death of Huey Long." www.c-span.org/video/?297015-4/death-huey-long.
"Death Valley Dorms." *Daily Reveille*, April 27, 2005. www.lsunow.com/death-valley-dorms/article_1acofa31-e203-50a4-aa6b-73ece032c835.html.
Federal Reserve Bank of St. Louis. "Federal Surplus or Deficit." fred.stlouisfed.org/series/FYFSD.
Franklin D. Roosevelt Day By Day. www.fdrlibrary.marist.edu/daybyday/.
"Georgia: Gov. Joseph Mackey Brown." *National Governors Association*. www.nga.org/governor/joseph-mackey-brown/.
Gideons International. "About Us." www.gideons.org/about (accessed November 5, 2018).

Hamblin, James. "A Mapped History of Taking a Train Across the United States." February 21, 2013. Map for 1930, www.theatlantic.com.

Holmes, William F. "Vardaman, James Kimble." *American National Biography Online*. www.anb.org/articles/05/05-00805.html.

Housing Works Bookstore Café. Tumblr. housingworksbookstore.tumblr.com/post/1205876553/this-might-be-the-coolest-book-inscription-weve.

"Hubert Humphrey's Year in Baton Rouge and How It Helped Shape our Civil Rights Laws." June 23, 2014. www.nola.com/opinions/index.ssf/2014/06/hubert_humphreys_year_in_baton.html.

"Huey Long and Father Charles Coughlin Speak 1935." Historycomestolife. www.youtube.com/watch?v=nfu_pLboswA.

"Huey Long Collection—Drinking and Talking." www.youtube.com/watch?v=X2ri3Tc4fEc.

"Huey Long Collection—Eulogy—1935." www.youtube.com/watch?v=j6GgrAQr6ss.

"Huey Long Collection—Hostility with T. Semmes Walmsley—1930–1935." 1:44, December 27, 2017. www.youtube.com/watch?v=WusvLhSoPdQ.

"Huey Long Collection—Huey and LSU." 1:03. August 10, 2019. www.youtube.com/watch?v=XtGPxL_n-mQ.

"Huey Long Collection—Making a Gin Fizz." www.youtube.com/watch?v=fqDSOPY3Jnw.

"Huey Long Collection—Senate Silence and Funeral Services." www.youtube.com/watch?v=Z4Nt44JC9kI.

*Huey Long*. Directed by Ken Burns. PBS, 1985. www.pbs.org/kenburns/huey-long/.

"Huey Long (1893–1935)." Historycomestolife. www.youtube.com/watch?v=-JJSrYa8v4o.

"Huey Long Praises the Official Reporters of Debates." Senate Historical Office. www.senate.gov/about/officers-staff/secretary-of-the-senate/huey-long-and-reporters-of-debates.htm.

"Huey Long Seen as Threat to FDR in 1930s." Danieljbmitchell. 5:54. July 26, 2007. www.youtube.com/watch?v=mdzAbxsjPRA

"Huey Long Speech at VFW, 1935." Old Is Best. www.youtube.com/watch?v=y2GBNMXCXzA.

"Huey Long Speech 1935." Old Is Best. 28:58. December 18, 2018. www.youtube.com/watch?v=8vf9x3fXlSw.

"Huey P. Long on the difference between Democrats and Republicans." Miscellus2. www.youtube.com/watch?v=8MKb35NKoFo.

Kauffman, Bill. "The Populist Patriotism of Gore Vidal." *The American Conservative*, November 20, 2006. www.theamericanconservative.com/articles/the-populist-patriotism-of-gore-vidal/.

King, C. R. "A Fresh Look at the Shooting of Huey P. Long." March 16, 2015. whoshothuey.yolasite.com/more-text.php.

Kirwan, Albert D. *Revolt of the Rednecks: Mississippi Politics: 1876–1925*. Lexington: University of Kentucky Press, 1951. hdl.handle.net/2027/uc1.b4485918.

LBJ to Claudia Alta "Lady Bird" Johnson (née Taylor), September 11, 1934. *Dear Bird: The 1934 Courtship Letters.* archives.lbjlibrary.org/items/show/383 (accessed June 12, 2015).

"List of advocates of universal basic income." Wikipedia. en.wikipedia.org>wiki>list_of_advocates_universal_basic_income#.

Long, Huey P. "Share Our Wealth." Pamphlet, 1934. xroads.virginia.edu/~ma01/Kidd/thesis/pdf/share_our_wealth.pdf.

Long, Russell. "Why I Am for Earl Long." Radio address. www.hueylong.com/legacy/russell-long-speech.php.

McCain, Charles. Post of October 15, 2015. www.Charlesmccain.com.

McSween, Harold B. "Huey Long at His Centenary." *VQR Online.* www.vqronline.org/essay/huey-long-his-centenary.

"Minsky's Moment." In "Economics Briefs: Six Big Economic Ideas." *The Economist,* July 30, 2016. www.economist.com/sites/default/files/econbriefs.pdf.

"President Roosevelt Reads Bonus Veto to Joint Congress." Footagefarm. www.youtube.com/watch?v=YPBJam20pJA.

Purdy, Elizabeth R. "Presidential Race of 1928." *Encyclopedia of Alabama.* www.encyclopediaofalabama.org/article/h-1517 (last modified February 18, 2015).

Rabalais, "The Kingfish, Biff & the Golden Thirties." www.google.com/books/edition/Greatest_Moments_in_Lsu_Football_History/-43SPTBE2hwC?hl=en&gbpv=1&dq=Rabalais,+The+Kingfish,+Biff+%26+the+Golden+Thirties&pg=PA66&printsec=frontcover.

Senate Historical Office. "Huey Long Praises the Official Reporters of Debates." January 24, 2019. www.senate.gov/about/officers-staff/secretary-of-the-senate/huey-long-and-reporters-of-debates.htm.

Sheire, James W. "Louisiana State Capitol." *National Register for Historic Place Inventory—Nomination Form.* National Park Service. focus.nps.gov/pdfhost/docs/NHLS/Text/78001421.pdf (accessed July 28, 2015).

Street, William B. "The Man Who Invented the Redneck." *Commercial Appeal Mid South Magazine,* March 21, 1965.

"Sugar Bowl." Wikipedia. en.wikipedia.org/wiki/Sugar_Bowl.

Telser, Lester Telser. "Lessons from the United States Great Depression and the German Hyperinflation." In *Selected Works of Lester G. Telser.* works.bepress.com/lester_telser/57/.

———. "The Reconstruction Finance Corporation and the Great Depression: How Good Intentions Led to Calamity." In *Selected Works of Lester G. Telser.* works.bepress.com/lester_telser/4/.

———. "The Veterans' Bonus of 1936." *Journal of Post Keynesian Economics* 26, no. 2 (2003). www.jstor.org/stable/4538871#:~:text=The%20bonus%20was%20paid%20to,253.

Traughber, Bill. "LSU parades into Nashville in 1934." September 8, 2010. www

.vucommodores.com/sports/historycorner/spec-rel/090810aao.html (accessed September 7, 2015).

Trotter, Michael C., MD. *Huey P. Long's Last Operation: When Medicine and Politics Don't Mix.* www.ncbi.nlm.nih.gov/pmc/articles/PMC3307515/.

U.S. Department of Labor, Bureau of Labor Statistics. *History of Wages in the United States from Colonial Times to 1928* by Estelle May Stewart and Jesse Chester Bowen. Washington DC: Government Printing Office, 1934. fraser.stlouisfed.org/content/?title_id=4126&filepath=/files/docs/publications/bls/bls_0604_1934.pdf.

Watts of Love. www.wattsoflove.org.

"What the Man Behind the 'American Dream' Really Meant." *Boston Globe.* April 16, 2015. www.bostonglobe.com/ideas/2015/04/16/what-man-behind-american-dream-really-meant/uni438RcM82Y3QDnkwRz5H/story.html (accessed February 19, 2016).

# Index